The Asbury Theologica
World Christian Revitalization Movements

Ruth Ann Tipton's study of Christian Union churches and missions in tension within the cultural context of Papua New Guinea presents a complex and many faceted narrative and analysis of missional initiatives at odds with local ecclesial interests. And this tension is exacerbated by the values imposed by traditional Melanesian religions still rooted in the local population. Following a carefully nuanced analysis of this complex of events, highlighted by differing cultural and economic expectations, constructive resolution to the problems on the field are explored in terms of facilitating Melanesians with a capacity for 'self theologizing.' This denotes a learned capacity for engaging the Melanesian culture directly with the scriptures to discern what Christian praxis might look like in that environment. A project of this depth and breadth of vision means this study may rank high among those providing an astute engagement of society and faith in a non-Western context. There can be no higher outcome for a project in Christian revitalization studies.

J. Steven O'Malley
General Editor
The Asbury Theological Seminary Studies in World Christian Revitalization

Intercultural Studies Sub-Series

The behavioral science approach to the study of revitalization movements has a long history that has developed several models. Anthropologists, among others, observed that people responded to colonialism and the expansion of the West in various ways: armed resistance, selective acceptance and passive resistance, among others. The problems of the colonial frontier led to a memorandum on acculturation written by Robert Redfield, Ralph Linton and Melville Herskovits in 1936. Elsewhere in the world, anthropologists observed "nativistic" or "cultural renewal" movements as well: cargo cults in Melanesia, messianic movements in South Africa, and political revolutions in Latin America. Anthony F. C. Wallace brought some order to this area of study with his 1956 article where he named the stages and subsumed the movements under the name of "revitalization movements." Harold Turner contributed the notion of New Religious Movements to focus on the indigenous responses to mission work seen in every continent. This can be seen as part of a larger development, from the 1960s on, to develop Social Movement Theory where people are seen as agents intentionally acting to renew and reform society by organizing others to resist or dethrone the powers that be. Such movements develop a culture and social organization that give meaning and impetus to action on behalf of the leader and/or the program.

In this book, Ruth Tipton presents a history of a specific mission over time. The Christian Union Mission began mission work among the Nembi soon after Australian colonial "pacification" in 1964, and spread their work to the Melpa people in 1983. Dr. Tipton herself was a part of that mission for over 37 years. Near the end of her time there, the leaders of the now local and indigenous church asked her to write a history of the church. As she reviewed memories, minutes, and interviews, she realized that there were two histories: one what the missionaries thought they were doing and the other what the people thought the missionaries were up to. These perspectives were not the same, and so Dr. Tipton has endeavored to bring us both sides of the story. In the process, she has produced a sensitive and nuanced history of mission that stands out as an account of conversion, revitalization, and growth of Christianity in the Highlands of Papua New Guinea.

Michael A. Rynkiewich
Editor for the sub-series on Intercultural Studies

Unrealized Expectations

*A History of Christian Union Mission
and World Gospel Mission's Work
among the Nembi and Melpa People of
Papua New Guinea*

Ruth Ann Tipton

*Asbury Theological Seminary Series:
The Study of World Christian Revitalization Movements in
Interculutral Studies*

EMETH PRESS
www.emethpress.com

Unrealized Expectations: A History of Christian Union Mission and World Gospel Mission's Work among the Nembi and Melpa People of Papua New Guinea

Library of Congress Cataloging-in-Publication Data

Names: Tipton, Ruth A., author.
Title: Unrealized expectations : a history of Christian Union Mission and
  World Gospel Mission's work among the Nembi and Melpa people of Papua
New Guinea / Ruth Ann Tipton.
Description: Lexington : Emeth Press, 2017. | Series: The Asbury Theological
  Seminary series in intercultural studies | Includes bibliographical
  references.
Identifiers: LCCN 2017031029 | ISBN 9781609471149 (alk. paper)
Subjects: LCSH: Christian Union Mission--History. | World Gospel
  Mission--History. | Missions--Papua New Guinea--Southern Highlands
  Province--History. | Mailu (Papua New Guinean people)--Missions--History.
  | Medipa (Papua New Guinean people)--Missions--History.
Classification: LCC BV3680.N5 T57 2017 | DDC 266/.023730953--dc23
LC record available at https://lccn.loc.gov/2017031029

Dedication

Dedicated

to the CUM and WGM missionaries

who worked among the Nembi and Melpa people of PNG

and

to the Nembi and Melpa people of CUC of PNG

who overcame trauma, fear, and unprecedented change

to build a strong Christian presence in their country

and want their story to be recorded in a written history.

Table of Contents

Chapter Three: Missionization / 55

Chapter Four: Indigenization / 113

Chapter Five: Nationalization / 141

Chapter Six: Maturation / 225

Chapter Seven: Frustration—The Spiritual Harvest Ministry / 263

Chapter Eight: Revitalization / 289

Figures

Figures

Tables

Maps

Abbreviations

ACE	Accelerated Christian Education
ANGAU	Australian New Guinea Administrative Unit
AUD	Australian Dollars
EA	Evangelical Alliance
CCCU	Churches of Christ in Christian Union
CLTC	Christian Leaders Training College
CMC	Churches Medical Council
CMCC	Church/Mission Coordinating Council
CMS	Church Mission Society
CUC	Christian Union Church
CUC of PNG	Christian Union Church of Papua New Guinea
CUM	Christian Union Mission
EBC	Evangelical Brotherhood Church
ESJ	E. Stanley Jones
IEA	International Education Association
LMS	London Mission Society
MAF	Missionary Aviation Fellowship
PANGU	Papua and New Guinea United
PMV	Public Motor Vehicle
PNG	Papua New Guinea
RBT	Region Board of Trustees
SHP	Southern Highlands Province
SIL	Summer Institute of Linguistics
SSEC	South Seas Evangelical Church
TPNG	Territory of Papua and New Guinea
USA	United States of America

USD	United States Dollars
WGM	World Gospel Mission
WMS	Wesley Mission Society

Glossary

Aron: The name refers to people living on the eastern side of a major river. It also refers to major fight alliances made up of people living primarily on the eastern side of the river.

Australian Territory of Papua: The name the Australians gave to southeast quadrant of the island of New Guinea when the British released the colony of British New Guinea to the Australians in 1906. It went by that name until World War Two.

Beche-de-mer: A large sea cucumber that is eaten as a delicacy in some parts of Asia.

Bilum: String bag. It can also refer to the loin cloths that the men wore in their traditional dress.

Blackbirding: An illegal labor (de facto slave) trade that developed in Melanesia.

Blackbirders: Illegal labor traders.

British New Guinea: When the British protectorate of Papua was annexed as a full British colony in 1888, its name was changed to British New Guinea.

Coastals: The people living in the coastal areas of Papua New Guinea. Their cultural patterns are distinct from those living in the interior mountainous regions.

Derestricted: When the people quit fighting among themselves and submitted to government control, the area was "derestricted" and outsiders were allowed to enter freely.

Divelopmen: A Pidgin term used to describe small scale projects that benefit local groups (Rynkiewich).

First Contact: The first time that the colonial administrators or explorers from the Western world met up with a new indigenous group.

German New Guinea: The northeast quadrant and the Bismarck Archipelago that Germany claimed as its colony in November of 1884.

Guria: A Pidgin term that means to shake, tremble, shiver or quake.

Gutpela sindaun: The good life that everyone enjoys when all things are in balance. In Melanesian religions all things are interrelated, interdependent and linked together. When things are in balance the cosmos is well ordered and the biological, spiritual, and material worlds all prosper.

Hap ten: The tenth part. It is the Pidgin term used for tithe.

Highlands: The mountainous interior of the island of New Guinea. Until the 1930s the various colonial administrations believed that it was uninhabited.

Highlanders: The people from the mountainous interior of Papua New Guinea. Their cultural patterns are distinct from the cultural patterns of the people from the coastal areas.

Karinj: The name given to people living on the western side of a major river. It is also used to refer to a major fight alliance made up primarily of groups living on the western side of the river.

Kepel: A pre-Christian Nembi cult. The ancestral spirits lived in stones and were considered to be a part of the family. Most men had some spirit stones that they looked after.

Kiap: The Pidgin word for patrol officer.

Kina: PNG currency. A kina consists of one hundred *toea*.

Mandated Territory of New Guinea: (Sometimes shortened to the Mandated Territory). In the treaties that were negotiated following World War One, the Germans lost their Pacific colonies. Australia was designated as the colonial administrators of the former German New Guinea under a mandate from the League of Nations.

Marita: The fruit of one type of pandanus or screw pine tree.

Missionization: The people had come under the influence of the Christian missions working in their areas.

Moga: The term refers to a system of competitive exchange that operates between groups or individuals and is prevalent in and unique to the Melpa people living in the Mount Hagen area. It is more commonly called *moka* in literature. The administration in the 1950s and 1960s used *moga* as an umbrella term for all compensation payments and exchanges. By 1978 the Nembi had redefined the term to mean primarily mortuary payments.

Neu Guinea Kompagnie: The New Guinea Company—a German business enterprise that claimed land on the island of New Guinea, pressured Germany to claim a colony in the South Pacific to protect German business interests and was the first colonial administrator of German New Guinea.

Pacification: the process of bringing the groups under government control. Many of the groups in Papua New Guinea were either engaged in warfare amongst themselves, resisted the advances of the colonial administration, or both.

PANGU Pati: Papua New Guinea's first political party formed in June of 1967. The members of this party led the push for independence. The acronym stands for Papua and New Guinea United.

Papua: The southwest quadrant of the island of New Guinea. It was claimed as a British protectorate in 1884.

Patrol Officers: Colonial administrative officials who were responsible for the exploration and pacification of newly contacted indigenous groups.

Peaceful Penetration: A policy established by Sir Hubert Murray in the administration of Papua prior to World War Two. When bringing new groups under the rule of colonial law, force was to be avoided if at all possible. Administrative officers were to refrain from using force against newly contacted groups unless they were attacked first.

Papa Tumbuna: Grandfathers, great uncles, or male ancestors.

Papua New Guinea: The name chosen when the territories became an independent nation in 1975.

Pidgin: Neo-Melanesian—one of the official trade languages used in Papua New Guinea.

Restricted: Only government personnel—patrol officer or local members of the constabulary—were allowed into restricted areas. The only way outsiders, including missionaries, were allowed to enter an area was to accompany one of the government patrols or to obtain a special permit.

Singsing: A traditional dance.

Spiritual Harvest Ministry: A millenarian cult based in the Nembi Valley that promises special blessings to people who support Israel and claims that the people in the Nembi Valley are a part of the lost tribe of Benjamin.

Tanget: Broad leaves that the men tucked into their bark belts to cover their posterior.

Temo one: Literally red spirit. It is the name that the Nembi gave to the patrol officers and missionaries when they first began working among the Nembi people. In some dialects the term was *tomo honpi*.

Territory or Papua and New Guinea: The name given to Papua and New Guinea after World War Two until independence when the two territories were joined and administered as one.

Tiagaso **oil**: The sap of a palm tree that was a highly valued trade item in the Highlands of Papua New Guinea during pre-colonial days.

Timp: A pre-Christian Nembi cult. There were two *timp* cults—*tundu timp* (short *timp*) and *sollu timp* (long *timp*). The cult was passed from one group to the next for a price.

Toea: PNG coins. It takes one hundred *toea* to make a *kina*.

Tumbuna: Grandparents and/or other ancestors.

Wanbel: Literally "one belly." It means to be at peace, in agreement or untied.

Yeki: The Nembi name for the high God. The terms Yekil, Yekikele, Seki, or Sekil are also used.

Preface

The Churches of Christ in Christian Union (CCCU) began working in what was then the Territory of Papua and New Guinea (TPNG) in 1963 where they established a mission known as Christian Union Mission (CUM). In 1997 they formed a partnership with World Gospel Mission (WGM) and have continued to work in Papua New Guinea (PNG) to the present. I tell the story of CUM and WGM's work in PNG.

I was a part of the story that I tell. In April of 1970, I joined the Christian Union missionaries working in the Territory of Papua and New Guinea, and I continued working there until July of 2007 when I completed my service as a career missionary and left Papua New Guinea. My primary responsibilities were translation, literacy, and cultural studies, but I was also involved in numerous other ministries. For a number of years, I served as the field recording secretary. I held several other field offices during my time of service in Papua New Guinea, and for years I was a member of the field executive committee. I returned to the USA every three to five years for furloughs that lasted from nine to fourteen months. My final furlough was an extended furlough that started in May of 2002 and lasted for three years.

My interest in writing this history came from two sources. First, I wanted to share with my missionary colleagues the cultural insights that I had gained by working extensively with a translation committee and by living among the Nembi and Melpa people. Because I wanted to write from a current missiological perspective, in the spring of 2004 I enrolled in Asbury Seminary as an unclassified student. At the outset I took on-line courses in mission history and missiology, but I spent the 2004-2005 school year on campus where I studied on a full time basis. In July of 2005 I returned to Papua New Guinea for a final two-year term as a missionary with CUM/WGM.

The second impetus came from CUC of PNG. Because the Nembi and Melpa people embrace orality, stories are important to them. As the church developed, the people wanted to learn more about the CCCU in the USA. They asked how the missionaries ended up in the Nembi Valley in the Southern Highlands Province of Papua New Guinea. The church leaders expressed a desire for CCCU's story along with their stories of first contact, colonization, and missionization to be preserved in writing for the sake of future generations. In September of 2005 at a regional church conference held in Mount Hagen, the delegates talked of their desire for a missionary to work with them on a history of CUM/WGM's work in PNG, and pressured the field director to appoint someone to work on the project.

None of the church leaders called my name, but they kept looking directly at me as they talked about the history, and made it clear that they wanted me to assist with the project because they had come to view me as "*meri bilong buk na pepa*" (a woman of books and paper). I agreed to assist with the project, and during my last two years in PNG I began collecting stories and archival materials that would help in writing a history.

When I began my research, I expected to discover events that were highly significant and write about those particular events from the perspectives of both the missionaries and the Nembi and Melpa people. However, when I conducted interviews with the people and with the missionaries, recurring themes emerged from the interviews, and the events the interviewees recalled were related to the recurring themes. During my interviews of the Nembi and Melpa people, themes that surfaced included early contact, education or lack of education and training, development such as the establishment of trade stores or micro businesses, the medical ministry, the church constitution and its appropriateness for PNG societies, Sunday schools, youth ministries, women's ministries, control issues, relationships, outreach, and finances. The themes that emerged when I interviewed the missionaries included cultural differences, the establishment of an indigenous church, law and order problems, finances, dependency, outreach, and the relationship with the people, the church, its pastors and its leaders. Any retelling of history is a selective process, the construction of a narrative. The Nembi and Melpa construct one version, the missionaries construct another, and I am negotiating between the two. In writing the history, I write about significant events, the themes that are reflected by those events, and the different perspectives of those who experienced the events.

CCCU and its missionaries emphasized their beliefs in the "oneness of the Church of Christ," that Christ was "the only Head," and that the Bible was "the only rule of Faith and Practice."[1] Missionaries went in response to the command to "go and make disciples of all nations," and they went with the goal of evangelizing and establishing an indigenous church which they defined as "self-governing, self supporting, and self-propagating."[2] They assumed that the goal of every missionary was to work himself or herself out of a job, but most of them knew little else about mission theory, anthropology, or cross-cultural ministry.

At first both the home board and the missionaries on the field seemed hesitant to rely too heavily on studies in mission, but over time they became more open to mission studies. By the mid-1980s, interest in missiology was growing. A number of missionaries returned to school at the end of their first term in order

---

[1]*Constitution and Bylaws of the Churches of Christ in Christian Union.* [Circleville, Ohio: The Advocate Publishing House, 1963], 8.

[2]The missionaries could not have named Rufus Anderson as the mission theorist who declared that the aim for Christian mission was to establish, a "self-propogating, self-governing, self-supporting" church, but they embraced the teaching. See Rufus Anderson and R. Pierce Beaver. *To Advance the Gospel: Selections from the Writings of Rufus Anderson.* [Grand Rapids: Eerdmans, 1967], 38.

to study linguistics or missiology. At least five of the missionaries attended extension courses that Fuller Theological Seminary offered at Christian Leaders Training College (in Banz). Four of the missionaries took extended furloughs to attend Fuller Theological Seminary, and three completed degrees. All four returned to Papua New Guinea for at least one more term of service. As I write this history, I ask what the missionaries knew about mission theory at that stage, and how what they learned changed their perspectives and their approach to their work among the Nembi and Melpa people.

My research has involved participant observation, library research, and interviews of both missionaries and the local people. I was a participant observer during the 37 year span that I was in Papua New Guinea. During my first two terms I was primarily a learner and an observer. I tried to participate in the daily activities of the people. I wrangled invitations from some of the women to stay overnight in their homes. I went to the gardens and asked them to teach me how to plant sweet potato vines with a digging stick only to have them replant the vines that I had improperly placed in the ground. I learned how to spin yarn on my knee, and the women taught me how to make a string bag.[3] When the people held a pig festival, I observed all of the activities leading up to pig kill as well as the pig kill itself. I watched as they settled their debts, welcomed guests from Lake Kutubu, and conducted a number of *singsings* (dances). I took notes, asked questions, and kept a journal of my observations of and participation in local events. Later I used those observations to prepare a cultural notebook divided into categories of ecology, technology, kinship, socio-political system, religion, and values.[4] I recorded and transcribed several Nembi myths and legends during the 1970s and first half of the 1980s. These personal records provided insights into the perspectives of both the missionaries and the Nembi people in 1970s and early 1980s.

I became more deeply involved in the translation program from the mid 1980s until the program was completed in 2002. I learned from my Nembi co-translators and the translation committee as we worked our way through the New Testament and from the literacy workers and teachers as we prepared literacy teaching materials. I also had extensive interaction with the church leaders and participated in many of the meetings between the missionaries and the church leaders.

For the library research, I located published ethnographies, books, and articles. There is a wealth of published sources, and I gained many valuable insights from the work of others who have studied Melanesian religions and/or the Nembi and Melpa people. I rely on the work of others to tell the story of exploration, colonization, first contact, and other events that occurred prior to World War Two.

---

[3]They never let me start the string bag because they said that it was too difficult for me to learn. After they completed the first row, it was easier, and they taught me how to complete the bag. I finished one, but it was far from perfect, and had holes in several places.

[4]I had no formal training in ethnographic research. I used the following book as a guide, and it suggested placing "anthropological notes" into those categories. Alan Healey. *Language Learner's Field Guide.* [Ukarumpa, Papua New Guinea: Summer Institute of Linguistics, 1975].

In addition, when the data pointed me in that direction, I searched websites such as NASA, the UN, the Australian Government, and others.

I began archival research in 2005 after I made the commitment to CUC of PNG to assist with a history project. On several different occasions between 2005 and 2007 I spent time in Port Moresby where I made daily trips to the PNG National Archives and read through stacks of post-World War Two patrol reports and made photo-copies of anything that referred to the Nembi area. For primary documents written before World War Two I searched the on-line collection of the Australian National Archives at http://www.naa.gov.au/col-lec-tion/search/. I looked at mission reports that included not only articles that missionaries wrote for the *Missionary Tidings* and the *Evangelical Advocate* published by the CCCU or the *Call to Prayer* published by WGM, but also unpublished documents including official minutes and correspondence of the CCCU General Missionary Board, the CUM field council, and the field executive committee. In addition, some of the missionaries shared with me personal journals, letters, pictures and e-mails.

I conducted open ended interviews of numerous Nembi and Melpa people. Many Nembi "old timers" who experienced colonization, pacification, derestriction[5] and missionization[6] are still living. I spent eleven weeks in Papua New Guinea in November and December of 2009 and January of 2010 during which I interviewed and recorded the stories of more than ninety of the Nembi and Melpa people. I interviewed the regional board of trustees and some of the district boards as a unit, and many of the church leaders and former church leaders individually. Some interviewees were elderly people who recalled their interaction with the colonial administrators during the 1950s, 1960s, and 1970s. A few were second and third generation people who have heard the stories of the older people, but did not live through the experience themselves. A number of the incidents that the interviewees recalled are corroborated in the Australian Officer's Patrol reports or in the mission records. These stories serve as primary sources that reflect the views of the Nembi participants. For the interviews I used the language of the interviewee's choice. A few chose to be interviewed in English, many used Pidgin, and some spoke in Nembi Angal Enen or used a strange combination of the three.

---

[5]The terms "pacification" and "derestriction" were used by the colonial administration to indicate the degree of control the colonial administration had over the local people. "Pacification" is defined as the process of bringing the groups under government control. Many of the groups in Papua New Guinea were either engaged in warfare amongst themselves, resisted the advances of the colonial administration, or both. As long as they were fighting among themselves and/or as long as they resisted the colonial administration's advances, they were not "pacified," and the area remained "restricted." Only government personnel—patrol officer or local members of the constabulary were allowed into "restricted" areas. The only way outsiders, including missionaries, were allowed to enter an area was to accompany one of the government patrols or obtain a special permit to allow them to enter. When the people quit fighting among themselves and submitted to government controls, the area was "derestricted" and outsiders were allowed to enter freely.

[6]The term "missionization" means that the people had come under the influence of the Christian missions working in their areas.

In December of 2013 and January of 2014, I returned to PNG and worked with the church's regional secretary to prepare a Pidgin history prior to a fifty-year celebration held in January. I conducted no formal interviews during that time, but had many conversations with various people. Some of the information that I learned from Rick Pombre, who worked with me on the history, and others was very helpful in writing Chapters Seven and Eight.

More than seventy-five people have served as missionaries for CUM and WGM in PNG. I interviewed all but seventeen of them. Three declined an interview, three were short term workers whom I have been unable to locate; seven are deceased, and four began serving in PNG after 2008. I was able to interview the spouses of three of the deceased missionaries. Most of the interviews were face to face open ended interviews which lasted anywhere from an hour and a half to three hours. I had two or more sessions with several of the interviewees, especially missionaries who served between 1963 and 1985. A few of the interviews were conducted by telephone and these lasted from forty-five to ninety minutes. I recorded all interviews on a digital tape recorder, and transcribed or summarized many of the interviews. The interviewees were very generous with their time and did their best to recall the events from the past, but much of the chronology and many of the details of the oral accounts had grown fuzzy. However, the oral records supplemented the written records and provided new insights into the events.

The historian's goal is to strive for as much objectivity as possible, but to be aware of his or her perspectives and biases and to guard against personal biases as much as possible in order to write the most objective and accurate story that he or she can produce.

Christian historians have been criticized for allowing their faith to interfere with good academic scholarship. Maxie B. Burch looks at contemporary evangelical historians, and the way that they integrate their faith with their commitment to academia. At times evangelical groups have sanitized their history to make it more acceptable to their constituency, causing the history to lose credibility in the academic world.[7]

Some Christian histories and biographies are little more than hagiography. Alan Neely defines missionary hagiography as "*sanitized* or *idealized* accounts of missionaries' lives that stress their goodness, sacrifice, success, suffering, and victories over temptation, self, sin, opposition, and death, while minimizing or ignoring altogether their frailties, mistakes, and not infrequent wrongdoing."[8] Neely says that many missionary biographies, journals, autobiographies, memoirs, articles, and correspondence are "indisputably hagiographical" and some historians have relegated them to the realm of folk tales, myths, and legends.[9]

---

[7]Maxie B. Burch, *The Evangelical Historians: The Historiography of George Marsden, Nathan Hatch, and Mark Noll.* [Lanham, Md: University Press of America, 1996], 36.

[8]Alan Neely, "Saints Who Sometimes Were: Utilizing Missionary Hagiography," *Missiology* XXVII, no. 4 [October 1999], 442.

[9]Neely, 441-442.

Like all historians, Christian historians' writings reflect their cultural values, and all historians must be aware of their worldviews, and acknowledge them. There is no such thing as an unbiased historian and those who acknowledge their own biases while striving to write as objectively and with as much integrity as possible may gain a hearing in the academic community.[10]

I have been a part of the history that I will write about Christian Union Mission's work among the Nembi and Melpa people. I have been a mission insider but an outsider to the Nembi and Melpa people, and I have written from a missionaries' perspective but tried to understand the perspective of the Nembi and Melpa people. The importance of owning my worldview, my perspectives, and biases, of writing with honesty and integrity and striving for as much objectivity as possible is magnified because of my participation in the events. I have tried to avoid sanitizing the history. I have not avoided writing about events that reflect unfavorably on the mission and I have not written to a particular audience, saying only what I think the home constituency, the mission leaders, the missionaries, or the Nembi and Melpa people want to hear. Writing honestly about the good, the beautiful, the bad, and the ugly gives greater honor to God who has worked through the human beings involved in the story to accomplish His purposes. At the same time, I have tried to be sensitive to the concerns of the people who have contributed to the history by sharing their stories. My goal has been to write honestly about the events and the various perspectives without malice or ill intent.

---

[10]Burch, 41-48.

Acknowledgments

The writing of this book has been a lifelong journey for me. I began working among the Nembi people in 1970 and ended my career as a full time missionary when I left Papua New Guinea in 2007. Writing the history has brought home to me the concept of *missio Dei*. Mission is God's mission. It is not the mission of CCCU or WGM or any other denominational agency. It is God's mission, and He works through the church to accomplish His purposes. The noted missiologist, David Bosch says, "Mission is…a movement from God to the world; the church is…an instrument for that mission. …To participate in mission is to participate in the movement of God's love toward people, since God is the fountain of sending love."[1] It is God who calls people to cross-cultural ministry, and it is God who fully understands the culture of the messengers and the receivers of the message. He understands all of the cultural understandings, misunderstandings, limitations, and miscommunications. He works through people to grow His church around the world. I am honored that He has allowed me to be a part of His mission.

I am grateful to Asbury Theological Seminary and to the E. Stanley Jones (ESJ) School of World Mission for accepting me into its program, providing scholarships, and giving me the opportunity to look back at the mission in which I participated and analyze its strengths and weaknesses. The faculty members have shown an interest in me and my work and have encouraged me not to give up.

I am extremely grateful to my mentor, Dr. Michael A. Rynkiewich who has taken a keen interest in my work and has patiently read, reread, critiqued, and recritiqued the volumes I have written. His advice has always been "spot on" and I am deeply indebted to him. I also appreciate the input that my readers, Dr. Lalsangkima Pachuau and Dr. Eunice Irwin have given me. The comments and insights that they have brought to the project have always been helpful. Dr. Irwin has been my neighbor and friend and has encouraged me never to give up.

The staff members of the Asbury Information Commons have helped me tremendously. Lisa Setters, and Linda Fleck were especially helpful in my quest for out-of-print books and articles and other library resources. They succeeded in finding nearly everything that I requested, which was no small feat!

I have been greatly encouraged by my fellow students in the ESJ school of World Mission. The ESJ sisters is a group of women enrolled in advanced study

---

[1]David Jacobus Bosch, *Transforming Mission: Paradigm Shifts in Theology of Mission.* [Maryknoll, N.Y.: Orbis Books, 1991], 390.

programs at Asbury Seminary. We met together regularly, and they have been a special source of encouragement as I worked and researched.

I am grateful to my missionary colleagues. Many welcomed me into their homes for overnight visits so that they could tell me about their experiences and their memories of their service in PNG. Others carved time out of their busy schedules to grant lengthy telephone interviews.

My brothers, John, Joe, and Dan Tipton, my sisters-in-law Emalie Hayes Tipton and Dixie Campbell Tipton along with my parents, Marion Luther Tipton and Audrey Dixon Tipton (until their demise) have always supported my life choices and assisted me in countless ways. I feel deep gratitude for the family that God gave to me.

Finally, I am profoundly indebted to the Nembi and Melpa people. When I returned to PNG for a research trip in 2009, they provided for me, took care of me when I visited their areas, and sought me out so that I could record the stories that they wanted to be included in "our" history. It is their stories that give the greatest substance to the history. I will be eternally thankful for the privilege I have had of living and working among them.

Chapter One

Background and Setting

Introduction

In January of 1963 the Churches of Christ in Christian Union (CCCU) sent James and Virginia Hummel to begin a work in what was then the Territory of Papua and New Guinea (TPNG). A year later the Hummels began working among the Nembi people living in the Nipa/Poroma area of what was then the Southern Highlands District (later Southern Highlands Province) under the name of Christian Union Mission (CUM).

When the missionaries entered their world, the Nembi people were curious about the strangers who came to work among them. The missionaries and the Nembi people did not understand each other, and each group had its own reasons for accepting or tolerating the other, as will be shown later. As I write the story of CUM's work among the Nembi people of the Southern Highlands Province and a group of Melpa people living on the fringes of Mount Hagen in the Western Highlands Province of Papua New Guinea, I show how the different perspectives of colonial administrators, the Nembi, the Melpa, the Euro-American missionaries, and even the sending church administrators shaped their interactions with each other. The story includes events that occurred between 1935 and the 2015. Although Christian Union Mission did not begin its work among the Nembi until 1964 and the Melpa until 1983, the time frame is expanded because events that occurred during the colonial administration's first contact with the Nembi people influenced the events that unfolded after 1964.

The missionaries and the Nembi people met and interacted with each other with no clear understanding of the other's perspective. People with an individualistic and dualistic perspective interacted with people with a group oriented and less dichotomized perspective. Because of their different cultural perspectives, the expectations that each held for the other stood in opposition, percipitated repeated conflict, and remained unrealized.

As I write, I consider the perspectives of both the missionaries and the Nembi and Melpa. In doing so, I acknowledge that as a mission insider and a Nembi/Melpa outsider, I can never fully understand the Nembi and Melpa perspective.

Everything I learn from them I filter through my own cultural lenses. Nevertheless, constantly I negotiate the tensions between the themes and events that were significant to the missionaries and those that were important to the Nembi and Melpa people, consider the differences in the ways they understood the events, ascertain how the events were related to the recurring themes, and determine why those particular themes were important.

I write about the conflict between two of the pioneer missionaries because of its impact on the work in its beginning stages and because many of the Nembi people whom I interviewed spoke about it. I have said little about other conflict between missionaries or between the missionaries on the field and stateside authorities. That occurred frequently, but conflict arising out of the different cultural perspectives of the Western missionaries and the Melanesian church leaders is more relevant to this history.

The history is divided into eight chapters. The first (current) chapter gives the background and describes the setting. It describes pertinent geographical and historical background for Papua New Guinea and describes the first contact[1] experience of the Nembi people and the follow-up visits that administrative officials made to the Nembi area prior to World War Two.

Chapter Two is entitled *Colonization*, and it tells the story of renewed contact with the Nembi groups following World War Two. The process of pacification and derestriction among the Nembi occurred during the 1950s and early 1960s, and they finally accepted the administrative presence.

Chapter Three is called *Missionization*, and it covers the years of 1963 to 1978. It tells the story of Christian Union Mission's initial outreach to the Nembi people. There is some overlap between chapters two and three, but I do not discuss the mission's work in detail until Chapter Three. Both chapters two and three will allude to the relationship between the mission and the colonial administration. In Chapter Three I discuss the missionaries' entrance to the Nembi area in 1964 and the various ministries that the mission started. Some of those ministries have continued to the present. The missionaries wrote the church's constitution and by-laws during this period with little input from the emerging PNG church. although the pastors were consulted about the by-laws. Papua New Guinea became an independent nation in 1975, and the Christian Union Church of Papua New Guinea was formally organized in 1978. The chapter ends with the church's first regional and district councils.

Chapter Four is called *Indigenization* and deals with the period from 1979-1982. During this period, the mission worked towards strengthening the newly founded church. The local church members were more involved in every phase of the work. Committees were organized for every ministry with both mission and church representatives serving on the committees. The committees made regular reports to the church boards and the mission council about the progress of the work and made recommendations about the work. Major changes took place in

---

[1]First contact refers to the first time that the colonial administration met a new group of indigenous people.

the medical ministry that the mission had begun in 1965. The Highlands Highway opened giving a road connection to the rest of the Highlands and the Northern Coast. The government set up its "work permit" system and required the submission of an organizational chart. Law and order issues began to surface. Fighting between local groups stopped during the colonial period, but it reemerged in 1981. For the first time a missionary's home was robbed as its occupants slept. The Bible school was reorganized several times. In December 1982 at the annual regional meeting a confrontation occurred which brought the indigenous church's dissatisfaction to the fore, forced the mission to reevaluate its approaches to mission, and started negotiations between the church and the mission about the work in PNG. This meeting was a watershed event as it began a new chapter in the church/mission history although the relationship between the two has often been rocky.

The fifth chapter is called *Nationalization*. I make the term *Nationalization* distinct from *Indigenization* because during this period the church came more into its own. It lasted from 1982 to 1998. A church representative visited the USA. The mission began to withdraw more, and the indigenous church and mission reached out to Mount Hagen and Port Moresby. The mission involvement in the medical work ended abruptly when the sister-in-charge was robbed and injured in her own home, and the mission withdrew from the medical work without giving the church or the local people a chance to respond to the situation. The church eventually assumed the total responsibility for the medical work. The mission became known as the "*guria* mission,"[2] a name that was applied even more widely after the mission left Farata and Ka.

The organizational structure was changed with the church and mission functioning as two separate autonomous bodies, and a church mission coordinating council (CMCC) was organized with the hope of coordinating the ministries of both bodies. Landowners at Ka began to move in on the mission ground. The relationship between the missionaries and the PNG church was often very tense, and the missionaries were frequently at odds among themselves. In 1995 at Ka station Rosemary Lawhun died suddenly of a heart attack. WGM and CCCU formed a partnership and WGM took over the administration of the field in January of 1997. There were numerous incidents of local warfare. Fighting at Farata closed the station in 1994. Fighting broke out between Utabia and Upa following the 1997 national election. It had far-reaching effects, and nearly closed the churches in Port Moresby. CMCC continued to meet, but it did not work well, and the churches began to declare that the church and the mission are not "*wanbel.*"[3]

---

[2]*Guria* is a Pidgin term which means to shake, tremble, shiver or quake. When *guria* was used to describe the mission, it meant a trembling, shaking, fearful mission.

[3]*Wanbel* means in agreeement or at peace. Throughout the church and mission history, and especially after the structure was changed so that the church and mission functioned as separated autonomous bodies, the statement that the church and mission are not *wanbel* was heard repeatedly.

Chapter Six is entitled *Maturation*. It began in 1999 and continued to 2015. I start there because that was the year that the mission finally left Ka. Tribal fighting in the Ka area was intense, making it very difficult to carry out any of the ministries effectively. The mission withdrew from Ka in April of 1999. The translation of the New Testament was completed in 2002. The Bible school opened in Mount Hagen in 2005. The relationship between the church and mission[4] oscillated between negative and positive. Missionaries returned to the Nembi area in 2011.

Chapter Seven is called *Frustration*. One of the church leaders started a movement called the "Spiritual Harvest Ministry." It developed into a millenarian cult with cargo expectations, and many people in Ka District followed his teachings. In 2009 Christian Union Church of Papua New Guinea voted to expel him and his followers from the church organization.

The eigthth and final chapter is *Revitalization*. It asks where we go now and what can be learned from the history. The church is moving towards a time of revitalization as some of the leaders examine their culture in the light of scriptures to see how the two interact. Finally, it challenges the sending church and mission to ask how to best relate to the Melanesian church rather than how to push it away from dependency.

Oceania and Melanesia Defined

Papua New Guinea is a part of the culture area known as Oceania, which is divided into Polynesia, Micronesia, and Melanesia. Melanesia is an oblong shaped area located south of Micronesia, west of Polynesia, and north and east of Australia. The name means "black islands" (referring to the people's skin color, not to the islands themselves). The area includes the island groups, from east to west, of the Fiji Islands, New Caledonia, Vanuatu (formerly the New Hebrides), the Solomon Islands, the Torres Strait, the Bismarck Archipelago, and New Guinea. The map shows the divisions of Oceania.[5]

Some experts say that Fiji is a part of Polynesia rather than Melanesia because, though Fijians are dark skinned, they speak a Polynesian language and share Polynesian culture and social structure. The Philippines lie to the west of Oceania and are considered to be a part of Asia.[6] Most of Indonesia, also a part of

---

[4]Throughout the paper "mission" and "church" refer to different entities. I use "mission" to refer to the missionaries and their agency, specifically Christian Union Mission. I use the term "church" to refer to the indigenous church, specifically Christian Union Church of Papua New Guinea" and its leaders.

[5]Darrell Tryon "Language Distribution in the Pacific" Australian National University. http://press.anu.edu.au/oceanic_encounters/mobile_devices/ch02s02.html [accessed on September 4, 2014].

[6]There are some who consider the people as Pacific islanders rather than Asians (Conversation with Andy Ponce).

Asia, lies west of Melanesia, however West Papua, the western half of the island of New Guinea, is a part of Melanesia culturally but is an Indonesian province.[7]

Although the prehistory of the people of Oceania can never be fully known, anthropological, linguistic, and archaeological research suggests that there were two major land masses in what is now known as the Pacific Ocean, and between the two continents was a chain of islands separated by narrow straits which allowed people to travel between them. It is believed that at the end of the last ice age, the ocean levels rose and much of the connecting land disappeared. Later, Austronesian speakers from Southeast Asia improved their sailing skills and developed canoes and/or rafts capable of going on long distance ocean voyages, and migrated to all of the islands in the South Pacific. The Austronesians settled in the Philippines, Malaysia and Indonesia, and these communities spawned other explorers who arrived off the coast of New Guinea about 4000 years ago. The Austronesians either absorbed the people already living on the islands into their own group or forced them to migrate to the more isolated inland regions of the island. Evidence of the migration is found in the differences in Austronesian and non-Austronesian languages of Melanesia and in the cultural differences of the Highlanders and the Coastal groups of New Guinea.[8]

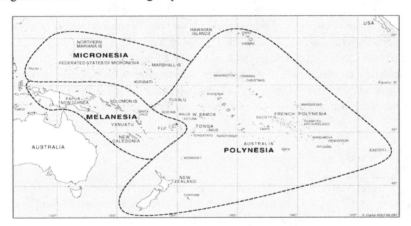

Map 1: Oceania

Pre-Colonial Contact with Westerners

Explorers, traders, labor recruiters, plantation owners, and missionaries worked throughout Melanesia before European nations formally established colonies in the region. Most of them approached the islands in well-armed ships and did

---

[7]Mapsouthpacific.com "Map South Pacific" http://www.mapsouthpacific.com/paci-fic/index.html [accessed on September 4, 2014].

[8]Michael A. Rynkiewich, *Cultures and Languages of PNG: The Story of the Origins, Migrations, and Settlement of Melanesian Peoples, Language, and Cultures.* [Goroka, Eastern Highlands Province, Papua New Guinea: Melanesian Institute, 2004], 17-27.

not hesitate to use their guns. Before the European colonial powers expressed an interest in acquiring colonies in the South Pacific, settlers including missionaries claimed land in New Ireland, New Britain, and the Duke of York Islands.[9]

Whalers, traders of sandalwood and *beche-de-mer*, and labor recruiters became active throughout Oceania, and their contact with the islanders was often violent.[10] When laws were passed allowing plantation owners in Fiji and Queensland to contract Melanesians as indentured workers for a period of three years, a *defacto* slave trade developed. Unscrupulous men engaged in illegal labor trade that became known as 'blackbirding.' They visited the Islands, kidnapped the Melanesians, and took them to Fiji and Queensland to work as plantation laborers with no promise of a return to their homelands. The practice depopulated the islands and sowed discontent and mistrust among the Melanesians who resisted the Europeans with increasing violence.[11]

The Melanesian code of justice held groups accountable for any wrong doing that a member of the group committed. Any one from the offending group could be held responsible for an offense that another member of the group committed. When persons of European descent exploited, killed, or kidnapped Melanesians, the Melanesians retaliated against any other European who came their way. From the Melanesian perspective, the Europeans all belonged to the same group, and any European could be held accountable for and pay the consequences of another European's wrong doing. Killing one European for another's crimes satisfied the Melanesian code of reciprocity, but it angered the Europeans who saw it as a gross miscarriage of justice when Melanesians took the life of an innocent person. As the tensions increased, European citizens who had settled in the South Pacific pushed the European powers to establish protectorates and/or colonies in the area.

---

[9]Michael A. Rynkiewich, "Land Acquisition during the German Period" in *Land and Churches in Melanesia: Issues and Contexts*, ed. Michael A. Rynkiewich [Goroka, EHP, Papua New Guinea: Melanesian Institute, 2001], 250.

[10]J. D. Legge. *Australian Colonial Policy; A Survey of Native Administration and European Development in Papua.* [Sydney: Angus and Robertson, 1956], 7-8.

[11]Edward Wybergh Docker. 1970. *The Blackbirders, the Recruiting of South Seas Labour for Queensland, 1863-1907.* [Sydney: Angus and Robertson, 1970], 180-190, 224. Docker documents the story of blackbirding in this book. A few of the labor recruiters tried to deal honestly with the South Sea islanders by making sure they understand the length of service they were committing to before they were taken to work on the plantations, but kidnapping was more common, and if a village the blackbirders visited failed to produce the number of laborers the captain of the ship demanded, it was not uncommon for the ship's crew to spray the village with gun shots and/or to burn the offending villages. Many of the blackbirders were also involved in illegal firearms trade with South Sea Islanders trading guns for laborers. Most labor traders did not keep a record of their activities. The exception is William T. Wawn who kept a log and later published a firsthand account of his work as a labor recruiter in a book published in 1893 entitled *The South Sea Islanders and the Queensland Labour Trade.*

Christian Mission in Oceania

Mission outreach to Oceania began first in Polynesia and spread from there to Micronesia and Melanesia. The Protestant mission to the South Pacific was initiated by three newly formed mission societies—the London Mission Society (LMS), the Wesley Mission Society (WMS), and the Church Mission Society (CMS), all of which originated in England and were influenced theologically by John Wesley and George Whitfield and the Evangelical Revival in England.[12] The London Missionary Society was the first to work in Oceania. It arrived in Tahiti in the Society Islands on Sunday March 5, 1797, on a ship called *Duff* with 30 missionaries on board.[13]

John Williams joined the mission in the Society Islands in 1817 and was based on the island of Raiatea. He had a vision for planting churches, and became convinced that Polynesians could be effective evangelizers, while the expatriate missionaries would never accomplish the task of evangelizing the South Pacific Islands on their own. Williams acquired a schooner named the *Endeavor* that he used solely for outreach to the islands.[14] In 1821 he sent out Polynesian teachers[15] from Raiatea to carry the message to other Polynesian islands where the chiefs were willing to accept them and offer them protection. Thus, John Williams developed a strategy that was repeated throughout the South Pacific for the next 160 years. The Gospel moved from Tahiti to the Cook Islands, and on to Tonga, Samoa and Fiji.[16] The stories of the indigenous missionaries will never be fully told, but two books, *The Deep Sea Canoe* by Alan Tippett and *Polynesian Missions in Melanesia* edited by Crocombe and Crocombe, focus on the role that the indigenous missionaries played in carrying the Gospel to the islands of Polynesia and Melanesia. Many of the Polynesian missionaries became missionary martyrs in Melanesia.

The first missionaries to settle permanently on mainland New Guinea were Cook Islanders working with the London Missionary Society and led by Ruatoka. After several unsuccessful attempts to establish stations elsewhere along the Papuan coast, Ruatoka and his associates established a permanent station at Port Moresby on November 26, 1873.[17] A year later William and Fanny Lawes and

---

[12]A. R. Tippett. *The Deep-Sea Canoe: The Story of Third World Missionaries in the South Pacific.* [South Pasadena, CA: William Carey Library, 1977], 13-16.

[13]John Garrett. *To Live Among the Stars: Christian Origins in Oceania.* [Geneva: World Council of Churches, 1972], 22-23.

[14]Garrett, 30.

[15]Ron Crocombe and Marjorie Crocombe, eds. *Polynesian Missions in Melanesia: From Samoa Cook Islands and Tonga to Papua New Guinea and New Caledonia.* Suva, Fiji: [The Institute of Pacific Studies, 1982], 1.

[16]Tippett, *The Deep Sea Canoe*, 18-21.

[17]Crocombe and Crocombe, 59-62.

their small son joined Ruatoka and the other Cook Islanders at Port Moresby.[18] In 1877 James and Jane Chalmers joined the Lawes family. After a brief visit at Port Moresby for initiation, Chalmers settled on the Island of Suau near the Southern tip of New Guinea. Jane died in February of 1879, and Chalmers relocated to Port Moresby in July, 1879.[19] Lawes and Chalmers became recognized for their knowledge of Southwest New Guinea, its people, and the Motu language. They were frequently asked to assist newcomers, interpret, or liaise between the Europeans and the local people.[20] They became participants in the move towards colonization.

Colonialization in Papua and New Guinea

Until the last quarter of the nineteenth century when tensions over territorial claims among the various colonial powers mounted, European colonial powers had no interest in claiming the Island of New Guinea as a colony. In the late 1800s, the French and Germans actively explored the South Pacific and claimed several islands, and the British and Germans haggled over islands where their citizens had established plantations. Citizens of Australia, a well-established British colony, wanted Britain to annex New Guinea to establish a buffer zone between Australia and Germany or any other power interested in the South Pacific. The British repudiated annexation, but Germany and Australia vied for the unclaimed portion of the island of New Guinea.

As early as 1880, Adolf von Hannesmann, a German businessman, declared that the South Pacific was wide open for colonization, and that Germany should stake her claim.[21] A German newspaper, the *Allgemeine Zeitung*, printed an article on November 27, 1882 calling for the "German nation to take in hand the colonization of New Guinea.[22] German planters and traders had plantations in the Bismarck Archipelago, but none on mainland New Guinea.

The Germans moved quickly to rectify the situation and create a "legitimate" claim to the northeast coast of mainland New Guinea. Otto Finsch, an anthropologist and ornithologist working for the *Neu Guinea Kompagnie* set out to acquire

---

[18]Oram, Nigel D. *Colonial Town to Melanesian City: Port Moresby 1884-1974.* [Canberra: Australian National University Press, 1976], 14; Langmore, Diane. *Missionary Lives Papua, 1874-1914.* [Honolulu: University of Hawaii Press], 3.

[19]Garrett 212-213.

[20]Langmore, Diane. *Missionary Lives Papua, 1874-1914.* [Honolulu: University of Hawaii Press, 1989], 211-213.

[21]Arthur J. Knoll and Hermann Hiery. *The German Colonial Experience: Select Documents on German Rule in Africa, China, and the Pacific, 1884-1914.* [Lanham, Md: University Press of America, Inc, 2010], 14.

[22]J. L. Whittaker, N.G. Gash, J. F. Hookey, and R. J. Lacey. *Documents and Readings in New Guinea History: Pre-history to 1889.* [Milton, Queensland: Jacaranda Press, 1975] 443. http://www.papuaweb.org/dlib/bk2/documents-ng/ [Accessed on September 9, 2014].

land for the company along the northeastern coast of New Guinea.[23] For about fifteen dollars in trade goods, he claimed that six men sold him all the nearby land and the rights to all of the "ownerless" land between the Dutch border and the Huon Gulf.[24] On October 17, 1884 he raised the German flag at his newly built house and in so doing established German's right to claim a colony on the Island of New Guinea.[25]

The Germans officially hoisted their flag in the Bismarck Archipelago on November 3, 1884, and on November 20, 1884, they raised their flag at the Friedrich Wilhelms (Madang) harbor on mainland New Guinea. The British raised their flag at Port Moresby on November 6, 1884 and claimed Papua, the Southeastern quadrant of the island, as its protectorate.[26] The island of New Guinea had been divided among the Germans, the British and the Dutch who claimed the southwest coast of New Guinea in 1828, and the entire Western half of the Island in 1848.[27]

Map 2: German and British New Guinea[28]

[23]Nikolaĭ Nikolaevich Miklukho-Maklaĭ, and C. L. Sentinella. *New Guinea Diaries, 1871-1883*. Madang, P.N.G.: Kristen Pres, 1975, 293

[24]Peter G. Sack. *Land Between Two Laws: Early European Land Acquisitions in New Guinea*. [Canberra: Australian National University Press, 1973].122-123.

[25]Sack, 123.

[26]Whittaker et al., 438-474.

[27]Gavin Souter. *New Guinea: The Last Unknown*. [Sydney: Angus and Robertson, 1963], 22.

[28]http://bookgainville.com/wp-content/uploads/2013/02/new-guinea.png [accessed on February 6, 2015]

The Germans claimed New Guinea to protect the commercial interests of German citizens.[29] They alienated vast tracts of land, assuming that any unoccupied land was ownerless and was theirs for the taking.[30] For the Germans it was all about land acquisition and the development of commercial enterprise, but for the New Guineans it led to the loss of land and the loss of freedom, and the implementation of forced labor. German people believed that a "protectorate for the benefit of Germany would ultimately benefit the natives by bringing the supposed advantages of German civilization."[31]

The British claimed Papua in part because Australian citizens wanted a buffer zone between Australia and the German colonies,[32] and in part to protect the Papuans from European exploitation. At first Lawes and Chalmers, LMS missionaries, resisted annexation. Nevertheless, when blackbirders victimized Papuans and land swindlers tried to snatch away Papuan land in 1883, the missionaries changed their thinking, and campaigned for Britain to take on the role of protecting Papuans from European exploitation. The missionaries favored a British protectorate over a colonial administration led by "Australian annexationists" who had treated poorly the indigenous people of Queensland.[33] The proclamation avowed that the protectorate's primary purpose was to protect the lives and properties of the Papuan people.[34] So, with vast colonies elsewhere, Britain was not really interested economically in Papua, but responded to pressure from missionaries and Queenslanders, in particular.

The German occupation of New Guinea was short lived. The Germans were in charge until the outbreak of World War One. After declaring War on Germany in August of 1914, the Australian military invaded the territory on September 11, 1914, and defeated the Germans in a single day.[35] The formal surrender of the German colonies to the Australian forces took place at Kokopo on September 21, 1914. The Australian military took over the administration of the colony without resistance from the German officials and remained in charge until after the war ended.[36] On December 17, 1920 the League of Nations officially designated the Commonwealth of Australia to be responsible for the governance of the Mandated Territory of New Guinea. Annual reports were to be sent to the League of Nations, and no changes could be made in the Mandate without the approval of the

---

[29]Sack, 73-74.

[30]Sack, 124.

[31]Miklukho-Maklaï and Sentinella, 332.

[32]Whittaker et al., 443-444.

[33]Langmore, 211-213.

[34]Whittaker et al., 464.

[35]S. S. Mackenzie. *The Australians at Rabaul: The Capture and Administration of the German Possessions in the Southern Pacific.* [Sydney: Angus and Robertson, 1941], 73-74. http://www.awm.gov.au/histories/first_world_war/volume.asp?levelID=67896[Accessed on September 12, 2014]

[36]De Groot, Nick. "Land Acquisition and Use During the Australian Period" in *Land and Churches in Melanesia: Issues and Contexts. Point Series No. 25.* edited by Michael Rynkiewich. (277-304). [Goroka, EHP, Papua New Guinea: Melanesian Institute, 2001], 283.

League of Nations.[37] The Japanese occupied the Mandated Territory on January 23, 1942, and the Australian civilians fled. During the war the territory became a battleground between the Allied and the Axis forces.[38]

Following World War One, the Territory of Papua remained a separate territory that was also under the control of Australia. After Papua was first declared a British Protectorate, it underwent several changes in administration. The Australians thought that making Papua a British protectorate would give Britain full authority over all persons living in the protectorate, regardless of their nationality or place of origin. However, the British courts declared that only British "subjects" would be under the authority of Great Britain. The protectorate established no jurisdiction over the indigenous people or foreigners who resided in the Papuan protectorate.[39] Not until the protectorate was annexed as a British Colony on September 4, 1888 did Britain claim full authority and jurisdiction over all who resided within British New Guinea's borders, regardless of their nationality.[40] The British annexed the colony with the understanding that the Australian colonies would assume responsibility for British New Guinea after Australia gained its independence. British New Guinea became the Australian Territory of Papua on September 1, 1906.[41]

John Hubert Puckett Murray became the acting administrator of Papua in 1907 and was permanently appointed to the position in 1908. He served as the lieutenant-governor of Papua for 32 years until his death on January 27, 1940.[42]

Exploration in both territories was difficult because of the rugged terrain and the resistance of many groups to outsiders. Slowly the administrative officials in both territories contacted the coastal groups and brought them under "administrative control." By 1930 "control" only "extended between ten and forty miles inland. The Australians were convinced…that the interior was largely uninhabited,"[43] and maps of the day showed that most of the interior remained unexplored. [44]

---

[37]League of Nations Mandate for the Territory of New Guinea 17 December, 1920. *Official Yearbook of the Commonwealth of Australia No 31-1938.* http://www.jje.info/lostlives/transcripts/D00044.html [Accessed on September 12, 2014]

[38]August Ibrum K. Kituai. *My Gun, My Brother: The World of the Papua New Guinea Colonial Police, 1920-1960.* [Honolulu: University of Hawai'i Press, 1998], 169.

[39]Whittaker et al., 494.

[40]Whittaker et al., 509-517.

[41]Stuart, Ian. *Port Moresby, Yesterday and Today.* [Sydney: Pacific Publications, 1970], 78.

[42]Brian Jinks, Peter Biskup, and Hank Nelson. *Readings in New Guinea History.* [Sydney: Angus & Robertson, 1973], 104; Stuart 88-89.

[43]Bob Connolly and Robin Anderson, *First Contact.* [New York, N.Y., U.S.A.: Viking, 1987], 11.

[44]See the map on the inside cover of James Sinclair's book, *Last Frontiers: The Explorations of Ivan Champion of Papua* published in 1988.

First Contact in the Highlands

First contact for the Highlands groups came in the 1930s. In the Mandated Territory of New Guinea the discovery of Gold in 1926 "only 35 miles inland from New Guinea's Northern coast"[45] brought an influx of gold prospectors from Australia. As the gold in the coastal areas played out, the gold prospectors moved deeper inland in hopes of discovering new deposits. Between 1930 and 1934 they made first contact with many of the Highlands groups living in the Mandated Territory of New Guinea and even crossed the border into Papua.[46] Much of the early contact in the Mandated Territory was violent. Most of the gold prospectors were quick to shoot, but even the patrol officers thought that violence was unavoidable.[47]

On the Papuan side first contact was generally more controlled than in the Mandated Territory. It occurred when the government sent out exploratory patrols that "discovered" the people living in the mountainous valleys of Papua. Sometimes it was violent, but fewer people died in Papua than in New Guinea. Murray developed a policy of "peaceful penetration." When bringing groups under the rule of colonial law, force was to be avoided. If attacked first, administrative officers could use force to accomplish the greater goal, but force was to be avoided if possible.[48] Western law and order would be introduced later after the people had become accustomed to the administrative presence.[49] The first goal was to establish a peaceful co-existence with the newly contacted groups. Fewer people

---

[45]Connolly, and Anderson, 10.

[46]The Leahy brothers, the Fox brothers, the Ashton brothers, the McKee brothers, and Ludwig Schmidt were among those who contacted new groups in the unexplored areas, but the Leahy brothers are the best known largely because they kept journals on their journeys. Michael Leahy, an amateur photographer, captured on film much of the journey and the people's reactions to first contact situations. A number of authors, including Michael Leahy have written books that document first contact in the Mandated Territory of New Guinea. They include Michael J. Leahy and Maurice Crain. [*The land That Time Forgot: Adventures and Discoveries in New Guinea.* New York: Funk & Wagnalls, 1937; Michael J Leahy, and Douglas E. Jones. *Explorations into Highland New Guinea, 1930-1935.* Tuscaloosa: University of Alabama Press, 1991 http://www.netlibrary.com/urlapi.asp?action =summary&v=1&bookid=20250 [accessed on September 26, 2014]; Gavin Souter. *New Guinea: The Last Unknown.* Sydney: Angus and Robertson, 1963; Bob Connolly and Robin Anderson, *First Contact.* [New York, N.Y., U.S.A.: Viking, 1987; and Bill Gammage. *The Sky Travellers: Journeys in New Guinea, 1938-1939.* Calton, Vic: Melbourne University Press, 1998.

[47]Bill Gammage, *The Sky Travellers: Journeys in New Guinea, 1938-1939.* [Calton, Vic: Melbourne University Press, 1998], 80-81.

[48]Hubert Murray, "The Scientific Aspect of the Pacification of Papua." in *Tribal Peoples and Development Issues: A Global Overview,* ed. John H. Bodley. [Mountain View, California: Mayfield Publishing Company, 1988], 42-51.

[49]James Patrick Sinclair. *Last frontiers: The Explorations of Ivan Champion of Papua: A Record of Geographical Exploration in Australia's Territory of Papua between 1926 and 1940.* [Broadbeach Waters, Gold Coast, Qld., Australia: Pacific Press, 1988], 238.

died in Papua, but when people resisted the patrols, the guns were just as deadly and contact was just as unexpected and traumatic for the Papuans as it was for the New Guineans.

During the 1930s, Jack Hides and Ivan Champion both led major exploratory patrols into the Papuan hinterlands. The stories of those and other patrols can be found in the writings of James Sinclair and Gavin Souter. Hides and Champion published books and articles about the patrols that they led. The books and articles by all of these men are included in the bibliography.

First Contact with the Nembi

First contact for the Nembi people occurred in May of 1935 when Jack Hides and James O'Malley led an exploratory patrol known as the Strickland-Puarari Patrol throughout much of what is now the Southern Highlands. They departed from Daru on January 1, 1935 on "the last major exploratory expedition to be carried out in nineteenth-century style, without benefit of prior aerial reconnaissance, without airdrops to replenish supplies, and without radio communications."[50] They carried food supplies, equipment for prospecting for gold, tents, lamps, matches, kerosene, ammunition and trade goods that would be used to purchase additional food. Hides had never encountered Papuans who were not eager to secure European steel knives and axes, and so he chose that as his main item for trading along with some cloth, beads, and small mirrors. He carried no shell with him. It was a major mistake because the Papuans he was about to encounter had no interest in European steel. They wanted only shell.[51]

The story of the Strickland-Purari patrol is well documented. Not only did Hides and O'Malley file the mandatory reports after the patrol had ended, in 1936 Hides published an account entitled *Papuan Wonderland*. James Sinclair wrote at length about the patrol in a biography of Jack Hides entitled *The Outside Man*. In the mid-1980s, Edward L. Schieffelin, who conducted research among the Kaluli people in the Mt. Bosavi area, and Robert Crittenden, who carried out research in the Nembi area, collaborated on a book about the Strickland-Purari patrol in which they sought to capture the perspective of the people whom Hides and O'Malley visited. The research took place in the late 1970s and the early 1980s almost fifty years after the patrol. It was carried out not only by Schieffelin and Crittenden but also by other scholars who had researched previously among the groups contacted during the patrol. In most areas, the researchers located and interviewed persons who experienced first contact, but in one or two areas none were still living.

The Wola people lived at the head of the Waga and Nembi Valleys, and the Nembi people dwelt further south all along the Nembi Valley system. The Nembi

[50]James Patrick Sinclair, *The Outside Man.* [Melbourne, Australia: Angus and Robertson Ltd, 1969], 118; Edward L Schieffelin and Robert Crittenden, eds. *Like People You See in a Dream: First Contact in Six Papuan Societies.* [Stanford, Calif: Stanford University Press, 1991], 52.

[51]Sinclair, *The Outside Man,* 125-127

and Wola were culturally and linguistically related; speaking languages that were partially intelligible to each other and having similar social systems organized around a complex exchange system. The groups were highly competitive; inter-clan rivalries were intense; violence frequently erupted; warfare was rife; and sorcery was widespread.[52] They had close trading links with the lowlanders of Lake Kutubu, and they considered the lowlands to be a "mysterious and danger-ous place."[53]

Although the Wola and Nembi had not yet met Europeans, and knew nothing of the Western world, they were well aware that a world existed beyond their borders.[54] The Nembi, Lai, Mendi and Kagua Rivers converge to form the Erave River, and in close proximity to the point of convergence was the Kuvivi ceremo-nial ground that belonged to some of the Nembi groups. It was a central trading junction for a number of major trade routes. The Nembi were known for being shrewd traders and men who knew how to drive a hard bargain. According to Crit-tenden, the Nembi people

> dominated the interchange between the Foi people of the Mubi Valley/Lake Ku-tubu area and the people of the Highlands valleys. This critical position made them widely desirable as exchange partners, and they had connections with people at all points of the compass. It was this rather than a highly productive agricultural system that supported their intense networks of competitive ceremonial exchange and enabled them to overcome many of the disadvantages of living in a marginal environment.[55]

By the time that the patrol reached Nembi and Wola country, the food supplies they carried were nearly exhausted, and the people were unwilling to accept the trade goods that Hides offered in exchange for food. On May 11, 1935, while still in Wola Country the patrol had a battle with Wola people at a place named Sez-inda and several men were killed. After the battle the people gave the patrol food and offered no further resistance.[56]

Crittenden says that a youth named Mombilal Nial lived with his maternal relatives at Merut[57] in Nembi country. He also had relatives among the Semin-al, another Nembi group. He was visiting his paternal relatives at Sezinda in Wola country and witnessed the battle and the deaths of several of his paternal relatives. Incensed, he hurried back to his place of residence at Merut. He informed the people of Semin-al and Merut of the patrol's approach and of the battle that had taken place at Sezinda and he urged them to revenge the death of his patrikin.[58]

On May 12, 1935 the patrol began its walk across the Nembi Plateau. It took the patrol six days to make its way through Nembi country. Its reception varied

---

[52]Schieffelin and Crittenden 125-128.
[53]Schieffelin and Crittenden, 136.
[54]Schieffelin and Crittenden, 128-135.
[55]Schieffelin and Crittenden, 130.
[56]Crittenden, "Across the Nembi Plateau," 154-166.
[57]The Merut are also known as the Tindom people.
[58]Robert Crittenden, "Across the Nembi Plateau," 176.

from group to group. Most resisted or antagonized the patrol, but the first group at Injip was undoubtedly aware of the battle at Sezinda. They sought to appease the patrol by welcoming them and feeding them well. The men collected sugar-cane and bananas along with sweet potatoes and other items and waited at their ceremonial ground for the patrol to arrive. Their strategy worked. When Hides saw the bounty and noted the friendly overtures of the local men, he camped there overnight.[59] Hides later wrote about the encounter, "Friendly men brought us plenty of food, and besides the usual banana and potato, we were given neat parcels of brown wood salt. ...They gave us bundles of cured ginger."[60] The group warned Hides that opposition lay ahead, but Hides assured them that the patrol was equal to any challenge it met.[61]

On May 13th the patrol passed through land belonging to the Semin-al and the Merut people. Both groups attacked the patrol. The Semin-al men mounted repeated attacks on the patrol. The patrol suffered no casualties although attackers wrestled one of the constables to the ground and would have killed the constable if Hides had not shot one of the assailants. By the time the patrol moved out of Semin-al territory at least six of the local men had been killed. When Crittenden did his research, the Semin-al no longer remembered exactly where the attacks had occurred, but they still recalled the names of the men who died.[62]

With no food and with no hope of purchasing it from the local groups, Hides instructed the carriers to harvest food from gardens as the patrol went along. In the Merut area, Hides decided to camp on a knoll that he thought would be defensible if an attack occurred. As the last of the patrol members arrived at the camp, they brought reports that men were approaching to stage a mass attack. A lone house stood in the clearing, and Hides sent the unarmed carriers into the house and instructed them to stay there. He and O'Malley and the ten police fought off their attackers.[63]

By the time that Crittenden carried out his research, the Merut stories of the attack were muddled. He says that the shouting men called for various courses of action. Some were concerned about the women and children who were in hiding. Some wanted to feed the patrol in an effort to appease it, and some wanted to attack. The voices of those who called for an attack proved to be the strongest.[64] O'Malley later recalled the shouts and yodeling of the men as they stormed the camp. The battle lasted for three hours—from around three in the afternoon until sundown.[65] Hides reported that there were six rushes during the three hours. He saw two dead bodies. Police Sargaent Orai testified that all of them would have died had they not defended themselves.[66]

---

[59]Crittenden, "Across the Nembi Plateau," 171-172.

[60]Jack Hides, *Papuan Wonderland.* [London: Blackie and Son, 1936], 124

[61]Hides, *Papuan Wonderland,* 127.

[62]Crittenden, "Across the Nembi Plateau," 176-180,

[63]Hides, *Papuan Wonderland,* 132-133

[64]Crittenden "Across the Nembi Plateau," 180.

[65]Sinclair, *The Outside Man,* 155

[66]Sinclair, *The Outside Man,* 155.

Sometime after the final rush had been repulsed, an old man appeared on a hill about 200 yards away, waved a fern and shouted a message three times.[67] Hides could not understand the message, but Crittenden says, "The old man was telling them to go away and leave the Merut in peace."[68] According to the Merut, fourteen men were killed and others were wounded.[69]

That night a sick carrier died, and the patrol members buried him in a grave hidden under leaves and ashes. By dawn the patrol had moved on and walked about a mile before unarmed men began to follow them in silence watching their every move.[70]

The Merut were stunned and devastated by what had happened. They were used to fighting, but they had never before encountered rifle fire. Crittenden says,

> The bodies...were collected together the next day after the patrol moved on and were hurriedly placed without funeral on ledges of the limestone cliffs of nearby pinnacles...The people in Merut and Semin-al were in a state of shock...They held no ceremony, no period of mourning over the dead. There were no mortuary payments of pearl shells and pigs to the clans of the mothers of the dead and no real thoughts of vengeance. On whom could they take revenge? Whether they were spirits or men, they were gone the next day.[71]

As the Merut were retrieving their dead, they discovered the hidden grave of the dead carrier but quickly buried the corpse again. Mombilal Nial circulated the story that he had killed the carrier.[72]

Slowly, the patrol made its way across the Nembi Plateau and out of the Nembi area. Men followed the patrol as it passed from the territory of one group to the next. The patrol bypassed several attempted ambushes. They asked repeatedly for food, but none was forthcoming.[73] At one point a self-appointed guide led them into an enclosure where about 300 men had gathered and were waiting with sugarcane and bananas. Hides noticed that the men had collected freshly cut saplings and rope, and convinced that the local men had set up a trap, he instructed police to stand guard at the entrances, and the patrol passed through without stopping to rest or accepting the proffered food.[74]

On another occasion, some Nembi men offered the patrol some poisoned sugar cane, but Hides suspected treachery and told the men not to eat it.[75] Twice warriors rushed the patrol, and four more Nembi men were killed. The only other Nembi group that opted to appease the patrol was at Mondomap where an elderly man befriended them. He assured Hides that he knew about the events of the day,

---

[67]Hides *Papuan Wonderland*, 135
[68]Crittenden "Across the Nembi Plateau," 183.
[69]Crittenden "Across the Nembi Plateau," 183.
[70]Hides, *Papuan Wonderland,* 136-138
[71]Crittenden, "Across the Nembi Plateau," 183.
[72]Crittenden, "Across the Nembi Plateau," 183-184.
[73]Hides, *Papua Wonderland*, 137-146.
[74]Hides, *Papuan Wonderland,* 142-143.
[75]Sinclair *The Outside Man,* 158.

but the patrol was now among friends and was welcome, and he invited them to stay. Numerous people visited the camp, but none of them carried weapons and they provided abundant food. The patrol stayed there for two days. The elderly man pointed out the "Elai" (Erave) River flowing in the distance.[76]

On May 16th the patrol approached Toiwara where they met the next to last Nembi group that they would encounter. The Mandamap and Toiwara groups were sworn enemies. When the patrol approached from Mandamap, the Toiwara people were wary. They offered minimal food and demanded high prices for the little food that they brought.[77] As the patrol was leaving Toiwara, the people set up two ambushes. At the first ambush, the men scattered at the sound of rifle fire. A little further on the patrol took one man as prisoner and made him their guide. For two days the patrol camped with their prisoner at Urida at the Southern-most edge of the Nembi area. As the patrol was leaving Urida with the prisoner, Hides realized that the local men planned a second ambush and avoided it by taking an alternate route. The prisoner led the patrol out of Nembi country to the Erave River where they built rafts. On May 23 when the patrol was ready to leave, Hides released the prisoner, gave him some gifts and told him to return to the safety of his people. The prisoner was the last Nembi person to have contact with the patrol.[78] The patrol passed through Kewa country on its way back to the coast. It arrived at Kikori government station on June 18, 1935. Hides was not a good map maker, and he could not pinpoint the exact locations of the places that he had visited.

The Nembi did not forget the first contact they had with Europeans. In 1970, shortly after I first arrived in the Nembi area, one of the missionaries was conversing with some of the local pastors when one of them said, *"Namba wan taim ol wait skin I kam long dispela hap, planti man ol I dai..."* (The first time white men came to this area many men died...). The others interrupted him before he could say more, telling him to be quiet. At that time, no amount of questioning could get them to say more about their first contact experience. Crittenden says that the Hides-O'Malley patrol made a lasting impression on the Nembi people, and that coupled with the quantities of shell that later patrols traded, gave them their "first impression of economic inferiority."[79]

When I interviewed Susi Tio, she recalled stories that her maternal grandmother told her about the "light skins" passing through the area "like tourists do today" but killing a lot of people. No one knew who the strangers were or where they came from, but most thought that the strangers were ancestral spirits returning from the dead. The Nembi called the light-skinned strangers *temo one* (red

---

[76]Hides, *Papuan Wonderland*, 150-152.

[77]Crittenden, "Across the Nembi Plateau," 170, 194

[78]Hides, *Papuan Wonderland*, 156-162; Crittenden, "Across the Nembi Plateau," 194-197.

[79]Robert Crittenden, *Sustenance, Seasonality and Social Cycles on the Nembi Plateau, Papua New Guinea.* [Canberra, Australia: Australian National University, 1982], 199.

spirits),[80] and after the massive killings on that first visit, the Nembi were thereafter afraid of the 'red spirits'.[81]

Follow-Up Contact with the Nembi

Subsequent patrols carrying an adequate supply of shell as their main trade item retraced Hides' journey, but it was several years before a patrol reentered the Nembi area. In 1936, Ivan Champion led the first follow-up patrol. In January of 1936, Champion, Hides, Taylor from the Mandated Territory, F. E. Williams the government anthropologist, and Lewis Lett took reconnaissance flights over the Mendi, Lai, Nembi, and Wage Valleys, as well as the Tarifuroro. They spotted a lake that Hides had missed on his trip. Hides named it Lake Marguerite after his wife, but when Ivan Champion, who made the first maps of the area, visited the lake a few months later, he learned the local name—Kutubu—and gave that name to the lake.[82]

The patrol that Champion led in 1936 traversed much of the territory that Hides had covered the previous year. Champion crossed the upper reaches of the Nembi Valley, but did not enter it. Some of the police officers had been with Hides on the Strickland-Purari patrol, and they recognized it as the valley that Hides had followed. Hides called it the *Wen* Valley, but Champion learned that *wen* meant presently, and that the people called the river the *Nembia*.[83] The next day the patrol crossed the Nembi River near its source on a log bridge and climbed to a nearby ceremonial ground "where ninety men were sitting in a line. Before them were sugarcane and sweet potatoes that "they signified belonged to us.""[84]

It was 1939 before patrols again visited the Nembi area, and most of the contacts were unsettling and/or violent. For the 1938-1939 fiscal year, patrol officers A. T. Timperley, O. J. Atkinson, and J. C. (Jack) Bramell joined Bill Adamson and Ivan Champion at Lake Kutubu. The government anthropologist, F. E. Williams spent six months in the area studying the culture and languages of the people at Lake Kutubu and in the Augu Valley.[85]

For the first time since Hides patrol in 1935, the government patrols entered the Nembi Valley where they found evidence of the Hides and O'Malley's 1935 visit to the area. A patrol led by Bill Adamson and A. T. Timperly visited the upper Nembi Valley.[86] They passed near Sezinda and the people showed them "the

---

[80]The term *temo one* means literally 'spirit red' or 'the red spirits'. The term changes according to the dialect. Some said *tem one, tom one* or *tomo one*.

[81]Susi Tio, interview by author, Mato, Poroma Census Division, Southern Highlands Province, Papua New Guinea, January 2, 2010.

[82]Sinclair, *Last Frontiers,* 130-133.

[83]Ivan Champion, "The Bamu Purari Patrol, 1936 (Continued)" *The Geographical Journal* 96, no. 4 [October, 1940]. 245. http://www.jstor.org/stable/1787580 [Accessed September 16, 2014].

[84]Ivan Champion, "The Bamu Purari Patrol, 1936 (Continued)," 245.

[85]Sinclair, *Last Frontiers,* 247-252.

[86]Sinclair, *Last Frontiers,* 256.

skull of one of the casualties...placed upon three sticks in the form of a shrine" and later Adamson reported seeing people wearing shell clips and cartridges as ornaments.[87]

As they traversed the Nembi Valley, shouting, yodeling, singing, and chanting Nembi men met the patrols. Adamson reported that as they passed through the upper Nembi Valley, they were "...accompanied by a vanguard of singing men who were all around. They kept up an ululating chant, the ones in front being answered by those behind...their ceaseless wailing chant gets on everyone's nerves."[88] As the patrol made its way down the valley they were met consistently with "cheerful, noisy tribesmen, celebrating the progress of the patrol" and trading "vast quantities of food for shell or handkerchief" which "the recipient would hold high above his head while the crowd would stamp upon the ground and yell. They would break into song" until Adamson's ears "positively sang with the noise, and the ground shook as if cattle were milling in a yard."[89]

When Champion and Bramwell visited the area where "Hides had his big fight,"[90] Champion carried a .22 rifle with him at all times, and gave daily demonstrations of the rifle's power by sticking a sweet potato on the end of a bow and shooting it off. He too commented on the constant yelling. "...at times one can get an uneasy feeling under the belt with a pack of screaming, yelling natives at the tail of the line...the whole idea is not to look round or be perturbed by their yelling when you are on the move."[91]

At several points the patrols witnessed tribal fighting and saw burned out houses, destroyed gardens, and casuarinas trees that had been debarked and/or cut.[92] Williams in his research among the Waga people in the Augu Valley learned how highly the people valued their casuarinas trees. An informant told him that during warfare, "After you have killed one or two of your enemies, carried off their pigs and burnt their houses, it is the crowning insult and injury to murder their beautiful casuarinas."[93]

When a seaplane picked up F. E. Williams on May 7, 1939, no groups had staged an attack on any of the patrols that entered their areas. Champion sent a report of the patrol that he and Bramell had just completed. Government influence was spreading, but Champion made no claim that the uncontrolled area was ready to be opened to non-government personnel. After receiving Champion's report,

---

[87]Schieffelin and Crittenden, 274.

[88]Sinclair, *Last Frontiers*, 257.

[89]Sinclair, *Last Frontiers*, 257.

[90]Sinclair, *Last Frontiers*, 258.

[91]Sinclair, *Last Frontiers*, 258

[92]Sinclair *Last Frontiers*, 258

[93]Williams, F. E. "Report on the Grasslanders: Augu—Wage—Wela" in Murray, Sir Hubert. *Territory of Papua Annual Report for the Year of 1938-1939*. [Canberra: Government of the Commonwealth of Australia, 1940], 42. Australian National Archives, Series Number M3816, Control Symbol 3 Item Bar Code 1182610 Page 362 of digitalized copy http://recordsearch.naa.gov.au/SearchNRetrieve/Interface/ListingRe-ports/ItemsListing. aspx [Accessed on October 7, 2014]

Murray declared the uncontrolled area would be open to European developers as of July 1, 1939.[94] Murray overstated the degree to which government influence had taken hold in the area,[95] but his decision to declare the uncontrolled territory "open" had little impact. Because of the political situation and increasing hostilities in Europe, no one was interested in entering the uncontrolled area.

Even as the ink was drying on Murray's proclamation, it became evident that the Nembi area was not under effective administrative control. Tribal fighting intensified, and some of the groups attacked the patrols. On May 15, 1939 Adamson and Atkinson left on a patrol that went to Urida in the lower Nembi area where they came across active fighting. One of the men shot arrows at the patrol. Adamson fired his gun first at the man's feet and then he fired two shots over the man's head before the man fled and the hostility towards the patrol ended. Later, on the same patrol, a group of about one hundred warriors shot arrows at the patrol, but scattered when shots were fired in their direction.[96]

At the same time, Champion and Timperley led a patrol to the Mubi, Erave, Iaro, Kagua, Akuru, Nembi and Wage Valleys surveying as they went. A crowd of men gathered for an attack. One youth rushed Champion, and Champion knocked him over, but an arrow grazed Champion's hat and a man was poised to fire a second arrow at Champion. When he did not withdraw, Champion shot and killed him, and the crowd of men quickly dispersed. Champion had been patrolling for years, and it was the first time that he had killed anyone.[97]

Ten days later Champion came across active fighting at the Kuvivi flats. Some of the warriors fired arrows at the carriers and were poised to shoot more arrows at the patrol until Champion ordered four of the police to shoot off their guns. The warriors fled, but at least two men were wounded.[98] Champion later wrote in his diary, "I think these people may be termed treacherous…This district would be an excellent position for a police camp, because it is central to the tribes who appear to carry on interminable internecine warfare."[99]

A few days later Adamson and Bramwell visited the Nembi Valley. The people no longer threatened the patrol. They were "quiet and orderly" and spread unverifiable rumors about people being killed in the lower Nembi Valley. Someone pilfered a knife, and Adamson fired at a limestone pinnacle some distance away. The people could see particles fly when the bullet hit the limestone. The knife was quickly returned. When they arrived at Kuvivi (Poroma), they saw two men who had been wounded during Champion's patrol, but the people did not resist

---

[94]Sinclair, *Last Frontiers*, 261

[95]Sir Hubert Murray. *Territory of Papua Annual Report for the Year of 1938-1939.* [Canberra: Government of the Commonwealth of Australia, 1940], 5-6. Australian National Archives, Series Number M3816, Control Symbol 3 Item Bar Code 1182610 Page 362 of digitalized copy http://recordsearch.naa.gov.au/SearchNRetrieve/Inter-face/ListingReports/ItemsListing.aspx [Accessed on October 7, 2014]

[96]Sinclair, *Last Frontiers,* 262, 266.

[97]Sinclair, *Last Frontiers,* 264.

[98]Sinclair, *Last Frontiers,* 266.

[99]Sinclair, *Last Frontiers,* 265.

their presence and provided them with plenty of food. When they moved to Urida where Adamson and Atkinson had faced resistance a few weeks earlier, the people were amiable, and did not appear to resent the earlier incident. Adamson thought the people were beginning to realize the power of the guns, and the damage they could inflict on the local people.[100]

The Adamson and Bramell patrol was the last to visit the Nembi area for some time. World War Two became a reality. The patrol officers at Kutubu received word that Great Britain had declared war on Germany on September 3, 1939, and Australia followed suit. The Papuan administration decided to cut the size of the Kutubu police camp for the 1939-1940 fiscal year because of the cost and the uncertainty of war.[101] Only Bill Adamson and Jack Bramell remained at the Lake Kutubu camp.

On May 23, 1940, the Papuan administration ordered Adamson and Bramell to evacuate the police camp at Lake Kutubu, and to carry the supplies overland to Kikori. They closed the camp; stored some supplies leaving them in the care of the local constable; and told him that the government would return some day and reward him for his service. Adamson and Bramell reached Kikori on July 24, 1940.[102] Nine years would pass before patrol officers returned to Lake Kutubu.

Reflections about Early Contact

Writing about early contact in the coastal areas of New Guinea, Clive Moore said, "Both sides tried to follow their own cultural rules."[103] During first contact in the Highlands of Papua New Guinea, neither Australians nor the Highlanders understood the other and each misinterpreted the other's actions, motives, and reactions, but both tried to control the situation in which they found themselves. The patrol officers thought that they knew and understood Papuans, and but the Highlanders were different from the Coastals. When Hides observed the Highlanders' homesteads and gardens, their burial practices, and their gardening methods that stood in stark contrast to the "lackadaisical farming methods of the average Papuans," and he concluded that 'these people are not Papuans as we know them."[104]

First contact shook the Highlanders' world. The Hides-O'Malley patrol carried no trade items that interested the newly contacted groups, but subsequent patrols carried a plethora of wealth in the form of abundant shell, steel, cloth, and other trade goods. The people witnessed displays of unprecedented power when the intruders fired off guns, instantly killing pigs or men who opposed them, but the Highlanders also learned that, if handled correctly, the patrols became a source of unprecedented wealth.

---

[100]Sinclair, *Last Frontiers,* 265-266
[101]Sinclair, *Last Frontiers,* 267, 274
[102]Sinclair, *Last Frontiers*, 274-276.
[103]Clive Moore. *New Guinea: Crossing Boundaries and History.* [Honolulu: University of Hawai'i Press, 2003], 162.
[104]Hides, *Papuan Wonderland,* 93.

Identity of the Patrols

For the Highlanders, the only logical explanation was that the strangers came from the spirit world. Some assumed that they were deceased relatives returning from the dead, and some even thought that they recognized their departed relatives among the patrol members.[105] Others believed that they were sky spirits that merited neither fear nor respect.[106]

The patrol officers knew that in first contact situations the people assumed they were from the spirit world and believed that the assumption gave them a distinct advantage over the newly contacted people, but through ritual the Highlanders believed that the spirits could be placated, controlled, and manipulated, so they tried to control the intruders. The people reacted with fear and curiosity, running to hide when they first saw the patrol coming and/or cautiously approaching the patrol if it lingered in their area.[107]

Attempts to actively resist patrols were met with gunfire, and the people suffered numerous, sudden, and devastating casualties. Some tried passive resistance by refusing to provide the patrol members with the things they demanded, but that created problems and ended up with the police and carriers foraging in their gardens and shooting their pigs.

Groups that opted to placate their visitors fared the best. They gave the patrol members whatever they requested, and quickly passed them along to the next group to get them out of their area. Thus, they protected themselves, and gained wealth because they were well paid for the food they brought, the pigs they surrendered. The people tried to minimize harm and maximize the benefits for themselves.[108]

An administrative patrol in the Mandated Territory spent some time at Tari. When it moved on, a Huli man named Hedzaba joined the patrol as a carrier. He stayed with it for almost a year. When he returned to his home he made a speech to the people who hoped he could tell them exactly who the visitors were. Hedzaba told his people that "he could not say...who these beings were and why they had come. He could say that for some reason they wanted to be thought human, and if fed it was safe to let them stay." Within two hours the people sold the camp "five thousand pounds of taro and sweet potatoes."[109]

Hedzaba's assessment had some merit. "If fed it was safe to let them stay." Two of the Nembi groups opted for placation and fed the patrol when Hides and O'Malley walked through their area. Men at Injip had bananas and sugar cane waiting for the patrol as it entered their clearing. Crittenden notes that those food items were used for both "common hospitality" and in rituals for the "appease-

---

[105]Connolly and Anderson, 89-91. See also the film "First Contact" where a bereaved mother tries to drag away a Coastal member of a patrol.
[106]Connolly and Anderson, 198-199.
[107]Gammage 1-2.
[108]Gammage 91, 93, 121, 128, 188.
[109]Gammage, 199.

ment of the spirits."[110] At Mandomap an old man met the patrol and invited them to stay. The people fed the patrol well and no one was harmed.[111] The following year when Champion and Adamson crossed the upper reaches of the Nembi River, ninety men met them with gifts of sugarcane.[112]

In 1939 the Nembi men greeted the first patrols to visit their area after Hides by bringing abundant food, and by chanting, singing, yodeling, ululating, and dancing. Adamson wrote that they celebrated the patrol's progress,[113] but it was more likely an effort to appease the unwelcome spirits than a celebration of their progress. The patrol members found the constant chanting, yodeling and yelling unnerving, but as long as the men provided food and did not resist, they came to no harm.

Resistance and Violence towards Patrols

Resistance was futile as the Merut learned when they attacked Hides and O'Malley. The Highlanders had never before seen guns. They could defend themselves well with bows and arrows and spears, but had no defense against the guns that the interlopers carried. Trompf says, "The love of killing for its own sake is not characteristically Melanesian."[114]

It is impossible to know why some groups attacked the patrols. The patrol officers were ignorant of the existing relationships that might affect the patrol's reception. O'Malley testified that the Merut attack on the patrol "was entirely unprovoked."[115] It never occurred to him that the provocation may have come from an incident that had taken place two days earlier, miles away from Merut. If, as Crittenden suggests, a Merut man had relatives at both Sezinda and Semin-al and had witnessed the death of some of his kinsmen at Sezinda,[116] then the Merut and Semin-al may have attacked in retaliation for the deaths at Sezinda. Likewise, subsequent hostilities or overtures of friendship depended in part on the relationship the succeeding group had with the preceding group, partly determined by the direction that the patrol came from. The people of Toiwara were wary when the patrol approached them from enemy territory.

For the Nembi, early contact had been traumatic. When the last patrol visited the area in 1939, the people opted for placation. They were calm, gave no sign of resistance, and provided the patrol with food.[117] The patrols stopped coming as suddenly as they began. Not until the 1950s did the patrols reenter the Nembi

---

[110]Crittenden, "Across the Nembi Plateau," 171.

[111]Crittenden, "Across the Nembi Plateau," 193-194.

[112]Ivan Champion, "The Bamu Purari Patrol, 1936 (Continued)," 245.

[113]Sinclair, *Last Frontiers*, 257

[114]G.W. Trompf. *Melanesian Religion.* [Cambridge [England]: Cambridge University Press, 1991], 26.

[115]Sinclair, *Outside Man*, 155.

[116]Crittenden, "Across the Nembi Plateau," 176.

[117]Sinclair, *Last Frontiers*, 265-266.

world. For the Nembi the re-entry was as disconcerting as the first contact. I now tell the story of renewed contact with the Nembi that took place in the 1950s.

Chapter Two

Post World War Two Colonialism

Introduction

The previous chapter ended with the outbreak of World War Two and the closing of Lake Kutubu in July of 1940.[1] After the Lake Kutubu base camp was evacuated, the administration restricted access to the Highlands. Australians (and other outsiders) were not permitted to go there. Thus, the Nembi and most other Highlanders were cut off from contact with European colonizers other than the military planes that flew overhead during the war. The Nembi people talk about the planes that passed overhead during World War Two. Stephen Andayo said that his grandfather had climbed high on a mountain and shot arrows at the planes flying overhead in hopes of bringing one of the big birds down. Kanj Mesmba said that his mother gave birth to him during the time that the planes flew overhead. An elderly woman became quite animated as she talked about seeing the planes as a young girl.

I begin this chapter by briefly mentioning the impact that World War Two had on the people of Papua and New Guinea. When the war was over, the former Territory of Papua and the Mandated Territory of New Guinea were administered as one and the combined territories were called the Territory of Papua and New Guinea. Immediately following the war, the administration concentrated on the rehabilitation and the reconstruction of the coastal areas, but by the end of the decade, the Australians once again turned their attention to the "closed" Highlands and sought to "open" it.

The process of opening the Southern Highlands began in 1949 when the patrol post was reopened at Lake Kutubu. When patrols reentered the Nembi area in the 1950s, the administration already considered the Nembi groups to be "arrogant" and "uncooperative." The Nembi greeted the return of the patrols with fear, apprehension, and resistance, and patrol officers could not understand why the Nembi had such an unfavorable impression of the administration. Eventually the Nembi

---

[1]James Patrick Sinclair, *Last frontiers: The Explorations of Ivan Champion of Papua: a Record of Geographical Exploration in Australia's Territory of Papua between 1926 and 1940.* [Broadbeach Waters, Gold Coast, Qld., Australia: Pacific Press, 1988], 276.

accepted the patrol officers and sought to learn the secret of the administration's obvious wealth and power, and the patrol officers strove to bring economic and political development to the Nembi area.

Christian Union Mission began working among the Nembi groups in January of 1964 before the administration had fully derestricted the area. I tell the story of missionization in chapter three, but there is some overlap between chapters two and three. As Jeffrey Clark, Chris Ballard, and Michael Nihill make clear in their analysis of colonialism in the Pangia area of the Southern Highlands, the administration expected missions entering restricted areas to have a "pacifying effect" on the people and to promote and assist the administration with economic development.[2] In this chapter I mention the role of Christian Union Mission in establishing trade stores because the impetus for opening the trade stores and later closing them was driven more by administrative expectations of the mission than by the mission's ministry goals.

World War Two

During World War Two, Papua and New Guinea became a battle ground between the Japanese and the Allied forces. The first of the bombs fell at Rabaul on January 4, 1942,[3] at Lae on January 21, 1942,[4] and at Port Moresby on February 3, 1942.[5] The Japanese occupied the Mandated Territory of New Guinea. For more than three years, sea, air, and land battles took place in both territories. Thousands of Papuan and New Guineans were evacuated from their homes to make room for military installations,[6] and many became refugees in their own land as they moved from one place to another to avoid the bombings and the fighting between the opposing forces.[7] The civilian administration left, and Australian New Guinea Administrative Unit (ANGAU), a military unit, took over the administration of both territories for the duration of the war.[8]

---

[2]Jeffrey Clark, Chris Ballard, and Michael Nihill. *Steel to Stone: A Chronicle of Colonialism in the Southern Highlands of Papua New Guinea.* [Oxford, UK: Oxford University Press, 2000], 97-98.

[3]August Ibrum K Kituai. *My Gun, My Brother the World of the Papua New Guinea Colonial Police, 1920-1960.* [Honolulu: University of Hawai'i Press, 1998], 169.

[4]Gavin Souter. *New Guinea: The Last Unknown.* [Sydney: Angus and Robertson, 1963], 193.

[5]N. D. Oram, *Colonial Town to Melanesian City: Port Moresby 1884-1974.* [Canberra: Australian National University Press, 1976], 65-66.

[6]Oram, 72-73; Lucy Mair. *Australia in New Guinea.* [Melbourne: Melbourne University Press, 1970], 202

[7]Ian Willis, *Lae, Village and City.* [Carlton, Vic: Melbourne University Press, 1974], 129.

[8]Geoffrey Gray. "Remembering the War in New Guinea," Australia War Memorial, 2000, 1. http://ajrp.awm.gov.au/AJRP/remember.nsf/Web-Printer/2BA56E46D717A65-2CA256A99001D9F10?OpenDocument [Accessed on September 16, 2014].

The loss of life and property during the war was unprecedented. The European centers and many of the coastal villages were totally destroyed in the melee.[9] All of the coastal areas were affected, but the northern coast and the islands in the former Mandated Territory of New Guinea suffered the greatest devastation. When the war was over, and the civil administration returned to Papua and New Guinea, the Australians felt they owed a debt of gratitude to the people of Papua and New Guinea.[10] For the first time, Australia was willing to pour substantial amounts of money into the development of Papua and New Guinea.[11]

The administration's first concern was rehabilitation, reconstruction, and the compensation of Papua New Guineans for their war losses.[12] By 1950 the task was fairly well complete,[13] and the administration turned its attention to the renewed exploration, pacification, and derestriction of the Highlands.

The Australians administered the Territory of Papua and New Guinea under a trusteeship agreement with the United Nations. Every three years, missions from the United Nations visited the territory and monitored Australia's work and pressured Australia to move the Territory as quickly as possible toward independence.[14] The 1960s were an era of decolonization in Africa and Asia, and there was a strong push to end worldwide colonization.

Opening of the Highlands

In 1950 the Australian minister for territories, P. C. Spencer, announced that the goal was to have the uncontrolled areas "fully controlled and administered within the next five years,"[15] but the process took more than twenty years. In 1968 there remained 670 square miles of restricted areas.[16] "Control" meant that the administration had contacted most of the people; established patrol posts to create a

---

[9]Kituai, 168; W. E. H. Stanner, *The South Seas in Transition: A Study of Post-war Rehabilitation and Reconstruction in Three British Pacific Dependencies.* [Sydney: Australasian Pub. Co 1953], 87-88. The destruction on the north shores and the islands was especially horrendous, but some of the villages along the south shore suffered the same fate. Villagers living near Port Moresby were relocated and the militray took over their land.

[10]Brian Jinks, Peter Biskup, and Hank Nelson. *Readings in New Guinea History.* [Sydney: Angus & Robertson, 1973], 322-333

[11]Peter Biskup, Brian Jinks, and H. Nelson. *A Short History of New Guinea, Revised Edition.* [Sydney, Australia: Angus and Robertson Ltd, 1968],128

[12]Jinks, Biskup and Nelson, 323.

[13]Jinks, Biskup, and Nelson, 341.

[14]Stanner, 113, 128-129, 150

[15]Jinks, Biskup, and Nelson, 341. Spencer made the announcement in June of 1950. In May of 1951, Paul Hasluck replaced Spencer as the Australian minister for territories, and he remained in that position until 1963. Hasluck realized it was impossible to meet Spencer's goal of gaining control of the Highlands within five years, but he kept the goal in place in order to pressure the administration to push ahead as quickly as possible (Hasluck, *A Time for Building,* 78-79).

[16]Lucy Mair. *Australia in New Guinea.* [Melbourne: Melbourne University Press, 1970], 41.

point of sustained contact; and taken a census. Pacification meant that the people had quit resisting the patrols that entered their areas; adopted the Australian idea of law and order; ceased inter-group warfare; embraced the Queen's peace; and settled their disputes through adjudication.

Only administrative personnel were permitted to enter uncontrolled areas. Others entered only with special permission and in the company of an official patrol. Once an area was controlled, the administration lifted the restrictions and allowed non-administrative personnel to enter the area on their own.[17] Under ANGAU and during the Provisional administration, the Highlands were amalgamated into one large district known as the Central Highlands District,[18] but in 1951 the Central Highlands was divided into the Eastern, Western, and Southern Highlands districts and each had its own district commissioner.[19]

The method of pacification was reminiscent of Sir Hubert Murray's peaceful penetration and his policy of the gradual extension of administrative influence. Regular patrols composed of one or two Australian Patrol officers, a contingent of the Royal Papua and New Guinea Constabulary, a medical orderly, and carriers went into new areas to establish or renew contact with people and to assert the administration's position of authority. The patrol officers negotiated with the people for the right to establish a new post. After they reached an agreement, the people worked alongside patrol members providing both volunteer and paid labor to construct temporary bush buildings and an airstrip. The newly established post became a center from which administrative influence radiated more deeply into uncontrolled areas.[20]

Some of the Australian patrol officers were experienced men who had been a part of the public service before World War Two, but most were inexperienced new recruits. They led the patrols, and their stories are revealed in the obligatory reports that they wrote after each patrol.[21] The patrols often faced resistance, and

---

[17]Paul Hasluck, *A Time for Building: Australian Administration in Papua and New Guinea, 1951-1963*. [Carlton, Vic: Melbourne University Press, 1976], 77.

[18]James Patrick Sinclair, *Last Frontiers: The Explorations of Ivan Champion of Papua: A Record of Geographical Exploration in Australia's Territory of Papua between 1926 and 1940*. [Broadbeach Waters, Gold Coast, Qld., Australia: Pacific Press 1988] 286-287.

[19]District and Division Boundaries: News Release for South Pacific Post, September 12, 1951, in *Administration New Release to ABC South Pacific Post,* {NB 59-54 HW 331}.

[20]Hasluck, *A Time for Building*, 79-80.

[21]See James Sinclair Patrick, *Kiap: Australia's Patrol Officers in Papua New Guinea*. [Bathurst: Brown 1984] for a published account of post-World War Two patrols. Sinclair uses "his own service as a framework" for telling the story of Australia's post-World War Two kiaps" (7).

sometimes deaths occurred.[22] Lives were lost on both sides, but with bows and arrows, spears, and axes matched against guns, the Highlanders were unable to defeat the administration.

Southern Highlands Province

The Southern Highlands, the only Highlands district in Papua, was one of the last areas to be pacified. In August of 1949 Assistant District Officer S. S. Smith, and Patrol Officer D. J. Clancy reopened the patrol post at Lake Kutubu.[23] For a year patrols from Lake Kutubu and Mount Hagen explored the Southern Highlands, continually searching for a site to construct an airstrip at least one thousand yards long.[24] The patrols looked at sites at Samberigi, the Nembi Valley, and the Kuvivi flats near Poroma. On Wednesday September 6, 1950, a Kutubu patrol led by S. S. Smith located a feasible site at Mendi.[25] Smith negotiated with elderly men whom he thought might be the land owners and appeared to exercise authority over the local people for the right to camp at Murumbu (Mendi) and build an airstrip.[26]

Mendi Patrol Post

The Mendi people demonstrated mixed attitudes toward the patrol. At first they refused to sell food, but after they saw the trade goods the other groups were acquiring, their competitive spirit came to the fore. In two days, the people at Murumbu sold enough food to the patrol to last for almost two weeks.[27] The patrols carried unprecedented wealth in the form of shell and trade goods, and demonstrated unparalleled power. Their guns splintered rows of wooden shields, shattered rocks, and dropped pigs with a single bullet.[28] Groups that accepted the patrol's presence acquired a share of the wealth that the patrol carried.

---

[22]An Administrative press release dated November 12, 1953 acknowledged that the Telefomin people killed two patrol officers (D. M. Cleland, Administrative Press Release: Policy in Regard to Uncontrolled Areas [Port Moresby, November 12, 1953], 1 {NB 49-54, HW 283}). Numerous other deaths occurred. An administrative patrol killed a Lai Valley man when it tried to intervene in a tribal fight, and the man's group attacked the patrol (A. L. Ford. Mendi Patrol Report Number 7, 1952-1953, 3, {NB 49-54, HW 283}). In the Augu Valley the people killed a member of the constabulary, and some of the people said that the government was weak because it did not revenge the policeman's death (Lake Kutubu Patrol Report Number One of 1953-54, 3, {NB 49-54 HW 352}). These are just a few of the incidents.

[23]James Patrick Sinclair, *Kiap: Australia's Patrol Officers in Papua New Guinea.* Bathurst: Brown, 1988, 111.

[24]Ivan Champion, 8th August, 1950, Department of District Services and Native Affairs, Port Moresby Memorandum to Assistant District Officer at Lake Kutubu in Kutubu Patrol Report Number 2 of 1950-1951 {NB 49-54 HW 56}.

[25]Lake Kutubu Patrol Report Number 2 1950-51, 7, {NB 49-54 HW 30}.

[26]Lake Kutubu Patrol Report Number 2 1950-51, 1-9 {NB 49-54 HW 23-32}.

[27]Lake Kutubu Patrol Report 2 1950-1951, 9, {NB 49-54 32}.

[28]Lake Kutubu Patrol Report 2 1950-1951, 9, {NB 49-54 32}.

Police and carriers began working on the Mendi airstrip on Sunday the 10th of September, 1950. A few of the local people joined in the work while hundreds more gathered to watch.[29] Before the airstrip was completed, hundreds of the Mendi people assisted with the construction of the strip. They were paid with various trade goods including tomahawks, knives, and mirrors.[30] The first small plane landed on the Mendi airstrip on Friday, October 20, 1950, and by December of 1950 regular weekly flights occurred between Mendi and Mount Hagen.[31]

It took a foot patrol five or six days to traverse the distance between Mendi and Hagen, but an airplane flight took thirty-five minutes.[32] The airstrip did not totally eliminate the need for foot patrols, but it lessened the demand and made the acquisition of supplies much easier.

In March of 1951 the administration negotiated with the people for the final purchase of the Mendi land,[33] and the people's attitude changed when they were about to receive compensation for their land. Allen Timperly, the officer in charge of the land purchase, found that the people were hard bargainers and unwilling to part with their land easily, and that numerous owners staked a claim. From Timperley's perspective, the administration had protected the Murumbu people from enemy attack and the people had acquired considerable wealth from their interactions with the patrols. Timperley was disgruntled with the "discontent" and "noncooperativeness" that surfaced when he tried to finalize the purchase of the land.[34]

In 2001 Bernard Narokobi wrote,

> For the biggest part of our colonial history and our post colonial history, Western conceptions of property and selling of land have dominated our thinking about the buying and selling of land. By and large, alienated land is stringently subjected to the Western, especially Anglo-Australian perceptions of ownership. On the one hand, Melanesian cultural perception or philosophies of ownership have not been considered, except in awarding *ex-gratia* payment for alienated land.

> …Alienated land, by definition, is land divorced from or taken away from the original owners. This alienation cuts off and separates men and women as the subjects from the land as an object. The land is removed and affixed to a new subject or master. This act of separation disregards the entire Melanesian cultural universe, with all spiritual, emotion, and *tumbuna* activities.[35]

---

[29]Lake Kutubu Patrol Report 2 1950-1951, 17-21, {NB 49-54 HW 44}.

[30]Lake Kutubu Patrol Report 2 1950-1951, 22-25, {NB 49-54 45-48}.

[31]George Greathead, 21st December, 1950, letter from District Office, Central Highlands District, Goroka, to The Director, Department of District Services and Native Affairs Port Moresby, in Western Highlands Patrol Report 4 of 1950-1951, PD 14 to 25 October, 1950, {NB 49-54 HW 67}.

[32]Lake Kutubu Patrol Report 2 1950-1951, 21-22, {NB 49-54 HW 44-45}.

[33]Mount Hagen Patrol number 6 of 1950-51, 7, 18 {NB 49-54 HW 123, 133}.

[34]Mount Hagen Patrol Number 6 of 1950-51, 8 (NB 49-54 HW 124).

[35]Bernard Narokobi, "The Wind is Blowing" in *Land and Churches in Melanesia: Issues and Contexts*, ed. Michael A. Rynkiewich, [Goroka, EHP, Papua New Guinea: Melanesian Institute, 2001], 5-7.

Large contingents of people from other areas arrived and promised full coop-eration if the administration would relocate to their areas, and, once again, Mendi competitiveness kicked in.[36] Trompf says that "in the midst of exchange complex-ities, men "jostled competitively for prestige and authority."[37] The Murumbu did not want to lose the wealth, status and prestige that the administrative presence brought to them, and when other groups tried to lure the administration away, the Mendi lowered their demands and agreed to sell their land. On March 16, 1951, the administration paid seventeen pearl shells, three axes, nine twelve inch knives, and three spades for the purchase of 292 acres at Murumbu in the Mendi River Valley.[38]

On the 4th of September, 1951, the Southern Highlands became a district and Mendi was designated the District headquarters,[39] and in October of 1951 Mendi started to send out regular patrols to extend administrative influence.[40]

Extension of Influence

When the groups began to accept the administration's presence, patrol officers selected an apparently influential man from each group to serve as a village con-stable and made him responsible for carrying out the administrative directives. The patrol officer relayed his instructions to the people via the village constable. The administration instructed groups to build rest houses and police barracks for patrols to use when they visited the villages; to dig and use latrines; to establish burial grounds; and to assist with road work that was to "proceed hand in hand with (the) extension program."[41] The administration theorized that time and en-ergy expended on roadwork reduced the time and energy available to engage in inter-group fighting.

A census identified the people who belonged to each group. The earliest of-ficial census in the Mendi sub-district took place in an area adjacent to the Mendi station in 1954.[42] Each man presented himself with all his wives and children, and the names were recorded in a census book. Not all of the people presented them-selves for the first census, but the patrol officers revised the census frequently. During each visit to an area, the patrol officers added the names of previous non-

---

[36]Mount Hagen Patrol number 6 of 1950-51, 8 {NB 49-54 HW 124}.

[37]G. W. Trompf, *Payback: The Logic of Retribution in Melanesian Religions.* [Cam-bridge, UK: Cambridge University Press, 1994], 114.

[38]Mount Hagen Patol Report Number 6, 1950-51, 8-10, {NB 49-54, HW 124-126}.

[39]Sinclair, *Kiap*, 111 and 113

[40]Mendi Patrol Report Number 1 for 1951-1952, 8, {NB 49-54 HW 168}.

[41]Robert Cole, 31 December, 1954, in a letter to the Department of District Services and Affairs, Port Moresby in Mendi Patrol Report Number 5 of 1954-1955 {NB 54 – 58 HW 65}.

[42]Robert Cole, 31 December, 1954, in a letter to the Department of District Services and Affairs, Port Moresby in Mendi Patrol Report Number 5 of 1954-1955 {NB 54 – 58 HW 64}.

attendees to the census book and recorded any deaths and births that had occurred since the previous census.

Patrols officers introduced the people to the law. Patrols were required to hear "court" cases in the villages. The patrol officer was the judge and jury and settled the cases according to his understanding of the administration's law.

Nipa Patrol Post

In 1959 the administration freed up staff to open a patrol post at Nipa for the express purpose of bringing the people in the Nembi Valley and on the Nembi Plateau under control.[43] A press release in February of 1960 reported that a patrol post had been established at Nipa where tribes were "engaged in sporadic inter-clan fighting" and noted that "the establishment of a patrol post there is the first step in bringing about peace in the valley, and providing the condition and services necessary to assist the people to progress out of primitive tribal standards." There would be difficulties before "the more belligerent groups settled down to living peacefully with their neighbors."[44]

Beginning in 1960, the administration conducted regular patrols to the upper and middle Nembi Valley and the Nembi plateau, and patrols from Erave and Kagua visited the groups living in the Lower Nembi and Emia[45] Creek areas. It was several years before the groups were brought under "partial control" Most of the groups resisted, some actively and others passively.

The Nembi

When the administration returned to the Southern Highlands in 1949, the Nembi already had a reputation for being "arrogant" and "parsimonious with food and assistance to patrols." Patrol officers in the 1950s seemed oblivious to the fact that the Nembi people had engaged in a lengthy battle with the Strickland-Purari patrol led by Jack Hides in 1935, but officials were aware that the pre-war Lake Kutubu patrols had not been well received in the Nembi area, and that the patrol officers in the 1930s considered the people of the Nembi area to be "contentious," "arrogant," "avaricious," and "uncooperative."[46]

---

[43]Nipa Patrol Report Number 1 of 1959-1960, {NB 58-61 HW 56}.

[44]Administration Press Release Number 7, Port Moresby, February 26, 1960 in Nipa Patrol Report Number 1 of 1959-1960, {NB 58-61 HW 56}.

[45]What I spell Emia is spelled Amia in many of the patrol reports.

[46]John S. McLeod, November 20, 1952, Letter to Director of District Services and Native Affairs in Mendi Patrol Report Number 4 of 1952-53, {NB 49-54 HW 196b}; Edward L. Schieffelin, and Robert Crittenden, editors, *Like People You See in a Dream: First Contact in Six Papuan Societies* [Stanford, Calif: Stanford University Press] 275.

The Administration's Perspective

In 1952 a Mendi patrol of seventy-three men led by B. R. Heagney entered a part of the Nembi Valley for the first time in thirteen years. Several groups refused to sell food, and the patrol foraged their gardens.[47] To feed everyone adequately, the patrol required daily four large copra bags each containing approximately 165 pounds of sweet potatoes. Pre-World War Two patrols paid one mother of pearl shell for each bag, but Heagney thought the price was too high. He offered beads, the accepted price in the Lai and Wage Valleys, but the people in the Nembi Valley wanted only pearl shells. Heagney blamed inefficient gardening methods for the "antipathy of the people of the Nembi Valley to parting with their sweet potatoes." He thought that "one of the main reasons for the lack of co-operation in this area is the natural greed or avariciousness here. Some gardens were just coming in, but there were certainly no lack of gardens in the advanced stage."[48]

In response to Heagney's report, John S. McLeod said,

The natives North-East of Kutubu, including the Mendi Valley, have never been noted for their co-operation. They are arrogant and have been continuously parsimonious with food and assistance to patrols. Mr. Champion always reported adversely on the Nembi, Wage, Lai, and Mendi peoples.

... Mr. F. E. Williams has stated in his paper "The Grasslanders" that they demand higher prices amongst themselves than they do from the Government, it was on this advise that Mr. Champion set the standard amount of one 'Goldlip' shell in his patrols before the War. It is very hard to change the standard set over so many years by various patrols.

The natives North-West (sic) of Kutubu are diametrically opposite to the Mendi in their attitude to the administration...(in) the Tari Basin...the natives are anxious to have the government in the area. To the North-East (sic) of Kutubu the locals appear very anxious to be rid of it. As yet they have no serious clashes with the forces of law and order, and to date, ignorance has been bliss as far as the consequences are concerned."[49]

What the administration interpreted as arrogance and uncooperativeness may have been an expression of fear. In October of 1953, J. A. Frew led a patrol from Mendi that camped at Huim (Wim) on the northeastern side of the Nembi River. Frew reports that men from Huim guided the patrol, calling to "various people, in the gardens and sitting on the hillside slopes, to go and hide as we were evil

---

[47]Mendi Patrol Report Number Four of 1952-1953, 2-3, {NB 49-54 HW 197-198}.

[48]Mendi Patrol Report Number Four of 1952-1953, 17, {NB 49-54 HW 212}.

[49]John S. McLeod, 20 November, 1952, Letter to The Director, District of Native Affairs, Port Moresby in Mendi Number Four of 1952-1953, {NB 49-54, HW 196b}.

people bent on harming them."[50] Upon hearing what the guides were shouting[51] Frew decided to camp immediately, but the

> guides, despite the fact that we were travelling through large garden areas, with much shouting and gesticulations, informed us that there was no food, no people, notwithstanding those that we could see now hiding in the cane grass and fleeing up the mountain slopes, and no villages or ceremonial grounds, three being in plain view at the time.[52]

Men armed with bows and arrows gathered. The patrol line closed up and the police were warned to be on their guard. When the patrol set up camp about eighty of the local men came and sold some food, but when Frew asked questions about walking tracks, the place, and the groups in the area, "a note of animosity was struck as a native butted in and told the few, with whom I was conversing, not to tell me anything least I return to sleep another night in the area."[53] The men deliberately answered questions falsely.[54]

Frew complained about the high prices that the Nembi demanded for food, the constant haggling over prices, and the Nembi's "contemptuous" refusal to sell when the patrol officer did not "acquiesce" to the owners demand.[55] Frew wrote,

> The process of bringing the areas visited, especially the Nembi Valley, under Government control will undoubtedly be lengthy and arduous. The people in the upper Nembi were found to be arrogant—being over proud and confident—and discourteous, often exceeding the bounds of decency in their remarks. There were, however, several places where we were made welcome, which at least bodes well for any patrol establishing a post in the area preparatory to the extension of control.[56]

The Nembi Perspective

In 2009 and 2010 the Nembi people, who had lived through pacification in the 1950s and 1960s, all spoke of the fear they had when the patrols entered their area. Susi Tio, who was a young girl at the time, said that they were afraid of the unknown. They saw that the intruders' light colored skin was different from their own, and they were afraid. The light skinned beings ate strange food and when they gave the people a taste of rice or salt by putting it in their hands or on their lips, the people were afraid but curious. Their fear was compounded by stories that "light skinned" beings had entered their world before and killed a lot of peo-

---

[50]Mendi Patrol Number 5 of 1953-1954, 4 {NB 1949-1954 HW 420}.

[51]Frew was unlikely to understand the guides' shouts, but interpreters and forty carriers accompanied this patrol and some of them would have understood what the guides were shouting and relayed the message to the officer in charge.

[52]Mendi Patrol Number 5 of 1953-1954, 4 {NB 1949-1954 HW 420}.

[53]Mendi Patrol Number 5 of 1953-1954, 4 {NB 1949-1954 HW 420}.

[54]Mendi Patrol Number 5 of 1953-1954, 13 {NB 1949-1954 HW 429}.

[55]Mendi Patrol Number 5 of 1953-1954, 16 {NB 1949-1954 HW 431}.

[56]Mendi Patrol Number 5 of 1953-1954, 15 {NB 1949-1954 HW 430}.

ple.[57] After the massive killings during the red spirits' first visit, the Nembi were afraid. Good things like hospitals and schools came later, but at first there was only fear and force.[58]

Map 3: *The approximate positions of the Nembi groups in 1963*[59]

Thomas Kas also spoke of the overwhelming fear and stories of earlier battles with the red spirits. They believed that red spirits came for the people when they died and led them away to the spirit world. Thomas told the story of the first

---

[57]The term *temo one* means literally 'spirit red' or 'the red spirits." The term changes according to the dialect. Some said *tem one, tom one* or *tomo one.*

[58]Susi Tio, interview by author, Mato, Poroma Census Division, Southern Highlands Province, Papua New Guinea, January 2, 2010,

[59]Nipa Patrol Number 8 of 1962-1963, {NB 62-63 HW 362}. The map is adapted from a patrol map drawn by Peter J. Barber. The names have been modified to reflect current usage.

encounter. A large group of *papa tumbuna* (grandfathers and great uncles) from several areas had gathered at a spirit house and were performing a ritual when they saw something like they had never before seen coming towards them. The men collected their bows and arrows and spears and prepared for battle, and when they saw the light skinned beings they said, "Our ancestors who died before are coming to eat us." The men attacked the strangers, and some of the arrows found their mark. The strangers fought with guns, and many people on both sides died.[60] Thomas's grandfather was killed in the ensuing battle. In the end the battle was lost and they all fled and went into hiding taking their families, their pigs, and what belongings they could carry with them.[61]

Kanj Mesmba from Utabia was a young unmarried man when the patrols visited the area in the 1950s and 1960s. He was a priest in one of the spirit cults, and performed rituals that were meant to heal the sick. When the patrols came, they were all afraid. According to Kanj, *"Ol kiap i kam na bagarapim sindaun bilong mipela"* (The patrol officers came and spoiled our way of life). They killed pigs, were quick to fire off their guns, and the police caned the people when they did not respond to the commands quickly enough. They believed that red spirits had come to eat them. The smell of the soap that the members of the patrol used was foul. The people liked the smell of pig grease, and the *tiagaso* oil that they traded up from Lake Kutubu, but found the strange smells of the patrol officers and their entourage unpleasant. They were afraid.[62]

Stories about first contact are well within the living memory of the Nembi people. Kevin Hovey says that living memory goes back "as many generations into the past as can be remembered by the living members of a community."[63] Many of the Nembi people living in the 1950s experienced the disastrous first contact, just as the older generation of today experienced the return of the administration in the 1950s and 1960s.

The Nembi lived with fear, a fact that Kanj Mesmba acknowledged. They feared their enemies, the unknown, and they especially feared the spirit world. Hiebert, Shaw, and Tiénou say that

> A...worldview theme that runs through nearly all folk religions belief systems is near constant fear and the need for security. In a world full of spirits, witchcraft,

---

[60]Several interviewees said that they had killed members of the administrative patrols. Although I found written records confirming that the people had attacked patrols and died as a result, I found no written confirmation that the local people in the Nembi area killed any member of a patrol. Thomas is talking about a battle that occurred in his grandfather's day which would have placed it in the 1930s.

[61]Thomas Kas, interview by author, Mato, Poroma Census Division, Southern Highlands Province, Papua New Guinea, December 31, 2009.

[62]Kanj Mesmba, interview by author, Port Moresby, Papua New Guinea, January 29, 2010,

[63]Kevin G. Hovey, *Before All Else Fails, Read the Instructions: Manual for Cross Cultural Christians*. [Brisbane: Harvest Publications, 1995], 101.

sorcery, black magic, curses, bad omens, broken taboos, angry ancestors, human emies and false accusations of many kinds, life is rarely carefree and secure.[64]

Trompf says that the Melanesian world was filled with spirits, both beneficent and malevolent, and fear of death was instilled into women and children, sometimes as a means of social control in male dominated societies, but the men also lived in fear of "encountering a deadly force. This was a fearfulness distinct from the despicable fear towards one's enemy or prey. It was a sense of awe, uncertainty, obligation, and sometimes plain terror in the face of unknown powers."[65] The Nembi feared inexplicable deaths and other events that they believed were caused by angry ancestors or by some unknown malevolent spirit that an enemy sorcerer had prompted to bring death or wreak havoc on wary victims. When the unknown became tangible in the form of a long line of strangers led by beings with light complexions who spoke a strange language; carried portable houses and a plethora of strange objects including guns; demanded food, firewood, and tent poles; helped themselves to what the people failed to provide; and shot guns to demonstrate their power, the only logical explanation was that they originated from the spirit world and the people were afraid.

The Nembi sought to control that which they feared. They used ritual and sacrifice to control the spirits, and when confronted with strange beings, they poised for an attack. They were warriors who faced their enemies in battle and some groups were so successful in battle that they had come to consider themselves invincible. They were constantly on guard against their enemies whom they feared, but they were strong and able to protect themselves and resist any foe. The colonial forces were unlike anything they had met in the past, but the Nembi people stood up to them until the "government made them weak," and forced them to concede defeat. "*Mipela birua wantaim gavman i go i go until ol i mekim mipela wik nau.*" (We were enemies with the government for a long time until they made us weak.)[66]

The Nembi Groups

The Nembi groups farthest to the north lived within four to six miles of Nipa, those farthest to the South are six to eight miles south of Poroma. Warfare among the Nembi was widespread, and the various groups formed numerous fighting-

---

[64]Paul G. Hiebert, R. Daniel Shaw, and Tite Tiénou, *Understanding Folk Religion: a Christian Response to Popular Beliefs and Practices*. [Grand Rapids, Mich: Baker Books 1999], 99.

[65]G. W. Trompf, *Melanesian Religion*. [Cambridge [England]: Cambridge University Press 1991], 38-39.

[66]Thomas Kas, interview by author at Mato in Poroma Sub-district of the Southern Highlands Province on December 31, 2009.

alliances. The *Aron* and *Karinj*[67] alliances were the largest, but they also formed many smaller alliances within the larger alliances. A. F. McNeill said that, *Aron* and *Karinj* are

> ...repetitive terms used to describe large groups of people, who form the largest existing alliances...The terms are more than a description of a group's location in relation to a river. They also define the largest extant fighting alliances. The Nembi people form the local Karinj alliance in association with the Poroma villages of Unjubia (Utabia) Kusa, Kesu, e.t.c. (sic). Their immediate enemies are the people to the Northeast of the Nembi River, those people around the Del (Det) village. The existence of these alliances do not prevent large scale tribal fighting between groups within the alliance."[68]

Beginning in 1960 patrols from Nipa, Mendi, Kagua and Erave visited the Nembi Valley and Nembi Plateau almost constantly. The patrols visited all groups, but the groups that were engaged in active fighting or previously had been under the administration's scrutiny received the most frequent visits.

All resisted the administration. Some fled when patrols approached; some refused to accommodate demands for food and firewood; and some shouted abuse at the patrols that visited their areas; and some launched attacks on the patrols. The administration said that the Nembi people were "difficult to deal with" and they required a "stern approach." The patrols were instructed not to back down in the face of opposition, show no sign of weakness, and clearly demonstrate that the administration was a powerful force.[69]

In Appendix Two I tell the story of the Nembi groups' resistance to the administrative patrols.

---

[67]The terms *Aron* and *Karinj* and variants surface in literature about various groups in the Highlands of Papua New Guinea (Reithofer, 20; Wiessner, Tumu, and Pupu 53; Sillitoe 1979, 28). *Karinj* means "west" and when used in reference to a group of people, refers to those living on the western side of a major river while Aron refers to the people living on the eastern side of the river (Silitoe 1979, 28fn, Reithofer, 20). In patrol reports, patrol officers began to discuss the terms as early as 1952 (Mendi patrol report Number 4 of 1952-1953, 13, {NB 1949-1954 HW 208}), but it was several years before the terms were clearly understood. Terrell defined *Aron* and *Karinj* as large clans or tribes (Kutubu Patrol Report Number 1 of 1953-1954, 12-13, {NB 49-54 HW 360-361}), but later the patrol officers realized that the terms referred to fight alliances. A. F. McNeill gave the clearest definition. N Wright, a patrol officer stationed at Poroma and Nipa in the late 60s and early 70s said that although the names referred to the groupings on the east and western sides of the rivers, Aron meant "on top or above" and Karinj meant "to the side and below" (N Wright, Poroma Patrol Number 5 of 1968-69, Area Survey—Nembi Census Division, 3 {NB 68-69, HW 177}; Poroma Patrol Number 7 of 1969-70, Area Survey, Nembi Valley Census Division, 4 {NB 69-70, HW 205})

[68]Nipa Patrol Report Number 3 of 1969-1970, 3 {NB 69-70, HW 95}.

[69]R. E. Focken, 29 September, 1964, letter to Assistant District Officer in Mendi in Nipa Patrol Report Number 1 of 1964-1965, {NB 64-68 HW 6}.

The administration required warring groups to make peace and seal the peace with a "*moga*"[70] exchange[71] that took place under administrative supervision. Patrol officers encouraged the groups to include any other rituals or exchanges that were traditionally used to make peace. The exchange was imposed on the people and did not fully satisfy the traditional requirements for peace, but the administration declared that it marked the end of all hostilities between groups, righted all wrongs, both past and present and set the land boundaries that were to be recognized in perpetuity. Once the "*moga*" had been paid, any further hostilities would be met with administrative wrath, and the imposition of punitive measures such as imprisonment or retaliatory raids against any group and/or individual who violated the imposed peace.

The administration believed that the fighting would not stop until the exchange had taken place, and they assumed that the preservation of honor was the primary reason for the fighting. The people would quit fighting if "honor were satisfied by the intervention of a more powerful third party."[72] Administrative intervention was a "sufficiently strong deterrent" for the people to realize "that the decision as to whether or not they will go to war no longer rests with themselves, and that the risks of incurring the official wrath are not balanced by the satisfaction of slaying their neighbours."[73]

However, the enforced payments ignored the past and failed to address a host of relevant issues and eradicate the underlying causes of the hostilities, especially when land disputes were at the heart of the conflict. The various claims and counter-claims were extremely difficult to judge, and so the administration adopted a policy that "the status quo with regard to land occupation and ownership, existing at the advent of the extension of Government control, should be maintained."[74] The group that occupied disputed land when the administration achieved effective control became, according to administrative policy, the permanently recognized owners of the land. The policy ignored underlying resentments, left the disputes

---

[70]"*Moga*." The term refers to a system of competitive exchange that operates between groups or individuals and is prevalent in and unique to the Melpa people living in the Mount Hagen area, and is more commonly called *moka* in literature. One group or individual initiates an exchange partnership by bestowing gifts on an exchange partner. At a later date, the recipient must give back more than he initially received from his exchange partner. There has been no *moka* exchange unless the amount that is given back exceeds what was received in the first place (Andrew Strathern *The Rope of Moka*, 10, 216). The Highlands groups of Papua New Guinea have different types of exchange systems which are widely discussed in the literature (See Weissners, Tumu and Pupu; Rubel and Rossman; Sillitoe, *Give and Take*: and Lederman), and no ethnography of the Highlands groups is complete without mentioning systems of exchange applicable to the groups being studied. However, the administration in the 1950s and 1960s used *moga* as an umbrella term for all compensation payments and exchanges.

[71]Mendi Patrol Report Number 4 of 1961-1962, 1, {NB 61-64 HW 43}.

[72]A. Roberts, 17 October, 1953, in a letter written to the District Commissioner of the Southern Highlands Dictrict in Mendi Patrol Number 3 of 1953-1954, {NB 49-54 HW 370}.

[73]Lake Kutubu Patrol Report No 1 of 1953-54, 12 {NB 49-54 HW 361}.

[74]Mendi Report No 4 of 53-54, 3 {NB 49-54 HW 411}.

unsettled, and left intact the traditional enmities that seethed under the surface and sometimes spanned generations.[75]

Alan Tippett theorized about change that occurs when the members of a society are confronted by outside forces that impose a new structure on the society. There is outward conformity to the imposed law, but at a deeper hidden level the members of society continue to follow the former practices. If the restraining forces are removed, the practices reemerge, and the members of the society return to their earlier practices.[76] At the insistence of the colonial administration, the Nembi groups quit fighting, but the underlying issues remained unresolved, and tribal fighting reemerged with a vengeance a few years later. A good example is a land dispute between the Injua and some of their neighbors.

In 1967, after the CCCU missionaries had arrived in the general area, trouble erupted at Injua where the people had fully cooperated with the administration for the last six years. The Injua people had some long standing land disputes with some of their neighboring groups including the Obua, Tegibo, and Karamela. When a patrol went out to investigate a land dispute, the Injua men were afraid they were going to lose their land, and became "uncooperative." Initially two men were arrested for riotous behavior and taken to the police barracks at Tegibo. About eighty Injua warriors advanced on the police barracks, but they "were stopped." They were all charged with "threatening behavior" and sent to Nipa where thrity-five of the men were sentenced to two months imprisonment. The patrol officer reported that the situation had "resolved itself" and that the dispute was dormant and that the groups were living in peace, but the situation required arbitration with the land commission.[77] However, the situation was never resolved, and fourteen years later in 1981 six years after independence, the dispute again erupted, and the first of many post-independence tribal fights broke out among the Nembi groups. The disputed land was still an issue in a fight that broke out between the Injua groups and their neighbors in 2010.

Imprisonment

The administration considered the prisons to be useful institutions for political education and the introduction of the new system of law and order. Captured prisoners were given short sentences, and when they returned unharmed, the administration expected that they would become "ambassadors of goodwill" after they had seen Mendi or other more developed centers.[78]

A number of the people that I interviewed told stories about being taken prisoner, or watching as their kinsmen were taken to prison. Each policeman had a pair of handcuffs attached to his uniform. When the prisoners were fewer than

---

[75]Schieffelin and Crittenden, 277.

[76]A. R. Tippett. *Introduction to Missiology.* [Pasadena, California: William Carey Library 1987], 163-168.

[77]Nipa Patrol Report Number 1 of 1967-1968, 1-2, 6-7 {NB 66-68 HW 261-262, 267-268}.

[78]K. W. Dyer, November 24, 1961, letter written to the Assistant District Officer at Mendi, in Mendi Patrol Report Number Four of 1961-1962 {NB 58-61 HW 41-42}.

the police, the police used their handcuffs to secure the prisoners. If they took a large number of prisoners and did not have enough handcuffs, they used rope and lashed one man to the next until there was a long line of prisoners. After walking to their destination under police guard, the prisoners served out their jail sentence at either Nipa or Mendi. Some of the men returned without their beards and minus the adornment that reflected their status within their group. They came back looking like youths without a name, and their wives, children, and close relatives cried when they saw the returnees stripped of their dignity.[79]

Mapunu, who was then a small boy living near Farata, recalled crying when his father (uncle), Pereyap, was led off to prison. He climbed up on the roof of a house that was under construction but had not yet been thatched and watched the police lead his father away. Until long after dark he sat on the roof crying, thinking that he would never again see his father.[80]

Thomas Kas from Mato recalled his prison experience. He and the other prisoners had been handcuffed one to the other and forced to walk to Nipa where they were sentenced to a prison term.[81] They were afraid of the police who were quick to cane them, and they especially feared the spit of the policemen who chewed betel nut.[82] The line of prisoners sat, stood and walked as one, had no way of escape, and if one fell down, they all fell down.[83]

Few wanted to repeat the prison experience. Ndipilli from the Lai Valley was sentenced to two months in jail after his sister claimed that he had taken her pig and contributed it to bride wealth for his brother. When Ndipilli refused to give his sister another pig, she went to the patrol officer who sentenced Ndipilli to two months in prison for taking the pig. Ndipilli says that in jail, they were given hard labor; the food was poor; the police treated them roughly; and they did not sleep well. The beds were bunked three high and they did not like having men sleep above and/or below them. They were cold. There was no fire, and they did not have enough blankets to keep warm at night. In Ndipilli's words, "*Mipela pilim pen nogut tru.*" (We bore a lot of pain and suffering.) When his time was up, he returned to his place, gave a pig to his sister, and was determined not to be sentenced to another jail term. He would follow the patrol officer's law.[84]

---

[79]Mapunu Pereyap, interview by author, Mato, Poroma Census Division, Southern Highlands Provimce, Papua New Guinea, January 1, 2010.

[80]Mapunu Pereyap, Interview by author, January 1, 2010.

[81]The jail terms varied, but usually they lasted from two to six months depending on the severity of the offense.

[82]The people in the Mendi, Nipa, and Mendi areas of the Southern Highlands did not chew betel nut prior to contact and pacification.

[83]Thomas Kas, interview by author, Mato, Poroma Census Division, Southern Highlands Province, Papua New Guinea, December 31, 2009.

[84]Ndipilli, interview by author, Mil, Lai Valley Census Division, Mendi, Southern Highlands Province, December 20, 2009.

Partial Control

After several years, the administration broke the resistance. By accepting the administrative presence, the Nembi admitted defeat and changed their tactics first to more passive forms of resistance and eventually to total cooperation. The Nembi wanted for themselves the power and the wealth that the administration possessed, and cooperation was more productive than resistance. Clark, Ballard, and Nihill write about the pacification of the Wiru people in the Pangia area of the Southern Highlands Province. "Acceptance of colonial control was a final confirmation of the direction from which power and wealth were flowing. It was as if Wiru...were ritually realigning themselves with the true source in the same way as people who engage in cargo cults."[85] They realized the futility of resistance, but "struggled to understand what pacification and submission to an external control entailed."[86] Their words are applicable to the Nembi.

After that the overt resistance to the patrols diminished. Patrol officers appointed village constables for each group. The patrol officers' words became the ultimate authority. Sometimes groups settled disputes quickly among themselves because they did not want the patrol officer to be involved. For example, when a dog belonging to a man from Kum killed a chicken belonging to the village constable from Upa who then killed the dog, tempers flared and the two groups were on the verge of an all-out war. They heard that a patrol officer was on his way to investigate, and the two groups quickly made peace. When the patrol officer arrived he found nothing to investigate.[87]

After 1961 patrols generally avoided making mass arrests. Individuals who broke the law either paid compensation to the offended party or received prison sentences. However, the area was not "fully" controlled, and some of the groups went into hiding whenever a patrol approached. Between 1963 and 1965, the people of Pomberel and Tobua tried "to use magic (sorcery) to make the administration leave them alone." [88]

When the groups showed signs of accepting the administrative presence, the patrol officers invited village constables and other leaders to Mendi. When the Utabia leaders visited Mendi, they were given rides in a car, shown the interior of an aircraft, and issued shovels to begin working on roads in their own area. After the headmen safely returned to Utabia, the people began working on the roads.[89] Tensions between groups continued to erupt and reports of intergroup fighting surfaced. Patrol officer Lucas reported that the "groups on the Nembi River were displaying odd attitudes" and "the Utabia group appear to be inherently evil! Al-

---

[85]Jeffrey Clark, Chris Ballard, and Michael Nihill. *Steel to Stone: A Chronicle of Colonialism in the Southern Highlands of Papua New Guinea.* [Oxford, UK: Oxford University Press, 2000]:66-67.

[86]Clark, Ballard, and Nihill, 67.

[87]Nipa Patrol Report Number 2, 1962-1963, {NB 61-64 HW 239}.

[88]Nipa Number 7 of 1968-1969, Area Study-Nembi Plateau Census Division, {NB 68-69 HW 153}.

[89]Mendi Number 7 of 1961-62, 1, 7, {NB 61-64, 105,110}.

though they are making a reasonable effort on roads and other village work, there is something unsavoury underlying their mien." Lucas had no doubt that "the Utabia group would be up to some mischief at the drop of a hat."[90] Jeffries agreed, saying that the Utabia were a "flagitious crowd" that respected only force, had to be "firmly handled" and would not withhold cooperation in the presence of a "strong police party."[91] In 1964 the people began to lay aside all resistance to administrative patrols, and by 1965, the people had accepted the administration and adopted "progressive" attitudes.[92]

Poroma Patrol Post

The groups living between Poroma and Toiwara were on the fringes of the areas patrolled by the Nipa and the Kagua/Erave patrol posts. Their fear of patrols continued for a number of years.

In 1965 Patrol officer, J. S. Hicks suggested that a patrol post be established at Poroma. He argued that the villages in the lower Nembi and upper Erave Valleys were on the extreme fringes of three different administrative areas—Nipa, Mendi, and the Erave, and it took two days of walking to reach the area from the established centers. The villages of Det, Paboronga, and Waramesa were currently under Mendi, the villages in the Toiwara area were administered from Kagua but most accessible through the Nembi Valley, and some isolated areas in the Wage Valley that were just beginning to come under administrative influence could all be administered by Poroma. A patrol post at Poroma would provide more immediate access to 16,000 people who would then be within a day's walk to an administrative center.[93] Hick's suggestions were strongly supported by A. J. Zweck, the District Commissioner, who thought that the area had good potential for economic development. [94]

Hicks went ahead with work on the proposed Poroma airstrip, and for almost two weeks in March and April of 1965, the people form Mato, Poroma, and Nenja worked on an airstrip at Poroma getting it ready for a Cessna aircraft to land on the strip. When the work was done, the groups held a dance to celebrate its completion.[95] The proposal did not receive final approval until 1967 after fighting

---

[90]Nipa Number 9 of 1961-1962, 9-10 {(NB 61-64 HW 166-167}.

[91]A. C. Jefferies, 17 May, 1962,letter to the Southern Highlands District, {NB 61-64 HW 158} in Nipa Number 9 of 1961-1962 {NB 61-64 HW 155-172}.

[92]Nipa Patrol Report Number 3 of 1969-1970:1969/70 Area Study-Nembi Plateau Census Division, 2, {NB 69-70 HW 94}.

[93]Nipa Patrol Number 8 of 1964-1965, 6-7, {NB 64-66, HW 141, 142}.

[94]A. J. Zweck, July 5, 1965, in a letter written to the Director of the Department of District Administration at Konedobu, in Nipa Patrol Report Number 8 of 1964-1965, {NB 64-66 HW 132-133}.

[95]Nipa Patrol Number 8 of 1964-1965, 4-5, {NB 64-66 HW 139-140}. The groups were competing to see who would get the first airstrip. While the Poroma people worked on the airstrip, Father Ben from the Catholic Mission at Det told the Patrol officer that the people at Det did not want the mission if they did not get an airstrip at Det.

erupted in the Det/Pabronga area among people living in the Undiri Census division on the fringes of the Mendi sub-district.

People from Pumi killed a man from Sumia named Putap and his wife and child. The woman was originally from Pabaronga. The people of Sumia reported the murder to the administration, but the administration failed to take firm action against the Pumi.[96] Subsequently, the people of Det/Pabaronga, Pambadl, and Sumia formed an alliance against the Pumi, One, Pororo, Iane, Iagen, Pinj, and Endowa groups in the Lai Valley. In November, they raided Pumi and killed ten people in what became known as the Pumi Massacre.

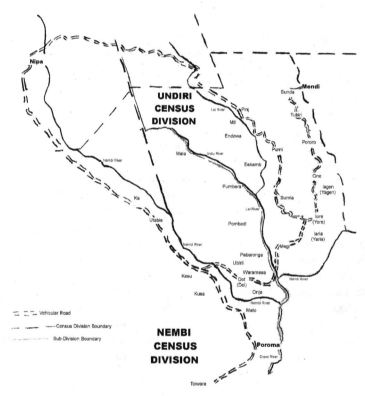

Map 4: *Groups involved in the Pumi massacre in late 1966*[97]

The administration reacted immediately and patrols from Mendi and Erave converged on the area, in search of the perpetrators on both sides. The administration was angry at the Pumi people for committing the original murders, and livid with the Pambadl/Sumia alliance for reverting to their own code of justice. In scenes reminiscent of the 1950s and early 1960s, attackers confronted the patrol

---

[96]Mendi Patrol Report Number 4 of 1966-1967, Appendix A, {NB 66-68 HW 47}.

[97]Map is adapted from C. P. Dangerfield Mendi Patrol Report Number 18 of 1966-1967, 18 {NB 66-68, HW 194}.

as it carried out its investigation. The people of Pabaronga fled before the patrol reached their territory, and other groups protected those who had gone into hiding.

The administration took a number of prisoners from both sides and by the middle of December captured all but three of the men involved in the Pumi killings.[98] Administrative officials acknowledged that they had not acted promptly or firmly when they first heard about the death of Putap and his wife and child. M. J. E. Anderson, the acting assistant District commissioner at Mendi remarked,

> There is no doubt in my mind that had we been able to take stronger action against the Pumi people following the original killing of Putap, the massacre that followed would not have occurred. The near relatives of Putap told me on the first day of investigations after Putap was killed, that unless we burned down the Pumi's houses, cut down their trees, and destroyed their gardens as a token of our wrath, (In addition to catching all of the offenders) the Sumia people would do it for us immediately (when) they got the opportunity. Our patrols eventually ended up protecting the perpetrators of Putap's killing instead of dealing severely with any breaches of the…law that could be found amongst the Pumi people.[99]

A standing patrol led by C. P. Dangerfield camped at Pombadl from February the 4th to May the 5th of 1967. Dangerfield had long talks with the people at Pambadl to learn why they had participated in the Pumi massacre. The people said that they understood the killing of the man in retribution for an earlier murder, but his wife and child were innocent victims. It was "ethically right to kill those who unjustly slew in revenge."[100]

The director of the Department of District Administration wrote that "this sort of thing may have been expected in 1960 or so in this area, but not in 1967." He opined that it happened because the administration had neglected the Det/Pabaronga area. He noted that there was "a heavy concentration of schools and aid posts in the immediate and west Mendi areas, but not much elsewhere."[101]

The incident at Pumi and the involvement of the groups living on the Eastern banks of the Nembi river confirmed the need for a patrol post at Poroma, and the administration agreed that the groups of Pombadl, Waramesa, Unja, Ubiril, Pabaronga, and Det would be transferred from Mendi to the nearby Poroma patrol post as soon as a bridge was built across the Nembi River and a road link between Det and Poroma was completed.[102]

---

[98]Mendi Patrol Report Number 8 of 1966/1967, 1-10 {NB 66-68 HW 133-142}.

[99]M. J. E. Anderson, 12 January, 1967, Letter to the Mendi District Commissioner, Southern Highlands in Mendi Patrol, in Mendi Report Number 8 of 1966-1967 {NB 66-68 HW 132}.

[100]Mendi Patrol Report Number 18 of 1966-1967, 8 {NB 64-68 HW 190}.

[101]J. K. McCarthy, 13 March, 1967, Director of the Department of District Administration, Konedobu in a letter to the District Commissioner of the Southern Highlands Province, in Mendi Patrol Report Number 8 of 1966-1967 {NB 66-68 HW 128-129}.

[102]M. J. E. Anderson. 12 January 1967, letter in Mendi Patrol Report Number 8 of 1966-1967, {NB 66-68 HW 132}.

In January of 1967 a patrol post officially opened at Poroma with patrol officer N. McQuilty serving as the first officer in charge. Along with routine administration of the area, plans called for the establishment of an administrative school, an aid post,[103] a local government council, and the promotion of economic development.[104] The people cleared the airstrip that had been built in 1965, and the administration opened Poroma station.[105]

In 1966 C. P. Dangerfield asked why the Nembi people had been more resistant to administrative influence than most of the surrounding groups and noted that the Tobua people "threatened the life of an officer in 1964." Even though they accepted the presence of the administration, "violent reactions" occurred whenever the administration "intruded into their traditional society." He said there were "two facts" that explained their strong resistance to administrative patrols. The first was that an "unfavourable view of the administration filtered through before the advent of regular patrolling." The second was the graded nature of the society where...the Head-Men are very powerful" and maintain their power and authority through competiveness.[106] I suggest an additional reason. In dealing with tribal conflict, the administration compromised its neutrality on more than one occasion. When its actions helped one side against the other, the administration became the other's enemy.

By 1967 the administration's emphasis for the Nembi groups changed from pacification and control to economic and political development.

Economic Development among the Nembi

The Nembi people prospered in the pre-contact society because of their position in the trade networks that existed between the Highlands and the Lowlands of Papua New Guinea. The only trade commodity that originated with them was a five-toed pig that other groups valued highly, but trade routes converged at the Kuvivi flats where the Nembi, Lai, Mendi, and Kagua Rivers join to from the Erave River, the Nembi were in a position to profit from the "flow of goods." They were persons in the middle, and valued trade items such as pearl shells, *tiagaso* oil, salt, and stone axe heads passed through their hands to the surrounding groups. The Nembi were "desirable as exchange partners and had connections

---

[103] An aid post provided rudimentary health care for the local people. The orderlies were trained to diagnose the more common illnesses and give first aid to injured persons, and transfer more serious cases that were beyond the expertise of the orderly to larger medical facilities with more highly trained medical staff at Nipa or Mendi.

[104] D. R. Marsh, 26 January, 1967, in a letter to The Director of the Department of District Administration in Konedobu, in Nipa Patrol Report Number 10 of 1966-1967, {NB 66-68 HW 80-81}.

[105] Nipa Patrol Report Number 10 of 1966-1967, 4 {NB 66-68 HW 92}.

[106] Nipa Patrol Report Number 10 of 1966-67, 6-7 {NB 66-68 HW 94-95}.

with people from all points of the compass" and "they became well known as canny traders and hard bargainers."[107]

When the administrative officials became aware of the Highlander's insatiable appetite for shell, they brought unprecedented supplies of shell into the area to purchase sweet potatoes, pigs, and labor from the local people. The new supply of shell "short-circuited the traditional process of trade." They were "bypassing and competing with traditional networks" and pacification "allowed Papuan traders to travel further along the trade routes themselves than previously," and "they too bypassed traditional middle men and neutralized traditional strategic trade positions."[108] The increased supply of shells also devalued them as tokens of exchange. The Nembi remained "in the middle" but it was no longer an advantageous position.

The administration believed that four things were necessary for economic development to occur. First, infrastructure, especially roads, had to be built. The second requirement was to introduce the people to a cash economy. The third requirement was for trade stores where people could use cash to acquire the goods they required. The fourth was for projects that would create a means for the local people to earn money. The administration worked to complete each of the steps, but in the Nembi area they were still a work in progress when Papua New Guinea became an independent nation.

By the time of independence, a road ran along the Nembi Plateau and through the Nembi Valley and connected Nipa and Poroma, but only a fair-weather road connected the Nembi groups to Mendi. It was 1976 before the all-weather Highlands highway reached Mendi, linking the Southern Highlands to the coast,[109] and it was 1978 before the highway began to make its way through the Nembi Valley towards Nipa and Tari.[110]

Road work provided a means of introducing the Nembi to a cash economy. In March of 1967, J. K. McCarthy called for the use of cash rather than trade goods in all transactions that the administration had with the Nembi people in order to hasten the process of changing from barter to a cash economy.[111]

---

[107]Schieffelin and Crittenden, 130-132. For a more complete discussion of the Nembi trade networks see Robert Crittenden, *Sustenance, Seasonality and Social Cycles on the Nembi Plateau, Papua New Guinea.* [Canberra, Australia: Australian National University, 1982], 194-255 and Schiefflen and Crittenden, 126-135.

[108]Scheiffelin and Criettenden, 134.

[109]Rena Lederman. *What Gifts Engender: Social Relations and Politics in Mendi, Highland Papua New Guinea.* [Cambridge [Cambridgeshire]: Cambridge University Press, 1986], 5.

[110]Bill Tolbert, "To Everything there Is a Season" *Missionary Tidings* XXIX, no 7 [February, 1978]:4.

[111]J. K. McNeill, 13 March, 1967, letter to the District Commissioner, in Nipa Patrol Report Number 10 of 1966-1967 {NB 66-68 HW 78}.

The Highlands labor scheme[112] played a significant role in bringing cash into the Nembi area. When the first recruits to plantation labor returned to the Nembi area after their two-year contracts ended bringing gifts and money with them and telling stories about the world beyond the Nembi borders,[113] the number of young men who wanted to be a part of the scheme increased significantly.[114] By 1970, older men encouraged the younger men to sign up for the Highlands labor scheme because there were few opportunities for employment within the district and it was a way to obtain money.[115]

The introduction of trade stores gave the people a place to spend their cash and secure items that they wanted. In the 1960s, the administration expected missions to assist with economic development and to run trade stores so the people had a place to spend the money they received from administrative contracts to acquire the goods they desired. At the administration's request, Christian Union Mission opened a trade store at Ka in 1965[116] that was "well patronized by the people."[117] The administration considered trade stores to be a work incentive for the people,[118] and they quickly became the people's primary source of European goods.[119] For about two years Christian Union Mission's trade store at Ka was the only trade store servicing the area.[120] When Christian Union Mission opened outstations at Montanda, Farata, and Embi, it established trade stores on the new stations.[121] The Catholics also opened trade stores on their stations, and in 1967 European companies opened trade stores at Poroma and Nipa.[122]

Trade stores caught on, and the local people soon wanted their own stores. In 1968 Pe at Upa opened the first trade store owned and operated by a Nembi person,[123] and other local entrepreneurs soon followed his example. In December of 1969, McNeill noted that the people in the Nembi were eager to establish trade stores. They built bush buildings and with a small investment of twenty dollars or so purchased a small amount stock to sell. The administration was concerned be-

---

[112]The administration recruited young men from the Highlands to work on plantations in the Coastal and Islands regions. The signed up for a two year contract after which they were repatriated to their home provinces.

[113]Nipa Patrol Report Number 3 of 1968-1969, Situation Report, {NB 68-69 HW 19}.

[114]Nipa Patrol Report Number 11 of 1967-1968, 1 {NB 66-68 HW 287}.

[115]Poroma Patrol Report Number 7 of 1969-1970, Appendix A, {NB 69-70 HW 217}.

[116]Telephone conversation with Betty Seymour held in May of 2005.

[117]Nipa Patrol Report Number 5 of 1965-1966, 2 {NB 64-66, HW 292}.

[118]Nipa Patrol Report Number 5 of 1965-1966, 2 {NB 64-66, HW 292}.

[119]Nipa Patrol Report Number 2 of 1969-1970, 11, {NB 69-70 HW 75}. Goods that were in high demand included steel axes, cooking pots, umbrellas, spoons, enamel plates, cloth and clothing, beads, fish line, fish hooks, soap, salt, sugar, and matches were popular items. At first canned fish and rice were not well received, and spades sold very slowly because people still preferred to use digging sticks for garden work.

[120]Nipa Patrol Number 10 of 1966-1967, 10 {NB 66-68 HW 98}; Mendi Patrol Number 18 of 1966-1967 9, {NB 66-68 HW 191}.

[121]Christian Union Mission Executive Committee Minutes, November 11, 1972, 2.

[122]Poroma Patrol Report Number 2 of 1966-1967, 12 {NB 66-68, HW 227}.

[123]Nipa Patrol Report Number 2 of 1968-1969, 3 {NB 68-69 HW 13}.

cause most of the people did not have enough cash or enough potential customers for the stores to become viable enterprises.[124] By 1973 eighty small trade stores operated in the Nembi Valley. Most of them were not profitable, but a few of them did well and benefitted both the owners and the customers.[125]

When the local people began operating their own trade stores, Christian Union Mission sold store goods wholesale to the new store owners. After roads improved and the local trade store owners could get a supply of wholesale goods from the other sources, and the laws changed making it illegal for missions with non-commercial land leases to be involved in the business, Christian Union Mission quit the trade store business. It closed its stores on the outstations in 1972[126] and at Ka in 1974.[127]

Finding a way for the Nembi people to earn money was difficult. At first the administration searched for large scale projects sponsored by European investors but found no suitable projects or investors. One of the hindrances was the lack of available Nembi land. The high population density meant that little undisputed land was available for economic development,[128] and with a growing population, land pressure increased. Because no land was available for large scale coffee plantations, the administration distributed coffee plants to small holders. The first coffee was introduced on the Nembi plateau in 1965,[129] but it was 1969 before most of the Nembi villages planted their first coffee seedlings. In 1971 the first five pounds of coffee was harvested, and production increased during the next two years.[130] For years most Nembi people, both men and women owned a few coffee trees which provided them with some cash income.[131]

In the late 1960s, the United Church at Nipa expressed an interest in developing a tea plantation in the Nipa Basin, and in February of 1969 A. F. McNeill said that the economic "future of the entire Nipa area depended on the establishment of a tea plantation by the United Church at Nipa."[132] In the end, the idea of a tea plantation was abandoned because of the difficulty in securing land, and because the United Church was unable to acquire the needed funding for the project.[133]

---

[124]Nipa Patrol Report Number 3 of 1969-1970: Situation Report, 2-3 {NB 69-70 HW 90-91}.

[125]Poroma Patrol Report Number One of 1973-1974, 10, {NB 70-74 HW 383}.

[126]C UM Executive Committee Minutes, November 11, 1972, 2

[127]CUM Field Council Minutes, October 26, 1974, 6

[128]Crittenden, *Sustenance, Seasonality and Social Cycles*, 239.

[129]Crittenden, *Sustenance, Seasonality and Social Cycles*, 239.

[130]Nipa Patrol Report Number 3 of 1969-1970, Situation Report, 3 {NB 69-70 HW 90}

[131]When I returned to the Nembi area in December of 2013, some of the people said that the youth are no longer interested in owning coffee trees because the trees require too much work for the income that they produce.

[132]A. F. McNeill, 14 February, 1969, letter to the Southern Highlands District Commissioner in Nipa Patrol Report Number 7 of 1968-1969 {NB 68-69 HW 144}.

[133]Nipa Patrol Number 2 of 1971-1972: Situation Report, 2 {NB 70-74 HW 220}.

The administration could not secure enough land for a large scale cattle project,[134] but it encouraged each group to free up six to ten acres that would support a few heads of cattle and create a source of income.[135] In August of 1968 the first cattle blocks were marked off at Injip, Injua and Upa where local men had accumulated enough funds to buy fencing for four or five heads of cattle.[136] Injua was the first Nembi group to stock its project,[137] and by November of 1971, three head of cattle grazed on five acres of land. Eight other groups, including Upa, Enip, Pomberel, Tobua, Karamela, Eskam, Tegibo, and Ulal were ready to start their projects.[138] The people wanted the cattle more for status and prestige than for the economic gain. The administration expressed concern that the people would slaughter the cows before their economic potential was realized.[139] The fear was well founded. As Schieffelin and Crittenden note, on the Nembi plateau

> in 1974 fighting broke out again between clan alliances over the ownership of cattle for a new project. Several cows were killed and a number of clansmen ended up in the Nipa jail. ... The Nembi never saw these projects as developmental, profit making ventures but rather as traditional attempts to gain renown and political advantage in the continuing rivalries between local clans and Big Men, using new means and object of exchange. Where cows are kept on the Nembi Plateau, they are viewed as large pigs to be displayed and killed at pig-killing ceremonies for the glory of the clans that owned them.[140]

Several companies explored the Nembi area for exploitable mineral and oil resources. After independence oil companies carried out extensive explorations throughout the Southern Highlands Province. As a result of those explorations, oil was discovered at Kutubu in 1986, and the Kutubu Oil Project began commercial production in June of 1992.[141] Gas was discovered at Tari in 1987 and the Hides Gas to Electric Project began producing gas in 1991. Subsequently, smaller oil fields were set up at Gobe in 1998, Moran in 2000, and Southeast Manada in 2003,[142] but not enough reserves have been found in the Nembi area to merit the establishment of large scale operations.

During the 1960s and early 1970s, the administration attempted to introduce a number of small scale development projects including fisheries, tea, chilies,

---

[134]M. P. D. Davies, 23 December, 1971, letter to the District Commissioner of the Southern Highlands District in Nipa Patrol Number 2 of 1971-1972 {NB 70-74 HW 214}

[135]Nipa Patrol Report Number 2 of 1971-1972, 3 {NB 70-74 HW 224}.

[136]Nipa Patrol Report Number 2 of 1968-1969, 1, 3 {NB 68-69 HW 11-13}.

[137]Nipa Patrol Report Number 1 of 1970-1971, Situation Report, 2 {NB 70-74 HW 21}.

[138]Nipa Patrol Report Number 2 of 1971-1972, Situation Report, {3 NB 70-74 HW 224}.

[139]Poroma Patrol Report Number 6 of 1970-1971, {NB 70-74 HW 99}.

[140]Schieffelin and Crittenden, 276-277.

[141]Our Activities: Kutubu http://www.oilsearch.com/Our-Activities/PNG/Kutu-bu.html[Accessed on April 22, 2013]

[142]"Our Activities: Hides GTE" http://www.oilsearch.com/Our-Activities/PNG/-Hides-GTE.html [accessed on April 22, 2013]

pyrethrum[143] and silkworms.[144] None of the projects were successful, and in the end the primary source of income for the Nembi people came from coffee or local produce such as food and firewood that they raised in their gardens or harvested from their land and sold to the missions and administration.[145]

As independence approached, the lament of the patrol officers was that in spite of their best efforts, there was no economic development in the area, and that except for the Highlands labor scheme, the Nembi people had only limited access to a cash income. The people still depended on the traditional exchange system. Money had been incorporated into the exchange system; pigs remained an important item of trade; pearl shells were becoming less important; and salt and smaller shells were no longer included in the bride wealth.[146] The people from the lower Nembi Valley and the Nembi Plateau area had strong pre-contact ties with the Kutubu people. After the discovery of oil at Lake Kutubu, those ties were strengthened when Kutubu men secured Nembi wives. The exchange of bride wealth brought some cash into the Nembi area.

To the present there has been little economic development. In 2000 Bryant Allen reported that the people living on the Nembi Plateau were among the most "disadvantaged people in the Southern Highlands" of Papua New Guinea.[147]

Local Government Councils

In 1967, a newly appointed Director of District Administration said that eighty-two percent of the people of Papua and New Guinea had council representation, and the time had come to make the system more efficient by consolidating councils rather than starting new ones. The director claimed that "the areas still not covered were those of such scanty population and poor resources that its extension there would be of little value."[148] However, the people from the Nipa/Poroma area of the Southern Highlands District come from an area that was densely populated,[149] but had no representation in local government councils.

The Nipa Local Government Council started with the people of the Wage and Nipa Basin Census Division forming the council core after the first council elec-

---

[143]Mendi Patrol Report Number 17 of 1966-1967, Situation Report Undiri Census Division, 4 {NB 66-68 HW 161}.

[144]Nipa Patrol Report Number 3 of 1969-1970: Situation Report, 2 {NB 69-70 HW 91}.

[145]Poroma Patrol Report Number 7 of 1969-1970, Area Survey – Nembi Valley Census Division, 6, 10 {NB 69-70 HW 207, 211}.

[146]Ronald Paul Hood "Melanesian Paradigm Shifting: Nembi Worldview Change and the Contextualization of the Gospel among Urban Immigrants." [PhD diss., Fuller Theological Seminary, 1999], 42.

[147]Bryant Allen, "The Setting: Land, Economics and Development in the Southern Highlands Province," in *Conflict and Resource Development in the Southern Highlands of Papua New Guinea*, eds. Nicole Haley and Ronald J. May [Canberra: Australia National University E Press, 2007], 44.

[148]Mair, 90.

[149]Crittenden, *Sustenance, Seasonality and Social Cycles*, 307-375; Nipa Patrol Report Number 7 of 1968-1969.

tions were held in from October 10 to Deccember 1, 1966.[150] In January of 1968, the first Nembi groups of Injua, Tegibo, Obua and Semin were incorporated in the Nipa Local Government Council,[151] but it was January of 1970 before the rest of the groups on the Nembi Plateau elected their first councilors and became a part of the Nipa Local Government Council.[152] A number of years after independence the Plateau groups formed their own council.

The people living in the Nembi Valley Census Division had no council representation until the Poroma Local Government council was opened in February of 1971.[153] In 1973 patrol officers reported that the council had "little effect" in terms of economic development, but the people liked the council and looked to it "for advice and assistance."[154] The Nembi people were only beginning to develop political awareness as the rest of the country was pushing for political independence.

In 1973 D. C. Ekins said the Nembi Plateau was "a complete political wilderness as far as comprehension of government machinery, both local and central." The Nembi people weren't too concerned about future developments,[155] and they were very "pro-administration" and patrol officers with a "white epidermis" were still a "big-deal" to them. Councilors were nearly all non-Pidgin speakers, and they attended the local government council meetings because of the allowance they received for attending the meetings. They did not take an active part in council proceedings, and they were merely the "front men" for the "real traditional leaders." The local government councils had "little effect on the majority of the people, and although a few of the councilors realized the potential of local government council, they did not communicate "this knowledge to their constituents." Other councilors thought the council was simply "another idea concocted by the patrol officer and that they might as well go along with it to humor him." Political enlightenment would only be "achieved by actually experiencing the changes as they occur."[156]

Papua New Guinea became an independent nation only ten years after the Nembi groups had accepted the colonial presence, laid aside all forms of resistance, and opted for full cooperation with the administration. The Nembi like other Highlanders wanted to delay independence, but educated Papuans and New Guineans from the Coastal and Islands Regions pushed to take over the government of their own country. I tell about the push for independence in Appendix Three.

---

[150]Nipa Patrol Report Number 10 of 1966-1967, 13 {NB 66-68 HW 101}.

[151]A. F. McNeill, 24 February, 1968, letter to the District Commissioner at Mendi in Nipa Patrol Report 13 for 1967-1968 {NB 66-68 HW 300}.

[152]Nipa Patrol Report Number 5 of 1969-1970 {NB 69-70 HW 190}.

[153]Poroma Patrol Report Number 5 for 1970-1971, {NB 70-74 HW 68}.

[154]Poroma Patrol Report Number 1 of 1973-1974, 3, 10-11 {NB 70-74 HW 374, 381-382}.

[155]The future developments he referred to was rapidly approaching self-government and independence.

[156]Nipa Patrol Report Number 2, 1972-1973, Area Study – Nembi Plateau {NB 70-74, HW 325}.

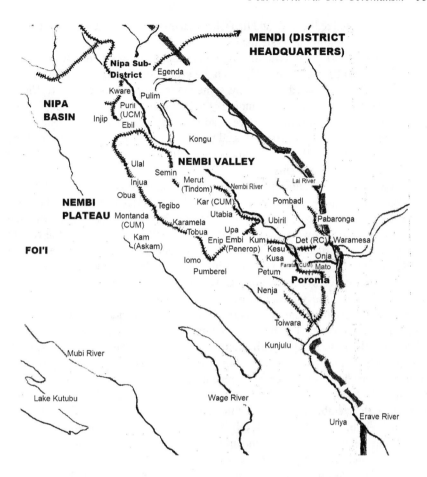

Map 5: *Nembi groups in 1973 showing completed roads*[157]

Reflections about Colonization

From the earliest days of colonial control in Papua New Guinea, British and Australian administrations depended on Christian missions to help them achieve their goals. The relationship between the colonial administrations and the missions was one of mutual dependency and a mutual awareness that each was using the other to achieve different objectives.[158] Sir Hurbert Murray encouraged Christian missions because he believed that the traditional belief systems with their "objectionable" practices had to be replaced by a new system that would assist the people to

---

[157]The map is adapted from G. Elimo, Poroma Patrol Report Number 1 of 1973-1974, {NB 70-74 HW 383}. It shows the roads that had been completed by independence. The spelling of place names has been changed to reflect current spellings. The map is not drawn to scale.

[158]Diane Langmore, *Missionary Lives Papua, 1874-1914* [Pacific Islands Monograph Series, no. 6. Honolulu: University of Hawaii Press, 1989], 216.

move from the old to the new, and that Christian missions played a significant role in replacing the traditional systems.[159]

Following World War Two, the Highlands administrators said that the Christian missions had a "pacifying effect" on the groups being brought under administrative control and issued to missions some of the first permits to enter restricted areas.[160] As they had from the beginning of colonialism, Christian missions helped provide health and education services and received administrative subsidies for the services they provided. Hasluck said the administration gave assistance to the missions for their medical programs because the "missions had staff and were already in touch with patients."[161]

Clark, Ballard, and Nihill say that the administration's willingness to allow the missions to enter the Wiru area before it was fully derestricted attested to the interdependence between administrators and missionaries.[162] Similarly, when Christian Union Mission began working among the Nembi in January of 1964, the Nembi area was still "restricted," and the missionaries and patrol officers depended on each other. The missionaries were answerable to the administration and had to satisfy the patrol officers' expectations. Christian Union Mission's entered the trade store business because of the administration's expectations for the mission, and the mission withdrew from the trade store business when the administration made it clear that it did not want the mission to compete with the local trade store owners.

During the process of colonization, the Nembi lost their advantageous position of coveted trade partners. The administration failed to introduce development projects that allowed the Nembi to regain some of the advantage and prestige that they had lost. The interdependency of the mission and the administration reinforced the Nembi perception that the mission and administration both had significant wealth. The failure to establish suitable economic development projects among the Nembi prior to independence set the stage for future conflicts between the church and mission. After the colonial administration was gone, the Nembi expected the mission to share its resources and promote economic development, but the mission prioritized the spiritual over the secular and considered the promotion of economic development to be a secondary concern. I now tell the story of missionization and the relationships that developed between the mission and the Nembi church.

---

[159]John Hubert Plunkett Murray, *Papua of To-day; or, An Australian Colony in the Making* [London: P.S. King. 1925] x, 222-233, 249; Sir Hubert Murray, *Native Administration in Papua.* [Port Moresby: Walter Alfred Black, Acting Government Printer, 1929]. 21, NAA: A518, 1850/1/5 http://record-search.naa.gov.au/scripts/Imagine.asp?B=108257 [Accessed on August 8, 2012]

[160]Warren R. Read, June 1, 1964, Nipa Patrol Report Number 15 of 1963 to 1964, 5 {NB 61-64 HW 401}.

[161]Paul Hasluck, *A Time for Building: Australian Administration in Papua and New Guinea, 1951-1963.* [Carlton, Vic: Melbourne University Press, 1976], 113.

[162]Clark, Ballard, and Nihill, 97

Chapter Three

Missionization

Introduction

In this chapter I look at Christian Union Mission's outreach to the Nembi people. When Christian Union Mission arrived on the scene, the people of the Nembi Valley were under "partial control." Most of the resistance to an administrative presence had been laid aside, but pockets of resistance remained. Some of the groups continued to engage in intermittent warfare. Three other missions were well established at Nipa and two of those missions expected to enter the Nembi Valley. The Protestant mission withdrew from the Nembi Valley in deference to Christian Union Mission. The missionaries who began working in the Nembi Valley were unprepared for the cultural differences between them and the Nembi.

The missionaries and the administration assumed that the people had no well-established religion but followed transient cults that found their expression in a number of superstitious practices that they would have to lay aside. Hiebert says that mission never takes place in a vacuum. When missionaries attempt to plant churches, they enter a social context and seek to communicate the gospel in a cultural context that must be understood[1] if mission outreach is to reach its fullest potential. Christian Union Mission missionaries had an inadequate understanding of the cultural context that they entered. On the other hand, the Nembi interpreted everything the mission and the colonial administration did according to their traditional beliefs. When they embraced Christianity, many of the expectations that they held for the former belief system were carried over to the new. Those expectations affected the relationship between the Nembi people and the missionaries. In this chapter I briefly discuss the Nembi belief systems as I understand them, and I include a more detailed analysis in Appendix Four.

A pioneer missionary began working in the Nembi Valley in January of 1964. Conflict arose between him and the home board. When other missionaries arrived on the field they were caught up in the conflict, and it deeply affected the work.

---

[1] Paul G. Hiebert. *The Gospel in Human Contexts: Anthropological Explorations for Contemporary Missions.* [Grand Rapids, Mich: Baker Academic, 2009] 18-19.

As the missionaries negotiated a complex set of relationships with the colonial administration, with other missions, with the Nembi people, with each other, and with the sending agency, they established a medical ministry, started schools and literacy classes, promoted economic development, began women's ministries, and carried out religious instruction. Through these ministries, they eventually won converts. After there were converts, they worked to develop an organized self-supporting, self-governing, self-propagating church. They wrote a constitution and received official governmental recognition for Christian Union Church of Papua New Guinea. In 1978 the Nembi converts voted to accept the constitution and formally elected their district and regional church leaders.

Mission Outreach to the Southern Highlands

The first two missions to enter the Southern Highlands District opened their work in 1950. The Unevangelized Field Mission[2] established itself in the Lake Kutubu area,[3] and the Methodist Overseas Mission,[4] out of Australia, entered the Mendi area. The Rev. Gordon Young of the Methodist Mission arrived at Mendi on October 25, 1950 with a patrol bringing laborers to assist with the construction of the Mendi airstrip and patrol post.[5] After two days he returned to Mount Hagen with an outgoing patrol, but one month later, on November 22, 1950, he returned with another patrol and started the first mission outreach to the Mendi area. He established a mission station one-half mile from the patrol post. When Allan Timberley finalized the purchase of land for the Mendi patrol post and air strip, he also purchased five acres of land for the Methodist Overseas Mission.[6]

The Catholics opened their work in the Southern Highlands in 1954 when Father A. Michellop and Brother J. Delaborre, who were associated with the Yule Island Catholic Mission, established themselves at Mendi during the July, August, and September quarter of 1954. Soon after that they applied for permits to enter other areas of the Southern Highlands.[7] They opened sub-stations in the Lai Valley and by 1956 they had established a school at Pinj staffed by a Papuan teacher and regularly visited by priests who were stationed at Mendi.[8] The East and West

---

[2]The mission later changed its name to the Asia Pacific Christian Mission and it spawned the church that is now known as the Evangelical Church of Papua.

[3]S. S. Smith, May, 1950, Kutubu Patrol Report Number 2 of 1949-1950, 34 {NB 49-54, HW 14}.

[4]This group was originally the Australasian Wesleyan Methodist Mission Society and later became a part of the United Church of Papua New Guinea.

[5]S. S. Smith, November, 1950, Lake Kutubu Patrol Report Number 2 1950-51, 21, {NB 49-54 HW 44}.

[6]Allan Timberly, 16 April, 1951, Mount Hagen Patrol Report Number 6 of 1950-1951, 18 {49-54 HW 133}.

[7]Robert R. Cole, 20 October, 1954, Southern Highlands District Quarterly Report, Period 1st July to 30th of September, 1954, 15 {NB 54-59 HW 182}.

[8]J. J. Pickrell, 12 June, 1956, Mendi Patrol Report Number 11 of 1955-56, 3 {NB 54-58, HW 277}.

Indies Bible Mission[9] began working in the Pabarabuk area near Mount Hagen in 1948,[10] and from there they moved into the Ialibu area in the early 1950s.[11]

Nipa

As they had in Mendi, the Overseas Methodist Mission arrived in Nipa while the newly established patrol post was still under construction. On December 2, 1959, a small administrative patrol escorted the Reverends Young and Keightly to Nipa. The officer in charge assigned the missionaries a temporary site by the airstrip and helped them search the surrounding area for a site suitable for a permanent station. Young left after a couple of days, but Keightly remained and the Methodist Overseas Mission started its work at Nipa.[12] In April of 1960, the missionaries selected Puril, a site located one and one-half miles south of Nipa, as the permanent location for the Methodist Overseas Mission Station.[13] The Australian missionaries, C. J. Keightley with his wife and three children were at Nipa along with John Teu from the Solomon Islands with his wife and children.[14] When the lease at Puril was finalized, a nursing sister, Helen Young, joined the Keightley and Teu families. She started a medical ministry while the rest of the staff worked on the construction of the mission station. At first little religious teaching took place.[15] The administration restricted the missionaries' movements to a one and one-half mile radius from their station but as the nearby groups accepted an administrative presence, the administration lifted the restrictions, and the missionaries expanded their influence and became more involved in religious instruction.

Not long after the administration opened the Nipa Patrol post, Catholic priests began visiting the area every three months and remained in the Nipa area for a

---

[9]I mention the East and West Bible Mission because James and Virginia Hummel had contacts associated with the East and West Bible Mission that later became the Evangelical Bible Mission and established the PNG Bible Church (World Mission Associates http://www.wmausa.org/page.aspx?id=83853 [accessed on July 19, 2013]). When James and Virginia Hummel first came to Papua and New Guinea, many of the indigenous pastors who first entered the Nembi Valley were associated with this group or with the Bible Mission, an offshoot of the East and West Bible Mission.

[10]Gerald T. Bustin, "The Papua New Guinea Bible Church" World Mission Associates http://www.wmausa.org/page.aspx?id=83853 [accessed on July 19, 2013].

[11]Robert R. Cole, July, 1955, Southern Highlands District Quarterly Report Period 1st of April to 30th of June, 1955, 11 {NB 54-58 HW 206}.

[12]J. Jordan, January, 1960, Nipa Patrol Report Number 1 of 1959-1960, 6-7 {NB 58-61 HW 58-59}.

[13]D. N. Butler, June, 1960, Nipa Patrol Report Number 4 of 1959-1960, 5 {NB 58-61 HW 82}.

[14]D. N. Butler, June, 1960, Nipa Patrol Report Number 4 of 1959-1960, 14-15 {NB 58-61 HW 91-92}.

[15]R. T. Fairhill, 7 November, 1961, Nipa Patrol Report Number 2 of 1961-1962, 13 {NB 61-64 HW 86}.

week to ten days on each visit.[16] By the end of 1961 they had located land that they hoped to acquire for a station, but they had not yet applied for the lease because they did not have enough personnel to staff the station.[17]

In March of 1962, Vic and Elsie Schlatter arrived in Nipa and began a work for the Apostolic Christian Church. His primary emphasis was Bible translation. He sought and obtained the permission of the leader of the Overseas Methodist Mission who encouraged him to settle at Nipa because of Shlatter's plans to translate the scriptures into the vernacular. Since the Methodist Overseas Mission was south of Nipa, Schlatter located north of Nipa.[18]

Christian Union Mission's appearance at Nipa is noted in a history of the United Church. "The arrival of another mission, the Christian Union Mission, with no prior consultation with the other missions already working there meant that here was an added danger of confusion in the people's minds as they heard the presentations of the gospel by the four missions."[19]

Nembi

The Overseas Methodist Mission was the first mission to patrol and start churches in the Nembi area. Working out of Puril, they opened churches among several of the groups in the upper Nembi Valley including Semin and Injua. In 1963 or early 1964 they established the first mission station in the Middle Nembi Valley when a Solomon Islands missionary and his wife moved to Togura near Utabia.[20]

By August of 1962, the Catholic Capuchin mission started patrolling the lower Nembi area from the Kagua sub-district,[21] and by March of 1963 they were conducting sporadic visits to the Nembi Plateau.[22] They gave pearl shells to village constables in recognition of their position of authority, and to Nembi groups to secure ground at sites where churches would eventually be located.[23]

---

[16]D. N. Butler, June, 1960, Nipa Patrol Report Number 4 of 1959-1960, 14-15, {NB 58-61 HW 92}.

[17]R. T. Fairhill, 7 November, 1961, Nipa Patrol Report Number 2 of 1961-1962, 13 {NB 61-64 HW 86}.

[18]Rosalie M Donais, *To Them Gave He Power: The Gripping Tale of God's Great Love For the Stone Age Waola Highlanders of Papua New Guinea* [Tremont, Illinois: Apostolic Christian Church Foundation, 1987], 27-34.

[19]Ronald G. Williams, *The United Church in Papua New Guinea and the Solomon Islands* [Rabaul, PNG: Trinity Press, 1972], 304.

[20]Mapon Ek, interview by author, at Mato near Poroma, SHP, Papua New Guinea, December 31, 2009. Don and Betty Seymour, interview by author, Avon Park, Fla, May 27 and 28, 2010.

[21]N. D. Lucas, 20th August, 1962, Nipa Patrol Report Number 2 of 1962-1963, {NB 61-64 HW 240}.

[22]Peter J. Barber, 25 March, 1963, Nipa Patrol Report Number 8 of 1962-1963, {NB 61-64 HW 360}.

[23]Alan C. Jefferies, July, 1963, "Native Situation" in Mendi Patrol Report Number 3A of 1962-1963a, 1-2, {NB 61-64 HW 206-207}.

Kanj Mesmba from Utabia, who later aligned himself with Christian Union Mission, joined a Catholic patrol that went from place to place buying ground for the future churches. According to Kanj, the Catholic priest who led the patrol paid groups from five to ten pearl shells for ground. The patrol went to the newly acquired Catholic station at Nipa where they stayed for several months and constructed the first bush buildings. After two or three months had passed, Kanj grew homesick and decided to leave. The priest encouraged him to remain and offered to send him to catechist training at Erave, but Kanj declined the offer and returned home. While Kanj was at Nipa, Jim Hummel arrived by aircraft to investigate the possibility of establishing a work in the Nembi area for Christian Union Mission.[24]

Jim and Virginia Hummel arrived in Papua New Guinea in January of 1963 to begin a work under the auspices of the Churches of Christ in Christian Union (CCCU). Details about James and Virginia Hummel's first year of service in Papua and New Guinea are sketchy,[25] but apparently, he did not enter the Nembi area until after Christian Union Mission received its certificate of incorporation on the 21st of November, 1963.[26] Hummel is first mentioned in the patrol reports on January the 29th, 1964, when joint patrols from Mendi and Nipa met Hummel at Kum. The patrol from Nipa went to Kesu, and the Mendi patrol and Hummel went to Utabia.[27] Based on that evidence, I assume that Christian Union Mission's outreach to the Nembi people began in January of 1964. I tell CUM and Hummel's story more fully later in this chapter.

Nembi Beliefs

It is impossible to comprehend the Nembi understanding of their world, their early perception of the administration and missionaries, and their view of Christianity without some understanding of their belief system. Hiebert says,

> As Christians we are often unaware that our beliefs are frequently shaped more by our culture than by the gospel. We take our Christianity to be biblically based and normative for everyone. We do not stop to ask what parts of it come from our sociocultural and historical contexts, and what parts come from Scripture. Missionaries are forced to deal with sociocultural differences, and therefore, with social and cultural contexts. But even then they may take little time to systematically study

---

[24]Kanj Mesmba, interview by author, at Port Moresby, Papua New Guinea, January 29, 2010.

[25]I contacted Jim and Virginia Hummel and requested to interview, but my request was denied. I rely on interviews with pastors from Ialibu who accompanied Hummel into the Nipa area, the Nembi people, and Hummel's missionary co-workers. I also gleaned from the *Missionary Tidings* and from the minutes of the CCCU general foreign missionary board.

[26]Relevant documents are held at CCCU headquarters in Circleville, Ohio, USA. A copy of the Certificate of Incorporation is included in Appendix One.

[27]Warren R. Read, 12th February, 1964, Nipa Patrol Report Number 12 of 1963-1964, (NB 61-64 HW 371).

in depth the contexts in which they serve, despite the fact that the effectiveness of their ministries is determined in large measure by how well they do this.[28]

The missionaries only partially understood the traditional Nembi belief systems, but even today some elements of the traditional beliefs find expression in the Christian beliefs of the Nembi people.

Melanesian religions, according to G. W. Trompf, are so varied that it is difficult to generalize about them, but they do share some broad themes.[29] They are primarily concerned with maintaining equilibrium between the spirit and the physical world that come together to form a single monistic whole. When a good balance is achieved, and a good relationship exists between the human and the "more-than-human," people enjoy prosperity and well-being. "Group wealth is taken as a reflection of good relationships between humans and the spirit order."[30]

Lawrence and Meggitt say that Melanesian belief systems conceived both an ordinary physical world or "natural environment" and a spirit world filled with spirits, ghosts, demons, and powers that were more powerful than ordinary human beings and existed either in some remote location that replicated the earth or attached themselves to the earth and were capable of assuming bodily form.[31] They believed in both a physical and a spiritual presence, but the two were not separated.[32] As Trompf makes clear, they existed together, in a monistic physical/spirit world without divisions.[33]

The Nembi thought that the patrol officers and missionaries came from the spirit world and that their unprecedented wealth and power originated with the spirits, but the Nembi were unsure exactly where the red skinned beings originated. They theorized that the strangers were ancestral spirits returning from the dead; that they came from the sky; or that they were descendants of a red skinned female spirit named *Ollep Yalin* who was the mother of all.

Several of the Nembi people whom I interviewed in 2009 and 2010 talked about the pre-Christian cults. Interviewees referred to a number of the cults by name, but they spoke most often of a fertility cult named *timb*—including *tundu*

---

[28]Hiebert, *The Gospel in Human Contexts*, 18.

[29]G. W. Trompf. *Melanesian Religion.* [Cambridge, England: Cambridge University Press, 1991], 12.

[30]Trompf, *Melanesian Religion*, 20.

[31]Peter Lawrence and Mervin J. Meggitt. *Gods, Ghosts, and Men in Melanesia; Some Religions of Australian New Guinea and the New Hebrides* {Melbourne: Oxford University Press, 1965], 9-10.

[32]The perception of a physical world and a spiritual world is a Western way of describing what, for the Melanesians, is one world without division.

[33]G. W. Trompf, *Melanesian Religion,* [Cambridge [England]: Cambridge University Press, 1991], 16-19.

(short) *timb* and *sollu* (long) *timb*—and another cult named *kepel*.[34] Matthew Werip, who was a youth in the early 1960s, recalled taking part in some of the *kepel* rituals. Most of the men had some spirit stones that they looked after. The spirits living in the stones were considered to be part of the family. The men constructed special houses in isolated areas for the stones, and laid them out on shelves. When there was illness, or things were not going well, the men gathered at the spirit house, sacrificed a pig, and fed the spirit by rubbing the stone with a mixture of pig grease, *tiagaso* oil, and/or wild edible greens. They would talk to the spirit as they rubbed the stone, telling it to eat, be satisfied, and go.[35] When they performed the rituals, the spirits would listen and depart, and things would return to normal. After the ritual ended, the men ate the pig that remained, but the women and children were not allowed to participate in the ceremony or eat any of the pork from the sacrificed pig. [36]

Today the people equate *temo* with Satan, and they say that the spirits were hard task masters. Tia Paik, an elderly man from Mil in the Lai Valley said, "The spirits had surrounded us in the Lai Valley, and finished off my fathers, brothers, mothers, and sisters. We were fighting, and we had nowhere to go, and so we were ready to receive a new talk that would allow us and our families to escape the tyranny of the spirits."[37]

Cults would come and go. The *timb* cults were sold from one group to the next. D'Arcy Ryan who wrote the first ethnography about the Mendi people in the 1950s, described the rituals associated with the purchase of the *timb* cults.[38] To the administration the *timb* cults were anathema because of the high price that donor groups demanded from the recipient group when they sold the cult's secrets and because of costly fines and severe punishments given to the uninitiated if they violated the cults' taboos or learned its secrets.[39]

---

[34]Several informants mentioned the *timb* and *kepel* cults, and they always specified that there were two distinct *timb* cults—*tundu timb* and *sollu timb*. They also named and described some of the rituals that were associated with the cults, including one called *ip temo* in which a pig was drowned and then eaten. Without an in-depth study it was difficult to tell if they were naming separate cults, or rituals associated with cults they had already named.

[35]Matthew, the interviewee, spoke in Pidgin, and said that they talked to the spirit in the following manner, "*Spuu* (a combined blowing and spitting sound), *Yu kaikai na pinis.* (You eat and desist). *Spuu! Yu no ken kam long ol pikinini bilong mipela!* (You cannot come to our children). *Spuu! Yu no ken kam long ol manmeri!* (You cannot come to the adults.) *Spuu! Mipela kilim pik na givim yu ya, na yu kaikai, na spuu, Yu go!* (We have killed pig and given to you, so you eat, and you go).

[36]Matthew Werip, interview by author, Semin, Southern Highlands Province, Papua New Guinea, December 26, 2009.

[37]Tia Paik, interview by author, Mil, Lai Valley, Southern Highlands Province, Papua New Guinea, December 20, 2009.

[38]D'Arcy Ryan. "Gift-exchange in the Mendi Valley: An Examination of the Socio-political Implications of the Ceremonial Exchange of Wealth among the People of the Mendi Valley, Southern Highlands District, Papua." [PhD diss., University of Sydney, 1961], 265-287.

[39]Alan C. Jeffries, 25 January, 1962, Mendi Patrol Report Number 7 of 1961-1962, 11-13 (NB 61-64 HW 114-116).

The Nembi belief that prosperity and power came from the spirits is widely shared among Melanesian and other folk religions. Trompf says,

> If anything distinguishes Melanesian religion from most, it is their apparent emphasis on the material results of rituals and of relationships of the more-than-human. Blessing is far less inward peace of the soul (as with western Christianity) or bodily health…than abundance in pigs or other foodstuffs and valuables. Group wealth is taken as a reflection of good relationships between humans and the spirit order…[40]

Hiebert, Shaw, and Tiénou define power in folk religions as

> the ability to make things happen. People see themselves engaged in constant struggles with spirits, other humans, and supernatural and natural forces that surround them. In such a world, everything can be explained in terms of competing powers and power encounters in which the stronger dominate the weaker.[41]

Ennio Mantovani contrasts theistic religions with biocosmic religions. Theistic religions, such as Christianity, recognize an ultimate God, who is the creator of the universe, the source of all things, and distinct from and above his creation. Human beings seek a relationship with the Creator.

Trompf argues that all Melanesian religions are theistic in that they "deal with gods of some kind,"[42] but Mantovani considers Melanesian religions to be biocosmic. The ultimate is the experience of life in which all things, biological, spiritual, and material are bound together in a cosmic whole. All things are interrelated and interdependent and linked together. When things are in balance, the cosmos is well ordered and the biological, spiritual, and material worlds all prosper. When things go awry, human beings work to restore the balance by appealing to the more powerful spiritual elements through ritual and sacrifice.[43] Mantovani calls the ideal condition for Melanesians *gutpela sindaun* (the good life), when a groups' relations with the spirits, with their allies, and with their enemies are all positive.[44]

When ritual and sacrifice failed to restore the proper balance, the Nembi searched elsewhere for the cause of the malady. Sorcery (*tom yop pu, nemong nemong llo, mend mend rup pu aelleme*) was common. Both men and women had the ability to create magic potions or make poisonous concoctions that could, when placed on the intended victim's food, alter behavior or cause illness or

---

[40]G. W. Trompf, *Melanesian Religion*, 20.

[41]Paul G. Hiebert, R. Daniel Shaw, and Tite Tiénou, *Understanding Folk Religion: a Christian Response to Popular Beliefs and Practices.* {Grand Rapids, Michigan: Baker Books, 1999], 84-85.

[42]Trompf, *Melanesian Religion,* 29.

[43]Ennio Mantovani, "What is religion," in Ennio Mantovai, *An Introduction to Melanesian Religions: a Handbook for Church Workers: Book Two of a Trilogy,* ed. Enniao Mantovani [Goroka, Papua New Guinea: Melanesian Institute, 1984b], 31-35.

[44]Ennio Mantovani, "Traditional Values and Ethics" in *An Introduction to Melanesian Cultures: A Handbook for Church Workers: Book One of a Trilogy,* ed. Darrel Whiteman [Goroka, Papua New Guinea: Melanesian Institute, 1984a], 201.

death. Others controlled spirits through chanted spells and could create havoc, cause illness or death, trigger anger, and incite violence and fighting.

The women were especially feared not only because of sorcery, but also because they were considered to be inherently evil,[45] dangerous, polluting and "inimical" to male vitality and power.[46] The people would look for a woman who might have caused the illness or death through sorcery or because of her polluting powers. Once she was identified, they offered her gifts of shell or pork to get her to cease her attacks on her victims.[47] If she persisted, she could be sentenced to death.[48]

The literature widely reports that the Highlands groups of Papua New Guinea believed in sky spirits and assumed that the outsiders who entered their world were from the sky.[49] The Nembi believed in sky people, and they had the concept of a high God, *Yeki*[50] who resided in the sky. He was benevolent but remote and not very involved in the daily affairs of the people. When things went wrong and the sacrifices and rituals failed to work, they would turn to *Yeki* the High God. Paul Embel recalled going with his father to a specially prepared place to call on the high God after all else had failed. In his words,

> The prayer to *Yeki* is without sacrifice of pig but only from a freshly built altar decorated with very special bush leaves. You stand in the middle of the place prepared with all your male siblings and cry out aloud and call on the perfect, clean or white god from above the white clouds. Subsequently, an immediate change to the environment follows, that is the garden, plants, domesticated animals and family members grow healthy.[51]

Some of the Nembi thought that the administrators and missionaries were associated with a cult called *Iso* or *Is Pandol*. It was a highly enigmatic cult whose

---

[45]Alan C. Jeffries, Mendi Patrol Report Number 7 of 1961-1962, 12 {NB 61-64 HW 115}.

[46]Edward L. Schieffelin and Robert Crittenden, editors. *Like People You See in a Dream: First Contact in Six Papuan Societies.* [Stanford, Calif: Stanford University Press, 1991], 137.

[47]Matthew Werip, interview by author, Semin, Southern Highlands Province, Papua New Guinea, December 26, 2009.

[48]When I first arrived in Papua New Guinea in 1970, missionaries were caring for two young siblings whom the group had rejected after their mother was buried alive for allegedly practicing sorcery.

[49]Bob Connolly and Robin Anderson. *First Contact: New Guinea's Highlanders Encounter the Outside World.* [New York, N.Y., U.S.A.: Viking, 1987], 199-198; Bill Gammage. The Sky Travellers: Journeys in New Guinea, 1938-1939. [Calton, Vic: Melbourne University Press, 1998], 1-2. For a more complete discussion of the belief in sky beings see Appendix Seven.

[50]The name of the high God varied, depending on the dialect. He was called Yeki, Yekil, Yekikele, Seki, or Sekil by most of the Nembi people. The Enga called the sky beings *Yalyakali* (Wiessner, Tumu and Pupu, 181). The Wiru have a sky God named *Yakili* (Clark, Ballard, and Nihill, 24-25). The Kewa term for the benevolent sky being is *Yaki* (Franklin and Franklin, 317).

[51]Paul Embel, e-mail message to the author, August 4, 2013.

secrets were known only to a few priests called *more*, who had been fully initiated and brought into the cult's core. Like most of the Highlands belief systems, it was confined to a particular area. The *Iso* cult was followed from Poroma to Margarima. Central to the cult was a light skinned female being named *Ollep Yalin*[52] from whom all people descended. She had lived in the area and bore children, but eventually she entered a blue pond near Injua.[53] The children she bore after she entered the pond all had light skins. The Nembi performed rituals to keep *Ollep Yalin* and her light skinned descendants inside the water.[54]

Whether the administrators and missionaries were returning ancestors, sky beings who had come to earth, descendants of *Ollep Yalin,* or originated in some other unknown place, the Nembi were convinced that they came from the spirit world and that their wealth and power originated with the spirits. Further, the Nembi wanted to tap into the power the outsiders possessed that enabled them to control the people and enforce a new system of law and order.

When Christian missions entered the scene, they were viewed as being the same as or at least related to the colonial administration. W. R. Patterson said in March of 1965 that "the missions as a whole" were "regarded as some sort of 'brother' to the administration,"[55] and when the missionaries came they were accepted for what they brought. Hans Reithofer reports that the Somaip who lived on the periphery of the Mendi and Kandep sub-districts went in quest of mission representatives for the wealth, power, and prestige they promised to bring.[56] In 1973 D. C. Ekins wrote in an area study for the Nembi Plateau census division. "The people are attracted to the missions for what they could get out of them and hence are quite pro-mission at the moment. They often equate the missions with the Administration by considering them another 'Department'."[57]

People I interviewed in 2009 and 2010 separated missions from the administration. Perhaps that is in hindsight. Nevertheless, Sara Ollie James' remarks were typical. The government came first, and brought with it law and order. The government treated the people harshly. The people had heard stories of the government's first visit to the area when men were killed. They had seen the scars from old bullet wounds on some of the men, and they were afraid. Government personnel enforced the law, took prisoners, and meted out punishment to those who disobeyed the law. The government came and went, but the missions stayed.

---

[52] Also called *Salin* depending on the dialect.

[53] Some of the legends say that she entered a hole in the ground near Injua.

[54] See Appendix Seven for a more complete discussion of *Iso* or *Is Pandol.*

[55] W. R. Paterson, March 3, 1965, Supplementary Report, 7 in Nipa Patrol Report Number 1 of 1964-1965 {NB 64-66 HW 17}.

[56] Hans Reithofer, *The Python Spirit and the Cross: Becoming Christian in a Highland Community of Papua New Guinea.* [Münster: Lit, 2006], 238-239.

[57] D. D. Ekins, 24 July, 1973, Area Study in Nipa Patrol Report Number 2 of 1972-1973, {NB 70-74, HW 324}.

The missionaries were less harsh than the government personnel. The government brought the law, and the missionaries brought God's word.[58]

When Christian Union Mission began its work among the Nembi and began to teach about a new belief system, the Nembi kept their beliefs hidden while they listened, evaluated, and tried to ascertain how everything fit together.

Solar Eclipse

The Nembi people I interviewed associated the arrival of Christian missions with a time when the sky became dark in the middle of the day. A total solar eclipse was seen in Indonesia, Papua New Guinea, and the Pacific on February 5, 1962.[59] Patrol officers warned the people of the coming eclipse and told them not to look at the sun when the darkness came. Different groups handled the phenomena in different ways, but today they associate the eclipse with the coming of the missions.

Ndipilli, an elderly man from Mil in the Lai Valley, reported that the people at Mil covered their eyes with cloth and sat quietly while it grew dark. The Catholics had a station at Pinj across from Mil on the Eastern side of the Lai River, but the people from Mil did not attend the services prior to the eclipse. After the eclipse, Ndipilli and his group began attending services at the Catholic station.[60]

Susan Tindal Jimi was a small girl living at Injua. When the darkness came, she and her mother hid in the house. The darkness frightened her and she cried. Her mother told her that *tomo honpi* (the red skinned spirits) had caused the darkness and it meant that the time of the red skinned spirits had come.[61]

According to Mapon Ek, who was a youth living at Utabia, the people carefully prepared for the darkness. They collected food and firewood and put it in their houses. They dug latrines close to their houses, and they agreed that, when the darkness came, no one but a woman's only child could go outside. Mapon associated the eclipse with the presence of Jim Hummel and John Ottway, Christian Union Mission's first missionaries, and with a fire that destroyed the home of Don and Betty Seymour at Tokura near Utabia which prompted their move to Ka.[62] The eclipse actually occurred almost two years before Hummel and Ottway began patrolling in the area, and the fire at Utabia occurred four years later, but Mapon

---

[58]Sara Ollie James, interview by author at Semin, Nipa Sub-District, Southern Highlands Province, Papua New Guinea, December 24, 2009.

[59]Fred Espenak, "Solar Eclipses:1961 -1970" *NASA Eclipse Web Site: GSFC Solar System Exploration Division.* http://eclipse.gsfc.nasa.gov/SEdecade/SEdecade1961.html [Accessed on August 3, 2012].

[60]Ndipili, Interview by author, Mil, Southern Highlands Province, PNG, December 20, 2009.

[61]Susan Tindal Jimi, Interview by author, Semin, Southern Highlands Province, PNG December 24, 2009

[62]Mapon Ek, Interview by author, Mato, Southern Highlands Province, PNG, December 31, 2009.

conflated those events with the eclipse. Kanj Mesmba from Utabia further associated the coming of the Bible with the eclipse.[63]

Christian Union Mission's Work among the Nembi

The Churches of Christ in Christian Union (CCCU) was founded in 1909, and had been supporting overseas mission outreach since 1913.[64] In 1960 the denomination worked in the West Indies where James and Virginia Hummel were serving in Dominica in association with Christian Union Mission.[65]

In September of 1961 the Hummels sent a letter to the CCCU general foreign missionary board stating that they were due for furlough in eight months and rather than return to Dominica they asked permission to go to Papua and New Guinea where Virginia had served as a single missionary with the East and West Indies Bible Mission. They wanted to establish a work there, set up a dispensary, and practice dentistry. The CCCU missionary board took seriously the command "to make disciples of all nations"[66] and believed that God was opening a door for them to begin a work in a new country. The board gave the Hummels a positive response.[67] Within a year the Hummels joined High Street Church of Christ in Christian Union in Chillicothe, Ohio[68] and were appointed to pioneer a work in Papua New Guinea. They planned to leave as soon as they raised their support.[69]

Christian Union Mission was not registered with the Australian colonial government, but because of Virginia Hummel's previous service, the Hummels contacted the East and West Indies Bible Mission. They informed the missionary board that Rev. A. Broughten had invited the Hummels to come to Papua and New Guinea as associate missionaries with his organization and suggested that after the Hummels were in Papua and New Guinea, then they could apply for Christian Union Mission to be registered in its own right. The board accepted the recom-

---

[63]Kanj Mesmba, Interview by author, Port Moresby, PNG, November 23, 2009.

[64]Kenneth Brown and P. Lewis Brevard 1980. *A Goodly Heritage, From Out of the Past: History of the Churches of Christ in Christian Union.* [Circleville, Ohio: Churches of Christ in Christian Union: Circle Press, Inc, 1980]. 173-174.

[65]Minutes of the Executive Committee of the General Foreign Missionary Board, CCCU, October 20, 1960, 1. Before they were married Virginia Hummel had worked in New Guinea with the East and West Indies Bible Mission. After her first term of service in New Guinea, she enrolled in a dental school in Texas where she met and married James Hummel. They then went to Dominica in the West Indies under the auspices of Bethany Fellowship that became associated with Christian Union Mission in Dominica, but they wanted to go to Papua and New Guinea (Interview with Don and Betty Seymour, Avon Park, Florida, May 27 and 28, 2013).

[66]Matthew 28:19.

[67]Minutes of the Executive Committee of the General Foreign Missionary Board, CCCU, Seotember 27, 1961.

[68]Don and Betty Seymour, interview by author, Avon Park, Fla, May 27 and 28, 2010.

[69]Minutes of the General Foreign Missionary Board, August 17, 1962.

mendation with the "ultimate goal" of achieving "full government recognition" for "our own organization."[70]

Hummel went to Ialibu where the East and West Indies Bible Mission had an established work. Missionaries associated with the East and West Indies Bible Mission agreed to release some of their pastors and pastoral trainees to accompany Hummel into a new area.[71] While at Ialibu, Hummel met John Ottway, a Bible school teacher who later joined Hummel in his outreach to the Nembi area. Hummel and a group of pastors settled near Kagua at Kwarelombo,[72] the East and West Indies Bible Mission's most remote station, while Hummel searched for an area to establish a permanent work.[73]

The first of many misunderstandings and miscommunications surfaced in August of 1963 when Broughten of the East and West Indies Bible Mission visited CCCU headquarters in Circleville, Ohio and met with the executive committee of the CCCU General Missionary Board. He claimed that Hummel had signed an agreement to work with his organization and expressed surprise that Hummel was working to secure formal recognition for Christian Union Mission.[74] The missionary board took no formal action during its meeting with Broughten, but at its next meeting the board opted to discontinue its association with Broughten because of doctrinal issues.[75] The CCCU general missionary superintendent, Rev. G. C. Johnson, visited the Territory of Papua and New Guinea in March of 1964. During his trip, he made contact with Broughten in Sydney, Australia. After that visit, by mutual agreement, the break with the East and West Indies Bible Mission was finalized.[76]

By then, the board was actively seeking additional personnel to send to Papua New Guinea. In February of 1964 Ottway[77] and Martha Jean Waugh, a nurse who had been serving on the Texas Mexican Border,[78] were both accepted as "tentative

---

[70]Executive Board Meeting, General Missionary Department, November 27, 1962.

[71]I do not have a complete list of the Ialibu men who joined Hummel in the outreach to the Nipa/Poroma area, but the names I have learned include Yoke, Rema, Tandako, Wakena, Longpela Nali, Wepo, Sotpela Nali, and Aiyale. (Aiyale in interview by author, Mt. Hagen, WHP, PNG, January 22, 2010).

[72]I use the name that Aiyale, one of the pastors who entered the Nembi area with Hummel, gave me when I interviewed him. Hummel in an article that he wrote for the *Missionary Tidings* said the name of the place near Kagua was Tawiti'anda. (James Hummel "Greetings from New Guinea," *Missionary Tidings* XV, no 1 [August, 1963], 3.

[73]Aiyale in interview by author, Mt. Hagen, WHP, PNG, January 22, 2010.

[74]Executive Board Meeting of the General Missionary Board, Circleville, Ohio, August 21, 1963.

[75]Executive Committee Meeting of the General Foreign Missionary Board, Circleville, Ohio, October 22, 1963.

[76]Executive Committee of the General Foreign Missionary Board, Columbus, Ohio, March 20, 1964.

[77]Ottway was already working with Hummel in Papua and New Guinea. He sent to the board an application for formal acceptance as a Christian Union Mission missionary.

[78]Martha Jean Waugh Blakeman, interview by author, Lockbourne, Ohio, USA, March 10, 2010.

candidates" for Papua and New Guinea.[79] On June 2, 1964 the missionary board placed Don and Betty Seymour under preliminary appointment to New Guinea,[80] and two days later the board placed the Seymours under full appointment.[81]

Move into the Nembi Valley

Hummel and Ottway, accompanied by pastors from Ialibu, Pangia, Kagua, and Tambul, began patrolling the Nembi Valley in early 1964.[82] When G. C. Johnson visited the field in March, Hummel recommended that Christian Union Mission base its work at Utabia in the Nembi Valley, and on March 20, 1964, the home board approved Hummel's recommendation.[83] Ottway settled at Tindom, and Hummel worked out of Utabia.[84]

Hummel's strategy was to make friendly contact with the Nembi people and secure their loyalty by giving gifts of beads, cloth, and other trade goods. Several of the men I interviewed recalled receiving lengths of cloth from the mission. Mapunu from Farata said that Ottway had invited the boys from the Poroma to come to Tindom where Ottway gave them lengths of black cloth. They removed their *tangets* and *bilums* (broad leaves and woven loincloths) and fastened the cloth around their waists. They went home thinking "*Mipela i wanpela luluai bilong gavman*" (We were representatives of the government.)[85] When Laki Nenis from Embi heard that Hummel was visiting Embi, he ran to see, and found a lot of young boys had received lengths of red cloth which they were now wearing instead of their *tangets* and *bilums*. The pastor gave Laki a length of cloth, and he joined the other boys who were marching around showing off. Later Pastor Kwale, who was assigned to work in the area, told the boys who had received the cloth to come to school. They went and started to learn to speak and read Pidgin.[86] Mapon Ek said that he and the other boys his age from Utabia were given blue strips of cloth.[87]

Later Hummel negotiated with each group and gave them pearl shells to cement their loyalty and to gain the right to build a church and place a pastor on

---

[79]Executive Board of the General Missionary Board, Circleville, Ohio, February 3, 1964.

[80]Special Meeting of the General Missionary Board, Circleville, Ohio, June 2, 1964.

[81]Meeting of the General Missionary Board, Circleville, Ohio, June 4, 1964.

[82]Warren R. Read, Nipa Patrol Report Number 12 of 1963-64, {NB 61-64 HW 371}. Hummel may have conducted preliminary patrols into the Nembi Valley prior to January of 1964, but the mission records suggest that he had no regular contact with the Nembi area prior to January of 1964.

[83]Executive Committee of the General Foreign Missionary Board, Columbus, Ohio, March 20, 1964.

[84]Executive Committee of the the the General Missionary Board, Columbus, Ohio, March 20, 1964.

[85]Mapunu Pereyap, interview by author, Farata, SHP, PNG, January 1, 2010.

[86]Laki Nenis, interview by author, Embi, Southern Highlands Province, PNG, January 6, 2010.

[87]Mapon Ek, interview by author, Mato (Poroma), Southern Highlands Province, PNG, December 31, 2009.

their ground. The number of pearl shells that Hummel gave each group varied according to the size of the groups with larger groups receiving more, and smaller groups receiving fewer shells.[88]

Tui Ori and Jeremaiah Kombap Kele were originally from Ka, but their group had been routed during tribal fighting in the mid-1950s. In 1963 they lived at Mil in the Lai Valley.[89] They were evidently among a large group of men from Mil who were sentenced to three months in prison for fighting in December of 1963.[90] While in prison they both learned Pidgin. When they were released from prison, Tui's uncle, who had heard that a white man associated with a mission was living at Tindom, told them to go work for the mission. Tui and Jeremaiah went to Tindom and found John Ottway, who hired them to work as laborers and interpreters. They were the first local youths to work for the mission.[91] The imported pastors and the Nembi people had no common language. Two youths who understood Pidgin and spoke the local language were a welcome addition to the mission staff.

Aiyale was one of the pastors from Ialibu who worked with Hummel and Ottway. He said that they circulated among the Nembi groups several times before they secured ground for churches. The Catholics were also working the area, and so the Nembi pitted CUM and the Catholics against each other to see who would offer more. Each group wanted to align itself with the mission that they thought would bring them the greatest material benefit.[92] The behavior of Hummel and the Catholic priests emulated the behavior of the Nembi big-men who use their resources to establish and maintain relationships based on exchange.

Once Hummel paid for the ground, the people built a church and a house for the pastor who established a "mini-station." When the pastors first asked the people to listen to the Gospel message, the people refused. They said that they had appealed to the spirits, and they believed that the shells that they received from

---

[88]Aiyale said that each group was given from thirty to forty pearl shells, depending on the size of the group. Tui Ori said in his first interview that each group was given twenty to thirty pearl shells, and in his second interview he said that each group was given eight, nine, or twenty pearl shells. Mapon reported that Utabia received 12 pearl shells for the land for a church and the first house that Hummels occupied. When I interviewed Benjamin Wang, the son of the head man, Wang, who had given the ground at Farata, he said that his father had been poorly paid for the ground, but Mapunu who was present at the interview said he had received 12 pearl shells, and it was a high price when the land was purchased. Whatever price that the mission paid to the various groups for land for churches was considered to be a generous amount at that time.

[89]Kanj Mesmba, interview by author, Port Moresby, Papua New Guinea, November 23, 2009; Tui Ori interview by author, Port Moresby, Papua New Guinea, January 29, 2010; Tia Paik, interview by author, Mil, Lai Valley, Southern Highlands District, Papua New Guinea, December 19, 2009.

[90]N. C. McQuilty, 1 April, 1964, Mendi Number 27 of 1963-64, 4-5 {NB 61-64 HW 458-459}.

[91]Tui Ori and Jeremaih Kombap Kele, interview by author, Mendi, 2007; Tui Ori, interview by author, Port Moresby, November 24, 2009.

[92]Aiyale, interview by author, Mount Hagen, Western Highlands Province, PNG, January 22, 2010

the mission came from the spirits.[93] The pastors asked young boys from each area who appeared to have an aptitude for learning Pidgin to work as their interpreters. The pastors taught their interpreters literacy, scriptures, and how to be a pastor.

In June of 1964, Hummel brought his family to live in the Nembi Valley.[94] At first they settled at Utabia and lived in a "grass" house that the people built,[95] but after a storm the house began to lean to one side. So, the Hummel family relocated to Tindom[96] where Ottway was living and the mission had built some sturdier bush buildings in anticipation of the arrival of Don and Betty Seymour.[97]

Acquisition of Ka Station

Between Utabia and Tindom there was a large tract of temporarily unoccupied land that the Ka people had vacated during tribal fighting. At first the administration thought that the land belonged to Tindom/Merut, but in 1962 a patrol officer realized that another group had claims to the land.[98]

In April of 1964 Hummel lodged an application on CUM's behalf for some land on both sides of the Nembi River. Patrol Officer Warren R. Read went with Hummel and Ottway to talk to the people about selling their land and making it available to the mission. The people on the eastern (Mendi/*Aron*) side of the river were not willing to part with their land, but the owners on the western (Nipa/*Karinj*) side wanted to sell twice as much land as the mission had requested.[99]

---

[93]Aiyale, interview by author, Mount Hagen, Western Highlands Province, PNG, January 22, 2010; Tui Ori, interviews by author, Port Moresby, PNG, November 24, 2009 and January 29, 2010.

[94]I do not know for sure when Hummel brought his family to the Nembi Valley, but when Hummel wrote a letter to the CCCU missionary board dated June 8, 1964, he used the Kagua address. The July issue of the *Missionary Tidings* listed Hummel's address as Nipa via Mendi. I am fairly certain that Hummel moved his family into the Nembi Valley in June or early July of 1964,

[95]Several of my interviewees told me that Virginia and the two children flew into Nipa where the mission had a house. There were no roads or airstrips in the valley, and anyone entering the Nembi Valley walked in. When they were ready to move into the Valley, a group of men from Utabia walked to Nipa with Jim, and carried Virginia Hummel to Utabia on a stretcher. I am not sure why she was carried in. She had given birth to their second child a few months earlier. Dale, the older child, rode on the shoulders of some of the men, and they carried Mark, an infant in a string bag.

[96]Mapon Ek, interview by author, Mato, (Poroma), Southern Highlands Province, PNG, December 31, 2010. Kanj Mesmba, interview by author, Port Moresby, PNG, January 29, 2010.

[97]Don and Betty Seymour said that the Hummels relocated from Utabia to Tindom because of tribal fighting, but both Mapon Ek and Kanj Mesmba who were from Utabia said they moved because the house leaned or collapsed. Tribal fighting was undoubtedly another reason.

[98]N. D. Lucas, Nipa number 9 of 1961-62, Native Affairs, 3, {NB 61-64 HW 168}.

[99]Warren R. Read, Nipa Number 15 of 1963-1964, 3, {NB 61-64 HW 399}.

In May of 1964 Read and Ottway spent three days surveying the land that the owners were willing to sell. The investigation revealed that

> the owners of the ground ... are from Mil and Mala and reside within the Undiri census division which falls within the Mendi Admiinistrative area.

> The land known as Ka ... lies approximately half way between Tindom and Ungabia (Utabia) on the Nipa side of the Nembi River. ...The owners on the Nipa side of the river...are more than willing to part with this land.[100]

In December of 1964 Read surveyed the land again and placed markers around all borders,[101] but the purchase of Ka for lease to Christian Union Mission was not completed until a year later. On December 19, 1965, the administration paid 105 pounds and fifteen shillings for the land. Afterwards John S. Hicks, the patrol officer who finalized the purchase reported,

> Ninety acres of land was purchased near Udjubia (Utabia) for lease to the Christian Union Mission. Little difficulty was had in making this purchase and the owners seemed pleased with the pay received. ...An airstrip for light aircraft is at present being constructed by Christian Union people at Ka. They have great plans for an agricultural station, school and fully staffed hospital. Whether these plans will see fruition apparently depends on the generosity of subscribers in the U.S. They have, however, ninety acres to play with and will certainly contribute to the overall development of the people in the area.[102]

The Ka people who censused at Mala approached Hicks with a

> request that they be censused in the Nembi Valley. They have land in the Nembi Valley, and want to build a rest house beside the Nembi road midway between Merut and Udjubia. The majority of the Ka group lives in the Nembi and visit Mala solely for census purposes.[103]

Hicks informed them they would have to wait, but he recommended that they be allowed to move from Mala to Ka.[104]

Thus, the Ka people worked for their own advantage. Each group had its own motivation for parting with land and inviting missions to establish themselves in their area. Jeffrey Clark, Chris Ballard and Michael Nihill say that the Wiru accepted the missionaries because they hoped it would bring development and allow them to acquire the same apparent wealth and benefits that the European colonizers possessed.[105] The Ka people saw it as a way to reclaim their land. By selling

---

[100]Warren R. Read, Nipa Number 15 of 1963-1964, 4-5, {NB 61-64 HW 400-401}.

[101]Warren R. Read, Nipa Patrol Report Number 5 of 1964-1965, 23-24 {NB 64-66 HW 103-104}.

[102]J. S. Hicks, Nipa Patrol Report Number 5 of 1965-1966, 7 {NB 64-66 HW 296-297}.

[103]J. S. Hicks, Nipa Patrol Report Number 5 of 1965-1966, 8 {NB 64-66, HW 298}.

[104]J. S. Hicks, Nipa Patol Report Number 5 of 1965-1966, 8 {NB 64-66, HW 298}.

[105]Jeffrey Clark, Chris Ballard, and Michael Nihill. *Steel to Stone: A Chronicle of Colonialism in the Southern Highlands of Papua New Guinea*. Oxford, [UK: Oxford University Press, 2000], 100-101.

part of their land, they established a relationship with both the administration and the mission and anticipated reaping future benefits. For the first time the administration acknowledged them as a separate group. Further, they regained the right to reoccupy the ground that they lost in the middle 1950s during tribal fighting.

Missionary Personnel

Don and Betty Seymour departed for Papua New Guinea on October 31, 1964[106] and arrived at Nipa a few days later. They had not been trained for cross cultural ministry, and knew little about Papua and New Guinea.[107] The administrative authorities were unwilling for Betty and the children to move into the Valley because of recent tribal fighting, but they did not object to Don joining Hummel on patrols. Therefore, the family lived at Nipa for about six months while Don went on regular foot patrols into the Nembi Valley. He was away from Nipa most of the time.[108]

The Seymours wanted fellowship and interacted freely with the missions that were already established in the Nipa area. They plied the established missionaries with questions about the area and how to relate to the people. Each had his or her own unique approach, and gave them different advice, but the time at Nipa became a time of orientation and learning for the Seymours.[109]

Shortly after the Seymours arrived at Nipa, Ottway left the field. Many of the Nembi people that I interviewed had vivid memories of Ottway patrolling with Hummel and holding church services with the people.[110] He worked closely with the pastors and the Nembi men, and was becoming proficient in the local lan-

---

[106]*Missionary Tidings* XVI no 5, [January, 1965], 1.

[107]Betty Seymour, interview by author, Avon Park, Florida, May 29, 2010. Betty's ideas about Papua and New Guinea had been formed by reading Russel T. Hitt's book *Cannibal Valley* about the opening of the Missionary Alliance work in Irian Jaya. She had also read some articles in the *Reader's Digest* about Papua and New Guinea, but she had no other exposure to Melanesia or Melanesian cultures.

[108]Don and Betty Seymour, interview by author, Avon Park Florida, May 27, 2010.

[109]Don and Betty Seymour, interview by author, Avon Park, Florida, USA, May 27, 2010.

[110]Some of the people had positive memories and others had negative memories. Tui Ori, who was Ottway's interpreter, had positive memories of his time with Ottway. Timb, a man from Tindom, credited Ottway with saving his life. He was a small boy when Ottway lived at Tindom. Timb's father, Swimb, who was a head man at Tindom and had been selected to be a village constable, became friends with Ottway. Timb became seriously ill. Ottway, while carrying a gun to ward off a possible attack, helped Timb's father carry the child through Semin, which was enemy territory, to a health center near Nipa. Timb was given medical treatment and survived.

Kibem and Sumim, who were young girls when Ottway resided at Tindom tell a different story. Sumim said that Ottway was a harsh man who insisted that the children and youth help him build houses at Tindom. Kibem said that she and some other girls had not worked to Ottway's satisfaction, and he made them sit on the ground until late afternoon. Her father became worried and came looking for them, and he was angry that Ottway had detained the girls.

guage. He patrolled a lot, and was responsible for supervising literacy classes that the pastors taught in the villages.[111]

The people of Tobua had been especially hostile towards the administration. As late as January of 1964, they had threatened one of the patrol officers who immediately withdrew and returned with reinforcements.[112] In November of 1964, one of Ottway's patrols took him to Tobua where he spanked a child. The spanking angered the Tobua men, and they threatened to kill Ottway. When Warren Read, the officer in charge at Nipa, learned of their threats, he told Hummel that Ottway had to leave immediately because in Read's words, "This place is just beginning to settle down, and the last thing that we need here is a dead white man."[113] Hummel sent Ottway to Wewak for a vacation, and then wrote to him and told him that he was to return to Australia and not come back to the Nembi Valley.[114]

Following a patrol through the Nembi census division in November of 1964, Read wrote about CUM,

> The Christian Union Mission is quite active in the Nembi area. For at every rest house the patrol visited they had stationed indigenous teachers of religion who seem to be exerting a certain pacifying influence on the local people. That is the teachers are stationed in the vicinity of the government rest house.

> The leader of the mission Mr. J. Hummel is at present living at Merut with his wife and family whilst awaiting for his lease applications of the land known as Ka to be approved and finalised.[115]

Martha Jean Waugh left the USA for PNG on January 9, 1965 and joined the Hummels at Tindom/Merut.[116] The patrol officers granted her permission to live at Tindom/Merut on the condition that she return to Nipa every two or three weeks. Martha said, "I don't know why, but they insisted that I come outside for a few days each month. I think the patrol officers felt that the local people were resistant to outsiders coming in." Seymour escorted her to and from Nipa where she stayed with the Seymour family for a few days until she was allowed to return to Tindom.[117]

---

[111]Don and Betty Seymour, interview by author, Avon Park, Florida, USA, May 28, 2010.

[112]Warren R. Read Nipa Patrol Report Number 5 of 1964-65, 16-17 {NB 64-66 HW 96-97}.

[113]Don and Betty Seymour, interview by author, Avon Park, Florida, USA, May 27, 2010

[114]Don and Betty Seymour had only been in Nipa for a short time when Ottway left. As soon as Betty and the children were settled into the house at Nipa, Hummel took Don on a tour of the area to visit all of the preaching points, and Read came across them while they were at Enip. Warren Read was leading a patrol through the Nembi census division. He was at Tobua on Thursday and Friday the 19th and 20th of November. The following week he arrived at Enip on the 24th of November, and departed Enip on the 26th. In his report, Read makes no mention of the plans the Tobua people had to kill Ottway, but the timing of that trip agrees with the information that Don Seymour gave in his interview.

[115]Warren R. Read, Nipa Patrol Report Number 5 or 1964 to 1965, 16-17, {NB 64-66 HW 102}.

[116]"Prayer Requests" *Missionary Tidings* XVI no. 6, [February, 1965], 7.

[117]Martha Jean Waugh, interview by author, Lockbourne, Ohio, USA, March 10, 2010.

With the arrival of Waugh, the group of pioneer missionaries was complete. The Overseas Methodist Church determined that it would not be in conflict with Christian Union Mission,[118] and so, except for some churches in the border areas of the Upper Nembi Plateau at Semin and Injua, they withdrew to the Nipa Basin and allowed Christian Union Mission to assume the responsibility for the Nembi area. To minimize the potential conflict between the two missions, the Methodist Overseas Mission sold the station that they had at Togura to CUM. The Seymours moved into it in April of 1965 when the administration gave its approval for the family to enter the Nembi Valley.[119]

The Seymours lived at Togura until April of 1966 when the bush house they were living in caught fire from an overheated cook stove and was totally destroyed along with most of their personal belongings.[120] The lease for Ka station had been finalized four months before the house burned, and the Seymour family moved into a house at Ka that he was building for Waugh so she could relocate the medical clinic from Tindom to Ka.[121]

The missionaries' goal was to establish a church among the Nembi people, but they juggled a complex set of relationships with the administration, other missions, the home board, each other, and the Nembi people.

Relationships

The missionaries came from a western society that stressed the autonomy of each individual. Hiebert says, "The modern missionary movement was based on the assumption that the gospel is addressed to individuals, calling them to an inner experience of personal conversion based on the cognitive affirmation that Jesus Christ is Lord."[122] The underlying assumption was that the group was less important than the individual.[123]

Both the patrol officers and the missionaries approached the Nembi from a paternalistic Western perspective. Mary T. Lederleitner, who is a cross cultural consultant serving with Wycliffe Bible Translators, says that paternalism acts for the benefit of "another person without that person's consent" and that it "advances peoples' interest at the expense of their liberty."[124] Lederleitner, who writes about the relationship between donors and recipients in global partnerships, says that western paternalism is rooted in feelings of superiority and trusts no system other than its own. There is an underlying feeling that the donor must retain control in order to ensure that the recipient acts responsibly and remains accountable for

---

[118]Don and Betty Seymour, interview by author, Avon Park, Florida, USA, May 27, 2010.

[119]Betty Seymour, telephone interview by author, Wilmore, Ky, USA, May 3, 2005.

[120]Meeting of the General Missionary Board, April 26, 1966. Circleville, Ohio, 1.

[121]Don and Betty Seymour, interview by author, Avon Park, Florida, USA, May 27, 2010.

[122]Paul G. Hiebert, *Transforming Worldviews: An Anthropological Understanding of How People Change* [Grand Rapids, Mich: Baker Academic, 2008], 173.

[123]Hiebert, Transforming Worldviews, 171.

[124]Mary T. Lederleitner, Mary T. *Cross-cultural Partnerships: Navigating the Complexities of Money and Mission.* [Downers Grove, IL: InterVarsity Press, 2010], 78.

what he or she does.[125] That description is equally applicable to the relationship that existed between the patrol officers and the Nembi people. Kituai says that patrol officers were convinced they were bringing to the people a "better life" that was free of tribal fighting and sorcery, and would have the benefit of improved health, freedom of movement, and more material goods.[126] Likewise, the missionaries believed that the Gospel would release the people from the tyranny of the spirits, assure them of eternal salvation, and give them a better life. The ethnocentric assumptions and the paternalistic approach to the Nembi affected the relationships that the missionaries built with the administration, with other missions, and with the Nembi people.

With the Colonial Administration

In the colonial setting missionaries were under the authority of the patrol officers. The missionaries and the colonial administrators were interdependent, to borrow Clark, Ballard, and Nihill's word in their description of mission outreach to the people in the Pangia area of the Southern Highlands.[127] The patrol officer depended on the missionaries to help "pacify" the people and bring health, education, and other services to the area. In 1966 after Christian Union Mission opened Ka Community School, the Southern Highlands district commissioner, wrote,

> The commencement of primary education by the Mission is extremely helpful. Because the educational programme for the next 5 years envisages only two additional administration schools in the whole of the Nipa Administrative Area, the education of the mass of the people is going to be up to the Christian missions.[128]

The patrol officers did not oppose the mission's message. They thought that the message would help bring peace and curtail some of the unwanted practices, but the administration welcomed the mission more for the services it provided than for its message.

The administration was firmly in control. The missionaries could only enter an area with the administration's consent, and they could only acquire land for a mission station or build an airstrip with the administration's approval. The relationship between Christian Union Mission and the pre-independence Papua and New Guinea colonial administration was much like the relationship that Langmore described between the missionaries and the administration in the 1880s. The missionaries saw themselves as distinct from the colonial officials, but the people perceived little difference between the two.[129]

---

[125]Lederleitner, 79-82,

[126]August Ibrum Kituai, *My Gun, My Brother: The World of the Papua New Guinea Colonial Police, 1920-1960.* [Honolulu: University of Hawai'i Press, 1998], 40-41

[127]Clark, Ballard, and Nihill, 97.

[128]D. R. Marsh, 3 March, 1966, in letter to the Department of District Administration, Konedobu in Nipa Patrol Report Number 7 of 1965-1966 {NB 64-66 HW 342}.

[129]Langmore, 216, 229-231.

With Other Missions

The relationship among the missions working in the Nembi area was strained and highly competitive. As an example, in 1964 at about the same time that CUM applied for land at Ka where they hoped to put an airstrip, the Catholics applied for land at Det with plans to build an airstrip, and the Overseas Methodist Church applied for land about one-half mile Det and said they wanted to build an airstrip. Patrol offices became frustrated that "three separate missions" wanted to build "three separate airstrips" within two miles of each other. The people wanted the strips because they were a "status symbol." One Patrol officer declared that "no mission would be given permission to build an airstrip...the people feel cheated about the whole thing...I think it is certain that no large scale conversions will take place within the Nembi for many years to come."[130] In the end the Overseas Methodist Mission withdrew, and the Catholics and CUM were both allowed to construct airstrips.

For a number of years, a great deal of animosity existed between Christian Union Mission and the Catholic Mission. The people were quick to recognize the competitiveness between the two missions and used it to get more from their benefactors.[131] Both the Catholics and Christian Union Mission established schools and provided health services and neither group wanted the other to infringe on its ministries or "steal its sheep."

Differences in the theology of the two missions were at the heart of the conflict. Christian Union Mission did not accept some of the tenets, teachings, and practices of the Catholic Church and did not want the Catholic Church to lead the people astray with unbiblical teaching. Similarly, the Catholic Church believed that CUM was teaching errant doctrines, and did not want the people drawn into heresy.[132] Neither side accepted the other as "brothers in Christ."

After the missions had established their base, and they began to concentrate on building their stations and their ministries, the tensions between the missions eased.[133] For several more years the competitiveness and tensions between the Catholics and CUM continued to ebb and flow, but they were less extreme than they had been during the 1960s.

---

[130]John Hicks in Nipa Patrol Report Number 8 of 1964-1965, 6 {NB 64-66 HW 141}.

[131]Nipa Patrol Report Number 1 of 1964-1965, 9, {NB 64-66 HW 144}.

[132]Vatican II was still in progress. The first session opened on October 11, 1962, but the closing session did not take place until December 8, 1965. The Documents of Vatican II had not yet been released. Prior to Vatican II Protestant believers were considered to be heretics, but after Vatican II they were recognized as "separated brethren" who had an errant theology but were genuine but misguided Christians. See (Felix Just, S.J., PhD, "The Second Vatican Ecumenical Council, (Vatican II)" Catholic Church Documents related to Biblical Resources. http://catholic-resources.org/ChurchDocs/Vati-canCou-ncil2.htm [Accessed on August 19, 2013] and "Decree on Ecumenism *Unitatis Redintegraito*."http://www.vatican.va/archive/hist_councils/ii_vatican_council/documents/vat-ii_decree_19641121_unitatis-redintegratio_en.html [accessed on August 19, 2013]).

[133]N. Wright, 19 January, 1970, Poroma Patrol Report Number 7 of 1969-1970, Area Survey – Nembi Valley Census Division, 8 {NB 69-70 HW 209}.

The Nembi followers of the two missions laid aside their competitiveness more quickly than the expatriate missionaries. In January of 1969 patrol officer Noel Wright reported that among the people the relationship between the missions and churches was "harmonious," but among the Euro-American staff members there tended to be friction as each group tried to extend its influence.[134] In August of 1969, A. F. McNeill reported that, on the Nembi Plateau, "the relationships among the followers of the various missions were excellent," but the people followed the missions for their materials and wealth more than their message.[135]

With the Nembi People

Tribal societies are group oriented. Hiebert says, "Individuals are important only because they are interconnecting nodes in the larger webs of kinship. Their well-being is dependent on the kin group's well-being, and their life has meaning only as it is shared."[136] The Nembi approached the missionaries from a group oriented perspective and sought to relate to them in a way that would bring the greatest benefit to the kin group. When they accepted pearl shells and allowed the mission to build a church and place a pastor on their ground, they established a relationship with the mission and expected to reap future material benefits from the relationship. Hummel expected to secure exclusive rights to establish and maintain churches among the Nembi groups.[137] However the acceptance of one mission did not prevent the acceptance of another. Individuals and sub-groups had the freedom to establish their own relationships and build their own exchange networks within the larger Nembi societies. They were free to invite other mission groups if they so desired.

Paul Sillitoe, who studied exchange among the Wola, says that group relationships were built on a network of individual exchange relationships. Individuals belonged to a group that acted collectively when the individuals decided that it was in their own best interests to cooperate in a particular activity. Individuals were free to participate or not participate in collective activities.[138] The exchange of gifts worked "not only to integrate Wola society but also to maintain the autonomy of the individual, because it is in the interests of men to excel in handling

---

[134]Noel Wright, 7 January, 1969, Poroma Patrol Number 5 of 1968-1969, Area Survey Nembi Valley Census Division, 7 [NB 68-69, HW 181}.

[135]A. F. McNeill, 24th September, 1969. Nipa Patrol Report Number 3 of 1969-1970, 1969/70 Area Study – Nembi Plateau Census Division, 15-16 {NB 69-70 HW 107-108}.

[136]Hiebert, *Transforming Worldviews,* 108.

[137]In April of 2010 I had a brief conversation with Jim Hummel during which I requested an interview. During that conversation, he told me that while he was there, he had maintained a tight control over the groups and had kept the Catholics from establishing churches in the area. He said that those who followed him, had been less firm, and other groups had entered the area. He wanted the groups to be loyal only to him and to Christian Union Mission.

[138]Sillitoe, Paul. *Give and Take: Exchange in Wola Society.* [New York: St. Martin's Press, 1979], 83-84.

wealth and so achieve renown, and it is in the interests of their society that they do this and so stimulate social cooperation."[139]

D'Arcy Ryan, who studied gift exchange among the Mendi people in 1954, said that Mendi exchange is made up of a complex system of individual (*twem*) and clan (*sem*) exchanges. Ryan reported that "*twem* can take place only between friends and all friends are expected to make *twem*."[140] Ryan concluded that

> all relationships between individuals, even within small, co-residential kin-groups are marked by some form of gift-exchange. …This same principle of gift-exchange is expended to create and maintain relations between progressively larger groups, up to alliances among the major political units.[141]

In the 1980s Rena Lederman took a second look at gift exchange in the Mendi area. She says that Mendi groups were made up of a number of sub-groups or "equivalent segments, each with strong and diverging loyalties outside the group."[142] Gift exchange was based on both group oriented and individual exchange and both personal and clan exchanges played a significant role in Mendi societies.[143] An exchange of gifts established a relationship between the donor and the recipient, and both partners incurred obligations in the exchange.[144] "*Twem* is most clearly viewed as a social relationship. *Twem* gifts create long term friendships that are maintained even in the absence of transactions; and when a gift is outstanding between partners, the quality of their social contact affects the recipient's obligation to repay."[145]

CUM opened its station at Farata in 1968. The people at Farata said that when they agreed to allow CUM to build at Farata they were making the mission a part of their group. From their perspective what was the mission's was theirs. The "purchase" of the ground was the establishment of a relationship and not the surrendering of land. It was for the mutual benefit of the mission and the kin group at Farata, and any development of the station belonged to both the mission and the people. The destruction of the station in tribal fighting and the consequences to the relationship of CUM and Christian Union Church of Papua New Guinea are discussed in Chapter Five.

The exchange of bride wealth establishes a relationship between the bride's and the groom's kin groups. Most of the pastors who entered the area with Hummel were single men, and many took local wives. Several interviewees told me that when the young women saw the soap, clothes, blankets, beads, food and cooking utensils that the pastors used, they were attracted to them, and entered

---

[139]Sillitoe, *Give and Take*, 289).

[140]Ryan, "Gift-Exchange," 68.

[141]Ryan, "Gift-Exchange," 75.

[142]Rena Lederman, *What Gifts Engender: Social Relations and Politics in Mendi, Highland Papua New Guinea.* [Cambridge [Cambridgeshire]: Cambridge University Press, 1986], 52.

[143]Lederman, 65-66.

[144]Lederman, 92-93.

[145]Lederman, 82.

into marriages without the customary exchange of bride wealth.[146] When the people became upset with Hummel for bringing in outsiders who violated protocol by taking wives without giving bride wealth, Hummel used mission money to purchase pearl shells for bride wealth.[147] He paid the bride wealth on the pastors' behalf.[148] From the perspective of the Nembi people, Hummel did no wrong. The people would have rejected the mission and its message had the bride wealth not been paid.[149]

Getting the pastors to take local wives was a part of Hummel's overall plan. He thought that if the pastors settled permanently in the Nembi area, it would, in the long term, strengthen the church.[150] The arrangement was satisfactory to the Nembi who, like the Enga, see marriage as a means of establishing an on-going relationship and gaining access to outside resources.[151]

With the Home Board and between Missionaries

Hummel's actions brought him into conflict with the home board. The General Missionary Board, located in Ohio, took a "hands-on" approach to the administration of its fields. It expected to be fully informed about the activities on each field and exercised a fair amount of control over field decisions, especially those related to finances.

The home board was generous with its support, but it had underestimated the cost of sponsoring a new work on a remote field, and did not have reserve funds in

---

[146]Kanj Mesmba, interview by author, November 23, 2009 and January 29, 2010. Kanj spoke of the illicit marriages in both interviews. He, and others who were present, said that the young women were attracted to the pastors and sought them out on their own. It is highly probable that the Nembi men encouraged the girls of marriageable age to seek husbands among the pastors, especially when word circulated through the area that Hummel paid bride wealth for the pastors.

[147]The implication in most of the interviews was that Hummel had paid the entire bride wealth for the pastors. However, when I inteviewed Aiyale, he said that the mission had given twenty pearl shells and two pigs to assist with his bride wealth, but his kin group helped him by giving an additional thirty-one pearl shells, twenty-five pigs and four cows.

[148]Mapon Ek, interview by author, Mato (Poroma), Southern Highlands Province, Papua New Guinea.

[149]Kanj Mesmba, interview by author, November 23, 2009 and January 29, 2010, Port Moresby, Papua New Guinea. In the interviews Kanj and others gave the names of many of the pastors and the wives that they had acquired with Hummel's assistance. These pastors were intensely loyal to Hummel.

[150]I found no written records that Hummel paid bride wealth for the pastors, but my interviews with Nembi pastors and church leaders and with Don and Betty Seymour confirmed that securing local wives for the pastors was a part of Hummel's overall strategy.

[151]Pauline Wilson Wiessner, Akii Tumu, and Nitze Pupu. *Historical Vines: Enga Networks of Exchange, Ritual, and Warfare in Papua New Guinea,* [Washington, D.C.: Smithsonian Institution Press, 1998], 99.

hand. The board had to raise the funds that it sent to Papua and New Guinea, and securing funds and equipment from the home constituency was a slow process.[152]

The board expected Hummel to use designated funds only for the stated purposes. Only projects that had received prior approval from the board were to be presented to the CCCU congregations. However, Hummel communicated directly with some of the state side congregations about some unapproved projects. He thought that the board had promised him some "cushion funds" that would allow him to meet unexpected expenses without having to wait for a response to special appeals. He never received the expected "cushion money," and he struggled with the delay between the submission of a request for funding and the receipt of the funds. From Hummel's perspective, the ministry was hampered because it took so long for funds to reach the field.[153]

In June of 1963 the board raised funds at a convention for CCCU pastors and ministers to purchase a shortwave radio.[154] When Hummel received the money for the transceiver, he used it as "cushion money" rather than to purchase the radio transceiver.[155] The conflict was magnified because Hummel was unwilling (or unable) to give a full account of expenditures from the funds that he had used as "cushion money." He reported that he had used it for the work, but did not itemize the expenditures. From Hummel's perspective, the CCCU missionary board had reneged on its commitment. From the board's perspective, it was irresponsible and poor stewardship to give money to someone who was unable or unwilling to fully account for the use of the funds he received.

An extensive exchange of letters between Hummel and the home office[156] only deepened the conflict. After G. C. Johnson, who was then the general missionary superintendent, visited the field in March of 1964, the tensions eased somewhat,[157] but the problem remained unresolved and soon resurfaced.

The conflict between Hummel and the home board set the stage for conflict between Hummel and Seymour. Hummel saw the CCCU mission board's sponsorship as a means to an end, and he thought of the work in Papua and New

---

[152]As an example, when Martha Jean Waugh requested funds for a kerosene refrigerator for medicines, a lay member of the church headed up a drive to collect 70,000 Betty Crocker coupons to pay for the refrigerator. The first appeal for coupons went out in August, 1965 (Thelma Meade, "Let's Help Our Nurse in New Guinea" *Missionary Tidings* XVII no 1, July, 1965, 10). Seven months later the funds for the refrigerator were in hand (G. L. Blankenship, "The Answer is Already on Its Way" *Missionary Tidings* XVII March, 1966, 12). Subsequently the funds for a gas stove for sterilizing instruments in the New Guinea clinic were also raised and sent to PNG (Thelma Meade Strouth, "Remember Those Coupons" *Missionary Tidings*, XVIII no 12, July, 1967, 8).

[153]The General Missionary Board Meeting Minutes, Circleville Ohio, December 15, 1966.

[154]"Prayer Requests" the Missionary Tidings, XV no 12 [July, 1963], 7.

[155]The General Missionary Board Meeting Minutes, Circleville Ohio, December 15, 1966.

[156]I did not have access to the correspondence between the home office and Hummel, but the correspondence is referred to frequently in the minutes of the general mission board.

[157]Executive Committee of the General Missionary Board, Columbus, Ohio, March 20, 1964.

Guinea as his work. When the Seymour family arrived on the field, they were caught in the middle of the conflict.[158]

Passing out the gifts in exchange for the friendship and loyalty of the group troubled Seymour.[159] He became convinced that "the people would have to believe the gospel for the gospel's sake, and not because of gifts." His preferred strategy was to teach and preach the scriptures from the beginning and allow the Holy Spirit to bring it home to the hearts of the people. He reasoned that the merchandise that the mission gave out obliterated the message, and the constant giving of gifts increased the likelihood of dependency and reduced the possibility of establishing a fully autonomous, self-supporting, self-governing, and self-propagating indigenous Nembi church.[160]

The people knew that there was a problem between the two men, but at the time they did not know why. Several of my interviewees told me that the relationship between Jim Hummel and Don Seymour was troubled. The typical comments were, *"Tupela i hevi liklik."* (The two had problems.) or *"Tupela i no wanbel"* (The two did not agree).

Rev. Grover Blankenship, who replaced G. C. Johnson as the missionary superintendent, visited Papua and New Guinea in 1966, but he was unable to resolve the conflict.[161] In late 1966, Hummel returned to the USA. He and the board met several times, but in the end Hummel resigned and did not return to Papua and New Guinea.

I interviewed Blankenship in 2012, and asked him about Hummel. He said that there had been problems, but he considered Jim and Virginia Hummel to be highly effective missionaries who had worked in a difficult situation and opened a work among people from a primal society.[162] On December 29, 1966, after Hummel left the field, the board appointed Don Seymour to replace him as the field superintendent.[163]

A number of interviewees told me that, just before Hummel left the field, he asked the pastors and their interpreters to declare their loyalty by standing either with him or with Seymour. The pastors were divided. Some thought that Hummel

---

[158]Interviews and conversations with Don and Betty Seymour, Leland and Pearlina Johnson and others.

[159]Seymour said that all of the missions including the Catholics and the United Church gave gifts when they first made contact with the people and negotiated for the right to start a church in a new area.

[160]Don and Betty Seymour, interview by author, Avon Park, Florida, USA May 28, 2010.

[161]I could not verify the date of Blankenship's visit. Mapon Ek, said that when Blankenship came to the field, he told Hummel to return to the USA (interview by author, Deccember 31, 2009). However, after Hummel returned to the USA, his first meeting with the board was on December 15, 1966 and at that meeting Blankenship briefed the board "on his recent trip to the New Guinea Mission Field" (General Missionary Board Meeting Minutes, December 15, 1966, Circleville, Ohio).

[162]Grover Blankenship, interview by author, Waverly, Ohio, April 2012,

[163]Meeting of the General Missionary Board Executive Committee, December 29, 1966, Circleville, Ohio.

was a good man and Seymour was sending him away unjustly, but others were convinced that Hummel had done something wrong and aligned themselves with Seymour.[164] Most of the pastors from the outside areas aligned themselves with Hummel who hoped to return to the field and take over the work in the Nembi area. The outside pastors continued to work for CUM for about a year, but when they learned that Hummel would not be returning to the field, most of them left.

When the people of Utabia heard that Hummel was gone, they grieved. They heard that the mission had dismissed him, and they did not know why. They mourned over his departure and wailed as they do when they lose a member of their group to death.[165]

After Hummel left and new missionaries arrived, the field policy on giving changed. In the early 1970s the field council prepared some "guidelines for missionaries" that included the following advice in regard to giving.

> Do not give gifts of money or other valuable items to individuals. It is against the culture of the people to give something for nothing.

> Giving things away is not a good practice. This country doesn't have beggars as many other countries, and we should not encourage it. A few cents must be charged for milk tins, old clothes, and other small items—and they keep their self-respect.

> If one missionary gives special favors, he is soon swamped with other requests. Also he is lifted above the other missionaries. When the favors stop he may be resented.[166]

The new policy was motivated by two factors. First, it was a reaction to the excessive giving that took place during the first three or four years that the mission worked in the area, but it demonstrated that the CUM missionaries did not understand the role that exchange plays among the Nembi. Second it wanted to establish a fully self-supporting church that would not develop long term dependency on overseas funds, both concerns of the mission but not of the Nembi people.

Establishment of Ministries

Christian Union Mission ministered holistically, promoting economic, health, educational, and other ministries with varying degrees of success, but the ultimate goal of each ministry was to bring people to faith in Jesus Christ. The missionar-

---

[164]Mapon Ek, interview by author, Mato (Poroma), Southern Highlands District, Papua New Guinea, December 31, 2009. A heard the story from a number of other interviewees as well. According to Mapon, Blankenship visited the field and told Hummel that he was being recalled. I found no written documentation, but the board instructed Blankenship to visit the field in June of 1966 (Meeting of the General Missionary Board, June 8, 1966, Circleville, Ohio). Several interviewees referred to Blankenship's visit in conjunction with Hummel's departure. His first meeting with the board after he returned to the USA took place on December 15, 1966.

[165]Kanj Mesmba, interview by author, November 23, 2009, Port Moresby, Papua New Guinea.

[166]Papua New Guinea Field Handbook, 1978, 8.

ies began the ministries as soon as they arrived in the territory, but it was several years before they won converts and developed a church among the Nembi people. I write about the ministries here. Some ministries were discontinued after a few years, but others have continued to the present.

Medical Ministries

The Hummels applied to go to New Guinea with the understanding that they would begin a medical work. After Martha Jean Waugh arrived on the field, she set up the first medical clinic at Tindom, and she and Virginia Hummel conducted medical patrols. The medical ministries grew, and for years the staff continued to run station clinics and carry out medical patrols to nearby areas. The administration considered Waugh's presence to be an asset but the people were reluctant to take the medicine.

In 1965 the life expectancy was 34 years of age. One-third of the babies died in the first twelve months, and forty percent died before the age of five.[167] Waugh saw medicine as "a door through which we pass to present Christ."[168] Hummel brought in a young man who had received some medical orderly training in Mendi to be Waugh's assistant. Waugh also selected three young girls named Ipnem, Sumim, and Kibem whom she trained to assist her. From the outset, Waugh taught that Christ was the Great Physician. She and her staff prayed with the people whenever they gave medicine. The administration kept her well-supplied with medications.[169]

One patrol officer wrote about the missions'[170] medical work

The Missions are doing a lot of good work in this way but the people are still show-ing fear and do not come in for treatment, others only come in when their illness has reached an advanced stage and little can be done for them. These fears are gradually being overcome by having Medical patrols constantly through the area and by the people seeing for themselves the results of medical treatment.[171]

In 1966 Waugh and the medical clinic moved from Tindom to Ka where the mission had constructed better bush facilities and housing for Waugh and other

---

[167]Martha Waugh, "Medicine – Stone Age or Modern" *Missionary Tidings* XVI no. 2, [September, 1965], 5. The article did not site Waugh's source, but Paul Hasluck, the Australian minister for territories reported that life expectancy in the Highlands was thirty-two years of age and in some places the infant mortality rate was as high as one in three (Paul Hasluck *A Time for Building: Australian Administration in Papua and New Guinea, 1951-1963.* [Carlton, Vic: Melbourne University Press, 1976] 102).

[168]Martha Waugh, "Medicine – Stone Age or Modern" *Missionary Tidings* XVI no. 2, [September, 1965], 5.

[169]Martha Waugh (Blakeman), interview by author, Lockbourne, Ohio, USA, March 10, 2010.

[170]Both Christian Union Mission and the Catholic Mission carried out medical minis-tries among the Nembi people.

[171]J. S. Hicks, 19 February, 1966, Nipa Patrol Report Number 7 of 1965-1966, 6 {NB 64-66, HW 350}.

medical staff members was separate from the clinic building. She trained local men to assist with the medical work. Additional missionary staff arrived in PNG and assisted with the medical work. Ted and Florence Meckes arrived in December of 1967, and after residing at Ka for a few weeks, they opened Montanda station and by February of 1968 CUM had an aid post there.[172] Shirley Ulman (Queen) arrived in the Nembi Valley on August 10, 1968,[173] and worked with Waugh for several months before Waugh returned to the USA for her furlough. Another nurse, Alice Jean Christie (Maher) joined the medical staff in July of 1969. The increase in medical staff enabled the nurses to engage in regular medical patrols and increase the emphasis on midwifery services.

As the people saw "the results of medical treatment," they became more interested in the mission's message. For them every illness had a spiritual cause, and the cures came from a spiritual source. When the missionaries gave medicine and prayed over the sick, many people who would have died in the past recovered. The Nembi wanted to know more about the power behind the healing. Hiebert, Shaw, and Tiénou caution that in primal societies, medicine and Christian prayers and rites may be understood as a more powerful way to "bribe" God or manipulate the spirits.[174] Such was the understanding that the Nembi had, but the success that the medical staff had in treating seriously ill adults and children made the people more receptive to the missionaries' message.

In September of 1969 Ulman began conducting patrols to the Upper Nembi Valley and the Nembi Plateau,[175] and Christie patrolled in the Lower Nembi Valley. When Waugh returned to the field in May of 1970, she conducted the clinics at Ka and the surrounding areas.[176]

The population density on the Nembi Plateau was high,[177] and the people welcomed the medical patrols. Ulman appealed to the field council for permission to live at Embi and open a permanent medical clinic there.[178] In a meeting held on October 31, 1970 Ulman was granted permission to open Embi station to carry out "evangelistic and...medical work."[179]

---

[172]D. Agg, 12 February, 1968, Nipa Patrol Report Number 13 of 1967-1968, 5, {NB 66-68 HW 307}.

[173]Shirley K. Ulman, "Anniversary Letters" *Missionary Tidings,* XXI no 4, [November, 1969]: 9.

[174]Paul G. Hiebert, R. Daniel Shaw, and Tite Tiénou, *Understanding Folk Religion: a Christian Response to Popular Beliefs and Practices.* [Grand Rapids, Mich: Baker Books 1999],162.

[175]Christian Union Mission Executive Committee Minutes, June 10, 1970

[176]Christian Union Mission Annual Field Council Minutes, March 19, 1971

[177]In 1975 the Nembi Plateau had a population density of 242 persons per square mile and was the second highest for the entire Southern Highlands District (Alice Jean Christie, "CUM Medical Report" in Christian Union Mission Annual Field Council Minutes, February 19, 21, and 28, 1976).

[178]Christian Union Mission Executive Committee Minutes, June 10, 1970

[179]Christian Union Mission Executive Committee Minutes, October 31, 1970

In October of 1970 CUM sponsored three of the locally trained assistants—Lapon, Somne and Suk—for three years of formal aid post orderly training in Pidgin at the Nazarene Kudjip Hospital. In exchange for the sponsorship, the three men agreed to work for the mission for at least three years after they competed their training.[180]

By the time that Martha Jean Waugh, the pioneer missionary nurse, left the field in June of 1974 the mission had medical clinics at Montanda, Ka and Embi, and the midwifery program and infant welfare clinics were well established. Eva Donahue joined the nursing staff in PNG October of 1972,[181] and Mary Hermiz a nurse with midwifery training arrived in the Nembi area in September of 1974 three months after Waugh's departure.[182]

In August of 1972, Carl E. Waggoner who had served as a missionary in Kenya under the joint auspices of the CCCU and WGM was elected as CCCU's general missionary superintendent. WGM operated a hospital at Tenwek in Kenya. When Waggoner visited TPNG for the first time in March of 1973, he equated Christian Union Mission's work in TPNG with WGM's work in Kenya 25 years earlier. He asked the field council to consider expanding the medical work to include a doctor and at least six nurses and to give greater emphasis to the spiritual ministry among the people who attended the clinics. He also insisted that CUM begin charging fees for treatments that the people received at its medical clinics. The home board approved his directive to charge fees.[183]

The introduction of fees was premature and ill-advised and contrary to the government policy of the day. In the end, the home board postponed the introduction of medical fees and increased the operational budget for the medical work in PNG.[184]

Dr. Richard Morse, one of the doctors serving at Tenwek Hospital in Kenya, visited the medical work in TPNG in January of 1974 on his way back to Africa following a furlough in the USA,[185] and Alice Jean Christie, one of the TPNG nurses, visited Tenwek hospital for six weeks before she returned to TPNG for her second term. They both concluded that the medical work and government policies in Papua New Guinea differed significantly from Kenya, and the TPNG medical staff would have to develop a medical program that was unique to and appropriate for its situation. In the meantime appeals had already gone out to the home constituency for a doctor to join the medical staff in TPNG.[186]

---

[180]Christian Union Mission Executive Committee Minutes, October 7, 1970.

[181]Eva Donahue, "Farewell Greetings," *Missionary Tidings,* XXIV no 5, December, 1972, 11.

[182]Carl E. Waggoner, "News Flashes," *Missionary Tidings* XXVI no 3, October, 1974, 3.

[183]Christian Union Mission Annual Field Council Minutes, March 8, 9, 13, and 17, 1973. 5; Christian Union Mission Executive Committee Minutes, November 10, 1973, 3.

[184]Executive Committee of the General Foreign Missionary Board, Churches of Christ In Christian Union, April 26, 1974. p 3.

[185]General Foreign Missionary Board Meeting, Churches of Christ in Christian Union, November 27, 1973, Appendix A, Reports, p 2.

[186]Alice Jean Christie, "Report on her visit to Tenwek Hospital in Africa" in her file held at CCCU headquarters in Circleville, Ohio, June, 1974.

When word got out that the CUM was considering upgrading its medical facilities and adding a doctor and more nurses to its medical staff, the competitiveness between the Catholics and CUM surged to the fore. The Catholics had plans
to establish a health center at Det, and they had opened a clinic at Pumberel about
the same time that CUM opened its clinic at Embi. Independence was rapidly
approaching, and while the administration depended on the missions to deliver
medical services to the Nembi, it had no tolerance for competitiveness between
missions.[187] The administration did not favor placing a doctor in the Nembi area
and indicated that any doctor who joined CUM's medical staff should be placed
at Nipa which was more central and would serve a larger area.[188] CUM was in
danger of losing its medical ministry and decided that it would cooperate fully
with the Catholics and the administration to help provide the best possible medical services for the entire Nembi area.

As independence approached, the colonial administration and later the PNG
government pushed to indigenize the medical ministry and to get the local people
more deeply involved in the administration of the health sub-centers. In October
of 1975, the mission launched medical boards of management for each of its three
sub-centers. Village councilors appointed one or two respected persons from each
of the areas to the health center's board of management. The health boards were
responsible for getting the local people to assist with the upkeep of the center's
grounds and buildings, to discuss the center's needs and the needs of the community, and to plan for the center's future. The sister-in-charge at each center
served as the board's advisor. Each board had a fair amount of autonomy, but was
answerable to the church/mission agency with whom it was to consult regarding
major decisions.[189] The committees were functioning by November of 1975,[190]
and at Ka the board quickly constructed a bush ward because it wanted inpatient
facilities.[191]

The mission joined the Churches Medical Council whose liaison officer negotiated with the government on behalf of all Christian churches and missions
in regard to the national health policies, and after numerous meetings with the
Catholics, United Church and provincial health authorities, the medical work in
the Nembi area was reorganized. The health center that the Catholics operated at
Det became responsible for all community health in the Nembi Valley, and Ka
was downgraded to an aid post.[192] CUM became the primary health agency on the

---

[187]In an effort to quell the competitiveness, the administration proposed placing a government center at Mesapaem half-way between Ka and Det and suggested that the center
be staffed by nurses from both Christian Union Mission and the Catholics. The proposal
was not adopted, but it was indicative of the administration's impatience with competitiveness between mission groups.

[188]Christian Union Mission Field Council Minutes, October 26, 1974, 3.

[189]Christian Union Mission Executive Committee Minutes, October 4, 1975, 5.

[190]Christian Union Mission Field Council Minutes, November 21, 1975, 7.

[191]Christian Union Mission Annual Field Council Minutes, February 19, 21, and 28,
1976, 34.

[192]Christian Union Mission Annual Field Council Minutes, February 9-10, 1978, 23

Nembi Plateau. It closed the clinic at Montanda, and the United Church opened a new clinic at nearby Tegibo. The CUM staff was asked to continue to conduct the child welfare clinics and offer midwifery services at Montanda for several more years. The Catholics closed their clinic at Pumberel and opened an aid post at Kum. Embi was upgraded to a health sub-center. Eventually the government built new health facilities for the Nembi Plateau at Ol less than a mile from Embi with the understanding that the Christian Union Mission would close Embi and provide the staff for Ol when the buildings were ready. The medical work transitioned from Embi to Ol in 1979 under Mary Hermiz's leadership.

Beginning in 1975, the expatriate nurses concentrated on recruiting trained indigenous staff from other areas of PNG to join the CUM medical team. The first indigenous nursing sister joined CUM medical staff in 1977. The qualifications for students enrolling in medical training were continually upgraded, and the Nembi candidates fell short of the new requirements. It was several years before Nembi students qualified to enter medical training. In 1977 CUM sent out four students to nurse aid training at Kudjip Nazarene Hospital and a few years later when other students completed grade ten and qualified to go to nurses' school, the mission trainees went to Kapuna Hospital in the Gulf Province or to Kudjip Nazarene Hospital in the Western Highlands Province.

One of the challenges that the medical staff faced was to maintain a strong spiritual emphasis in the medical ministry. From the beginning the nurses and their staff prayed with the persons that they treated,[193] and when the nurses started conducting regular well-child clinics, they had devotions before the clinic began.[194] However, most of the nurses felt that the spiritual emphasis given in the medical ministry was weak. The comment that Waugh made in the 1974 report to the field council was typical, "The spiritual ministry in the medical work is lacking. Services are held at times, but there is no daily consistent ministry."[195]

The medical staff instituted two programs to enhance the medical program's spiritual outreach. First they started a chaplaincy program for the inpatients at each of the health sub-centers. The nurses met with the church leaders and asked them to appoint a pastor for each of the health sub-centers who would regularly visit the inpatients, pray for them, counsel them spiritually, encourage them to commit to Christ, disciple those who did, and make follow-up visits to their homes once they were dismissed from the clinic. The church leaders agreed that it was a good idea, but they were not sure who they could appoint to be a clinic chaplain, and they did not know how they could pay the chaplain for his services.[196] By February of

---

[193]Martha Jean Waugh, interview by author, Lockbourne, Ohio, USA, March 6, 2010.

[194]Shirley K. Ulman, letter to the PNG Field executive committee, in Christian Union Mission Executive Committee Minutes, June 10, 1970.

[195]Martha Jean Waugh, "General Medical Report" in Christian Union Mission Annual Field Council Minutes, February 15-16, 1974, p 12.

[196]Christian Union Mission Executive Committee Minutes, October 4, 1975.

1976, a clinic chaplain had been appointed to serve at Ka and Embi clinics,[197] and it functioned for a while, but in time it faded away.

The second spiritual outreach involved women in a witness program at the monthly infant welfare clinics held in each area. Christian women were invited to accompany the medical personnel on patrols to participate in services held before the clinic began and to witness one on one with the women who were waiting with their children to be seen at the clinic. The program caught on quickly and became a precursor to the current women's ministries of Christian Union church which are discussed in greater detail later.

The nurses may have felt that the medical work did not give enough emphasis to "the spiritual side of the ministry," but the people had a different perspective. They did not separate the physical from the spiritual. Traditionally they had turned to the spirits in times of illness. When the mission taught better hygiene, offered western medicine, and prayed over those they treated, some who would have faced certain death in the past recovered, and the people believed that the medicine and the healings came from God.[198] Even in the face of possible death, some chose not to sacrifice to the spirits for their healing. For the people, with or without medicine, all healing had a spiritual source.

The mission has not been involved in health ministries since April of 1985 when it withdrew from Embi and surrendered its role as agency for Ol health center following a traumatic home invasion. I tell that story in Chapter Five. Christian Union Church wanted to reclaim the role of health agency. The Catholics, who took over the agency after CUM left, withdrew from the agency role at Ol as of January 1, 1990 and relinquished it to Christian Union Church. The Catholics agreed to help provide staff for the health center and CUC could appeal to other church groups for trained medical workers until the church had its own personnel. The mission appointed a health secretary to assist the church until it found a qualified person to serve as the church's health secretary.[199] One year later, in January of 1991 the mission gave the regional board of trustees six months to find a health secretary who would be responsible for managing the health ministries that were to be fully administered by the regional board of trustees.[200] Temon Embel became the church's health secretary and served in that position until his death in 2016. Under his leadership, the church has added aid posts and reclaimed the health center at Tegibo. Presently, Christian Union Church administers health services at Ol, Tegibo, Ka, Askam, Mont, Tula and Poroma.

---

[197]Christian Union Mission Annual Field Council Minutes, February 19, 21, and 28, 1976.

[198]Several interviewees said that they believed that the medicines and the healings came from God. A comment by Ndipilli in the Lai Valley was typical, "We took the medicine and we prayed and we recovered more quickly than we had before. We prayed when we took the medicine, and we got better because we chose God."

[199]Christian Union Mission Field Council Minutes, December 28, 1989 and January 1, 1990, 16-17.

[200]Christian Union Mission Field Council Minutes, January 15, 1991, 6.

Educational Ministries

From the earliest days of the work, CUM was involved in educational programs. Missionaries organized literacy programs, conducted pastoral and Bible school training programs, established the first English school in the Nembi area in February of 1966, and held religious instruction classes for the community as a whole. Only the English schools received formal recognition from the administration, but the informal training impacted the area, and for some Pidgin literacy was a precursor to entering English school. Later the mission developed a vernacular literacy program for kindergarten age children so they could learn to read in their vernacular before they entered English school. The Pidgin schools and vernacular literacy programs for children were forerunners to the system later adopted in Papua New Guinea in which the first two years of each child's formal education are taught in the vernacular or the trade language.

Pidgin Literacy

The early pastors began Pidgin literacy classes as soon as they were settled into their assigned place of service. John Ottway organized and supervised the first literacy classes,[201] and a number of Nembi interviewees talked about attending literacy classes conducted by the outside pastors.

Later as each mission station opened, the missionaries started Pidgin literacy classes that were well attended by the youth and the children. For teenagers and young adults who were too old to be selected for English school classes, the Pidgin literacy classes were their main alternative. Pidgin literacy classes were soon turned over to indigenous teachers. At first the church leaders became teachers in the Pidgin school, but as the church developed, the church selected literacy teachers from among English school-leavers or the more accomplished Pidgin readers.

Until the late 70s, most of the Bible school students were recruited from the Pidgin literacy classes.[202] As more English schools opened, the demand for Pidgin schools diminished. By 1978, the only station Pidgin school that continued to function was at Farata. The other Pidgin schools had closed in part because there were no "teachers of people qualified to train as teachers."[203] An underlying cause for the lack of teachers was the discontinuation of the mission subsidy for literacy teachers. For the first 15 years the missions subsidized the literacy teachers, paying them a token amount for their services. When the mission withdrew the subsidy and asked the church to be responsible for the teachers' pay, several of the Pidgin literacy classes closed.

---

[201]Don and Betty Seymour, Interview by author, Avon Park, Florida, USA, May 27, 2010.

[202]Ron Hood, Annual Report in PNG Annual Field Council Meeting Minutes, February 19, 21 and 28, 1976, 30.

[203]Bill Tolbert, Annual Report for Director of Christian Education, in PNG Annual Field Coucil Meeting Minutes

Vernacular Literacy

Betty Seymour started the first vernacular literacy classes. She adapted lessons from primers that the Apostolic Christian Mission had prepared and taught literacy in women's classes that she had organized. These classes came to an end when she returned to the USA for furlough in 1968.[204]

Later on, I was responsible for the development of the vernacular literacy program. Three approaches were taken to vernacular literacy. We developed transfer literacy for those who could already read Pidgin or English, literacy programs for preliterate adults, and pre-school literacy for children old enough to learn to read, but not yet enrolled in English school. The community schools allowed vernacular literacy teachers to conduct transfer literacy classes for grade six students for one hour each week. In addition, we held workshops in each district for literate youth who wanted to learn to read and write stories in the vernacular. The attendees reproduced the stories they wrote and produced booklets using a silkscreen.

We trained literacy teachers to teach preliterate adults, but the program had only limited success. Teachers, mostly school leavers whom the church appointed, organized classes for adults that met for one to three hours per week. They received little or no pay and few taught for more than six months. It was more successful when literate individuals worked with non-literate individuals on a one-on-one basis until the other person learned to read.

The classes for children not yet enrolled in English school ended in the 1990s when the PNG government passed new legislation whereby the government sponsored elementary schools in each community. Each local community chooses teachers who instruct the children in the language of the community's choice, either Pidgin, Motu, or the vernacular. The government trains the teachers that the community selects.

Community Schools

On February 21, 1966, Christian Union Mission opened the first English school in the Nembi area with an enrollment of 30 children in a preparatory class.[205] The administration fully recognized the school,[206] and provided it with the necessary books and supplies. Virginia Hummel was the first teacher, and the first students came from throughout the Nembi area. The students who lived

---

[204]Betty Seymour, "Godon Angal for New Guinea" *Missionary Tidings*, XIX no 4, November, 1967, 11

[205]A preparatory class was like kindergarten. At that time the elementary schools had seven classes—a preparatory class and six grades. New schools took in a new class of students each year so it took seven years for the community schools to have all the grades and be ready to send students to high school. In the 1970s the high schools began with grade 7, and nearly all of the students were boarding students.

[206]John S. Hicks 21, February, 1966, in letter to Assistant District Commissioner in Nipa Patrol Report Number 7 of 1965-1966, (NB 64-66 HW 344).

too far away to walk to school each day boarded at Ka during the week and went home on weekends.

School was new, and some of the parents wanted their children to enroll while others did not. Nenis Laki from Embi said that when he heard that children were screened for the school at Ka, he told his mother that he was going, and left without talking to his father. He was accepted into the school and was enrolled for one week. When his father heard that Nenis had gone to enroll in the school, he was disturbed and went to Ka to get his son back. Hummel pleaded with the irate man, asking him to allow his son to remain in school, but the father refused and threatened to drown himself in the Nembi River if Nenis did not come with him, and so Nenis returned with his father and lost the opportunity to attend school at Ka.[207] In contrast, Ronald Upiap from Injua, who was accepted into the first class, walked to school early on Monday morning and stayed there until Friday afternoon when he returned to his home. At the mid-week, his mother would bring a load of sweet potatoes to the halfway point, and hide them for him. After school ended for the day, he went to the agreed upon hiding place, retrieved the sweet potatoes and walked back to school at Ka.[208]

Elsie Conley arrived at Ka in December of 1966, just a few days after Virginia Hummel left the field. Conley began to teach immediately to finish out the first year.[209] By 1970 there were four grades in the school. Missionaries taught the classes, and each teacher taught two grades.

In 1970 new legislation gave missions the option of operating their own schools and or being part of the national education scheme. Those that opted to maintain their own schools apart from the national education scheme would receive no assistance from the government. Those who became a part of the national education schemes would receive books and supplies from the government, follow a government approved curriculum, and have government appointed and paid teachers. The church/mission remained the agency for the school and was responsible for providing housing for the teachers. Each school was to have its own board of management made up of representatives from the sponsoring church/ mission and representatives selected by the communities that the schools served.

The Evangelical Alliance (EA) had a representative on the national education board who liaised on behalf of the member missions and churches. The education department agreed that only teachers whose churches or missions belonged to EA churches would be appointed to EA schools. Christian Union Mission did not have enough qualified expatriate personnel to adequately staff the school and decided that the best long term solution was to become a part of the national education scheme and secure indigenous teachers for Ka School. The mission joined

---

[207]Nenis Laki, interview by author, Embi, Southern Highlands Province, PNG, January 6, 2010.

[208]Ronald Upiap, interview by author, Mount Hagen, Western Highlands Province, PNG, December 4, 2009

[209]Elsie Conley, interview by author, Circleville, Ohio, USA, March 25, 2010.

the Evangelical Alliance in October of 1970[210] and appealed to the EA liaison officer to help locate indigenous teachers for the school. The first indigenous teacher,
Gideon Pranis from Manus Island came for the 1971 school year.[211] He taught the
upper grades, and one of the missionaries, taught the lower grades.

In 1971 seventy students were enrolled in Ka community school in grades
two to five. Because there were only two teachers, the school did not take in a
class in 1971. In compliance with the education ordinance of 1970, a board of
management comprised of five village representatives, Pranis, and two mission
representatives was formed. The board of management decided that, in the future,
Ka Community school would enroll only students from Ka, Tindom, Utabia, and
Wim. No new boarders would be accepted at Ka community school. For the first
time the school charged a fee for children to enroll in the school, and 98.5% of the
students paid their fees.[212]

By then several other English schools had opened in the Nembi area. The
Catholics opened a school at Det in 1968,[213] and the administration opened one at
Poroma in 1969.[214] The first schools on the Nembi Plateau opened in 1970 when
the administration started a school at Pumberel, and the United Church began one
at Injua.[215] In 1972 the Catholics opened a school at Kum[216] and Christian Union
Mission opened a school at Poi near Montanda in 1973.[217] The administration
opened Semin school in the early 70s.

Beginning in 1973, Ka school was fully staffed by indigenous teachers,[218] a
move that made it less dependent on the mission and allowed it to function consistently in the absence of expatriate missionary staff. After the first few years,
indigenous church leaders rather than the missionaries became the agency representatives on the Ka school board of management. The school has functioned
uninterrupted since its beginning in 1965 although during tribal fighting in the 80s
and 90s student enrollments dropped significantly at times. Today the first eight
grades are taught at Ka Community School and many of its graduates completed

---

[210]Christian Union Mission Executive Committee Minutes, October 31, 1970, 1.

[211]Christian Union Mission Executive Committee Minutes, December 19, 1970, 1 and
Christian Union Mission Executive Committee Minutes, January 1, 1971, 2.

[212]Ruth McClain, Education Department Report in Annual Field Council Minutes, February 19, 1972, 4.

[213]C. P. Dangerfield, 6, June, 1967, Mendi Patrol Report Number 18 of 1966-1967, 10
(NB 66-68, HW 192).

[214]Noel Wright, 12th February, 1969, Area Study Nembi Census Division, in Poroma
Patrol Report Number 5 of 1968-1969, 1, (NB 68-69 HW 172).

[215]Noel Wright, 5 April, 1971, Situation Report, 7 in Nipa Patrol Report Number 2 of
1970-1971, (NB 70-74 HW 136).

[216]G. Elimo, 6th December, 1973, Poroma Patrol Report Number 1 of 1973-1974, 5 (NB
70-74 HW 376).

[217]Ted and Florence Meckes, Montanda Report for Annual Field Council and Meckes
Personal Report in Christian Union Mission Annual Field Council Minutes, February 15
– 16, 1974

[218]Leland Johnson, 1974 Annual Report in Christian Union Mission Annual Field
Council Minutes, February 15-16, 1974, 11.

high school and tertiary level education, entered numerous professions, and found good employment. During the 2013 school year it had twenty teachers with an enrollment of 778 students.

Missionary Children's School

Until the first missionary children's teacher, Ruth McClain, arrived in Papua New Guinea in 1970, missionary parents either home schooled their children or sent them to a boarding school. McClain opened the school for missionary children in 1971 with an enrollment of six children in several different grades.[219]

The programs that the missionary children's school used varied from year to year and teacher to teacher. For several years beginning in 1981, the missionary children's school used The Accelerated Christian Education (ACE) program for homeschoolers.[220] The parents assisted the teacher and helped monitor the children's studies. After several years the mission dropped the ACE curriculum in favor of other programs.

In the meantime, some other missions established ACE schools that enrolled both expatriate and Papua New Guineans. They employed an extractionist approach to education. They selected the most gifted students in their ACE and English Bible schools in Papua New Guinea, found overseas sponsors, and sent them to the USA for college and even high school training. They sent college students to Kentucky Mountain Bible College, God's Bible school in Cincinnati, Hobe Sound Bible School in Florida, and other conservative Wesleyan schools. The school of choice for high school students was Mount Carmel High School in Kentucky.

Kanj Mesmba said that when he heard that Christian Union Mission had started an ACE school for the missionary children, he approached the mission with a request that the children of the church leaders and pastors be allowed to attend the ACE school for missionary children and that the mission arrange for the children of the church leaders and pastors to attend the same high schools that the missionary children attended. The parents would pay the fees, but they wanted their children to have the same opportunities and attend the same schools that the missionary children attended. The missionaries told Kanj that the mission did not have the personnel or the financial resources to establish an ACE school large enough to accommodate the children of pastors and church leaders. The pastors and church leaders should sponsor their children at the community schools and send them to high schools in Papua New Guinea.[221]

When I interviewed pastors and leaders of Christian Union Church of Papua New Guinea in 2009 and 2010, several of them told me that Christian Union Mission had done a disservice to Christian Union Church when it failed to enlarge its

---

[219]The enrollment in the missionary children's school was always small and catered to several grades. Most years six or seven children attended the school, and the enrollment rarely exceeded ten children.

[220]Christian Union Mission Field Council Minutes, April 30 and May 1, 1982, 21.

[221]Kanj Mesmba, interview by author,

ACE school and open it to the children of the pastors and church leaders in the PNG church and denied them the opportunity to enroll in Ukarumpa International High School or attend high school in the USA. Several acknowledged that their children had completed high school and received tertiary education in Papua New Guinea and were now teachers, nurses, policemen, and other professionals employed in both the public and private sector, and earning a good income. However, from their perspective, Ka Community School was a "government" school, and the mission had done little to promote education among the children of its adherents, and their children did not support the church.

The church leaders say that, compared to the churches spawned by missions that had opted to sponsor the children of its adherents at schools in the USA, Christian Union Church of Papua New Guinea is poorly supported. Students who have been sponsored to attend overseas schools find high paying jobs when they return to Papua New Guinea. They give generous offerings to the sponsoring churches. My interviewees held CUM responsible for their lack of support because "CUM came without a plan" and made no provisions for the overseas education of the children of its adherents. Other groups "came with a plan," provided for the overseas education of the children of its adherents, and now the other churches prospered.[222]

Pastoral Training and Bible Schools

From the outset, the mission sponsored regular training for the pastors and interpreters. Missionaries or the more educated pastors taught literacy to preliterate pastors and interpreters, and used simple pictures and drawings as teaching aids for the pastors to use when they instructed the local people.[223] Hummel was in charge of the pastoral training until he left the field, and after that Seymour assumed the responsibility.[224] When mission stations opened at Montanda, Farata, and Embi, the resident missionaries held pastors' classes in their areas, following the same basic format for classes that missionaries had used from the beginning.

---

[222]A number of the individuals and groups that I interviewed criticized the mission for its lack of a plan and its failure to sponsor their children, youth, and church leaders for an overseas education. These included among others, Kanj Mesmba, Timothy Pe, William Wop, the CUC Port Moresby District Board, and the CUC Regional Board. The CUC church leaders, pastors and members had discussed the issue widely, and when I interviewed them, they reported the consensus that they had reached. Some of the groups that sent its adherents overseas for high school and college training, had started churches on the Nembi Plateau and other areas where CUC churches dominated. The CUC church leaders said that pastors of the new groups kept telling the people of Christian Union Church that Christian Union Mission had entered the area without a plan, and failed to provide a proper education for its youth and leaders.

[223]Several of the elderly men who had served as pastors spoke of the pictures and simple drawings that they were given to help them recall the story they had learned during the training session and teach it to the people when they returned to their place.

[224]Don and Betty Seymour, interview by author, Avon Park, Florida, May 28, 2010,

The mission sent the first full time trainees to schools operated by other groups. Rema and Yoke were from the Ialibu area and had come to the area with Jim Hummel. The mission sent them to Lapalama, a school that tutored Papua New Guineans in English, and after they completed the course at Lapalama they went to Christian Leaders Training College (CLTC) at Banz in 1969. Rema dropped out of school after two years to return to his home place and work with the church in his home area.[225] Yoke completed his course, and in 1972 he married and joined the Nembi Bible School staff where he worked for a year and one-half before he left the mission.[226]

In 1970 the mission sent out the first three local male students—Simon En from Montanda, Tui Ori from Ka, and John Esup from Farata—for Bible school training. By then Lapalama had upgraded its standards and would accept only students who had a fifth grade education and further required that the potential students had served their church as an evangelist or pastor for several years.[227] No Nembi person qualified to go to Lapalama. Instead, the mission sent its students to Lae Bible School operated by the Swiss Evangelical Mission. Additional students were sent to Lae in 1971 and 1972.[228] The Nembi students returned to the Nembi area and served the church after they completed their schooling. Some left after a few years, but others became leaders in the church and several have served until the present.

The mission started a central Bible school at Ka in 1970 that met three days per week. It was open to both pastors and youths who wanted to become pastors.

---

[225]Christian Union Mission Executive Committee Minutes, March 6, 1971, 1.

[226]Betty Yoke Lapa, interview by author, Mount Hagen, Western Highlands Province, January 22, 2010. According to Betty, Yoke's wife, they went to Ka as newlyweds where Yoke worked for a year and one-half in the Bible school. When the mission planned to give Yoke oversight over the pastors, some of the local people said they did not want him to have authority over them and threatened to harm him if he remained. He left and went to work for Missionary Aviation Fellowship (MAF). After a year's employment at MAF they along with SIL (Summer Institute of Linguistics) sent him to Australia for a two-year course. When he returned to PNG, he enrolled at CLTC for further training and graduated with a diploma degree in 1979. The mission at Ialibu planned to send him to God's Bible School in Cincinnati for further training and had finalized all of the arrangements. Sponsors from the US sent money to Yoke's bank account. They were given two weeks to go to Ialibu and Pangia (Betty's home) to say good-bye to their kin groups before leaving for the USA. During that time, Yoke went to Mendi, and invested the money that he had been given for school in a business and opted not to go to the USA. In Mendi he began drinking heavily, and he along with two other men raped a girl from Mendi. He was given a two-year prison sentence for his crime. When he was released from prison, he resumed his heavy drinking and died about six months later.

[227]Christian Union Mission Executive Committee Minutes, July 30, 1971, 1

[228]In 1971 Mapon Ek, Jeremaih Kombap Kele, Pangia Waista became the second group to go to Lae Bible school for training (Christian Union Mission Executive Committee Minutes, March 6, 1971, 1) and in 1972 six more young men went to Lae.

In 1973 the mission expanded the Ka Bible school program to a three-year full time course.[229]

In 1971 the mission sent six girls to a Bible school at Yagrumbak near Wewak operated by the Southseas Evangelical Mission,[230] and the following year the mission sent an additional ten girls to Yagrumbak.[231] The second group completed two years of training at Yagrumbak, but the pastors' student committee did not want the girls to return to Yagrumbak for another year. The committee asked that they be enrolled in a school in the Nembi area.

Several of the women I interviewed told about a trip that they took to Wewak under the school's supervision during one of their term breaks. They had raised sweet potatoes in their gardens and went to sell them at the market and visit the stores in the town of Wewak. While waiting for the school vehicle to come pick them up, the girls met some policemen from Mendi who lived at the Wewak police barracks. One of the girls claimed that she was related to one of the policemen, and when the men invited the girls to their house, several went with them while others waited for the school vehicle. No harm came to the girls who had gone off on their own, and the men returned them safely to the guest house in Wewak, but they were reprimanded for their meandering. There is no mention of the incident in the field minutes, but I think it may have been the reasons that the pastors did not want the girls to return for their third year of training.

The mission opened a girls' school at Farata[232] on February 5, 1975. Eleven girls were enrolled in the school, and five of the eleven had completed two years of training at Yagrumbak.[233] The schools ran consistently for several years. The mission prioritized the Bible schools and always freed up mission staff for the Bible school. Both missionaries and indigenous personnel staffed the schools. The indigenous male teachers were graduates of either CLTC or Lae Bible School, and the indigenous female teachers were graduates of the girls' school.

In June of 1979, the two schools merged, and the women's school moved to Ka and became known as the Girls' Division of the Nembi Bible Training Center.[234] By 1978 an increasing number of Nembi youth had completed grade six. The school transitioned from a Pidgin curriculum to an English curriculum and added English classes to the Bible and pastoral training courses, and by 1981 most classes were taught in English.

---

[229]Don Seymour, "Field Superintendent's and Ka Area Report" in Annual Field Council Minutes, February 15 – 16, 1974, Appendix, p 6.

[230]Christian Union Mission Executive Committee Minutes November 12, 1970, 1. The names of the girls who went the first year were Sumim and Kibem from Ka and Laim, Hosea, Kidem and Midon from Montanda.

[231]Christian Union Mission Executive Committee Minutes, February 12, 1972, 1. The ten girls sent out the second year are not recorded, but they included Wepeli, Koreyaem, Tindal, Pombre, Susi Kibem Tio, Pore, Mapu, and several others.

[232]Christian Union Mission Annual Field Council Minutes, February 15-16, 1974, 5-6.

[233]Elsie Conley, "Farata Girls' School Report" in Annual Field Council Minutes, March 6, 1975.

[234]Christian Union Mission Annual Field Council Minutes, May 2-3, 1980

The year 1981 brought the first major disruption to the Bible school. There had been no major tribal fighting in the Nembi area since the late 1960s, but on May 6, 1981 it reemerged with a vengeance.[235] On June 11, 1981 the school closed for a two-week term break, but because of the fighting the students did not return to the school at the end of the break.[236]

The Bible school reopened in February of 1982, but the Christian Union Church of Papua New Guinea was dissatisfied with the Bible school program. The Regional Board of Trustees recommended that "that the present school be closed at the end of the school year 1982 and that a pastoral training school in Pidgin be started." The mission council accepted the board's assessment and agreed to redesign a program in Pidgin for the Bible school with major input from the regional board.[237]

Tribal fighting and a shortage of both expatriate and indigenous staffing again disrupted the Bible school program. In 1983 eleven students enrolled in the Bible school, but when tribal fighting broke out on the Nembi Plateau, three of the students dropped out of school leaving an enrollment of eight by the end of the school year.[238]

In January of 1984 the Bible school started a new year with thirteen new students and eight returnees bringing the total enrollment to twenty-one.[239] The director of the Bible school and the missionary teacher both left the field in February of 1984. At first the mission director and the national teacher kept the Bible school going,[240] but later the Bible school closed because of inadequate staffing. New missionary recruits who arrived on the field in November of 1984 were appointed to work in the Bible school, but they left the field after only fifteen months of service. When Dean and Shirely Queen returned to PNG in July of 1987 following a prolonged furlough, they reopened the Bible School that had been closed for over two years. They spent the first six months cleaning up the facilities, getting ready for the reopening and securing indigenous teachers for the school. Under their tutelage, with the aid of one indigenous teacher, the school reopened in February of 1988.[241] Except for a few months in 1995, it ran consistently, and from 1991 to 1993 the Wesleyan church sent some of its trainees to Nembi Bible School and provided a teacher for two years.[242] The school closed in 1998 because of tribal fighting and never reopened in that location. I tell the story of its relocation to Mount Hagen in Chapter Seven.

---

[235]Christian Union Mission Annual Field Council Minutes, January, 15-16, 1982, 37,

[236]Christian Union Mission Annual Field Council Minutes, January 15-16, 1982, 39.

[237]Christian Union Mission Field Council Minutes, April 30-May 1, 1982, 6.

[238]Elsie Conley, "Nembi Bible School Report" in Christian Union Mission Annual Field Council Minutes February 3-4, 1984, p 18.

[239]Elsie Conley, "Nembi Bible School Report" in Annual Field Council Meeting Minutes, January 25, 1984, p 17-18.

[240]Don Seymour, "Frontlines" *Missionary Tidings* XXXV no 7 [April, 1984]: 2.

[241]Dean Queen, "Annual Report," in Christian Union Mission Annual Field Council Minutes, January 13, 1989.

[242]Christian Union Mission Field Council Minutes, June 20-21, 1991, 8.

Economic Development

The colonial administration depended on the mission to assist with the overall economic development of the area. Christian Union Mission opened the first trade stores in the area at the administration's request. In addition, the mission worked with various development projects with varying success. The missions and the administration were the primary employers as the administration paid people for road work and the missions developed their stations.

Soon after the Ka lease was finalized, CUM acquired some calves to begin a cattle project. The goal was to train pastors and church members in the care of cattle and assist them in the acquisition of cattle for their own projects.[243] Cattle were also maintained at Montanda station for several years from the late 60s to the mid-1970s. However, the cattle projects did not work well in the Nembi area in part because of the land pressure that made it difficult to find enough unused land to develop a project, and partly because the people wanted cattle for prestige and status, and never saw them as a means of economic gain. They treated the cows like pigs, using them for bride price and killing them at pig feasts, without allowing enough time for the project to become a profitable venture.[244]

In 1967 the mission acquired an agricultural lease at Montanda[245] which was developed by Ted and Florence Meckes. The people gave the mission a swampy piece of land that they thought was useless. It was covered by thick bush and the mud came up to their knees when they tried to walk through it. When the Meckes came, they asked the people to clear the land, and the people worked hard and did it. They dug drainage ditches, built a house, planted gardens and turned the useless bit of ground into a productive garden site. In the process they introduced some new garden techniques and crops to the people.[246] Trompf says that missions frequently built their stations on land that the people considered to be unusable. Once the land was reclaimed, the people looked to the mission for employment and further exchange.[247] The missionaries who followed the Meckes at Montanda lacked the expertise to maintain the gardens like the Meckes did, but the people continued to find some employment with the mission, and they grew many of the new crops in their own gardens. The church eventually inherited a well-drained piece of land that became its district headquarters.

In 1983 the mission started a sheep project with the goal of training youth and supplying sheep to locally owned community projects. Amos Almap, who was

[243]Conversation with Don Seymour.

[244]Schieffelin, Edward L. and Robert Crittenden, editors. *Like People You See in a Dream: First Contact in Six Papuan Societies.* [Stanford, Calif: Stanford University Press, 1991], 276-277.

[245]A. F. McNeill, 16 September, 1967, letter to the Southern Highlands District Commissioner in Nipa Patrol Report Number 1 of 1967-1968, (NB 66-68 HW 258).

[246]Sara Olli James and Susan Tindal Jimi, interview by author, Semin (Nipa), Southern Highlands Province, PNG, December 24, 2009.

[247]G. W. Trompf, *Payback: The Logic of Retribution in Melanesian Religions.* [Cambridge, UK: Cambridge University Press, 1994], 398.

the lead shepherd, had been taking care of the sheep at Ka for two and one-half years. In the middle of 1987, he fled from Ka in fear of his life because a man from Wim wanted to kill Amos in retaliation for the death of a brother who had been killed assisting Amos's kin group in a tribal fight. Amos could no longer safely live and work at Ka, so he fled to the protection of his own group.[248] The sheep project continued for several years after Amos left. By January of 1989 five local sheep projects had been started.[249] However, because both the mission and church lacked personnel to consistently oversee the sheep project, the mission after consulting with the church leaders sold the sheep and discontinued the project.[250]

In 1984 the church and mission considered setting up a community business with the church and mission as the principal shareholders that would be open to outside investors, but controlled by the church.[251] Church and mission representatives contacted the commerce department in Mendi with a request to carry out a feasibility study. The department estimated that the church and mission would have to raise eight thousand kina to start the business, and asked the church and mission how they intended to raise the required funds.[252] In December of 1984 when Don Seymour, the general missionary superintendent, visited the field he cautioned that "the field, both church and mission, need to be aware of the high risk involved in a business venture. Also, it is important not to undermine the concept of Biblical stewardship."[253] For reasons unknown, the planned business venture never got off the ground.

Women's Ministries

In the Nembi pre-Christian world, the women were excluded from the cults. They had only limited access to the spirits, and depended on the men to intercede on their behalf. Some of the women rued their exclusion from the cults and wanted more direct contact with spiritual powers. They secretly approached the spirits on their own. They were responsible for taking care of the pigs, and sometimes they would hide the runt of a litter, take it to an isolated place where they developed and performed their own rituals, and sacrificed the piglet in an effort to contact the spirits without male mediators.[254]

Outreach to the women began when Betty Seymour started a weekly Bible class for the women at Ka. Twenty-two women showed up for the first class, and

---

[248]Butch Jenkins, "Report for Community Development" in Christian Union Mission Annual Field Council Minutes, January 25. 1988.

[249]Butch Jenkins, "Annual Report for 1988" in Christian Union Mission Annual Field Council Minutes, January 13, 1989.

[250]Christian Union Mission Field Council Minutes, January 15, 1991, 6.

[251]Christian Union Mission Field Council Minutes, May 4 and 5, 1984, p 7.

[252]Christian Union Mission Field Council Minutes, August 3-4, 1984, p 3 and 15.

[253]Christian Union Mission Field Council Minutes, December 13, 1984, p 3.

[254]Alice Jean Christie Maher, interview by author, Wilmore Kentucky, USA, August 13, 2010.

the second week there were forty.[255] When Seymour left for furlough other missionaries took over the classes, and by August of 1969 eight hundred women from throughout the Nembi area were attending the classes.[256] Some of the women walked up to three hours to be able to attend the classes. The classes were soon divided. One was held for the enquirers who were interested in learning about the Christ and Christianity, but were not ready to commit to being baptized. Another class was held for those who wanted to be baptized. The Nembi women were never quiet about their new found faith, and carried the lessons they learned back to their homes, sharing it with their husbands and with anyone else who would listen and living out their newly found faith in their daily contacts with others.[257] They became the church's first evangelizers.

Christianity for the women was empowering. It offered them direct access to God. They were no longer dependent on the men to intervene with the spirits on their behalf. Instead they could now go directly to God through their own prayers. In addition to attending weekly classes held on the mission stations, they were free to participate in worship in their own villages. Christianity was open and inclusive. Men, women, and children all attended the services, and partook in the prayers and heard the scriptures read. Even those who had not adopted Christianity were free to attend the Christian services. It contrasted with the traditional cults that carefully guarded its secrets, exacted a price from everyone, but allowed only the male initiates to participate in the rituals, and threatened harm to any uninitiated person that violated the cults' protocol.

Beginning in 1975 the medical staff asked some of the Christian women to accompany them on patrols to conduct well-child clinics held every month in each area. They became known as *witnes meri* or *tenael paengen llo angal llaopalleme ten* (witness women). The vast majority could not read or write. To help prepare them for their task of evangelization, missionary women taught them Bible stories using a "stick figure Bible story book" which helped them remember the lessons they had been taught. They attended a weekly class to learn the stories, and then two or three women would accompany each medical patrol to witness to those who were waiting to be seen by the medical staff.

The mission outstations developed into districts, and each of the districts had an active corps of witness women. The women's husbands empowered them, releasing them to accompany the medical patrols even if it meant the women would not be able to go to their gardens and collect food on the days they went on patrol and the men would have to help their wives with the pigs. The ministry was ef-

---

[255]Betty Seymour, "Godon Angal for New Guinea" *Missionary Tidings,* XIX no 4, November 1, 1967

[256]Rose Gurwell, "Highlights Mount of Praise Missionary Services" *Missionary Tidings,* XXI no 3, October, 1969.

[257]Martha Jean Waugh "Women's Meetings" *Missionary Tidings,* XXIII no 7, [February, 1972]: 5.

fective, and many of the people that the women contacted made Christian commitments.[258]

When the women went on medical patrols their purpose was twofold. First, they wanted to evangelize, and second, they wanted to pray for and encourage those who were struggling with issues in their lives. The witnessing team members prayed for anyone in need. They prayed for each other. They prayed for the non-Christians. They prayed for women who were troubled and shared their concerns with the witnessing women. The women did not limit their witnessing to the clinics. Two or three would get together and go looking for women working in their garden and witness to them. They went to the hamlets and held impromptu services. Even the men would stop and listen to the witnessing women as they testified to what God had done in their lives.[259] They organized Sunday school classes for the children and taught them stories from the Bible.

With the help of the nursing staff with whom they worked most closely, annual retreats were organized for the leaders of the witness women from all districts, but later it was opened to all women who wanted to attend. I am not sure what year the first retreat was held, but almost 90 women attended the retreat in 1978.[260] The retreats became an annual women's camp organized for renewal, fellowship, and prayer.

Today for the women of Christian Union Church of PNG, the annual camp is the highlight of the year. Women from all of the districts come together for a week of services. In each service representatives from each district plan dramas, give testimonies, sing, or quote memorized Bible verses.

Men are marginalized during the women's camp, but without the men's empowerment, the camp could not take place. The attendees must have their husbands' approval before they can come to the camp. While the women are at the camp, their husbands perform the duties normally assigned to the women such as looking after the older children, harvesting food, and looking after the pigs. Second, the church leaders and a number of pastors from each district come to the camps with the women both for the women's protection and to cook for the women during the camps, freeing up the women to attend the camp services.

Today the women's ministries of CUC of PNG reflect the values of the larger culture. Women remain under the authority of the men, but they are recognized for their own achievements. The anthropological literature says a lot about "big-men" and much less about "big-women," but the Nembi recognize "big-women" and give higher status to women who have performed well. Annette Weiner writes about the women who are valued among the Trobriand Islanders and given pub-

---

[258]Sandy Tolbert, "Patrols for Christ" *Missionary Tidings,* XXVII no 5 [December, 1975]: 8.

[259]Eva Donahue, "Congregation Unwanted" *Missionary Tidings* XXVII no 7, February 1976, 12.

[260]Dorothy Wood, "Bung Bilong Witnis (Witnesses Retreat)" *Missionary Tidings* XXIX, no 11 [June, 1978]: 8.

lic recognition for their achievements.[261] M. Strathern says that a Hagen woman earns status and prestige as producer of pigs and as an intermediary between her kin group and her husband.[262] It is similar for the Nembi. A woman's status is recognized for gardening skills, pig husbandry, child rearing, and her ability to mediate between her own group and her husbands. At least one "big-woman" usually stands behind a "big-man."

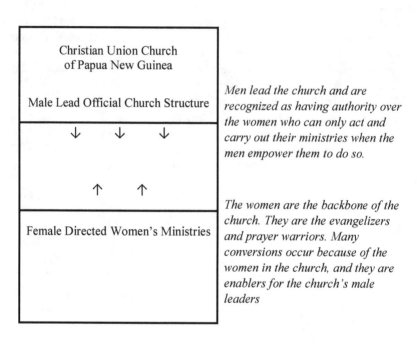

Figure 1: Women's Position in CUC of PNG

Women have been and continue to be a driving force behind CUC of PNG. Many have influenced their fathers, husbands, brothers, and children to become Christians, a fact which is readily acknowledged by the current pastors and church leaders. Women have never held an official position on the regional church board, but some have served on district boards, and many have and continue to serve on the boards of their local churches. The above figure represents the position of the women in CUC of PNG. The lower line represents the women, and the men are represented by the upper line. The men maintain authority over the women who can only carry out Christian ministry when the men release them and empower

---

[261]Annette B. Weiner, *Women of Value, Men of Renown: New Perspectives in Trobriand Exchange.* [Austin, Tex: University of Texas Press, 1976].

[262]Marilyn Strathern, *Women in Between: Female roles in a male world: Mount, Hagen, New Guinea.* [New York: Seminar Press, 1972], 139.

them to do so. Having been released by the church for ministry, the women have become the major force that makes the church work. In Nembi culture the women are the providers and the producers. The men depend on the women to help them initiate and maintain their relationships. In the church culture, the women are the evangelizers, and the growth of the church has depended largely on the efforts of the "witness women" who remain a vital force in the church.

Language Learning and Cultural Studies

When I interviewed former CUM missionaries to PNG and asked them what mistakes the mission had made, almost all of them said that we did not learn the language or understand the culture well enough. The policy handbook of the CCCU missionary department said,

> The first task of the new missionary is to learn the language. ...The general missionary board requires each missionary to learn the language of his area. A missionary must pass a prescribed course of language study before being admitted as a voting member of the mission. Exception may be made only by the general missionary board. ...During the first year there should be at least five hours of language study daily. Periodic examinations are given. Study should be continued until the missionary has a thorough grasp of the language.[263]

In the early days neither the imported indigenous pastors nor the missionaries spoke the Nembi vernacular. They used Pidgin as their language of communication. The pastors from Kagua district spoke a language that was closely related to Nembi Angal Enen and readily learned the Nembi vernacular, but other pastors and most of the missionaries, never learned the local language. Pidgin was new to the people, and it was as foreign as English. Tui Ori, one of the mission's first interpreters, said that at first he did not understand much of what he was asked to interpret. "*Mi tanim tok nating i go i go.*" (I kept interpreting without understanding.)[264]

Later, the field's official policy was that all missionaries must learn Pidgin first and once they were fluent in the Pidgin, they should learn the vernacular. There was always a shortage of personnel on the field and only a few of the new and/or returning missionaries were given time for language study.

The missionaries' attitude towards learning the local language kept changing. During my first term on the field from 1970 to 1974, the missionaries were deeply involved in various ministries, but they wanted lessons in the vernacular. I set up a series of language workshops when all the missionaries laid aside their regular responsibilities and gathered at Ka for a week or weekend of language study. Between the workshops, the missionaries completed assignments on their own stations. The lessons and the workshops ended when I went on a year's furlough in 1974, and they were never resumed. I always thought the effort had been futile,

---

[263]Foreign Missionary Department of the Churches of Christ in Christian Union, "Co-Laborers Together With God: Handbook of Policy 1980 Revised Edition, 21.

[264]Tui Tandopen Ori, interview by author, Port Moresby, PNG, November 24, 2009.

but one of the former missionaries told me that he had learned a lot during that time, and rued the fact that the program had not continued.[265]

Five years later a couple who asked to be given a full year to study the vernacular was denied because the field did not have" adequate vernacular study materials for them to use."[266] However in 1984 under different field leadership, the council decided to prioritize language study and give each new and returning missionary a year for language study. Pidgin was a prerequisite to vernacular study, but as soon as the missionary passed the Pidgin test, he or she was to study the vernacular under the supervision of a tutor.[267] The reaction of the missionaries who participated in the tutorial program varied. One person refused to write down anything because she was just going to absorb the language, but she "absorbed" very little. Another felt that the requirement to study the vernacular had deprived him of ministry for a whole year. A field crisis cut the program short and it was never reinstituted.

Most of the former missionaries did not study missions, missiology, or anthropology before they went to Papua New Guinea. When confronted by a new culture, they learned about its surface aspects, but did not comprehend the underlying forces that drove the society. A number of missionaries realized that they were inadequately prepared to work cross-culturally and when they returned to the USA on furlough they sought training that would enable them to work more effectively in a cross-cultural setting.[268]

Among the CCCU missionaries who served in PNG, cultural studies were sporadic at best, and they were sparked by the interests of individual missionaries rather than by a concerted effort of the mission as a whole to understand the Nembi culture. A few of the missionaries were intensely interested in the culture and tried to learn as much as possible about the it. In the late 1970s during my second term and Dennis Brown's first term, we worked together on a "culture committee" to learn about the culture and local perceptions. We met numerous times with some of the church leaders and local men and women just to talk and

---

[265]Bill Tolbert, Interview by author, Circleville, Ohio USA, June 19, 2010.

[266]Christian Union Mission Field Council Minutes, December 14, 1979, 3.

[267]Christian Union Mission Field Council Minutes, May 4-5, 1984, 1, 11.

[268]When Seymour went on furlough in 1968, he wanted to study missions at Fuller Seminary, but the home board said they would investigate "schools closer to Ohio where concentrated courses were available" (General Foreign Missionary Board Meeting, Churches of Christ in Christian Union, February 4, 1969). Evidently no schools were found, and Seymour returned to the field without taking further studies. Later on a number of missionaries did study at Fuller during their furloughs following their first term in Papua. The board fully supported some during their studies, and others resigned so they could attend Fuller and submitted applications for renewed missionary service after they completed their courses. Two earned MA degrees from Fuller, one earned a PhD in cross cultural studies, and a fourth completed all required course work but never wrote his thesis. When Fuller Theological Seminary offered extension courses at Christian Leaders Training College at Banz in the Western Highlands Province of Papua New Guinea, I along with three others from our mission enrolled in the courses.

ask questions about the culture and local perspectives. Even some of the local headmen indulged us and took time to answer our questions. At mission gatherings, we talked a lot about the culture. On one of his visits to the field, the CCCU general missionary superintendent said that he had heard more about the culture than about the Holy Spirit. He feared that our study of the culture would overshadow divine guidance, but we believed that God had inspired our interest in the culture, and that the two were not mutually exclusive.

By the late 1970s church growth theory had come to the fore, and the CCCU missionary department required furloughing missionaries to take an intensive course on church growth for credit at Ohio Christian University. It was the first time that most of the PNG missionaries were exposed to church growth theory. When I interviewed Bill Tolbert, he spoke about how little of the culture and mission theory he understood when he went to Papua New Guinea. He said, "We did not know there was such a thing as group conversion until we studied McGavaran" and he said, "We may have stifled a people movement" when following an evangelistic service an entire group said, 'We want to follow Jesus.' We told them that it did not work that way. Each individual had to decide for himself or herself."[269]

McGavran defines a people movement as "a joint decision of a number of individuals which enables them to become Christians without social disorientation."[270] He says that they are multi-individual decisions in that many persons participate in the decision that is mutually interdependent because the people decide together. Many individuals participate in the act, but their decision is based on what the others do. The group together make a decision to follow Christ.[271] The decision must be followed by careful teaching and discipleship. Tippett says that a group decision allows Christianity to replace the former religion at the center of the society.[272] The missionaries did not understand the dynamics of a group oriented society and responded according to their individualistic Western perspective. They did not know how to deal with a group decision to convert to Christianity.

Translation Ministry

The pioneer missionaries were convinced that the New Testament must be translated into the vernacular. The first appeals for someone to go to Papua New Guinea to work on a translation went out in 1967.[273] I had just completed my second summer of training at the Summer Institute of Linguistics at the University of North Dakota, and had decided that I wanted to work in Bible translation

---

[269]Bill and Sandy Tolbert, interview by author, Circleville, Ohio, June 19, 2010.

[270]Donald A. McGavran, *Understanding Church Growth*. [Grand Rapids, Mich: Eerdmans, 1980], 335.

[271]McGavran, *Understanding Church Growth*, 340.

[272]A. R. Tippett, *Introduction to Missiology*. [Pasadena, California: William Carey Library, 1987], 161-163.

[273]Betty Seymour, "Godon Angal for New Guinea" *Missionary Tidings*, XIX no 4, November, 1967, 11.

and literacy. I was considering applying to Wycliffe Bible Translators, but when my denomination appealed for a translator and literacy worker for Papua New Guinea, I applied and was accepted. I arrived on the field in April of 1970. After teaching for a year in the community school at Ka, I concentrated on learning the language, but was also involved in numerous other ministries.

When I returned for my second term, Ron Hood joined the translation team, but he was assigned to teach at Ka Bible School during his first year on the field. After one year he was released from the Bible School and concentrated on language learning and translation. He, too, had to juggle his translation time with numerous other mission responsibilities. We divided the work, and I became responsible for literacy and Ron was responsible for the translation. He had a better knowledge of the biblical languages and was more suited to the translation than I was. After his second term, Ron enrolled in Fuller Theological Seminary where he earned both an MA and a PhD in intercultural studies. At first the translation program was put on hold, and I continued to concentrate on the literacy programs, but in 1986 the general missionary superintendent told me that I should work on the translation instead of waiting for Hood to complete his studies. I felt forced back into the translation, and Hood said that he felt like he was forced out of it.

The method was to work through an initial draft with a full time translation assistant. After my translation assistant and I completed the initial draft, a translation committee made up of church appointed representatives from each of the CUC districts, from the Catholic Church and from other denominations reviewed and revised the initial draft. From eight to fifteen men served on the committee. Most were pastors or catechists. As long as the work was centered in the Nembi area, the men came together on Monday and returned to their homes on Friday. Each committee session lasted from eight to twelve weeks with eight to twelve weeks between committee sessions.

There were many interruptions to the work. In Chapter Five I tell the story of the traumatic events that caused interruptions, and in Chapter Six I tell about the completion of the project and the dedication of the Angal Enen New Testament.

For the CUM missionaries, the purpose of all the ministries that they established was to bring people to Christ and to develop a self-governing, self-supporting, self-propagating church. I now consider the early development of the PNG church.

Church Development

For the CUM missionaries, there was no church until there were converts. The mission did not expect unconverted people to support a pastor, and so the mission supported the first pastors who came from other areas. At each place congregations of interested persons grew up around the pastors, but several years passed before there were converts.

Conversions and Baptisms

The pioneer missionaries thought that because the Nembi society was male dominated, it was important to baptize men before the women. Twenty-two men were baptized at the first two baptisms—ten at the first and twelve at the second. There were no local converts at the first baptism. Some of the outside pastors had not been baptized before they entered the area, and they were the first to receive the rite of baptism.[274]

The third baptismal service included both men and women. It took place at Montana in December of 1968, and fifty-seven people were baptized.[275] Subsequently baptisms were held regularly on all the stations, and there was a steady increase in the number of converts and baptized Christians. Baptismal candidates attended a "believers' class" for at least a year where they learned basic Christian concepts. Prior to the baptism, a committee of missionaries, pastors, and/or church leaders questioned the candidates[276] about their understanding of Christian concepts such as law, grace, sin and salvation. Each candidate gave his or her testimony, and the committee asked the candidate's kinspersons to verify the accuracy of the testimony. The committee told candidates who did not grasp the basic concepts or had been involved in quarrels or disputes to wait until the next baptism.

Church Organization

Baptism became an accepted prerequisite for church membership. As the number of baptized converts increased, the missionaries deliberated about how and when a local congregation became an organized church that became responsible for its own finances and fully supported its own pastor. The missionaries decided that a church was "intermediately organized" when at least two men who regularly attended church had been baptized or were attending baptismal classes. At that point the local church should appoint a financial committee comprised of two men. A church would be fully organized after fifteen people had been baptized; it had a baptized pastor; and at least two baptized men "qualified maritally[277] to be

---

[274]Don and Betty Seymour, interview by author, Avon Park, Florida, May 27, 2010.

[275]Ted and Florence Meckes, "Montanda" *Missionary Tidings* XX, no. 8 [March, 1969]: 7.

[276]Betty Seymour, "Thursday Church at Ka Station" *Missionary Tidings,* XXIV no 8 [March, 1973]: 8, 11. Pastors and missionaries were a part of the committee for the first few baptisms, but church leaders replaced the missionaries. Graduates from the Lae Bible School became the first Nembi church leaders, and after they had completed their training replaced the missionaries on the baptismal examination committees.

[277]Because the society was male dominated, the missionaries assumed that only men could serve as elders. The marital requirement was that they have only one wife. Men with more than one wife could be baptized and become members of the church, but they were not to be selected as a church elder. When some of the local churches chose women as their elders, co-wives were not prohibited from serving as an elder in the local church.

elders." An organized church was to have elected elders and a finance committee that collected offerings and paid the pastor. The pastor and elders would serve as a "discipline committee" and handle any problems that came up within the local congregation, and the church would be "fully responsible" for its pastor's support.[278] Until the church was "organized" the mission paid the pastor, but kept the pay scale at a level that they thought the church could afford to pay when it took over.[279]

By 1971 four distinct areas had formed around the mission stations—Ka, Farata, Montanda, and Embi. By then most of the pastors were local men, and they had little contact with pastors from other areas. Until 1972 the missionaries and/or their interpreters organized and taught all of the classes that were held on the mission stations. When the first local men graduated from Lae Bible School[280] and returned to the Nembi area in December of 1972, the mission assigned them to work as area ministers. They took over the classes that the missionaries had been teaching and supervised the pastors. The mission pushed for each area to become self-governing, self-propagating, and self-supporting.

As a first step towards that goal, the missionaries appointed a committee of pastors called the 'area committee' to work with the area minister in the oversight of the churches. The area minister and one other pastor from each area served on a general pastors' committee that was responsible for setting the pay scale for the area ministers and handling any other issues about the area ministers.[281] Each area took up offerings to support the area ministers and sent the offerings to Ka. If the offerings were insufficient to pay the area ministers, the mission was prepared to provide a hidden subsidy for up to three years on a diminishing scale. After three years, the mission expected to phase out the subsidy. The mission opted to keep the subsidy hidden because the mission feared that if the subsidy were known, "the church would not do its best."[282]

Beginning in 1970, the mission sponsored an annual pastors' conference at Ka where all of the pastors came together for services and fellowship. Missionaries planned the first two conferences, but included an indigenous representative on the conference planning committee for the first time in 1972. The stated purpose of the conference was to "to give a sense of unity in Christ in the whole area and to charge with the responsibility to fulfill the great commission."[283]

At the 1972 pastors' conference, the pastors chose a student committee to be responsible for screening and recommending all persons who applied for a Bible school whether at Ka, Farata, Lae, Yagrumbak, or CLTC. The following year the pastors chose Menger En as the first indigenous spokesperson for the church

---

[278]CUM Field Executive Committee Meeting Minutes, October 31, 1970, 2.

[279]Field Council Meeting, October 26, 1974, 5.

[280]As I noted in the previous chapter, the first fulltime trainees were sent to a Bible school in Lae operated by the Swiss Evangelical Brethern.

[281]Field Council Minutes, September 13-14, 1974, 4.

[282]CUM Field Executive Committee Meeting Minutes, January 13, 1973, 7.

[283]CUM Field Executive Committee Meeting, May 13, 1972, 3. The committees plans were appended to the minutes, but there was no page number.

and chairman of the pastors' conference.[284] His sole responsibility was to chair the 1974 conference. These were the first steps towards formally organizing the church.

Church Constitution

In 1975, the CCCU general missionary superintendent, Carl Waggoner, directed the field to draft a constitution for Christian Union Church of Papua New Guinea, a requirement for the church to receive recognition from the PNG government. In compliance with the directive, the field council appointed a constitutional committee comprised solely of missionaries to draft the constitution. The committee used as a model a constitution that the West Indies church had adopted recently. It also referred to the constitution of the Churches of Christ in Christian Union in the USA and to constitutions belonging to other denominations in Papua New Guinea. The committee completed the first draft of the constitution by November of 1975 and sent it to Port Moresby for a lawyer to review.[285]

The missionaries wrote the constitution from a Western perspective using western structures. The concepts were foreign to Nembi society. It did not occur to anyone to ask how a Melanesian church using Melanesian structures would be organized.[286]

The constitution said that Christian Union Church of PNG was a regional member of the Churches of Christ in Christian Union whose international headquarters are in Circleville, Ohio, USA. It specified that the highest governing body in PNG was a regional conference that was to elect a regional superintendent and assistant superintendent by majority vote, to appoint boards it deemed necessary, and to discuss issues concerning the church. The regional conference was comprised of all regional and district officers, all certified pastors and deaconesses, and delegates from the local churches. It was to meet every two years. Between sessions a regional board made up of the regional superintendent, the assistant regional superintendent, and all district superintendents was in charge.

The organization of the districts paralleled the region, but the district conferences were to meet annually rather than every other year. Each member church was to have a board comprised of the pastor and three lay elders who could be either male or female members of the church. The district board appointed the pastors, but the church members were to elect their lay leaders.

---

[284]New Guinea Field Council Minutes, June 15, 1973, 2.

[285]Field Council Minutes, November 21, 1975, p. 5.

[286]Traditional alliances were formed on the basis of kinship and friendships that had been established through exchange. An individual within a group used his influence to persuade others to join him and his group in an alliance. Group decisions were made by consensus after prolonged discussions during which all interested parties could voice their opinion. See Sillitoe, *Give and Take* and Lederman, *What Gifts Engender.* Both write about the formation of groups and alliances among the Wola and the Mendi people. The missionaries did not consider either Nembi social structures or forms of decision making when they drafted the constitution.

On June 19, 1978, the church leaders met at Ka for a four day meeting during which the constitution committee members and the church leaders reviewed the constitution item by item, and discussed the by-laws that would be written to complement the constitution. The missionary chairman of the constitution committee then went to each district and taught the pastors about the constitution.[287]

The church leaders, pastors, lay delegates from each church, and missionaries voted to accept the constitution at a church conference held at Ka on August 10, 1978.[288] Within the next four months each district held a council and selected their district boards. Finally, on December 18, 1978, the first Regional Conference was held at Ka to elect the Regional Board, and the Christian Union Church of Papua New Guinea was formally organized.[289] The Regional conference elected Mapon Ek to be regional superintendent and Tui Tandopen Ori to be the assistant regional superintendent.[290] At the first regional conference, the delegates grappled with issues of contextualization as it discussed and voted on the by-laws that would go with the constitution. The missionaries wrote the by-laws with limited input from the church leaders and pastors. As a result, some were a poor cultural fit, and became problematic for the church. These are discussed in Chapter Four.

Conclusion

Clark, Ballard and Nihill write about colonization and missionization among the Wiru in the Pangia area during the 1950s and 1960s. The Catholics, Lutherans, East and West Indies Bible Mission,[291] and Wesleyans worked in the Pangia area in the early 1960s. While the missions were establishing themselves, they were highly competitive. and gave gifts such as "blankets, axes, and shells" to ensure that they secured a following. Clark, Ballard, and Nihill say that this contrasted with the way that traditional cults made their entrance into Wiru society. Traditionally the receptor group of a new cult paid the donor group to reveal its secrets. When Christian missions made their debut, the missionaries brought a new belief

---

[287]Field Council Minutes, July 29, 1978, 10-11.

[288]Bill Tolbert, "The Christian Union Church in Papua New Guinea" *Missionary Tidings,* Vol XXX no. 3 [October, 1978]: 4.

[289]Field Council Minutes, January 20, 1979, 9.

[290]Sandy Tolbert, "First Regional Conference," *Missionary Tidings,* Vol XXX, no 11, [June, 1979]: 7.

[291]Clark, Ballard and Nihill, 96-106. The East and West Indies Bible Mission began working at Kaupena in the Western Highlands Mission in 1948. They entered the Ialibu area in the 1950s and from there moved into the Pangia and Ialibu areas. At some point the East and West Indies Bible Mission evidently divided their work and spawned the Bible Mission and the Evangelical Bible Mission. Clark, Ballard, and Nihill mention the name change from East and West Bible Mission to the Evangelical Bible Mission, but they make no distinction between the Bible Mission and the Evangelical Bible Mission that became two distinct groups. The Wesleyans, according to Clark, Ballard, and Nihill, purchased a station from the "overextended" Evangelical Bible Mission in 1963 and began working in the area.

system to the people and gave gifts to solicit a following. "New cults were evaluated in terms of their ability to produce the goods" and initially the Wiru were attracted to the mission because of the goods that they brought, and the "more generous a mission was with presents, the more likely it was to be accepted. Patrol officers working among the Wiru thought that "material gain, or the belief that it would ensue," motivated the Wiru to accept Christianity.[292]

Clark, Ballard, and Nihill say that it was "inconceivable" to the evangelistic missionaries that worked among the Wiru that conversion could be credited to anything other than the "intervention of the Holy Spirit," but economic motivations played a role in the acceptance of Christianity. The Wiru accepted Christianity as true in part because of the perceived European power and wealth that came with it.[293] By following the teachings of the Christian missions and working at the development projects that the administration introduced, the Wiru expected development to come their way and to acquire the same kind of power and wealth that the patrol officers and the Euro-American missionaries possessed. Their expectations of development were not fulfilled, and the result was disillusionment.[294]

Similarly, among the Nembi, mission groups gave gifts to win the loyalty and acceptance of the people. In so doing, they raised the expectation that Christianity would bring development and unprecedented prosperity to the Christians. The Nembi listened to the message in part because of the means that it promised to deliver. Missionaries assumed that when they acquired land for stations, they obtained the right of exclusive ownership, but the Nembi believed that they retained rights to the land and were establishing an on-going reciprocal exchange relationship with the mission. When the missionaries wrote the constitution and by-laws they did not understand Melanesian structures or the cultural implications of some of the by-laws. All of these set the stage for future misunderstandings that came to the fore as the Nembi church leaders took over the governance of the church.

---

[292]Clark, Ballard and Nihill, 96-106.
[293]Clark, Ballard and Nihill, 109-113.
[294]Clark, Ballard and Nihill, 87-89.

Chapter Four

Indigenization

Introduction

Chapter Four covers the period from 1979 to 1982. Less than twenty years had passed since the colonial administration began to "pacify" the Nembi groups and introduce them to Western law. During that time, the Nembi had gone from actively resisting the colonial presence to accepting it and finally embracing the new system of law and order. They set out to learn all they could from the patrol officers and wanted the development that the patrol officers promised to bring, but the patrol officers walked away when Papua New Guinea became an independent nation on September 16, 1975. The expected development remained unrealized, and in the absence of the patrol officers the people expected the missions to bring the development.

The mission had been working with the Nembi people for fifteen years. It had been ten years since local converts began seeking baptism and joining the church in significant numbers.[1] The mission worked to strengthen the growing church as its members continued to cope with unprecedented change. Church leaders became more involved in the mission ministries, and they evaluated the mission's work in the light of their cultural understandings. In time, they found the mission lacking.

I begin the chapter by discussing the different perspectives of the missionaries and the Nembi people. Neither understood the other well, and each judged the other in the light of their own cultural understandings. It became evident that the missionaries did not understand Nembi cultural nuances when the members of the

---

[1]As reported in Chapter Three, ten outside pastors were baptized at the first baptism, and at the second 12 men were baptized. It is not clear how many of the twelve were from outside the Nembi area and how many were Nembi men. The third baptism was held at Montana in December of 1968. Both men and women were baptized. After that baptismal services were held regularly on all stations and there was a steady increase in the number of conversions and baptisms.

regional conference and the church leaders discussed the constitutional by-laws that related to cultural issues.

After the Highlands Highway opened, the people became more mobile and law and order problems developed. Some were both a part of and a result of social change, and others such as tribal fighting were a reversion to their earlier practices after the restraining hand of the colonial administration was removed. The colonial experience, however, had weakened the leadership of the traditional big-men, and both war and peace became unmanageable.

The PNG government established a work permit system for all expatriates working in the country. The new law required the mission to submit an organizational chart to the central government in Port Moresby. That forced the mission to define in writing its relationship to the church. The organizational chart reflected the mission's understanding that the church and the mission were two separate but parallel entities. That view became problematic for the church because the people believed that the two were one.

At the end of the time period, the church found its voice, and some of the pastors and church leaders informed the mission about what they perceived to be the mission's failures.

Perspectives

Most of the CCCU missionaries could not have named John Nevius, Henry Venn, or Rufus Anderson as the mission theorists behind their thinking, but the missionaries embraced the idea that the ultimate goal was to establish a fully independent self-governing, self-supporting, self-propagating church. The missionaries also believed that "the object and work of the missionary are preeminently spiritual"[2] and the missionary should avoid as much as possible being involved in business and other secular endeavors. Both of these stances would become problematic.

Behind the story lay two different worldviews. I find Paul Hiebert's approach to worldview to be helpful in trying to understand the perspectives of the missionaries and the Melanesian church leaders. Hiebert defines worldview as "the foundational cognitive, affective, and evaluative assumptions and frameworks a group of people makes about the nature of reality which they use to order their lives."[3] One's knowledge and understanding of the world, one's feelings, and one's moral judgments are centered in his or her worldview. According to Hiebert, "worldviews are part of cultures. They are the structures on which cultures are built," and to understand cultures one must consider not only the surface structures but also the deep underlying cultural structures in the "cognitive, effective, and evaluative" aspects of culture.[4]

---

[2]Rufus Anderson and R. Pierce Beaver. *To Advance the Gospel: Selections from the Writings of Rufus Anderson.* [Grand Rapids: Eerdmans, 1967], 77.

[3]Paul Hiebert, *Transforming Worldviews: An Anthropological Understanding of How People Change.* [Grand Rapids, Mich: Baker Academic, 2008], 25-26.

[4]Hiebert, *Transforming Worldviews,* 80.

Hiebert says that all people have a concept of self. People who belong to group-oriented societies define the individual in terms of each person's relationship to the group as a whole. Each person is a part of the greater whole, and without the group there is no identity. Their world is built around the group to which they belong, and the group's identity is more significant than the individual's identity. Other people have an autonomous concept of themselves. Their identity is centered in themselves, and the groups to which they belong are identified in terms of the individual. The individual is more important than the group.[5]

Rynkiewich says that the West assumes that "individuals are ontologically prior to society." Individuals create the society. This contrasts with Melanesian thinking where relationships exist prior to persons. The relationships create persons who are, in turn, defined in terms of their relationships. Having multiple relationships with kin, enemies, and spirits is part of becoming a big-man.[6]

Similarly, Richard A. Shweder and Edmund J. Bourne say that persons from more holistic societies tend to be defined in relationship to their groups. They have a socio-centric identity. In contrast, those from Western societies tend to be more individual-oriented and find their identity within themselves. They have an ego-centric identity.[7]

The missionaries had an ego-centric identity and the Nembi people had a socio-centric identity, and each group responded to the other on the basis of its own understanding of the world. Hiebert writes about conflicting worldviews and the impact that it has on mission. The Western worldview stresses order. It values structure, "punctuality, efficiency, and organization" and assumes order must prevail if progress is to take place. Westerners associate "order with good and chaos with evil." In contrast, the traditional worldview values relationships over order, but "true relationships are inherently chaotic." According to Hiebert relationships are "unpredictable," plans are always "tentative." Decisions are made by consensus, and "there is little hierarchy." "For Christians in many non-Western societies, the central issue in Christianity is not order but right relationships."[8]

CUM missionaries thought in terms of hierarchical structures, dichotomized between sacred and secular, separated the spiritual from the physical, and wanted the church to be independent. The mission perceived itself as a brother to the church[9] who was there to assist and develop a self-reliant church that was not dependent on foreign resources. Missionaries used paternalistic language to describe the mission's relationship to the church and spoke of the day when the

---

[5]Hiebert, *Transforming Worldviews,* 80.

[6]Michael Rynkiewich, "Person in Mission: Social Theory and Sociality in Melanesia" *Missiology* XXXI, no. 2, [April, 2003]; 156, 161.

[7]Richard A. Shweder and Edmund J. Bourne, "Does the Concept of Person Vary Cross-Culturally." In *Cultural Conceptions of Mental Health and Therapy*, eds. Anthony J. Marsella and Geoffrey M. White [Dordrecht: Reidel, 1984], 97-133.

[8]Paul G Hiebert. *Anthropological Reflections on Missiological Issues.* Grand Rapids, [Mich: Baker Books, 1994], 139-143.

[9]"Konstitusen Bilong Christian Union Church of Papua New Guinea" (Draft one), in CUM Annual Field Council Minutes, February 9-10, 1978, p 37.

church would stand on its own without the aid of the mission. When CUC voted to accept its constitution in August of 1978, a missionary reported to the home constituency,

> Pray for the church. Christian Union mission had mothered this child for fifteen years. Now it tries to stand alone. Like a mother watching her first-born taking its first steps, we watch and wait, standing ready to help, yet knowing that we must not interfere as it stumbles. We must allow it to grow and mature—once a child, but now a sister.[10]

Lederleitner notes that scriptures use paternalistic language. In Galatians 3:7 Paul called believers the children of Abraham and in First Timothy 1:2 Paul called Timothy his true son in the faith. Paternal language creates problems "when one person uses the term but the other person does not feel that it is fitting."[11]

I suggest that problems also occur when the same term used by both persons raises different expectations for the two sides. The church also used paternalistic language. It called the mission its "father,"[12] but from their perspective, a father would never abandon a son, or push him away insisting that he must stand on his own. A Southern Highlands' father endeavors to keep his son close and help in any way he can. Even after the son becomes an independent adult, a father shares his resources to ensure both his and his son's wellbeing. E. Ogan, who carried out research among the Nasioi people of Bougainville in the early 1960s, reported that among the Nasioi feelings of dependency on "more powerful beings for all good things in life" prevailed.[13] Consequently, the people of Bougainville did not want independence because they wanted to depend on the Australians to bring them greater economic development and a better way of life.[14] Likewise, the Nembi church wanted to depend on the mission to ensure its well-being.

The Nembi people had a worldview that conceived a world where spiritual and physical were so intertwined that they could not be separated. They had a monistic worldview and did not separate the sacred from the secular. The church and mission had entered into an on-going relationship and CUC of PNG considered the mission to be brother who was responsible for sharing resources and ensuring that the church prospered. In their view, God sent the mission to them to bring both spiritual and material blessings.

---

[10]Bill Tolbert, "The Christian Union Church of Papua New Guinea," *Missionary Tidings*, [XXX no 3, October, 1978], 4.

[11]Mary T. Lederleitner, *Cross-cultural Partnerships: Navigating the Complexities of Money and Mission.* [Downers Grove, IL: InterVarsity Press, 2010], 77.

[12]The mission usually used the term father or brother when referring to its relationship with the church. However, the author of the article quoted above spoke of the relationship between a mother and child rather than a father and child. Most of the time, the missionaries talked about the mission being the "papa" of the church.

[13]E. Ogan, *Business and Cargo: Socio-Economic Change Among the Nasioi of Bougainville.* [Port Moresby: New Guinea Research Unit, Australian National University, 1972], 70.

[14]Ogan, 89-90.

The mission used hierarchical structures. Authority passed from the missionary board in the USA to the mission and then to the indigenous church. This view was illustrated in the charts that the mission drew up to symbolize the relationship between the mission and church. In contrast, the Nembi society built a complex web (not hierarchical) of relationships between both groups and individuals. At the center of each group is a "big-man" who earns his status because of his ability to maintain exchange relationships with many persons both within and outside of his own group. The 'big-man' is not at the top of a hierarchy as much he is at the center of a network; his strategy is not as much about power as influence; and his control not authoritarian as much as persuasion. Groups relate to other groups as a unit, but individuals within the group form relationships with other individuals both within and outside of their own group. Thus, loyalties can overlap, and political alliances, often short-lived, arise out of the exchange relationships between groups and individuals.[15] The following diagrams show the hierarchical structures that the mission visualized, and illustrates the network of exchanges that the Nembi used.

---

[15]See Ryan who researched exchange relationships among the Mendi in the 1950s, Sillitoe who researched exchange relations among the Wola in the 1970s and Lederman who researched gift exchange among the Mendi in the 1980s.

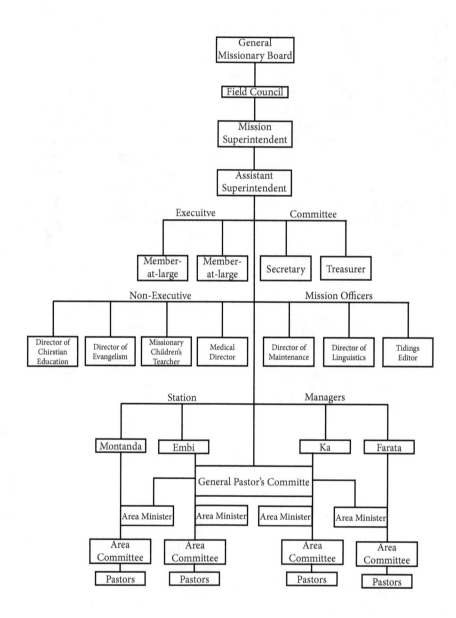

Figure 2: Mission's View of Church/Mission Organization 1976
(Before the Church was Recognized as an Entity in Its Own Right)

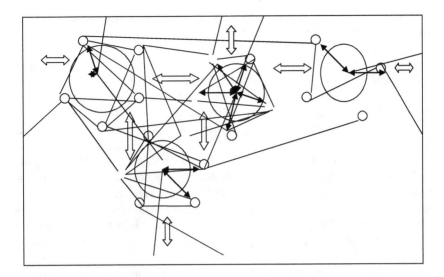

The diagram represents the relationships that exist among close knit groups and the individuals who belong to each group. The large circles represent the groups. The double arrows show the relationships maintained between groups. At the center of each group is a big-man. He maintains multiple relationships both within and without his group as do the individuals who support him. The result is a network of exchanges and a complex web of relationships that are used to form economic and political alliances. The groups and individuals belonging to each group do not limit their relationships only to persons belonging to their central groups. They maintain relationships with other groups and individuals who may be called upon for economic or political assistance.

Figure 3: Nembi Network of Exchange Relationships

The By-laws

The differences in the Melanesian church leaders' and the Western missionaries' decision making processes and the missionaries' limited understanding of Nembi culture became evident when the church discussed its by-laws at the first regional conference. The by-laws related to cultural issues were controversial.

At the time, there were seventy-four churches in the Nembi area with a total of membership of 2,118 people. There were 140 registered voters at the conference. Christian Union Church of PNG had six ordained ministers, four licensed ministers, seventy certified pastors, and two certified deaconesses.[16]

The by-laws that were approved in 1978,[17] dealt with organizational issues such as the requirements for baptism and membership; reporting and account-ability; qualifications for and responsibilities of officers at the local, district, and regional levels; duties of pastors and other church officials; the resolution of con-flict; and financial support for the region and the districts; and with cultural issues such as participation in pig festivals; death compensation payments; and bride wealth.

The registered voters had little to say about the by-laws relating to the organi-zation of the church, but the attendees discussed at length the by-laws relating to cultural issues such as bride wealth and death compensation payments. All agreed that members of Christian Union Church should give and receive bride wealth for a man's first wife, but there was prolonged discussion about whether a member of Christian Union Church should participate in the exchange of bride wealth for a man's second wife.

Rena Lederman says that for the Mendi, "the most important single context for building up an exchange network is marriage."[18] Sillitoe says that for the Wola "helping a relative to marry strengthens the relations between individuals."[19] If a member's daughter, sister, or other close female relative married a man who

---

[16]Sandy Tolbert, "First Regional Conference" *Missionary Tidings*, [XXX no 11, June, 1979], 7. The term ordained minister was later changed to regional minister. It was open to men who had served as licensed minister for at least seven years and his marriage complied with the biblical standards for church leaders (1 Timothy 3:2 and Titus 1:16). The term licensed minister was later changed to district minister. The requirements were that he had served as a pastor or evangelist in a local church for at least two years, he had completed a prescribed course of study at an approved Bible school and his marriage complied with the biblical standards for church leaders. A certified pastor was to complete a course of study as required by the district board, to have held a local witness certificate for at least two years, and to have a good name in his community, and his marriage was to comply with the bibli-cal standards for church leaders. The local church decided who was to receive a witness certificate. Any man or woman who was a committed believer, witnessed to others about his or her Christian faith, and had a good reputation within the community was qualified to receive a witness certificate which was issued by the district. The requirements for women to become district and regional deaconesses paralleled the requirements for licensed (dis-trict) and ordained (regional) ministers.

[17]I could not find a written copy of the requirements laid out in 1978, so I referred to *Konstitusen Bilong Christian Union Church Bilong Papua New Guinea (Na Ol Bailo na Sakremen)* issued in May 2002. Although the terminology has changed, the basic require-ments for church licenses remained the same in subsequent editions of the church's consti-tution.

[18]Rena Lederman. 1986. *What Gifts Engender: Social Relations and Politics in Men-di, Highland Papua New Guinea.* [Cambridge (Cambridgeshire): Cambridge University Press, 1986], 74

[19]Paul Sillitoe. *Give and Take: Exchange in Wola Society.* [New York: St. Martin's Press, 1979], 177.

already had one or more wives, and the church member did not participate in the exchange of bride wealth, that member would be cut off from the long term relationships that the exchange established. The regional conference voted not to participate in the exchange of bride wealth for a man's second wife.[20]

There was also prolonged discussion over the exchange of *"moga"*[21] which was understood to refer to mortuary payments. Some objected because the payments were made in part to appease the spirits of the ancestors so that they would not create havoc among the living. Sillitoe said that the Wola believed that if the ancestral spirits were dissatisfied with the exchange of mortuary payments, they might become angry and attack those responsible for making the payment.[22] The missionaries and some of the pastors argued that any who believed in Christ, the Omnipotent, need not fear the wrath of the spirits. In Deuteronomy, God commanded the Israelites not to practice sorcery, engage in witchcraft, cast spells, consult medians or psychics or call on the spirits of the dead, [23] and Isaiah told the Israelites to place their trust in God rather than seeking the dead on behalf of the living.[24]

The problem was that the appeasement of the spirits was only one element in the mortuary exchange, and the other elements were either ignored or not understood. These exchanges were also used to maintain relationships between the paternal and maternal kin of the deceased. These sentiments do not seem to be against the values of the Christian church. With some reinvention, the Nembi might have been able to continue in this important social exchange.

Mortuary payments had economic implications for both the donors and the recipients. The ultimate recipients of the mortuary payments were the deceased person's maternal relatives. Gifts were first given to the closest relatives of the deceased partly as an expression of grief and sympathy over the loss they had experienced and partly in expectation that it would eventually be reciprocated. The

---

[20]Christian Union Mission of Papua New Guinea, Field Council Meeting Minutes, January 20, 1979, p. 9.

[21]During the colonial era, the administration misused the word *"moga."* The term refers to a system of competitive exchange that operates between groups or individuals and is prevalent in and unique to the Melpa people living in the Mount Hagen area. It is more commonly called *moka* in literature. One group or individual initiates an exchange partnership by bestowing gifts on an exchange partner. At a later date, the recipient must give back more than he initially received from his exchange partner. There has been no *moka* exchange unless the amount that is given back exceeds what was received in the first place (Strathern 1971, 10, 216). The Highlands groups of Papua New Guinea have different types of exchange systems which are widely discussed in the literature (See Weissners and Tumu, Rubel and Rossman, Sillitoe, and Lederman), and no ethnography of the Highlands groups is complete without mentioning systems of exchange applicable to the groups being studied. The administration in the 1950s and 1960s used *moga* as an umbrella term for all compensation payments and exchanges. By 1978 the Nembi had redefined the term to mean primarily mortuary payments.

[22]Sillitoe, 202.

[23]Deuteronomy 18:11.

[24]Isaiah 8:11-19.

paternal relatives then collected the wealth they had received and redistributed it to the deceased person's maternal relatives. After several years, the maternal relatives gave a reciprocal gift to those who had participated in the original mortuary payment.

Lederman says that the Mendi recipients usually returned to the original donors more than they had received,[25] and Sillitoe says that the Wola recipients returned three items for every item they received.[26] Participation in death mortuary payments was not obligatory. Persons had the right not to participate, but a person who never participated in mortuary payments lost prestige and status and risked becoming a social recluse.[27] So, the *moga* exchanges had several functions and were intertwined with the structure of traditional society. The threat that ancestors would create havoc may have served only as a way of encouraging people to participate rather than being a central feature of the exchanges.

The regional conference voted not to participate in death compensation payments.[28] Some of the Christians argued that the mortuary payments sparked disputes and fights among people who thought that they had been slighted in the distribution of the goods. Others argued that it was not right to make a profit and enhance one's wealth and status by participating in mortuary payments.

The church was divided over both issues. The votes were taken before the conference participants reached a consensus thus short-circuiting the normal way for the Nembi people to make decisions. More than fifty percent of the registrants voted not to accept bride wealth for a second wife or participate in mortuary payments, but both the issues were passed by only a small margin. The church leaders were as divided over the question of "*moga*" as the general church constituency. In a subsequent meeting, the regional board of trustees had a "long discussion" about "*moga*" and they remained so divided over the issue, that they discontinued the discussion until a later date without making a decision.[29]

The introduced method of decision-making conflicted with the traditional method of decision-making. In the traditional society, decisions were not finalized until everyone accepted a negotiated settlement. If the church conference had been held in traditional style, then the discussion about *moga* would not have been cut short. The conference would have delayed the decision until a later time, and no by-law would have been included in the constitution. The issue would have been brought up at each subsequent conference until the church reached a consen-

---

[25]Lederman, 162.

[26]Sillitoe, 209, 211.

[27]Sillitoe, 198-199; D'Arcy Ryan, "Gift-exchange in the Mendi Valley: An Examination of the Socio-political Implications of the Ceremonial Exchange of Wealth among the People of the Mendi Valley, Southern Highlands District, Papua." [PhD diss., University of Sydney, 1961], 161.

[28]Christian Union Mission of Papua New Guinea, Field Council Meeting Minutes, January 20, 1979, p. 9.

[29]Regional Board Quarterly Meeting, April 18, 1979 in Christian Union Mission of Papua New Guinea Field Council Meeting Minutes, July 28, 1979, p. 14.

sus. In the meantime, the members would have continued to exercise their individual rights to participate or not participate without violating a controversial rule.

Even though the missionaries discussed the by-laws with the pastors before writing them, they did not understand the culture well enough, or allow sufficient time for the church to evaluate their practices in the light of scripture. They were outsiders who observed surface phenomena but did not understand the inner workings of the culture. Hiebert says,

> In trying to understand another culture, the outsider can observe human behavior and products but cannot see beliefs and worldviews. These can only be inferred from the acts and comments of the people. There may be no informant who will, or even can, verbalize the worldview of the culture, for it exists largely implicitly in the minds of the people.[30]

Luzbetak defines Christian contextualization as "the various processes by which a local church integrates the Gospel message...with its local culture." The two "must be blended into that one God-intended reality called Christian living"[31]

Hiebert, Shaw and Tiénou suggest a four-step process for Christian contextualization. The first step is to study the culture and find out the significance of every aspect of culture. The second is to critique the culture and determine what conflicts with scriptures and what does not. At this point the missionary and the members of the local culture work together, but the missionary must be keenly aware of his or her cultural bias.

The third step is the evaluative response. Under the leadership of the Holy Spirit the members of the local culture decide how each aspect of the culture will be handled in light of scripture. Some will be rejected, others will be modified, some things will be substituted and some will be newly created. The missionaries may help guide the members of the local culture through this process, but the local people must make the final decision. The fourth and final step is transformation, and it changes not only individuals but also the social and cultural systems.[32]

Considering this recommended process, it seems that the CUM short circuited the procedure. The missionaries failed to understand all aspects of the culture, and they failed to recognize their own cultural biases. Their attempt to guide the church through the third step was flawed. The discussion was cut off by a premature vote. An ill-advised policy was instituted by a simple majority of registered voters before the church had reached a final consensus.

---

[30]Paul G. Hiebert. *Transforming Worldviews: An Anthropological Understanding of How People Change.* [Grand Rapids, Mich: Baker Academic, 2008], 89.

[31]Louis J. Luzbetak. *The Church and Cultures: New Perspectives in Missiological Anthropology.* [Maryknoll, N.Y.: Orbis Books, 1988], 69.

[32]Paul G. Hiebert, R. Daniel Shaw, and Tite Tiénou. 1999. *Understanding Folk Religion: a Christian Response to Popular Beliefs and Practices.* [Grand Rapids, Mich: Baker Booksd, 1999], 20-29.

David J. Bosch, a respected missiologist said, "The gospel must remain the Good News while becoming, up to a certain point, a cultural phenomenon."[33] Andrew Walls, a noted historian of the Christian movement, identifies two principles at work in the process of contextualizing the Gospel. He calls the first the "indigenizing principle" which says

> God accepts us as we are, on the ground of Christ's work alone, not on the ground of what we are or are trying to become...God accepts us together with our group relations...our 'dis-relations'...those predispositions, prejudices, suspicions, and hostilities whether justified or not, which mark the group to which we belong. He does not wait to tidy up our ideas any more than he waits to tidy up our behavior before he accepts us sinners into his family.[34]

As Bosch puts it, "the Gospel is at home in every culture, and every culture is at home in the Gospel."[35]

Walls calls the second principle the "pilgrim principle." It stands "in tension with the indigenizing principle" and recognizes that "not only does God take people as they are: he takes them in order to transform them into what he wants them to be...The pilgrim principle warns him (the Christian) that to be faithful to Christ will put him out of step with his society."[36] The Gospel confronts culture and challenges society by revealing aspects of society that must change to make it what God wants it to be.

Mortuary payments were a part of the Nembi culture that the Gospel challenged, but the issues were not cut and dried. The situation was similar to that found in First Corinthians chapters eight to eleven where Paul discusses the issue of eating meat that had been sacrificed to idols. Paul did not write a hard and fast rule, but advised the Corinthians to "do all for the glory of God...and not to cause anyone to stumble."[37] During the next twenty-five years the church leaders and missionaries worked together on numerous revisions of the constitution and by-laws. It was and still is an on-going process. At one point, all of the regional and district church leaders met together with three mission representatives of which I was one, and spent several days discussing and modifying the entire constitution and by-laws. Hours were spent discussing the church's stance on mortuary payments.

The group said that the subject was deep and had a lot of hidden innuendos. Christians had an obligation to show their sympathy to the bereaved by giving food and firewood and maybe even money during their time of mourning. They decided that Christians should not participate in or contribute to rituals to deter-

---

[33]David Jacobus Bosch. *Transforming Mission: Paradigm Shifts in Theology of Mission.* [Maryknoll, N.Y.: Orbis Books, 1991], 454.

[34]Andrew F. Walls, "The Gospel as Prisoner and Liberator of Culture" in *Landmark Essays in Mission and World Christianity,* eds. Robert L. Gallagher and Paul Heritg, [Maryknoll, New York: Orbis Books, 2009], 137-138.

[35]Bosch, 455.

[36]Walls, 139.

[37]1 Corinthians 11:31-32

mine who was responsible for the death of the deceased person. They should not give money or other items to appease the spirit of a deceased person. They should not borrow money in order to contribute to mortuary payments, and they should not contribute to a mortuary payment as an investment anticipating a profitable future repayment.

However, this has not settled the matter. The mortuary payment issue is still being discussed. The final statement was poorly worded. It says that a member of Christian Union Church "*i no ken mekim wanpela samting bilong wok bisnis bilong daiman*" (cannot participate in a business transaction over a person's death). Some Christians are asking if they can be paid for digging a grave and burying a corpse and if it is acceptable for Christians to sell a coffin or run a mortuary.

There will be further discussion and further modifications on what a Christian should do during a time of mourning. However, the church now needs to focus on the positive rather than the negative and decide how a Christian can participate in the community's grief, honor the dead, sympathize with the mourners, and strengthen the relationships with the maternal relatives of the deceased without compromising their Christian faith and integrity.

Social Changes

Colonization and missionization brought very rapid change to the Nembi people. The changes they were facing challenged every aspect of their culture and deeply affected the relationship between the church and mission and the larger community. When the restraining hand of the patrol officers was removed, there was a breakdown in law and order.

Anthropologists no longer assume that cultures are self-contained and not overly affected by outside influences. Rynkiewich defines culture as

> …a more or less integrated system of knowledge, values and feelings that people use to define their reality (worldview), interpret their experiences, and generate appropriate strategies for living; a system people learn from other people around them and share with other people in a social setting; a system that people use to adapt to their spiritual, social, and physical environments; and a system that people use to innovate in order to change themselves as their environments change.[38]

Rynkiewich says that culture is contingent. It is influenced by and adapts to new ideas, persons, pictures, and objects that come from without and stretch their boundaries. Culture is constructed. It changes as people adjust their culture to accommodate new information and ideas that come their ways. Culture is contested. Persons constantly challenge and redefine their cultural perceptions. Without that understanding, missionaries "fail to grasp the missionary situation and to communicate the gospel properly."[39]

---

[38]Michael A. Rynkiewich *Soul, Self, and Society: A Postmodern Anthropology for Mission in a Postcolonial World.* [Eugene, OR: Cascade Books, 2011], 19.

[39]Rynkiewich, "The World in My Parish," 316.

In 1978 the Nembi struggled to cope with the tremendous change that had come their way. In holistic societies, every change is religious change. For the CUM missionaries as well as the Nembi and Melpa people, the driving force was their religious beliefs. The goal of the missionaries was to introduce Christianity to the Nembi people that they might become followers of Christ. Alan R. Tippett calls religion the integrator of society. In primal societies, everything that happens passes through the religious grid. It is at the core of society, permeates every aspect of the society, and serves as the force that holds the society together. Religious changes occur during times of "stress" when forces from without or within disturb the society's equilibrium making the society open to change and ready for conversion.[40] The decision to accept Christ begins a process that occurs over time and allows Christianity rather than the former religious system to become the integrator of the society and the force that holds society together.[41] Tippett draws on Anthony F. Wallace's theories of revitalization to develop his own theory of conversion and revitalization.

Wallace defines revitalization as "a deliberate organized conscious effort by members of a society to construct a more satisfying culture."[42] It occurs when the members of a society are dissatisfied with their cultural system and set out to establish a "new cultural system."[43] Revitalization according to Wallace is a process that has five stages which moves from a "steady state" to a "period of increased individual stress" to a "period of cultural distortion" to a "period of revitalization," during which the change becomes established and finally a "new steady state."[44]

The parallels between Wallace's and Tippett's theories are apparent. Tippett identifies four types of religious change. The first is demoralization which occurs when the society is challenged by outside sources such as military conquest, colonialism, unfair trade practices, exploitation of a society, or mission outreach, and that which has worked in the past, no longer works. If nothing replaces the former, a cultural void is created.[45]

The second type of religious change is submersion. Outside forces bring a sudden end to one system and impose a new structure upon the society. There is outward conformity to the new imposed laws or religion, but at a deeper, hidden level, the members of society continue to follow the former practices. If the outside restraining forces are removed, the hidden practices reemerge.[46]

Conversion is Tippett's third type of religious change. It involves a group decision to make the change and it can only occur at a time when the society is ready

---

[40]A. R. Tippett, *Introduction to Missiology.* [Pasadena, California: William Carey Library, 1987],161.

[41]Tippett, *Introduction to Missiology,* 175-178.

[42]Anthony F. C Wallace, "Revitalization Movements" in *American Anthropologist* 58, no 2 [April 1956]: 265.

[43]Wallace, 265.

[44]Wallace, 158-166.

[45]Tippett *Introduction to Missiology,* 163-168.

[46]Tippett *Introduction to Missiology,* 168-167.

for a change. The group debates the pros and cons of the proposed change, and as a group decides to accept or reject the new religion. If there is a group decision to accept Christianity, then Christianity can replace the old religion at the center and become the force that unites the society.[47] Tippett's fourth type of religious change is revitalization and often develops out of conflict or decline.[48]

In *Solomon Islands Christianity*, Tippett analyzes the anthropological impact that colonialism and Christian mission had on the Solomon Island's cultures. All cultural practices, including those that Western observers found despicable such as head-hunting, cannibalism, human sacrifices, and slavery, served a sociological function within the society, uniting it and enabling the people to defend themselves from their enemies and achieve success. When they were abolished without providing a functional substitute, it created a cultural void at the very heart of the society that opened the way for cults and nativistic movements to develop among the Solomon Islanders.[49]

At the time of the first regional conference, Papua New Guinea had been an independent nation for three years and three months. Indigenous public servants had replaced the expatriate patrol officers. The public servants staffed the former patrol posts and advised the local government councils, but no longer regularly visited each area. The Highlands Highway was under construction in the Nembi Valley. It followed the road that patrol officers had built in the 1960s. Hundreds of Nembi people—men, women, and youth—found employment working on the road, but this time they were assisted with heavy equipment as the road was widened and upgraded to an all-weather, all-vehicle road.[50]

With the road came greater mobility, a greater awareness of the world beyond the Nembi Valley, more economic activity, and easier access to Mendi and Mount Hagen. A pattern of in and out migration developed. Public motor vehicles (PMVs) began to operate in the area. Many people, both men and women, traveled to Mount Hagen and found employment on the coffee plantations in the Western Highlands during the annual coffee picking season. Law and order problems increased as youth resisted village authorities and, for the first time, alcoholic beverages were readily available.

Amidst these changes, both the church and the larger community began to voice their discontent with their relationship with the mission and the mission's way of doing things.

---

[47]Tippett *Introduction to Missiology*, 175-178.

[48]Tippett, *Introduction to Missiology*, 179-182.

[49]Tippett *Solomon Islands Christianity*, 139-200.

[50]Bill Tolbert "To Everything There Is A Season" *Missionary Tidings*, XXIX no 7, February, 1978, 4.

Community Relations

Hans Reithofer notes that during the colonial days, missions were considered to be "on a par with other development projects" and brought "power and prestige" to the group where it located.[51] Similarly, Clark, Ballard and Nihill say one of the reasons the Wiru accepted the colonial presence, embraced Christianity, and rejected their past was because they expected the change to bring them development, wealth, power, and prestige.[52]

As I mentioned in the previous chapter, the Ka group sold part of their land because the sale brought them recognition and allowed them to reoccupy land from which they had been routed during tribal fighting a few years earlier. They expected to benefit from the jobs and training that the mission offered. The mission, however, wanted to reach out to the entire Nembi area and not just to the people of Ka. The mission gave on-the-job training to its workers, and taught them the skills that they needed to do their jobs. The Ka group became dissatisfied when the majority of the people that the mission hired were from groups other than Ka.[53]

The mission's primary concern was for the development of a spiritual ministry, the growth of the church, and the evangelization of the Nembi people. Everything else was secondary. The mission could not allow the "secular" to detract from the "sacred." In Acts chapter six, the apostles expressed a similar attitude when they gathered the church to select seven men to be responsible for distribution of food among the Christians because they wanted to give their full attention to "prayer and the ministry of the word."[54] The church in Acts solved the problem by choosing representatives of the complaining groups to take care of the "secular" details.

Hiebert describes the attitude of the missionaries well when he writes,

> Conservative theologians affirmed the reality of miracles but often accepted a naturalistic view of the world. Many of them drew a line between evangelism and the "social gospel," thereby reinforcing the dualism that had led to the secularization of the West. For them, evangelism had to do with the supernatural salvation of the soul. The social gospel involved ministry to human bodily needs, such as good, medicine, and education. This they dismissed as of secondary importance.[55]

An early complaint about Christian Union Mission came in October of 1974, when the Ka councilor told the Poroma local government council that CUM was

---

[51]Hans Reithofer, *The Python Spirit and the Cross: Becoming Christian in a Highland Community of Papua New Guinea.* [Münster: Lit, 2005], 238-239.

[52]Jeffrey Clark, Chris Ballard, and Michael Nihill. *Steel to Stone: A Chronicle of Colonialism in the Southern Highlands of Papua New Guinea* [Oxford, UK: Oxford University Press, 2000], 87-88, 109-110.

[53]Knowledge is a property, and once one acquires it, there is no obligation to share it with others, particularly outside of community. This works against the idea that education will spread knowledge. Likewise, relationships are a means to a commodity, and so there is no obligation to let others outside community share in the benefits of a relationship.

[54]Acts 6:1-4.

[55]Paul G. Hiebert. *Anthropological Reflections on Missiological Issues.* [Grand Rapids, Mich: Baker Books, 1994], 220.

not doing enough to train the local people as drivers, carpenters, mechanics, and sawmill operators. The mission hired few local laborers, taught none of the local people to drive or repair cars or motorbikes, and had not trained anyone to operate the sawmill. Instead of hiring local people, the mission taught the Bible School students to care for the cows and paid them nothing for their work.

In contrast, according to the councilor, the Catholics offered training in all of those areas and also hired many of the local people living near their station to be laborers. He said that the Christian Union Mission needed to follow the example set by the Catholics and teach the local people the skills they needed to take care of cows, workshops, sawmills, and stores so that when the missionaries departed the local people would have the skills to carry on the work because in the councilor's words, "this is our country and we must run our own country."[56]

Implied in the councilor's complaint was the expectation that the workshop, sawmill, and cattle project would belong to the Ka people when the mission departed. The Ka people wanted to take over, but they depended on the mission to equip them with the skills to do so.

The mission did not want to promote a particular Nembi group. The CUM missionaries saw every ministry as a means to an end. The ultimate goal was to bring people to Christ. In I Corinthians 9, Paul writes about living incarnationally among the groups that he visits. He became all things to all people so that he might win some.[57] This was the attitude of the CCCU missionaries. Every ministry had as its ultimate goal the evangelization of the people, and/or the growth and development of the church as a whole, not one particular Nembi group. When the mission departed, it expected the church and not the Ka people to take over, and this was at odds with Ka expectations.

Law and Order

A breakdown in law and order was one of the effects of rapid change. It was both a part of and a result of social change. From the time that the mission first began working in the Nembi area, minor incidents of petty thievery occurred. Occasionally someone took laundry from a clothes line, sneaked into a pantry and pilfered canned fish or rice, took nails or tools at a building site, snatched a chicken, or snitched garden produce. Few missionaries had fences around their houses, and people were free to approach the houses without restraint. The missionaries kept their houses locked when they were not home, but they were never threatened personally. After the Highlands highway came through, breaking and entering increased, and missionaries felt that their safety was threatened. The first home invasion occurred in October of 1980 when someone broke into the home of Bob and Sara Jones while they slept and stole a motorbike and some money. A few days later the home of Mary Hermiz, who was then living at the Ol Health Sub-Center, was broken into. After those two incidents, the mission made mis-

---

[56]Christian Union Mission, Field Council Meeting, October 26, 1974, 1

[57]I Corinthians 9:19-22.

sionary homes more secure by placing security wire over all windows of all mission houses.[58]

At about the same time, tribal fighting broke out among some of the Nembi groups. As I mentioned above, Tippett's theory says that when the members of a society are confronted by outside forces that impose a new structure on the society, the people conform outwardly to the imposed law, but at a deeper hidden level they continue to follow the former practices. If the restraining forces are removed, the practices reemerge, and the members of the society return to their earlier practices.[59] The reemergence of tribal fighting in the Highlands of Papua New Guinea affirms his theory.

The colonial administration forced an end to tribal fighting, and the entire Nembi area lived in peace for fourteen years. After independence, both the traditional social control in the hands of the big-men, and the introduced social control in the hands of the Australian patrol officers were gone and no restraining force remained. In May of 1981 when someone began to clear ground for garden on some disputed land, tribal fighting broke out anew on the Nembi Plateau.[60] The fight lasted for more than three years. The men said that they were independent now, and no longer had to obey the patrol officer's law. They would fight if they wanted to.[61]

The tribal fighting interrupted the church and mission ministries. The Bible school closed for a two week break in June and did not reopen because the students were afraid to return to school.[62] Almost all of the in-patients at the Pumberal Health Center fled and refused to sleep at the clinic although they did return to be treated as out-patients. Fewer women came to the clinic to deliver their babies, and several nights a week the clinic staff spent hours removing arrow heads and treating wounds that had been inflicted during the days' fight.[63]

The mission established Poi school in 1973.[64] Because of the fighting, the school closed in July of 1981 and the teachers departed. "Persons unknown" van-

---

[58]Christian Union Mission of Papua New Guinea, Field Council Meeting Minutes, November 1, 1980, p. 1,

[59]A. R. Tippett. *Introduction to Missiology*. [Pasadena, California: William Carey Library 1987], 163-168.

[60]Mary Hermiz, Health Secretary's Report in Christian Union Mission Annual Field Council, January 15, 16, 1982, p 36.

[61]Not only I, but other missionaries received a similar response when they questioned the men about their reasons for fighting. They first talked about the land that both sides claimed and ended by saying that they had a right to fight, and they would.

[62]Sara Jones, "Personal Report" in Christian Union Mission Annual Field Council, January 15, 16, 1982, p. 50.

[63]Mary Hermiz, Health Secretary's Report in Christian Union Mission Annual Field Council, January 15, 16, 1982, p 36-37.

[64]Leland Johnson, 1974 Annual Report in Christian Union Mission Annual Field Council Minutes, February 15-16, 1974, 11.

dalized the teacher's houses. After checking with the education department, the mission dismantled the houses, and the school never reopened.[65]

That same year tribal fighting broke out in the Lai Valley where Christian Union Church had eight member congregations. By the end of the year, only three pastors remained at their churches, and two of the churches had been burned down during the fighting.[66]

The re-emergence of tribal fighting in the Highlands of Papua New Guinea was widespread. In January of 1982, the government organized a workshop in Mount Hagen for church and mission leaders to discuss how they could work with the government to address the issue of fighting in the Highlands. The regional and field superintendents represented Christian Union Church and Mission at the conference. Sir Julius Chan, who was then prime minister of Papua New Guinea, was a guest speaker. During 1981 throughout the entire Highlands region, 416 wounded men had been treated in clinics. Another 174 men had been killed. A total of 614 had been arrested, and 800,000 men had engaged in fighting. Chan said that more police were not the answer. The fact is that the police force did not have the extra manpower, vehicles, or equipment they needed to control the fighting. Chan asked the churches to preach the gospel of truth and peace and to join with the police and government in negotiating with the fighting groups and helping them reach a settlement.[67]

Church/Mission Organization

In the midst of all the change and turmoil, the mission pushed to make the church more independent. The mission viewed the church and mission as two separate but parallel entities. It visualized the church as an autonomous body that had the right to make its own decisions. The mission no longer would exercise authority over a self-governing, self-supporting, and self-propagating church. The mission could advise and assist the church, and it should involve the church in all ministries, but it should not, did not, and could not control the church.[68]

That view was formalized in 1980 when the PNG government, in an effort to promote greater indigenization of both businesses and missions, required all expatriates working in Papua New Guinea to secure a work permit. All organizations with expatriate employees were required to submit an organizational chart to show the relationship between expatriate and indigenous employees and to demonstrate that the organization was indigenizing the positions that were filled

---

[65]Christian Union Mission, Executive Committee Meeting Minutes, September 13, 14, 1982, p. 3.

[66]Bob Jones, "Combined Ka District Advisor and Personal Activities Report" in Proceedings of the Annual Field Council, January 15, 16, 1982, p. 43.

[67]Bill Tolbert, "Church Report" in Christian Union Mission of Papua New Guinea Field Council Meeting Minutes, April 30-May 1, 1982, p. 18.

[68]Bill Tolbert "The Christian Union Church in Papua New Guinea," *Missionary Tidings,* [XXX no 3, October, 1979], 4.

by expatriates. The chart was to be reviewed and updated every three years, and the government would monitor the rate of indigenization.

A mission committee drew up the required chart showing parallel structures. On the mission's side, committees headed departments that were responsible for particular ministries.[69] All but two departments[70] worked with the district and regional boards in developing their ministries. Church representatives served on the departmental committees. (See chart at the end of this chapter.)

The indigenous church, in contrast, visualized a single entity where the church and mission shared resources. As the mission cut the church subsidy, the church questioned if the church and mission were *wanbel* ('one belly', but in English: united, in agreement, of one mind, or at peace). From the church perspective, unless the church and mission shared the resources sent from overseas, they were not *wanbel*. They reasoned that CCCU in America had sent the missionaries to the Nembi people to establish a church, and the offerings that came from the church in America were intended to aid and bless[71] the church in Papua New Guinea. Withholding resources suggested to them that the mission was diverting for itself resources that were intended for the PNG church.

The idea that outsiders may be commandeering goods intended for the people of Papua New Guinea was not unique to the Nembi. Albert Mauri Kiki, who was one of the leaders in the movement for independence, reported that during the colonial era, the people of the Gulf province thought that the expatriates had appropriated for themselves goods that their ancestors had intended for the Papuan people.[72] Cargo cults commonly make similar assertions. Yali, the leader of a cargo cult in the Madang area, believed that Europeans waylaid cargo meant for the New Guineans.[73] Similarly, following World War Two, a cargo myth developed in the Port Moresby area that said that on cargo ships the white people changed the labels and kept for themselves goods that dead Motuan relatives shipped to their living Motuan kin.[74]

The difference in the way the church and mission viewed their relationship lay behind most of the issues that the church brought to the mission.

---

[69]Organizational Chart, Christian Union Mission, p. 12 in CUM Field Council Meeting Minutes, December 6, 1980.

[70]A publications department that was responsible for sending articles to the *Missionary Tidings* and the department that oversaw the missionary children's school had no indigenous employees and did not relate to the regional and district boards.

[71]When the Nembi use the word bless, it refers to "material" blessings as much as "spiritual" blessings.

[72]Albert Maori Kiki, *Kiki: Ten Thousand Years in a Lifetime, a New Guinea Autobiography.* [New York: F.A. Praeger, 1968], 52.

[73]Peter Lawrence, *Road Belong Cargo: A Study of the Cargo Movement in the Southern Madang District, New Guinea.* [Manchester: Manchester University Press, 1964], 121, 164, 187, 189, 191.

[74]G. W. Trompf, *Payback: The Logic of Retribution in Melanesian Religions.* [Cambridge, UK: Cambridge University Press, 1994], 170.

Church Issues

The mission separated "mission" owned assets from "church" owned assets, but the church considered all assets to be "mutually" owned. Geert Hofstede, an organizational anthropologist, has spent a lifetime studying cross-cultural relationships in the corporate world. His son, Gert Jan Hofstede, and Michael Minkov, another specialist in cross-cultural relationships joined him in publishing the third edition of *Cultures and Organizations; Software of the Mind.* They discuss the differences between individualistic societies where individual concerns take precedence over group concerns and group-oriented societies (or to use their term, collectivist societies) where group concerns take precedence over individual concerns. Group oriented societies speak of "us," "we," or "ours" rather than "I," "me," or "mine," and things are jointly owned with all members of the group having access to jointly owned objects when they need them. Individualistic societies stress "I," teach the children to make it on their own, and stress private rather than joint ownership.[75]

Lederleitner discusses the two perspectives and finds biblical support for both views. She says the parable of the ten virgins and the parable of the talents found in Matthew 25 call for individual responsibility and accountability. However, in Second Corinthians 8:13-14 Paul calls for the sharing of resources. In Acts 2:41-47 the early believers held all things in common and James 2:14-17 calls for the believers to help those who are in need.[76]

Training, Vehicles, and Infrastructure

In Chapter Three, I wrote about the formation of area committees and a general pastors' committee that predated the formal organization of the church. Almost as soon as the general pastors' committee and the area committees were organized, they began to submit requests to the mission for training, vehicles, infrastructure, and finances and to call into question the relationship between the church and mission.[77] On September 16, 1975, PNG became an independent nation, and the expatriate patrol officers left the country. The church thought the missionaries might leave and wanted training and resources that would enable them to take over mission assets when the mission departed. The mission considered the requests on a case by case basis.

One of the early requests for assistance from the mission came in February of 1975 from the Ka area committee. They sent a letter to the mission saying that the church lacked workers and asking for training as drivers and mechanics. The area leaders wanted a car. They were concerned that if they hired a driver or a

---

[75]Geerte Hofstede, Gert Jan Hofstede, and Michael Minkov, *Cultures and Organizations: Software of the Mind: Intercultural Cooperation and Its Importance for Survival* 3rd ed. [New York: McGraw Hill, 2010], 90-91.

[76]Lederleitner, 38-39.

[77]Christian Union Mission Annual Field Council Minutes, Febrauary 11, 18 and 19, 1977, p. 41

mechanic, he would demand high wages, and the church would not have enough money to pay a driver or hire a mechanic.[78]

Vehicles and drivers' training became a "hot topic" between the church and the mission. The church repeatedly asked the mission to give it vehicles but the mission insisted an outright gift would increase the church's dependency on the mission. If the church wanted a vehicle it should use its own resources to acquire, operate and maintain it, but the church lacked the resources for a vehicle. The church saw the mission's unwillingness to share its resources as selfish, insensitive, and unchristian.

The church leaders wanted to learn how to drive. They reasoned that if they learned to drive, they could use mission vehicles to carry out their ministries. When the regional board first requested that the mission teach the church superintendents how to drive, the mission hesitated because the church owned none of its own vehicles.[79] In 1979, after repeated requests, the mission council agreed to teach the regional and district superintendents and a medical worker to drive with no strings attached because driving had become an "important issue" for the church.[80]

Periodically, the workshop offered training in general maintenance, building, and mechanics to trainees selected by the church districts.[81] However, trainees seldom worked for the church after their training was complete, but found more profitable employment elsewhere. The "secular" training programs were never consistent. They changed whenever there was a turnover in mission personnel.

The mission and church found ways to cooperate in the building of the permanent church structures. Generally, the people provided timber for the churches and the mission cut the lumber and assisted with the construction and gave some assistance with building supplies or money.[82]

The difference in the housing standard for expatriate and indigenous personnel became an on-going issue. When the regional board of trustees wanted im-

---

[78]Ka Eria Komiti, "Letter from Church Leaders" in Field Council Meeting Minutes, February 21, 1975, p 9. When the district asked for training, it did not have a vehicle, but was thinking ahead to the day when they would have one. Two and one-half years later by saving money from district funds and securing contributions from district churches, Ka district had enough money to buy a car. With the approval of the regional board of trustees, the district sought the mission's approval. The mission did not oppose their securing a car, but insisted that the car be used strictly for the church and not for business and the district be fully responsible for the cost of operating and maintaining the vehicle (Annual Field Council Minutes, February 9-10, 1978, p 16). The project ultimately failed. Contributors demanded free rides to Mendi and to the health center, but were unwilling to give additional funds for the operation and maintenance of the vehicle.

[79]Annual Field Council, February 11, 18, and 19, 1977, 18.

[80]Christian Union Mission Field Council Meeting Minutes, October 27, 1979, 6.

[81]Annual Field Council, February 11, 18, and 19, 1977, 17.

[82]Christian Union Mission Executive Committee Meeting Minutes, July 31 and August 5, 1976, p. 5; Christain Union Mission of Papua New Guinea Field Council Meeting Minutes, August 12, 1976

proved housing for the workshop foreman, who was also the assistant regional superintendent, the mission informed the regional board that housing was "not a church matter but a mission matter."[83] The mission placed on the project list a request for funding for a new house for the workshop foreman, [84] but mission policy said that no project could be started until the funds were received from the US. The wait for funding delayed approved projects, and if the funds never came in, the projects were never started. When the mission failed to carry through with an approved project because of the lack of funding, in the church's eyes it became another broken promise.

Finances and Church Subsidy

To force the church away from dependency, the mission planned to eliminate the subsidy that it gave to the church. However, the financial system outlined in the constitution failed to generate enough funds to meet the needs of the church, and the church leaders could not understand why the mission wanted to eliminate the subsidy. In the 1960s, the mission fully supported the pastors. By the mid-1970s the mission wanted to phase out the pastors' subsidy. Mission attempts to wean the church off the subsidy were never successful. A policy instituted on January 1, 1974 said that no existing church was to remain on subsidy for more than two years.[85] Instead, each area received a small subsidy that was used to pay the area minister.

In 1977 the mission divided the subsidy among all four areas according to the number of churches in each area, but each year it planned to cut back one-third of the amount. The expectation was that the subsidy would be totally eliminated after three years.[86] Five years later in 1982, no local congregations received subsidy, but each district continued to receive a subsidy that was used primarily to pay the district superintendents.[87]

The by-laws of the constitution said that member churches would collect their own offerings and pay the pastors. The churches were to keep ninety percent of all receipts for themselves, and they were to give ten percent of all receipts to the district. Each district in turn was to keep ninety percent of its total receipts and forward ten percent to the region. The money the region received did not meet its needs. Most people depended on subsistence agriculture for their livelihood and had no paid employment. The church/mission taught that every Christian was to

---

[83]Regional Board of Trustees Meeting, April 14, 1980, in Proceeding of the Annual Field Council of the Christian Union Mission of the Papua New Guinea Region, 2-3 May, 1980, p. 17.

[84]Christian Union Mission of Papua New Guinea, Field Council Meeting Minutes, October 23, 24, and 31, 1981, p 11.

[85]Christian Union Mission Executive Committee Meeting Minutes, November 10, 1973, p. 6.

[86]Annual Field Council of Christian Union Mission of Papua New Guinea Region, February 11, 18, and 19, 1977, p. 5.

[87]Proceedings of the Annual Field Council, January 15 – 16, 1982, p. 20.

give their tithes and offerings to support the church. Persons who did not have money to give could give garden produce or even a pig or piglet, and they did. However, in the entire Nembi area there was never an abundance of cash and that was reflected in the church offerings.

In 1980 the regional board of trustees suggested that all churches should bring all of their offerings to the district board, and the district boards would then re-distribute the funds back to the churches and equalize the pay of all pastors in the district.[88] Their suggestion was never followed, but it would have been more culturally appropriate than the system implemented in the church's constitution. It is worth noting that years later when churches were started in the Port Moresby area, all churches combined their offerings, and the leaders of the Port Moresby area distributed it back to the Moresby churches according to their needs.

The mission wanted to eliminate the subsidy for two reasons. First, although its resources were greater than the church's resources, it struggled financially, and did not have the funds to supply many of the church's requests for assistance with buildings, vehicles, and increased subsidy. Second, it wanted the church to become an independent self-supporting entity. It theorized that withholding funds would keep the church from becoming dependent on the overseas resources. The missionaries adopted the thinking of Glenn Schwartz, a proponent of withhold-ing Western funds as a means of avoiding unhealthy dependency and promoting healthy independent churches. He says that overseas funding stifles the initiative of the local people to give, leads to outside manipulation, and promotes foreign leaders over local leaders.[89]

John Rowell suggests a different approach. He defines dependency as "the unhealthy patterns of reliance on Western financial support that are presumed to be encouraged when missionaries readily offer support for indigenous workers, for ministry projects, or for facilities development in pioneer situations."[90] Un-healthy dependency develops when outsiders give funds in such a way that they do not allow the indigenous leaders to develop their own vision or they relegate the indigenous leaders to a subordinate position. Rowell suggests that "biblical generosity" is appropriate and dependency grows out of the strings that Western-ers attach to their giving rather than the giving itself. He insists that outside fund-ing can assist local churches without creating dependency[91]

Rowell says that the Bosnian Christians use the metaphor of a family when they reflect on the relationship between Christians from more affluent societies and those from economically deprived societies. All are members of God's fam-ily, and as such, those with a surplus have a Christian duty to help meet the needs

---

[88]Christian Union Mission, Field Council Meeting Minutes, September 27, 1980, p. 5.

[89]Glenn Schwartz, "Cutting the Apron Strings" *Evangelical Missions Quarterly* 30 no 1, [January, 1994]; 37-42 reprinted in *Mission Frontiers: The Bulletin of the U. S. Center for World Mission*, January-February, 1997, http://www.missionfrontiers.org/issue/arti-cle/cutting-the-apron-strings (accessed on November 4, 2013).

[90]John Rowell, T*o Give or Not to Give: Rethinking Dependency, Restoring Generosity, and Redefining Sustainability.* [Tyrone, GA: Authentic Publishing, 2006], 14.

[91]Rowell, 15-18.

of the brothers and sisters who lack, a duty to show humility one to the other, a duty to avoid double standards, a duty to honor one another, and a duty to avoid selfish interest. Westerners express concerns about dependency from the perspective of "missiological dangers" and non-Westerners are more concerned about "biblical duties."[92]

Many of the Nembi church leaders that I interviewed in 2009 and 2010 expressed a view that paralleled the Bosnian perspectives. They said that the Nembi church would never stop asking the mission for financial assistance because they believe that the mission and the church in America are wealthy, and have an obligation to assist their poorer brothers in Christ. I suggest that both views whether from a perspective of "missiological dangers" or one of "biblical duties," can be used to mask underlying motives such as greed or a desire for control, power, prestige and status.

Lederleitner critiques both Rowell and Schwartz. She says that the setting affects the approach that should be taken to funding, and what is appropriate in eastern European countries like Bosnia may be inappropriate in rural Africa. Foreign funding may weaken local giving and accountability and create dependency, but when approached in the right way, it does not necessarily do so.[93]

Church/Mission Relationship

The relationship between the mission and the church was increasingly dysfunctional, and neither fully trusted the other. The dysfunction grew out of the different worldviews and the different expectations that the church and the mission had for each other. The mission withheld funds to force the church to become more independent, but the church saw the withholding of funds and the insistence that the church pay its own way as a denial that the church and mission were one in Christ. Both sides wanted to form a partnership, but each side had a different understanding of what 'partnership' meant.

Mapon Ek recalls that the church leaders and missionaries disagreed over projects and finances. In spite of their differences, the two kept working together. The church leaders had contact with leaders from other denominations with whom they swapped stories. They compared the way that Christian Union Mission related to them with the way that other missions related to their churches. The church leaders were convinced that other missions allowed the church men to use their vehicles, were more generous with financial support, assisted with major projects, and provided better training for their church leaders. When CUC leaders complained to the missionaries, arguments between the church leaders and the missionaries ensued.[94]

---

[92]Rowell, 18-22.

[93]Lederleitner, 89-91.

[94]Mapon Ek, interview by author, Mato (Poroma), Southern Highlands Province of Papua New Guinea, December 31, 2009.

A regional conference took place on December 16, 1982. Some of the church leaders and pastors felt that the mission was giving too little assistance to the church, and decided that it would be best for the mission to leave. They reasoned that if the missionaries left, they would have full access to mission resources and the work would be fully localized. They would be free to use mission vehicles, equipment and funds for the benefit of the church as they saw fit.[95] They wrote a paper detailing their dissatisfaction and presented it at the conference. They waited until all of the delegates were registered and had gathered at the church, and then they told the missionaries who were seated at the back that the church wanted them to leave Papua New Guinea and informed them of the mission's failures and short comings.[96]

The paper said that the most important work of Christian missions was to develop local churches, but Christian Union Mission had not done enough to develop Christian Union Church. It had not obeyed the laws of Papua New Guinea, the host country, because the work was not sufficiently localized. The mission had no indigenous teachers in the Bible school, and had no other church workers.[97] The church's constitution did not work well for the PNG church, and was unacceptable. The mission had not carried out its God-given task, and Christian Union Church wanted to find another mission to assist them.

The mission's failures in three areas were especially odious to the church. The first was that the church did not know how much money CCCU in America sent to the field. They suspected that the mission was withholding funds that the church in America intended for the PNG church. They had no representatives on the mission council, and no say in how the money from the USA was allocated or what projects were approved for the field. The church wanted their representatives to attend the mission council and executive committee meetings. They wanted to have direct access to the council rather than have the district advisors and the regional superintendent serve as go-betweens for the church and mission.

The second was that the mission had made a number of promises that it had not kept. The mission had failed to support the church's evangelistic efforts to the extent that it had promised. No missionary had been sent to the Lai Valley, and several of the churches had closed. The mission had promised to send three men to a training course for senior pastors at CLTC, but had not carried through.

The mission planned to send some senior pastors to a six-month course that CLTC held for Pidgin speakers, but CLTC cancelled the course.[98] The mission

---

[95]At the time the PNG government was pushing business and other organizations to localize their work. They wanted Papua New Guineans to have the positions that expatriates held.

[96]Letter from Christian Union Church of PNG to Christian Union Mission, December, 1982.

[97]The mission had employed a number of indigenous Bible school teachers, but none stayed for more than a few years. By "other church workers" they meant drivers, mechanics, carpenters, bookkeepers, sawmill operators, and the like.

[98]Christian Union Mission Annual Field Council Minutes, March 16, April 4 and April 16, 1981, p 17.

was open to assigning expatriate missionaries to work in both the Iapi area and the Lai Valley, but the shortage of mission personnel and finances and the frequent changes in field leadership kept the mission from carrying through with their stated intentions. Tribal fighting in the Lai Valley led to the closure of the churches.

When the plans failed, the mission read Revelation 3:7-8 and concluded that God was closing the door and drew back. The church, in contrast, concluded that the failure to carry through was an unfulfilled promise. The Nembi church read Ephesians 4 where Paul talks about Christian unity and admonishes the Christians to put off falsehoods and speak truthfully for all belong to the body of Christ,[99] and found the mission lacking.

The third was that the mission started projects but failed to see them through to completion. One example the church used was the Bible School. The mission had started a Pidgin Bible school, and then changed to English, and then reverted back to Pidgin.[100] There was no consistency. In addition, the houses that the mission built for the church leaders and other mission workers were only partially finished.

The paper concluded that, if Christian Union Mission did not change its ways, then the mission could leave Papua New Guinea and the church would either find another mission to work with them or stand on their own.[101] For four hours the missionaries listened as the disgruntled leaders and pastors[102] elaborated on the charges against the missionaries.

Afterwards the missionaries gathered for a time of debriefing, soul searching, and earnest prayer for unity between the church and mission. At their next field council meeting held on January 14, 1983, they summarized the major complaints that they had heard at the regional conference as they understood them and considered what they could do to mend the broken relationship. In a history of struggle, this was the biggest crisis that the mission had faced. The confrontation forced the mission to critique itself and ask how it could improve its relationship to the church. That story is told in the next chapter.

---

[99]Ephesians 4:25.

[100]The mission went back to using Pidgin as the language of instruction because the regional board of trustees was not satisfied with the English program and requested that the mission go back to teaching in Pidgin.

[101]Letter from Christian Union Church of PNG to Christian Union Mission, December, 1982.

[102]Many of the church leaders, pastors and delegates did not openly join those who had taken over the conference. They did not speak up either for or against the charges. For some their silence may have been consent. For others, it may have meant they wanted to listen and process the accusations before forming an opinion.

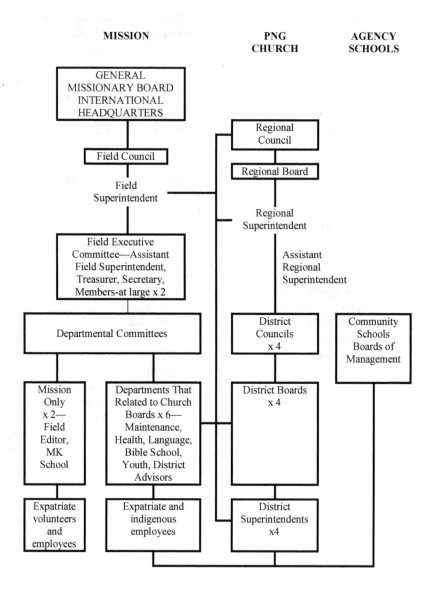

Figure 4: Organizational Chart 1980

The mission chart was expanded to show a position for every employee under the committees, but that is not shown here.

Chapter Five

Nationalization

Introduction

When the church confronted the missionaries with its discontent and frustration on December 16, 1982, the root of the conflict lay in the different worldviews of the Western missionaries and the Melanesian people and in the different expectations that the church and mission[1] had for each other. The missionaries came from a society that promoted the interests of individuals above the interests of the groups to which the individuals belonged. In the Nembi society, on the other hand, individuals' concerns took second place to their groups' concerns. The missionaries considered each person to be an autonomous individual, but the Nembi defined each person according to his or her relationships. As Rynkiewich says, group oriented societies define each person in terms of the groups to which he or she belongs, and the relationships, "especially the exchange relationships," that each maintains.[2]

The mission expected the church to become fully self-supporting without depending on overseas funds to run its programs and carry out its ministries. In contrast, the church expected to depend on and eventually control the overseas funds that the churches in the USA provided for the mission. The Nembi church thought that the mission had failed to meet the obligations that it incurred when it established relationships with the Nembi groups and planted churches. In Nembi society when a group initiated a relationship, it was expected to grow like sweet potato vines to link the two groups in more and more ways. Thus, the missionaries expected the relationships that they developed to diminish leaving the partners as independent individuals, while the Nembi entered into relationships in order to

---

[1]In this chapter, and throughout the paper, when I write about the church and the mission I am referring to two distinct entities. "Mission" refers to the missionaries and their agency (Christian Union Mission), and "church" refers to the indigenous church (Christian Union Church of PNG) and its leaders.

[2]Michael A. Rynkiewich, "Person in Mission: Social Theory and Sociality in Melanesia" *Missiology: An International Review,* Vol XXXI, No 2 [April 2003]: 156.

become more intertwined in reciprocal exchanges and thus more interdependent. These cultural differences set the stage for the conflicts between the church and mission.

In this chapter I write about the church/mission relationship and the opposite expectations that the church and the mission held for each other. In spite of their differences, the church and mission worked together to promote ministries, revise the constitution, and develop church leadership. The Christians of CUC of PNG expect their pastors and church-leaders to be different from the traditional big-men, but the expectations that the society holds for its traditional leaders shapes the expectations that the Christians hold for their pastors and church leaders.

The church and mission functioned as two separate autonomous bodies. A church/mission coordinating council (CMCC) was organized with the hope of bringing the two sides together and promoting greater cooperation between the two. The church subsidy and the sharing of mission resources were the issues that caused the greatest tensions between the church and mission. Whenever the mission attempted to cut the subsidy, the church objected and tensions rose.

When CCCU and WGM formed a partnership and WGM took over the administration of the PNG field in January of 1997, the church leaders anticipated having greater access to mission resource, but that did not happen.

Beginning in 1983 a number of missionaries urged the mission to withdraw from the Nembi area. The missionaries took the lead in starting a work in the Mount Hagen area, and Nembi migrants to Port Moresby started holding fellowships in their homes in the absence of a church. That led to the establishment of churches in the Port Moresby area.

There were a number of traumatic events that affected the church and mission's work. Hold-ups and home invasions occurred more frequently. After the sister-in-charge at Ol Health center was injured during a home invasion, the mission withdrew from Embi immediately and the mission's involvement in the medical work came to an abrupt end. The church eventually took over the medical ministry. Tribal fighting led to the closure of Farata station, and to the mission's withdrawal from Ka in 1999.

Conflict

Conflict is ever-present. Duane Elmer, a professor of international studies, says that Western individualism lends itself to conflict because it easily "sacrifices community for personal preferences" and "splinters churches, friendships, family, and groups rather than struggle for ways to bridge differences, reconnect, forgive reconcile, and heal."[3] A similar critique could be made of Melanesian group oriented societies. The groups are prone to conflict as each group strives for prestige and status under the leadership of its "big-men," and each group is quick to ridicule, belittle, and combat other groups that threaten its interests. The church

---

[3]Duane Elmer, *Cross-Cultural Conflict: Building Relationships for Effective Ministry,* [Downers Grove, Illinois; InterVarsity Press, 1993], 25.

came to see the mission as a hindrance to its development and even its primary adversary as the mission reduced the aid it was giving to the church in an effort to make it more self-reliant and self-supporting and less dependent on overseas funds. In other words, the Nembi perceived that they had held up their end of the group-to-group contractual (but not written) relationship, but that the missionaries had failed to reciprocate. No amount of talk about trust, faith, love, giving, forgiving, and caring could overcome the perceived lack of action in these areas.

Cross-cultural ministry increases the possibility of conflict. Elmer says "Most cross cultural conflicts are...inadvertent, occurring because underlying cultural values and corresponding rules are not understood. What is surprising is not that we have so many conflicts but that, given everyone's cultural centeredness, there are not more conflicts."[4] Rynkiewich says, "Communication of the gospel is handicapped if we do not know with whom we are communicating, what they are thinking and feeling, and how we are being heard."[5] Not only is the communication of the gospel handicapped, the probability of cross-cultural conflict increases and the possibility of cross-cultural church planting decreases. Neither the CUM missionaries nor the CUC church constituency understood the culture and thinking of the other.

The New Testament church was no stranger to cross-cultural conflict. In Acts chapter fifteen the council at Jerusalem was called to consider a dispute that arose between Jewish and Gentile Christians about whether or not it was necessary for all new converts to follow the Mosaic Law.[6] In Galatians we read that Paul rebuked Peter when, in the presence of Jewish visitors, Peter, who had been eating with the Gentiles, withdrew and separated himself from the Gentiles. Paul was concerned because the actions implied that something more than Christ's atoning death on the cross was necessary for people to become Christians. This theology emphasized the Jewish laws and thus made the cultural differences between the two groups a stumbling block to the unity that came through faith in Christ.[7]

The church's perspective on ministries, its approach to evangelism and outreach to new areas, its view of unexpected and often traumatic events such as home invasions, hold-ups, fires, death, tribal fighting, and its perception of the mission's departure from the mission station at Ka differed from the mission's. At times the conflict between church and mission overshadowed the greater goal of growing a church in PNG.

Church/Mission Relationship

After the confrontation that took place on December 16, 1982 and before the missionaries held their next council meeting on January 14, 1983, the mission leaders met with the church leaders several times. At the January meeting of the mission

---

[4]Elmer, 22.

[5]Rynkiewich, "Person in Mission," 155.

[6]Acts 15:1-35.

[7]Galatians 2:11-16.

council, the primary discussion was about the church/mission relationship and the steps that the mission could take to restore unity with the church. The missionaries, working from their own perspective, created a list of church complaints[8] and then tried to figure out how to respond to the concerns without compromising the goal of establishing a self-supporting church.

The church believed that the mission was withholding funds that the church in the USA intended for the PNG church and rued the mission's failure to give the church control over mission assets. The indigenous church wanted direct contact with the sending denomination in the USA, and it wanted to gain control over mission resources, especially the finances. The missionaries believed that the church needed to support itself with funds that were generated within PNG, and felt that giving the church financial assistance would create dependency and in the long run hurt the church. The mission wanted the church to be independent, but the church wanted to depend on outside resources and pushed for dependency.

In an attempt to improve the impasse, the mission decided to give the church representation on departmental committees, to provide training for the church leaders, and to begin working with the church leaders on the revision of the church's constitution.[9] The mission council increased the district church subsidy from $69.50 per month to $100.00 per month and the regional church subsidy was increased from $30.00 per month to $50.00 per month. It set aside an additional $50.00 per month to be placed in a village church development fund that was used to assist the local congregations with the construction of permanent church buildings.[10]

In February of 1983, the mission council drew up a statement of mission[11] and hammered out a five-year plan that was meant to address the church's issues. The plan emphasized formal and informal training, the production of Christian litera-

---

[8]Christian Union Mission Field Council Minutes of January 14, 1983, p.1. First, the mission did not carry out its promises. Second, the missionaries started work that they did not finish. Third, the missionaries did not follow the PNG constitution because they had not indigenized the work. Fourth, the mission did not tell the church how the mission used the money that it received from America. Fifth, the mission had a double standard for church and mission buildings. Sixth, the missionaries did not work with the church. Seventh, the mission had not taught the PNG church about the church in America. And finally, the mission was not concerned about people who were lost and did not care if they went to hell. In addition, the church had complained about the constitution, saying that it was not a good "fit" for the PNG church.

[9]Christian Union Mission Field Council Meeting Minutes, January 14, 1983, 1-2.

[10]Christian Union Mission Annual Field Council Meeting Minutes, February 10 – 12, 1983, 32.

[11]The statement of mission said, "Being redeemed through faith in Christ, we are children of God, devoted servants of Christ and his church, debtors to all men, and committed to his cause and the Oneness of His Body.

In willing submission to Christ's commands, we are dedicated to the furtherance of His Kingdom by ministering to the needs of the whole man.

To this end, we pledge ourselves." (Christian Union Mission Annual Field Council Meeting Minutes, February 10 – 12, 1983, 13.)

ture, evangelism, development and establishment of the church, encouragement, and incarnational living by sharing in the personal needs and lives of the people.

Among other things, the missionaries pledged to send one man to Christian Leaders' Training College (CLTC) at Banz, conduct in-service courses for Bible school graduates and church leaders, and provide drivers' training for church personnel. The church saw the failure to secure a lease in Mendi as one of the mission's broken promises. The mission agreed to secure a lease for land in Mendi for a church, and planned to promote Christian stewardship and accountability, and teach church leaders, pastors, and lay persons about CUC church structure. Missionaries, especially the district advisors who worked most closely with the pastors and church leaders, were to visit regularly the homes of pastors and church leaders, sharing their fire and food. The missionaries were to reciprocate by planning times of food and fellowship in their own homes for pastors and church leaders. All missionaries were to make a greater effort to participate more fully in the lives of the people by attending wakes and weddings and visiting mothers who had recently given birth.

The plan did not list the steps that would be taken during 1984 and 1985, but it included a bridging statement that said, "We are committed to continue all that we began to do in 1983, and we agree that we must formulate specific and measurable goals in conjunction with the Regional Board of Trustees for evaluation of our work and progress during this period."[12]

Long term goals called for the role of the missionaries to diminish, and the role of indigenous personnel to increase. By 1990 the plan called for a merged field structure with the missionaries working under the direction of the church. The goal of having a single church structure was in line with the church thinking. They wanted a single organization. But again, the church and mission had opposite understandings of what a single field structure would mean. For the missionaries, a single structure meant that missionaries would work under the authority of the church, the mission would become smaller, and the church would be less dependent on overseas funds. For the church, it meant that the church would receive increased funding and greater control of mission funds.

The mission had no plan to surrender mission financial resources to the control of the church. In the mission's thinking when the missionaries left, the financial assistance that the mission gave the church would end. According to the mission's plan, by 1995 Nembi Bible School was to be fully nationalized except for the principal. By the year 2000 all the work, including the Nembi Bible School, would be fully nationalized, and CUM was to be fully phased out. Any missionaries remaining on the field would be working under Christian Union Church of Papua New Guinea, and the church and Bible school would be fully supported by funds generated from within Papua New Guinea.\

The plans reflected the missionaries' limited understanding or misunderstanding of what was bothering the church. The mission wanted the church personnel

---

[12]Christian Union Mission Annual Field Council Meeting Minutes, February 10 – 12, 1983, 15.

to assume full responsibility for governing the organized church, evangelizing its own people, and supporting the church's pastors, leaders, and institutions. In contrast, the church's primary concern was to gain access to the missionaries' resources and assets. They told the missionaries to move out and let the church carry out the work, but they fully expected money, vehicles, and other assets to be left behind for the church to manage and control and for the money from the church in America to continue to flow into the church coffers.

On the one hand, the relationship between the church and mission seemed to improve during 1983 for several reasons, First, there was more dialogue between the missionaries and the church leaders. Second, the church representation on departmental committees made the church more aware of the financial arrangements for each department; led to the development of a church mission coordinating council that fostered dialogue between the church and mission; gave the church a greater voice in mission ministries; and made some mission funds available to the church. Third, the mission agreed to send a church representative to the USA.

On the other hand, the improvement was short lived. For one thing, there was a large turnover in mission staff. By April of 1984 all but five of the fifteen missionaries who had been present at the 1982 confrontation had resigned, left the field for health reasons, or taken extended furloughs. The field superintendent who led the church through the crisis left the field in December of 1983 and enrolled in Fuller Theological Seminary. The new superintendent had served one term in PNG, but he had been away from the field for five and one-half years. A diminished commitment to the five-year plan came with the turnover in mission staff, and even greater determination on the part of the missionaries to reduce church dependency. For the church, it meant that the mission ignored its desire for greater access to mission resources and that the mission was once again failing to keep its promises.

Money was the issue behind much of the church's discontent. The requests for representation on the mission field council, for information about the church in America, and for a church representative to visit the church in the USA were rooted in the desire for an increased share of the funding that came to the mission from the church in the USA. The church suspected that the funds that the church in America was sending to the field were really intended for the church in PNG, but the missionaries were greedy, wanted to keep the money for themselves, and held back or waylaid the funds meant for the church. The church assumed that if a church representative went to the USA and had direct contact with the churches, he would bring goods and/or money back to the PNG church.

The church leaders asked, "How can the missionaries come to PNG and not have money to give to the church?"[13] Clark, Ballard, and Nihill say that for the Wiru in the Pangia area, Christianity brought money, and their commitment to Christianity

> is based on the control of money…and mediates…the relationship between people and spirits (church donations are not a sacrifice). A wealthy man has more suc-

---

[13]Timothy Pe, interview by author, Mendi, Southern Highlands District of Papua New Guinea, January 15, 2010.

cessful relations with God, an idea not totally alien to some Western churches. The power of Christianity, God's benevolence is released through the control of money...[14]

As I mentioned previously, the church's thinking paralleled the thinking of other groups in PNG. Lawrence reports that the people in the Madang area thought that the Europeans, and especially the missionaries, were withholding cargo or the secrets to obtaining cargo from them.[15] He says that a cargo ideology was intrinsic to the cultures in the region and that the Australian administration thought that economic, political, and educational development was the key to combating the thinking.[16]

Church Autonomy

Some of the missionaries developed greater missiological awareness. Four of the missionary families took extended furloughs to study at Fuller Theological Seminary. All four families returned to the field during and/or after their studies at Fuller for two or more years of service, and three of the four men served as the field superintendent after they returned to the field. In addition, Fuller offered extension courses at Christian Leaders Training College that were open to both missionary and indigenous personnel who had completed an undergraduate degree. Several missionaries took the courses. The studies at Fuller, both on and off the field affected the thinking of the CUM missionaries, especially in the area of finances.

Some missionaries were convinced that the mission was hurting the church and causing it to be dependent on the overseas resources rather than supporting itself and taking its place as a sending church. They referred to Roland Allen's book, *Missionary Methods: St. Paul's or Ours, A Study of the Church in the Four Provinces.* The book which was first written in 1912 was a critique of the Western missionary methods of his day. In regard to finances, Allen said that the method used to support the missionary and the way the church finances were organized is of relative unimportance. Rather,

> the primary importance of missionary finance lies in the fact that financial arrangements very seriously affect the relations between the missionary and those whom he approaches. ...what is of supreme importance is how these arrangements...affect the minds of the people, and so promote, or hinder, the spread of the Gospel.[17]

Allen said that Paul sought no financial support from others, accepted no per-

---

[14]Jeffrey Clark Chris Ballard, and Michael Nihill. *Steel to Stone: A Chronicle of Colonialism in the Southern Highlands of Papua New Guinea.* [Oxford, UK: Oxford University Press, 2000], 165-166.

[15]Peter Lawrence, *Road Belong Cargo,* [Melbourne: Melbourne University Press, 1964], 134, 176

[16]Lawrence, *Road Belong Cargo,* 269-275.

[17]Roland Allen, *Missionary Methods; St. Paul's or Ours?* [Grand Rapids: Eerdmans, 1962], 49.

sonal financial assistance from those to whom he preached, and did not administer church funds. He did not establish large compounds or saddle the churches that he planted with business enterprises, property, or large mission compounds that the church had to maintain after he left.[18] Paul established churches not missions. At each place, he stayed long enough to start a church, usually five or six months, and then he moved on, leaving behind a congregation that he expected to function on its own. He kept contact through writing letters and by sending messengers to visit the churches that he established. His converts and the churches he started became involved in missionary outreach to their nearby communities.[19]

Rufus Anderson made similar statements. He said that it was the missionary's job to establish churches (congregations) and train competent pastors, and then move on to new areas where the church had not yet been established. The missionary's job was "to preach the gospel where it has not been preached."[20]

The current trend in missiology, whatever it may be, tends to take over all missionary thinking regardless of whether or not it is appropriate for a particular context.

Self-Supporting

For the CUM missionaries, self-supporting meant that the church would raise its funds from within Papua New Guinea. World Gospel Mission's handbook of policy says that a church is self-supporting when it "solicits and administers tithes, offerings, and grants, as well as local and foreign donations, in a responsible manner."[21] The missionaries were convinced that the church now depended on the mission for its support and that mission subsidies must be phased out for the good of the church.

Glenn Schwartz, who was a former missionary in Africa, and an administrator at Fuller Theological seminary during the 1970s, articulates the views that most of the CUC missionaries held. Schwartz says that when churches rely on foreign resources rather than looking to their own members to secure the resources they require, they exist with an unhealthy dependency that hinders the development of a truly indigenous church. The goal is to develop "spirit-led self-reliance" that allows the church to draw on local resources to carry out its ministries.[22] Until the church sees the work as its own, makes its own decisions, and funds its own

---

[18]Allen, *Missionary Methods,* 49-60.

[19]Allen, *Missionary Methods,* 82-93. One critique of Allen's statements is that it is hard to tell the difference between a church and mission because Paul expected the church to become a mission.

[20]Rufus Anderson "The Theory of Missions to the Heathen" in *To Advance the Gospel: Selections from the Writings of Rufus Venn,* R. Pierce Beaver ed. [Grand Rapids Michigan: William B. Erdman's Publishing Company, 1967], 76.

[21]*World Gospel Mission Manual on Missionary Procedures,* November 2005, 16.

[22]Glenn Schwartz, *When Charity Destroys Dignity: Overcoming Unhealthy Dependency in the Christian Movement : a Compendium.* [Lancaster, Pa: World Mission Associates. 2007], xxxvi.

ministries, it will be dominated by the outside supporting mission.[23] Because they are often hidden, overseas funds increase distrust, enhance the possibility that money will be misappropriated, hinder accountability, and lead to less local funding for the church.[24] According to Schwartz, culturally appropriate local economic development projects for the members of the church accompanied by the practice of Biblical stewardship will allow the church to move away from dependency to "spirit-led self-reliance."[25] It frees up the foreign resources that can then be used to take the Gospel to new areas while the church assumes the responsibility for evangelizing the local areas.[26]

The missionaries thought that church ministries should be supported through "Biblical stewardship," and rely on the tithes and offerings from its adherents to support the church rather than church-run business ventures. Rynkiewich distinguishes between 'development' as a Western project designed to enhance economic, political, and educational structures in non-Western countries, particularly former colonies, and the Pidgin term *divelopmen* that represents the way the locals expect the project will benefit the local group. He says that church leaders "are expected to provide *divelopmen* for their followers"[27] while the missionaries and others are trying to provide development. The Nembi church leaders expected the mission to provide *divelopmen* for the church, a project more focused on resources than on structural change.

The mission made several attempts to assist with the economic development of the Nembi area and to introduce projects with the goal of training and assisting pastors and church members with their own projects. The expectation was that project owners would give tithes and offerings to support the church. In addition, the mission made several failed attempts to start projects in which the church would have a vested interest. Mission attempts to promote development projects are described later in this chapter.

The mission based its teaching about tithes on scriptures. In the Old Testament law Moses said that one-tenth of everything belonged to the Lord.[28] The prophet Malachi said that the people of Judah were robbing God because they were not bringing in their tithes and offerings to the storehouse.[29] The missionaries taught that one-tenth of all the people owned belonged to God. If they had ten mounds of sweet potatoes, one belonged to God. If they had ten pigs, one was God's. If they

---

[23]Schwartz, *When Charity Destroys Dignity*, 12.

[24]Schwartz, *When Charity Destroys Dignity*, 35.

[25]Schwartz, *When Charity Destroys Dignity*, 13-14, 153-162.

[26]Schwartz, *When Charity Destroys Dignity*, 47.

[27]Michael A. Rynkiewich, "Big-man Politics: Strong Leadership in a Weak State," in *Politics in Papua New Guinea: Continuities, Changes and Challenges: Point Series no 24*, eds. Michael A. Rynkiewich and Roland Seib. [2000]: 28, 32.

[28]Leviticus 27

[29]Malachi 3:6-17

had had one *kina*, ten *toea* belonged to God.[30] In Pidgin the term for tithe is *hap ten*, and some of the people say that they understood the *hap ten* to mean ten *toea* rather than one tenth of all they had. I recall one missionary reporting that one of the church leaders informed him that the "tithe system" would never work in Papua New Guinea. The missionary was appalled because to him it was a Biblical mandate. The church people responded better to giving an annual thanksgiving offering.

The church took up the first thanksgiving offering on the Sunday before Christmas in 1984. Other denominations took up annual thanksgiving offerings, and it was a style of giving that seemed to resonate with Melanesian cultures. The church and mission spent several months teaching about biblical stewardship. Don Seymour, the general missionary superintendent of CCCU wrote,

> One of the goals of the indigenous church is to become self-supporting. A comprehensive stewardship plans is being developed by national church leaders and missionaries for the Christian Union Church of Papua New Guinea. A "Thanks Offering" on Christmas Sunday will be given and the plan will be fully initiated. Many weeks of prayer and teaching have already taken place and your earnest prayer are requested that national believers will truly understand and practice Biblical stewardship.[31]

A combined total of five thousand *kina* was given. It was the largest offering that the church had ever taken. Ron Priest wrote about the first Thanksgiving offering and claimed that the generous offering was a result of the intensive teaching on stewardship that had taken place in the months leading up to the offering.[32]

Simon Papon, who was the Embi district superintendent at the time, tells a different story. He recalls attending a course on Christian stewardship at Puril sponsored by the Evangelical Alliance. The people agreed to give the first offering, but they did not view it as an offering of thanks to God. They said that God had given them Jesus who had suffered much on their behalf, and they had to compensate Jesus for his sufferings. The people collected money, pigs, pearl shells, bananas, sugar cane, sweet potatoes, and firewood and gave it to compensate Jesus.[33] Embi District gave K1096, seven pigs, three pearl shells, and a large food offering.[34] Later the Nembi came to view the annual thanksgiving offering as a way to thank

---

[30]Currently the currency in Papua New Guinea is *kina* and *toea* and it is counted like dollars and cents. It takes 100 *toea* to make one *kina*. Before Papua New Guinea got its own currency, it used Australian currency which was dollars and cents. When money was first introduced to the Nembi area, the Australian currency was pounds and shillings, but in 1966 Australia changed to dollars and cents.

[31]Don Seymour, "Frontlines of Information and Intercession" *Missionary Tidings* XXXVII no 3 [November, 1984], p 2.

[32]Ron Priest, "The Shaping of the Church: Stewardship" *Missionary Tidings* XXXVII no 7, [April, 1985], 5.

[33]Simon Papon, interview by author, Mendi, Southern Highlands Province, January 15, 2010.

[34]Ron Priest, "The Shaping of the Church: Stewardship" *Missionary Tidings* XXXVII no 7, [April, 1985], 5.

God for giving them life, and bringing them to prosperity during the past year. Clark, Ballard, and Nihill say that the Wiru people also give offerings to thank God for his benevolence.[35] The CUC thanksgiving offerings have increased, and the money received in the annual thanksgiving offering is now one of the main sources of income for the church.[36]

G. W. Trompf defines retributive logic as "the way people think about rewards and punishments" and that "Melanesians interpret affairs in terms of requital or basic principles of retribution"[37] The logic of retribution is found in all known Melanesian religions. It finds expression negatively in revenge killings and positively in reciprocal exchanges.[38] Trompf defines compensation as the giving of "an appropriate 'equivalence' to make amends either for wrongdoing or for being forced to deprive someone of their life and liberty."[39] It involves either making restitution for a wrongdoing or paying a kin group for a loss, especially the loss a male relative during war. In traditional Melanesian societies compensation was rarely paid between enemy groups. Instead it was given to allies for the losses they suffered while assisting with a fight.[40] "The 'paying back' involved in daily exchanges…entails for givers and takers the sense of fulfilling obligations, and thus the heightened awareness that their (economic) activity is conditioned by social and more than human experiences."[41]

Retribution involved both the human and the spiritual spheres and there was "a relative comparability and indigenous parallelism between dealings in the two spheres."[42] In traditional Melanesian belief systems, spiritual forces made things go right when they were pleased and wreaked havoc when they were angered. Sacrifices and offerings were given to the spirit beings to set things right and induce the spirits to make things right.[43]

In Chapter Three I mentioned Mantovani's analysis of religions. Biocosmic religions consider the ultimate to be the experience of life in which all things, biological, spiritual and material are bound together in a cosmic whole. When things are in balance, then the cosmos is well ordered and the biological, spiritual, and material worlds all prosper. When things go awry, human beings work to restore the balance by appealing to the more powerful spiritual elements of the cosmos

---

[35]Clark, Ballard, and Nihill, 166.

[36]Simon Papon, interview by author, Mendi, Southern Highlands Province, January 15, 2010.

[37]G. W. Trompf, *Melanesian Religion*. [Cambridge, England: Cambridge University Press, 1991], 51.

[38]G. W. Trompf, *Payback: The Logic of Retribution in Melanesian Religions.* [Cambridge, England: Cambridge University Press, 1994], 24.

[39]G. W. Trompf, *Payback*, 107.

[40]G. W. Trompf, *Payback*, 107.

[41]G. W. Trompf, *Payback*, 114-115.

[42]G. W. Trompf, *Payback*, 117.

[43]G. W. Trompf, *Melanesian Religion*, 66.

through ritual and sacrifice. [44] When balance is achieved, the entire community enjoys the good life or *gutpela sindaun* that is, according to Mantovani, the highest Melanesian cultural value. [45]

What Mantovani calls *gutpela sindaun,* Trompf call blessings. He says that in Melanesian thinking blessings include spiritual, physical, and economic wellbeing and they come when persons maintain good relationships with their fellow human beings and with the spirit world. [46] Melanesians sacrificed to the spirits not only to placate and appease them, but also to honor the spirits and seek their blessings. People gave to the spirits in the hope that the spirits would reciprocate and the group would prosper and be blessed, [47] and exchanges "between humans and the spirit-world" were understood "to be analogous to those between (living) humans," and they nearly always involved "rituals of redress" and that were intended to bring things back into balance. [48]

The same logic of retribution that affected the way they related to the spirits in their traditional belief system has been adapted into their Christian belief system. They see God as one who both rewards and punishes. He gives blessings and brings *gutpela sindaun.* On the other hand, if he is displeased, then trouble and *taim nogut* (bad times) come their way, and they seek Him to make things go better. Today they give the large offering annually, in part to honor God and demonstrate submission to His will, and in part to ensure that He will continue to bless them and bring them the *gutpela sindaun* they hope to enjoy. Although they no longer think they are giving compensation to Jesus, retributive logic continues to influence their giving. If they honor God by giving generous offerings, He in turn will bless them personally and the church and its ministries. When that does not happen, the source of the blockage must be found. In this case, it is thought to be the missionaries.

Mantovani says that religion can be viewed as both a system and a personal attitude held by the adherents to a particular belief system. As an attitude, it varies between acceptance and manipulation. Typically, religions that use rituals and spells to relate to the spirits are considered to be manipulative, and prayers are "seen as symbols of acceptance." However, through their prayers some Christians attempt to force God to do their bidding, and some people use rituals and spells to express their submission to a divine will. [49]

---

[44]Ennio Mantovani, "What is religion," in Ennio Mantovai, *Point Series No. 5: An Introduction to Melanesian Religions: a Handbook for Church Workers: Book Two of a Trilogy.* [Goroka, Papua New Guinea: Melanesian Institute, 1984], 31-35.

[45]Ennio Mantovani, "Traditional Values and Ethics" in Darrel L. Whiteman, *Point Series No. 6: An Introduction to Melanesian Cultures: A Handbook for Church Workers: Book One of a Triology.* [Goroka, Papua New Guinea: Melanesian Institute, 1984

[46]G. W. Trompf, *Melanesian Religion,* 73.

[47]G. W. Trompf, *Payback,* 117-119.

[48]G. W. Trompf, *Payback,* 123-124.

[49]Montovani, "What is religion," *Point Series No. 6,* 26-28.

Self-Governing

The mission considers the church to be self-governing when it "has a legally recognized governmental structure and process designed and directed" by indigenous church personnel.[50] For the mission that meant the church must have a constitution and qualified leaders. From the mission perspective, a major step towards establishing a self-governing church was taken when the church voted to adopt the constitution on August 10, 1978.[51] Christian Union Church of Papua New Guinea was duly registered with the PNG government, but the first constitution, written by the missionaries, was not a good cultural fit. Complaints about the constitution surfaced quickly. I recall being at the regional conference in 1980 when the church leaders, pastors, and church delegates complained about parts of the constitution, saying that it did not follow their customs. After much discussion, the missionaries told them they were free to change it, as long as they followed the procedures that were outlined in the constitution.

Constitution revision

Serious work on the constitution's revision began in January of 1983.[52] It took almost twenty years to complete. Both the mission and church personnel appointed to work on the revision of the constitution kept changing. Missionaries left for furlough and/or resigned from the field requiring that another person be appointed to work with the church leaders on the revision. Church leaders who worked on the constitution were voted out of office and others replaced them.

In November of 1998, church leaders from each of the districts met with Tim Bennett and me in Mount Hagen along with former church leaders who had previously served on the constitution revision committee to study the proposed revisions and finalize recommended changes. In December of 1998 a regional assembly comprised of male and female leaders from all districts along with pastors and lay representatives and three missionaries examined the proposed revisions and made some final changes. Church and mission leaders then met with district assemblies and the local congregations who reviewed the new constitution and gave their final endorsement.[53] The revised constitution was finally approved and printed in May of 2002, and the mission paid to have it printed.[54]

When I was in PNG in January of 2014, I learned that the missionaries and church leaders were working on further revisions of the constitutions. I asked what they were changing. I expected to hear that they did not like some of the by-laws, especially those that talked about *moka*. I was surprised when the missionaries told me that they wanted to reinstate term limitations for church leaders.

---

[50] *World Gospel Mission Manual on Missionary Procedures*, November 2005, 16.

[51] Bill Tolbert, "The Christian Union Church in Papua New Guinea" *Missionary Tidings*, Vol XXX no 3, October, 1978, 4.

[52] Christian Union Mission Field Council Meeting Minutes, January 14, 1983, 1-2.

[53] Ruth Tipton "Tipton Tidbits," a newsletter sent to supporters, December 1998.

[54] Papua New Guinea Field Council Meeting Minutes, April 20-21, 2001, 14-01.

The original constitution said that no regional or district leader could hold an office for more than eight consecutive years, but when the constitution was revised the term limitations were removed. When I asked the regional secretary about the changes, he said that he did not like term limitations. If a person had been elected to an office and was doing a good job, he or she should be allowed to stay in his or her office as long as the people wanted him or her. The two conversations left me wondering who was pushing for the changes—mission or church personnel.

Church leadership

The constitution retained the Western hierarchical forms of church government. Jacob Til and Daniel Kor wrote a history of the Wara Lai District complete with pictures, statistics, and diagrams. They included a diagram of the district's hierarchical structure in their history. In January of 2014 when Rick Pombre, the regional church secretary, and I were working on a Pidgin history of the church in preparation for the fifty-year celebration, he brought with him diagrams showing the hierarchical church structure of CUC that he wanted to be included in the history. He said, *"Em i bikpela samting na em i mas i stap long histori bilong yumi."* ("It is important, and it must be included in our history.") Below are the diagrams that the regional superintendent and the men who wrote the history of the Wara Lai District wanted to include in their histories.

Structures of Christian Union Church of Papua New Guinea

(As prepared by Rick Pombre, CUC regional secretary)

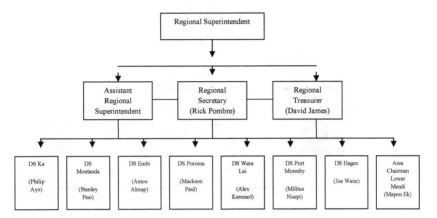

Figure 5: Regional Structure

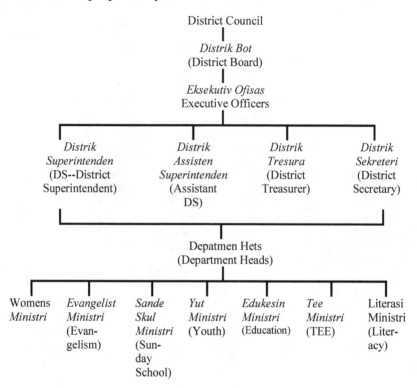

Figure 6: District Church Structure

(As prepared by Jacob Til and Daniel Kor)

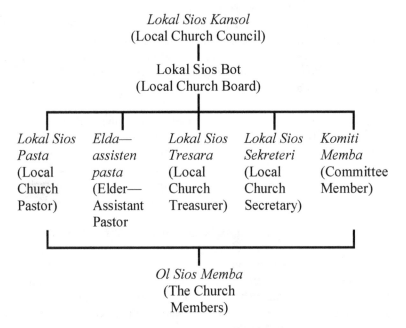

Lokal Sios Kansol
(Local Church Council)

Lokal Sios Bot
(Local Church Board)

| *Lokal Sios Pasta* (Local Church Pastor) | *Elda— assisten pasta* (Elder— Assistant Pastor | *Lokal Sios Tresara* (Local Church Treasurer) | *Lokal Sios Sekreteri* (Local Church Secretary) | *Komiti Memba* (Committee Member) |

Ol Sios Memba
(The Church
Members)

Ol Arapela Kristen na Lotu Lain
All Other Christians and Church Attendees

Wanwan ofisa bilong distrik i stap aninit long distrik bot. Distrik bot i gat pawa long rausim wanpela ofisa husait ol i ting i no wok gut na i no laik aninit long distrik bot. Distrik bot i stap aninit long distrik kansol. Ol kansol i gat pawa long senisim na makim nupela man long wok taim wok term bilong ol i pinis.

(Each district officer is under the authority of the district board. The district board has the authority to remove any officer that they think is not performing his/her duties well and is not subordinate to the district board. The district board is under the authority of the district council. The council has the authority to change and select a new officer when the term of service for the sitting officer expires.)

Figure 7: Local Church Structure

The current church leaders accept the Western hierarchical structures, but their role is defined partly in terms of the role that a Melanesian big-man was expected to fill. Rynkiewich says that "The success of a big-man depended on his ability to create a following, keep it together, and put it to use to further the cause of his local constituency."[55] Although the traditional big-man no longer exists, Rynkiewich argues that the dynamics that created the big-man continue to operate in the political, religious, business, and social arenas in PNG. Politicians, church leaders, and business men depend on the support of the group or constituency from which they come.[56]

In 1963, Marshall D. Sahlins, who compared Melanesian and Polynesian systems of leadership, stressed that a big-man achieves rather than inherits his position. First, he develops reciprocal exchange relationships within his own group until he becomes the groups' "center man." Once he has built up a following within his own group, he uses the goods he acquires from them to set up reciprocity with other "center men," earning increased status and prestige for himself and his followers.[57]

The big-man system, according to Paula Rubel and Abraham Rosman who compared thirteen New Guinea societies, has an internal and an external structure. The internal structure is comprised of the big-man and his followers who help and support their leaders by providing him with the goods that he requires to maintain an exchange relationship with other big-men from other groups. The external structure involves the competitive exchanges made between big-men for the benefit of himself and his followers.[58]

Sillitoe says that the traditional Wola big-men were known for their ability to manipulate wealth and excel in exchange and social relationships. Through persuasion rather than force, they became respected men of status, renown and influence.[59] Thus, although the system varied somewhat from group to group, at the center of each group was a big-man. He maintained multiple relationships both within and without his group as did the individuals who support him. The result was a network of exchanges and a complex web of relationships that were used to form economic and political alliances. The groups and individuals belonging to each group did not limit their relationships only to persons belonging to their core groups. They maintained relationships with other groups and individuals whom they could ask for economic or political assistance.

Rubel and Rosman say, "the most important personal quality essential to attain

---

[55]Michael A. Rynkiewich, "Big Man Politics," 18-21.

[56]Rynkiewich, "Big man Politics," 28-31.

[57]Sahlins, Marshall D. "Poor Man, Rich Man, Big-Man, Chief Political Types in Melanesia and Polynesia," *Comparative Studies in Society and History* 5, no 3 [April, 1963]: 288-293.

[58]Rubel, Paula G., and Abraham Rosman. *Your Own Pigs You May not Eat: A Comparative Study of New Guinea Societies.* [Canberra: Australia National University Press, 1978], 291-302.

[59]Paul Sillitoe, *Give and Take Exchange in Wola Society* (New York: St. Martin's Press, 1979), 108-111.

the position of Big-man…is the ability to organize, plan, and manage production and exchange."[60] In customary societies the big-man's success belonged not only to himself, but also to his followers who were his enablers, and he worked for the benefit of his entire group, and from his group of followers he obtained the goods that he used to establish exchange relationships from those outside of his group.[61] If one substitutes these criteria to the missionaries, it is clear why, in the eyes of the people, the missionaries failed to "organize, plan, and manage production and exchange."

During the fifty-year celebration of CUM and CUC in PNG, one of the church leaders said, "We are the church's big-men." So how are the church leaders the "big-men" of the church, and what do they have to achieve to be the church's big-men? Rynkiewich says that "in the religious hierarchy, church leaders are expected to provide *divelopmen* for their followers."[62] Like the politicians, they look for outside sources that they can bring into the church to help its development, and the mission is considered to be a viable source of assistance.

I used open-ended questions when I interviewed the past and present church leaders. When I asked them to tell me about their time as regional or district superintendents, they spoke about the assistance that they had or had not been able to secure for the church while they held their positions. Kanj Mesmba visited the USA in 1986 for three months when he was serving as the church's regional superintendent.[63] The CUC churches in Papua New Guinea raised the money to send him to the USA where he visited many churches—both large and small. He went with the expectation that he would bring some significant gifts back for the church. He saw the money that was put into the offering plates in the churches that he visited. When he left the country, he expected to receive a generous gift to take back to the PNG church, but he was given nothing except one suitcase filled with new clothes. He was disappointed and felt that he had failed the churches.

His experience paralleled the experience of Yali who started a cargo cult in the Madang area. During World War Two, Yali remained loyal to the Australians during the Japanese occupation. The Australians sent him and other loyal New Guineans to Australia for training in jungle warfare. During one of his trips he was shown an aircraft repair shop, large stores, and warehouses. He came back convinced that there were plenty of goods for everyone, but none of it made its way to New Guinea.[64]

According to Kanj, when representatives from other churches such as the Evangelical Bible church, the Wesleyan church, and the Pentecostal churches visit the churches in the sending country they always return with gifts from overseas. He named Mapunu, who started out in Christian Union Church, but later joined

---

[60]Paula G. Rubel and Abraham Rosman, *Your Own Pigs*, 293.

[61]Michael A. Rynkiewich, "Big-Man Politics," 18-21.

[62]Michael A. Rynkiewich, "Big-Man Politics" 28.

[63]Betty Seymour "Welkam Bek (Welcome Back)" *Missionary Tidings,* Volume 39 Number 5, January, 1987 p 6-7.

[64]Lawrence, *Road Belong Cargo*, 123-129.

a Pentecostal group, as an example. He pointedly recounted that when Mapunu visited the church in the sending country,[65] he brought a large tent back with him. Others who have visited the overseas churches talk about the gifts they have received and chide Kanj because he came back with nothing.[66]

The CCCU missionary department did send money to the field for the PNG churches as a result of Kanj's visit. The mission put the money into a Village Church development fund and used it to assist several of the local congregations with the construction of permanent churches.[67] Kanj did not realize that the money for church development had been pledged as a result of his visit, and he felt that he had failed. He also charged that the mission had let him down by not providing assistance for the PNG church as a result of his visit.[68] Undoubtedly, had he known that the churches in America sent money as a result of his visit; he would have insisted that the church rather than the mission should have decided how it would be used.

Simon Papon, a former Embi District superintendent, was briefly the acting regional superintendent. While he held the position the mission was engaged in an active building program to construct permanent churches in several of the districts, and he takes credit for getting the building program started.[69] Sengi Iruwa was the Regional superintendent from 1990 to 1992. Under his leadership, the mission provided the church with a vehicle and the church's first tent.[70] Also, Timothy Map went to the USA to study at Circleville Bible College while Sengi was the regional superintendent.[71] Tope Pesi who served as the Montanda District superintendent for years takes credit for securing the health agency for Tegibo health center back from the United Church.[72]

The church leaders expect to promote not only the spiritual growth and development of the church but also financial and material benefits. They do not separate the two. When asked to talk about their contributions as a leader, they emphasized material growth and said little about the spiritual.

Church members expect their leaders to lead by a different standard than the

---

[65]Mapunu visited Finland where the Pentecostal group that he joined has its base.

[66]Kanj Mesmba, interview by author, Port Moresby, January 29, 2010.

[67]Field Council Meeting Minutes, October 20, 1987 3, and Field Council Meeting Minutes, November 17, 1987 p 4.

[68]Kanj Mesmba, interview by author, Port Moresby, Papua New Guinea, January 29. 2010.

[69]Simon Papon, interview by author, Mendi, Southern Highlands Province, Papua New Guinea, January 15, 2010.

[70]A visitor from the USA promised to give a tent to CUC of PNG. The project did not have prior approval of either the field council or the home board, but to maintain credibility with the church, the mission felt that the promise had to be honored. One of CCCU's member congregations in the USA took on the project, purchased a tent, and sent it to PNG.

[71]Sengi Iruwa, interview by author, Mendi, Southern Highlands Province, Papua New Guinea, January 11, 2010.

[72]Tope Pesi, Interview by author, Mendi, Southern Highland Province, Papua New Guinea, December 17, 2009.

village leaders and politicians. I asked members of the Mount Hagen local congregation if a church leader should be like a local big-man. The unanimous response to the question was "No." They argued that a church leader has to be different from tribal leaders who manipulate wealth and people to achieve their purposes. They said that a good church leader did not consider himself or herself to be more important than others. He or she places himself or herself last and has the heart of a servant. Good church leaders do not shame others. They do not address issues in public before they have talked to the person in private. A good Christian leader identifies with the people. He or she will pray for those who are sick and cry with those who mourn. Good church leaders work with everyone in the church, give counsel based on the scriptures, live according to their own words or no one will follow them.[73] They talked about their ideal, but the reality is less than the ideal.

They said nothing about the expectations that remain the same for pastors and church leaders. Melanesians expected big-men to bring status and prestige to their followers, and today voters expect big-men politicians to bring benefits to the groups that put them in office. Similarly, church leaders are expected to bring material benefits to the church. The missionaries pushed the church leaders to support the church through tithes and offerings, but as the people gave their offerings, they expected to reap benefits.

Nevertheless, the church's ideal for church governance and leadership differs from the cultural view of leadership. When I asked John Kingal, a former pastor of the Mount Hagen church, about the differences, he said that Biblical values are incompatible with cultural values. In Matthew, Jesus said that the leader should lead with humility and have a servant's heart.

> You know that the rulers of the Gentiles lord it over them, and their high officials exercise authority over them. Not so with you. Instead, whoever wants to become great among you must be your servant, and whoever wants to be first must be your slave—just as the Son of Man did not come to be served, but to serve, and to give his life a ransom for many.[74]

The culture says that the leader is a "big-man." He is the most important person in the tribe, and others must cater to his wishes. The two are in conflict, and can be an area of struggle for a pastor and a church leader.[75]

Even those who have not aligned themselves with the church expect the pastors and church leaders to show a different style of leadership from the politicians and the big-men. Andrew Inja said that the successful big-man politician is dishonest and uses a lot of "double talk" in order to gain his following and maintain

---

[73]I interviewed several members and leaders in the Mount Hagen Congregation in 2006, and these remarks are an amalgamation of their responses. I interviewed both men and women and both younger and older people. Some asked to remain anonymous, and so I have not included the names of the people who made the remarks. They were talking about the leaders in their local congregation, but I think that their words were equally applicable to the district and regional leaders.

[74]NIV Matthew 20:25b-38

[75]John Kingal, interview by author, Mount Hagen, 2006.

his position of power. Successful politicians have to be deceptive and dishonest to be elected to office. They have to "work the system"[76] or they will be forced out of office. Pastors and church leaders must be men of "one talk" or they will lose respect and people will no longer follow them.[77]

Christian Union Church of Papua New Guinea is a self-governing entity, and the governance of the church centers on the church leaders who are elected at the regional and district assemblies. The introduced hierarchical Western system, the Melanesian big-man system, and scripture all influence the expectations that the church has for its leaders. The Christians point to some of the former leaders as the antithesis of a good church leader. When I asked them why they elect persons who they know will not make good leaders, they say that politics has entered the church and the system has corrupted the church and its leaders.[78]

The church takes the scriptures seriously and do not idealize the traditional style of leadership for the church. However, the traditional cultural values and forms of leadership are embedded deeply in the hearts and minds of the Christians and their cultural perspectives affect the way that the scriptures are applied. The diagram illustrates the point.

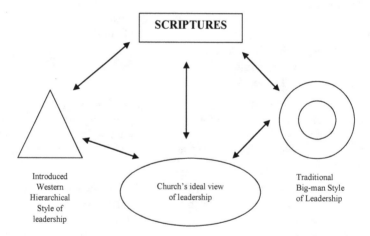

Figure 8: Systems Affecting CUC's View of Church Leadership

---

[76]"The system" refers to the practice of using bribery, deception, fraudulent votes, and empty promises to entice and manipulate people so they will vote for a politician and keep him in power.

[77]Andrew Inja, Interview by author, Mendi, Southern Highlands Province, Papua New Guinea, January 19, 2010.

[78]I asked this question of several of the people that I interviewed in January of 2009 and 2010, and they all said that the "system" was in the church. Even in casual conversations, the pastors and church members say that some of the church leaders have used the system to attain their position.

The church leaders are caught between two political systems—the big-man system and the western system that the missionaries introduced. Rynkiewich says,

> God instituted governments…and every system serves purposes for the society and is not to be…dismissed lightly. It is also true that every system is a fallen system because men and women are involved. While the particular system of government may not matter to God, the results of governance do.[79]

As such, Rynkiewich says, every system "is subject to prophetic critique based on kingdom values."[80] He also says that "without a theology of politics and law, justice and reconciliation, as well as contextualization, missionaries risk imposing Western concepts and practices where they will not work."[81]

Self-Propagating

Evangelism and church development were the ultimate goals of every ministry that the mission established including the medical ministry, translation, education, youth, women's ministries, evangelism, and community development. The mission expected the church to eventually assume full responsibility for the ministries. Christian Union Mission said that the "real work of a missionary" was to work himself or herself "out of a job as soon as possible." Indigenous workers were to "be trained to take over the duties of spreading the Gospel in order that a truly indigenous church may be established."[82]

World Gospel Mission's policy today says that missionaries are to work "to establish a truly indigenous" work that will eventually be led by indigenous Christians who would "ultimately assume full responsibility for the "maintenance, management, and growth of the work." The missionaries are to work cooperatively with the indigenous Christians to "establish and develop an indigenous church that views itself as a church of its own culture, not a foreign transplant." WGM's policy adds self-functioning and self-ministering to the three-self model. It defines self-propagating to mean that the indigenous church is "carrying out the Great Commission locally, nationally, and internationally." Self-functioning means that the church has "assumed responsibility" for the "daily operation of its ministries" at all levels, and self-ministering means that the church "identifies needs in its society and plans and carries out ministries of compassion to alleviate those needs."[83]

---

[79]Rynkiewich, *Soul, Self, and Society*, 128.

[80]Rynkiewich, *Soul, Self, and Society*, 128.

[81]Rynkiewich, *Soul, Self, and Society*, 128

[82]*Policy Handbook Foreign Missions Department of the Churches of Christ in Christian Union*, 1980 revised edition, (900.1), 32.

[83]World Gospel Mission Mannual on Missionary Procedures, November, 2005, 16.

Development of the Church Mission Coordinating Council

I have shown that from the mission's perspective, the mission and church were two separate parallel entities, but from the church's perspective, they were one. The mission wanted the church to assume the ultimate responsibility for both the financial support and the administration of ministries that the mission maintained. It asked how those ministries could be shifted from the mission to the church.

In 1985 the mission proposed the formation of a Church Mission Coordinating Council (CMCC) made up of an equal number of representatives from the mission and the church.[84] The goal was to give the church a greater voice in administering the departments and ministries that it would eventually take over, and to create a venue where the church and mission would come together to discuss mutual concerns. The departmental committees were placed under the authority of and became accountable to the CMCC rather than the mission. These included the health, language, women's ministries, education, and youth departments. In addition, the mission created a new department of evangelism and church growth that was under CMCC and committed to carrying out "evangelistic efforts and the planting of new churches." The mission had its own department of outreach ministries that was to plan and initiate "evangelical outreach and church planting in areas where the church lacked the funds and the personnel to pursue the outreach."[85] I have already mentioned Rufus Anderson whose writings influenced the missionaries' thinking. They were convinced that it was the mission's job to open new works, and leave the existing ministries in the hands of the church.[86]

The mission reviewed its budget and allocated funds to the mission, CMCC, and the church. All of the CMCC departments were given some mission funds to work with, but they were expected to generate other funds to support their ministries. Theoretically, the CMCC controlled the funds designated for the departments that had been placed under CMCC, but in reality, as long as missionaries remained in charge of those ministries, the funds remained under mission control.

From the mission perspective, the CMCC had no real authority over the church or the mission. Its authority was limited to that which was delegated to it by the church and mission, and its primary purpose was to coordinate the activities of the two separate bodies. The regional board remained the authority over the church, while the mission council remained the authority over the mission. Both bodies were answerable to the General Missionary Board in the USA as was the church mission coordinating council.

Conversely, the church expected the CMCC to be the final authority in all matters, and they thought that both the church and the mission would comply with decisions hammered out in the CMCC. The mission drew up a chart to demonstrate the relationship between the church, the mission, and the coordinating council as three parallel structures. In the mission's view, all three were answerable to the

---

[84]A diagram of the CMCC structure is included in Appendix Nine, p 604.

[85]Christian Union Mission Field Council Meeting Minutes, February 8-9, 1985 p 8-11.

[86]Rufus Anderson, "The Theory of Missions to the Heathen," 75-76.

home board; however, the CMCC was also subject to both the mission council and the church's regional board. This, as you can see, was just the opposite of the indigenous leaders' view.

The first CMCC meeting was held in April of 1985.[87] At first, the CMCC meetings improved the relationship between the church and the mission as both sides entered into more open discussions about their differences and their expectations, but in the long run, the expectations that each side held for the other could not be reconciled. The church expected to be given greater access to mission resources, while the mission expected the church to take over the ministries that the mission had begun and to generate the funds that were needed for those ministries. The most divisive issue was money. Both sides thought that the other should provide more funds for the ministries. CMCC became the place where the church and mission voiced their discontent and the on-going conflict found its greatest expression.

Church Subsidy

The mission subsidized the ministries that were under the control of CMCC. About one-third of the mission budget, a total of $819.00 per month was placed under the control of CMCC. This included funds for a church subsidy, the translation program, Bible school, the sheep project, women's ministries, youth, and evangelism and church growth. The mission retained control of a monthly budget of $1656.00 that was used for evangelism, fellowship, labor and station upkeep, the MK school, the workshop, the operation of vehicles and generators, language learning for missionaries, and a general contingency fund.[88]

The church and mission remained on opposite ends of the spectrum. The mission tried to push the church away from dependency while the church pressed the mission for more money. The church considered assets such as vehicles and generators to be jointly owned, but the mission thought that the mission exclusively owned mission assets. Problems developed when the mission cut the funds the church was receiving and removed furniture and generators from Embi and Montanda stations. In September of 1988, three and one-half years after CMCC was started, the field council voted to cut the CMCC budget by twenty-five percent beginning on July 1, 1989 and by an additional twenty-five percent each year thereafter with the goal of terminating the CMCC budget within four years."[89]

The mission expected the church to make up the funds that were taken away because of the CMCC budget cuts. The church expected the mission to leave the generators on the stations that it vacated, but the mission was struggling financially. From the mission perspective, good stewardship required the mission to liquidate assets that the mission was no longer using. It decided to sell the genera-

---

[87]Christian Union Mission Field Council Meeting Minutes, February 8-9, 1985 p 22

[88]Christian Union Mission, Executive Committee Meeting Minutes, May 1 and 7, 1985, 4-5.

[89]Christian Union Mission Field Council Minutes, September 16, 1988.

tors on Embi and Montanda stations where missionaries no longer lived.[90] The mission council gave the church districts and the regional board of trustees the option of purchasing the generators at fair market value within thirty days,[91] but the church had no funds to purchase the generators. By March of 1990 the mission had removed the generators from the stations, and the church leaders became increasingly frustrated and discontented with the mission.

The mission allowed the church to use mission vehicles, but expected the church to pay mileage.[92] The church leaders wanted the mission to either give them their own vehicles or allow them to have free access to mission vehicles without charging them mileage.

In 2010 I interviewed both Sengi Iruwa, who was the regional superintendent in 1991, and Timothy Pe, who was the regional treasurer. Both men spoke of the conflict between the church and the mission over money and the mission's insistence that the church pay mileage whenever it used mission vehicles. The church leaders thought that they should be able to use the vehicles free of charge. Some of the church leaders voiced again the belief that the money that the churches in the USA sent to support the work in PNG was intended for the church. It followed that the missionaries were misappropriating the funds by keeping the money for themselves rather than giving it to the PNG church as the church in the USA intended. They did not understand the system under which the missionaries worked and believed that things came easily to all white people including missionaries who had easy access to money, vehicles, equipment, and an abundance of other resources.[93]

The church leaders were convinced that the mission had money, but the missionaries did not trust the church leaders to manage the money well. When I interviewed Timothy Pe, he said that it was true that they do not manage their money well, but noted that, at the time, the church leaders did not understand why the missionaries accused them of being poor money managers.[94]

The church grew increasingly frustrated with the mission, and in 1990 they expressed their concerns at meetings of the CMCC and in a series of letters sent to the mission council. The mission council appointed a committee called the "*stretim*" (correcting) committee to meet with the church leaders and find ways to correct false impressions and to improve the deteriorating relationship.[95] The dichotomous church/mission structures and finances were the core of the problems.

---

[90]Christian Union Mission Field Council Minutes, December 28, 1989 and January 1, 1990, 17, 19.

[91]Christian Union Mission, Annual Field Council Meeting Minutes, March 10, 1990. 2.

[92]Christian Union Mission, Annual Field Council Meeting Minutes, March 10, 1990, 5; Christian Union Mission Executive Committee Meeting Minutes, February 14, 1991, 2-3.

[93]Sengi Iruwa, interview by author, Mendi, Southern Highlands Province, Papua New Guinea, January 11, 2010.

[94]Timothy Pe, interview by author, Mendi, Southern Highlands Province, Papua New Guinea, January 15, 2010.

[95]Christian Union Mission of Papua New Guinea, Field Council Meeting Minutes, October 1, 1990, 6.

The church wanted the church and mission to merge into a single organization, and they wanted all church and mission finances to be placed in a single account with the church and mission having equal access to all funds and other church and mission assets, including vehicles.[96]

In January of 1991 the field council presented the mission's entire budget to the church mission coordinating council. The mission released two hundred and fifty dollars from its monthly budget to the regional board to assist with funding of evangelism, community development, women's ministries, youth, and health. The regional board of trustees would be free to distribute the funds as it saw fit. The subsidy funds would be terminated as of the end of December, 1995.[97] In addition the mission gave the regional board of trustees the funds for the maintenance of Montana and Embi stations and made them responsible for the maintenance of those stations.[98]

The church was not satisfied with the new arrangements. During 1991 the regional board sent a series of requests to the mission for funding for buildings, vehicles, evangelism, and other ministries. The missionary board provided the church with funds to purchase a car,[99] but the majority of the requests were denied. At the end of the year, the church sent a seventeen point letter to the mission detailing the mission's short-comings and saying that if the problems could not be worked out, then the missionaries should return to the USA for one year and develop a plan that was acceptable to the church and leave the church in charge while they were gone. The implication was that the missionaries would go, but the funds and all other mission assets would remain.

When the church and mission came together, they agreed to try to work out their differences. The mission proposed giving the church a subsidy of $100.00 for every adult missionary who was on the field or on furlough preparing to return to the field. At that time there were eleven missionaries on the field and two on furlough who were preparing to return to PNG making a total of thirteen. The first month's subsidy would be thirteen hundred US dollars. From those subsidies, the mission expected the church to be responsible for funding new works, church subsidy, evangelism, youth ministries, women's ministries, the literacy program, and Embi and Montana station maintenance. The mission proposed that the regional board rather than the mission respond to all requests for financial assistance from the local churches, church departments, the districts, and the region. If the church's regional board of trustees accepted the mission's proposal, the church would begin receiving the subsidy as of January, 1992.

In addition to the monthly subsidy, the mission agreed to give three hundred dollars to assist village churches that were building their first permanent church.

---

[96]Christian Union Mission Executive Committee Minutes, December 7, 1990, 3.

[97]Christian Union Mission Field Council Minutes, January 15, 1991, 6

[98]Christian Union Mission Field Council Minutes, January 15, 1991, 7.

[99]Christian Union Mission Field Council Minutes, June 20-21, 1991, 7; Sengi Iruwa, interview by author, Mendi, Southern Highlands Province, Papua New Guinea, January 11, 2010.

Every three years the regional board could propose a project for starting a new work in a new area for the General Missionary Board to consider. If the General Missionary Board approved the project, it would help provide funding for the new work and missionary labor for the new work.[100]

I recall missionaries being divided over the proposal, but the majority agreed to it. Some thought that it was time to pack up and go home. Others thought that it created dependency and that the increased subsidy would mean that the mission was trying to buy from the church the right to remain in Papua New Guinea. Others thought that the mission had an obligation to improve the church/mission relationship and believed that an increased subsidy would make a difference.

In an effort to ensure financial accountability, the mission and church were to jointly prepare a letter and let the district boards and all pastors know that the money was being received from the mission. Mission and church leaders would travel to the district explaining the plan to all pastors and district superintendents. The hope was that the church people would hold the church leaders accountable for the way that they used the funds.[101]

The church accepted the mission plan, and it remained in effect for several years. When the CCCU general council in the USA elected a new general missionary superintendent, he and the General Missionary Board wanted to be sure that the subsidy money was being used "properly" and to the "best advantage" for "the building of the church" and they wanted to hold the PNG church accountable for the way they used the funds.[102]

With the subsidy in place, the church pushed for the church and mission to merge into a single organization. The church wanted equal access to all mission resources and a greater say in the placement of missionaries.[103] The mission gave a large portion of its ministry funds to the church, and as a result, the mission was short of funds and lacked the financial resources to fulfill additional church requests. In March of 1995, the church again wrote to the mission saying that they were not united. Added to the previous grievances was a statement that the mission had not given adequate assistance to Sengi Iruwa during the Farata fight or to the regional superintendent when his son had a prolonged illness and died. They charged that the mission failed to carry out the ministries that it had started. They concluded that the missionaries could leave, but the support that came for the churches in the USA should continue to come to CUC of PNG.[104] In the midst of the conflict between the church and mission, the Churches of Christ in Christian Union formed a partnership with World Gospel Mission.

---

[100]Christian Union Mission Annual Field Council Minutes, November 5-6, 1991, 48-53.

[101]Christian Union Mission, Annual Field Council Minutes, November 5-6, 1991 42-53.

[102]Christian Union Mission, Annual Field Council Minutes, January 11, 1993, 1.

[103]Christian Union Mission Field Council Minutes, June 23, 1993, 2.

[104]Christian Union Mission Field Council Minutes, March 1, 5, 6, 1995, 6-7 and Appendix VI.

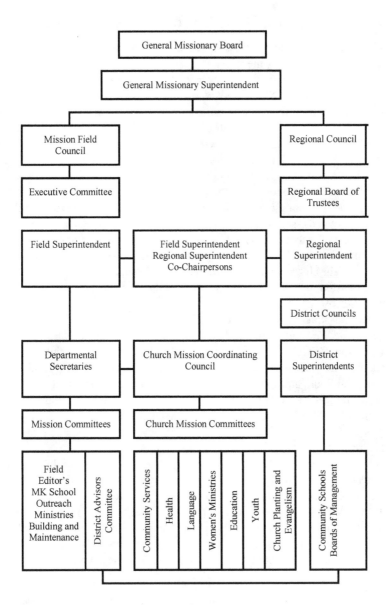

Figure 9. Structure of the Church/Mission Coordinating Council

Partnership with World Gospel Mission

In 1994 the devaluation of the kina led to a high inflation rate in PNG. Although the monthly budget that the mission received in US dollars generated more kina, still the mission's purchasing power declined because of high inflation. Tribal fighting in the lower Nembi Valley led to the closure of Farata station and unexpected expenses for the mission. Political unrest was evident throughout all of Papua New Guinea.[105] With all of the uncertainties in Papua New Guinea, the nationwide political and financial crisis, and the mission's on-going conflict with the church, the missionaries' morale dropped to an all-time low. Some said that the mission had slipped into "maintenance mode" and was unable to carry out any real ministry. Some began to talk about leaving the field, and suggested that it might be time for CUM of PNG to liquidate its assets and return to the USA. After prolonged discussion, the mission council prioritized its ministries and gave the highest priority to the Bible School, second priority to the completion of the translation of the New Testament, and its third priority to having a missionary work with the church leaders. The council decided that it could not afford to maintain a mission in Port Moresby and recalled the Port Moresby missionaries to the Highlands by July of 1995.[106]

The missionary department of CCCU struggled financially. It administered work in the West Indies, on the Texas Mexican Border, and in Papua New Guinea. In addition, CCCU sponsored a number of individual missionaries who had dual appointments through CCCU and World Gospel Mission (WGM) and worked in Africa and South and Central America. For years CCCU operated a school on the Texas-Mexican border, but the school became cost prohibitive and was closed at the end of the 1993-94 school year. In Papua New Guinea, the country's financial crisis led to a demand for increased funding beyond what had been raised for the PNG field.[107]

In June of 1995 the General Missionary Board and the General Board of Trustees of CCCU held a joint meeting to discuss the future of the CCCU mission fields, and at that meeting the two boards agreed to seek a closer relationship with WGM in the administration of the CCCU fields.[108] Within a year, the CCCU General Board of Trustees, the CCCU General Missionary Board, and the WGM Board of Directors, unanimously approved an agreement between the two organizations and implemented it on August 1, 1996.[109] The WGM Board of Directors

[105]Ruth Tipton, "Uncertainty, ...One Certainty!" *The Evangelical Advocate*" 90, no. 9 [May, 1995], 18.

[106]Christian Union Mission Field Council Meeting Minutes, March 1, 5, 6, 1995.

[107]R. L. Sayre, "General Missionary Superintendent's Address Councils, *1995" in 1995 Year book churches of Christ in Christian Union, Council Addresses and Reports*, [Circleville, Ohio: Churches of Christ in Christian Union, 1995], 13-14.

[108]David Lattimer, "A New Partnership Agreement With WGM," *The Evangelical Advocate* 91 no. 9 [May, 1996]: 11.

[109]David Lattimer, "Why...The New Partnership Agreement With WGM," *The Evangelical Advocate* 91 no.11 [July, 1996]: 11.

gave all CCCU missionaries who continued to serve beyond January 1, 1997, a career appointment with WGM, and they were given full credit for their years of service with CCCU.

In January of 1996, during the negotiations for the CCCU/WGM partnership, Don Hohensee, the WGM Vice-president of Field Ministries and David Lattimer, the CCCU General Missionary Superintendent visited the PNG field together and met with both the missionaries and the church leaders about the impending partnership.

The CUC church leaders hoped that they would receive greater assistance from the partnership. They told Hohensee and Lattimer that they wanted more funding from overseas, assistance with the construction of buildings, a change in the Bible school curriculum to include both Pidgin and English, and more missionaries to work with youth, women's ministries, outreach, medical, and support ministries. They asked for greater contact with the church in the USA. They wanted to send a representative to the USA for the purpose of raising funds for the church in Papua New Guinea, and they wanted their representative to speak directly to the missionary board in the USA. They asked to send an evangelistic team to the USA,[110] and they wanted another man to attend Circleville Bible College for further training.[111]

Both of the overseas leaders told the church that once the partnership was formed, any requests that came from the church would have to first be approved by the regional board of trustees and then the field council before it could be forwarded to WGM's headquarters. WGM's priorities were evangelism, church planting, and the training of church leaders. WGM also sponsored medical and education ministries, but they were not the mission's top priority. WGM administered the missionaries, and the missionaries administered the field.[112]

The church leaders were disappointed when the mission council did not agree for them to have more direct contact with the church in the USA and stateside officials. The mission denied the request because it thought that the church wanted to by-pass the field council and to approach the home board directly with its requests for assistance,[113] which is exactly what the church wanted most. The missionaries did agree to place on the project list a request for money to assist the church with its evangelistic efforts.

After WGM officially took over the administration of the field on January 1, 1997, the mission continued to struggle financially. A change in the financial system made it less likely the mission would receive unplanned assistance from overseas. Under CCCU, the funds that the missionaries raised to support their fields were pooled. Each year the field prepared a budget that was based on the

---

[110]At the time, Timothy Map was the regional evangelist, and he wanted to take an evangelistic team to the USA. The RBT's expectation was that such a team would bring back funds that the PNG church could use for evangelism.

[111]Church Mission Coordinating Council Meeting Minutes, January 15, 1996.

[112]Church Mission Coordinating Council Meeting Minutes, January 15, 1996.

[113]Christian Union Mission Field Council Minutes, January 18, 1996, 5-6.

estimated expenditures for each ministry, subject to approval by the CCCU missionary board and financed from the pooled funds.

Under WGM, missionaries had individual ministry accounts. Each missionary was responsible for raising enough funds for his or her personal support as well as his or her ministry. Also, from their individual ministry accounts the missionaries contributed allotted amounts to the mission budget. When WGM first took over the administration of the PNG field, the amounts that were needed for the field administration were underestimated. It soon became evident that it was not enough, and in 1999 the field council requested that the amount that each missionary was raising for field support be increased.[114]

A second change was the way that visitors from headquarters related to the church. Under CCCU's administration, whenever the general missionary superintendent or other officials from the USA visited PNG, they made it a priority to meet with the regional board of trustees and the CMCC during their visits. As a result, they often made concessions to church demands. WGM's policy said that "the mission on the field is...distinct from the national church on that field... (and) functions as the connecting link between the national church on that field and the administration at headquarters through the regional coordinators and the vice president of field ministries."[115] Thus, exactly what the church did not want to happen, happened anyway. Any requests from the churches on the field had to come through the missionaries. When officials from the USA visited the fields, they prioritized meeting with the missionaries. They met with the church leaders and the CMCC when requested, but their primary concern was the missionaries. As a result, the church had fewer meetings with the overseas visitors than it had in the past, and from the church's perspective, the meetings were less productive than they had been in the past.

In spite of their intrinsic differences, the church and mission worked together to start new ministries and reach out to new areas. The joint effort of the church and the mission led to the establishment of camp meetings and the promotion of other ministries.

Camp Meetings

Camp meetings are a genre that caught on quickly with the Nembi church. The first camp meeting took place at Ka from January 11 to January 16, 1994 to celebrate thirty years of missionary service in Papua New Guinea.[116] When I returned to Farata following the camp, Christians were still talking about the camp. More than one person said to me, "*Mipela wokim samting tru, ya!*" (We did something real.)

Before the first camp meeting, the women of CUC held annual retreats for the leaders of the women's groups, but after the first camp meeting, they held

---

[114]Field Council Meeting Papua New Guinea, December 1, 2, 3, and 4, 1999.

[115]*World Gospel Mission Missionary Policy Handbook,* March, 2005, 2.

[116]Robert Sayre, "First Camp Meeting of the Christian Union Church of Papua New Guinea," *The Evangelical Advocate* 89 no. 7, [March, 1994]: 12-13.

camps for any woman who wanted to attend.[117] Each year a different district hosts the camp, and in 2010, Port Moresby district hosted the camp at Taurama, a Port Moresby suburb, where a business man with Nembi ties had acquired a block of land. After the camp he deeded one-half of his land to the Port Moresby District, and they started a new church.

Youth camps are held annually at the district levels, and in December of 2013 a regional youth camp took place in Mount Hagen. The districts sponsor frequent camps, and often have baptisms in conjunction with the camps. Most of the camps conclude with a pig feast.

The camp meetings with their accompanying pig kills (and at the district level, baptisms) have an important social function for the members of Christian Union Church of PNG. Lederman says that the people living in the upper Mendi area viewed the pig kills "as historical events…and as such, their most important characteristic…is a complex articulation of particular people, interests, and ambitions in social situations constrained by past events."[118] The people refer to particular camps as pivotal events in the church's story or in their own Christian journey. Members of the Awaranda in the Lower Mendi area church report that they started holding fellowship meetings after they attended the first regional camp held at Ka in January of 1994, and their fellowship meeting grew into a full congregation. When Jacob Til and Daniel Kor wrote a history of the Wara Lai District, they included the story of a district camp meeting held from December 27 to 31, 1999, to celebrate the arrival of the year 2000.

Lederman says that the purposes of the pig kills among the upper Mendi were for gifting, exchange, the building of renown, prestige, and status, competiveness, and a way to augment the entire alliance's reputation for strength and the ability to amass and distribute wealth.[119] Sillitoe says that pig kills bring renown to those who stage it. Individuals sometimes stage their own pig kill at a time of their own choosing, but they reap greater benefits when more men kill their pigs at the same time by attracting more people and earning greater prestige and glory.[120] Christian Union Church of PNG gains an element of prestige and status from the camp meetings that it holds.

When I ask the members of CUC why they go to camps, they say it is for spiritual renewal and fellowship. They say that they have formed strong friendships with some of the Christians from the other districts, but they rarely see them except at the camps. It is a time to come together and renew friendships. They recall the purpose of the camp, the camp speakers, the messages they heard, the people who were baptized, and the number of pigs that were killed.

---

[117]Anna Timothy Map, "Christian Union Mission's National Women's Convention." *The Evangelical Advocate,* 90 no. 12 [August, 1995], 11.

[118]Rena.Lederman. *What Gifts Engender: Social Relations and Politics in Mendi, Highland Papua New Guinea.* [Cambridge [Cambridgeshire]: Cambridge University Press, 1986], 205.

[119]Lederman, 181.

[120]Paul Sillitoe. *Give and Take: Exchange in Wola Society.* [New York: St. Martin's Press, 1979], 91.

Outreach to New Areas

One of the criticisms that the church leveled against the mission in the meeting of December, 1982 was that the mission had not carried the work beyond the Nembi area.[121] A number of missionaries also were convinced that the mission had remained in the Nembi Valley too long and was failing to fulfill a Biblical mandate to move out to new areas and allow the church to take the responsibility for evangelizing in the Nembi Valley. Both the church and mission wanted to expand the work, but expansion was hindered because each waited on the other to take the initiative.

Mendi is the provincial headquarters for the Southern Highlands Province. For the first fifteen years that the mission worked in the Nembi area, access to Mendi was limited. The Highlands Highway did not reach Mendi until 1976 well after PNG had become an independent nation,[122] and not until the late 1970s did it make its way through the Nembi Valley on its way to Nipa and Tari.[123] With easier road access, some Nembi people relocated to Mendi for school or employment. By 1977 all of the schools in the Nembi area were graduating students from grade six each year, and a number of the students qualified to attend high school at Nipa, Tari, or Mendi. The church pushed the mission to expand its ministries to other rural areas and to urban areas.

Rural Areas

From the time it first entered the Nembi area, the mission had contacts with the people living near Mil in the Lai Valley and those at Iapi across from Toiwara on the eastern side of the upper Erave River. People in both locales asked for a missionary to be assigned to their area.

Iapi was on the fringes of the Kagua District. It was in an isolated area that could be reached by a fair weather road that passed through Ialibu and Kagua and took about six to eight hours to drive from Mendi. It could also be reached by going to Toiwara, and crossing the upper Erave River and then walking about an hour to the station. The missionaries and church personnel usually crossed the river.[124]

In both the Lai Valley and the Iapi area, indigenous persons developed the

---

[121]The complaint was not included in the written paper, but it was a part of the four hour discussion and was seen as one of the promises that the mission had failed to keep. The church had been pushing for the mission to establish a presence in Mendi for several years, but no presence had been established in Mendi.

[122]Lederman, 5.

[123]Bill Tolbert "To Everything There Is A Season" *Missionary Tidings*, XXIX no 7, February, 1978, 4.

[124]Until the Highlands Highway reached the Nembi Valley, the people at Toiwara maintained a vine bridge across the river. After the Highlands Highway opened, the Sugu Valley Cattle Ranch that was located near Iapi constructed and maintained a cable chair that crossed the river at Toiwara. It was easier and more dependable to bring in cargo and personnel via Toiwara than it was to use the fair weather road that passed through Ialibu and Pangia.

work and planted several churches with minimal aid from the mission. Tio Andayo completed his studies at Lae Bible college in 1974, and when he returned to
the Nembi Valley he married Susi Kibem who had completed two years of training at Yagrumbak and was enrolled in the girls' Bible school at Farata for her final
year of study. She dropped out of school and married Tio. They were assigned
to carry out mission work in the Iapi area. Susi and Tio walked to their assigned
area, crossing the Erave River on a vine bridge. They were there for three years,
and they started five churches at Iapi. At the end of three years they returned to the
Nembi Valley and began working in the Farata District as pastors.[125]

The Lai Valley was more accessible than the Iapi. The Ka people had relatives
at Mil in the Lai Valley. From the beginning, CUM missionaries patrolled the area
and started several churches. Two of the men from the Lai Valley, Tia Paik and
Kondul, walked to Ka for the weekly inquirers' classes. They liked the talk they
heard and appealed to Don Seymour, *"Givim mitupela spun long kaikai rais, na
sol long putim long kaikai."* ("Give the two of us a spoon to use to eat the rice and
salt to put on our food.")[126] They were asking the mission to assign a missionary or
a pastor to go to the Lai Valley to teach them so they could understand God's word.

In 1973 James Perek, a youth from Tobua on the Nembi Plateau, graduated
from Nembi Bible School, and he sensed God calling him to work in the Lai
Valley that was then a part of Ka District. Tia and Kondul walked to Ka to meet
James, and they escorted him back to Mil in the Lai Valley to begin his ministry.
They gave him the patrol officer's rest house that was no longer used, and supported James with "food, firewood, and other necessities." He won converts, and
he along with the new converts visited numerous areas in the Lai Valley, starting
churches. James became the area coordinator and organized classes for the growing number of converts. He married a woman from the Lai Valley, settled at Mil
and has remained there to the present. In 1991 the Lai Valley became a district
in its own right, and James Perek became the first District Superintendent for the
"Wara Lai District."[127]

In 1977 the general pastors' committee requested that the mission place missionaries in both the Iapi and the Lai Valley areas.[128] At the time the mission lacked both
personnel and resources to open new stations, but mission and/or church personnel
made regular visits to both areas for classes and/or week-end visits for evangelism
and outreach. Both areas believed that the mission had promised to assign them a
missionary. In 1979 the pastors in the Iapi area threatened to secede from Christian
Union Church unless the mission assigned a missionary to work in their area full time.

Clark, Ballard, and Nihill say that the Wiru welcomed missionaries because of

---

[125]Susi Tio, interview by author, Mato Youth Camp, January 2, 2010.

[126]Jacob Til and Daniel Kor, "Stori Bilong Kristen Union Sios Wara Lai District 1963-
2007" in *Histori Bilong Christian Union Church of Papua New Guinea 1963 to 2014* eds.
Rick Pombre and Ruth Tipton [Unpublished Mission Document], 160.

[127]Til and Kor, 163.

[128]Christian Union Mission Annual Field Council Minutes, February 11, 18, and 19,
1977, p 18, 41.

the material benefits that they brought, encouraged the missionaries to establish themselves in their areas, and turned away from one mission if it appeared to them that another mission would bring them greater benefits.[129] Among the Nembi the call for an expatriate missionary was prompted more by a desire for the material benefits that a missionary would bring than for the message that was already being taught. The threat from the Iapi area to secede from Christian Union Church if the mission did not assign a missionary to their area was designed to pressure the mission to send a missionary and establish a station.

In 1981, the mission sent Don and Dorothy Wood to open a station in the Iapi area.[130] By mid-1981 the family had relocated to Iapi and planned to replace the temporary bush buildings with permanent structures.[131] In August of 1982, the field superintendent resigned and unexpectedly left the field, and the mission did not have enough personnel to cover the work.[132] At the same time, the home office advised the field to reevaluate the move to Iapi in consideration of the need to establish urban ministries in PNG.[133] The church leaders warned that if the mission withdrew its missionaries from Iapi, the churches in that area would be lost to Christian Union Church,[134] but the council decided to withdraw the Wood family from the Iapi and place them at Farata with the understanding that Wood would travel to Iapi via Toiwara each week to make contact with the Iapi churches.[135] Plans were made for someone to return to the Iapi as soon as personnel became available,[136] but in the end the plans were scrapped.[137]

The mission never agreed to send a missionary to the Lai Valley, but in January of 1982, the mission made plans to build a bush house at Pumi for church and mission personnel to use when they visited the area. The mission purchased poles and other supplies for the building.[138] About that time tribal fighting became very active in the Lai Valley. During the fighting two of the churches were burned and only three out of eight pastors remained at their churches.[139]

Urban Outreach

The church and mission first considered moving into the urban areas in the late

---

[129]Jeffrey Clark, Chris Ballard, and Michael Nihill. *Steel to Stone: A Chronicle of Colonialism in the Southern Highlands of Papua New Guinea.* [Oxford, UK: Oxford University Press, 2000], 100-113.

[130]Christian Union Mission Annual Field Council Minutes, March 16, April 4 and 15, 1981, p 11-12

[131]Christian Union Mission Field Council Minutes, July 16-17, 1982, p 4.

[132]Christian Union Mission Field Council Minutes, August 27, 1982, p. 1.

[133]Christian Union Mission Field Council Minutes, October 8, 1982, p. 1-2.

[134]Christian Union Mission Field Council Minutes, October 8, 1982, p. 9.

[135]Christian Union Mission Field Council Minutes, October 8, 1982, p. 1-2.

[136]Christian Union Mission Annual Field Council, February 10-12, 1983, p. 16.

[137]Christian Union Mission Executive Committee Minutes, December 13, 1983, p. 2.

[138]Christian Union Mission Field Council Minutes, January 4, 1982, p 2.

[139]Bob Jones, "Combined Ka District Advisor and Personal Activities Report" in Christian Union MIssion Annual Field Council, January 15, 16, 1982, p. 43.

1970s. In 1978, the mission had some contacts in Port Moresby and investigated the possibility to starting a work there,[140] but nothing opened up and the mission found the possibility to be cost prohibitive and delayed the move into Port Moresby for several years.[141] After the Highlands Highway opened, Christian Union Church repeatedly asked the mission to establish a work in Mendi.[142] The Regional Board of Trustees decided that opening a work in Mendi was more important than opening one in the Lai Valley.[143] One of the criticisms that the church leveled against the mission in the meeting of December, 1982 was that the mission had not carried the work beyond the Nembi area.[144] A number of missionaries were convinced that the mission had remained in the Nembi Valley too long and was failing to fulfill a Biblical mandate to move out to new areas and allow the church to take the responsibility for evangelizing in the Nembi Valley. They pushed to establish a work in Mendi, Mount Hagen, and other areas outside the Nembi Valley.

The Move Towards Mendi

Beginning in July of 1981, the church pushed the mission to open a work in Mendi, and the mission agreed to their request.[145] In 1983, the council recommitted itself to opening a work in Mendi, and set aside funds that could be used to develop the Mendi work.[146] The mission field superintendent and the church regional superintendent made many trips to the lands office in Mendi trying to procure a land lease in or near Mendi where the church and mission could open a work, but no land opened up before the field superintendent returned to the USA for an extended furlough and a new man took his place. The mission council repeatedly reaffirmed the commitment to find land in Mendi,[147] but the effort failed.

The church had the contacts in Mendi, but they had no money to put towards

---

[140]Christian Union Mission Field Council Minutes, July 29, 1978, p 8.

[141]Christian Union Mission Annual Field Council, January 15-16, 1982, p. 11.

[142]Requests from the church to start a work in Mendi are recorded in the minutes of the Christian Union Mission Field Council meetings held on July 25, 1981 (p 5), October 23, 24, and 31 1981 (p 14), and January 4, 1982 (p 2) and the Executive Committee Meeting Minutes, May 31, 1982 (p 1).

[143]Christian Union Mission Field Council Minutes, July 16-17, 1982, p. 11.

[144]The complaint was not included in the written paper, but it was a part of the four-hour discussion and was seen as one of the promises that the mission had failed to keep. The church had been pushing for the mission to establish a presence in Mendi for several years, but had not yet moved into Mendi.

[145]Requests from the church to start a work in Mendi are recorded in the minutes of the Christian Union Mission Field Council meetings held on July 25, 1981 (p 5), October of 1981 (p 14) and in January of 1982 (p 2) and Christian Union Mission Executive Committee Minutes of May 31, 1982 (p 1).

[146]Christian Union Mission Annual Field Council Minutes, February 10-12, 1983, 14.

[147]Christian Union Mission Field Council Minutes, May, 4-5, 1984, 7; Christian Union Mission Field Council Minutes, August 3-4, 1984, 7, 15-16; Christian Union Mission Field Council Minutes, September 16, 1988, 11; Christian Union Mission Executive Committee Meeting Minutes, February 14, 1991, 11-15.

starting a work there. They felt they could or would not establish a church in Mendi unless the mission helped them obtain and develop a lease. In writing about dependency, Schwartz says that "Buildings and programs aren't the church."[148] Had the church pursued its Mendi contacts more aggressively, they could have started a church in Mendi without waiting for the acquisition of a lease and for the mission to commit to a building program. As it was, instead of forming partnership as Lederleitner proposes and recognizing their interdependency, to use Rowell's term, the church and mission waited on each other to take the lead and then each blamed the other for failing to start a church in the town of Mendi.

Beginning on December 1, 1994, the mission rented a house from MAF and placed its field director in Mendi for one year. They instructed him to work with the lands department to try and secure a piece of property large enough to relocate the Bible school to Mendi.[149] Missionaries planned to relocate the Bible school during the next two years to either Mendi or Mount Hagen wherever enough land was procured first. In July of 1995, the mission had located two potential lots in Mendi that were available for lease. The field council decided to try to obtain both lots,[150] but in the end the lots went to someone else. In December of 1995, the field director moved back to Ka to work with the Bible school, and for the next two and one-half years, the mission had no presence in Mendi.

Following the 1997 national elections, tribal fighting intensified throughout the Nembi area, making it impossible to carry out either the translation or Bible school ministries at Ka. In 1998 the missionaries searched for rental properties in Mendi where they could relocate mission staff. CUM rented a house from the Lutheran mission that the Bennett family occupied when they returned to the field in August of 1998. The Evangelical Church of Papua had a house that became available for rent in October of 1998, and the mission agreed to rent it as soon as it became available.[151] The mission used the Lutheran house for about eight months, but it rented the house from the Evangelical Church of Papua for eleven years.

Church people from the Wara Lai District rather than missionaries were instrumental in planting the church at Tupiri near Mendi. They had kinship ties with some of the people at Tupiri, and asked the regional board to appoint a pastor for the church. Simon En, the appointed pastor, moved to Mendi in 1998 when the mission acquired the ECP rental. The mission hired him to work as security at the rented property while he served as pastor at the Tupiri church. He had been instrumental in starting the Mount Hagen church, and was equally effective in Mendi. At this writing, the Tupiri church is the only CUC church in the Mendi area. I continue the story of the church/mission's time in Mendi in Chapter Seven.

---

[148]Schwartz, "Cutting the Apron Strings." http://www.missionfrontiers.org/is-sue/article/cutting-the-apron-strings (accessed on November 4, 2013).

[149]Christian Union Mission Field Council Minutes, June 29, 1994, 1, 4; Christian Union Mission Field Council Minutes, November 9, 10, 13, 1994, 2-3.

[150]Christian Union Mission Annual Field Council Minutes, July 29-30, 1995, 4.

[151]Christian Union Mission Field Council Meeting, May 13, 1998, 106-98.

The Push to Mount Hagen

Mount Hagen is located in the Western Highlands of Papua New Guinea, has a population of over 29,000,[152] and is central to the seven Highlands' provinces—Eastern Highlands, Chimbu, Jiwaka, Western Highlands, Enga, Southern Highlands and Hela Provinces. Daily, except on Sundays when the vast majority of businesses are closed, thousands of people from the surrounding areas converge on Mt. Hagen to buy supplies; to sell coffee and other produce; to visit *wantoks*; to seek medical attention; and to take care of other business affairs. There are numerous squatter settlements scattered throughout the city, and a number of tea and coffee plantations are found near Mount Hagen in the Western Highlands and Jiwaka provinces.

The Mount Hagen Missionary Home is a guest house especially for missionaries and church workers. In November of 1983, the guest house board searched for a new host family. The position provided the family with room and board but no salary. The mission agreed that Bill and Becky Benner should apply for the position, and if accepted they would relocate to Mount Hagen and look for opportunities for Christian Union Mission to begin a work in the Mount Hagen and on the nearby plantations.[153] The Benner Family was accepted to the position of host family at Mount Hagen Missionary Home,[154] and on January 2, 1984, they moved to Mount Hagen.[155]

Hagen Plantation Ministries

In the 1980s many Nembi people traveled to and from Mount Hagen to find work on the coffee plantations during the coffee picking season. When Bill Benner looked into the possibility of beginning a work on the coffee plantations, he learned that plantation ministries were closed to expatriates, but wide open to indigenous pastors. The mission consulted with the regional board of trustees to find a pastor to assign to the plantation ministries in the Mount Hagen area.[156] Jeremaiah Kele who had been serving as the superintendent of the Farata District left his position in August or September of 1984 to become the indigenous leader of the Mount Hagen area plantation ministry.[157] By April of 1985 Jeremaiah, with the help of two men who worked on the plantations, held regular services at Kudjip and Kurumul plantations. John Kua, a pastor from Montanda District, held services at Koban plantation, and Wesa Lun, a pastor and former church leader from Ka District, held services at Kendeing plantation.[158] The pastors were not paid for

---

[152]Thomas Brinkoff, "City Population, Papua New Guinea," http://www.citypo-pula-tion.de/PapuaNewGuinea.html [accessed on February 26, 2014].

[153]Christian Union Mission Field Council Minutes, November 4, 1983, 1.

[154]Christian Union Mission Executive Committee Minutes, December 13, 1983, 2.

[155]Becky Benner, "From Bush to Town" *Missionary Tidings* 36 no 10 [July, 1984]: 9.

[156]Christian Union Mission Field Council Minutes, May 4-5, 1984, 6.

[157]Don Seymour "Frontlines For Information and Intercession," *Missionary Tidings*, XXXVII no. 2, October, 1984, 2.

[158]Christian Union Mission Annual Field Council Minutes, April 28-29, 1985, 12.

their pastoral work but found employment and housing on the plantations. The mission provided Jeremaiah, the area leader, with a motorbike for transport[159] and gave him eighty kina per month to assist with the plantation ministries.[160] The plantation ministries ran consistently in the Mount Hagen area for five or six years in spite of tribal fighting that broke out between July and October of 1985 leading to a mass exodus of workers who fled to their home provinces.[161]

When the Hagen town church was well established, it assumed the responsibility for the plantation ministries, and the mission was less directly involved in the oversight of the plantation churches. Eventually most of the plantation churches closed. As the oil fields developed. many of the Nembi people found employment elsewhere and fewer sought employment on the plantations. One church continues to function on Kimil Plantation, and it is now a part of Hagen District.

Hagen Town Ministries

Bill Benner located lots in New Town that were available for lease,[162] and by April of 1985, the mission acquired a lot and the property was ready for development.[163] The Benner family was due to leave on furlough in June of 1985, and in anticipation of their departure, the field council assigned Dennis and Juanita Brown to move to Mount Hagen by May of 1985 to further develop the work in Mount Hagen.[164]

In April of 1985 before the Brown family moved to Mount Hagen, the mission unexpectedly withdrew from Embi station, and Roger and Dianna Miller replaced Bill and Becky Benner as the host family at Mount Hagen Missionary Home. The Brown family also relocated to Mount Hagen as planned to a house that the mission rented from the Nazarene Mission located in the Tarangau area of Mount Hagen.[165] The core ministries for the families working in Mount Hagen were to be field administration, town church planting, plantation church planting, and ministry to CLTC students.[166]

The missionaries believed that it was the mission's responsibility to evangelize and start churches in new areas and assumed the responsibility for developing any property that it acquired and assisted the indigenous pastors who worked alongside the mission with transport and ministry funds but not with personal support.[167]

Missionaries invited Simon En, who had served as the Montanda District Superintendent for eight years, to move to Mt. Hagen and help plant a church. Simon said that he had been praying about a new ministry for a year. When he

---

[159]Christian Union Mission Field Council Minutes, February 8-9, 1985, 4.

[160]Christian Union Mission Field Council Minutes, December 19, 1986, 4.

[161]Christian Union Mission Field Council Minutes, October 4-5, 1985, 6.

[162]Christian Union Mission Field Council Minutes, August 3-4, 1984, 6-7.

[163]Christian Union Mission Annual Field Council Minutes, April 28-29, 1985, 12.

[164]Christian Union Mission Field Council Minutes, August 3-5, 1984, 6-7.

[165]Christian Union Mission Executive Committee Minutes, May 1 and 7, 1985, 1.

[166]Christian Union Mission Field Council Minutes, December 13, 1984, 13.

[167]Christian Union Mission Field Council Minutes, February 8-9, 1985, 4.

was invited to help plant a church in Mt. Hagen, he agreed and relocated to Mount Hagen in early 1986. He became the key person in a successful church plant. He first came without his family, and for six months the mission provided his accommodation. He was given no salary for his work as a church planter, but he secured a job at Mount Hagen Missionary Home and worked there for four years to support himself and later his family until the church had grown enough to pay a pastor.[168]

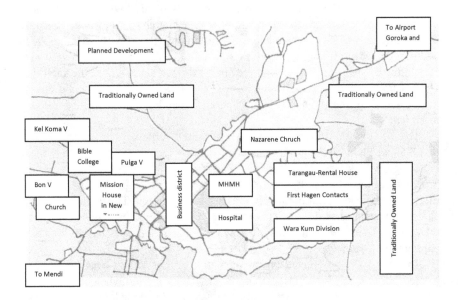

Map 6. Mount Hagen

Near the house that the mission rented from the Nazarenes in the Tarangau area of Mount Hagen was a squatter settlement where Denny Brown made the initial contact with people living in the Hagen. By September of 1985, the attendance varied, but a core group of six people from the squatter settlement participated in weekly services and a few children attended Sunday school at the missionary's home.[169]

Simon En made contact with a nurse from Goroka who belonged to the Evangelical Brotherhood Church (EBC) and was working in Mount Hagen but was not attending church regularly. When she learned that he had graduated from her church's Bible school in Lae, she agreed to attend the services with her family and became a strong supporter of the new church plant for several years until her

---

[168]Simon En, Interview by author, Mendi, Southern Highlands Province, Papua New Guinea, December 18, 2009.

[169]Denny Brown, "Hagen Church Planting Report" in Christian Union Mission Field Council Minutes, October 4-5, 1985, 4.

employment took her away from Mount Hagen.[170] Simon also contacted Southern Highlanders living in Mt. Hagen who were willing to meet together for worship services.[171] The congregation grew to seventy-five.[172]

For a short time the congregation rented the Nazarene church building in Mount Hagen and held services there on Sunday afternoons.[173] Manuel Ortiz in his book *One New People* says that renting is one of the methods for developing multiethnic congregations, but it rarely works well because disagreements tend to rise between the host congregation and the renting congregation over issues such as building maintenance and opposing goals of the two congregations.[174] The arrangement between CUM and the Nazarene church was short lived because disagreements arose over the power bill and holding the key to the building. In addition, the group from CUM was not free to hold its Sunday services until 1:00 P.M. after the Nazarenes had finished their services and vacated the facilities, and as Simon put it, "*Em i no fit taim long holim lotu.*" (It was not a good time to have a service.) Many missed services because they had other plans for Sunday afternoon.[175]

The mission finalized the acquisition of the lot in New Town, and by March of 1986 had enclosed the property with a fence. As soon as the fence was in place and the growth cleared, the congregation began holding services on the vacant lot. They endured wet grass, the blazing sun, rain, and muddy ground, but they kept meeting in the open air until the missionary home was built. The open air services caught the attention and led to the opposition of the people from the surrounding area. Most of them were active in the Catholic Church and saw no need for a new church to enter the area.[176]

The first building erected on the vacant lot at New Town was the pastor's house.[177] Simon had been in Hagen for about six months, and when his house was complete, his family joined him. Traditional land bordered the lot that was located just within the town limits. Simon and his family began to form relationships with

---

[170]Simon En, interview by author, Mendi, Southern Highlands Province, Papua New Guinea January 19, 2010.

[171]Simon En, interview by author, Mendi, Southern Highlands Province, Papua New Guinea, December 18, 2009.

[172]Denny Brown, "Activity Report for Denny Brown" in Christian Union Mission Annual Field Council Minutes, March 6, 1986, 5.

[173]Simon En, interview by author, Mendi, Southern Highlands Province, Papua New Guinea, December 18, 2009.

[174]Manuel Ortiz, *One New People: Models for Developing a Multiethnic Church* [Downers Grove, Illinois, InterVarsity Press, 1996], 66-69.

[175]Simon En, Interview by author, Mendi, Southern Highlands Province of Papua New Guinea, December 18, 2009.

[176]Simon En, Interview by author, Mendi, Southern Highlands Province of Papua New Guinea, January 19, 2010.

[177]Gene Lawhun, "Personal Report for Gene Lawhun" and Rosemary Lawhun, "Personal Report for Rosemary Lawhun in Christian Union Mission Annual Field Council, March, 1987, 9-10.

people from Pulga and Bon Villages that were located near the mission property. These newly formed relationships attracted the local people to come to the services that Pastor Simon was holding. Filling water containers for a woman from Pulga village during a dry spell when the village water source had dried up began a long term friendship with one woman who became the first to attend the church. Another friendship was formed when the pastor sent his young daughter with 30 *toea* to buy sweet potato vines from a woman who was working in her garden. Her conscience and culture said that you don't sell sweet potato vines. Instead you give them away. She refused the money and gave the vines along with some newly harvested sweet potatoes to the little girl and a friendship was formed. She started to attend regularly the open air services that Simon held each Sunday.[178] Walter C. Wright says, "Leadership is a relationship of trust. We listen to people we trust. We accept the influence of a person whose character we respect. Leadership that produces fruit is rooted in the character of the leader. It is impossible to provide consistent leadership out of insincerity."[179] The Hagen people accepted Simon as a pastor because he befriended them and won their trust.

Construction began on the missionary house in October of 1986. It was completed by March of 1987,[180] and the Miller family left their position as host family at Mount Hagen Missionary Home and moved into the newly completed missionary's house at New Town. Gene and Rosemary Lawhun, moved to Mount Hagen in June of 1987 when the Millers returned to the USA.[181] The people of Mount Hagen Christian Union Church remember Gene and Rosemary Lawhun and Pastor Simon as the persons who started the Hagen church.

The mission house was built on stilts. After it was constructed, the congregation placed temporary walls made of woven cane around the perimeter, threw tarps on the ground, and met under the house for two years[182] until the permanent church was built on traditional ground just up the road.[183]

Like Pastor Simon, Gene and Rosemary Lawhun worked at building relationships with the Hagen people. Paka Kor and Ana Aisik, who were among the first local women to attend the Hagen church, recalled going with Rosemary to visit the local women in their gardens. Gene went to the villages to contact the men, and almost daily he went to town so he could visit with people on the streets.

---

[178]Simon En, interview by author, Mendi, Southern Highlands Province, Papua New Guinea, January 18, 2010; and Paka Kor, interview by author, Mount Hagen, Western Highlands Province, Papua New Guinea, January 24, 2010.

[179]Walter C. Wright, *Relational Leadership: A Biblical Model For Leadership Service* [Carlisle, Cumbria, CA3 0QS, UK: Paternoster Press, 2000], 15.

[180]Butch Jenkins, "Personal Report by Butch Jenkins" Christian Union Mission Annual Field Council Minutes, March, 1987, 8.

[181]Gene Lawhun, "Personal Report" Christian Union Mission Annual Field Council Minutes, January, 25, 1988.

[182]Gene Lawhun, "The Mount Hagen Church Papua New Guinea" *Missionary Tidings* 41 no 1 [August-September, 1988]: 7.

[183]Rosemary Lawhun, "From then…to Now" *Missionary Tidings* 44 no. 1 [August/September, 1991]: 7.

Today the people remember Gene and Rosemary because of those visits. Never before had a white person sought them out and befriended them like Gene and Rosemary did.[184]

The congregation meeting under the house grew. A young man from Bon Village was opposed to the idea of a new church entering the area. He came to a service listened to the message, was intrigued, and returned the next week with one of his "cousin brothers"[185] in tow. They were soon joined by another woman from Bon Village and became full members of the new congregation. Pastor Simon used the mission van to pick up Southern Highlanders who had migrated to Mount Hagen for employment or education. Each Sunday he went to the various settlements in the Hagen area and to Hagen Technical College and other schools looking for people from the Nembi, Nipa, and Mendi areas who were from the same language family and interested in attending the services. The average attendance during 1987 increased to 115.[186] In May of 1988, the church baptized eight people at its first baptism.[187]

In September of 1987 Rosemary started a Sunday school in her living room that met while the adults gathered under the house for the Sunday morning service. She started with ten children, but by January of 1988 forty-five to fifty children attended each Sunday.[188] Some of the children from Pulga village attended Sunday school. At home they would sing the songs, rattle tin plates as though they were playing the tambourine, and recite verses that they learned in Sunday school. This attracted their mother who began attending the adult services, and found spiritual fulfillment that she had not found in the Lutheran church that she had been attending. She became one of the leading members of the new church plant.[189] As adults many of the children who attended the first Sunday school class became members of the Mount Hagen Christian Union church.[190]

About a quarter of a mile from the mission house, Andrew Kuawa, who was the pastor of the Wesleyan church in Hagen, owned some land just outside the

---

[184]Paka Kor, interview by author, Mount Hagen, Western Highlands Province, Papua New Guinea, January 24, 2010; Ana Aisik, interview by author, Mount Hagen, Western Highlands Province, Papua New Guinea, January 24, 2010.

[185]In many Melanesian societies, cousins are considered brothers and sisters. Many PNG English speakers refer to their cousins as "cousin brother" or "cousin sister" to indicate that they do not have the same parents, but they are closely related. In most, but not all, cases the fathers of the "cousin siblings" had the same father.

[186]Christian Union Mission Annual Field Council Minutes, January 25, 1988, 6.

[187]Rosemary Lawhun "Annual Report" in Christian Union Mission Annual Field Council Minutes, January 13, 1989, 20; Gene Lawhun "Annual Report" in Christian Union Mission Annual Field Council Minutes, January 13, 1989, 19.

[188]Rosemary Lawhun, "Annual Report" in Annual Field Council Meeting Minutes, January 25, 1988.

[189]Ana Aisik, interview by author, Mount Hagen, Western Highlands Province, January 24, 2010.

[190]Ana Aisik, interview by author, Mount Hagen, Western Highlands Province, January 24, 2010.

town limits. When he observed the church meeting underneath the missionary's house, he offered to sell a piece of property to the congregation so they could build a church. Negotiations for the church property began in January of 1988. The mission council paid a total of ten thousand kina for the ground. The payment included a vehicle (Suzuki) valued at thirty-five hundred kina.[191] The purchase of the land became final in January of 1989.[192] The property had old coffee trees and a lot of overgrowth that had to be cleared. As soon as the purchase of the land was finalized, the entire congregation and the missionaries worked together and cleared the land.[193] Before Gene and Rosemary Lawhun left for furlough at the end of May, 1989, the construction of the church building was nearly complete and the congregation was using it for services.[194]

Under Pastor Simon's leadership, the church sent students who were interested in ministry to Nembi Bible Training Center. John Kingal, Andrew Koki and Simila, the first to go to the school, enrolled in 1989[195] and completed their training at the end of 1991.[196] Others soon joined them and several of those who attended Nembi Bible Training Center became leaders in the Mount Hagen area.

Bill and Becky Benner returned from an extended furlough in 1989 and remained in Mount Hagen until Gene and Rosemary Lawhun returned to the field in June of 1990. The pastor's house and the mission house shared the same lot. In February of 1990 the mission moved the pastor's house from the mission property to the church property just down the road.[197]

In 1991 the Hagen church had grown to the point that it was able to support a full time pastor, and Simon En quit his job at the Mount Hagen missionary home.[198] The church supported not only its pastor but also the students that they were sponsoring at Nembi Bible Training Center.[199]

The mission struggled financially during the early 1990s. In 1989 the mission acquired a house in Port Moresby and placed a missionary family there. In 1991 it became clear that the field did not have enough financial resources to fund Port

---

[191]Christian Union Mission Annual Field Council Minutes, January 25, 1988, 6. The council agreed that the cash value of the Suzuki would be deducted from the total amount of cash given to the land owners. In the end the mission gave seven or eight thousand kina plus the Suzuki to purchase the land for the Hagen church.

[192]Christian Union Mission Annual Field Council Minutes, January 13, 1989 p 4-5.

[193]Paka Kor, interview by author, Mount Hagen, Western Highlands Province, January 24, 2010.

[194]Christian Union Mission Annual Field Council Minutes, March 10, 1990, 16.

[195]Dean and Shirley Queen, "Nembi Bible Training Center of Papua New Guinea" *Missionary Tidings* 42 no. 1 [August September, 1989]: 4

[196]Rosemary Lawhun "From then…to Now" Missionary Tidings 44 no. 1 [August/ Septmber, 1991]: 7-8.

[197]Bill Benner, "Personal Activities report in Annual Field Council Minutes, March 10, 1990, 16.

[198]Rosemary Lawhun, "From then…to Now" *Missionary Tidings* 44 no. 1 [August/ September, 1991]: 7.

[199]Bill Benner, "Personal Report", in Annual Field Council Minutes, November 5-6, 1991, 38.

Moresby, Mount Hagen, and the Nembi Bible Training Center. One of the three ministries would have to be left open in 1992. By then the Mount Hagen church was well established, and the field agreed that the Mount Hagen ministry could be left open more readily than the other two.[200]

In January of 1992 the regional assembly voted for Simon En, the church's founding pastor, to be Christian Union Mission's regional Superintendent.[201] He returned to the Southern Highlands to take up the responsibilities of his new role.[202] The next two pastors were early converts from Bon Village. John Kingal served as the church pastor from 1992 to December of 1997 when he left to pursue studies at CLTC in Banz.

The Outreach to Port Moresby

In 1981 tribal fighting broke out on the Nembi Plateau and the Sikirpao people of Karamela village of the Nipa District[203] in the Southern Highlands Province were defeated and routed from their homes. They scattered all over the country. Some established themselves at Erima settlement in Port Moresby and some went to work on Doa and Veimauri Plantations a few miles from Port Moresby. The group at Erima settlement did well. They acquired and operated a PMV route in Port Moresby for several years. They became the support network for other migrants from the Nembi area who began to migrate to Port Moresby for education, employment, or other personal reasons.[204] They spoke various dialects of the same language.

In 1983 a group of transplanted Nembi Christians led by a woman named Margaret began attending a Nazarene church at Five Mile on Sunday mornings. Traveling to Five Mile at night was not a good option, and so the group held night fellowships at Erima settlement in their homes. For a while the Nazarene pastor visited them in the settlement and the Nazarene missionaries gave the group some assistance, but the impetus for the church plant came from members of the Nembi Christian Union Church. Even though they had no pastor and only limited assistance, they met regularly for fellowship, worship and prayer and became a fledgling church plant without a pastor.

The fellowship of Christians had been meeting for about two years before outreach to Port Moresby is mentioned in the mission records. When Don Seymour visited Papua New Guinea in December of 1984, he reported that both the

---

[200]Christian Union Mission Executive Committee Minutes, February 14, 1991, 16-17.

[201]R. L Sayre, "Mission Links" *Advocate* 88 no. 6 [February, 1993] 10.

[202]The record of Simon En's election to serve the chruch as regional superintendent was a hand-written paper indicating that he had been voted into that office. It was included in a folder that contained the mission field minutes for 1993. The regional elections would have been held in late 1992 or early in 1993.

[203]Nicholas Nembo gave the name of the group in an appeal letter he wrote requesting for funds to assist the group and the church after a fire destroyed a home and severely damaged the church.

[204]Interviews with the Port Moresby church leaders on November 24, 2009 and January 29, 2010 at MAPANG guest house in Port Moresby.

missionaries and the PNG church had a vision for outreach to the cities of Papua New Guinea. They had already established a presence in Mount Hagen and on the nearby plantations, and they were carrying out "prayerful research" about outreach to Port Moresby.[205] In 1986 the mission leaders began traveling to Port Moresby regularly to contact the Nembi people living in the area,[206] and funds were allocated to give limited assistance to the Nembi church leader for travel to Port Moresby.[207] Don Seymour reported to the home constituency that a congregation had been started in Port Moresby in November of 1986.[208] In his 1987 annual report the field superintendent reported that mission personnel became excited about "the starting of a church in the nation's capital—Port Moresby, (and said that the move)...required not only prayers but dollars."[209] The Moresby fellowship had already been active for several years without involvement from the mission or the church in the Nembi area.

In January of 1989, the mission field superintendent reported that a congregation had been meeting in Port Moresby for two and one-half years without the benefit of a pastor or a missionary.[210] That changed when Tui Tandopen Ori from Ka became the first designated pastor and went to Port Moresby.[211] Both the church and the mission gave him some assistance, but it was not a living wage. He was a licensed driver, and supported himself first by driving a public motor

---

[205]Don Seymour "Frontlines" *Missionary Tidings* 37 no 5 [January, 1985]: 2

[206]Christian Union Mission Annual Field Council Minutes, March 6, 1986, 5.

[207]Christian Union Mission Budget Committee Meeting, December 19, 1986, 4.

[208]Don Seymour, "The Year in Review" *Missionary Tidings*, 40 no. 1, [August-September]: 5.

[209]Roger Miller, "Annual Personal Report" in Christian Union Mission Annual Field Council, March, 1987, 11.

[210]Gene Lawhun, "Superintendent's Report" in Field Council Meeting Minutes, January 13, 1989.

[211]"Tui's Story" (as translated by one of his son's in 1994) *Evangelical Advocate* 89 no 10 [June, 1994]:13. In an interview with Tui Tandopen Ori held on November 24, 2009 at MAPANG guest house in Port Moresby. Tui said that he went to Port Moresby in 1985, but in telling his stories, the specific dates were not always accurate. He said he had gone to Bible school in 1975, but his graduation certificate showed that he had attended the Bible school from 1970-1972. Tui said that he went with no assistance from the church or mission, but mission executive committee meeting minutes from May of 1987 say Tui Tondopen Ori felt called to become the pastor at Port Moresby. The mission expressed a willingness to assist him by paying for his air fare and giving him K100.00 for the first two months pending the approval of Church Mission Coordinating Council. There is no record of the outcome of the June meeting or what assistance was actually given to Tui. Mission records show that he served as a Bible school teacher in 1988, but in 1989 he gave up his role as Bible school teacher to become the pastor of Ka church (Dean and Shirley Queen "Nembi Bible Training Center of Papua New Guinea," *Missionary Tidings,* 42 no. 1, [August-September, 1989]: 4). I think that he went to pastor in Port Moresby in 1990. When he arrived in Port Moresby he became the pastor at the church in Erima settlement.

vehicle, and later by driving a garbage truck.[212] The group held house fellowships, Bible studies, women's fellowships and prayer meetings in several settlements and on nearby plantations. When they first started holding services at Erima, the people met outside in an open area, using umbrellas to shield them from the hot sun. Soon after that they were able to erect a church building with a corrugated iron roof and open sides offering shelter from the sun and allowing the building to be cooled by any breezes that were blowing. In July of 2007 fire damaged the building but a congregation continues to meet at Erima and use the damaged building.[213]

During 1990 the church purchased a house for the pastor at Erima from a man who was leaving the settlement. Until the pastor's house became available, Tui's family remained in the Southern Highlands, but after the church purchased the house, the mission assisted with the air fare to allow Tui's wife and children to join him at Erima settlement in Port Moresby.[214] A number of Nembi people moved into Eight Mile Settlement, and when Tui acquired a block of land at Eight Mile, he and his family relocated there. Some of the settlers at Eight Mile gave land so that a church could be established at Eight Mile, and Tui began holding fellowships there.[215]

In 1993, Kanj Mesmba replaced Tui Ori as the pastor at Erima while Tui conducted fellowships at Eight Mile.[216] Kanj served as pastor in Port Moresby for two years, and he and his family lived in the pastor's house at Erima settlement. At about the same time, the regional board appointed Daniel Pe to become the first pastor at Doa Plantation. Daniel found work at Doa plantation to support himself and his family, but the mission gave some assistance to both Kanj Mesmba and Daniel Pe when they first started working in the Port Moresby area. At a CMCC meeting held on November 7, 1994, the mission said that it was discontinuing the subsidy that it had been providing for Kanj and Daniel and urged the regional board of trustees to send them monthly support.[217] In 1996 Stanley Pesi replaced Kanj as the pastor at Erima.[218]

The mission purchased a home in Gordons in late 1989, and expatriate mis-

---

[212]Interviews with Tui Tandopen Ori held on November 24, 2009 and January 29, 2010 at MAPANG guest house in Port Moresby.

[213]Conversation with Miletus Nuepi

[214]Christian Union Mission Field Council Minutes, July 3, 1990, 2; Christian Union Mission Field Council Minutes, October 1, 1990, 1.

[215]Dean Queen, "Port Moresby Report" Christian Union Mission Field Council Minutes, June 23, 1993; Church Mission Coordinating Council Meeting, November 7, 1994

[216]I could not find records that indicated exactly when Kanj became the pastor in Port Moresby. However in June of 1993 Dean Queen, who was the missionary serving in Port Moresby, said in a report that he made to the field council that Tui was the pastor at Erima, but he had been ill and unable to visit the plantation work outside of Port Moresby. In that same meeting the field council agreed that pastors for Port Moresby should be an agenda item at the next CMCC meeting.

[217]Church Mission Coordinating Council Meeting Minutes, November 7, 1994, p 1.

[218]Stanley Pesi, conversation with author, December, 2013.

sionaries serving with Christian Union Mission resided in Port Moresby from 1990 to 1995 for the express purpose of assisting the church plant. Ron Hood, who was working on his PhD at Fuller Theological Seminary, returned to PNG for two years to assist the churches and conduct research. The Hood family arrived on January 24, 1990[219] and remained until December, 15, 1991.[220] Miriam worked as a teacher at the Port Moresby International School, and she surrendered her salary to support the work in Port Moresby.[221]

As Hood's time in Port Moresby was coming to an end, he wrote a detailed report about his work with the Port Moresby church. He had witnessed "real indigenous growth of the Erima church" whose leaders had shown "maturity, foresight and surprising restraint in handling money matters."[222] The church people had visited in "hundreds of settlement homes, invited people to a Billy Graham crusade and had started home fellowships and plantation outreach" The church had an active youth group which was attended by more than 90 youth and they had been given contracts to clean the city markets to earn money for the group.[223] He concludes,

> Port Moresby has been a great experiment in indigenization. Since, in the early days, they had no missionary, and they got little help from the Highlands, they learned to expect more of themselves...I try to keep a low profile and let them lead...the PNG urban experiment is unique and has much to teach us. This is a truly indigenous work, probably because of our distance from rather than our presence in this work.[224]

During the next four years, three other missionary families were assigned to work in Port Moresby. Bill and Becky Benner were in Port Moresby for about two months during December 1991 and January 1992.[225] The Queen family was based in Port Moresby from January 1992[226] until their term ended in September of 1994, and Gene and Rosemary Lawhun replaced them.[227]

The mission was struggling financially and found it difficult to maintain a missionary in the national capital. The Lawhun family worked in Port Moresby for about ten months until the mission rented the Port Moresby house and reassigned the Lawhun family to Mount Hagen in July of 1995. After their departure, the mission assigned no other missionaries to reside in Port Moresby.

---

[219]Christian Union Mission Field Council Meeting Minutes, December 28-29, 1989, 1.

[220]Christian Union Mission Field Council Meeting Minutes, June 20-21, 1990, 4

[221]Christian Union Mission Field Council Meeting Minutes, December 28-29, 1989, 1.

[222]Ron Hood "Port Moresby Urban Ministries Coordinator's Report and Personal Report of Ron Hood" Christian Union Mission Annual Field Council Minutes, November 5 and 6, 1991, 17.

[223]R. Hood, "Urban Ministries and Personal Report," November 5 and 6, 1991, 17.

[224]R. Hood, "Urban Ministries and Personal Report," November 5 and 6, 1991, 18.

[225]Christian Union Mision Field Council Meeting Minutes, June 20-21, 1991, 5.

[226]Dean Queen, "Annual Report for Dean Queen and Port Moresby" in CUM Annual Field Council Meeting Minutes, January 11, 1993, 14.

[227]Gene Lawhun, "My Over View of the PNG Field" in Field Council Meeting Minutes, March 1, 5, and 6, 1995.

Tension in the home provinces spill over to the urban settings. After the 1997 elections, the church was deeply affected when fighting broke out between Nembi groups living on the Nembi plateau and in the Nembi Valley of the Southern Highlands Province. People from both sides attended the Erima church. Some people left the church and the attendance at Erima dropped to less than ten persons.[228] Pastor Pius Kopap was assigned to serve the church at Doa Plantation for a short time, but he returned to the Highlands, and the church closed. Another group began using the buildings that Christian Union Church had built on the plantation.

In 1993 the church was given a piece of ground at Eight Mile,[229] and in 1998 the leadership team built a church at Eight Mile where many of the original members had migrated. This allowed people living at Eight Mile to avoid the increasing criminal activity at Erima. However, by 2000 the attendance at all congregations had dropped, partly as a response to the fighting in the Highlands among the various Nembi groups.

The Port Moresby church had effective lay leadership teams from the beginning. When the people tell the church's story they consistently mention several lay leaders who contributed to the church's development. The first leadership group included a policeman, Henry Map and his wife Betty, who worked in the women's program for years. Two young men named Samuel Mulpe, an accountant, and Stoney Kumalo, a public servant, were very active in the church during its beginning days, but they have since left the church. Stoney's wife Nancy, a nurse, is currently a member of the Erima Congregation and serves as the District Treasurer. Marilyn, the wife of Philemon Embel, who was the Nipa/Kutubu member of parliament, faithfully attended the church at Erima for several years. She quit attending because of repercussions from the tribal conflict that erupted after the 1997 elections. Another influential woman in the church was Mapa Wap. She was active in the women's groups, gave significant input to the decisions that the board made, and served as the area treasurer for several years.[230]

Luke Moni Kowi, a man from the Lai Valley lived and worked in Port Moresby for several years and was very active in the Erima church along with his wife Delilah. He served as a church elder and helped establish the first congregation at Erima. He returned to the Lai Valley in 1996 and now actively supports the churches in the Lai District.[231]

Nicholas Nembo, who works for the national literacy awareness secretariat, participated in the church's leadership team for many years, but has now become a part of another movement. Paul Embel earned a degree in theology, and he studied law at the University of Port Moresby. He is a gifted person and a good speaker

---

[228]Interview with Nicholas Nembo held on Januarey 29, 2010 at MAPANG guest house in Port Moresby.

[229]Dean Queen, "Port Moresby Report January-June, 1993," Field Council Meeting Minutes, June 22, 1993.

[230]Port Moresby District leadership team, Interview by author, January 29, 2010 at MAPANG guest house in Port Moresby.

[231]Conversation with Miletus Nuepi, Port Moresby, December 6, 2013,

and has made valuable contributions to the leadership of the Port Moresby area churches and often assists by speaking at the churches and currently serves on the Port Moresby District Board.[232]

Reflection about Outreach to New Areas

The mission and church succeeded in planting churches and opening new districts in Hagen and Port Moresby, but not in Mendi. In Chapter Seven I tell the story of the establishment of Port Moresby and Hagen Districts. Conflict over the expectations that the church and mission had for each other lay at the heart of the failure to acquire land in Mendi. The mission and church waited on each other to take the lead in locating land. The church had no money to develop a property and wanted the mission to locate land, fund the purchase, and develop it with the expectation that the property would be jointly owned by church and mission and eventually turned over to the church. The mission expected the church to take the lead and contact their *wantoks* in the Mendi area to build a nucleus for a church plant.

Some missionaries considered Mount Hagen and Port Moresby to be more strategically located and prioritized them over Mendi. The mission lacked enough resources to develop more than one area or project at a time. Development of property in Mendi took a back seat to other projects.

When the work in Mount Hagen started, the missionaries made the first move. They then asked the regional board to provide Nembi pastors to network with Nembi Christians and open preaching points on the Mount Hagen plantations.[233] In town they invited a key pastor to help them start a church. Both the missionaries and the pastors networked with Southern Highlanders, but the Western Highlanders eventually formed the nucleus of the town church and district.

When asked why Mount Hagen Christian Union Church lasted when other attempts to plant a church failed, Simon En, the founding pastor, gave two main reasons. First, he was there because God called him there, not because the missionary had invited him to come. Second, people from the local area became involved in the church. Had the church been built around only Southern Highlanders, it would have failed because the people from the Southern Highlands are not rooted in Mount Hagen. They follow their education, their employment, their *wantoks*, and their whims, and then move on. Because the Hagen people became involved in the work, it has lasted. They have been committed to the church from the time they first began to attend. They truly own the church.[234]

From the outset, the mission involvement with the Port Moresby district has been less than it has with the other districts. The nucleus of the church was formed when Christian migrants from the Nembi area began meeting together for fellow-

---

[232]I have known both of these men for years and had repeated contact with them and numerous conversations about their role in the church at Port Moresby.

[233]Christian Union Mission Annual Field Council Minutes, April 28-29, 1985, 12.

[234]Simon En, interview by author, Mendi, Southern Highlands Province, Papua New Guinea, May, 2006.

ship without the direct involvement of either the church or mission. They knew other Nembi migrants who had relocated to nearby settlements and plantations and established networks that led to the establishment of churches in the Port Moresby area.

For almost six years from January of 1990 to July of 1995, the mission placed missionaries in Port Moresby. The missionaries worked closely with the church, but avoided taking control of the churches. Although the mission provided some funds to subsidize the church plant in Port Moresby, the financial assistance that the mission gave was minimal. In November of 1991 at the end of his two-year term, Hood, who was the first CUM missionary to reside in Port Moresby, reported that Erima church was "financially self-sufficient" although mission funds often "provided the initial impetus to get things going."[235] Hood said, "The national church here in Port Moresby doesn't want us to carry them; they do want someone nearby to offer a hand when it is needed."[236]

Traumatic Events

Between 1983 and 1999 numerous traumatic events occurred. These include home invasions, fires, the death of a missionary, and tribal fighting. I now tell the traumatic stories that deeply impacted the Nembi people, the church, and the mission's relationship with the church and the larger community.

The Nembi people assume that there is an underlying spiritual cause for whatever happens. In their traditional belief system, when things went awry, they believed that the spirits were displeased and wreaking havoc, and they performed rituals of appeasement to make things right. In their Christian belief system when things go wrong they assume that God is taking punitive measures because of some sin in their lives. The Nembi look at scriptures such as Nahum's oracle against Ninevah that says, "The Lord is slow to anger and great in power; the Lord will not leave the guilty unpunished."[237] In Romans, Paul instructed the Christians to love their enemies, and he said, "Do not take revenge, my friends, but leave room for God's wrath, for it is written: 'It is mine to avenge; I will repay,' says the Lord."[238] As Hiebert puts it, the God of scriptures "not only heals (Luke 4:40); He punishes (Acts 5:1-10; Rev19:11-16)."[239] When traumatic events occur, the Nembi people look for the underlying causes.

In contrast, the missionaries initially explained the trauma in terms of natural causes, but they explained repeated trauma in terms of spiritual warfare. For example, when a fire started from an overheated cook stove, the missionaries saw it

---

[235]Ron Hood "CUM Annual Report For 10/91 Annual Field Council POM Urban Ministry's Coordinator Report" Annual Field Council Minutes, November, 5-6, 1991 18.

[236]Ron Hood "Annual Report for 10/91 Annual Field Council POM Urban Ministry Coordinator's Report" Annual Field Council Minutes" November 5-6, 1991, 18.

[237]Na 1:3.

[238]Ro. 12:13

[239]Hiebert, *Anthropological Reflections on Missiological Issues*. [Grand Rapids, Mich: Baker Books, 1994] 211.

as a natural occurrence. However, when four fires occurred on the same station in seven years, the missionaries began to speak in terms of spiritual warfare.

Hiebert speaks of the flaw of the excluded middle. Western missionaries are trained in science and religion and separate the sacred and secular. They exclude the spirit world from their worldview. They have no explanation for disasters, calamities, illnesses, catastrophes, and other traumatic events other than "it just happened." He says that two-thirds of the people in the world believe that the cause for such events originate in the spirit world and turn to demons, witches, sorcerers, ancestors, magic, and astrology for answers. In contrast, the scripture offers a third worldview that takes "spiritual realities…the natural world and human beings very seriously" but focuses primarily on the relationship between God and human beings.[240] In Ephesians 6:12 Paul says that "our struggle is not against flesh and blood, but against the rulers, against the powers of this dark world and against the spiritual forces of evil in the heavenly realm."[241]

Regardless of the cause, the missionaries believed that God was in control and was omnipresent, and that He would use any and all circumstances to advance His kingdom. They focused on the words of Jesus who, when instructing his followers to love their enemies, reminded them, "He (the Father in heaven) causes his sun to rise on the evil and the good, and sends rain on the righteous and the unrighteous."[242] When Jesus told his disciples, "As the Father has sent me, I am sending you,"[243] it meant that there would be difficult times, but God would be with them. Jesus warned his disciples just before his arrest, trial, and crucifixion, "In this world you will have trouble. But take heart! I have overcome the world."[244] When home invasions, hold-ups, fires, tribal fighting, and death interrupted the mission's work, the missionaries believed that God was with them, protecting and guiding them,[245] even though they could not say why God allowed some events to occur. As Roman 8:28 says, "And we know that in all things God works for the good of those who love him, who have been called according to his purpose."

Home Invasions and Hold-ups

The law and order problems worsened in the Nembi area after the Highlands Highway opened up. The first home invasions occurred in 1980, when someone broke into the home of Bob and Sara Jones as they slept and stole a motorbike and some money. A few days later, someone broke into the home of Mary Hermiz at Ol, but no one suffered physical harm in either of these incidents.[246] The law and order problems throughout the country continued to escalate. Robberies, home

[240]Paul G. Hiebert, *Anthropological Reflections*, 189-201.
[241]Eph 6:12.
[242]Mt. 5:45.
[243]Jn. 20:21.
[244]Jn. 16:33.
[245]Isaiah 43:2
[246]Christian Union Mission Field Council Minutes, November 1, 1980, 1,

invasions, rapes and hold-ups occurred frequently in urban areas. The first major crime to touch the CUM missionaries happened on Thursday, April 25, 1985. The mission reacted without considering the repercussions to its actions.

Robbery at Knife Point

An annual field council meeting was scheduled to be held at Ka on Friday and Saturday, April 26th and 27th, 1985. All of the missionaries except for the Miller family and Eva Donahue, who planned to come to Ka early on Friday morning, had already gathered in the Nembi Valley at Ka and Farata stations in anticipation of the next day's meetings. During the day on Thursday, April 25th, some of the missionaries had gone to Mendi to pick up the mail and had taken payroll money to Eva Donahue who was the sister-in-charge at Ol Health Center.

That night as she was getting the payroll ready, two men armed with knives entered her home and robbed Eva of approximately seven hundred kina in cash and threatened to rape her, and in the process they stabbed her, severely wounding her hand. After Eva was robbed, the mountains reverberated with the calls of people shouting out the news of the event. The Miller family and Eva headed for Det as quickly as possible to get medical attention for Eva. At two different points the people had closed off the road, and they were delayed for about 15 minutes at each roadblock.[247]

The missionaries assumed that the road blocks had been put in place to assist the criminals, but according to Simon Papon, who was then the District Superintendent at Embi District, Christians had gathered at Embi station as soon as they heard people shouting out about the robbery. They were upset and felt that "rascals" had wronged them as well as Eva and the missionaries. They believed they had an obligation to right the wrong, but no one knew for sure what had happened. The missionaries left without talking to the church leaders or anyone else, and so they stopped the car because they wanted to hear a first-hand account of what had happened.

The missionaries who were gathered at Ka and Farata reacted swiftly when they learned of the incident. The next day the missionary men took all of the vehicles to Embi and Ol for an immediate evacuation of the two stations while the women and children waited at Ka where they were instructed to gather in the houses on one side of the airstrip. The evacuation created an immediate housing crunch for the mission as displaced families moved in with other families living at Ka. Eva left within a few days for a medical leave that lasted eight and one-half months. Christian Union Mission's involvement in the medical ministry came to an abrupt halt.

The missionaries left Embi without giving the people a chance to make things right. The people dubbed the mission the "*guria* (shaking, trembling, fearful) mis-

---

[247]Eva Donahue, "Medical Report 1985" in Christian Union Mission Annual Field Council Minutes, March 6, 1986, 4. In her report Eva does not say that the men threatened to rape her, but I and two of the missionaries I interviewed remembered her reporting the threat to the missionaries immediately after the incident.

sion." After the missionaries had gone, the people investigated the incident and eventually identified the persons responsible for the theft. One was from the Toiwara area, and the other was from Kongip near Embi.

Within the next few days the assistant provincial health officer and the nursing supervisor for the Southern Highlands Province went to the health center and closed it for an indefinite period of time. In May of 1985 the mission was due to negotiate a new three-year contract with the government effective as of April 1, 1986, to serve as the agency for Ol Health Center, but the mission opted not to renew its contract. With Eva's sudden departure the mission lacked adequate staff for the medical ministry. Prior to the home invasion two expatriate and two indigenous nurses worked at the health center. One of the expatriate sisters was scheduled to leave for furlough six weeks after the incident, and her replacement was no longer willing to work at Ol. One of the indigenous nurses had given notice that she was planning to get married and seek employment elsewhere, and the second indigenous nurse was a recent graduate who still needed to work under the supervision of experienced nurses. Some of the provincial and local government council members pushed for the government rather than the mission to run the health center.[248]

Some of the local men immediately began to collect money for a compensation payment to give to Eva and the missionaries, but the effort came to an unexpected end when a man who called himself Pineapple and was heading up the effort to raise the compensation was killed in a car accident.

When I interviewed both the Embi people and missionaries about the incident in 2009 and 2010, their memories of the incident were unclear. The Embi people said that everything changed for them in a single night. One day missionaries were living at Embi, and they had health services at Ol Health Center, but the next day the missionaries were gone and the health center was closed for an indefinite period of time. First the government and then the Catholics took over the administration of the health center until Christian Union Church reclaimed the agency in the early 1990s.

The majority of the missionaries said that they no longer recalled the details.[249] When one of the missionaries heard the term "guria mission," he said, "Well, we were afraid." Another said that in hindsight "over-blown, over react, and too quick" described the mission's reaction to the incident. One of the missionary men vividly recalled the outrage that he felt when he learned that someone had robbed and threatened one of the missionary women. The missionaries reacted out of fear and anger and a desire to protect themselves. As one missionary said, "It was a very 'expatriate' reaction." At the time some of the missionaries strongly objected to the swift reaction and the immediate evacuation of Embi station after Eva was robbed, and others insisted that it was the only course of action open to the mission. Regardless of their individual views, all missionaries participated in the withdrawal and the action has to be collectively owned.

---

[248]Eva Donahue, "Medical Report 1985" in Christian Union Mission Annual Field Council Minutes, March 6, 1986, 4.

[249]Some of the missionaries did not want their names to be used when they talked about this incident, and so I am not citing particular interviews in this section.

Within a year of the incident, the missionary staff was reduced from eighteen to six. Nine, including Eva went on medical leave, and only Eva returned to the field to complete her term. Three families left for furlough, and one of those families chose not to return.

The missionaries would have left Embi within a few weeks of the incident, even if there had been no abrupt evacuation of all personnel. Eva left immediately for medical leave, and the second expatriate nurse and her husband were scheduled to leave for furlough about two months after the incident occurred. Even before the robbery took place, Roger and Dianna Miller were considering leaving Embi and moving to Mount Hagen to help plant the church in there.[250]

The abruptness of the withdrawal did not allow mission personnel time to negotiate with the Catholics, the government, or the Embi people and find replacements to minimize the disruption to the medical services in the area. It also magnified the shame that the people felt over the incident. Denying them the opportunity to make amends created a scenario whereby they would live with the shame for decades to come.

In December of 1985 I moved to Embi after the CCCU general missionary superintendent and a member of the missionary board visited the field, and granted me permission to return to Embi for three or four months for the purpose of testing primers and other literacy materials. In March of 1986 when I was ready to resume work on the translation I moved back to Farata, but for the next four months I commuted to Embi most weekends for the purpose of visiting literacy classes and testing primers.[251] No other missionary lived at Embi until Butch and Leatha Jenkins returned in 2011. They continue to reside at Embi although they

---

[250]The Millers had first arrived in PNG nine months earlier on July 23, 1984. However, Dianna was pregnant, and after complications developed with her pregnancy, they went to Brisbane Australia on December 4th to await the birth of their son. They had been back at Embi with their baby for about three weeks when the attack occurred. They were still perfecting their Pidgin language skills and had very limited exposure to the vernacular (Dianna Miller, "Personal Report" in Christian Union Mission Annual Field Council Minutes, April 28-29, 1985). Their annual reports written before the robbery occurred, suggested that they had already applied to become the host family at Mount Hagen Missionary Home when Bill and Becky Benner went for furlough. Dianna said that while she and Roger were in Brisbane, God had provided extra indigenous nurses to keep Ol Health Center operable reinforcing the idea "of us (missionaries) working ourselves out of a job such as the *haus sik* (health work), so the Lord can use us in other areas." Because of her and Roger's time in Brisbane, "God opened our eyes to the needs of urban ministries throughout the world." She concluded her report by saying, "God is opening doors for different types of ministries for our lives, and we are open and accepting of the changes that he has in store for us" (Dianna Miller, "Personal Report" in Christian Union Mission Annual Field Council Minutes, April 28-29, 1985). Similarly, Roger concluded his report with the statement, "He is now leading us into new directions and we will continue to be obedient to his voice" (Roger Miller, "Personal Report" in Christian Union Mission Annual Field Council Minutes, April 28-29, 1985). They were being wooed away from the Nembi Valley to work in Mount Hagen.

[251]Ruth Tipton "Personal Report for Ruth Tipton" in Christian Union Mission Annual Field Council Minutes, March 6, 1986, 13.

travel to Mount Hagen every few weeks and return to the USA for short furloughs every two years.

In January of 2014, the church held a fifty-year celebration at Embi, commemorating the birth of Christian Union Church of Papua New Guinea. It was a time of looking back as well as looking to the future. I gave a presentation on the history during which I mentioned the robbery and the mission's immediate withdrawal from Embi and the closure of Ol Health Center. I acknowledged the mission's failure to give the people a chance to make amends for what had happened. After I was finished speaking, a pastor from Toiwara came forward and said that as a youth he had been involved in criminal activity and that he had committed the robbery. He said that he had been converted and had been a pastor for a number of years. He made a public apology for having committed the crime. When he had finished speaking, Robby Kopele, who is a pastor and the son of one of Embi's first pastors, also apologized. He wept as he spoke of the shame that he felt. He said that he and his entire clan carried the shame and deeply regretted the incident because one of their own had participated in the robbery.

Stateside visitors and some of the missionaries asked why Robby was apologizing for something in which he had no part and for which was in no way responsible. Michael Rynkiewich's article on *Person in Mission* says that Melanesians define persons in terms of relationships rather than seeing them as autonomous, self-directed individuals, and they "make decisions on the basis of how it will affect their relationships, not as if they were an island unto themselves."[252] When the man from Toiwara apologized, some of the Embi people said that they had carried the shame from that incident for twenty-nine years. The shame had been exacerbated by the fact that they had been unable to pay compensation and make amends and repair the relationship that had been damaged because the missionaries involved left so quickly. The mission had been so concerned about protecting its missionaries that it failed to consider the long-term effect that its hasty withdrawal would have on the relationship between the church and mission and with the people of the Embi area.

Rynkiewich says guilt is "the feeling one has when a rule is broken" and shame is a "failure of character." Guilt is paid for through punishment or recompense, but shame requires that a person be transformed from "a failure to success."[253] Paul Gilbert, who has studied shame, says that scholars have long linked shame to a sense of falling short and failing to measure up to the ideal, but some studies have suggested that shame occurs when persons feel that they have become what they do not want to be.[254] It is possible for people to

> have a sense of shame for actions that they were not involved in or responsible for.
> … It does not matter if one is rendered unattractive by one's own or other people's

---

[252]Michael Rynkiewich, "Person in Mission," 164.

[253]Michael Rynkiewich, *Soul Self, and Society* [Eugene, Or: Cascade Books, 2011], 74.

[254]Gilbert, Paul, "What Is Shame? Some Core Issues and Controversies." In *Shame: Interpersonal Behavior, Psychopathology, and Culture*, ed. Paul Gilbert and Bernice Andrews, [New York, Oxford University Press, 1998] 3-38.

actions; what matters in the sense of personal unattractiveness—being in the social world as an undesired self, a self one does not wish to be. Shame is an involuntary response to an awareness that one has lost status and is devalued.[255]

Shame may have an external source when a person feels that he or she is unable to "create positive images in the eyes of others," or it may come from within if a person sees himself or herself as defective and unacceptable and in a place he or she does not want to be.[256]

At Embi, the mission's immediate withdrawal was seen not only as a condemnation of the crime that had been committed, but also a censure of the entire community and a deeply rooted sense of shame emerged. The Nembi community also experienced both guilt and shame. There was no question that a wrong had been committed, and upon investigation it was clear that one of their own participated in the act.

Robbery at Gun Point

Seven years later a home invasion occurred on Ka station. Gene and Rosemary Lawhun were living at Ka when a gang of ten masked men invaded their home at 2:15 A.M. on February 10, 1992. Five were armed with shotguns and the remaining five had bush knives and axes. Gene distracted the men while Rosemary grabbed their younger daughter and slipped into the older daughter's room in hopes that she could protect them both. The men demanded money, and Gene gave them all he had, but they wanted more. One of the men entered the room where Rosemary and the girls were cowering, locked the door behind him and demanded money, but he left the room when the youngest daughter began to sob. When the gang was finally convinced that Gene had no more money to give, they ransacked the house taking many of the Lawhuns' personal belongings. They left at 2:45 A.M. telling Gene that if he reported what had happened, they would be back.[257]

The mission made arrangements for Gene and Rosemary to fly to Ukarumpa, the main base for the Summer Institute of Linguistics, where there was a counselor who specialized in working with missionaries who had been traumatized.[258] The Lawhun family considered returning to the USA, but after their counseling sessions, they decided to remain and finish out their term.[259] They opted to leave Ka station and move to Farata as soon as a house became available.[260]

None of the other missionaries living at Ka wanted to leave the station where Ka Community School, the workshop, and the Bible school were all located. The

---

[255]Gilbert, 22

[256]Gilbert, 17

[257]Rosemary Lawhun, "Terror at Night" *Missionary Tidings 44*, no. 5 [April/May, 1992]: 4.

[258]Rosemary Lawhun, "Terror at Night" *Missionary Tidings* 44, no. 5 [April/May, 1992]: 4.

[259]Don Seymour "Frontlines" *Missionary Tidings* 44, no. 5 [April/May, 1992]: 2.

[260]Christian Union Mission, Executive Committee Minutes, March 31, 1992, 1.

mission council had prioritized the Bible school over the town ministries, and was deeply committed to a joint Bible school venture with the Wesleyan mission that had just started.[261] The missionaries tried to improve the security of their homes by installing, security fences around their homes, security wire on all windows and heavier locks on all doors. They began keeping dogs for security both inside and outside their homes, but none left Ka out of fear for their own personal safety.

Reports about the home invasion were lodged with the police, but there was little response, and the culprits were never found. There was little reaction from the local community although some suspected that at least some of the gang members were from Ka. Later when Rosemary heard a young man from Ka talking, she said she recognized his voice as the voice of the gang's spokesperson during the home invasion. However, there was no proof, and although the family remained wary of him, no one made formal accusations.[262]

The Lawhun family was not physically harmed during the home invasion, but the emotional trauma that they experienced was equal to the trauma that Eva and the Millers experienced during the previous event.

Hold-Ups

During the late 1980s and the 1990s an increasing number of holdups occurred, especially in areas where there had been active tribal fighting. A number of CUM missionaries working in both rural and urban areas were held up as they traveled the roads. There were numerous incidents, but although the CUM missionaries were traumatized by the hold-ups, none suffered major physical harm.

Following tribal fighting in the Nebilyer area of the Western Highlands Province, travel between Mendi and Mount Hagen became difficult for all vehicles. Wherever fights occurred throughout the Highlands areas, gardens and homes were destroyed during the fight leaving the war victims without adequate food or shelter. The crime rate soared as local men held up any vehicle passing through the fight zone in order to get food for their families and finances for their fight. In the late 1980s or early 1990s Butch Jenkins was held up as he returned to Ka from Mount Hagen. Some time after the home invasion at Ka as Gene Lawhun was traveling to Mount Hagen, he was stopped by some men who attempted to steal the vehicle, but he succeeded in getting away with the vehicle. In 1991 Tim and Diane Bennett were held up near Nipa in an area where there had been heavy tribal fighting, but the men let them go when they learned they were missionaries.[263] In July, 1992, Dean Queen who was living in Port Moresby was dropping people off one night following a service at the church at Erima when a gang of men assaulted him and tried to steal the van.[264]

A couple of days after Christmas of 1994, Jim and Becka Johnson and Esther

[261]Christian Union Mission Field Council Minutes, June 20-21, 1991, 8-9.

[262]Personal conversation with Rosemary Lawhun.

[263]Diane Bennett "Protection in Time of Trouble" *Missionary Tidings* 44 no. 2, [October/November, 1991]: 6, 11.

[264]Don Seymour "Frontlines" *Missionary Tidings* 45 no. 1 [August/September, 1992]; 2.

Tipton and I were returning to Ka from Mendi. There had been active fighting at Farata, and a group of men with guns stopped the car. When they saw us, they said they thought the car belonged to someone else, and they let us go without taking anything.[265] In August of 1997, Dean and Shirley Queen and Darin and Lisa Stambaugh and two of the teachers from Ka Community school were returning to Ka from Mendi when a group of six to eight men had pulled a log across the road in an effort to stop the car. When Dean did not stop they stoned the truck, and hit passengers who were sitting in the back of the truck, but they got safely away.[266]

In the year 2000 Tim and Diane Bennett were in Port Moresby during some work on the Port Moresby house, negotiating a rental contract for some new renters, and conducting courses for the Port Moresby church leaders. They stayed at New Tribe Mission guest house while there, and used a vehicle that New Tribes rented to its guests for a modest fee. One evening, they made a trip to the mission house in Gordons, and they were held up as they stopped to open the gate to the mission property. The gang took the car and some of their belongings, but did no physical harm to Tim or Diane.

Missionaries and expatriates living in PNG were not the only victims of rascal gangs. Papua New Guineas frequently became the victims of violent crime as they traveled the roads and went about their daily affairs. I moved to Mount Hagen in 1998 to finish the translation of the New Testament because tribal fighting was so prevalent in the Nembi area that there was no place that I could safely convene the translation committee. After I moved to Mount Hagen, the translation committee members traveled there by a circular route that enabled them to avoid enemy territory. That route took them through Nipa.

During one of the sessions Dick Mune, the Southern Highlands Provincial Governor was killed in an automobile accident in the Lai Valley on his way to Mount Hagen to secure a flight to Port Moresby. Dick Mune was from Semin on the Upper Nembi Plateau near Nipa. After his death intense tribal fighting broke out at Nipa,[267] making it unsafe for the translator workers to travel home via their normal route. When the session ended I made alternate arrangements for a PMV from Kagua owned by a member of the Bible Missionary Church to take them to a place across the Erave River from Toiwara southwest of Poroma. From there they could have made their way safely through the bush to their home areas. The committee members refused to accept the arrangements that I had made because they did not know the people of Kagua, and they did not know that the owner of the PMV was trustworthy. They preferred to take their chances with the route they usually travelled through Nipa.

On their way home, they were held up and robbed near Nipa. They left their belongings and fled for their lives. Pastor Roman took off running with the others, but he fell, and he was surrounded by enemies. He cried out, "Oh Jesus, they are

---

[265]Personal recollection.

[266]Dean Queen "Missionary Mama" *Evangelical Advocate* 94 no 10, [May, 1999]: 12-13.

[267]Michael A. Rynkiewich, "Big-Man Politics: Strong Leadership in a Weak State," *Point Series no 24* [2000]: 14-45.

going to kill me now." However, the men let him go, and he along with all of the other committee members returned safely to their homes minus their money and their possessions. Pastor Roman said that Jesus had power. When it was time for those from the Nembi Plateau to return to Hagen for the next session, a policeman agreed to take them to Mendi. They left in the middle of the night, but the car broke down in the middle of enemy territory. Again they left their belongings and ran in fright through the bush to the safety of their own villages.[268]

Reflection about Home Invasions and Hold-Ups

Missionaries who were held up always thanked God for his protection. After the Bennetts were stopped at Nipa in 1991, Diane wrote to her supporters in the USA, "As we pulled away, I thanked God for His protection. Now I would like to thank those at home who have been supporting us with their prayers. God had given you an important ministry. Please don't give up. We need your prayers!"[269] Rosemary Lawhun said after their home was invaded that she wanted her daughters "to know beyond a shadow of a doubt that God was there and he protected them." She further admonished their supporters to keep praying for them saying, "We cannot continue to be effective for Christ without your intercessory prayers!"[270]

In March of 1992 after the Lawhuns were robbed and missionaries had been held up several times on the road, the home board asked the PNG missionaries how they felt about remaining in Papua New Guinea in light of the rascal problem. At a special meeting of the field council, the missionaries agreed to issue the following statements,

> We as a field do not feel that our work in Papua New Guinea is finished. Given the law and order situation in PNG, we realize the possibility of and even anticipate further incidents in which missionaries are targeted and victimized by rascals. In view of this, we earnestly desire that the home constituency be made aware of the situation in PNG so that we can be blanketed by volumes of unceasing prayer. In addition, we feel that certain practical preventive measures should be taken to help deter further attempts. The board should be advised that this will require immediate funding for the purpose of making our homes more secure by installing alarm systems, security doors, and iron bars on windows.[271]

There were increasing number of gang rapes occurring throughout the country, and the council was asked how it felt about having single women missionaries in PNG. They agreed on the following statement,

> We as a field do not say we can say no to anyone who strongly feels that God is calling them to PNG, but they should be fully informed of the probability that they

---

[268]Ruth Tipton, "Tipton Tidbits," March, 2000.

[269]Diane Bennett, "Protection in Time of Trouble" *Missionary Tidings* 44 no. 2 [October/November, 1991]: 11.

[270]Rosemary Lawhun, "Terror at Night" *Missionary Tidings* 44 no 5 [April/May, 1992]: 4.

[271]Christian Union Mission Field Council Mintues, March 20, 1992, 1.

could become a victim of violent crime. It is especially important to inform all young women, both married and single, and all parents of pre-teen and teenage daughters of this possibility.[272]

Protection came from the local people among whom the missionaries lived. For several years I was the only missionary living at Farata. The Farata men came to me more than once and told me that I was safe at Farata. They were my protectors. They would look after me the way that they looked after their sisters. As long as the Farata people were there, I felt safe. In Mount Hagen, too, the people made sure that I was safe. One night, not long after I moved to Mount Hagen in 1998, Pastor Marcus of the Mount Hagen church came to the house to warn me that he had heard that a rascal gang from a nearby village was planning to break into the house that night even though a man from the church lived in a room under my house for security purposes. He told me not to be afraid. A group of men would stay at the church all night and watch, and if they saw or heard anything amiss, they would be there to protect me. Nothing happened, and the next day Pastor Marcus and some other men from Bon village talked to the leaders of the gang's village. He informed them that I was their missionary, and under their protection, and if anything happened to me, it was happening to the whole village, and they would have to answer to all of Bon Village. There were no more threats against me or the mission property.

During the home invasion at Embi and the one at Ka, the feeling that the local people would provide protection was compromised. The mission's reaction to the two home invasions and the effect on the local communities was vastly different. At Embi, the mission abruptly withdrew from the station and did not give the local people a chance to investigate the incident or respond to it. The entire community owned the incident and felt shame but never dealt with the shame and remorse that they felt and the mission gave them no opportunity to make amends through compensation according to their custom. At Ka there was no suggestion that all of the missionaries should withdraw from the station. The local community never owned the incident or made any moves to recompense the Lawhuns or the mission for the goods they lost.

At Embi the mission's immediate withdrawal was seen not only as a condemnation of the crime that had been committed, but also a censure of the entire community and a deeply rooted sense of shame emerged. Even though a number of missionaries disagreed with the abrupt reaction to the crime and the immediate withdrawal from Embi, they all participated, and the Nembi community experienced both guilt and shame. There was no question that mission personnel had been wronged, and when the Embi community investigated the wrong it became clear that one of their own participated in the act. At Ka the missionaries condemned the crime, but did not censure the community as a whole in spite of suspicions that at least some of the perpetrators of the act were from Ka. The suspicions remained hidden, and no sense of shame developed among the larger community.

---

[272]Christian Union Mission Field Council Mintues, March 20, 1992, 1.

Farata Fires

On Farata station four houses burned between 1984 and 1990. Yako Sikap, my translation assistant was living in a small two room house. On November 4, 1984, the house caught fire from an overheated cook stove. No one was injured, but Yako and his family lost all of their personal belongings in the fire.[273]

The second fire took place on Friday night, the 25th of July, 1986. I was sharing the house with Eva Donahue. I had just finished a translation committee session, and I had gone to Embi for the week-end to test primers, so I was not home when the fire started. We had just purchased a new bottle of propane gas and leaned it against the side of the house so that we could connect it when the old tank ran out. Early in the evening, Eva heard a hissing sound and went out to investigate. Gas was leaking from the bottom of the new tank, but it stopped after a few minutes, and Eva assumed that all of the gas had leaked out of the tank. A couple of hours later just as the station pastor came to shut off the power, the tank started leaking again, and this time it caused a flash fire. The pastor shouted out to the people of Farata who came immediately. Eva and the Farata people saved some of the contents of the house and most of the contents stored in a nearby shed, but the house and most of our personal belongings were lost.[274]

The Nembi people responded to the fire by showing sympathy and taking up offerings to compensate Eva and me for our losses. There was some looting, but most of the Farata people had worked hard to save all they could from the fire. The people from Embi and Ka Districts and the officer in charge at Poroma raised funds on our behalf.[275] Sengi Iruwa, the Farata District Superintendent was gone when the house burned. When he heard about it, he rushed home and came immediately to Ka to see Eva and me. As he walked into the house he said my name, grabbed my hand, and burst into tears. For the people of Farata, the loss of the house was not just the mission's loss or something that Eva and I had lost. It was their loss as well. They had invited the mission to establish the station, and they accepted the responsibility for the missionaries who stayed there. Because the buildings were on their ground, they saw them as theirs, and when the house burned, they mourned the loss.

The third fire occurred a few months later. Yako Sikap had moved into an older house that had been vacated by the Farata district superintendent and the mission was planning on replacing. The cause of that fire is unknown, but it may have started from an over-heated wood stove.

---

[273]Christian Union Mission Field Council Minutes, November 23, 1984, 2. The minutes do not mention the date of the fire, but it happened on November 4, the day before the regional conference was scheduled to take place.

[274]Ruth Tipton and Eva Donahue, "Fire at Farata," *Missionary Tidings* 39 no. 3 [November, 1986], 4-5.

[275]Ruth Tipton and Eva Donahue, "Fire at Farata" *Missionary Tidings* 39 no. 3 [November, 1986]: 4-5.

The fourth and final fire happened in 1990 at the end of one of the committee sessions. The men used a bush building to cook and they had lined the perimeter of the fire pit with stones, and then laid dried sword grass near the stones. A spark from the fire ignited the dried grass near the fire pit, and in a matter of minutes, the entire building burned.

Each of the fires drew a crowd. After the fourth house burned down, on elderly man from Farata walked away, muttering to himself, "*And te, and te, and te. Su ngo por, nimi and ombun tiyaelleme.*" ("Burn houses, burn houses, burn houses. At this place, they burn all their houses."). After the fourth fire, the people said that Yako and I must have had some hidden sin in our lives, and God was punishing us for our sins.

The missionaries considered spiritual warfare to be the root cause. At a field council meeting held in October of 1990 after the fourth fire, the missionaries cited Ephesians 6:12 and noted that

> During the past few years…a number of events…could indicate that Farata Station has been under satanic attack. Four houses have burned to the ground, and a number of missionaries who have lived on the station have had physical and emotional problems. It has become evident that there is a spiritual dimension to these problems, and we are truly engaged in spiritual warfare.[276]

The missionaries and the Farata District church leaders and pastors, walked around the entire station perimeter stopping every few feet to pray and ask God to break Satan's power and protect the station from further attack.

In January 2014, when Rick Pombre, CUC's regional secretary and I wrote a Pidgin history for Christian Union Mission and Christian Union Church of Papua New Guinea, we talked about the fires at Farata. I told him that the Farata people said that the fires had occurred because Yako and I had hidden sin in our lives, and the missionaries' belief that they were engaged in spiritual warfare. He said that he agreed with the people. God must have been punishing Yako and me for some sin in our lives.

Death of Rosemary

Gene and Rosemary Lawhun first came to Papua New Guinea in July of 1981, and completed three full terms of service. During those three terms, they worked in both the Nembi area and in Mount Hagen. Rosemary worked in the medical ministry and assisted with women's ministries and the Bible school. Gene worked as a church advisor, assisted with the building and maintenance program, and worked in the Bible School. When they returned for their fourth term of service, they were based in Port Moresby where they lived from September of 1994 to July of 1995. The field council recalled the Lawhun family to the Highlands, and they relocated to Mount Hagen in July of 1995. The council then asked Gene and Rosemary to return to Ka to work in the Bible school. They moved back to Ka in November of 1995, but Rosemary died suddenly of a heart attack on Friday, December 1, 1995. Her unexpected death sent shock waves through the mission and the church.

---

[276]Christian Union Mission Field Council Minutes, October 1, 1990, 6.

Everything came to a standstill on Ka station as everyone, missionaries, church leaders, station staff, and teachers worked together to administer CPR, arrange for a medical evacuation through MAF via the station's radio transmitter, and let their daughters know that Rosemary had fallen. The older daughter, age 15, was at Ukarumpa High School and had to be reached via the radio transmitter. The younger daughter, age 11, was at Ka. She was still asleep, and we had to wake her up, and help her pack a bag for her and her dad to go to Hagen as soon as the plane came.

One of the workshop staff took a car and drove to the Catholic station at Det and brought back Sister Gaurdencia, a nurse and a Catholic Sister who assisted with CPR and flew to Mount Hagen with the Lawhun family. Someone else grabbed a chainsaw and cut trees that had grown so tall at the foot of airstrip that a plane could not land safely. When the Lawhun family and Sister Gaurdencia took off for Mount Hagen, the Johnsons and I promised to go to Hagen as quickly as we could. After contacting Ukarumpa High School and telling the school officials to let the older daughter know about her mother and make arrangements for her to fly to Mount Hagen, the Johnsons and I left for Mendi. The Bennett family was living in Mendi, but had their house packed up for a move to Hagen within the next few days, and they knew nothing of Rosemary's collapse.

The station staff, church leaders and teachers stood by at the scheduled radio times, to learn the final outcome. After we were gone, they raised money to give to the Lawhun family. All contributed, and when they received confirmation that Rosemary had died they set up a road block on the highway that passes through the station, and asked passing motorists to contribute as well.

In Mendi we learned that a doctor from Kudjip had arrived at the air strip and seen Rosemary shortly after the plane landed at Mount Hagen, and he had pronounced Rosemary dead on arrival. The Bennetts and Johnsons and I made arrangements to join the Lawhun family in Mount Hagen later that day.

Gene wanted to repatriate Rosemary's body to the USA. The next few days the missionaries, the people from the Hagen church, other missions and the business community helped secure the coroner's report, prepare Rosemary's body for transport to the funeral home in Port Moresby where it could be embalmed and made ready for repatriation, made travel arrangements for Gene and his daughters to return to the USA as quickly as possible. The missionaries agreed that Jim and Becka Johnson should travel with them to the USA. About three hundred attended a memorial service at the Hagen church on Sunday, December 3, 1995.

On Tuesday the missionaries returned to Ka so that the Lawhuns and the Johnsons could prepare for their trip back to the USA. Everyone worked together to get the Lawhun family and Jim and Becka ready to leave on Thursday. On Wednesday, December 6th there was a memorial service for Rosemary Lawhun on Ka station. The church leaders had spread the word of Rosemary's death to all of the districts, a total of five to six thousand people walked in from all of the districts to attend the service. Many of them had their bodies smeared with white clay as a sign of mourning. Rosemary had never isolated herself from the people.

She spent time with them; visited them in their gardens; and welcomed them into her home. She liked and respected them, and they reciprocated.[277]

When a Nembi person dies, the people hold a wake (*omnda*) for the deceased that lasts for several days, the corpse is on display as mourners come from far and wide to show their sympathy to the relatives of the deceased and wail and keen over the body. Many come bearing gifts that were traditionally combined and used in morturary payments.

According to Sillitoe, the Wola claim that the relatives of the deceased give as an expression of their grief, and others give as an expression of sympathy, but other factors such as the relationship they have with the relatives of the deceased, and their proximity to the deceased person's place of residence also affect the amount that is given at the time of death. [278] They give with the expectation that the gift will be reciprocated, but sometimes they give for "nothing" (*paeme*).

Ledermen, who studied the Mendi people, says that gifts that are given for nothing are unsolicited and are given in times of need such as when a youth is raising bride wealth or when someone dies. There is no formal arrangement between the parties, but there is an expectation that when the giver is in need, the recipient will assist as he or she is able.[279] She notes that in pre-colonial times people were expected to give *paeme* gifts to the relatives of the deceased before the burial took place, but the custom has changed because some missions disapproved of the exchange of wealth during times of mourning.[280] Among the Nembi, Christians now bring rice, fish, firewood, and money that is used to help feed the people who have gathered for the wake as a way of showing their sympathy to the relatives of the deceased. The Ka District church leaders, teachers, and staff took the lead in collecting funds to give to the Lawhun family as a show of solidarity and sympathy.[281]

On Thursday, December 7, 1995, the Lawhun family and the Johnsons started on their journey back to the USA. John Kingal who was one of the early converts at the Hagen church travelled with them. Kingal and the Johnsons returned to Papua New Guinea about two months later.

After the plane took off from Ka, the Bennett family returned to Mendi to finish packing up their belongings and move to Ka four days later. The Bible school was a ministry priority, and the missionaries agreed that without Gene

---

[277]I have written much of this section from memory, but verified it from articles that her missionary colleagues wrote for the *Evangelical Advocate* in her honor. The articles include Gene Lawhun, "God is in Control" *Evangelical Advocate* 91, no. 7 [March, 1996]: 10-11; Becka Johnson, "In His Hands" *Evangelical Advocate* 91, no. 7 [March, 1996]: 16, 20; Ruth Tipton, "I Will Never Forget" *Evangelical Advocate* 91, no. 7 [March, 1996] 14 and Evangelical Advocate 91, no 8 [April, 1996] 9, 11, 14; and Jim and Becka Johnson and Ruth Tipton, "It Just Happened" *Evangelical Advocate* 91, no 8 [April, 1996]: 12, 14.

[278]Paul Sillitoe, *Give and Take: Exchange in Wola Society,* [New York: Saint Martin's Press, 1979], 195

[279]Lederman, 35-36.

[280]Lederman, 160.

[281]Timothy Pe, interview by author, Mendi, Southern Highlands Province, Papua New Guinea, January 15, 2010.

and Rosemary Lawhun, the Bennett family should return to Ka and assume the responsibility for the Bible school. The next few days were among some of the most difficult days I had in PNG. Janie, the Lawhuns' housekeeper, and I worked and grieved together as we packed up the Lawhuns personal belongings according to the instructions that Gene had given us and emptied out the house so that the Bennett family could occupy it when they returned to Ka.

Tribal Fighting

During the colonial era, the administration forced a halt to tribal fighting, but after 15 years of peace, fighting reemerged on the Nembi Plateau on May 6, 1981.[282] From that time to the present, there have been periodical outbursts of tribal fighting in the Nembi area, and it affects every aspect of Nembi life.

The tribal fighting that broke out in 1981 died down by the end of the year and 1982 was relatively calm. It broke out again on the Nembi Plateau on March 8, 1983 after a head man at Obua was killed. Between March 1983 and February of 1984, thirty-seven people were killed. Government, mission, and headmen's intervention brought no resolution to the fighting.[283] There were temporary lulls in the fighting, but the underlying issues were not resolved, and peace was not formalized.

By the early 1990s tribal fighting had spread to the Nembi valley. It could break out suddenly with little or no warning. First one or two houses would be burned, and then if the groups could not reach an agreement, arrows would fly. In January of 1991, during one of Don Seymour's visit to the field, all of the missionaries had gathered at Ka for a field council meeting. It was a class day, and hundreds of Christians had gathered at Ka to attend their weekly classes. The people of Ka were in the middle of negotiations over a compensation payment when a scrimmage broke out at the head of Ka airstrip, and arrows were flying back and forth between the two groups. Dozens of people including pastors, men, women, and missionaries walked between the two warring groups shouting for the men to stop fighting. The rain of arrows ceased and the disputing factions negotiated and asked everyone to contribute to a compensation payment to help restore peace. Everyone including the church and the mission contributed, and a fight was averted, but tensions remained high for some time to come.[284]

Tribal Fighting at Farata

During the 1980s and the early 1990s, the bows and arrows and spears were the weapons of choice, but by the mid 1990s, guns became more prevalent. In March of 1994, fighting erupted at Farata after a teen-age girl died. Just a few

---

[282]Mary Hermiz, Health Secretary's Report Christian Union Mission Annual Field Council Minutes, January 15, 16, 1982, p 36.

[283]Gene Lawhun, "Combined Report" in Christian Union Mission Annual Field Council Minutes, February 3-4, 1984, 13.

[284]Christian Union Mission Field Council Minutes, January 15, 1991, 5-6.

weeks before her death, she had attended a wake for a child near Toiwara. While there a youth from Wasup near Toiwara, who was interested in her, gave her a cigarette that she smoked. After the burial she returned to her place. She was pregnant, and two weeks later she died due to complications from her pregnancy. The people of Farata blamed the youth who had given her the cigarette for using sorcery to kill her and demanded compensation.[285] Negotiations over compensation payments broke down, and a fight ensued.

Some interviewees said that the benefits that some of the groups had received from an oil company that was opening up the Kutubu oil fields was an underlying reason for the fight. The company upgraded the Poroma road and extended it to Moro near Lake Kutubu, passing through land belonging to groups from Mato to Toiwara. The land belonging to the Farata people bordered the Highlands Highway, and extended slightly beyond the Poroma road junction, but the upgrade had hardly touched Farata land. The oil company paid the people from Mato to Toiwara for the upgrade, but Farata was left out. They felt they had been slighted. [286]

Other interviewees disagreed and said that although some people think that business and the road compensation was an underlying cause, it had not been discussed during the negotiations over the death of the girl. When the negotiations broke down a fight broke out between Farata and Mato, two villages that were less than one-half mile apart. [287]

The first death occurred on Saturday, March 26th when someone from the Mato side secured a high-powered rifle with a scope and shot and killed a man from Det who had come to assist the Farata people with their fight. He was hiding in a clump of bamboo at a distance that an arrow could never have reached. After the first death, both sides prepared for a prolonged fight.

On Sunday evening, Wang, the headman from Farata knocked on my door. He told me that things were serious, and he was doing his best to stop the fighting, but a lot of people were angry and determined to fight. If he could not stop it and their enemies crossed onto Farata land, he would join the fight and defend his ground.

On Monday March 28th, tensions were extremely high, but some attempted to renew the negotiations. I had a vehicle at Farata. Sengi Iruwa, the Farata district superintendent who was a part of the Farata kin group came and requested to bor-

---

[285]I interviewed several people from both sides about the fight. All agreed that the fight broke when negotiations over compensation for the death of the young girl broke down. Some said that the Wasup youth had shared a cigarette with her, and she became ill after she smoked it. One interviewee said they had fornicated and later she died. Another said the people of Farata believed that the youth from Toiwara had performed sorcery to cause her death. At the time of the fight I heard that she was pregnant and had died from complications after a miscarriage.

[286]Susi Tio, interview by author, Mato, Southern Highlands Province, January 2, 2010; Napu Ker, interview by author, Farata, Southern Highlands Province, December 31, 2009; Thomas Kas, interview by author, Mato, Southern Highlands Province, December 31, 2009. The road may have passed through a few hundred feet of Farata's land, but very little.

[287]Sengi Iruwa, interview by author, Mendi, southern Highlanda Province, January 11, 2010.

row the car so that he could take his family and his possessions to safety at Ka. I did not want to remain at the station without a vehicle even for a short time. It was a couple of hours before I could talk to Ka on the radio transceiver, but I told him I would ask someone from Ka to come get him, his family and their belongings and take them to Ka when I talked on the radio. It was a mistake I have always regretted. The fight exploded before the radio time arrived, and the enemies from Mato crossed onto Farata's ground. When the men from Mato broke the Farata line of defense, I tried to find Sengi, but it was too late. He had already fled. Later all of his personal belongings were lost.

Both sides promised that they would harm no buildings on the station, but when they broke through Farata's line of defense, they swarmed the station and burned a chicken house at the station's entrance. Yako, my language assistant believed that he was in no danger, but even though he told the invaders that he was from Pomberel and had no part in the fight, they pointed a gun at him, and he fled, not stopping until he had reached the other side of the Nembi River. Rex, one of the Farata youths was shot in the face with a homemade shot gun, and the people asked me to take him to Det for treatment. I did that, and then went to Ka to let the other missionaries know that serious fighting had erupted at Farata.

The missionary men returned to Farata with me, and we arrived back about an hour after I first left. We learned that Wang, carrying a piece of roofing iron as a shield and a bow and arrows as weapons had joined the fight. When his enemies recognized him, they ran him down with a car, killing him, and then they axed him almost beyond recognition. The battle was over. The Farata people were routed, fleeing in fear of their lives. The few who remained collected Wang's body, and some were rolling on the ground in anguish over the loss of their headman. They carried Wang's body off to a place of hiding, so that their enemies could not come and further mutilate the body, and Farata was totally deserted.

The Farata people were my protectors, when they were routed, there was no security. The missionary men agreed that it would be unwise for me to stay at Farata without the protection of the local people. I grabbed a few personal belongings, packed up my computer, and translation work, and went to Ka for the night.

The missionaries at Ka were in transition. One family had just completed a three-year term and was starting their journey back to the USA on Tuesday, March 29th. Another family had just arrived and was scheduled to take the departing family to Mount Hagen to catch their flights to the USA, and to be gone for about a week while they purchased personal and ministry supplies. Another missionary residing at Ka was on vacation in Lae and would not return to Ka for a couple of weeks. That left just one family and I in the Nembi area for about a week.

On Wednesday morning, March 30th, I returned to Farata to meet Yako, my translation assistant who had returned to Farata the previous day. As I drove onto the station, I met Yako and two or three other men making a hasty exit. They told me that the enemies were coming, but that I should park my car near my house, and stay inside my house. Nothing would happen to me. I drove a few more feet and met the enemies, mostly youths carrying torches. They told me they thought that I was not around. I informed them that I had just arrived. They said I should park my car and go into my house, and they would not hurt me. They were going to burn out Farata Village. For the next couple of hours, I watched as they ransacked the village, burned houses, and destroyed gardens. They had promised not to harm anything that belonged to the mission, but they broke into Yako's house and into the district superintendent's house and looted both. As I saw them carrying off Yako's things, I told them that they belonged to Yako who worked for the mission and had nothing to do with Farata. One older man snatched a sleeping bag from a boy about 12 years of age and returned it to me. The boy threw himself onto the ground and had a temper tantrum screaming, kicking, and thrashing around because the sleeping bag had been taken away.

Someone started to break in the door to the storage shed, and I called out informing him that nothing belonging to the Farata people was in the shed, and they left it alone. Some women went into the gardens belonging to the translation committee, but they left when I told them that they were my gardens. A teenager came to the office door saying that he wanted to buy a Bible. I was incredulous and said, "You want to buy a Bible now, while you are ransacking gardens, looting, and burning houses?" When he said yes, I showed him one, and then I realized he was just checking the office to see if it held anything belonging to the Farata people. I told him to look around. Everything in the office belonged to me or the mission. He turned to leave and said, "Okay, I will take this." I was so angry that I snatched it out of his hands. I said, "You, will not! You will pay me two kina or you will not have it!" He left quickly.

A little later some older men from Mato came bringing a Coleman lamp and some other things that belonged to Yako. They gave them back to me, saying, "Here! Take these! They belong to the mission. We are not thieves. Our quarrel is not with you, your worker, or the mission." They left as quickly as they came.

By 11:30 a.m. the raiders were gone. But, it was clear that I could not safely continue to live at Farata. I went to the storage shed and collected storage drums, boxes, and suitcases and began packing everything up. There would be radio contact with Ka at 3:45 p.m. I was afraid that if I left the station my home and the office would be looted in my absence, and so I waited until the regularly scheduled radio time to inform the Johnsons at Ka that the village had been burned out and I thought we needed to evacuate the station. They brought all of the available mission vehicles, hired some local Public Motor Vehicles and brought workers who helped pack up everything and move out. We left the Farata around 1:00 a.m. leaving very little behind.

Eight hours later, around 9:00 the next morning, Jim Johnson returned to Farata to pick up the few things that had been left behind. In our absence, someone had broken into the houses, helped themselves to what they could find, and even pulled mirrors off the bathroom walls.

Everything we did was observed by people on both sides. I learned later that even while I was packing up with no one else nearby, the men from Farata had not forsaken their role as protector. They were hiding on a nearby mountain watching everything that happened. They had an M16 and some other weapons, and they had agreed that if anyone attacked or harmed me in anyway, they would rush in and fight my attackers. The other side claims that their battle was not with the mission, that they did not want the mission to leave, and that the houses had been broken into by "rascals" of a third group that was not involved in the fight. In short, they created the conditions where lawless men could do what they said they would not do.

Sengi could no longer stay at Farata, and he went to Ka and asked that the missionary men and the district superintendents stay at Farata to look after the station. Sengi said that the missionaries and the church leaders from Ka, Embi, Montanda, and the Lai Valley were not involved in the fight, and they could have stayed at Farata safely, and no one would have damaged the buildings if they had been occupied. They would not have killed church leaders or pastors from other areas because that was their custom. People on both sides of the fight had close ties with Christian Union Mission and Christian Union Church, and they say that no one would have disturbed the mission buildings because they belonged to God. In the buildings that were unoccupied, rascals from other areas may have come in and taken some of the window louvers, but the buildings would have remained intact.[288]

Farata was at the heart of the fight zone. None of the church leaders were willing to stay there, and the mission staff was small. At that time, there were only three male CUM missionaries in PNG. One was based in Port Moresby, and the other two were at Ka. For two months after we evacuated Farata, the missionaries made frequent day trips to Farata to check on things, but no one stayed at night, and the church leaders showed no interest in organizing a team to stay there to protect the station and the buildings. Someone began to vandalize the unoccupied buildings. Window louvers, plywood, and roofing iron were disappearing from the buildings a few pieces at a time.

Both the station and Farata village had a lot of large casuarinas trees. The mission paid to have the trees on Farata station planted after it first acquired the lease. Someone barked all of the trees both in the village and on the station, and then someone on the Mato side borrowed a chain saw from the oil company, and cut down all of the trees in Farata Village. Farata youth formed a gang and began holding up vehicles as they drove through the battle zone. They especially targeted vehicles belonging to the oil company because it owned the chain saw that had been used to cut their trees.

The missionaries wanted to practice good stewardship. The trees on the station were large enough to be sawn for lumber, and after they had been barked, the mission did not want to let "all that good lumber to go to waste." The mission cut down the trees and carried them to Ka where they were sawn into lumber, but it was exactly this action that turned out to be an insult to the people of Farata who believed that the mission had sided with their enemies. The Farata people became angry, disillusioned, and disenchanted with the mission because the people said that the final act that the victors in a tribal fight perform after they have vanquished their enemies is to destroy their trees.[289]

---

[288]Sengi Iruwa, interview by author, Mendi, Southern Highlands Province, Papua New Guinea, January 11, 2010.

[289]Sengi Iruwa, interview by author, Mendi, Southern Highlands Province of Papua New Guinea, January 11, 2010.

The mission added insult to injury by dismantling the buildings at Farata. To the missionaries, it made no sense to allow persons unknown to carry off the buildings piece by piece until nothing was left, and so the mission decided to dismantle the buildings and bring them to Ka where they could be sold or used in other building projects as needed. The materials from the district superintendent's house and the church were given to the regional church. The church leaders sold the materials and put the money in the regional treasury. The materials from the houses belonging to the mission were either sold or stored and used in subsequent building projects.

Most of the interviewees acknowledged that "rascals" from groups not involved in the fight were coming to Farata station and vandalizing the buildings, but they still insisted that the buildings would have remained intact if the mission had not dismantled them. The one exception was Susi Tio from Mato who lost her home, gardens, pigs, and money during the fight. She believed that the mission was wrong to cut the trees and dismantle the houses, and said that on one hand she struggled to understand the mission's actions, but on the other hand she knew that rascals would have taken it all if the mission had not removed the buildings.[290]

Church leaders later condemned the mission for leaving Farata too quickly and then further damaging its relationship with the people by cutting the trees and dismantling the houses. If the mission had allowed the enemies to burn the houses, or if rascals had carried off the houses, that would not have hurt the mission's relationship with the people of Farata. But when the mission dismantled the houses and cut the trees, it destroyed the relationship that the church and mission had with the people of Farata. The people say that, because of my gender, they understand why I left Farata when it became a battle ground, but they criticize the mission for leaving the station too quickly, denuding Farata station of its trees, and dismantling the buildings.[291]

The fight lasted for seven years, and many people on both sides including a number of headmen were killed. It wreaked havoc on the churches in the area. Susie Tio, who was from Mato, was a leader among the women's groups. After the fighting broke out, most of the men were involved in the fight, took no part in church services and even ridiculed the women who continued to meet for prayer every Sunday. Susie and four other women scattered during the week and went into hiding, but they gathered at Mato every Sunday to pray. They did not go to the church for their time of prayer, but they never failed to meet at Mato until all of Mato village was burned out. Then they moved to Poroma where they continued to hold their Sunday prayer meetings. Other women joined the group.[292] They met at Poroma for two years, but eventually, the fight spread to Poroma, and they moved further down river and were scattered.

---

[290]Susi Tio, interview by author, Mato, Poroma District, Southern Highlands Province, Papua New Guinea, January 2, 2010.

[291]Timothy Map, interview by author, Ka, Poroma District, Southern Highlands Province, Papua New Guinea, January 13, 2010.

[292]Susie Tio, interview by author, Mato, Poroma District, Southern Highlands Province, Papua New Guinea, January 2, 2010.

In 1999 the women of CUC decided to hold their annual camp at Poroma that had been laid waste by the fight. The women came from all of the church districts—Kar, Embi, Farata, Montanda, the Lai Valley, even Ialibu—and a lot of men came with the women. The women say that many of the men repented during the camp, and the fighting slowed after the women's camp at Poroma.[293] At first there were temporary truces, but in 2001 the two sides made a more permanent peace.

A few men refused to join the fight, and they became the leaders of the church remnant. Farata District was reorganized as Poroma District. Peter Rapu was elected as the District Superintendent and Peter Yaki was elected to serve as the assistant superintendent. They renamed the district Poroma District and began to rebuild it.[294]

Thomas Kas said that no outside group such as the police or the government stopped the fight. The people themselves decided they were ready to make peace in response to some of their own local leaders. They performed a peace ceremony. Each side killed five pigs, and exchanged the meat from the pigs that they had killed. They shook hands and then each side gave the other side two casuarinas trees that each side then planted on its ground. In 2010, the two trees that the Mato people received and planted were growing well. One of the trees that the Farata people planted died, but the other was thriving.[295]

Peace between the people of Farata and Mato has reigned since 2001, and the people of both sides have resettled their land. However, there remains a deeply rooted sense of "us" and the "other." One of my interviewees concluded his remarks about the fight by saying, "We hurt ourselves because we broke God's law, but on this side we are good people, and we like the other side. They are not. They are 'big headed', conceited, and jealous, and they don't like others."[296]

I found during my research that F. E. Williams who was the first anthropologist to study the grasslanders (as the Highlanders were then called), affirmed the significance of casuarinas trees during tribal warfare. For a few weeks during February and March of 1939, he lived among a group of people in the Augu Valley who were culturally and linguistically related to the Nembi people. He noted that each place had casuarinas trees and remarked on the pleasure the people took in the trees that "made the place good." He observed that "the ring-barking of the casuarinas trees" was a "feature" of local "warfare." An informant told him, "After you have killed one or two of your enemies, carried off their pigs, and burnt their houses, it is the crowning insult and injury to murder their beautiful

---

[293]Susie Tio, interview, January 10, 2010; Jenny Pe, conversation with author, December, 2009.

[294]Susie Tio, interview, January 2, 2010.

[295]Thomas Kas, interview by author, Mato, Poroma District, Southern Highlands Province, Papua New Guinea, December 31, 2009. I failed to ask him about the significance of the trees and what would happen if both of the trees died on either side.

[296]I interviewed a number of people at Mato and Farata from December 30, 2009 to January 2, 2010. They all alluded to "us" and "the other," but only one person put it so succinctly. I have chosen to withhold the name of the person who spoke.

casaurinas."[297] The missionaries were unaware of the significance that the Nembi people assigned to the cutting of trees in a fight zone.

The church leaders and people on both sides condemn the mission for cutting down the trees and dismantling the buildings on Farata station. They say adamantly that the mission and not the people destroyed the station. The people on both sides wanted the mission station to remain undisturbed. They claim that they cannot understand why the mission destroyed the station. The people say nothing about warriors swarming the station when they broke through Farata's line of defense, about burning a chicken house that was on the station, or about breaking into and looting houses on the station occupied by indigenous staff members. They insist that they would not have harmed the station trees, but someone had already barked the trees before the mission cut them down.

The missionaries assumed that the buildings they built and the gardens and trees they planted or paid someone to plant on their behalf belonged to the mission and that the mission had the right to use its assets as it saw fit. The Farata community assumed that they shared in the ownership of the buildings and the trees and that the mission had an obligation to protect the station and the trees. The trees and the station embodied the relationship between the mission and the people, and when the mission cut the trees it hurt the relationship.

The Farata people no longer welcome Christian Union Mission and Christian Union Church at Farata. When the fight ended and they reclaimed their land, they invited the Evangelical Church of Papua to build a church on the station site. They say that if the mission apologizes and pays compensation for destroying the station, they will welcome the mission back, but until that happens, they do not want Christian Union Mission or Christian Union Church at Farata.[298]

When I left Farata, I moved to Ka. The fighting in the Nembi area became more frequent. Five years later, in April of 1999, the missionaries left Ka during another time of tribal unrest.

Tribal Fighting at Ka

Following the 1997 national elections, fighting intensified in the Nembi area. When asked what sparked the fight between Utabia and Upa in 1997, the people say that a big-man from Upa was ill, and when his kinsmen tried to take him to the health center at Det, men from Utabia blocked the road and would not allow the car to go to Det. The fight broke out after the big-man died. If questioned fur-

---

[297]F. E. Williams "Report of the Grasslanders Augu Wage Wela" in Sir Hubert Murray. 1940. *Territory of Papua Annual Report for the Year of 1938-1939*. Canberra: Government of the Commonwealth of Australia, 42. Australia National Archives, Series Number M3816, Control Symbol 3 Item Bar Code 1182610 Page 362 of digitalized copy http://recordsearch.naa.gov.au/Search-NRetrieve/Interface/ListingReports/ItemsListing.aspx [Accessed on April 7, 2014]

[298]Mapunu, interview by author, Farata Station, Poroma District, Southern Highlands Province, January 1, 2010; Sengi Iruwa, interview by author, Mendi, Southern Highlands Province, January 11, 2010.

ther, the people admit that the refusal to allow the car to go to Det was politically motivated.[299]

When I left for furlough in May of 1997, the translation program was based at Ka, and the Bible school was in session. The elections took place in July of 1997, and fighting broke out in September.[300] By October of 1997 there was intense fighting between the groups in the Nembi Valley and the Nembi Plateau, and the Bible school was closed because of the fighting. Neither the students nor the indigenous teachers who were from the Nembi Plateau could safely remain at Ka. When I returned to Ka in March of 1998, the fighting made it impossible to convene the translation committee at Ka. The literacy coordinator who was from Utabia had lost two houses and his gardens had been destroyed. The translation assistant who was from the Nembi Plateau could not come to Ka.

Some of the people at Ka aligned themselves with the people of Utabia. The fighting never came onto the station even though the land belonging to one of the fighting groups bordered the station. The people of Tindom, who lived a mile or so beyond the station, were not a part of the fight. They put a marker at the lower end of the airstrip where the station bordered ground belonging to the one of the fighting groups; informed the groups involved in the fight that no one was to bring the fight onto the station; and patrolled the station. If either group brought the fight beyond the marker, the Tindom men said that they would join the fight on the opposite side. They also informed me that the missionaries were under their protection, and that we would be safe at Ka. They were watching out for us, and would not allow anyone to harm us.[301]

We lived within earshot and we frequently heard the sounds of battle, and at times we could see warriors gathered in the distance. The sounds of nearby fighting made it difficult to concentrate on any kind of work or carry out any effective ministry. Four missionaries were on the field, and we were all based at Ka. Dean and Shirley Queen were scheduled to leave for furlough in June of 1998, leaving only Linda Bell and me on the field for a few weeks until Jim and Becka Johnson returned to the field in July, and Tim and Diane Bennett came back in August.

In May the field council agreed to rent the house belonging to the Evangelical Church of Papua when it became available in October of 1998. In the meantime, those of us living at Ka kept a bag packed so we could evacuate quickly if the need arose,[302] and we moved mission records to Mendi for safe keeping. When given an opportunity to house sit in Mendi for MAF for six weeks, Linda Bell accepted and went to Mendi on May 25th, temporarily escaping the tensions.[303] When we learned that the Lutherans had a house that they were willing to rent immediately,

---

[299]Conversation with Rick Pombre, January, 2014.

[300]Timothy Map, interview by author, Ka, Poroma District, Southern Highlands Province, January 13, 2010. The fight was deeply rooted in politics. Timothy Map had contested the seat and lost. He came in fourth. According to Timothy the election was held in July and the fighting broke out in September of 1997.

[301]Ruth Tipton, E-mail to David Lattimer, May 22, 1998.

[302]Christian Union Mission Field Council Minutes, May 13, 1998.

[303]Dean Queen, e-mail to Don Hohensee, May 26, 1988.

the mission rented it, and when the Bennett family returned to the field in August, they lived at Mendi rather than Ka. In July of 1998, the Johnsons family returned from furlough and settled in at Ka, and Linda Bell returned to Ka.[304]

Sometime between October of 1998 and April of 1999, the mission and church made an effort to bring an end to the fighting between Utabia and Upa. The mission leaders held numerous meetings with the church leaders from all areas including those from Ka and Embi districts. They decided to try to forge peace between the fighting factions by carrying iron crosses to the fight zone and erecting them on both sides of the battle ground. On the appointed day, Jim Johnson and I trekked up the mountain from Utabia with a handful of church leaders and pastors who carried the cross to the battle zone where we waited for the contingent from the other side to arrive on the opposite side of the fight zone.

Tim Bennett and John Kingal loaded the second cross on a mission truck and drove along the plateau road to the fight zone where they hoped to erect the cross on the Upa side. They drove very slowly across the plateau road, and the church leaders carried megaphones and announced to the people what they were hoping to do. As they made their way across the Plateau, thousands of Christians from CUC and other churches lined up and walked behind the truck until "it looked like a human snake." When they arrived at the fight zone, they were met by a group of very determined men with guns who would not allow the procession to proceed any further. They were the fight leaders on the Upa side, and they were not ready to make peace. The men said that the mission and church had brought nothing to give them "*bel kol*"[305] and without that they would not allow the church and mission to erect the crosses on the fight zone. Timothy Pe, who was one of the church leaders, was driving an ambulance that belonged to Pumberel Health Center, and when he edged the ambulance forward beside the truck, the men thought that Timothy was trying to pass the mission truck and proceed to the battle ground. They attacked the ambulance, breaking out the lights and windows, and ripping out the wires under the car's hood. Tim Bennett laid the cross on the ground near the fight zone, and the procession turned back. Someone came to the edge of the battle ground and called out to those of us waiting on the other side that they were not coming, and we left the other cross laying near the Utabia side of the battle ground and returned to Ka. The church and mission failed in its effort to forge peace that day.

Although the mission had extended discussion with the church leaders before attempting to erect the crosses, it had failed to have discussions with the fight leaders on the two sides. In November of 2009 I interviewed the leaders of Port Moresby district, and some of them had participated in the attempt to erect the crosses. Stephen Kelle said that the people were divided. Sone wanted to join the Christians and stop the fight, but others said they still had lives to avenge and they

---

[304]Jim and Becka Johnson, interview by author, Tarlton, Ohio, October 15, 2010.

[305]*Bel kol* means literally "cold stomach." It means to be at ease or at peace. They were not willing to reconcile unless they received some kind of compensation for the losses they had suffered.

could not stop fighting.[306] Sillitoe says that among the Wola, fighting ends when the casualties on both sides are fairly even and the majority are ready to call a halt to the hostilities and return to a more "natural flow of life."[307] Trompf notes that in Melanesian warfare, the side that is winning will push for peace while the losing side will resist because they want the opportunity to avenge their losses.[308] When the mission and church carried the crosses, no matter how many people wanted peace, the effort was premature, and no peace could be established until the score between the two sides was evened out. The fighting continued for several more years. When I interviewed the Port Moresby District leaders, several of the board members agreed that the fighing had ended and the people now travel freely between the Nembi Valley and the Nembi Plateau. However, one man, who is from Utabia, said that they had not received all of the reparations payments that they had been promised, and "*lain bilong mi i gat belhevi i stap.*" (My kin group is still troubled or worried or dissatisfied.)[309]

Reflection about Tribal Fighting

The devastating effects of the tribal fighting cannot be overstated. At Farata, the station was in the middle of the fight zone and there was no one to act as the protector of the station. At Ka, the fight zone did not surround the station. The Tindom people who were not aligned with either side in the fight, became the protectors of Ka station and the missionaries living there. The district superintendent of Farata District pleaded with the missionaries and the church leaders to send a group to the station to act as its protectors, but they were unable and/or unwilling to fulfill his request.

During tribal fighting in the Nembi area, the church has been a restraining force. Church attendance drops off during a fight, partly because it is not safe to meet together, and partly because many leave the church to join the flight. Some men refuse to fight because they fear God and think that it is wrong to kill other people. The translation committee members were either pastors or committed members of the church.[310] They talked about the role that Christians played in the tribal fights. First, they refuse to fight, but some do go to

---

[306]Port Moresby District Board Member, interview by author, Port Moresby, National Capital District, Papua New Guinea, November 23, 2009.

[307]Sillitoe, *Give and Take*, 81.

[308]G. W. Trompf, *Payback: The Logic of Retribution in Melanesian Religions.* [Cambridge, UK: Cambridge University Press, 1994], 98.

[309]Port Moresby District Board, interview by author, Port Moresby, National Capital District, Papua New Guinea, November 23, 2009.

[310]All of the members of the translation committee were men. They were selected by their districts and sent to serve on the committee. Several times I asked the church leaders to appoint women to serve on the committee, but they never did. Christian Union Church and the Catholic sent men to serve on the translation committee, and occasionally, but not consistently, the United Church sent a representative to the committee.

the battle ground, stand at a distance and watch the fight.[311] They carry water and food to give to the fighting men if they need it. They also run onto the battlefield to retrieve a kinsman who has been killed or injured in the fight. They refuse to knowingly give money to buy guns or ammunition for the fight, but admitted that money they give for compensation may be diverted to purchase weapons. They contribute to compensation payments for the death or injury of an ally who has been injured in the fight, because the only way to stop the fight or keep it from becoming worse is to give compensation. The Christians give in hopes of stopping the fighting. The Christians pray. The women, especially, are the prayer warriors, but the men who refuse to fight also pray for the fight to end.

Departure from Ka

For years, the mission made plans to move out of the Nembi Valley. From the time that the mission first talked about leaving Ka, the missionaries kept the church leaders informed about its intentions to leave Ka. The local land owners were aware that the missionaries intended to leave at some point. The discussions with the church leaders prompted rumors about the mission's departure from Ka, and the landowners moved to reclaim their land. At one point one of the local land owners threatened the field superintendent, after the land owner built a house on mission ground and the field superintendent asked him to remove it. In January of 1993 the field superintendent[312] reported that he had spent hours trying to "smooth over relations" with the local people regarding land.[313] The church leaders considered the landowner problems to be the mission's problem rather than their own. I recall missionaries discussing the issue with church leaders at the church/mission coordinating council. When asked to assist with the landowner problems, the church leaders said that it was "*samting bilong misin*" (the mission's concern), and did not assist or intervene.

The mission kept the church leaders informed about its plans to eventually withdraw from Ka. The church leaders voiced no objections, but they expected the mission to leave its assets behind. The mission, on the other hand, had no plans to leave all of its assets behind. The buildings would be turned over to the church, but other assets would be required to begin a work elsewhere. Vehicles and equipment that the mission no longer required would be sold at fair market value. The church would have the first chance to purchase the items, but if the church did not

---

[311]Those who were watching the fight, but not participating in it, were sometimes killed if they got caught in the cross fire or if they got too close to the active fighting.

[312]The field superintendents changed frequently. Each time one field superintendent returned to the USA on furlough, the home board appointed another man to serve as the field superintendent. Most of the field superintendents held their position for no more than two years. The frequent change in field leadership hampered the mission's ability to carry through with its established plans.

[313]Butch Jenkins, "Field Superintendent and Personal Report" in Christian Union Mission Annual Field Council Minutes, January 11, 1993.

come up with the money then they would be sold elsewhere. It was a matter of good stewardship in the mission's eyes.[314]

The fighting after the 1997 elections made it impossible to carry out ministries at Ka, and the mission planned to relocate as soon as possible. Even while the missionaries still remained at Ka, the land owners occupied some of the empty buildings. The translation committee could not gather at Ka, and all of the language buildings were locked. One day I discovered that someone had broken the lock on the *haus kuk* (bush kitchen) and fastened his pigs inside. I was angry. I released the pigs, and then I went looking for their owner. When I found him, I informed him that he had no right to break into a locked building and fasten his pigs inside. I had released his pigs and put a new lock on the cook house. He was furious, and picked up a piece of lumber and was ready to hammer me on the head, but one of the bystanders stepped in between us and he dropped the plank. He informed me that Ka was his ground, and the houses on that side of the air strip belonged to him. I had no right to be there, and I should get out and go to Mendi, or Hagen or anywhere away from Ka.[315]

After that encounter, I was ready to leave Ka as soon as I could. The translation committee could not convene anywhere in the Nembi area, and even Mendi was off limits to some of the committee members because of fight alliances.

In August of 1998, the missionaries decided to withdraw all missionaries from Ka as soon as they could find housing for everyone elsewhere.[316] I moved to Mount Hagen in September of 1998, and a week or so later the other single woman missionary living at Ka moved to Mendi, leaving only Jim and Becka Johnson and their young daughter at Ka. Jim began to shuttle the missionaries' personal effects to Mendi and Mount Hagen.[317]

From the beginning of the fight, the missionaries asked the people not to bring weapons onto the station. When Jim saw some men with guns and told them not to bring their guns on the station, they told him that it was their ground and they would carry their guns wherever they wanted. They said that they watched him, and they knew he was gone a lot, and they threatened to harm his wife and daughter when he was gone. At that point Jim knew that it was time for him and his family to leave Ka. After that Jim insisted that Becka and their daughter travel with him whenever he left Ka station.[318]

---

[314]Christian Union Mission Field Council Minutes, April 26, 1996, p 1-2.

[315]Later I had amicable contact with the land owner. He never gave a verbal apology for breaking into the building or for telling me to leave Ka, but when I saw him a couple of years after I left Ka, he made a point of coming to me and shaking hands and being friendly. When we shook hands, I interpreted his actions as a non-verbal apology, and I think he interpreted my willingness to shake hands as acceptance of his apology and possibly as an apology for releasing his pigs. I never gave a verbal apology for letting out the pigs. When I returned to PNG in 2009 to do research, he sought me out when he heard that I was back, and he introduced me to some other people as "his missionary."

[316]Christian Union Mission Field Coundil Minutes, August 26, 1998, 110-98.

[317]Jim Johnson, "A Lae Adventure," *Evangelical Advocate* 94 no. 5 [December, 1998], 12.

[318]Conversation with Jim Johnson,

Before the mission left Ka, the missionaries decided to discuss with the RBT the possibility of dismantling some of the former Bible school building and using the materials to build district superintendents' houses at Poroma and in the Lai Valley.[319]   Subsequently, a church mission coordinating council meeting took place at Montanda sometime before the plans for the mission's final departure from Ka were solidified. At the meeting the mission discussed the possibility with the church representatives. The Ka district superintendent was in the meeting, and he reported the discussion to the people at Ka. Tim Bennett, the field director, lived in Mendi. He slept at Ka after the meeting and planned to return to Mendi the next day. Early the next morning a large crowd of people gathered outside the Johnsons' house where Tim Bennett stayed. A man named Tefnas, who was the local government councilor, served as the spoke person. He informed Tim and Jim that the mission was not going to dismantle any building on Ka station. If the mission started to tear down any buildings, the landowners were going to kick the missionaries off Ka station right then, and the mission would leave the place naked (*lusim dispela ples as nating*). After that the missionaries knew that if they revealed their plans to leave Ka, they would leave "with just the shirt on our backs and have nothing to start over with somewhere else."[320]

The mission located a compound at Ialibu that was available for rent and had a workshop and adequate housing for the Johnson family and other missionaries. The council agreed that Jim and Becka Johnson should leave Ka as soon as arrangements for the final departure could be made. Because of the tribal unrest and the landowners' threats the missionaries decided not to inform the local people or the Ka District church leaders that its planned departure was imminent.[321] The mission did hold a meeting in Mendi with the church leaders from the other district to inform them of their plans. They agreed to the mission's plan at that meeting, but afterwards denied having any prior knowledge of the move.[322]

The mission withdrew from Ka on April 15, 1999.[323] The mission hired trucks from a trucking company to carry cargo and equipment to Ialibu, and it hired policemen to stand guard to make sure the landowners did not interfere with the move. Both the landowners and the church leaders were taken by surprise and said, "*Misin i hansapim mipela.*" (The mission held us up.) Tensions were high when the mission packed up and moved out. It took several days to complete the move. Tensions became so great that the mission decided not to take the generator in order to avoid a confrontation between the police and the local people.[324]

---

[319]Christian Union Mission Field Council Minutes, August 26, 1998, 110-98.

[320]Jim Johnson, interview by author, Tarlton, Ohio, October 15, 2010.

[321]Field Council Minutes, Papua New Guinea, Attachment 1, Notes on Preliminary Planning Session Papua New Guinea Field, February 5, 1999. The decision to move to Ialibu was by common consent, and there is no record in the minutes of the field council taking a formal vote on the move. However, the rental property had been located by February of 1999 and the departure from Ka was being planned.

[322]Jim and Becka Johnson, interview by author, Tarlton Ohio, October 15, 2010.

[323]Ruth Tipton, e-mail to Dan Tipton, April 16, 1999.

[324]Diane Bennett, e-mail to Dean Queen and M. Hohensee, April 9, 1999.

Andrew Inja is from Ka, and was one of the local landowners. He had two years of training at CLTC, but he dropped out of school to get married. He became deeply involved in the leadership of Ka district, and in early 1996 the regional conference voted him in as regional superintendent. His three years in office were marked by controversy.[325] When the regional board removed him from office, he left the church and demanded that the mission pay him seven or eight thousand kina to compensate for his early termination from office. His demands and threats were relentless. The mission was getting ready to leave Ka, and the council agreed to give him the largest house on Ka station in lieu of a cash settlement.[326]

All other buildings were designated either for Ka Community School or for Ka District church. Missionaries gave the keys to the buildings to Simon Map who was a member of the Ka District board and told everyone that the houses belonged to the district. Local landowners who were not a part of the church wrestled the keys away from Simon, and occupied the vacated buildings.[327] When one of the local landowners insisted that the buildings belonged to the church, he was badly beaten by some of his brothers who occupied the houses and claimed them as their own.[328]

Rumors about the mission's departure from Ka abounded. One rumor that persists to the present was that people on the Nembi Plateau had acquired a bomb, and the mission was afraid that they were going to drop the bomb at Ka, and so the mission left.[329] This is an unfounded rumor. The missionaries left because it was impossible to carry out any kind of ministry at Ka at that time, and because landowners threatened the personal safety of the missionaries who remained at Ka.

After the mission left, Ka landowners said that the mission shamed them and it

---

[325]Several times during Andrew's three years in office, the regional board put Andrew on probation, and his assistant acted as the regional superintendent. Andrew wanted to go to the USA as a representative of the church, and in February of 1997 the field council said that if he went to the USA, he must first get a letter of approval from the regional board of trustees with a guarantee that they would cover his full expenses, that he had to follow the guidelines of WGM and CCCU while in the USA, that he would return any of the money left from his trip to CUC of PNG, that any money that he received from the churches in the USA was to be turned in to CCCU or WGM, and that his kin group must agree not to ask for compensation if he was injured or killed during his trip. He never received the approval from the regional board of trustees, and he never went to the USA. Andrew blamed the missionaries.

[326]Kanj Mesmba, interview by author, Port Moresby, National Capital District, January 29, 2010; Field Council Minutes, Papua New Guinea, February 5, 1999, 22-99; Conversation with Rick Pombre, January, 2014.

[327]Simon Map. I did not get to interview Simon Map as I had planned, but he was present when I interviewed Timothy Map, and when Timothy talked about the missions' withdrawal from Ka, Simon said that the missionaries handed him the keys when they left Ka.

[328]E-mail to M. Hohensee, John Muehleisen, and CCCU missionary department, April 17, 1999.

[329]Timothy Map, interview by author, Ka, Poroma District, Southern Highlands Province, Papua New Guinea, January 13, 2010. A number of other people I interviewed mentioned the rumor about the bomb.

was wrong to carry off the cargo and equipment that had been kept at Ka. Therefore, the mission owed them compensation, and if the mission refused to pay compensation, none of the missionaries would be allowed to travel through Ka. The mission felt that it had done no wrong and refused to pay the Ka landowners any compensation.[330]

Rynkiewich says that in the past Melanesians who surrendered land to missionaries did so "in the hope that the newcomers would be a help to the community."[331] When the Ka people surrendered the land to the mission, they were not giving up their ownership rights. They were establishing a relationship that they expected to benefit their group, and they assumed co-ownership of the resources that the mission brought and the buildings that the mission constructed. The mission considered the houses, equipment, vehicles and other resources to be its own, and assumed that it had the right to dispose of its resources as it saw fit. The mission expected the buildings to go to either the church or the school, but the landowners believed that their claims to the buildings superseded the rights of the church.

During the fight, the people from Utabia and Tindom told us missionaries that they were glad we were there because our presence helped provide security for the station and ensure that the property would not be destroyed during the fight. We found it impossible to carry out effective ministry, and none of us thought that we should remain just to secure a piece of ground. The Christians from Ka District say that we abandoned them during hard times. Almost all of the people that I interviewed from Ka District started their story by saying, "*Misin i lusim mipela long taim bilong trabel, na misin i rong long go long taim mipela i stap long hevi.*" ("The mission left us when there was trouble, and the mission was wrong to leave when we were struggling.")

In sum, for us missionaries the move was about safety, good stewardship, and the diminished ability to carry out the ministries that we felt God had called us to. For the people it was all about fraternal relationships, economic *divelopmin,* and political alliances; and the mission's withdrawal of personnel and assets undermined all three.

Conclusion

Christian Union Church of Papua New Guinea is a self-supporting, self-governing, self propagating, self-ministering, and self-functioning church. It struggles financially and does not understand why the mission resists giving them a monthly subsidy, but it continues to carry out ministries. The mission gives some assistance to the church, in response to specific requests, but the church and mission are at odds over finances. Christian Union Church was birthed in the Nembi area of the Southern Highlands Province, one of the less developed areas in PNG. Bryant Allen reports that in 2000 more than seventy-five percent of the people in the

---

[330]Christian Union Mission Field Council Minutes, August 5, 2000, 21-00.

[331]Michael A. Rynkiewich "Introduction: The Land and Churches Research Project," in *Land and Churches in Melanesia: Issues and Contexts*, ed. Michael A. Rynkiewich Goroka, [EHP, Papua New Guinea: Melanesian Institute], 9.

Southern Highlands live on "poor to medium quality land," and have been unable to generate significant cash incomes. In 1996 the majority of people living in the Southern Highlands received an annual cash income of less than twenty kina. The Southern Highlands is considered to be a "disadvantaged" province because of its "poor environment, low cash income, and poor access to markets and services.... The most disadvantaged people in the SHP are those on the Nembi Plateau and in the higher fringes of the Mendi Basin, where agricultural pressure on land is strong, incomes are very low, and the population densities are high."[332]

The cry of the church leaders is that the church has little because the people have little to give. Like the politicians who seek to bring outside income to their areas to promote *divelopmen*, the church leaders seek outside funds to promote the development of the church. They expected the mission to provide money to allow them to carry out its ministries. The church consistently over-estimates the amount of resources available to the mission and can not understand why the mission insists that the church should rely on resources generated from within the country.

The tensions between the church leaders and the mission parallel the tensions between Australia and Papua New Guinean leaders during the struggle for independence. The political leaders looked to Australia for a large portion of its revenue, but they did not want Australia to control their country. Sir Albert Maori Kiki, one of the men who pushed for independence from Australia said, "The fact that Australia provided the largest share of our revenue did not entitle it to domination. It is a false and out of date idea that grants in aid must have strings attached."[333] It was the expectation of the PNG political leaders who pushed for independence in the early 1970s that the Australia government would continue to provide them with substantial aid after the territory became an independent nation.[334] In other words, they wanted to continue to be dependent on their relationship with someone who had the resources that they needed.

Frequent tribal fighting has aggravated the church's lack of adequate resources. The Nembi Christians become victims of the fighting. In the heat of battle, they lose gardens, houses, property, and other personal assets. In addition, their group expects them to contribute to compensation payments or other obligations that the group incurs because of the fighting. As a result the offerings they give to the church diminish.

When the mission withdrew from Ka taking with it vehicles, equipment, furniture, and other belongings, both the Ka landowners and the Ka District church leaders felt the mission was abandoning them during its time of need and stripping

---

[332]Bryant Allen, "The Setting: Land, Economics and Development in the Southern Highlands Province," in *Conflict and Resource Development in the Southern Highlands of Papua New Guinea*, eds. Nicole Haley and Ronald J. May [Canberra: Australia National University E Press, 2007], 40, 41, 44.

[333]Albert Maori Kiki. *Kiki: Ten Thousand Years in a Lifetime, a New Guinea Autobiography.* [New York: F.A. Praeger, 1968], 154.

[334]Michael Somare, *Sana: An Autobiography of Michael Somare* [Port Moresby: Niugini Press Pty Ltd, 1975], 145.

them of assets that they had come to consider to be their own. During the next few years the fighting grew worse throughout the Southern Highlands Province. At first the mission maintained a presence in Mendi, but when the mission temporarily withdrew its personnel from Mendi in 2002 because of political instability, most of the Nembi church leaders also expressed feelings of abandonment. I tell that story in the next chapter.

Chapter Six

Maturation

Introduction

Chapter Six tells the story from April of 1999, when the missionaries withdrew from Ka and relocated to Mendi, Ialibu, and Mount Hagen, to 2015, when CUM missionaries (two families) were located in Mount Hagen.[1] The relationship between the church and mission went on a downward spiral when the mission phased out the church's monthly subsidy, withdrew missionaries from Mendi, sold the mission property in Port Moresby, and used the funds from the sale to develop the Bible school property. Relations improved after the Bible school reopened, the mission leadership changed, and a missionary family returned to the Nembi area. The relationship plummeted again in 2013 when the field council sold the original mission property in Mount Hagen to secure funds to further develop the Bible school property. Whenever the mission assumed the right to act alone without collaboration with the church, the relationship suffered.

When the mission first left Ka, the field director lived in Mendi, other missionaries lived in Ialibu and Mount Hagen, and the mission's top priority was the reopening of the Bible school in a new location. I begin the chapter by telling the story of the completion of the Angal Enen New Testament and its dedication in 2002. I then briefly tell the story of the mission's time in Mendi and the relocation of the Bible school to Mout Hagen, and I conclude the chapter by writing about the events that most profoundly affected the church/mission relationship. Although tensions dominated this relationship, at times the church and mission came together in a very positive way. The church/mission dedicated the Angal Enen New Testament in March of 2002, and the districts started new churches. The church formally recognized Mount Hagen and Port Moresby as districts. A church leader and pastors who had been displaced during tribal fighting established a new area now called the Lower Mendi Area. The church reached out to new areas and established new districts.

---

[1] A family was based at Embi on the Nembi Plateau until they left for an early furlough during the first week of February, 2015.

The Dedication of the Angal Enen
New Testament

There were many interruptions to the translation work. The translation ministry was based at Farata from the mid 1980s until March of 1994 when tribal fighting led to dismantling of Farata station. It was then based at Ka. When I left for furlough in May of 1997, the translation program was based at Ka. When I returned to PNG in March of 1998, I lived at Ka, but tribal fighting had erupted between Utabia and Upa. It was impossible to safely convene the translation committee at Ka. My translation assistant could no longer come to Ka because his group was aligned with the people of Upa.

At the end of May I started commuting to Montanda to meet with my translation assistant for two or three days each week to work on the translation. At the time the mission had only one operable vehicle, and so I traveled to and from Montanda on a PMV that dropped me off about a mile from the station. I walked in and camped out in the former missionary house where I carried my water, cooked on a single burner kerosene stove, and used a Coleman lamp and candles for lighting. My translation assistant walked to Montanda from Embi, and we worked together. The arrangement did not work well. We were expending a lot of energy, and little translation was completed. I was soon convinced that I needed to move out of the Nembi area if the translation were to be completed. At first I planned to relocate to Mendi, but a man from near Mendi joined the fight, aligning himself with the people of Utabia. He was killed in the fight, and his gun was seized. His group sent out word that they would payback their kinsman's death by killing someone from the Nembi Plateau, and it was no longer safe for the translation committee to meet in Mendi.

I moved to Mount Hagen in September of 1998. The translation committee members traveled there by a circular route that enabled them to avoid enemy territory when they came to Mount Hagen. The men slept in a Sunday school room at the church in Mount Hagen, and they cooked, showered, and worked under my house. They stayed at the house until it was time to go sleep, and the entire group made their way back to the church for the night. Some rarely went to town because they feared that they would be spotted by some of their enemies and attacked even though they were on "neutral" ground.

The Angal Enen New Testament was ready for typesetting by February of 2001, and the dedication took place at Poroma during the third regional camp meeting that was held from March 25 to 29, 2002. The fighting between the Nembi Valley and Plateau had eased. The tribal war between Mato and Farata had raged for seven years, but about six months before the dedication of the New Testament, the two sides reached a peace agreement. Still, the people had not yet returned to their abandoned ground and homes. Poroma was a government station filled only with vacant buildings that remained intact. The church/mission got permission to hold the camp at Poroma and to use the vacant buildings to house those attending the camp.

The New Testament dedication took place on Good Friday, March 29, 2002, the last day of the camp. The morning began with a pig kill, and the dedication service took place while the pigs were roasting in the pit. The service concluded with a ceremony of presentation[2] before people came forward and purchased the New Testaments. The pits were opened and the pig meat distributed to the people who walked back to their districts where they held Easter services.

One of the Highlights of the dedication camp was a special offering that was taken for the Bible school in Mount Hagen. The church leaders agreed to take up the offering, and John Muehleisen, who was then WGM's vice-president of field ministries, promised that World Gospel Mission would triple the amount that the church raised for the Bible school.

When Daniel Pe, who was the acting regional superintendent announced that they were ready to take the special offering, one pastor stood and said the church wanted the mission to fund the Bible school because they were too poor, and could not assist. Several others voiced similar sentiments. After the naysayers voiced their objections Daniel Pe and several others spoke in favor of taking the offering, and asked for people to give or pledge whatever they could to help get the Bible school started. People stood, gave offerings, and made commitments to support the Bible school. Even the pastor who spoke first and said they were too poor to give anything to the school pledged to give one hundred kina. When the offering was counted, the total in kind, cash, and pledges came to K17,700 and seven pigs.

The next day all of the members of the regional board of trustees stood before the people and pledged to use the money that came in for the Bible school only for the Bible school.[3] Not everybody paid the pledges they made at the camp, but in January of 2004, the regional board of trustees had K6700 to use towards the cost of running the school when it opened.[4]

---

[2]At the beginning of the ceremony Tim Bennett, the field director opened a carton of New Testaments and handed a stack of New Testaments to the CCCU general superintendent who had come from the USA for the New Testament dedication. The general superintendent passed them to me, and I placed them in a string bag that the members of the translation committee were holding. They marched around and sang a song about God's word and then the CUC regional superintendent removed the Bibles from the string bag, and handed a copy to each of the district superintendents, leaders of the Catholic Church, and CUC women's leaders.

[3]David Lattimer, "A God Moment at Poroma" *Evangelical Advocate* 98 no 10 [June, 2002], 9-10; Jim and Becka Johnson, "Look What God is Doing in Papua New Guinea" *Evangelical Advocate* 98 no 12 [August, 2002], 12; Diane Bennett, "A Story to Tell" *Evangelical Advocate* 99 no 3 [November 2002], 16.

[4]Christian Union Mission Field Council Minutes, January 30, 2004.

Mendi

As I said in Chapter Five, from October of 1998 until August of 2010, the mission rented a complex in Mendi that belonged to the Evangelical Church of Papua (ECP). In 1999 the church appointed Simon En to plant a church at Tupiri on the outskirts of Mendi. The mission employed him to work as security for the compound and provided him with housing. Thus, the rental property provided housing for the missionaries and the Tupiri pastor, a place to hold meetings, and an office for the church. The drive for starting the church at Tupiri came from the Wara Lai District and the regional board of trustees, but the mission assisted with the church plant. I now tell the story of the mission's decision to withdraw from Mendi.

Political unrest escalated in the Southern Highlands Province leading up to and following the 2002 national elections and the subsequent supplementary elections held in 2003. At first the fighting was sporadic. It would erupt and be very active for a few weeks and then die down. Things would return to normal only to have the fighting reemerge with greater vengeance a short time later. The fighting first broke out in Mendi in December of 2001. The fighters destroyed businesses, homes, and school buildings,[5] and within a week more than fifty people had been killed. The Mendi hospital closed its doors because the warring factions on both sides threatened to burn the hospital down if the staff gave any kind of medical assistance to any of their enemies.[6] An entire section of town near the market and along the road leading to Mendi high school and the hospital became a fight zone. The fighting died down during the political campaigns, but it started up again with a vengeance after the elections were over.

The fighting was severe during the second half of 2002. Nichole Haley and Robert J. May, researchers who were associated with the Australian National University, reported that in December of 2002 fire destroyed fourteen government offices in Mendi. Travel throughout the Southern Highlands Province was dangerous, and because of the turmoil, airlines cancelled their regularly scheduled passenger flights into Mendi. Most expatriate workers including missionaries, volunteers, and aid workers withdrew from the Southern Highlands Province. Few public servants remained at their posts although many continued to collect their pay. Australian travel authorities warned visitors to avoid Mendi.[7]

In June or July of 2002, the mission temporarily withdrew its missionaries from Mendi because of the mounting violence but continued to rent the property. During the peak of the unrest the missionaries did not make regular visits to the Southern Highlands Province. The Tupiri pastor continued to live on the rented property, and the church leaders used an office, but they complained that the mission had abandoned them. By July of 2005 when I returned to Mendi, the political tensions had eased, and I lived in Mendi on the rented compound for two

---

[5]Dean and Shirley Queen, e-mail to friends and supporters, December 18, 2001.

[6]Dean and Shirley Queen, e-mail to friends and supporters, December 22, 2001.

[7]Nicole Haley and Ronald J. May, *Conflict and Resource Development in the Southern Highlands of Papua New Guinea,* [Canberra: Australia National University E Press, 2007], 1-2.

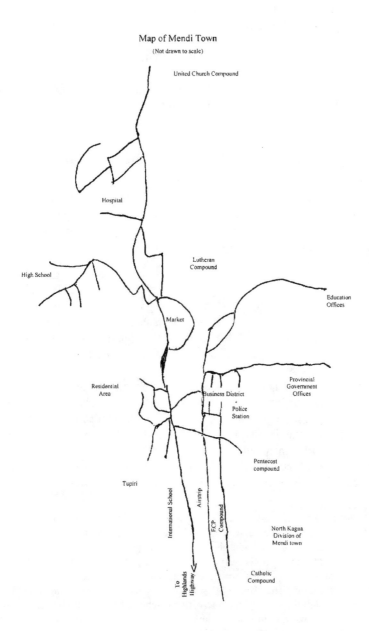

Map of Mendi Town
(Not drawn to scale)

Map 7: *Mendi* (Not drawn to scale)

years. After I left the field, missionaries made more frequent trips to the Southern Highlands, and used the rental as their base in the Southern Highlands. In 2010 the demand for rental properties in Mendi skyrocketed as companies developing gas and oil projects in other areas of the Southern Highlands looked for housing in Mendi. ECP raised the rent on its property, and the church/mission could no longer afford the rent and vacated the premises. Although they had looked for property in Mendi, the church and mission failed to find property that suited both parties.[8]

The Relocation of the Bible School

Finding ground to relocate the Bible school as quickly as possible became the mission's top priority after it left Ka in 1999. For two years, the church and mission visited several sites in Mendi, Ialibu, and Mount Hagen, and the missionaries and church leaders agreed that the school would be placed at whatever suitable property first became available at any of the three locations.[9]

Land Acquisition

In February of 2002 the mission began negotiations for the purchase of a site in Mount Hagen located on traditional land a short distance up the road from the Hagen CUC church.[10] At a CMCC meeting the regional board of trustees agreed to purchase the property, saying that they wanted the Bible School and it did not matter where it was located.[11]

The mission and land owners agreed to finalize the purchase of the ground in Mount Hagen on November 10, 2002, but the church also wanted the mission to reestablish its presence in Mendi. At CUC's regional conference held in September of 2002, the delegates voted that Tim Bennett, the mission director who was then on furlough, should live in Mendi when he returned. Mendi was more central to most of the CUC churches and the cost of travel to Mount Hagen made it difficult for the church leaders to have regular contact with the field director.[12]

---

[8]In 2001 the Mendi lands office granted a church/mission lease on a piece of property at the edge of Mendi in the Tupiri area. The mission planned to deed one-third of the land to the church and to proceed with the development as soon as possible (Christian Union Mission Fuield Council Minutes, April 20-21, 2001, p, 1), but the church leaders rejected the lease because some of them were traditional enemies with the Tupiri people and were afraid to go there (Christian Union Mission Field Council Minutes, September 14, 15, and 17, 2001, 4). I tell the story of the international school later in this chapter. In August of 2010 William Kowi, the provincial administrator offered the church a piece of property near the Mendi public market (Jim and Becka Johnson, interview by author, Tarlton, Ohio, October 15, 2015), but in the end the church failed to acquire the property (Jim and Becka Johnson, e-mail to Ruth Tipton July 31, 2014).

[9]Christian Union Mission Field Council Minutes, September 14, 15, and 17, 2001, 57-01.

[10]Christian Union Mission Field Council Minutes, February 13-14, 2002, 02-02.

[11]Christian Union Mission Field Council Minutes, November 9, 2002.

[12]Daniel Kor, Regional Secretary, "Letter from the RBT to the CMCC meeting in De-

The regional board of trustees sent a letter to Tim Bennett informing him of the regional conference's action. Tim Bennett responded to the letter saying that his family would not live in Mendi and explained why.[13]

The regional superintendent and the assistant regional superintendent were to be among the signatory parties on the Bible school land agreement. When the two men came to Mount Hagen for the final purchase of the land, they refused to sign the land agreement unless the field director agreed to live in Mendi.[14] This delayed the purchase of the land for the Bible school,[15] and prompted a series of e-mail messages and phone calls among the missionary families on the field, the missionaries on furlough, the WGM field director, and the CCCU leaders. Stateside leaders called a special meeting of the WGM and CCCU leaders with the PNG missionaries in the USA to discuss the situation. Tim Bennett, who was on furlough, the WGM director of field ministries, and the newly appointed WGM regional director, traveled to PNG in December of 2002 to meet with the church leaders and the missionaries in PNG.[16]

The meeting with Tim Bennett and the overseas officials took place on December 11, 12, and 13, 2002. The regional board of trustees learned that the property belonging to the former international school at Mendi was up for sale. They investigated the property and decided that it would be suitable for the Bible school and came to the meeting with the contact information for the person in charge of the sale. They favored placing the Bible school at the international school in Mendi because it was already "government titled" and was more central to most of the CUC churches. They believed "that God had opened Mendi just in time" and they would avoid landowner problems that would surface if the Bible school was located on customary land near Mount Hagen. They brought several other requests to the meeting, but everything else was secondary to the purchase of the Mendi property. [17]

---

cember 2002" in Papua New Guinea field Council Minutes and CMCC Summary", December 11, 12, and 13, 2002.

[13]Christian Union Mission Field Council Minutes, Novemver 9, 2002. The correspondence between the regional board of trustees and Tim Bennett was the only item on the agenda. The regional board insisted the Tim must live in Mendi when he returned. Otherwise, the RBT did not want him to come back to PNG. Tim's reasons for refusing were that Mendi was not a safe place to live at that time, and travel out of Mendi to Port Moresby and the other provinces was difficult. In addition, two of his children were attending Ukarumpa High School, and by living in Mount Hagen, the road trip to Ukarumpa was shortened by four hours.

[14]Jim and Becka Johnson, e-mail message to PNG missionary staff, WGM headquarters, and CCCU missionary headquarters, November 11, 2002.

[15]Becka Johnson, e-mail message to Queens, Bennetts, Ruth Tipton, Neals, D. Johnson, and Kevin Zirkle, December 6, 2002.

[16]Dennis Johnson was the WGM vice-president for field ministries, and Kevin Zirkle, a missionary to Japan, was the newly appointed WGM regional director

[17]Daniel Kor, Regional Secretary, "Letter from the RBT to the CMCC meeting in "Christian Union Mission Field Council Minutes," December 11, 12, and 13, 2002. The other requests were for the mission to be responsible for building pastors' houses and

During the negotiations with the church, the mission agreed to pursue the purchase of both properties. The Bible school would be placed in Mount Hagen, and the property in Mendi would be used as the regional headquarters for CUC, a training-conference center for the church, and a base for missionaries working in the Southern Highlands.[18]

The church leaders were elated at the prospect of acquiring the international school property in Mendi, and although they still wanted a missionary to live in Mendi to work with the church, they no longer insisted that the field director had to be placed in Mendi.[19]

In July of 2003 the mission signed an eighteen-month lease with the International Education Association (IEA) for the school property in Mendi. The property required a lot of maintenance to the fence, the water tanks, and especially to the main house. The security guard who worked for the IEA had occupied the main house.[20] He refused to move out because he claimed that the IEA owed him forty-five thousand *kina* in compensation for a broken arm and some gardens.[21] By the end of September, 2003 he continued to live in the main house. The mission placed its own security guards on the premise, paid part of the electric bill, and kept the grass cut, but because of the IEA security guard, the church/mission could not occupy the property.[22] As promised, the missionaries placed a bid of 120,000 *kina*, the original asking price, for the purchase of the Mendi International School property, but in the end, the mission was out-bid and someone else purchased the property.[23] The failure to acquire the Mendi property, from the point of view of the church, became another of the mission's broken promises and a point of contention between the church and the mission.

The church/mission finalized the purchase of the land for the Bible school in Mount Hagen on December 23, 2002 during a ceremony held on the property in the presence of church leaders, land owners, mission representatives, and govern-

---

purchasing land for "new works," and for the mission to start ACE (Accelerated Christian Education) schools for the children of pastors and church leaders. This was the first time that the church mentioned ACE schools. The PNG Bible Church sponsors ACE schools for Papua New Guineans. They select their most gifted students and send them to the USA for college and even high school training. Many never return, but those who do become well-heeled business men, public servants and politicians and some give generous contributions to the churches that helped them get their start. The church leaders reasoned that if CUM helped them start ACE schools for the children of pastors and church leaders, many of those children would be able to go to the USA to complete their education. They would return and generously support CUC, and the church would have adequate funds to carry out its ministries.

[18]Christian Union Mission Field Council Minutes, December 11, 12, and 13, 2002.

[19]Dennis Johnson, e-mail message to Dale Dorothy and Hubert Harriman, December 12, 2002.

[20]Christian Union Mission Field Council Minutes, July 26, 2003, 43-03.

[21]Dean Queen, e-mail message to Ruth Tipton, Dennis Johnson and Kevin Zirkle, July 28, 2003.

[22]Dean Queen, e-mail to Ruth Tipton, Dennis Johnson, and Kevin Zirkle, July 28, 2003.

[23]Christian Union Mission Field Council Minutes, January 19-25, 2007, Appendix 1B.

ment officials.[24] The mission began immediately to clear the land, landscape, and fence in the land in preparation for the construction of buildings, but these were only cosmetic solutions to real underlying problems.

Problems with the Land

The customary landowners had previously sold the property to another man, but he had not maintained a good relationship with the landowners or developed the land. Consequently, the landowners decided to sell the property to the mission, without providing clear title. The mission checked with the landowners and with lawyers about the rights that a previous owner had to land after it had been sold to another buyer.[25] It appeared that everything was in order when the mission purchased the land, but when the church/mission began to clear the land, the previous landowner and others made their discontent known. As Rynkiewich says regarding church land matters: there are "original landowners (a group) who assume that the land is ultimately still their own...(and) there are always other claimants to church land, some legitimate and many false, and they will make their claims known at a time that they choose."[26]

In February of 2003, a work team came from the USA to Mount Hagen with the goal of building a storage building on the new property and assisting with the landscaping and fencing.[27] The previous buyer showed up with two truck loads of men and tried to stop the work. The police came and intervened and the work was allowed to start.[28] A group of the original landowners then came and demanded that the mission pay for the right to use the road to the building site.[29] The provincial government built the road years before the mission purchased the property and it was supposed to be open to the public. The original landowners claimed that they had never been paid for the road and they wanted the mission to pay to

---

[24]Christian Union Mission Field Council Minutes, December 11, 12, and 13, Update on Land Purchase. John Kua was the regional superintendent at the time that the agreement was signed. When I interviewed him in December of 2009, he said that he refused to sign on the church's behalf because he thought it was a mistake to purchase the land in Mount Hagen. Instead Kanj Mesmba who was the assistant regional superintendent and William Wop who was the regional treasurer signed on the church's behalf. Kua did not want the mission to purchase the land in Hagen because he thought that the landowners would make additional demands after the papers were signed. He had worked on the plantation in the Hagen area for years and the Hagen people customarily demanded more after agreements were finalized. He wanted the Bible school to be located on government titled land in either Mendi or Ialibu rather than purchase new property in Mount Hagen.

[25]Christian Union Mission Field Council Minutes, October 12, 2002, 28-02.

[26]Michael A. Rynkiewich "Some Practical Advice on Church Land Matters" in *Land and Churches in Melanesia: Issues and Contexts*, ed. Michael A. Rynkiewich, [Goroka, EHP, Papua New Guinea: Melanesian Institute 2001], 340-341.

[27]Don Seymour, "Let's Go to New Guinea!" *Evangelical Advocate* 99 no 9 [May, 2003], 12-13.

[28]Diane Bennett, "Road Blocks," *Evangelical Advocate* 99 no 9 [May, 2003], 12-13.

[29]Diane Bennett, "Road Blocks," *Evangelical Advocate* 99 no 9 [May, 2003], 13.

use the road. The mission refused and told the landowners to take up the problem with the provincial government rather than the mission. The landowners lodged a lawsuit against the mission, and the mission hired lawyers who handled the negotiations with the landowners over the use of the road.[30]

Problems with Utilities Right-of-way

By September of 2003, the property was fenced in, most of the landscaping was completed, and the first house was under construction. Houses on the opposite side of the road were serviced by PNG Power, and the electric company agreed to extend the lines to the Bible college property. The local landowners, however, would not allow the electric or the telephone companies to put up new poles on their land or let power or telephone lines pass through their airspace, denying the mission those services on the Bible College property.[31] The mission installed a generator to supply the Bible school property with electricity a few hours each day.

Four years after the mission purchased the Bible school property, the Hagen churches held an evangelistic campaign early in January of 2007. John Kingal, who was one of the local landowners and the principal of the Bible College, participated in the campaign. As the final service was closing, he told the group that he was having some "discouraging times." Several of the pastors from area churches questioned him about his "discouraging times" and three offered to serve as mediators between the landowners, the mission, and the church for the utilities right of way. After several weeks of negotiations, the mission paid the landowners for the right of way.[32] In addition the mission gave gifts to the villages, the village counselors, John Kingal and the three area pastors who had led the negotiations,[33] but it was another six years before power was installed at the Bible College property.[34]

Rynkiewich writes about the relationship between churches and landowners in Melanesia and suggests that for cultural reasons, a church will never be the sole claimant for a piece of land. People launch claims against the church when they feel they are no longer in relationship with the church. In Western thought, autonomous persons exist prior to relationships. Each individual must develop his or her set of relationships. This is contrary to Melanesian thinking that says the relationships exist prior to persons and that "relationships develop the person." Relationships are formed through exchange, and objects, knowledge, or secrets that are surrendered in a relationship are not alienated from the person who surrendered them but are thought to be "safe in the relationship," that is, neither per-

---

[30]Christian Union Mission Field Council Minutes, April 9, 2003, 22-03.

[31]Dean Queen, e-mail to Tim Bennett, Ruth Tipton, Dennis Johnson, Kevin Zirkle, and George Neal.

[32]Becka Johnson, "Utility Right-of-way Update," *Evangelical Advocate* 103 no 5 [May/June 2007], 21.

[33]Christian Union Mission Field Council Minutes, January 12, 2007, 1-07; 2-07.

[34]Christian Union Mission Field Council Minutes, January 31, 2013, 2-13.

son has exclusive ownership, but both have claims that are secure as long as the object or land is not alienated from the relationship. Things that are given away are separated rather than alienated from the giver. When landowners surrender land, they are not alienating the land and giving up all future claims to it. They are establishing a relationship between themselves, and those who receive the land. The "buyers" or receivers of the land are entering into a relationship with the givers of the land. The land is safe in that relationship because it belongs to both the giver and the receiver.[35]

Problems surface if the church (or mission) denies the rights of the giver and the obligations of the receiver of the land. Rynkiewich says, the

> Church administrator would like to have legal ownership and free use of the land... as in other countries. However, church leaders will never have a solitary claim to land in Melanesia. There will always be other claimants and confusing complications. Therefore, the church is advised to be more realistic...and to enter into and work with the system as it is. While clear and uncontested title...is not a likely outcome, the church can have a high degree of security of tenure on the land. However, the work of sustaining claims on land will be a never-ending process for the church, as it is for all Melanesians.[36]

The problems that surfaced over the power lines came in part because some of the landowners felt they had been slighted when the mission first purchased the land and, therefore, were not included in the relationships that had been formed between the mission and other landowners. The excluded landowners would not allow the power lines to pass through their gardens or over their coffee trees. During the negotiations in January and February of 2007, the mission, church, and landowners held several meetings to discuss the situations. All expressed their concerns, and misunderstandings were cleared up. The relationship was accepted and everyone signed an agreement for the utilities right of way in the presence of lawyers.[37]

The mission has worked to gain a clear title to the Bible College land, but even if it holds a piece of paper saying that the land belongs to the church, the landowners will not go away and future claims are likely to surface. Rynkiewich says that the church should work to strengthen the relationship that it has with the landowners and recognize the landowners for the gift that they or their ancestors bestowed on the mission. "The heart of the church is relationship, relationship with God and relationship with brothers and sisters. In Melanesia, it is possible to acquire land on which to stand and be in ministry. It is not possible to extract the land from relationship and expect the community to live."[38]

---

[35]Rynkiewich, "Some Practical Advice," 336-338.

[36]Rynkiewich, "Some Practical Advice," 339.

[37]Becka Johnson, "Utility Right-of-way Update," *Evangelical Advocate* 103 no 5 [May/June, 2007], 21.

[38]Rynkiewich, "Some Practical Advice," 342-343, 346.

Development of the Bible School

After getting off to a rocky start, the development of the Bible school pro-
gressed quickly. Jim Johnson and his team of PNG workers were initially responsible for the work. During 2003 and 2004, numerous work teams from the USA
assisted with the landscaping, fencing, and building that had to take place before
the Bible school could be launched. Before Jim and Becka Johnson returned to
the USA for furlough in September of 2003, the mission terminated its lease on
the property in Ialibu, and moved the workshop to the Bible college property near
Mount Hagen.

In June of 2003, Benji and Erica Jenkins came to work as volunteers for eight
months. They served as the host family at the Mount Hagen Missionary Home,
and Benji headed up the building program at the Bible College after Jim Johnson
left on furlough. The first house was completed by November of 2003, and when
the Bennett family returned from furlough, they moved into the first house built
on the Bible school property. They lived there for six months.[39]

The missionary staff grew smaller. Benji and Erica Jenkins completed their
eight months of volunteer service and returned to the USA in January of 2004
with plans to return later as career missionaries.[40] Two of the missionary families
left the field unexpectedly. They both had large deficits in their ministry accounts,
and they also had other personal reasons for leaving.[41] Neither family returned to
the field. For more than a year, Tim and Diane Bennett were the only CUM/WGM
missionaries in Papua New Guinea.

Plans called for the Bible school to open in 2005. The mission expected the
church to be deeply involved in the Bible school by making financial contributions and by appointing a Bible school director and a Bible school board made
up of pastors and church leaders with missionary advisors.[42] The missionaries
prepared the Bible school curriculum, created a student handbook, and made financial plans for the school.[43] Some of the church leaders wanted English to be
the language of instruction or at least a part of the Bible school curriculum. The
missionaries thought that Pidgin should be the language of instruction because
most of the youth in the Nembi area had no training in English. During the 1990s
and the early 2000s, schools in the Nembi area closed because of tribal fighting
and very few Nembi students completed their primary and high school education.

When I interviewed Temon Embel, the officer in charge at Pumberel health

---

[39]Diane Bennett "Moving Again" *Evangelical Advocate* 100 no 12 [August, 2004], 13-
14. They opted to move out of the house on the Bible college campus to the mission house
in town that was serviced by PNG power.

[40]Mary Estle "The Desires of Our Heart" *Evangelical Advocate* 100 no 6 [February,
2004], 9.

[41]David Lattimer, "Mission Links" *Evangelical Advocate* 100 no 10 [June, 2004], 12.

[42]Christian Union Mission Field Council Minutes, January 30, 2004.

[43]Christian Union Mission Field Council Minutes,, January 30, 204; Bible School
Meeting, February 5, 2004 and February 6, 2004; Christian Union Mission Field Council
Minutes, February 13, 2004.

center, he spoke about a "chain of education" that tribal fighting in the Nembi area had broken. Schools closed and the children had no opportunity to complete their primary education or go to high school or university. The chain remained broken for ten to fifteen years. Finally, they started to create a new chain, but the broken chain set back the entire area. He said that the Bible school should offer training in both Pidgin and English. He also claims that the mission failed because it did not give adequate English training to church leaders. If the church leaders had been offered training in English, then the church would have grown faster and be stronger today.[44]

The church leaders appointed John Kingal to be the Bible school director, and pledged to help the students secure their fees.[45] The Bible school opened in 2005 with John Kingal, Tim Bennett, and Diane Bennett teaching classes in the school

Work teams built a double story classroom in 2006 a year after the Bible College started classes. The windows on the class room building were quite small and many of the church leaders complained that the windows were out of proportion to the rest of the building. The primary complaint was that the church had not been involved in developing the plans for the buildings and the landscaping. After the mission agreed to lengthen the windows on the building the complaints eased off.[46]

When I interviewed Tim and Diane Bennett, they recalled the controversy over the windows in the class room building and considered it to be a trivial matter.[47] Timothy Pe who was the regional superintendent at the time also recalled the controversy. For him it was not so trivial; in fact, it was symbolic of the problems between the church and the mission. The mission did not give the church leaders the opportunity to decide on what the mission considered to be mission issues and then assumed that the church would accept the mission decisions as final. The building with the small windows did not measure up to the standards that the church leaders expected to find in a town setting. The church wanted the buildings that the mission constructed to be as nice as the buildings that the churches have in the missionaries' home countries.[48]

Bible School Finances

The mission expected the church to finance CUBC primarily through offerings and school fees. From the outset, the church made an effort to give funds for the Bible school. The first effort came during the camp held at Poroma for the dedication of the Angal Enen New Testament. As I said earlier in this chapter, the

---

[44]Temon Embel, interview by author, Embi, Southern Highlands Province, Papua New Guinea, January 7, 2009.

[45]Diane Bennett "A Meeting with PNG Leaders" *Evangelical Advocate* 101 no 2 [October, 2004], 15.

[46]Christian Union Mission Field Council Minutes, June 29, 2006, 12-06.

[47]Tim and Diane Bennett, interview by author, June 24, 2009.

[48]Timothy Pe, interview by author, Mendi, Southern Highlands Province, Papua New Guinea, January 15, 2010.

church leaders agreed to take up a special offering for the Bible school, and John Muehleisen, who was then the WGM vice-president of field ministries, promised that World Gospel Mission would triple the amount that the church raised for the Bible school.

When the offering was counted, the total in kind, cash, and pledges came to K17,700 and seven pigs. Not everybody paid the pledges they made at the camp, but in January of 2004, the regional board of trustees had K6700 to use towards the cost of running the school when it opened.[49]

The annual women's camp in 2006 took up a special offering for the Bible College. The women gave cash, clothes and string bags to support the school. After they sold the clothes and string bags, and added the proceeds to the cash offering, they had K1695 to give to the Bible College.[50]

The special offerings for the Bible school helped, but they were infrequent and did not provide enough for the daily operation of the school. The regional board of trustees decided that each district should give ten percent of its annual thanksgiving offering to the Bible College, but most of the districts do not send in their ten percent. In 2013, the Bible school received only two hundred *kina* from the thanksgiving offerings.[51]

Tuition fees were to be the second major source of income for the Bible school. The first year the mission gave scholarships for each student who enrolled in the program and additional scholarships for those who excelled academically.[52] With a small missionary staff, and fewer scholarship contributions from the USA, the mission was unable to continue the scholarship program beyond 2007. It also gave fewer grants to the Bible school.

Today some of the districts assist their students with tuition, but the student is responsible for raising his or her school fees. When the mission receives overseas funds for the Bible school, the money is placed in the school's account, and it helps keep the school fees down for all students. Some students work for the mission to help pay their school fees. The missionaries pay them for their labor and apply their earnings to the student's school account. The missionaries do not contribute directly to the school's operational funds, but they will buy supplies and equipment for the school and pay for it out of their ministry accounts.[53]

The plan to fund the Bible school primarily from church contributions and tuition fees did not work well. In 2012, the mission started a piggery project,[54] and by October had expanded the project to include layer chickens and the sale of

---

[49]Christian Union Mission Field Council Minutes, January 30, 2004.

[50]Ruth Tipton "2006 PNG Women's Camp (unlike any others!)" *Evangelical Advocate* 103 no 4 [March/April, 2007], 19.

[51]Benji Jenkins, interview by author

[52]Christian Union Mission Field Council Minutes, June 13, 2005, 4-05. The boarding student received scholarships of up to eight hundred kina per year and day students received up to five hundred kina per year. The mission deposited the scholarship funds into the school accounts on behalf of the students.

[53]Benji Jenkins, interview by author, Circleville, Ohio, June 14, 2014.

[54]Christian Union Mission Field Council Minutes, September 14, 2012, 12-12.

produce raised in school gardens.[55] The projects hit some snags when the pigs quit producing well and when the school was unable to purchase new layer chickens in a timely manner and the egg production dropped. Nevertheless, the projects have helped fund the school's operations. Some of the indigenous Bible school staff members and Bible school students work on the projects under the missionaries' supervision. The goal is to generate enough funds that the Bible school will become financially self-sustaining while providing training for the Bible School students. [56]

Christian Union Bible College has been the mission's primary ministry since the school opened in 2005. The Bible school had an indigenous principal until October of 2007 when John Kingal left to take further studies in the Philippines. He had not been paid for his work during the 2005 school year, and so the mission paid him his back wages and termination pay.[57] When Kingal left the school, the board asked the mission to appoint a missionary to serve as the Bible school director. The mission appointed Benji Jenkins to be the Bible School director until the Christian Union Bible College Board chose to appoint someone else.[58] He continues to serve as the Bible school director, and when he is gone on furlough, another missionary serves as the acting director until Benji returns to the field.[59]

Timothy Pe, the church's regional superintendent from 2004 to 2006, said that the PNG church wanted a missionary to be the director of the school because the missionary has greater access to overseas resources. If the school has a financial need, an expatriate director will appeal to the overseas constituency and raise funds to meet the school's needs. If an indigenous person serves as director of the school, he or she will not have access to the overseas resources, and will have to appeal to the PNG church that has fewer resources and will be unable to meet the need.[60] Thus, the theme of how to get access to financial resources from the home church in America resurfaces. As it was in the 1970s, the church desires the missionaries' presence as much or more for the resources than for the expertise that the missionary brings.

---

[55]Christian Union Mission Field Council Minutes, October 9, 2012, Old Business.

[56]Benji Jenkins, interview by author, Circleville, Ohio June 19, 2014.

[57]Christian Union Mission Field Council Minutes, October 15, 2007, 45-07; 44-07.

[58]Christian Union Mission Field Council Minutes, October 15, 2007, 47-07.

[59]Benji and Erica Jenkins returned to the USA in August of 2008 leaving Jim and Becka Johnson as the only CUM/WGM missionaries in PNG until Shawn and Bethany Waugh arrived on the field in January of 2010. Jim was the acting field director and the Bible school director, but Becka did more to keep the school going than Jim. The Johnsons felt that they were unable to "do justice" to the school while they were the only missionary family on the field and should have closed it until they had more staff on the field (interview by author, Tarlton, Ohio, October 15, 2010). When Shawn and Bethany Waugh arrived on the field, he took over as Bible school director until Benji Jenkins returned. For about three months during 2010, from the time that that Johnsons left in August to the time that Benji and Erica Jenkins returned in November, the Shawn and Bethney were the only family on the field, and the Bible school was their primary responsibility.

[60]Timothy Pe, interview by author, Mendi, Southern Highlands Province, Papua New Guinea, January 15, 2010.

With the assistance of indigenous staff,[61] the school has remained open. Several of the church leaders expressed their gratitude for the new Bible school.[62] Temon Embel said that the church realizes that school is there because of the hard work of Tim and Diane Bennett and Jim Johnson.[63] The church leaders also expressed concerns about the Bible school and said that the mission has failed to listen to the wishes of the church in regard to the Bible school. That has negatively affected the relationship between the church and the mission.

Church/Mission Relationship

The relationship between the church and the mission oscillated between better and worse depending on events that were taking place. The mission's withdrawal from Mendi, the discontinuation of the church subsidy, the perceived failure to share mission resources, the sale of mission property, and the location and support of the Bible school all became points of contention between the church and the mission. Changes in mission leadership, increased contact with all districts, and the reassignment of a missionary to the Southern Highlands helped improve the relationship. The discontinuation of the church subsidy was undoubtedly the source of the greatest tension between the church and the mission.

The Church Subsidy

In chapter five I wrote about the subsidy that the mission agreed to give the church beginning in January of 1992. Each month the region received one hundred US dollars for each adult missionary who was on the field or on furlough preparing to return to PNG for another term of service. Some of the missionaries adopted the views of Glenn Schwartz who writes of "missiological dangers" and says that overseas funding stifles the church and promotes "unhealthy dependency." According to Schwartz, the church would only achieve full ownership of its ministries when it no longer relied on overseas funding.[64]

---

[61]Robby Kopele served as a teacher at the Bible school in 2007. He was followed by Stephen Andayo, Peter Rapu, and the current teacher, Martin. Sara Kon and Christina Tep graduated with the first class in 2007, and they returned to teach the students' wives. David James taught a class at CUBC in 2008 while he was the TEE coordinator. Richard Wolwa has also worked at CUBC.

[62]Temon Embel, interview by author, Embi, Southern Highlands Province, Papua New Guinea, January 7, 2010; John Kua, interview by author, Mendi, Southern Highlands Province, Papua New Guinea, December 21, 2009; Timothy Pe, interview by author, Mendi, Southern Highlands Province, Papua New Guinea, January 1, 2010; William Wop, interview by author, Mendi, Southern Highlands Province, December 7, 2009; and others.

[63]Temon Embel, interview by author, Embi, Southern Highlands Province, Papua New Guinea, January 7, 2010.

[64]Glenn J. Schwartz, *When Charity Destroys Dignity: Overcoming Unhealthy Dependency in the Christian Movement* [Lancaster, Pa: World Mission Associates, 2007], 12, 303.

Some of the missionaries were convinced that the mission was hurting the church by giving the monthly subsidy. In the words of one missionary,

> The church is dwarfed spiritually because the mission has always been there to give. The church has missed out on untold blessings from God because they have viewed the mission as the main source of income and have not had a vision of what God's people, from their own local churches contribute. We (the mission) are just going to have to let the church go through "withdrawal" pains.[65]

In 1999, the mission sent the church mixed signals. On the one hand the mission began to cut the subsidy with a goal of phasing it out in a few years.[66] On the other hand, the mission agreed to provide the church with a used vehicle after the tribal fighting in the Southern Highlands ended.[67]

The church was frustrated with the cut in the subsidy and said that the mission was wrong to take away the church's money. As in the past, the cut in subsidy was followed by a series of stormy meetings between the church and the mission. The church insisted that the subsidy be increased rather than cut and that the mission provide the region with a new rather than a used vehicle.

At a confrontational CMCC meeting held in February of 2001, Timothy Map, who was not a member of the regional board, showed up along with all the members of the RBT. The missionaries and stateside officials who were also at the meeting did not allow Timothy to speak because he was not a part of the RBT. In addition, the mission denied all of the church's requests. Afterwards, the regional board of trustees wrote a letter to the mission council dated February 12, 2001. The letter said that if the mission did not give the region a new car and increase the church subsidy to $1000.00 per month, then the RBT would stop all mission programs and fully exclude the missionaries from all church programs.[68]

---

[65]Dean Queen, e-mail to Tim Bennett, Ruth Tipton, Dennis Johnson, Kevin Zirkle, and George Neal, September 25, 2003.

[66]For the 1998-1999 fiscal year, the subsidy was $800.00 per month (Christian Union Mission Field Council Minutes, November 25, 1998), and for the 1999-2000 fiscal year it dropped to $600.00 per month (Christian Union Mission Field Council Minutes, February 14, 1999) and the monthly subsidy was cut to $564.00 per month for the 2000-2001 fiscal year (Christian Union Mission Field Council Minutes, December 1-4, 1999). For the 2001-2002 fiscal year. the monthly subsidy was dropped to $400.00 per month, but only $200 a month was given directly to the church and the other $200 was held for approved church projects (Christian Union Mission Field Council Minutes, December 4-8, 2004).

[67]Christian Union Mission Field Council Minutes, February 5, 1999, 21-99. Periodically the church requested that the mission provide it with a vehicle. The mission did help the region secure a vehicle in 1991, but subsequent requests for another vehicle were flatly denied until the church brought a request for a vehicle to a CMCC meeting in 1999. The Nembi area was embroiled in tribal conflicts. The mission agreed to provide the church with a used vehicle after the tribal fighting ended. The church pushed the mission for a new vehicle rather than a used one. Also, the church leaders were unwilling to wait for the cessation of hostilities for their vehicle.

[68]Christian Union Mission Field Council Minutes, February 13-14, 2001, Attachment One. The letter said that the RBT would terminate the translation program and not allow

The field council met the next day and prepared a response to the letter from the regional board of trustees. First, the mission was going to circulate a copy of the letter and call for a meeting of all district leaders on February 26, 2001 at a place of the church's choosing. Second, the subsidy would not be raised. Third, the mission would provide the church with a vehicle as promised,[69] but it would not be a new vehicle. If CUC or PNG felt that it could no longer work with the mission, the missionaries were prepared to leave.[70] There is no written record of what happened at subsequent meetings, but the missionaries remained and continued to work with CUC of PNG.

In May of 2001 one of the furloughing missionaries resigned, and the funds that she had been contributing to the field budget from her ministry account were no longer available. The budget for the 2001-2002 fiscal year had to be reworked. Beginning in April 2002, the $400.00 subsidy was cut to $200.00, and as of April, 2003, the mission would no longer give a subsidy to CUC of PNG. The council agreed that there would be no reversal of its decision.[71] When the church leaders learned that the mission had cut the subsidy and intended to eliminate it completely by April of 2003, the church said that the region would "die" if the mission no longer gave a monthly subsidy to the church.[72] It is significant that they did not say that the church would die. The region was based on the western hierarchical structures that the missionaries introduced, and it was not a good cultural fit.

The regional board of trustees informed the missionaries that the PNG church would no longer be responsible for evangelism or outreach to new areas. They were returning those responsibilities to the mission. Those statements, however, were inconsistent with what the church was doing because in that year it started fifteen new churches in the Southern Highlands Province, and the regional board

---

the Angal Enen New Testament to be dedicated. They would provide no information from the church to the WGM or CCCU headquarters. No missionary would be allowed to take pictures or videos or send reports to the mission headquarters in the USA. In addition, the RBT did not believe that Timothy Map's presence in the meeting was the reason for the mission's refusal to approve the RBT's requests, and they were offended when one of the missionaries passed a note to one of the overseas visitors. If the mission failed to give a positive response to their requests, they would send an official letter to all CUC congregations informing them of the CUM missionaries' total exclusion from CUC church activities.

[69]The mission offered to give a vehicle to the RBT, but it was an older car, and the RBT did not want that particular vehicle. The mission then offered to sell the car and give them the money from the sale of the vehicle so the region could get a vehicle of their own choosing (Christian Union Mission Field Council Minutes, September 14, 15, and 17, 2001, 46-01). Eventually the regional superintendent accepted the car, but it broke down shortly after he took it. The RBT felt it had been insulted by the "trashy" car that the mission had given them, and reprimanded the regional superintendent for accepting it (Timothy Pe, Interview by author, Mendi, Southern Highlands Province, January 15, 2010).

[70]Christian Union Mission Field Council Minutes, February 13-14, 2001, 05-01

[71]Christian Union Mission Field Council Minutes, May 23, 2001, 21-01.

[72]Christian Union Mission Field Council Minutes, September 14, 15, and 17, 2001, 43-01.

of trustees appointed Militus Nuepi to minister in Port Moresby. Under his leadership several new churches were started in the Port Moresby area.[73]

Apart from the monthly subsidy, the mission and individual missionaries gave assistance to the church for various projects.[74] When the monthly subsidy ended, the mission set aside funds to assist the church with "small capital projects" that the mission called "small wins for the church." The regional board of trustees reviewed and approved the requests before bringing them to CMCC meetings. The mission then evaluated the requests and approved several of them.[75]

From the mission's perspective, it was pushing the church away from dependency toward greater self-reliance. From the church's perspective, the church and mission should be one, and the church should have full access to the mission's resources. When I interviewed John Kua who was the regional superintendent from 2000-2004 and 2006 to 2008, he asked why the church and the mission were two separate entities. He said that the mission was not following scripture when it said that mission assets belonged to the mission, and church assets belonged to the church. He cited Acts 2:44, "All the believers were together and had everything in common." Acts 4:32 says, "All the believers were one in heart and mind. No one claimed that any of his possessions was his own, but they shared everything they had."[76] Peter and John both preached, but they held all things in common, and many people were converted. The mission was hindering the growth of the church by cutting the subsidy and keeping its resources separate from the church's resources.[77]

---

[73]Dean Queen, e-mail to Tim Bennett, Ruth Tipton, Dennis Johnson, Kevin Zirkle, and George Neal, September 25, 2003.

[74]Christian Union Mission Field Council Minutes, December 1, 2, 3, and 4, 1999, 77-99.

[75]Various requests were honored: $300.00 was given for Toiwara District needs; $500.00 was given to assist with the construction of the Tupiri church near Mendi; $800.00 was given to assist with the construction of a church building at Eight Mile in Port Moresby; $200.00 was given to buy a PA system for a church in Port Moresby (Christian Union Mission Field Council Minutes, December 1-4, 1999, 77-99); and $500.00 was given to build a bush guest house at Tupiri (Christian Union Mission Field Council Minutes, February 18-19, 2000, 09-00). When the work on the revision of the constitution was complete, the mission paid to have it printed (Christian Union Mission Field Council Minutes, April 20-21, 2001, 14-01). It rented the tent that was used for the regional camp and the New Testament dedication, and paid for the printing of letterhead stationary for the church (Christian Union Mission Field Council Minutes, September 14, 15, and 17, 2001, 37-01). While the Bible school was not functioning, the mission provided scholarships for several students to attend Bible schools operated by other churches (Christian Union Mission Field Council Minutes, November 22, 2001, 60-01). It built district superintendent's houses for the Toiwara and Wara Lai Districts (Field Council Meeting Minutes, (Christian Union Mission Field Council Minutes, May 4, 2002, 09-02).

[76]NIV.

[77]John Kua, Interview by author, Mendi, Southern Highlands Province, December 21, 2009.

Return to the Southern Highlands

As mentioned previously, the mission withdrew from the Southern Highlands in June of 2002 because of political tensions and tribal unrest. The mission believed that it acted prudently, but having consistent contact with church leaders was difficult. As the missionaries concentrated on the development of the Bible school, the tribal unrest became worse. The mission staff dropped to just one family, and the number of trips to the Southern Highlands lessened. I lived in Mendi from 2005 to 2007, but after I left the field in August of 2007, no other missionary resided full time in Mendi. The absence of missionaries in Mendi and the failure to acquire property there were problematic to the church.

In 2007 and 2008, Benji Jenkins took ministry trips to the Southern Highlands with the year two and three Bible school students. The group travelled to a district and stayed there for a weekend. The students preached in several different services according to a schedule that the district superintendents had worked out.[78] The trips improved the church/mission relationship and made the churches more receptive to the Bible College.[79] A number of people applied to attend the school as a result of the ministry trips.[80]

The thinking of the missionaries towards the Southern Highlands changed. In 2002 the missionaries had little interest in returning to the Southern Highlands. By 2010, they were looking for ways to go back. They wanted to take training to the districts, but operating the Bible College was an expensive proposition, and finances were short.[81]

Butch and Leatha Jenkins had served as missionaries in PNG from 1981 to 1994. In July of 2008 they submitted an application to return to PNG.[82] They settled at Embi station on the Nembi Plateau in May of 2011. They were the first missionaries to live long term at Embi since April of 1985 when the mission withdrew from Embi station and the medical ministry after Eva Donahue was injured in a home invasion. When I visited Butch and Leatha Jenkins in January of 2014, they spoke of the warm welcome they received when they returned to Embi.

After repairing the mission house at Embi, they worked closely with all of the districts in the Nembi area. They visited all of the church districts and have helped with *divelopmen* projects.

Rynkiewich defines *divelopmen* as small scale projects that benefit local groups. Politicians and church leaders are expected to provide *divelopmen* for their constituencies.[83] The government, or more accurately, the politicians pro-

---

[78]Benji and Erica Jenkins, interview by author, Washington Court House, Ohio, July 11, 2010.

[79]Jim and Becka Johnson, interview by author, Tarlton, Ohio, October 15, 2010.

[80]Benji and Erica Jenkins, interview by author, Washington Court House, Ohio, July 11, 2010.

[81]Jim and Becka Johnson, interview by author, Tarlton, Ohio, Octover 15, 2010.

[82]*Missionary Tidings Newsletter,* August, 2008.

[83]Michael A. Rynkiewich, "Big-Man Politics: Strong Leadership in a Weak State," *Politics in Papua New Guinea: Continuities, Changes and Challenges: Point Series* no 24 [2000]: 28, 32.

vided sawmills for the Nembi area churches (all denominations). Butch had the expertise to set up the sawmills, train operators, and ensure that each district set up committees responsible for the supervision of the project. After the districts organized committees responsible for the oversight of the sawmills, he turned them over to the districts. In this case the sawmill project satisfied the expectations of all concerned—the politicians, the church leaders, the mission, and the local people.[84]

Butch also assisted Embi district with the construction of a station church and has started a chicken project on the station. Leatha has worked with the distribution of Bibles and has spear-headed an effort to record the Angal Enen New Testament and produce audio-Bibles for the Nembi people.[85] Except for an eight-month furlough that they took from November 2012[86] to August of 2013, the Jenkins have lived at Embi.[87] Their return to the Southern Highlands helped improve the relationship with the church, and they have had an effective ministry.[88]

The mission has agreed to place a missionary family at Montanda in the near future. Seth and Veronica Porter joined the PNG missionary staff in September of 2012. They returned to the USA in May of 2014 and are hoping to return to PNG in a year or so. The church requested that a missionary return to Montanda. In January of 2014. the field council agreed that they would go to Montanda when they return to provide vocational training in carpentry and possibly mechanics for people from the Nembi area.[89] Seth anticipates taking the courses from one district to another, so that trainees can attend the course in their own area and the mission will not have to set up accommodations for the trainees. The mission is not planning to establish a "full-blown" vocational school, but simply offer a series of courses. William Powi, the provincial governor is from Semin near Montanda. He wants the mission to set up a vocational school and has offered to fund it, but the mission is not ready to commit to that.[90] As in the past, it appears that the church and community expect far more than the mission expects to deliver.

Tribal fighting is another potential problem. There was major fighting in the area in 2010. The fight did not reach Montanda station, but nearby Injua School sponsored by the United Church was burned down during the fight. There has been no active fighting since early 2011, and the two sides supposedly made peace at the end of 2012 or 2013, but some people say that the matter is not settled yet.

---

[84]Butch Jenkins, "Report for Sawmill Project, in Christian Union Mission Field Council Minutes, October 9, 2012.

[85]Leatha Jenkins, e-mail to LR scripture use, 15, August, 2013.

[86]*Missionary Tidings Newsletter*, December, 2012.

[87]*Missionary Tidings Newsletter,* August, 2013. At the beginning of February, 2015 the Jenkins left Embi for an early furlough for health reasons and family concerns. As I write this, no missionary resides at Embi.

[88]Kevin Zirkle, e-mail to Ruth Tipton, July 9, 2014.

[89]In 2016 Seth and Veronica returned to Papua New Guinea and currently reside at Montanda.

[90]Benji Jenkins, interview by author, June 19, 2014.

The Sale of Mission Property

As the mission worked to develop the Bible College property in Mount Hagen, it was strapped for funds. In order to secure the funds it needed for the development of the Bible school property, the mission sold two of its properties—one in Port Moresby and one in Mount Hagen. The sale of mission properties in urban centers became one of the church's major complaints.

The church leaders' concept of ownership stood in opposition to that of the missionaries. The missionaries assumed that the buildings they built, the vehicles they purchased, and the gardens and trees they planted or paid someone to plant on their behalf belonged to the mission and that the mission had the right to sell its assets as it saw fit. The church leaders assumed that the assets the mission acquired were owned jointly by the mission and the church, and the mission had an obligation to consult the church before it made any major decisions about the sale of mission assets. The church believed that the property that the mission had acquired would be the church's when the mission no longer required it.[91]

In May of 2001, the mission council approved the sale of the house in Port Moresby,[92] and used the funds received from the sale to develop the Mount Hagen Bible School.[93] Subsequent to the sale, Dean Queen and Jim Johnson informed the pastors at a conference that was held at Ialibu that the house had been sold.[94] When the church leaders learned that the property was sold, they thought that the Port Moresby area churches had been cheated out of property that was rightfully theirs.[95] A number of the church leaders that I interviewed in 2009 and 2010 including the Port Moresby District Board members said that the mission had been wrong to sell the Port Moresby house rather than deed it over to the Port Moresby churches.

In 2013 the mission sold its original house in Mount Hagen. The original property was about one-half mile from the Bible college property. The mission had a good relationship with the local people, and the women and children often walked between the mission house and the Bible school property. However, law and order problems developed[96] that made them feel less safe, and the missionaries established a policy that no women, young girls, or children could walk from the mission house to the Bible school property. The women felt the policy was a hindrance to their ministries.[97]

---

[91]Jim and Becka Johnson, interview by author, Tarlton, Ohio, October 15, 2010.

[92]Christian Union Mission Field Council Minutes, May 23, 2001, 24-01.

[93]Christian Union Mission Field Council Minutes, September 14, 15, and 17, 2001.

[94]CMCC Meeting Minutes, January 19, 2007 Appendix 1B in Christian Union Mission Field Council Minutes, January 19-25, 2007.

[95]Port Moresby Regional Board, interview by author, November 23, 2009.

[96]In 2008 a short time before Benji and Erica Jenkins left the field for furlough, a youth from Bon Village tried to snatch Erica's string bag as she walked from her house to the CUC church to meet with the church women. She did not let the youth have the bag, and he knocked her down. She was not injured, but after that incident the missionaries thought that their safety was compromised (Benji Jenkins, interview by author, Circleville, Ohio, June 18, 2014).

[97]Christian Union Mission Field Council Minutes, September 9, 2011.

The original Newtown property became more vulnerable to thievery,[98] and the mission was in debt. In 2010, the missionaries began to discuss the possibility of selling the house in Newtown and using the money to build another house at the Bible College and pay off the mission's debt.[99] Early in 2012 the PNG field council began to negotiate with the WGM headquarters for permission to sell the house.[100]

Rumors circulated among the pastors and church leaders that the mission was considering selling the Newtown house. The pastors, church leaders, and even the church's regional council voiced their opposition to the sale of the house. The members of the Mount Hagen Christian Union Church were also opposed to the sale of the house in Newtown because that was where the church started. The story of the mission coming to Mount Hagen and acquiring that property was tightly interwoven with their story. If the house were sold, a part of the church's story would be snatched away from them.[101]

At an RBT meeting held sometime during 2012, Peter Rapu, who was the assistant regional superintendent, asked if there was any way that the church could get the mission to do something. Benji responded that there was no way to force the mission or individual missionaries to do something, but he wanted to talk with the church leaders and learn their ideas so the mission focused on things that the church wanted the mission to focus on. He suggested that they bring a list to the next CMCC meeting that was to be held in January of 2013 so they could discuss it. As is common among the Highlanders of PNG, the terminology that both Peter and Benji used was vague.

It was a case of major miscommunication. When Peter asked his question, he was thinking in terms of mission property and resources, but when Benji answered he was thinking in terms of ministries that both the church and mission could focus on. The members of the RBT interpreted Benji's answer to mean that the mission had decided to give the church either the house in Newtown or the money from the sale of the property.

The church leaders wanted to use the house as a central office for the region, and they came to the CMCC meeting in January of 2013 expecting the mission to give them "something big." By then the WGM officials had agreed that the mission could proceed with the sale of the house. Benji informed the church leaders that neither he nor the mission field council had the authority to give the property to the church. Only the WGM board had that authority. The board approved the

---

[98]During one year, persons unknown stole three water pumps. One went missing while the family was at church on Sunday morning. The gate was locked, a security fence surrounded the property and a dog guarded the property, but someone scaled the fence and snitched the water pump. The house was located within the city limits and was far enough away from the village that it was more vulnerable to break-ins and theft than the Bible College property that enjoyed the protection of the nearby villagers. (Benji Jenkins, interview by author, Circleville, Ohio, June 18, 2014).

[99]Benji Jenkins, interview by author, Circleville, Ohio, June 18, 2014.

[100]Christian Union Mission Field Council Minutes, March 23, 2012.

[101]Conversation with Erica Jenkins, December, 2013.

sale on the condition that the funds would be used to build another house on the Bible College property. He agreed to discuss the issue in the field council.[102] The field council formally considered the church's request at a meeting held on January 31, 2013 and rejected it, saying they could not afford to give the house to the church for free and that the mission did not think that Mount Hagen was a good location for the church's central office.[103]

Much to the consternation of the church, the mission sold the house by August of 2013. None of the money went to the church. Instead, the mission used it to build a new house on the Bible College campus and liquidate debt.[104] The relationship between the church and mission plummeted. In subsequent CMCC meetings, the church leaders reminded the missionaries of the missions' past "wrongs" and "broken promises." They included, among other things, the cutting of the subsidy, the failure to acquire the international school in Mendi, and the sale of the Port Moresby and the Hagen houses.

Church/Mission Coordinating Council

The meetings of the church mission coordinating council (CMCC) again became highly dysfunctional. The entire regional board of trustees attended the CMCC meetings. When CMCC was first formed, the mission and the church had an equal number of representatives at the CMCC meetings. As the missionary staff grew smaller, fewer missionaries attended the CMCC meetings, and as the church started new districts the regional board of trustees grew in number.

Some of the church leaders said that the CMCC meetings were counterproductive. Culturally when a group meets with a headman or leader they expect to get something as a result of the meeting. When the church leaders come to a CMCC meeting, they come with the expectation that they will receive some kind of gift during the meeting. The church leaders bring requests to the meeting, and when the missionaries deny the requests it causes frustration and ill will for both the church leaders and the missionaries. Some of the church leaders suggested that CMCC be disbanded,[105] but others questioned the mission's right to do so.[106]

As of January, 2014, the mission disbanded CMCC. The missionaries told the church leaders that they were discontinuing CMCC meetings, not because the mission did not want to work with the church, but because they hoped to avoid the constant friction between the church and the mission that the meetings created. In lieu of holding CMCC meeting the missionaries committed to meet with the

---

[102]Benji Jenkins, interview by author, June 18, 2014.

[103]Christian Union Mission Field Council Minutes, January 31, 2013. At the time, most of the CUM/WGM missionaries were in the USA. Only two families were on the field and one of the two families was new to the field. The missionaries in the USA met and discussed the request and denied it.

[104]Christian Union Mission Field Council Minutes, August 14, 2013.

[105]Benji Jenkins, interview by author, Circleville, Ohio, June 18, 2014.

[106]When I was in PNG for the fifty year celebration, some of the church leaders told me that Benji had disbanded CMCC, and they wanted to know if he had the authority to do so.

four regional officers so they can update each other and talk about their mutual concerns and to visit the districts and where they will meet with the district superintendents and the district boards.[107]

Mission Leadership

In Chapter Five I wrote about church leadership, the church's expectations for its leaders, and the church's perception that the leaders of Christian Union Church of Papua New Guinea have not been adequately trained. Here I discuss the mission leadership and its impact on the church/mission relationship.

The policy of both the CCCU and WGM was that the mission leaders were appointed by the General Missionary Board under CCCU and the Board of Directors under WGM. Until 1994 the mission changed field leaders frequently. The General Missionary Board appointed field leaders to serve until they reached the end of their term. When they returned to the USA for furlough, someone else was appointed to the position. Several served as field superintendent only once during their missionary career. Some of the field superintendents were well liked by the church leaders, and the church wanted them to return to the position, but the church leaders were ready for others to move on at the end of their term.

After CUM became a part of WGM, the policy changed. The field director retained his position even when he was on furlough in the USA. Tim Bennett was the field superintendent when the mission became a part of World Gospel Mission. His title was changed to field director and he retained that position until he resigned from the field in 2008. The change gave greater continuity to the ministry programs, but the church blamed him for the conflict between the church and mission. According to the WGM handbook of policy, the field director "is directly responsible to (WGM) Field Ministries."[108] His primary responsibility is to carry out WGM policies first, and the directives of the field council second. The church leaders looked at the mission director as the mission's big-man, and they believed that he had a great deal of influence over the other missionaries and the stateside officials. They considered him to be primarily responsible for the decisions that the mission council made. From the mission perspective, the director was responsible for carrying out the council's directives even when they did not reflect the director's personal views, and he did not have the authority to side-step mission policy established by stateside authorities.

I have already mentioned several mission decisions that were unpopular with the church leaders. They thought that if the mission had a different field director, the responses to the church's requests would be closer to the church's expectations. In December of 2006 about six months before the Bennett family's term ended, the church sent the mission a letter about what they considered to be the mission's wrongs and failures under Bennett's leadership. These included the failure to acquire the international school in Mendi, the sale of the Port Moresby

---

[107]Benji Jenkins, interview by author, Circleville, Ohio, June 18, 2014

[108]*World Gospel Mission Missionary Policy Handbook,* March, 2005, 6.

property, and the permanent departure of several missionaries from PNG. In addition, the RBT believed that the mission had hidden in a secret account, one hundred and twenty thousand kina for the purchase of the Mendi international school. The RBT believed that the field director was responsible, and they did not want him to return to the field as the director or even as a missionary.[109]

The CMCC discussed the letter at a meeting held on January 19, 2007 while Kevin Zirkle, the WGM regional director, was visiting the PNG field. The RBT believed that a change in mission leadership would lead to more favorable responses to church requests, and the relationship between the church and the mission would improve.[110] At that meeting the missionaries thought the church leaders came to understand that the mission had no hidden accounts.[111] Nevertheless, when, in December of 2009, I interviewed John Kua, who was the regional superintendent in 2007, he told me that the mission held one hundred and twenty thousand kina and would use it to buy another property in Mendi.[112]

During the meeting, it became clear that the church was experiencing financial pressure. When Zirkle asked the church leaders what areas they felt that they could do on their own without the mission's assistance and where they needed help. They said that the reason the church was there was to bring others to Jesus Christ. They were good at witnessing and sharing Christ with others. Their efforts to evangelize were going well. They used indigenous men and women as speakers at their camps. They knew how to bring people to Christ. The regional board said that its primary concerns were the Bible school with training at all levels, the health work, and outreach to new areas. The church wanted the Bible school, but did not have enough money to support it adequately. They struggled to keep the school supplied with teachers and to find money to pay the teachers. The church also wanted assistance with the medical work at Embi. They had run the medical work for fifteen years and did not want the mission to take over the ministry, but they needed medical supplies and equipment for the health center. They wanted an expatriate doctor or nurse to come and assist with the work.[113] The region's total income came to about ten thousand kina per year, and they did not have the money to fund "those things."[114]

---

[109]Christian Union Church of PNG letter from RBT to Mission, December 8, 2006 in Appendix 1A, Christian Union Mission Field Council Minutes, January 19-25, 2007

[110]Christian Union Mission Field Council Minutes,, January 18, 2007, 1 in Appendix 1B, Christian Union Mission Field Council Minutes, January 19-25, 2007.

[111]CMCC Meeting Minutes, January 18, 2007, 2 in Appendix 1B, Christian Union Mission Field Council Minutes, January 19-25, 2007. The mission planned to take a loan to purchase the international school property.

[112]John Kua, interview by author, Mendi Southern Highlands Province, Papua New Guinea, December 21, 2009.

[113]CMCC Meeting Minutes, January 18, 2007, 2-4 in Appendix 1B Christian Union Mission Field Council Minutes, January 19-25, 2007.

[114]CMCC Meeting Minutes, January 18, 2007, 3-4 in Appendix 1B, Christian Union Mission Field Council Minutes, January 19-25, 2007. The minutes do not specify what things, but they undoubtedly meant run the Bible school, improve the health center facili-

At the end of the CMCC meeting, the regional board of trustees retracted its letter asking Tim Bennett to resign, and they apologized to Tim for blaming him for making decisions that the field council and the overseas officials made.[115] The Bennett family left the field in June of 2007. After they returned to the USA, they decided not to return to PNG for several reasons, but the letter the RBT had sent to them was not among their reasons for not returning.[116] They resigned from the PNG field in October of 2008.[117] They returned to the field for a short trip to pack up their belongings and say their good-byes. While they were there, three members of the regional board of trustees brought them a letter requesting that they return to the field, but the Bennetts said that it was time to move on.[118]

When the Bennetts left the field in June of 2007, Jim Johnson became the acting field director. He was the mission's builder and mechanic and made frequent trips to the districts with his team of builders to assist with the construction of permanent churches and other projects that the districts wanted. After he became the acting field director, he devoted most of his time to working with the church leaders, and little time was left over for building and maintenance. He spent hours in meetings listening to the church leaders' concerns, and came to better understand their point of view.

At first the church leaders expected everything to change because they had a different field director. They expected him to give what others had denied them, but that did not happen. They repeatedly asked that the subsidy be reinstated and asked for money from the sale of the property in Port Moresby, and Jim repeatedly informed them that the subsidy was dead and the sale of the house was final and he could not change decisions that the council had already made.[119] Slowly even though mission policies did not change, the relationship with the church appeared to improve. Zirkle said, "Jim Johnson did a lot of talking with the church leaders, and the attitude toward the mission seemed to get better."[120]

In August of 2008, the WGM office of international ministries decided that

---

ties, and open work in new areas, especially if it involved the construction of new facilities.

[115]CMCC Meeting Minutes, January 18, 2007, 2 in Appendix 1B, Christian Union Mission Field Council Minutes, January 19-25, 2007.

[116]Tim and Diane Bennett, interview by author, Circleville, Ohio, June 24, 2009. The Bennetts gave several reasons for their decision not to return to PNG. The missionaries in PNG are under a lot of pressure and the Bennetts were not handling pressure as well as they had in the past. Their children were young adults who were enrolled in colleges and starting families, and if they returned to PNG it would be difficult to maintain good contact with their children. Their last big assignment was to get the Bible school up and running, and they had succeeded in doing that, and they sensed that their ministry in PNG was finished. Diane felt that her spiritual gifts did not fit well with the PNG ministries. When they were offered work on another WGM field that fit better with her gifts and natural abilities, they were ready to move on.

[117]Christian Union Mission Field Council Minutes, October 31, 2008, 29:08.

[118]Tim and Diane Bennett, interview by author, Circleville, Ohio, June 24, 2009.

[119]Jim and Becka Johnson, interview by author, Tarlton, Ohio, October 15, 2009.

[120]Kevin Zirkle, e-mail to Ruth Tipton, July 9, 2014.

because of the small missionary staff in PNG, Zirkle, the WGM regional director, would be the field director for PNG.[121] A missionary on the field would be the acting field director, or the field manager. The hope was that when the field council made decisions that were unpopular with the church, it would take some of the pressure off the missionary in resident who served as the acting field director.[122] Jim Johnson was the acting field director until he left for furlough in August of 2010.[123] Benji Jenkins was then appointed to be the acting field director and served in that position from the time that he arrived on the field in November of 2010[124] until he left PNG and returned to the US in May of 2014 for a furlough.[125] In his absence Shawn Waugh served as the field manager.[126]

From WGM's perspective, Kevin Zirkle is the PNG field director. In contrast, from the perspective of the church leaders in PNG, the acting field director or the field manager is the field director, and they hold the missionary in residence accountable for the field decisions. For the church, the face they can see is the person in charge rather than the official field director who visits the field only periodically.

When I asked about the current relationship between the church and the mission, Zirkle reported that it was much better than it was when he began as regional director in 2002, but there are still concerns.[127] Benji Jenkins said that in recent years the relationship with the church had been great until the mission sold the house in Mount Hagen. The sale of the Hagen house reignited the feelings that the mission has all of the money, the church has little, and the mission does not share its resources with the church.[128]

In January of 2014 it became evident that the church leaders considered the acting field director to be primarily responsible for field decisions. The regional board of trustees (all PNG church leaders) held a meeting at Embi on January 15, 2014, and decided to "revoke" Benji Jenkins as a missionary to Papua New Guinea when his term ended in May of 2014. The letter said that Benji had asked the church to list its "priority needs," only to have them rejected when the church brought them to the meeting. In addition, he had not held CMCC or Bible College board meetings, and he had not visited the districts while he had been the field director. The letter said there were "many more" but they "only mentioned the

---

[121]Christian Union Mission Field Council Minutes, October 31, 2008, 28-08. Kevin Zirkle is a WGM missionary to Japan. He was appointed to the position of regional director of Asia, Europe and the Pacific Rim in 2002. His first trip to PNG was in December of 2002, and from then on he made periodic visits to PNG. After he was appointed to the position of field director, he visited PNG more frequently—at least annually, and sometimes more.

[122]Kevin Zirkle, e-mail to Ruth Tipton, July 9, 2014.

[123]*Missionary Tidings Newsletter,* August 2010.

[124]*Missionary Tidings Newsletter*, December, 2010.

[125]*Missionary Tidings Newsletter,* June, 2014. When Benji left PNG in May of 2014, Shawn was designated to be the field manager until Benji returns to the field.

[126]Benji Jenkins, interview by author, June 18, 2014.

[127]Kevin Zirkle, e-mail to Ruth Tipton, July 9, 2014.

[128]Benji Jenkins, interview by author, June 18, 2014.

four."[129] The main point of the letter was the "priority needs," and that referred to the Mount Hagen house. The RBT thought that Benji had promised to give them the house and reneged on his promise.[130]

After Benji received the letter from the regional board of trustees, the missionaries, like those in the past, called a meeting with the regional board of trustees to discuss the letter. The meeting took place at Embi, and all but one of the missionaries participated. The missionaries told the regional board of trustees that they did not have the authority to "revoke" Benji as a missionary. However, the regional board said they had taken similar action against Tim Bennett when he was the field director, and Tim had not returned to the field.

Once again, the conflict arose over the sharing of mission resources, and the different perspectives of the missionaries and the church leaders. The mission's present emphasis is on training for pastors and church leaders, and Benji expected the church leaders to bring requests for training or for assistance with outreach to new areas such as Kimbe. He was not thinking about requests for mission resources. The church leaders thought immediately of resources. The church believes that the mission has more resources than it does, and cannot understand the mission's reluctance to share its resources with the church. They find scriptural confirmation in their belief that the church and mission should be one and share all things in Acts chapters two and four.[131] They believe that the mission hurts the church because it does not support the church financially. They forget the later chapters in Acts where Paul "abandoned" every church that he planted, even taking up a collection among them for the home church, a reverse of what the PNG church has in mind. As Rolland Allen pointed out in his classic, *Missionary Methods: St. Paul's or Ours*, at each place Paul stayed long enough to start a church, usually no more than six months. He then moved on leaving behind a congregation that he expected to function on its own. He kept contact by writing letters and by sending messengers to visit the churches that he established, but the churches were on their own. His converts and the churches he started became involved in missionary outreach to their nearby communities.[132]

The missionaries want to avoid church dependency on overseas funds and assistance, but the church thinks it should be able to depend on the mission to provide it with resources so that the church can grow. The church leaders ask for outside resources to contribute to the development of the church and believe that the mission hinders the development of the church when it withholds resources from the church.

---

[129]Letter from Christian Union Church regional office to Christian Union Mission Field Council dated 24 January, 2014. Although the letter said that Benji had held "no meetings over the years" and had "never visited the respective districts," Benji said that he had in fact held CMCC and Bible College meetings and visited the districts. The RBT may be referring to a particular meeting or a particular visit to the district that he missed and/or to the council's decision to disband CMCC.

[130]Benji Jenkins, interview by author, Circleville, Ohio, June 18, 2014.

[131]Acts 2:42-47 and Acts 4:32-36.

[132]Roland Allen, *Missionary Methods; St. Paul's or Ours?* [Grand Rapids: Eerdmans, 1962], 82-93.

Another source of discord was the expectations that the church leaders hold for the mission leaders. Melanesian societies are competitive, and big-men constantly vie for position and status. They do this by attracting followers and supporters who find it to their advantage to be associated with a particular big-man.[133] Sillitoe says that among the Wola, traditional big-men attained and maintained their power, status, and position of influence through persuasion and their ability to manipulate wealth and excel in exchange and social relationships.[134] Similarly, Lederman reports that for the Mendi people, "a big-man's success depends on securing broad popular cooperation—which is never assumed—and on the willingness of people to ratify publicly his personal judgments."[135] If the big-man does not meet the expectations of his followers, they turn away from the big-man and pledge their allegiance to someone else who will. When the mission failed to live up to the church leaders' expectations, they blamed the field leaders and sought someone else who might be more open to their demands.

Despite the dysfunctional relationship with the mission, the church has established new districts and reached out to new areas.

The Establishment of New Districts and New Areas

The constitution of Christian Union Church of Papua New Guinea says that when an area has established four congregations, it is eligible to become a district in its own right. In November of 2008, the Port Moresby area was recognized as a district in its own right, and the Mount Hagen area became a district in January of 2013. I now tell their stories.

Port Moresby District

The Port Moresby churches began to rebuild in 2003 when Miletus Nuepi came to Port Moresby to serve as the pastor at Erima. In 2003, there was a church building at Eight Mile, but no active congregation. A small congregation was meeting at Erima. Miletus held services for two Sundays at Erima, and then he told the congregation that they would begin holding services at Eight Mile rather than Erima. The combined total number of persons attending all congregations were twelve to fifteen, but the group had a vision for starting new churches and reopening others.

In 2005 Stephen Kele came to Port Moresby and joined the pastoral team. Miletus became the pastor at Eight Mile, and Stephen became the pastor at Erima,

---

[133]Michael A. Rynkiewich, *Soul, Self, and Society: A Postmodern Anthropology for Mission in a Postcolonial World*, [Eugene, Oregon: Cascade Books, 2011], 122-123.

[134]Paul Sillitoe, *Give and Take Exchange in Wola Society* [New York: St. Martin's Press, 1979], 108-111.

[135]Rena Lederman, *What Gifts Engender: Social Relations and Politics in Mendi, Highland Papua New Guinea* [Cambridge: Cambridge University Press, 1986], 207.

making two active congregations. The district purchased a tract of titled land near the settlement at Eight Mile. So far it remains undeveloped, but the district hopes to develop it in the future.

Miletus formed a strong leadership team made up of pastors and lay leaders. Henry and Betty Map had been effective lay leaders in the church when it started in the 1980s, but in 2006 they were living near Baruni and not regularly attending either Erima or Eight Mile. The leadership team decided to purchase ground at Baruni and start a church there. It opened in October of 2006, making three active congregations in the Port Moresby area.

Some CUC church members lived and worked on plantations a fair distance from Port Moresby. One of the plantations was Veimauri, and two sisters, Rose Don and Jenny Imu, asked the Port Morseby team of pastors to start a fellowship there. In 2006 Titus Almap from Embi district joined the pastoral team and remained in the area for two years. As requested, the pastors started the fellowship at Veimarui, and it grew into a full congregation. They secured ground from the company, started holding services, and built a church.

The Moresby area CUC owned a church building and a pastor's house at Doa plantation a few miles beyond Veimauri but had not been using the buildings for several years. A woman named Rose Alik from the Solomon Islands moved in and was using the buildings to "minister the word of God."[136] Miletus Nuepi and Cliff Kiru wrote letters to Rose Akik and the company telling them of their wish to reclaim the buildings and begin holding services at Doa again. Miletus contacted Christina Martin who lived at Doa and asked her to find out how many people wanted to revive the CUC at Doa. When she brought a list of fifteen names, one of the Port Moresby pastors moved to Doa to reopen the church there.

By November of 2008 Port Moresby had five active congregations, and it became a district. The regional board sent the regional superintendent, William Wop; the regional secretary, Rick Pombre; and the regional treasurer, David James to Port Moresby to formally recognize Moresby area as a full district. Kanj Mesmba was elected as the district superintendent for the Port Moresby District and Stephen Kele was the assistant district superintendent.

In Chapter Seven I tell the story of Timothy Map and a cult that he started in the Nembi area. A number of the people attending the Baruni church were related to Timothy Map and sympathetic to his teachings. When Kanj who was the district superintendent and belonged to Timothy Map's kin group, was caught up in the teachings and released the Baruni pulpit to Timothy Map, the regional board suspended him from the office of Port Moresby district superintendent and appointed Miletus in Kanj's place. Stephen Kele remained the assistant district superintendent. The Baruni congregation left the CUC churches and no longer takes part in the district activities.[137]

In 2010 the CUC women held their annual camp in Port Moresby. Women

---

[136]Conversation with Miletus Nuepi on December 6, 2013.

[137]Conversation with Miletus Nuepi, Port Moresby District superintendent, December 6, 2013.

from all of CUC's districts traveled to Port Moresby for the event. Stanley Wap whose wife is an influential leader in Port Moresby district owned a tract of land at Taurama and allowed the women to hold their camp on his land. After the camp Stanley deeded one-half of his land at Taurama to the Port Moresby District, and it started a new congregation at Taurama with Miletus Nuepi as the pastor. Stanley Wap constructed a church building, and has plans to build a pastor's house at Taurama.[138]

In 2012 Pastor Luke Tiri from Montanda and Pastor Lamech Pima from Poroma District joined the pastoral staff in Port Moresby District. They have committed to remain in Port Moresby through 2015. The District Board appointed a layman, John Nenja, to be the pastor at Doa.[139]

Before Port Moresby was officially organized into a district in November of 2008, a pastoral/lay leadership team assumed the oversight of all the churches. When the area first became a district, the leadership rued the fact that they were now a district. They said the constitution interfered with the system that they had used prior to being recognized as a district, and for them the church's constitution was a major problem.[140] The constitution says that each local church may keep eighty percent of the offerings, but they must send twenty percent to the district. The district keeps eighty percent of the money they receive from the local church and sends twenty percent to the region.[141] Prior to becoming a district, each church sent all of its offerings to the church leadership team in Port Moresby, and the leadership team redistributed the money back to the churches as needed. It had provided enough to meet the needs of the local churches, and had allowed them to establish churches in new areas of Port Moresby. They built accountability into the system by not allowing the pastor(s) to handle the money and by relying on a leadership team rather than one person to make decisions about the church affairs. In addition, before they became a district, they occasionally received assistance from the region and the mission for some of their building projects. From their perspective, being a district meant that they would be expected to "stand on their own" and would no longer receive assistance from the region or the mission.[142]

The district board is now the district's primary leadership team. Miletus Nuepi is the district superintendent; and Luke Tiri is the assistant district superintendent; Alfred Omel serves as the district secretary; and Nancy Kumalo is the district

---

[138]Conversation with Miletus Nuepi, Port Moresby District Superintendent, December 6, 2013. I did not formally interview Miletus when I was in Port Moresby, but took me to visit the churches at Eight mile and Taurama while I was in town.

[139]Conversation with Miletus Nuepi, December 6, 2013.

[140]Port Moresby District leadership team, Interview by author, January 29, 2010 at MAPANG guest house in Port Moresby.

[141]Konstitusen Bilong Christian Union Church Bilong Papua New Guinea, Me 2002, 55-56. Earlier drafts of the constitution said that the churches and district would forward ten percent of their offerings, but in later editions the ten percent was changed to twenty percent.

[142]Port Moresby District Board, interview by author, Port Moresby, National Capital District, Papua New Guinea, November 23, 2009.

treasurer. Paul Embel also serves as a member of the Distrtict board. The Port Moresby District Board has established a policy that every pastor who comes to Port Moresby will enroll in CLTC for four years in either its Pidgin or its English course. CLTC is based at Banz in the Jiwaka province, but it has opened an extension campus in Port Moresby. Under this plan, Miletus enrolled in the Pidgin course for four years. He graduated in 2012. He then applied for and is now midway through the English program. Pastors Lamech Pima, Luke Tiri, Stephen Kele, and John Nenja are in the third year of their CLTC Pidgin Course and will graduate in 2015.[143]

One of the concerns that the Port Moresby district board has is that Christian Union Church has no pastors with advanced degrees. Many other denominations have well-trained men who have earned masters and doctorate degrees including the United Church, the Evangelical Church of Papua, the Nazarenes, the Lutherans, the Anglicans, and the Evangelical Bible Church. Port Moresby City is a developing city that is growing in size and is the home of many highly educated persons. In Christian Union Church the missionaries brought God's word, but they failed to provide advanced education for the pastors. The board members said that if Christian Union Mission would have consistently provided advanced training for its pastors, some would have left the church, but others would have remained faithful, and Christian Union Church would have educated pastors today.[144]

John Kua says that Papua New Guineans start churches according to their cultures. They follow their *wantoks* or they form new friendships and create new *wantoks* and start churches. The core congregations of most of the churches in Port Moresby have strong ties with the Nembi area.

As I was departing from PNG in February of 2014, I spent an extra day in Port Moresby so that I could visit more of our churches. Yana Kumalo took me to Veirmauri Plantation to see the church there. It was a Saturday, and no one was at the church, and so she took me to a nearby market where she said the people would be gathered. They were originally from the Nembi area and asked me to converse with them in Angal Enen. I did, much to their delight. The majority of the people attending the Port Moresby churches come from the Southern Highlands, but some are from other provinces. The district leaders hope that the people from the other provinces will carry the church back to the other provinces when they leave Port Moresby and return to their homes. The Christians in Port Moresby use what John Kua calls "the system"[145] to establish churches.

Mount Hagen District

Even in its infancy, Mount Hagen Christian Union Church took steps to plant other churches in the Hagen area. They participated in the plantation ministries.

---

[143]Conversation with Miletus Nuepi, Port Moresby District Superintendent, December 6, 2013.

[144]Conversation with Miletus Nuepi, Port Moresby, December 6, 2013.

[145]John Kua, interview by author, Mendi, Southern Highlands Province, Papua New Guinea, December 21, 2009.

Most of the plantation churches no longer exist but one at Kimil plantation continues to function. Under John Kingal's leadership, the Hagen people started a church at Dei Kaunsil near Mount Hagen. They attempted to start a church at Ialibu while some CUC/CUM missionaries were temporarily located there, but it never came to fruition. They also started a church in the Nebileya district near Mount Hagen, but when tribal fighting broke out, enemies burned down the church building; the people scattered; and the church died.

Between 2009 and 2012, the pastors and lay persons started six new churches and by 2013 there were nine churches in the Hagen area.[146] On the 15th of January, 2013, Mount Hagen area was formally recognized as Mount Hagen District of the Churches of Christ in Christian Union.[147] They elected a district board, and appointed district leaders for the youth, Sunday school, women's and prayer ministries. Each local church is encouraged to incorporate those four ministries into their programs. Joe Wane, the District superintendent, said that the district has dreams of going out to other areas of Papua New Guinea and starting other churches.[148]

New Areas

Poroma district was formerly called Farata District, but after the fighting between Mato and Farata during the 1990s, the district was renamed Poroma District. The people in the Farata area blamed the mission for dismantling Farata station and cutting the trees on the station, and some invited the Evangelical Church of Papua (ECP) to establish churches in the area, and so ECP started several churches. Some of the people were dissatisfied with ECP, and wanted CUC to restore its churches. Similarly, in the 1980s and 1990s there was extensive fighting among some of the groups in the Lai Valley. Some of the churches in the lower Lai Valley withdrew from the Wara Lai District and became a part of the Ka District. They were rather far from Ka, and the district assigned area pastors to work with those churches. When in 1991 Ka District appointed Mapon Ek to work as the area minister in the Lower Lai Valley, he lived at Sumia for two years, and got to know the people in the area. He left at the end of 1992.[149]

In 2000 Mapon Ek worked as a land mediator,[150] and he visited the people in

---

[146]Conversation with Joe Wane, current Hagen District Superintendent, December 19, 2013 I was unable to learn the exact location of all of the churches, but the names of the churches are Hagen Town, Ketakori, Kimil, Rumbrumb, Rulna, Kala, Pagl, Tiki, and Raimp.

[147]While visiting Papua New Guinea in December of 2013 and January of 2014 I was shown the certificate that the district was given when it was formally formed.

[148]Conversation with Joe Wane, current Hagen District Superintendent, December 19, 2013.

[149]Mapon Ek, interview by author, Mato (Poroma), Southern Highlands Province of Papua New Guinea, December 31, 2009.

[150]The government appoints respected men to be land mediators. They visit areas where land is in dispute, listen to the stories of all concerned and help negotiate a settlement that

the area to discuss their concerns over land disputes. His work as land mediator brought him into contact with the displaced churches from the Farata area and the lower Lai Valley,[151] and he learned of their desire to reestablish CUC churches.

Problems developed with the annual Thanksgiving offering. The districts collect the offering and divide it among the district, the Bible school, and the region. After Timothy Map began his Spiritual Harvest Ministry (discussed in Chapter Seven) Ka District started splitting the offering between the District and the Spiritual Harvest Ministry. The churches that had formerly been a part of the Wara Lai District and Farata were dissatisfied and felt that they received nothing in return for supporting the district. District officials seldom visited them or gave them assistance. They objected to the Spiritual Harvest Ministry and wanted no part of their offerings to support it. Most of the churches in Ka district joined the Spiritual Harvest Ministry, but those formerly associated with the Wara Lai and Farata Districts opposed it. They withdrew and took steps to form their own area. In 2008, Ka District appointed Mapon to serve as the area pastor[152] for the churches in the Lower Mendi Area.[153]

The church recognized the area as separate from Ka, Poroma, and the Wara Lai Districts. In 2014 eight churches were associated with the area.[154] They have an area board,[155] and when they come to regional functions they are recognized as a distinct area not directly associated with the other districts.

The story of the Lower Mendi area is awash with cultural innuendos. First, when tribal fighting breaks out, it deeply affects the churches. The churches in the Lower Mendi were displaced from their districts because of tribal fighting. Even after they made peace, they were unable or unwilling to align themselves with their former districts. The church districts and areas are primarily made up of the groups that formed traditional fight alliances in pre-colonial times. It is worth noting that in the Montanda District fighting broke out in 2010. The fighting has stopped, but half of the churches in the district do not participate in district functions at Montanda station. They have formed their own group, and are pushing to have their own area headquartered at Injua or Semin. The break away groups parallel one fight alliance, and the groups that remains loyal to Montanda District parallel another alliance.[156]

---

is agreeable to all parties.

[151]Lower Mendi Area pastors, conversation with author, Mount Hagen, December, 2013.

[152]Mapon Ek, interview by author, Mato (Poroma), Southern Highlands Province of Papua New Guinea, December 31, 2009.

[153]Lower Mendi Area pastors, conversation with author, Mount Hagen, December, 2013. The pastors informed me that the area had gone by several names. At first they called it the *San Kamap* (Sun Rise) area. Later they changed its name to the Central Poroma Area. Finally they settled on the Lower Mendi Area.

[154]The names of the churches are Sumia, Pitrekendo, Pun 1, Pumbule, Awaranda, Kusa, Kopa, and Pun 2.

[155]In January of 2014 the members of the area board were Mapon Ek, area chairman, Robert Sis, assistant area chairman, Stephen Tolopu, treasurer, Winsom Yepi, secretary, and Ira member.

[156]When I was in PNG in December of 2013 and January of 2014, I heard several

Mapon Ek networked with the churches in the Lower Mendi area. His role as land mediator required him to visit all of the groups frequently, and the question about the land belonging to the churches naturally came up. When he learned that the people wanted CUC churches in the area, he arbitrated with the districts and the region to get the churches reopened and to establish a new area. He became the man at the center of a new network of churches that is now recognized as the Lower Mendi area.

The second area is Kimbe. The island of New Britian is divided into two Provinces—East New Britain Province and West New Britain Province. Rabaul is located in East New Britian on the Northeastern tip of the island. Kimbe is located along the Northern coast in the West New Britain province. Many of the Nembi people have gone to Kimbe and Rabaul to find work on the nearby plantations. Some settled at Kimbe permanently and started two congregations—Kombongo and Griri.[157] The core groups at both congregations are Nembi people, but people from a number of other provinces including Morobe, Sepik, Kimbe, East and West New Britain, Chimbu, and others attend the churches.[158] The regional board and several of the district boards have sent pastors to work with the churches in Kimbe, and some have ministered effectively.[159] The regional board of trustees has repeatedly asked the mission to send missionaries to Kimbe.[160] Both mission and church leaders have visited Kimbe several times during the last 20 years. Most recently, Benji Jenkins, Seth Porter, and Peter Rapu visited the churches on Easter weekend in 2012.[161]

The regional board wants to develop the work in Kimbe, but they feel they lack the resources to develop a strong work in a new area, and so they ask the mission to help develop the work. The mission has lacked the personnel and the resources to develop a work at Kimbe while other areas such as Port Moresby and Mount Hagen and other ministries such as the Bible school were being developed. The missionaries who have visited Kimbe speak of the potential for effective ministry in Kimbe, the diversity found in the two congregations and the possibility for outreach from Kimbe to other areas in PNG.[162] In 2001 the mission wanted

---

people talk about the push to divide Montanda district. No official moves have been made to divide the district, but people are talking about it.

[157]Field Council Minutes Papua New Guinea, September 5, 1999, 58-99.

[158]Benji Jenkins, interview by author, Circleville, Ohio, June 19, 2014.

159   Rick Pombre, personal conversation, Mount Hagen, Western Highlands Province Papua New Guinea, January, 2014.

[160]CMCC Meeting minutes, January 15, 1996; Papua New Guinea Field Council Meeting Minutes, September 5, 1999, 26-01; WGM Papua New Guinea Field Council, January 13, 2013.

[161]Benji Jenkins, interview by author, Circleville, Ohio, June 19, 2014. Rick Pombre, conversation, Mount Hagen, Western Highlands Province Papua New Guinea, January, 2014.

[162]Many of the CUC/WGM missionaries have visited the Kimbe area during the last twenty-five years and all have come back with similar reports including Benji Jenkins who visited the area most recently.

the church to take the lead at Kimbe; encouraged the RBT to send pastors to work with the Kimbe congregations; and offered to assist with purchasing ground for Kimbe on the condition that the Kimbe churches and the RBT contribute towards the purchase price. The Kimbe churches and/or the RBT never came up with their share, and the mission used the funds for other ministries. [163]

After years of waiting on the region and the church to purchase property in Kimbe, the people bought a piece of property located on the main highway just outside of Kimbe town. One of the churches meets on the new property and the other meets on a plantation.[164]

Thus, despite the discord, the church has not lost sight of its responsibility for evangelizing and starting new churches.

Conclusion

In the 1960s, the Nembi people first accepted the missionaries as much for their merchandise as for their message. Presently, the church leaders continue to say that they need the missionaries as much for their resources as for their expertise, but they express an appreciation for the message that the missionaries brought. In the frank discussions that the missionaries and the church leaders had in January of 2007, the church leaders said that the church's primary purpose was to bring others to Christ, and they knew how to do that. The problem is that for people who approach life with a holistic worldview, medical, educational and developmental ministries cannot be separated from evangelistic and spiritual ministries. They are so intertwined that they cannot be pulled apart. For the most part the church and the mission have continued to work together in spite of their differences and their frustrations with each other. However, after the mission left Ka in April of 1999, a prominent church leader from Ka District pulled away from the mission and missionaries. In his eyes, the mission had lost all credibility, and he looked elsewhere for the material blessings that had failed to come. When other church leaders did not follow his lead, he started a cult. Almost all of Ka district followed his cult and left CUC of PNG, but the other districts rejected his teachings. He did not accept the missionaries or their counsel about his unorthodox teachings. In the end, CUC of PNG and its leaders confronted him and told him to either give up his unsound teachings or leave the church. I tell that story in Chapter Seven.

---

[163]Papua New Guinea Field Council Meeting Minutes, May 23, 2001, 26-01. At that time the land was available for six thousand kina. The mission set aside three thousand kina towards the purchase of the land that would only be released if the Kimbe churches contributed one thousand kina and the RBT contributed three thousand kina towards the land purchase.

[164]Benji Jenkins, interview by author, Circleville, Ohio, June 19, 2014.

Chapter Seven

Frustration: The Spiritual Harvest Ministry

Introduction

Adherents of the Spiritual Harvest Ministry date the beginning of their religious movement to June 27, 1999, when Timothy Map, the movement's prophet, claims that he heard God speak in an audible voice anointing Timothy a prophet with divine authority. The missionaries had departed from Ka two months earlier, leaving Timothy as the de facto leader of Ka District. At first his teachings were in line with the doctrines of CCCU, but as time passed Timothy's teachings became less and less orthodox. He claimed the authority of a God-ordained prophet. The missionaries had failed to bring the expected development to Ka District and had departed from Ka taking their assets with them. Consequently, he rebuffed the missionaries, and they lost any influence they had over him. The church leaders from other districts became increasingly frustrated with his teachings, questioned his doctrine, confronted him, and eventually expelled him from the church.

How are we to understand the emergence of this cult? In *Solomon Islands Christianity* Alan R. Tippett analyzes the anthropological impact that colonialism and Christian mission had on the Solomon Island's cultures. Head-hunting, cannibalism, human sacrifices, and slavery served a sociological function of uniting the societies, enabling them to defend themselves from their enemies and achieve success in warfare. When cultural practices were abolished without providing a functional substitute, it had far reaching repercussions related to trade and every aspect of island life. This cultural void at the very heart of the society opened the way for cults and nativistic movements to develop among the Solomon Islanders.[1] Tippett discusses *Etoism*, a cult that developed under the leadership of a Solomon Islands Methodist pastor named Silas Eto, which eventually led to a schism in

---

[1]Alan R. Tippett, *Solomon Islands Christianity: A Study in Growth and Obstruction* [South Pasedena, California: William Carey Library, 1967] 147-153.

the Methodist church in the Western Solomon Islands.[2] When I read the story of the cult, I saw numerous parallels to the development of Timothy Map's Spiritual Harvest Ministry.

Millenarian movements are common in Melanesia. They have been variously called cargo cults, messianic movements, nativistic movements, and apocalyptic movements. In the last one hundred and fifty years, more than two hundred such movements have been documented in Melanesia.[3] Trompf says that millenarianism is the acceptance of a set of beliefs that anticipate some "spectacular, unsurpassable" events in the future and millenarian movements apply to groups of people who wait in anticipation of the approaching events.[4] Cargo cults anticipate receiving "material blessings" from "non-empirical forces." The definitions of cargo cultism and millenarianism intersect, but they are not identical in meaning. Not all millenarian movements carry with them the expectation of cargo, and not all cargo movements anticipate future cataclysmic events.[5] Zocca uses the term messianic movement, defining it as "a movement whose principal aim is to await a collective salvation which is imminent (coming very soon) definitive (will happen only once) and earthly."[6] Cargo cults emerge when people are dissatisfied with their present existence and desire a better life that will bring them an abundance of both material and spiritual blessings.[7] In writing about the Spiritual Harvest Ministry, I use the term millenarian cult, but it has both millenarian and cargo expectations. It awaits the return of the Glory of God, and it promises God's blessings to those who give offerings to help support Israel.

Zocca says that most millenarian cults begin with a prophet who has some kind of special vision or revelation. When people hear about the prophet's revelation, they follow him/her and follow his/her instructions in hopes of receiving the promised goods or blessings. Contact with the western world and the accompanying rapid socio-cultural changes coupled with the traditional beliefs that prosperity came from the spirits who were controlled through ritual create the Melanesian propensity for cult activity.[8] Tippett says that cults develop when a "situation" and a "personality" come together. A group is dissatisfied with its situation and an individual recognizes it and takes advantage of the situation to promote his or her views or message. A prophet advocates the new doctrine, but the real "innovators" are the people who accept the prophet's message. The group creates the prophet by accepting the prophet's message.[9]

I now look at the situation in which the cult known as the Spiritual Harvest

---

[2]Tippett, *Solomon Islands Christianiity*, 212-216.

[3]Franco Zocca, *Melanesia and Its Churches: Past and Present.* [Goroka, Papua New Guinea: Melanesian Institute, 2007], 164.

[4]G. W. Trompf, *Cargo Cults and Millenarian Movements: Transoceanic Comparisons of New Religious Movements.* [Berlin: Mouton de Gruyter, 1990], 1.

[5]Trompf, *Cargo Cults and Millenarian Movements*, 11.

[6]Zocca, 164.

[7]Zocca, 173-175.

[8]Zocca, 175-177

[9]Tippett, *Solomon Islands Christianity,* 241.

Ministry emerged, the prophet who leads the cult, the message that the prophet proclaims, and the consequences for Christian Union Church of PNG.

The Situation

In 1997 Timothy was a candidate for the Nipa-Kutubu Member of Parliament in the national elections. I recall having a conversation with him when he decided to run for election. The church struggled financially, and he thought that if he could win the seat in parliament, he would be in a position to give significant financial assistance to the church.

One interviewee[10] said that the church and mission asked Timothy not to run for parliament. If he did run for parliament, he was not to use church or mission vehicles, and they did not want him to preach in the churches or use the church logo or the church name in any of his campaigning. Timothy disregarded those directives. He continued to preach in the churches during his campaign and he placed the church logo on his campaign vehicle.

Prior to his candidacy, he had a strong following among the Christians in all of the districts, and he anticipated receiving the votes of most of the Christians. One interviewee said that some of the Christians found themselves in a dilemma. They wanted to vote for Timothy because of his Christian beliefs, but their kin group supported a different candidate. The campaign divided the church and, when the region sponsored a camp meeting at Ka in 1997, the Plateau people did not participate because they favored the sitting member over Timothy. My interviewee said that voting in PNG does not follow "democratic rights." The voters cast their votes as the kin group dictates. The Christians divided their votes according to their kin group and not according to their Christian beliefs. Each candidate received the votes of his own kin group.

The elections took place in July, and Timothy Map came in fourth. In September of 1997, tribal fighting broke out between the groups on the Nembi Plateau and those in the Nembi Valley.[11] The fight was politically motivated, and the tensions continued for several years.[12] It was impossible to carry out effective ministry at Ka, and on April 15, 1999 the last of the missionaries left Ka.[13] I interviewed a number of people from Ka District in January of 2010, they all said that the mission was wrong to leave during "*taim bilong hevi*" (when there was trouble). The mission should have waited until the fighting had ended and left when the area was at peace. Timothy Map told me that the mission should have waited until four or five years after the fight ended to pull out of Ka. Their traditions condemn a man who deserts his group and forsakes his land in the midst of a fight.[14]

---

[10] I am choosing to withhold the names of my interviewees in this section.

[11] Timothy Map, interview by author, Ka, Poroma District, Southern Highlands Province, Papua New Guinea, January 13, 2010.

[12] The vast majority of the people I interviewed said that the fight started over politics, although a few downplayed the role that politics played in the fight.

[13] Ruth Tipton, e-mail to Dan Tipton, April 16, 1999.

[14] Timothy Map, interview by author, Ka, Poroma District, Southern Highlands Prov-

One interviewee said that the mission's unexpected departure from Ka was one of the reasons that Timothy gained the following that he did in Ka District. The people were disturbed because the mission left without informing the people of its intended departure. The mission gave one of the houses to Andrew Inja, and the other landowners said that the church had no claim to the ground or the other houses at Ka. Many Christians in Ka District were frustrated with the mission and were ready to listen to Timothy's revelations.

The Prophet

Timothy Map was a young child when the mission started working in the Nembi Valley. He recalled attending the Sunday school that Elsie Conley started on Ka station in 1967 or 1968.[15] Elsie Conley said that some of the older children who had not been accepted at the English school came to her and asked her to teach them to read. Timothy was among them. In response to their request, she started teaching Pidgin literacy classes to interested youth, and Timothy learned to read in her Pidgin class.[16]

In 1970, the mission arranged with the one of the school teachers at Poroma to hold special English classes for some of the pastors. They stayed at Farata station, and went to Poroma each afternoon and attended English classes for two hours after the school day ended. Timothy attended those classes. In 1971 the pastors came back to Ka to enroll in the Bible school. Timothy, who was younger than most of the pastors, did not enroll in the Bible school because of his youth. Instead he enrolled in the English School where he was accepted into second grade.[17]

While he attended Ka Community School, he taught Sunday school on Ka Station. He completed grade six in 1977 and went to Nipa High School in 1978 where he entered grade seven. After spending four years at Nipa High School, he enrolled in Dauli Teachers' College at Tari and graduated from there in 1983. He entered the teaching service and taught at Kaupena Community School for one year, and then he returned to his place and taught at Ka Community School for two years.

While Timothy was still in high school, God called him to worldwide evan-

---

[15]Timothy Map, interview by author, Ka, Poroma District, Southern Highlands Province, Papua New Guinea, January 13, 2010.

[16]Elsie Conley, interview by author, Circleville, Ohio, April 17, 2010. Elsie Conley first went to PNG in 1966, and she was the English school teacher. After the youth asked her to teach them to read, she held Pidgin classes in the afternoon after the English school was dismissed.

[17]Timothy Map, interview by author, Ka, Poroma District, Southern Highlands Province, Papua New Guinea, January 13, 2010. Timothy said that he was about ten years old when he enrolled in Ka Community School. Elsie Conley estimated that he was between twelve and fourteen years of age when he came with some others who asked her to teach them to read. When he started English school he was older than most of the other children.

gelism.[18] When Christian Union Church was invited to send representatives to Australia for a conference on evangelism, Timothy Map and Apollos Kemp were selected to go.[19] Later Timothy attended the International Conference for Itinerant Evangelists sponsored by the Billy Graham Evangelistic Association and held at Amsterdam from July 12 to 21, 1986.[20]

Timothy and his family went to Australia at Christmas time in 1986. They stayed there for six months and Timothy spoke at several smaller churches associated with a number of different denominations. After he came back to Papua New Guinea he worked with the church for several years as the regional evangelist.[21] He travelled throughout Papua New Guinea doing evangelistic work and starting churches. He worked the Nembi area, but he also travelled to Port Moresby, Hagen, and Kimbe.[22] One interviewee said Timothy was a good man and that he was an effective evangelist in the 1980s and the first half of the 1990s. He was a good preacher, who based his messages on the scriptures, and many people were converted under his ministry, but his messages became increasingly occupied with the "end times."[23] He won the respect of the people throughout the Nembi area. He visited those who mourned a death, brought them food and firewood, and ministered to them. When tribal fighting broke out, he travelled freely among the warring groups and tried to negotiate peace.

In 1989 the mission offered to promote Timothy for study at Circleville Bible College in the USA. The regional board agreed, and they wrote a formal letter of request to the home board. The mission sent a letter of support asking that Timo-

---

[18]Timothy Map, "A Papua New Guinean's Testimony" *Missionary Tidings*, XXXIV, no 8 [May, 1983], 5.

[19]Timothy Map, interview by author, Ka, Poroma District Southern Highlands Province, Papua New Guinea, January 13, 2010. Timothy said that he and Apollos attended a satellite crusade. The neetings were held in Hong Kong and piped into Australia. I checked a Wheaton College website that list a chronology of many of the events that have been sponsored by the Billy Graham Evangelistic Association. The list does not include all of the events sponsored by the Billy Graham Evangelistic Association. There is no of mention a crusade held in Hong Kong and carried to other nations via Satellite. It does list a "Sydney Celebration '85" that took place from September 15 to 29, 1985 (Billy Graham Center Archives http://www2.whea-ton.edu/bgc/archives/bgeachro/bgeachron02.htm)

[20]Timothy Map, interview by author, Ka, Poroma District, Southern Highlands Province, Papua New Guinea, January 13, 2010; "Amsterdam 86, International Conference for Itenerant Evangelists, We Were There" Missionary Tidings, 39 no. 3 [November, 1986], 7.

[21]Timothy Map, interview by author, Ka, Poroma District, Southern Highlands Province, Papua New Guinea, January 13, 2010. Timothy said that he and his family were in Australia first, but the written records suggest that the Amsterdam conference took place before he and his family went to Australia for six months. Timothy described the churches he visited as family fellowships rather than fully organized churches. They were associated with the Church of Christ, Church of God, Pentecostals, United Church, Harvest Ministry, Nazarene, Assembly of God and some others.

[22]Timothy Map, interview by author, Ka, Poroma District, Southern Highlands Province, January 13, 2010.

[23]Name withheld.

thy be allowed to study in the USA.[24] The home board approved the request on the condition that the PNG churches pay for his airfare and his pocket money while he was in the USA. The home board would cover the cost of tuition and accommodation.[25] Timothy raised enough money from the PNG churches to bring his family to the USA with him. They arrived in Columbus, Ohio in August of 1992, and Timothy enrolled in classes at Circleville Bible College.[26] Timothy studied for two years and earned an associates degree from the college in May of 1994.

After he completed his studies, the family returned to Papua New Guinea. In an article published in the *Evangelical Advocate,* Timothy spoke of his expectation to be involved in fulltime evangelism, counseling and church planting. He had a goal of starting twenty to thirty churches and winning four to six thousand converts by the year 2000. He thanked the churches in the USA for the financial assistance that the missionary department gave to his family for his schooling and their living expenses. He requested that the stateside constituency support his evangelistic outreach with their prayers and finances.[27]

Timothy said that his time at Circleville Bible College had been profitable and he had learned a lot about church history, homiletics, and the scriptures, but his questions about unfulfilled prophesies, especially those about the return of the Jewish people to Israel, remained unanswered.[28]

When Timothy returned to PNG he resumed his role as regional evangelist. For two years, he worked as he had before he went to the USA, but the church and mission both struggled financially, and he received only limited support from them. Both the regional board of trustees and Timothy pushed the mission to give greater financial support to the church's evangelism ministry that Timothy led, but the mission struggled financially; was transitioning to World Gospel Mission; wanted the church to assume greater responsibility for the financial support of its ministries; and gave no regular support to the church's evangelism program beyond the monthly subsidy.

In 1996 Victor Schlatter recruited Timothy to make a trip to Jerusalem. Schlatter had been a missionary with the Tiliba Christian Church based at Nipa. He translated the New Testament into the Wola language spoken by groups living near Nipa,[29] and was well-known throughout the area. After he left Papua New Guinea, he settled in Australia, made numerous trips to Israel, and became associated with the International Christian Embassy Jerusalem, a Christian Zionist organization.

---

[24]Christian Union Mission Field Council Minutes, December 28-29, 1989, 17.

[25]Christian Union Mission Field Council Minutes, July 3, 1990, 2-3.

[26]Timothy had one son, Moses when the family arrived in the USA. His wife, Ana was pregnant. Their daughter, Miriam was born on January 8, 1993.

[27]Timothy Map, "Return to Papua New Guinea," *Evangelical Advocate*, 89 no 10 [June, 1994], 12.

[28]Timothy Map, interview by author, Ka, Poroma District, Southern Highlands Province, Papua New Guinea, January 13, 2010.

[29]Schlatter uses the spelling Waola, but Paul Sillitoe used the spelling Wola. I have used Sillitoe's spelling Wola throughout this paper rather than Waola.

Schlatter has written his theological perspective in a book entitled *Where Is the Body?* The major theme of his book is that redemption has come to the world through the Jewish people. According to Schlatter, the entire Bible is based on God's interaction with the Jewish nation. The Jews who follow the Old Testament law and yearn for their Messiah are saved even if they do not recognize Christ as their Messiah. The Jews have been scattered around the world, but the Bible promises to re-establish Israel and restore the Jews to Israel. According to Schlatter, the restoration is a major theme in the Old Testament books of Isaiah, Zechariah, and Ezekiel and that every Old Testament prophet except Jonah at least mentions the theme. Christians have an obligation to respect, love, bless, assist and support the Jewish people. God's plan is to ultimately bring the Jews and genuine Gentile Christian believers together in one body. Schlatter travels throughout the South Pacific teaching Christians in established churches about Israel and urging them to develop an "appropriate relationship" with the Jewish people.[30]

The International Christian Embassy Jerusalem sponsors an annual Christian celebration of the Feast of the Tabernacles.[31] Schlatter recruits Papua New Guineans to go to Jerusalem,[32] and in 1996 Timothy Map was among the group that went to Israel for the celebration.[33]

Historically, the International Christian Embassy Jerusalem has had two primary goals. The first is to be a channel through which Christians around the world "could show their love and support to Israel." The second is to proclaim that God would "ultimately restore the children of Israel to their rightful land and sequentially to a right relationship with their God, the God of Israel."[34]

On its website, the embassy lists eight primary objectives based on scripture. They are to show concern for the Jewish people and the nation of Israel;[35] to interpret current events in Israel in the light of scripture;[36] to provide a place for Christians to come to a "biblical understanding of Israel" and learn how to relate to Israel;[37] to encourage Christians to pray for Israel;[38] to motivate Christian leaders worldwide to promote Israel and the Jewish people;[39] to help bring the Jews

---

[30]Victor Schlatter, *Where Is the Body: Discovering the Church in the Heart of Israel* [Shippensburg, PA: Treasure House, Destiny Image Published, Inc, 1999], 69, 66, 63, 135, 141, 134.

[31]"International Feast of the Tabernacles Presented by the International Christian Embassy Jerusalem" http://feast.icej.org/about [accessed August 19, 2014].

[32]Schlatter *Where Is the Body*, 16.

[33]Timothy Map, interview by author, Ka, Poroma District, Southern Highlands Province, Papua New Guinea, January 13, 2010.

[34]"History: The ICEJ's Story and Purpose" International Christian Embassy Jerusalem, http://int.icej.org/history [accessed August 19, 2014].

[35]Isaiah 40:1

[36]Psalm 102:13-16

[37]Ephesians 2:12-14

[38]Isaiah 62:6-7

[39]Genesis 12:1-3

back to Israel;[40] to support Israel;[41] and to bring reconciliation between the Arab and the Jew.[42] These eight objectives are the embassy's "founding principles."[43]

Timothy was deeply impressed with the teachings of the International Christian Embassy Jerusalem and Schlatter. When he returned from his trip to Israel in 1996, he began to teach about Israel and said that the Nembi Christians should take up offerings to support Israel. He began to talk a lot about the end times. He preached from scripture, but he took proof texts without reading them in context, and he talked a lot about death, tribulation, and the judgment. People responded to Timothy's messages out of fear. A few continued to follow their new-found faith, but many who converted soon lost their fear, gave up their new beliefs, and returned to their old lives. Some returned to the church that they had left to follow Timothy, while others relied on other spiritual forces and on cunning and stealth to bring them the power, wealth and prestige that they covet.[44]

Timothy reported that the first time that God spoke audibly to him was on June 13, 1978 at 5:00 in the morning while he was in high school. Timothy was staying on Ka station with Pastor Sengi Iruwa when he heard a voice coming from the ceiling of the house. He got up, and then a light came and wrote on the wall and told Timothy, "All of the people in this area and this electorate and this province and this country are not ready. I want you to get up and witness in my name to the world."[45] Timothy said that he did not see a vision. It was like a vision, but it was real. God spoke to him and wrote on the wall and called him to be a worldwide evangelist.

Timothy claims that on June 27, 1999, God appeared to him in his home, spoke audibly to him and declared that Timothy was His (God's) prophet.[46] God inspired Timothy to ask the people, "What do all of you see now?"[47] Timothy says that at a

---

[40]Isaiah 49:22

[41]Matthew 25:40

[42]Isaiah 19:25

[43]"Objectives: The ICEJ's Founding Principles" International Christian Embassy Jerusalem, http://int.icej.org/about/objectives [accessed August 19, 2014].

[44]My interviewee mentioned three of Timothy's proof texts. One is Daniel 9:27 which says, "He will confirm a covenant with many for one 'seven.' In the middle of the 'seven' he will put an end to sacrifice and offering. And on a wing of the temple he will set up an abomination that causes desolation, until the end that is decreed is poured out on him" (NIV). Another is Revelation 13:8 which says, "All inhabitants of the earth will worship the beast—all those names who have not been written in the book of life belonging to the Lamb that was slain from the creation of the world" (NIV). A third text is Hebrews 9:27 which says, "Just as man is destined to die once, and after that to face judgment..." (NIV).

[45]Timothy Map, interview by author, Ka, Poroma District, Southern Highlands Province, Papua New Guinea, Janaury 13, 2010.

[46]Cliff Kiru, "A Critical Evaluation of the Spiritual Harvest Ministry in Poroma, SHP" [Essay for R:604.803 Contextualization of the Gospel in Primal Societies, Laidlaw-Carey Graduate School, CLTC Delivery, Banz, Western Highlands Province, Papua New Guinea, 11 August, 2009].

[47]Timothy Map, interview by author, Ka Station, Poroma District, Southern Highlands Province, Papua New Guinea; conversation with Rick Pombre, January 2014. When I in-

service held later that morning, all of the songs, dramas, testimonies and even the sermon were on the same theme. It was the beginning of the "Spiritual Harvest Ministry"[48] that has become a millenarian movement with expectations of cargo. It emphasizes the words of the prophet over scripture, is overly concerned about the end times, venerates and supports Israel, and stresses the relationship the people in the South Pacific and especially those in the Nembi Valley have with Israel. Although Timothy still considered himself to be a part of Christian Union Church, he claimed that he had a special relationship with God and was not accountable to the Christian Union Church's district and regional councils and boards.[49]

The Message

After visiting Israel, Timothy urged the Christians to give special offerings to support Israel. The International Christian Embassy Jerusalem appeals to Christians to give financially to assist Jewish people who are in need and to help restore them to Israel.[50] Schlatter says that the first responsibility that the Gentiles have towards the Jews is to love the Israeli people, and the Gentiles should "confirm their love with material assistance."[51] Timothy was convinced of the validity of those positions and urged the Christians to take up special offerings to support Israel. He prominently displayed the flag of the nation of Israel in the services he conducted, and many of his followers began to wear the Star of David on their clothing.

Timothy taught that God would bless those Christians who supported Israel, meaning the current Israeli state. In the Abrahamic Covenant in Genesis 12:1-3, God says to Abraham, "I will bless those who bless you, and whoever curses you I will curse."[52] Timothy said that Galatians 3:8[53] and Romans 15:27[54] prove that spiritual blessings came to the Gentile world through the Jews, and hence the Gentiles must share their material blessings with the Jews. At the time that I

---

terviewed Timothy, he mentioned June 27, 1999 as a pivotal day in his ministry. He said that Ka District had invited him to speak at a service on a Sunday morning when all of the congregations in Ka District came together at Ka for a service. He told me that God "inspired him," but he did not say that God had spoken to him audibly. A pastor who is from Ka and has heard Timothy speak many times told me that Timothy claims that he heard God's voice speaking audibly to him on that day.

[48]Timothy Map, interview by author, Ka Station, Poroma District, Southern Highlands Province, January 13, 2010

[49]Name withheld.

[50]"Mandate; ICEJ's Scriptural Directive" http://int.icej.org/about/mandate [accessed August 21, 2014].

[51]Schlatter, *Where Is the Body,* 135.

[52]Genesis 12:3.

[53]Galatians 3:8 says, "The Scripture foresaw that God would justify the Gentiles by faith, and announced the gospel in advance to Abraham: 'All nations will be blessed through you' So those who have faith are blessed along with Abraham, the man of faith" (NIV).

[54]Romans 15:27 says, "They were pleased to do it, and indeed they owe it to them. For if the Gentiles have shared in the Jews' spiritual blessings, they owe it to the Jews to share with them their material blessings" (NIV).

interviewed Timothy, he had sent money to the International Christian Embassy Jerusalem three different times. The first time he sent two thousand *kina*. The second time he sent fifteen hundred *kina* and the third time he sent nine hundred *kina*. It had been about three years since he sent money because of many problems. Timothy said that the International Christian Embassy Jerusalem uses the money received from the people of the Pacific to help the Jews from Ethiopia return to Israel and assists them with their physical needs.[55]

I asked Timothy and several of my interviewees what Timothy meant when he said that people who supported Israel would receive blessings from God. Timothy evaded the questions, but one of my interviewees said that Timothy did not specify what kind of blessings they would receive. The people understood it to mean that they would prosper. Before now, the coffee has not been very productive, but if they give something to Israel, then the coffee trees will be more productive. The branches of the coffee tree will break under the weight of the coffee it bears. Before the *marita*[56] plants produced little fruit, but if they give to Israel, *marita* will grow in abundance. Instead of a plant growing just one fruit, it would grow four or five pieces of fruit. If they gave to Israel they believed that they would prosper materially.

One of my interviewees said that he personally had not gone to hear Timothy's new teachings. He never attends the services, but he hears reports from those who have attended the services. Between 1999 and 2001 some of Timothy's followers reported that they were going to do DNA testing on the people living in the Nipa-Kutubu electorate to see if they were descendants of the tribe of Benjamin.[57]

---

[55]Timothy Map, interview by author, Ka, Poroma District, Southern Highlands Province, Papua New Guinea, January 13, 2013.

[56]*Marita* is the fruit of one type of pandanus or screw pine tree.

[57]Schlatter says that after the Assyrians invaded Israel in 722 B.C. ten tribes were scattered and "with little or no precise historical records" were "lost from the ledger." Various cults "whose credibility is somewhat distanced from reality" have surfaced around the world including the Southern Highlands of Papua New Guinea with claims that they are one of the lost tribes of Israel. Recent DNA testing has identified men who descended from the tribe of Levi, and he speculates about what further DNA testing may reveal in the future (Schlatter, *Where is the Body*, 75-77). I was curious about the DNA testing that Schlatter spoke about, and googled it to see what I could learn. According to tradition, the Cohanim (Cohen singular) are direct descendents of Aaron, the brother of Moses. The study was prompted after a doctor from Eastern Europe who is a Cohen, went to the synagogue and heard a man from North Africa who also claimed to be a Cohen read from the Torah. The doctor hypothesized that if he and the man from North Africa descended from a common ancestor, they should share a common genetic marker. That led to two studies to test the hypothesis. Scientists collected DNA examples from 188 male Jews living in England, Israel, and North America who were asked to indicate if they were Cohanim or non-Cohanim. The study showed that 98.5% of the Cohanim shared a common genetic marker. The percentage of non-Cohanim Jews who shared the marker was significantly lower. A second study tested 106 Cohanim and found that 97 of the 106 had common genetic markers. The study is on-going, but it suggests that it could have "ramifications for the search" for the ten lost tribes of Israel ("The Cohanim/DNA Collection" aish.com http://www.aish.com/ci/

If the tests prove that they belong to the tribe of Benjamin, then they along with all other Jews worldwide will be repatriated to Israel. The planes or ships will come from Israel or the International Christian Embassy Jerusalem or somewhere and take all of those who are descendants of Benjamin to Israel. It does not matter if they are Christians or not, they will all go to Israel. Kiru says that they assume that the tribe of Benjamin is the only tribe that has not yet been restored to Israel, and when they go back to Israel the end of the world will come.[58]

In addition to the International Christian Embassy Jerusalem, Timothy's cult associates with the All Pacific Prayer Assembly led by Michael Maeliau, who is from the Solomon Islands. Maeliau is a self-proclaimed prophet who was formerly an ordained minister of the South Sea Evangelical Church of the Solomon Islands.[59] He is one of the founders of the All Peoples Prayer Assembly[60] and a member of the Jerusalem House of Prayer for all Nations led by Tom and Kate Hess.[61] The prophets associated with the All Pacific Prayer Assembly held a meeting at Tari in 2008 during which they affirmed that the people of the Nembi Valley belonged to the lost tribe of Benjamin. For Timothy's staunchest followers, that was adequate confirmation that they were from the lost tribe of Benjamin.[62]

Timothy Map had a strong following among all of the Christian Union Churches until the 1997 elections. After the elections, the fighting restricted his travel and he was no longer able to visit all of the districts. He was very active in Ka District, and after the mission left, he became the de facto district leader even though he was not the elected leader. He was upset with the missionaries when they left Ka, and his anger increased when the mission cut the subsidy to the church. He had no official position on the regional board, but he continued to hold the title of "regional evangelist." Even though he did not hold a position on the RBT, he attended the CMCC meetings, and often served as a spokesperson for the RBT.

---

sam/48936742.html [accessed on August 21, 2014.]).

[58]Kiru, "A Critical Evaluation," 4-5.

[59]The South Sea Evangelical Church of the Solomon Islands severed all ties with Michael Maeliau and his teachings on August 19, 2009. ("South Sea Evangelical Church Position Paper on the Teaching of Rev. Michael Maeliau" August 19, 2009 http://64.37.52.84/~ssecorgs/wp-content/uploads/2013/06/Position-Paper.pdf [accessed on August 22, 2014].

[60]The All Pacific Prayer Assembly grew out of the first World Prayer Assembly that was held in Seoul, Korea in 1984. A regional prayer assembly called the South Pacific Prayer Assembly was started in the Solomon Islands in 1991. In 2003 at a meeting of the assembly held in Vanuatu, the name was changed to the All Pacific Prayer Assembly. In 2013 the name was changed again, and it is now called the All Peoples' Prayer Assembly. (Miloalii Siilata, "The Prayer Movement Behind the Deep Sea Canoe Vision," http://www.ipcprayer.org/upload/resources/items/The_Deep_Sea_Canoe_Vision_1.pdf [Accessed on August 22, 2014]).

[61]Jaep Timmer, "Straightening the Path from the Ends of the Earth: The Deep Sea Canoe Movement in the Solomon Islands" in *Flows of Faith: Religious Reach and Community in Asia and the Pacific*, edited by Lenore Manderson, Wendy Smith, and Matt Tomlinson, [Heidelberg: Springer, 2012], 207-208

[62]Kiru, "A Critical Evaluation," 4.

In Chapter Six I wrote about a confrontational CMCC meeting held in February of 2001 in Hagen when the RBT demanded that the subsidy be increased. Timothy along with the all the members of the RBT came to the meeting, but the missionaries and stateside officials did not allow Timothy to speak because he was not a member of the RBT. One of my interviewees said that when Timothy returned to the Nembi Valley, he reported that WGM headquarters wanted to give one million kina to the church, but the missionaries would not allow it. Timothy said that the missionaries were hurting the church and the missionaries were condemned to be lost. During the dedication of the Angal Enen New Testament held in March of 2002, my interviewee approached John Muelhiesen[63] to learn if there was any truth to the story that the missionaries had prevented WGM from giving one million *kina* to the church. Muelhiesen told him, "We of the World Gospel Mission give support to the missionaries around the world. WGM supports only the missionaries. WGM does not give support to the church."[64]

In the 2002 national elections, Timothy was again a candidate for the Nipa-Kutubu Open Electorate, even though the regional board had asked him not to run. He again lost the election, and some of my interviewees claimed that politics corrupted him. There was a lot of political unrest in all of the Southern Highlands following the 2002 elections. In March of 2003, Timothy wrote a letter to the RBT asking if they and the mission wanted to reemploy him as a regional evangelist. He asked that the church/mission support him financially and that he be given a tent. He said that if they did not employ him to be a regional evangelist, "*Mi bai givim kaikai long Ka District tasol.*" (I will give food only to the people of Ka District.) The RBT waited six months to bring the request to the meeting to the CMCC meeting, but the meeting ended before the letter was revealed. When asked why they had waited so long to bring the letter to the missionaries' attention, they responded, "We don't know how to answer him."[65]

The missionaries assumed that the lack of finances lay behind the church's reluctance to respond to Timothy's request. The subsidy had been eliminated, and the church leaders told the mission that they could no longer evangelize or reach out to new areas without the subsidy. I suspect that the church leaders had begun to question Timothy's ethics and his theology. Several of my interviewees told me that politics in PNG are corrupting. It is almost impossible for a pastor to run for office and maintain his integrity. For several years, Timothy had been urging the Christians to support Israel and rumors about DNA testing were circulating. Many of the pastors questioned the validity of those teachings. None of these reasons were stated in the written records, but members of the RBT would have been fully aware of the concerns.

Timothy was not reinstated as the regional evangelist, and he confined his

---

[63] At the time Mulhiesen was the WGM director of field ministries.

[64] My interviewee said that Timothy is disillusioned with the missionaries and uses stories like that to encourage his followers to avoid the missionaries.

[65] Dean Queen e-mail to Tim Bennett, Ruth Tipton, Dennis Johnson, Kevin Zirkle, and George Neal, September 25, 2003.

teachings to Ka District. He says that God has talked to him repeatedly. When I interviewed him, I asked him to tell me about the times that he heard God's voice speaking directly to him. He told me that it would be impossible to tell about all of the times God has spoken to him. He keeps a written record of God's communications with him. I asked him if I could make photo copies of those records, but he did not share them with me. He did tell me about one of the times that God had spoken to him. It was on Wednesday May 7, 2008 at 6:34[66] and God said, "No matter how many servants and how many prophets are raised at the end times, from different regions and areas, they and you will come to one point which goes to Jerusalem at last." He said that meant that Christians from every church on earth will go to Jerusalem in Israel before the second coming.

Timothy's teachings became less and less orthodox, and increasingly concerned with eschatological themes, and he became increasingly involved with Michael Maeliau,[67] whom I mentioned earlier. In 1986 Maeliau had a vision that he considered to be a revelation from God. He saw a flood of crystal clear water make its way through a valley and flow over the bank of a dam and then change into cloud that traveled around the South Pacific, to the Americas, to Europe, to Africa and to Asia. It went to all parts of the earth and then formed a perfect circle around Jerusalem after which it shot into the sky and flooded the entire earth. Then a voice spoke from heaven and said, "And the glory of the Lord shall cover the earth as the waters cover the sea."[68] The meaning of the vision came to him slowly and was not fully revealed until he was in Papua New Guinea in 2004 and 2005 and at a prayer assembly in Singapore in 2005. It means that there will be a third great invasion[69] of the "manifest presence" or Glory of God that will begin in the uttermost parts of the earth (the South Pacific Region) and sweep around the

---

[66]He did not say whether it was A.M. or P.M.

[67]It is not clear how or exactly when Timothy formed an association with Maeliau, but Maeliau made frequent trips to PNG. In November of 2004 Maeliau was in Port Moresby and in April of 2005 he was in Maprik. When I went to PNG for my research trip from November to February of 2009 and 2010, the CUC regional board of trustees was evaluating and dealing with the issues that Timothy's teachings raised for the church. By then Timothy Map was an established associate of Michael Maeliau. They had copies of e-mails that had passed between Michael Maeliau and officials of the South Sea Evangelical Church while they were investigating Michael's teachings. In those e-mails Maeliau mentions those trips to PNG and the revelations he received while in Port Moresby and Maprik.

[68]Michael Maeliau, "The Deep Sea Canoe Vision" http://www.ipcprayer.org/upl-oad/resources/items/The_Deep_Sea_Canoe_Vision_1.pdf [accessed on August 22, 2014]. Maeliau has written a book about his vision and the movement that it started, but I was unable to get a copy through the libraries, and did not purchase a copy although it is available on-line. The citation for the book is Michael Maeliau, *The Deep Sea Canoe Movement: An Account of the Prayer Movement in the Pacific Islands over the Last Twenty Years.* [Canberra: B & M Pub, 2007].

[69]Michael Maeliau, "The Third Great Invasion of Planet Earth by God in Person" attached to a letter to Ken Taylor, The General Secretary South Sea Evangelical Church, 26th September, 2005.

earth and reach its climax in Jerusalem at the Feast of the Tabernacles.[70] Maeliau says that the first great invasion was the coming of Christ to earth. The second great invasion was when the Holy Spirit came on the Day of Pentecost, and the third great invasion is yet to come. He acknowledged that the doctrine of a third great invasion of God's presence on earth was new to the church, but justified it as a revelation that came from God.

He called his vision the "Deep Sea Canoe Vision." Maeliau has obviously borrowed the term "Deep Sea Canoe" from Alan Tippett who wrote about South Pacific Islanders and their missionary outreach throughout the South Pacific in a well-known book entitled *The Deep Sea Canoe*.[71] Tippett would not have sanctioned the teachings of Maeliau and his fellow prophets.

The influence that Michael Maeliau has over the thinking of some of the leaders of Papua New Guinea is evidenced by a proclamation that Michael Somare, who was then the prime minister of Papua New Guinea, made on August 26, 2007. He declared a covenant between the people of Papua New Guinea and the God of Israel. The written covenant begins by quoting Jeremiah 31:33-34 which says,

> "I will put my law in their minds and write it on their hearts. I will be their God, and they will be my people. No longer will a man teach his neighbor, or a man his brother, saying, 'know the Lord', because they will all know me. From the least of them to the greatest," declares the Lord, "For I will forgive their wickedness and ill remember their sins no more."[72]

Somare then concurs "with the Terms and Conditions of this Covenant" and

> entreats the Lord on behalf of the people of Papua New Guinea, that God would fulfill the stated intent of this Covenant to become applicable to my nation and peoples who today join me in declaring that the God of Israel is also their God.[73]

Somare, as prime minister of Papua New Guinea, signed the covenant at the Sione Kami Memorial Church (a United Church affiliate), and Michael Maeliau was one of the witnesses who signed the covenant. Papua New Guinea now celebrates an annual covenant day.[74]

The All Peoples Prayer Assembly has established a presence in New Zealand,

---

[70]Maeliau, "The Third Great Invasion" attached to a letter to Ken Taylor.

[71]Alan R. Tippett, The Deep-Sea Canoe: The Story of Third World Missionaries in the South Pacific. South Pasadena, CA: William Carey Library, 1977.

[72]The scripture reads "I will put my law in their minds and write it on their hearts. I will be their God, and they will be my people. No longer will a man teach his neighbor, or a man his brother, saying, 'know the Lord', because they will all know me. From the least of them to the greatest," declares the Lord, "For I will forgive their wickedness and will remember their sins no more." These words are quoted in their entirety in Hebrews 8:10-12, and in part in Hebrews 10:16-17\.

[73]https://masalai.files.wordpress.com/2013/08/covenant_day_somare_2007.jpg [accessed on June 4, 2015

[74]Conversation with Michael A. Rynkiewich who visited Papua New Guinea in March of 2015.

Australia, Papua New Guinea, and Hawaii.[75] Its primary purpose is to "track the Deep Sea Canoe Vision, outlining the move of God's glory from the ends of the earth back to Jerusalem, for its official launching to the world."[76] Timothy Map has associated himself with the All Pacific Prayer Assembly, as it was then called, and its leaders. He has embraced its teachings and has begun to instruct the people in Ka District about the return of the Glory. Many of Timothy's followers testified to having dreams and visions about the end times and the return of the Glory.[77]

When I interviewed Timothy,[78] he was reluctant to talk about some of his beliefs, and claimed to have no knowledge of some teachings that many of my interviewees told me were prevalent among his followers. He did explain his understanding of the coming "Glory." The Glory meant the presence of God. In the Old Testament, it led the Israelites through the wilderness in the form of a cloud by day and a pillar of fire by night.[79] After the temple was built at Jerusalem, the Glory dwelt there in the temple, but the Glory departed Jerusalem in 70 AD when the Roman government destroyed the second temple. According to Timothy, Ezekiel 11:23;[80] Exekiel 20: 47, 49;[81] Ezekiel 43:2-6:[82] and Revelation 15:8[83] were unfulfilled prophesies that prove that the Glory of God has to return to Jerusalem and enter the temple by way of the Eastern Gate before the end of time.[84] The people in

---

[75]Timmer, "Straightening the Path," 208.

[76]Miloalii Siilata, "The Prayer Movement Behind the Deep Sea Canoe Vision," http:// www.ipcprayer.org/upload/resources/items/The_Deep_Sea_Canoe_Vision_1.pdf [Accessed on August 22, 2014].

[77]When I asked Timothy about the dreams and visions, he said that many of his followers testified to having dreams and visions, but he never had dreams or visions. He preached the words that God told him to preach. They were not dreams and visions.

[78]Unless otherwise cited, I gleaned the information from the rest of this section from my interview with Timothy Map at Ka, Poroma District, Southern Highland Province of Papua New Guinea, January 13, 2010.

[79]Exodus 13:21-22.

[80]The glory of the Lord went up from within the city and stopped above the mountain east of it. (Ezekiel 11:23 NIV)

[81]Say to the word of the southern forest: 'Hear the word of the Lord. This is what the Sovereign Lord says: I am about to set fire to you, and it will consume all your trees, both green and dry. The blazing flame will not be quenched, and every face from south to north will be scorched by it.'... Then I said, "Ah, Sovereign Lord! They are saying of me, 'Isn't he just telling parables?'" (Ezekiel 20:47, 49).

[82]...and I saw the glory of the God of Israel coming from the east. His voice was like the roar of rushing waters, and the land was radiant with his glory. The vision I saw was like the vision I had seen when he came to destroy the city and like the visions I had seen by the Kebar River, and I fell facedown. The glory of the Lord entered the temple through the gate facing east. Then the Spirit lifted me up and brought me into the inner court, and the glory of the Lord filled the temple. While the man was standing beside me, I heard someone speaking to me from inside the temple... (Ezekiel 43:2-6).

[83]And the temple was filled with smoke from the glory of God and from his power, and no one could enter the temple until the seven plagues of the seven angels were completed. (Revelation 15:8)

[84]When Timothy gave me the above references, he first said Ezekiel 40:47 and 49, but

the Pacific and Asia countries were talking a lot about the return of God's Glory, and were responsible for moving the Glory of God and making it go.

When I interviewed Timothy, he had moved away from Ka station and was living on his own land about one-half mile away at a place that he called the Blessing Center. On his land, he built a complex of many houses that he called the Kingdom Leadership Institute. Representatives from the Asia Pacific region were going to come and hold courses and have discussion about how they could hasten the coming of the Glory. In 2007 and 2008, God had shown Timothy that 2010 was going to be the Glory year.

The Kingdom Leadership Institute was officially opened on December 16, 2009, and Michael Maeliau came for the opening. The prophets had been searching for the place where the Glory (presence) of God dwelt and had narrowed it down, first to the Pacific area, then to Papua New Guinea, then to the Southern Highlands of Province, and finally to the Nembi Valley. In the Nembi Valley the people feared and respected God and worshiped him daily. On December 16, 2009, by revelation, the prophets declared that the Nembi Valley was the core center where the Glory of God was hiding. All else would be revealed according to God's plan and in God's own time, but God had told Timothy that 2010 would be the Glory year. When the Glory of God returns it will be a cataclysmic event that will be reported worldwide, and people from all over the world will participate in the event. Before the Glory returns to Jerusalem, the third temple must be built.

Timothy made his second trip to Israel in September of 2009. When he told me about his second trip to Israel, he mentioned three ancient trade routes—the gold road, the spice road, and the incense road—that had gone from the Asia Pacific region to Jerusalem.[85] According to Timothy, the gold for Solomon's temple came from the Solomon Islands. One of the roads followed the same route that Solomon's ship had used when it came to the Solomon Islands and then returned to Jerusalem with gold for the temple.[86]

Beginning in 2007, the church's regional conference and the regional board of trustees carefully scrutinized Timothy's teachings and questioned whether he should remain a part of CUC of PNG. The regional council discussed the issue in 2007 and again in 2008, but delayed making the final decision until the regional conference held at Montanda in September of 2009. Timothy's followers came to the 2009 regional conference, but Timothy did not. His followers informed the council that Timothy was out of the country. He had gone to the Solomon Islands.

They further explained his views. When the Israelites left Egypt and went to Canaan, God wanted to give Glory to all of Israel. However, the Israelites were proud and defiant, and God took the Glory and hid it somewhere else. Timothy

---

quickly corrected himself and said Ezekiel 20:47 and 49. I am not sure if he gave the wrong reference, or if he is interpreting the fire mentioned in verse forty-seven to refer to glory.

[85] The prophets have redefined the original trade routes that went from Asia to Europe.

[86] Timothy said that the gold road went from the Solomon Islands to Jerusalem, but some of the written documentation that I have (cited below) said that the spice road went from the Solomon Islands to Jerusalem.

and Michael Maeliau and their associates had gone out. Some had gone to Singapore; others went to the Pacific Island countries; and still others went to Japan; and they would all meet at Jerusalem at the Eastern Gate. The prophets were searching for the Glory, and they would find the "hidden treasure" and bring it back on December 19.

I did not understand what they were searching for until I read a paper by Pastor George Annadorai from Singapore who is one of the prophets associated with the All Pacific Prayer Group. He and two other prophets—Maeliau from the Solomon Islands, and Andrew Chang from Taiwan—had a revelation that the ancient paths spoken of in Jeremiah 6:16-20[87] were the incense road, the spice road, and the silk road and they had all converged at Jerusalem that was then the ancient crossroads and "the center of the earth."[88]

They argue that the Eastern gate had three portals known as the Golden Gate, the Lion's Gate, and the Bethany Gate. The silk route went from Japan to the Lion's Gate. The Incense route went from Singapore to the Golden Gate, and the spice route went from the Solomon Islands to the Bethany Gate. The prophets said that Jerusalem was God's first born son, and the islands from which the goods originated were God's last born son. They organized a prophetic journey called 'J616' to take place in 2009. Three different groups would conduct a prayer voyage following the three ancient paths. The three groups would meet at the Eastern Gate in Jerusalem on September 19, 2009. They believed that tremendous wealth passed along the ancient routes to Jerusalem, but the people of Judah became greedy, and God closed the ancient paths and everything came to an abrupt end.[89]

The prophets believed that, according to Isaiah 45:1-3,[90] God had hidden treasures at the Eastern Gate in Jerusalem, and they expected to regain the hidden wealth when they arrived at the Eastern Gate at the end of the 'J616' prophetic journey. "God from heaven will give us 'keys' to these hidden treasure chests resulting in millions and billions of dollars (cash and convertibles) being trans-

---

[87]This is what the Lord says: "Stand at the crossroads and look; ask for the ancient paths, ask where the good way is, and walk in it, and you will find rest for your souls. But you said, 'We will not walk in it.' I appointed watchmen over you and said, 'Listen to the sound of the trumpet!' But you said, 'We will not listen.' Therefore hear, you nations; you who are witnesses, observe what will happen to them. Hear, you earth: I am bringing disaster on this people, the fruit of their schemes, because they have not listened to my words and have rejected my law. What do I care about incense from Sheba or sweet calamus from a distant land? Your burnt offerings are not acceptable; your sacrifices do not please me." (Jeremiah 6:16-20)

[88]George Annadorai, "J616 Prophetic Launching," attached to e-mail from Brian Watts to the Solomon Islands Chruch, nd, 1-2.

[89]George Annadorai, "J616 Prophetic Launching," 2-3.

[90]"This is what the LORD says to his anointed, to Cyrus, whose right hand I take hold of to subdue nations before him and to strip kings of their armor, to open doors before him so that gates will not be shut: I will go before you and will level the mountains; I will break down gates of bronze and cut through bars of iron. I will give you hidden treasures, riches stored in secret places, so that you may know that I am the LORD, the God of Israel, who summons you by name." (Isaiah 45:1-3)

ferred to God's people over the next seven years (2008-2015)."[91] They believed, further that the "wealth of the unrighteous" would be given to the "righteous." They thought it had to happen before the return of Christ and they were trying to "hasten the coming of the Lord." The world was "about to witness the great fall of Babylon" as "the church took over her rightful place in the financial market taking over Babylon's assets and bringing it into the kingdom of God."[92]

During my research trip, a number of people told me that 'J616' was a code word for Timothy and his followers. Based on the report that Timothy's followers gave to the Regional conference, he participated in the 'J616' prophetic journey. When I interviewed Timothy, I asked him about 'J616', but he claimed to have no knowledge of it. He looked up Jeremiah 6:16[93] and said that it was not something that he used in his teaching, and that I should ask the person who uses the verse about its meanings. He thought that it might be related to the trade routes.

A number of Timothy's followers were listening to the interview, and they also feigned ignorance. The idea may not have originated with Timothy, but the research evidence suggests that they knew more about 'J616' than they wanted to disclose. Further, it suggests that the blessings they seek by supporting Israel and the coming Glory that they await includes significant material blessings.

It is very difficult to discover Timothy's teachings. When I interviewed him, he evaded some of my questions, and when I questioned his followers they told me to ask the prophet. I do not know what new teachings have emerged during the five years that have passed since I interviewed him. One of the missionaries, Butch Jenkins, interviewed Timothy, but learned little. Timothy has prepared a constitution for his cult and is in the process of registering the Spiritual Harvest Ministry with the PNG government.[94] Timothy told me that he was not changing the teachings of Christian Union Church or bringing a new church into the area. He had associated himself with an international prayer group and sent money to support the International Christian Embassy Jerusalem, and that was all. He did not dispute the teachings of Christian Union Church of PNG.[95]

---

[91]George Annadorai, "J616 Prophetic Launching," 8.

[92]George Annadorai, "J616 Prophetic Launching," 8-9.

[93]Thus says the Lord: 'Stand in the ways and see, and ask for the old paths, where the good way is, and walk in it; then you will find rest for your souls.' (Jeremiah 6:16)

[94]Butch Jenkins, personal conversation, January, 2014.

[95]Timothy Map, interview by author, Ka, Poroma District, Southern Highlands Province, Papua New Guinea, January 13, 2014.

The Consequences

As Timothy's teachings became increasingly radicalized, the missionaries and church leaders talked to him several times to tell him that they saw errors in his teachings, and that he should quit teaching his new doctrines. He refused to quit. As mentioned previously, three consecutive regional councils held at Poroma in 2007, at Hagen in 2008, and at Montanda in 2009 discussed the teachings and found that they were inconsistent with the doctrines and beliefs of Christian Union Church of PNG. In 2009 the regional council voted that unless Timothy Map gave up his teachings about Israel, he could no longer be a part of Christian Union Church, could not speak in CUC churches or use any CUC properties.

Disputed doctrines included the following. First, Timothy had compromised the integrity of the scriptures. He says that God talks to him, and consequently he has a special relationship with God. The revelations that he receives cannot be Biblically substantiated but he claims that they come from the Holy Spirit and his declarations take precedence over scripture. "The Bible is no longer necessary... for the Holy Spirit teaches and reveals everything."[96]

Second, they were concerned about his teachings on the Holy Spirit. His followers are afraid to speak out against Timothy and his teachings. He tells them that God will not forgive the sins of anyone who speaks against the Holy Spirit. Because his revelations come from the Holy Spirit, anyone who speaks against Timothy speaks against the Holy Spirit, and his or her sins will "stick to him or her like coal tar" and that person will be lost.[97] Timothy also teaches that the Holy Spirit must return to heaven before the Glory comes and everything ends. At one point Timothy announced that the Holy Spirit informed him (Timothy) that He (the Holy Spirit) had departed from CUC of PNG.[98]

The CUC logo shows a dove descending to represent the coming of the Holy Spirit on the day of the day of Pentecost. On one of his trips to Port Moresby Timothy changed the logo to show the dove ascending rather than descending. The church leaders adamantly opposed Timothy's action. The church had discussed the existing logo, agreed on it, and adopted it. No individual had the authority to change the logo. The Bible does not say that the Holy Spirit has left the church. "How could Timothy make that claim?" The church leaders saw it as an act of insubordination.[99]

---

[96]Kiru, "A Critical Evaluation," 4-7.

[97]I am withholding the name of the interviewee. He is referring to Matthew 12:31-32, Mark 3:29 and Luke 12: 10.

[98]Timothy Map, interview by author, at Ka, Poroma District, Southern Highlands Province, Papua New Guinea, January 13, 2010.

[99]Several pastors talked about the changing of the church logo. Two of my interviewees were especially adamant about their opposition to the change. I have based this chapter on their comments, but have opted to withhold their names.

Figure 10:
CUC of PNG Logo

A third concern was that Timothy refused to submit himself to the authority of the regional council and the regional and district boards. They repeatedly asked him to quit teaching about Israel, about the people of the Nembi Valley belonging to the tribe of Benjamin, about being transported to Israel before the last day, about the departure of the Holy Spirit, and about the coming of the Glory of God, but he refused to stop. He is the sole leader in the services that he holds, and does not allow other pastors or church leaders to speak.[100]

Fourth, Timothy misinterpreted and misapplied scriptures such as Micah 2:12[101] and Jeremiah 29:14[102] that talk about the restoration of the Jews to Israel.[103] Every church leader who talked about the *Spiritual Harvest Ministry* during their interviews objected strongly to the teaching that the people in the Nembi Valley

---

[100]Nearly all of the church leaders that talked to me about Timothy, spoke of his unwillingness to submit to the authority of others.

[101]"I will surely gather all of you, Jacob; I will surely bring together the remnant of Israel. I will bring them together like sheep in a pen, like a flock in its pasture; the place will throng with people." (Micah 2:12).

[102]"I will be found by you," declares the LORD, "and will bring you back from captivity. I will gather you from all the nations and places where I have banished you," declares the LORD, "and will bring you back to the place from which I carried you into exile." (Jeremiah 29:14)

[103]Kiru, "A Critical Evaluation," 8.

belonged to the tribe of Benjamin and would be transported back to Israel before the end of the world. They found no scriptural or historical evidence to support the claim. Some said that that the teaching links the Christians' ultimate salvation to their relationship to the Jewish people and their willingness to support Israel rather than to their relationship to Christ and his death on the cross.[104]

When the regional council voted to expel Timothy and his followers, Timothy was out of the country and the regional council instructed the regional board to confront Timothy after he returned to PNG. The meeting took place at Ka on December 8, 2009.[105] When the RBT arrived for the confrontation Timothy and his followers were already gathered at the church. In a very tense atmosphere, the regional board of trustees took over the meeting. All of the regional church leaders spoke first. Afterwards they invited Timothy to speak and gave all of the Ka District church members and the leaders of the youth and the women a chance to speak. Even some of the non-Christians spoke up, but the church leaders told them it was a church meeting, not a village court, and only the Christians had the right to speak at the meeting. As the regional council had instructed, the RBT told Timothy that he and his followers were no longer a part of CUC. He should register his church under another name. Timothy objected, but in the end, he and his followers left CUC and held their services at the International Leadership Institute that Timothy had built at the Blessing Center at Utabia.

Some of Timothy's followers were incensed, and that night they torched a house that belonged to a pastor from Ka who did not follow Timothy. They thought that the pastor was responsible for Timothy's expulsion from CUC.[106]

The regional board told all of the pastors in Ka District to choose between Timothy and CUC. If they accepted Timothy's teachings, they could not be a part of CUC. One of the church leaders said that all of Timothy's kin group and close associates would follow him because "*bilip i bihainim blut*" (belief follows the blood lines). Many of the pastors in Ka District belong to Timothy's kin group. Others belong to groups that have strong political and fight alliances with Timothy's kin group. Except for those who joined the newly formed Lower Mendi Area, only one or two remained with CUC.[107]

In January of 2014, several people told me that a number of Timothy's followers are thinking about returning to CUC for several reasons. Timothy asks his

---

[104]Kiru, "A Critical Evaluation," 7.

[105]There were no missionaries at the confrontation. At the time, only one missionary family was on the field, and the church leaders handled the confrontation on their own.

[106]The pastor said that he had not reported Timothy to the RBT. At the regional council he had voted against the expulsion. During the meeting some had accused him, but when he responded to his accusers, most of the people accepted his denials, but some of Timothy's followers did not, and burned his house that night. He believed that they acted on their own without Timothy's knowledge or approval.

[107]When the church held its regional youth camp in Mount Hagen in December of 2013, only four youth from Ka District attended. Compared to Timothy, the District Superintendent is a weak leader, but he says that he has not accepted Timothy's teachings. One church remains in the district, and one or two others claim loyalty to both sides.

followers to contribute a lot of money to the support of Israel and other causes. Some say they are tired of the constant requests for money, and are thinking about returning to CUC where the demands are less. Some complain that Timothy is accountable to no one. He has no board and limits the participation in the services that he leads. One woman I talked to said that she used to attend Timothy's services, but now she stays away because everything is centered around one man. His followers bow in front of him before they give a testimony or take part in a service. She wanted no part of it because Christians should bow to no one but God.[108]

Reflection about Spiritual Harvest Ministry

As I stated above, the Spiritual Harvest Ministry or "*Israel Lotu*" (Israel Church), as the Nembi call it, is a millenarian cult with cargo expectations. The primary emphasis of the cult is two-fold. It looks at the so-called "unfulfilled prophecies" in the Old Testament, re-interprets them out of context, and seeks to reconcile isolated proof texts with current events. One of the primary concerns is the restoration of the Jewish people to Israel and the need for Christians to support Israel and assist poverty stricken Jews so they can return to their homeland and thus hasten the return of Christ. Before Christ returns and all things come to an end, the Holy Spirit must return to heaven, and the presence or Glory of God which departed from the earth in 70 AD, when the second temple was destroyed, must again manifest itself on earth in a third great invasion. When the Glory of God reveals itself, it will sweep around the earth beginning in the Nembi Valley, going across the Pacific, the Americas, Europe, Africa, and Asia, and ending up at Jerusalem where it will reenter the third temple that must be built before all things can conclude. In the meantime, Christians must support Israel and God in turn will "bless" them. "Blessings" mean that their gardens will produce well, and they will prosper. Jesus was a Jew, and God would not desert his chosen people, and he would bless those who helped the Jews.

Trompf says that cargo cults vary, and so does the amount of cargo that cultists expect to receive.[109] Annadorai's report about the prophetic journey to Jerusalem in 2009 to search for the "hidden treasure" concealed at the Eastern Gate of Jerusalem,[110] and Timothy's participation in the prophetic journey, suggest that the cult has expectations of great "blessings" in the form of significant wealth.

The second primary emphasis is the relationship of the people in the Nembi Valley to the Jewish people. The prophet says that God has revealed that they belong to the tribe of Benjamin. They wait for DNA testing that will prove that they belong to the lost tribes of Israel. That will allow them to go to Jerusalem before everything comes to an end, and their salvation will be assured because they are a part of God's chosen people.

---

[108]Name withheld.

[109]G. W. Trompf, *Melanesian religion.* [Cambridge, England: Cambridge University Press, 1991], 197.

[110]Annadorai, 3, 8-9.

It is worth noting that, as suggested by Somare's declaration of a covenant between Papua New Guinea and the God of Israel mentioned earlier, similar cults have developed elsewhere in Papua New Guinea. I do not know the situations that led to the development of the other cults, the stories of the prophets who lead the cults, or the details the messages they proclaim, but the groups prominently display the flag of Israel in their services and wear the Star of David on their clothing, give money to support Israel, and march on Covenant Day. Recently a member of parliament from the Eastern Highlands of Papua New Guinea gave K40,000 towards the support of Israel.[111]

This raises the question, what insights can the writings of scholars who have studied millenarian movements give about the development of the Spiritual Harvest Ministry and similar cults? Scholars have formed various explanations for the outbreak of cargo cults.

One of the earliest was F. E. Williams, who studied cargo cults that occurred along the Gulf coast of Papua beginning at the end of 1919 into the first half of the 1920s. The people expected deceased relatives to return on a ship bringing an abundance of European goods. The people exhibited strange behavior. Williams' explanation was that rapid cultural change caused the emergence of craziness and that the desire for cargo drove the people to "madness."[112] Kiki who was from the Gulf Province takes strong exception to Williams' assessment and says that cargo may have been one element of the movement, "but the main purpose of the strange behavior was an attempt to contact the dead."[113]

Peter Lawrence, who studied cargo cults in the Madang area from 1871 to 1950, argues that there was no "madness." When the values and the epistemology of the traditional system are applied to cargo cults, they have an "almost unassailable logic." Colonization and missionization brought changes to the people's way of life and to the material culture, but the changes were superficial. They did not "affect the basic principles of traditional behaviour and relationships."[114] In other words, they did not change the underlying worldview of the Madang people. The cargo movements were an attempt to control the changes that came their way and they were an expression of the belief that ritual produces cargo and well-being.[115] They were "strongly conservative in character" and could be attributed to "too little rather than too much change."[116]

---

[111]Conversation with Michael A. Rynkiewich who visited Papua New Guinea in March, 2015.

[112]F. E. Williams, *"The Vailala Madness" and Other Essays.* [Honolulu: University Press of Hawaii, 1977], 331-395.

[113]Albert Maori Kiki, *Kiki; Ten Thousand Years in a Lifetime, A New Guinea Autobiography.* [New York: F.A. Praeger, 1968], 51.

[114]Peter Lawrence, *Road Belong Cargo; A Study of the Cargo Movement in the Southern Madang District, New Guinea.* [Manchester: Manchester University Press, 1964], 223.

[115]Lawrence, *Road Belong Cargo,* 224.

[116]Lawrence, *Road Belong Cargo,* 223.

Peter Worsley, who studied numerous cargo cults throughout Melanesia, argued that cargo cults were burgeoning political movements rebelling against colonialism. They were, according to Worsley, an early expression of nationalism.[117]

Vittorio Lanternari, who studied cults around the world, says that cargo cults developed primarily for economic reasons. The cargo cults were a "reaction of people living in cultural and material poverty to the sudden appearance among them of new and unimagined riches."[118] In Melanesia people assumed that the material goods came from the spirits, and the cult movements occurred because the people expected the spirits to enable them to move out of poverty.[119]

More recently Franco Zocca, drawing on the work of Friedrich Steinbauer, a German anthropologist, said that the reasons for the development of cargo cults can be placed into five different categories. First, cargo cults sometimes develop for socio-political reasons. They are the result of a confrontation with a more powerful foreign culture and a determination not to be relegated to a position of inferiority. This was Worsley's argument. He saw the cult movements as embryonic political movements.

Second, ethical-Christian reasons may lead to the development of a cult. There is a deep-seated desire for the good life and a plentitude of spiritual and material blessings and they create rituals to help them acquire what they want. This was Lawrence's premise. People wanted their share of the material goods the Europeans had, and tried to obtain them according to their local beliefs.

The third reason is related to historical-cultural reasons. During a time of crisis, they return to their traditional myths to help them cope with sudden change. This hints at Anthony Wallace's theory of revitalization that I discussed in chapter four. People are dissatisfied with their cultural system and set out to change it.

The fourth explanation has to do with economical-rational reasons. People cannot explain where the wealth comes from, and lacking an adequate understanding of economics, technology, and science, they formulate a hypothesis to explain how it originates and from whence it comes. This resonates with Lawrences' theory as well.

Finally, Zocca says, most cults do not start for a single reason, but they develop when several of the above reasons come together to create the cult.[120]

Trompf says that theories about cargo cults that most scholars have developed discount religious reasons, but cargo cults cannot be adequately accounted for unless they include religious reasons. "Social scientists are going to have to shift out of those mindsets that disallow religion any explanatory function in the analysis of social life which westerners too often compartmen-

---

[117]Peter Worsley, *The Trumpet Shall Sound; A Study of "Cargo" Cults in Melanesia.* [New York: Schocken Books, 1968], 228-256.

[118]LanteVittorio Lanternari. *The Religions of the Oppressed; A Study of Modern Messianic Cults.* [New York: Knopf, 1963], 229.

[119]Lanternari, *The Religions of the Oppressed*, 232-235.

[120]Zocca, 173-175.

talize into non-religious spheres."[121] The cults embrace the Melanesian view of reciprocity and the logic of negative and positive retribution. Some erupt into violence, but others create "the perfection of reciprocal relations" that leads to the "total resolution of material, human and human-spirit relationships."[122]

> Cargo cults will never be understood through hermeneutics made cock-eyed by 'secular' university disciplines. For, perhaps more arrestingly than any other social phenomena, they gather up physically sublimated collective vindictiveness, the deep human desire for material security and community harmony, and the concerns for right relationships with the spiritual 'realm' into 'total visions' of the cosmos.[123]

So, what insights do these theories give concerning the development of the Spiritual Harvest Ministry? They all say cults develop when there is an element of dissatisfaction with the situation as it is. The cult developed in the midst of political discontent and a desire for the good life that was slipping away from the cult's adherents. The cult acknowledges June 27, 1999, as its founding day. During the previous two years, the prophet had been a candidate in the 1997 elections and lost and as a result the community was involved in a tribal war. Two months earlier, the mission had withdrawn during "*taim bilong hevi*" (a time of trouble), leaving the people disillusioned and dissatisfied. Tribal fights drain the groups of their assets. They must equip their warriors with weapons and ammunition. They must compensate their allies for any deaths or injuries that occur while fighting on their behalf. Enemies destroy gardens, burn houses, kill their pigs. Everyone loses major assets whether they belong to the victorious or vanquished groups.

The fight started because of politics. One man from Utabia said that during the fight, thousands of dollars were lost on businesses, PMV trucks, and other property. Before the fight, Utabia prospered, but during the fight it was destroyed. When the cult started, the prophet's kin group had not yet paid compensation for a number of the men who had died. If the cult is stopped, then there will be a lot of trouble at Utabia, and the people will demand that the prophet and his kin group pay large compensations for those who died in the fight. The cult leader and many of his followers are driven by the hope and expectation that their religious beliefs and practices will bring them to prosperity.[124]

As I wrote in Chapter Four, traditional Melanesian religions performed rituals to ensure that they maintained a good relationship with the spirit beings that made them prosper. It is an expectation that has been brought into the present, and the Christians believe that Christ has brought them prosperity. In January of 2014 at the fifty-year celebration, one of the leading women from the Port Moresby District told me that God made the Christians prosper. She told me to look at those who were not Christians. They wasted their money on foolish things that those who followed God avoided, and the Christians had more. God made them prosper.

---

[121]Trompf, *Melanesian Religion*, 202.

[122]Trompf, *Melanesian Religion*, 203.

[123]Trompf, *Melanesian Religion*, 205.

[124]I am withholding the name of the interviewee and the person that he was quoting. The statement came from a member of Timothy Map's kin group who has withdrawn from the cult.

The people from Ka District embraced the cult because of the "blessings" that it promised to bring to them. They do not think that they turned away from Christ or denied their faith. They trust the misguided prophet to give them new insights; show them how to improve their relationship with God and his chosen people; and lead them to greater prosperity and the end times. They reason according to their traditional group-oriented thinking and their expectations of reciprocity. God is their father, and a father never abandons his children. As descendants of the lost tribe of Benjamin, their ultimate prosperity and their eternal salvation is assured. In the meantime, they give fully expecting God to reciprocate by making them prosper.

Some of the leaders of Christian Union Church think that the cult's adherents will become disillusioned by the cult leader's unfulfilled prophesies and empty promises and will return to the more orthodox teachings of Christian Union Church. Cliff Kiru, a member of CUC of PNG now studying at CLTC, says that "sound biblical teachings" that are appropriately contextualized can be used to "correct, educate, and lead" the cult's adherents away from their "cultic culture" into authentic scriptural holiness.[125]

I now consider what can be learned from the story of Christian Union Mission and Christian Union Church of Papua New Guinea.

---

[125]Kiru, "A Critical Evaluation," 8.

Chapter Eight

Revitalization

Introduction

I have told the story of the missionaries who through their dedication and sacrifice preached the gospel and planted churches in the Southern and Western Highlands Provinces of Papua New Guinea, and the story of the people who overcame oppression, fear, misunderstanding, tremendous upheaval, and unprecedented change to help build a strong Christian presence in the two provinces. I have also shown that the church and the mission were often in conflict that grew out of the different cultural perspectives of the missionaries and the church leaders and the expectations that each had for the other. The conflict was fueled by the lack of economic development in the Nembi area. In this chapter I look at the cultural differences that caused the conflict, the lack of economic development that fueled it, and the expectations that remain unrealized. I then discuss the concerns that some of the church leaders express for the church's renewal, for better educated church leaders, and for the contextualization the gospel. Finally, I ask, "What's next?" I suggest that both sides need to examine themselves and ask how they can come together in an interdependent relationship and together do far more to advance the Kingdom of God than either could do on their own.

Worldview, Cultural Perspectives and Expectations

Hiebert said people from different cultures differ in their underlying beliefs and "basic assumptions" that "they use to organize their conceptual worlds. Hiebert said further,

> In trying to understand another culture, the outsider can observe human behavior and products but cannot see beliefs and worldviews. These can only be inferred from the acts and comments of the people. There may be no informant who will, or even can, verbalize the worldview of the culture, for it exists largely implicitly in the minds of the people.[1]

---

[1]Paul G. Hiebert. *Transforming Worldviews: An Anthropological Understanding of How People Change.* [Grand Rapids, Mich: Baker Academic, 2008], 89.

Both the missionaries and the Melanesian church leaders struggled to make their worldview known to the other and to understand the worldview of the other.

Worldview and Perspectives

The missionaries and the church leaders approached events and issues from opposite perspectives and neither understood the other. A simple table illustrates the differences between the missionaries and the church leaders.

Table 1: Cultural Perspectives	
Missionaries	*Nembi and Melpa Church Leaders*
Western worldview	Melanesian worldview
Ego-centric	Socio-centric
Dualistic	Monistic
Individual first	Group first
Separation of sacred and secular	No separation of sacred and secular

The missionaries view the world from a Western dualistic perspective that dichotomizes between sacred and secular. They prioritize what they consider to be spiritual ministries and view social ministries that promote health, education, or economic development as a means to an end and not a priority. The missionaries have an ego-centric world view. They see each person as an autonomous self-directed individual who is solely responsible for the decisions that he or she makes, builds his or her relationships out of individual contacts, and creates groups out of the individual relationships that he or she builds.

The mission used familial language to describe its relationship to the church. When it called itself a father to the church it meant that it was there to birth a fully independent, self-reliant church. Later it said it was a brother to the church. It was there to assist if needed, but it was to push the church away from dependency. The missionaries were deeply committed to the idea of developing an independent and fully autonomous entity that supported itself with funds that were generated within PNG. They believed that giving the church financial assistance created dependency and in the long run hurt the church.

The church leaders, on the other hand, view the world from a Melanesian monistic perspective that sees no separation between sacred and secular. The two are so intertwined that one cannot be separated from the other. The church leaders have a socio-centric world view. Each person is defined by the groups to which he or she belongs. Relationships create the individual, and the group's concerns take precedence above the concerns of the individual.

When the church used familial language to describe its relationship to the mission, its meaning was the opposite of the mission's meaning. From the church's perspective, a father would never abandon his son but strives to remain closely connected and is always ready to share his resources with his son. Brothers work together to advance the interests of both, and they do not forsake each other. The church expected the church and mission's relationship to become so tight that they functioned as one. When the Nembi and Melpa accepted the missionaries into their midst and converted to Christianity, they were entering into a long-term, on-going relationship with the missionaries and the sending church. They were one in Christ, and as such the mission was obligated to share its resources with the church. When the church lacked resources, it believed it should be able to depend on the mission to give them assistance. In short, the church wanted to depend on the mission to provide it with resources, but the mission wanted to avoid any suspicion of dependence on the part of the church.

The church's expectation for the mission to share its resources has its roots deep in the Melanesian worldview, and is reinforced by the Melanesian church leaders' reading of scripture. Melanesian societies are basically egalitarian. In the traditional society, a big-man was viewed as a person of status, prestige, and wealth; but the status was achieved, the prestige translated only into persuasion, not power, and the wealth was all borrowed and redistributed. He received a lot of goods, but he was expected to redistribute his wealth, and ultimately, he was expected to give it away and keep little for himself. He received goods from his followers and used those goods to establish exchange partnerships with people outside his own groups. The outsiders reciprocated by giving goods back to the big-man, usually in excess of the original gift, but the big-man was then obligated to redistribute the goods with profit to his followers who originally gifted him and enabled him to make the initial exchange. Another name for a 'big-man' is 'center man' because he was at the center of exchanges, but he was not the final recipient of the goods. Failure to reciprocate hurt the relationships that he needed to maintain to continue as a big-man.[2]

Expectations

The expectations that the church and mission held for each other were diametrically opposed. The following table illustrates the point.

---

[2]Paula G. Rubel and Abraham Rosman, *Your Own Pigs You May Not Eat: A Comparative Study of New Guinea Societies,* [Canberra: The Australia National University Press, 1978], 300-302.

Table 2: Opposite Expectations	
Mission	*Church*
Independent fully autonomous church	On-going relationship with mission
Withdraw resources to avoid dependency	Brothers in Christ share resources—depend on mission
Church stand on its own	Permanent reciprocal relationship
Father pushes off-spring towards independency	Father never abandons his son, keeps him close
Families separate	Families have permanent reciprocity that lasts even beyond death

At the heart of Melanesian worldviews is what Trompf calls retributive logic. There is an expectation of reciprocity that is expressed negatively in payback killings and positively in exchange relationships.[3] When the people gave ground so that the mission could set up its stations, they were establishing a relationship rather than surrendering their rights to the ground. They expected to share in the mission's resources, and they were establishing an open-ended enduring relationship when they made an initial gift of land; while the missionaries saw the deal as a cut-and-dried economic contract.

In *Road Belong Cargo*, Lawrence said that the attitude that the local people had towards the Europeans who settled the north coast near Madang varied according to whether the Europeans "upheld or repudiated the principles of reciprocity and equivalence."[4] Maklaï, who was the first European to establish a presence in the Madang area more than ten years before the Germans claimed it as a colony, practiced reciprocity and the people adopted him into their pattern of relationships.[5] The Germans ignored the "principle of reciprocity" and the relationship deteriorated. The Lutheran and Catholic missionaries better understood reciprocity, and when the people accepted Christianity, they sought to reestablish

---

[3]G. W. Trompf, *Payback: The Logic of Retribution in Melanesian Religions.* [Cambridge, UK: Cambridge University Press, 1994], 24.

[4]Peter Lawrence, *Road Belong Cargo*, [Melbourne: Melbourne University Press, 1964], 233.

[5]Rufus Pech. 1991. *Manub and Kilibob: Melanesian Models for Brotherhood Shaped by Myth, Dream and Drama.* [Goroka, Papua New Guinea: Melanesian Institute, 1991], 57.

their friendship with the Europeans. Later the colonial government again became more repressive, and the people became more hostile towards the Europeans.[6]

The fluctuation in the relationship between the church and mission can be traced to similar causes. When the mission tried to make the church more independent by withholding funds or cutting the subsidy, and when it sold houses or liquidated other assets without seeking input from the church or sharing the money that it received from the sales, the church leaders saw it as a denial of egalitarianism, equivalence, and reciprocity. The mission believed it was practicing good stewardship and the best practice in mission, but the church considered it to be a refutation of the relationship that the church and mission shared.

Previously I mentioned the work of Jeffrey Clark, Chris Ballard, and Michael Nihill who say that the Wiru people rejected their traditional culture in favor of Christianity because of the material benefits that they expected Christianity to bring to them. In the beginning the missions' practice of giving gifts to secure the loyalty of the people reinforced the perception that Christianity would bring prosperity.[7] Clark, Ballard and Nihill report that one Wiru pastor said "that money, not God, was the most important thing in the world."[8] Clark, Ballard, and Nihill say that for the Wiru people, Christianity is based on the control of money. Clark, Ballard, and Nihill compare money to the cult stones that were used in the traditional religions. According to the Wiru understanding of Christianity, money provides a way to "release the power of the spirit domain." People give offerings to thank God for his blessings and to mediate their relationship with God.[9]

The Nembi belief that prosperity and power came from the spirits was shared widely among traditional Melanesian religions. Trompf says, Melanesian religions are distinguished by their emphasis on the material benefits that ritual brings to the practitioner. Blessings from God (or the spirit domain) include all types of valuables. "Group wealth is taken as a reflection of good relationships between humans and the spirit order"[10] These expectations have carried over to Melanesian Christianity.

Among the Nembi the older generation says that God has blessed them with abundance. Their lives improved when they turned away from their pre-Christian cults and followed God. In the Lai Valley I interviewed three elderly brothers, Tia Paik, Ndipili, and Jacob Tia. According to the brothers, before Christianity came, the spirits were hard task masters. There was much sickness and many people died. They sacrificed nearly all of their pigs to the spirits, but people kept dying. There was continual warfare and they did not have a good life. Prosperity came after they decided to follow Christ. They no longer sacrifice the pigs to the spirits,

---

[6]Lawrence, *Road Belong Cargo,* 233-234.

[7]Jeffrey Clark, Chris Ballard, and Michael Nihill. *Steel to Stone: A Chronicle of Colonialism in the Southern Highlands of Papua New Guinea.* [Oxford, UK: Oxford University Press, 2000], 100.

[8]Clark, Ballard and Nihill, *Steel to Stone,* 151.

[9]Clark, Ballard and Nihill, *Steel to Stone,* 165-166.

[10]G. W. Trompf, *Melanesian Religion.* [Cambridge, England: Cambridge University Press, 1991], 20.

and now they have many pigs. There is less tribal fighting than there was in the past. When they do fight, they make peace more quickly and fewer people die. The brothers reported that in the old days the infant mortality rate was high, but now most babies survive to adulthood. Before they were few, but now they are many. Their ground has filled up with houses and people, and their gardens prosper. It is because they decided to follow Christ. He has blessed them abundantly.[11]

On the other hand, Tia Paik, one of the brothers, said that for the youth it is different. "The youth are dissatisfied, restless, strident, and unable to settle down." (*Sekel sekel pu taoll yu onu piyamom ngorup piyamom pupur aond saim*).[12] The difference is that the older generation remembers the life they had when they followed the pre-Christian cults and they do not doubt that they have received abundant blessings because of their decision to follow Christ. The younger generations, with their cell phones, access to the internet, and computers, have leapt into the age of technology. They do not recall life as it was before. Instead they look at the world, find themselves lacking, and think that they have been short changed.

Economy

The PNG economy fueled the conflict. Papua New Guinea as a whole ranks low in the worldwide economy, and as I noted in Chapter Five, the Southern Highlands is the least developed province in PNG and people on the Nembi Plateau are among the most disadvantaged people in the Southern Highlands Province.[13] Papua New Guinea is rich in mineral deposits, including gold, copper, natural gas, and oil and the export of these commodities has significantly strengthened the PNG economy during the last decade. The problem is that although the groups living nearest to the projects gain some financial benefits, most of the benefits generated by the mineral resources do not reach most of the people. Forty percent of the people live below the poverty level.[14] The per capita income grew from $1,279 in 2009 to $2,138 (USD) in 2014,[15] but the per capita income for PNG ranks 179th among

---

[11]Jacob Til, Tia Paik, and Ndipili, interview by author, Mil Southern Highlands Province of Papua New Guinea, December 20, 2009.

[12]Tia Paik, interview by author, Mil Southern Highlands Province of Papua New Guinea, December 19, 2009.

[13]Bryant Allen, "The Setting: Land, Economics and Development in the Southern Highlands Province," in *Conflict and Resource Development in the Southern Highlands of Papua New Guinea,* eds. Nicole Haley and Ronald J. May [Canberra: Australia National University E Press, 2007], 40, 41, 44.

[14]Australian Department of World Affairs and Trade. "Overview of Australia's Aid Program to Papua New Guinea" http://aid.dfat.gov.au/countries/pacific/png/Pages/default.aspx [accessed January 17, 2015].

[15]Australian Deparment of World Affairs and Trade. "Papua New Guinea Fact Sheet" Australian Government. http://www.dfat.gov.au/geo/fs/png.pdf [accessed on January 19, 2015.

267 world entities. Eighty-five percent of the people continue to earn their living through subsistence farming.[16]

The Nembi area, where the bulk of CUC churches are located, has not gained much financially from development. As they have always been, the Nembi people are in the middle. Large mineral and oil deposits have been discovered and major development projects have taken place among groups who surround the Nembi people, but nothing has been found in the Nembi area. In pre-colonial days, the Nembi position in the middle of major trade routes was an advantage for the Nembi people,[17] but the position in the middle is no longer an advantage.

The church members and other adherents give generous offerings to Christian Union Church. Each district takes up an annual thanksgiving offering and raises thousands of *kina* that is divided among the district, the region, and the Bible school, but the money is not sufficient to adequately support the church's ministries. The following quote taken from a letter that church leaders sent to the mission in 1991 expresses the church's frustration.

> We try to raise our own money, but our people of PNG do not have enough money like the people of America and other countries. Many of the people of PNG do not work for money. Only a few of our people have money. All of the other people have money only when the sell a pig or receive bride wealth or something like that. The rest of the time, they eat the food from their gardens and they have no money. And so our people put only ten or twenty toea in the offering, and it is not enough money for the church to carry out its work.[18]

Thus, the church leaders want development (or *divelopmen* to use Rynkiewich's term[19]) and look for outside resources to supplement the church's income. The mission appears to be the most likely source.

One of the church leaders told me that they would never stop asking the mission for money, because they believe that the mission is wealthy and has an obligation to share its resources with the church. Although the mission has greater resources than the church, it is far less wealthy and has far fewer resources than the church envisions. Christian Union Mission has always struggled financially to support its ministries in Papua New Guinea, and the church's frequent requests for additional funding have become overwhelming to the missionaries. Missionaries are required to raise funds for personal, ministry, and mission support as well as

---

[16]Central Intelligence Agency, "The World Factbook" Central Intelligence Agency of the US Government Library, https://www.cia.gov/library/publications/the-world-factbook/geos/pp.html [accessed on January 19, 2015].

[17]Edward L. Schieffelin, and Robert Crittenden, editors. *Like People You See in a Dream: First Contact in Six Papuan Societies.* [Stanford, Calif: Stanford University Press, 1991], 128-131.

[18]Regional Board of Trustees letter to Christian Union Mission, November 11, 1991. A copy of the letter is in Appendix Ten.

[19]Michael A. Rynkiewich, "Big-Man Politics: Strong Leadership in a Weak State" in *Politics in Papua New Guinea: Continuities, Changes and Challenges,* eds. Michael A. Rynkiewich and Roland Seib, 17-43. Goroka, Papua New Guinea: Melanesian Institute, 2000.

for any support that the mission gives to the church. More than one missionary has been recalled from PNG because he or she was unable to maintain adequate funds in his or her ministry account. However, as Jonathon Bock points out in his book, *Missions and Money*, the people from the majority world "greet with incredulity" the Western missionary's claim that he lacks money.[20]

Concerns of the Church Leaders

The church leaders give Christian Union Mission and its missionaries a mixed review. On the one hand, they express appreciation for the message and the missionaries who brought the message. On the other hand, they criticize the missionaries for not ministering more holistically and for not understanding the culture. The church leaders say that the mission failed because they came "without a plan." They did not minister well to the physical needs of the church and its adherents, leave the church with adequate resources, or provide an adequate education for the church's leaders.[21] According to the church leaders, the church now lacks because of the missionaries' failures and shortcomings. In this section I look at the church's call for renewal or revitalization, for contextualization, and for higher education for its leaders.

Renewal

Cliff Kiru, a member of CUC of PNG who is currently studying at CLTC, says that God has left markers in the Nembi culture that will lead people to Christ, but the people have not yet come into a clear understanding of who Christ is. In an article that he wrote for one of his classes, Kiru critiques the missionaries because they did not understand the Nembi culture and missed opportunities to use the Nembi concept of a high God to make the God of scriptures clear to the Nembi people. In Chapter Three and Appendix Four, I wrote about the Nembi concept of a high God whom I call *Yeki* but Cliff calls *Yekikele*. He says that the people understood *Yekikele* to be the "maker and owner of heavens and earth." That understanding was like a set of footprints that God had placed in the Nembi culture to lead the people to knowledge of the Triune God revealed in scriptures. Kiru says that scriptures must scrutinize every aspect of Nembi culture until God "takes the center stage."[22]

Kiru says that he was converted and was brought into a deeper understanding of Christ when he studied Paul's writings in Colossians about the image of God. In his words,

---

[20]Jon Bonk. *Missions and Money: Affluence As a Western Missionary Problem.* [Maryknoll, N.Y.: Orbis Books, 1991], 66.

[21]John Kua, interview by author, Mendi, Southern Highlands Province, Papua New Guinea, December 21, 2014..

[22]Cliff Kiru, "Footprints of God in Nembi Valley Culture in Light of Acts 17:22-23," [Major Essay: Christian Leaders Training College, Term Four 2014], 6-15.

My conversion to faith in Jesus as 'the Jesus I never understood before', after a study of Colossians, when in fact, I was supposed to have been fully aware of who Christ is, as a trained theologian, rings a bell loud and clear that there are uneducated Christians out there, who need to know the Christ of Colossians. Jesus Christ, as Emmanuel and not proxy to God, needs to be adequately preached, because a thorough knowledge of Christ will draw Christians out of their spiritual poverty, and will eventually lead them to renounce any intermediary of supplementary beings they may have, as stand-by alternatives, for use when calamities strike.[23]

Kiru was revitalized when he came to understand the supremacy of Christ after he delved into the meaning of the "image of God" in Colossians 1:15. He recognizes the need for the people of Christian Union Church to experience revitalization, and says that will occur by studying scripture and coming to a better understanding of who Christ is.

Higher Education for Church Leaders

Only by self-theologizing and allowing the scriptures to interact with the Melanesian culture will the people be brought into a deeper understanding of what it means to be a Melanesian Christian. Hiebert, Shaw, and Tiénou say that the members of the local culture must evaluate their culture in the light of scriptures. The missionaries can guide during the process, but they cannot make the decisions for the local people. The people must do it for themselves. The result is the transformation not only of the individuals but also the social and cultural systems.[24] Kiru and others are looking at their culture and beginning the process of contextualization.

Some of the church leaders, especially those working in urban areas, are frustrated because the church does not have enough well trained leaders to lead the Christian Union Church of PNG. During 2011 Paul Embel who is on the Port Moresby District board wrote about the church in PNG. He lamented the fact that the CUC church lacked qualified leaders, and said that Christian Union Bible College had to be strengthened so that it could adequately train leaders who could "stand the season." He said that the church leaders need to be trained to the master's level and beyond.[25]

The regional and district councils elect the church's leaders and the members of the regional and district boards. The superintendents lead their districts, but

---

[23]Cliff Kiru, "Christ Supreme—An Exposition of the Theological Meaning of 'Image of God' in Colossians 1:15—Its Implications and Significance, Then and Now." *Melanesian Journal of Theology* 30-2 [2014]. 19.

[24]Paul G. Hiebert, R. Daniel Shaw, and Tite Tiénou. 1999. *Understanding Folk Religion: a Christian Response to Popular Beliefs and Practices.* [Grand Rapids, Mich: Baker Booksd, 1999], 20-29.

[25]Paul Embel, e-mail to Ruth Tipton, March 7, 2011.

they are constantly under the scrutiny of their boards,[26] and if the board thinks that the leader has acted inappropriately scripturally, culturally, and/or politically, they address the issue and they invoke sanctions against him. That is usually done by giving him a specified period of probation during which he is expected to attend church, but take no part in leading or directing services or other church activities. On the positive side, it calls the church leaders into accountability, but on the negative side, probation can be imposed unfairly, and the practice leads to frequent changes in church leadership. The competitiveness that is built into the big-man system comes to the fore, and has a negative effect on church governance. Reasons for giving probation include the misuse of funds, the abuse of power, or the attempt to expand one's base by making unauthorized promises or commitments to the church constituency, participating in tribal fighting, and inappropriate conduct.

In 2011 the regional board gave probation to the elected regional superintendent during his third year in office. The regional council of 2011 asked missionary Benji Jenkins to serve as the acting regional superintendent while the elected superintendent was on probation. He held the position for one year until the next council of 2012 elected a new regional superintendent. Paul Embel said that the regional council was of the opinion that missionaries had failed to train suitably qualified leaders to lead the church into the 21st century, and consequently the missionaries should serve as the regional superintendent until they trained suitably qualified leaders.

> The council members lament that America is the leader in every way and why American missionaries never foresaw the need of leadership in the twenty-first century. The frustration is very real. The uneducated leadership is always bringing the church into question. They go up the church hierarchy and come tumbling down again.[27]

Paul Embel sees education as a solution to the problem. He wants training in English which is the official language of Papua New Guinea. The PNG constitution and all other government documents are written in English. English is the language of instruction in the schools and universities. The scriptures have been translated into Pidgin (one of PNG's two trade languages) and the vernacular, but the materials that are available in the vernacular languages and the trade languages are limited. Church leaders and pastors who want to gain a deeper understanding of the scriptures and/or read the writing of past theologians require an understanding of English. It is not unlike pastors and church leaders who speak English as their mother tongue and have an abundance of materials to study, but

---

[26] The district boards monitor the district officials including the district superintendents, local church boards, and pastors. The regional board is made up of four elected officials—the regional superintendent, assistant regional superintendent, the secretary and the treasurer—and all district superintendents. It monitors the activities of the elected regional officials, the district councils, and the district boards.

[27] Paul Embel, e-mail to Ruth Tipton, June 27, 2011.

they study Greek and Hebrew so they can gain new perspectives by studying the scriptures in the original biblical languages.

Embel says that other denominations have leaders who have earned MA and PhD degrees, and belittle the undereducated leaders of Christian Union Church.[28] He says further that the first missionaries came to preach the gospel and plant a strong national church. They should have built the church in every aspect so that, when the missionaries go, the indigenous leaders can take control without feeling that they are limited in their ability to run a church. Other denominations have well-educated leaders, and the leaders of Christian Union Church feel that the missionaries have misled them. They question the mission's methods and wonder why they are left without well-educated leaders. The church needs to expand, but to do so; it needs a "broader mindset."[29]

Other church leaders, even those who have little formal education, have expressed similar sentiments. John Kua said that the church wants a strong educational institution that the church will be able to "stand on." A strong school will produce well-educated Christian men and women who will bring their tithes and offerings to the church and help the church spread out to other provinces. They want the youth to be trained not only as pastors, church leaders, and evangelists but also as carpenters, mechanics, health workers, teachers, and other professionals.[30] William Wop informed me that the church wants qualified church leaders to have the opportunity for advanced training.[31]

The church leaders and missionaries agree that training for pastors and church leaders is a top priority, but they disagree about the type of training that should be prioritized. The mission concentrates on training in Pidgin for pastors for the rural setting where most of the CUC churches are located. The church leaders feel that the advancement of the church is slowed because the mission does not give more emphasis to higher level training.

I asked Benji Jenkins if the mission had any plans to transition into higher level training. He said that at this point the mission has no plans to provide training in English although the mission recognizes the need for it and some of the missionaries have discussed the possibility. However, the missionary staff is small, and the school funding is unreliable. The enrollment is too low to generate enough tuition funds to support the school, and the church funding is undependable. The missionaries struggle with deficits in their ministry accounts and lack the funds to give to the school.[32] Kevin Zirkle gave a similar response. He said that he had not heard that the church wanted more training in English, and with

---

[28]Paul Embel, interview by author, Embi, Southern Highlands Province, Papua New Guinea, January 6, 2010.

[29]Paul Embel, interview by author, Embi, Southern Highlands Province, Papua New Guinea, January 6, 2010.

[30]John Kua, interview by author, Mendi, Southern Highlands Province, Papua New Guinea, December 21, 2009.

[31]William Wop, interview by author, Mendi, Southern Highlands Province, Papua New Guinea, December 7, 2009.

[32]Benji Jenkins, interview by author, Circleville, Ohio, June 19, 2014.

the current staff, they cannot operate the school in Pidgin and do something in English as well.[33]

From the church's perspective, the mission lagged behind when it did not provide advanced theological training in English.[34] The church leaders feel that the church has not kept up with the rest of PNG society. In the Nembi area after years of tribal fighting, the schools are functioning again. Some who missed out on the opportunity to complete their primary education because of the tribal fighting are enrolling in the community school as adults.[35] A number of students qualify for high school each year and more and more Nembi students are accepted into the universities. The students who qualify for high school education no longer want to attend the CUC churches with partially educated pastors. The parents are pushing their children to do well in school and get a good education in hopes that they will find employment and support their parents and the church, but the youth are turning away from the church because they see no hope for advancement in the church.[36]

One reason the church leaders push for English education is the Melanesian expectation that Christianity will bring them prosperity. The church looks at some of its sister denominations that use an extractionist policy for the education of their most gifted youth. They find sponsors in the USA and send the brightest students to schools in the USA for their college and even high school education. When the students return to PNG they become well-heeled church leaders and/ or business men who give generous offering to their churches. From the Nembi perspective those churches prosper because of their emphasis on English education. Christian Union Mission came "without a plan" that would bring prosperity to the PNG church.

A second reason is a genuine desire for theological education. Kiru says that traces of animism linger in "the hearts and minds of professed Christians," and that more biblical teaching is needed to lead them to a deeper understanding of

---

[33]Kevin Zirkle, e-mail to Ruth Tipton, July 9, 2014. I found it interesting that the current field leadership had heard nothing about the church's wish for English training, because most of the church leaders that I have talked to, even when I returned to PNG at the beginning of 2014, spoke of their desire for the church leaders to have training in English. English is the official language of Papua New Guinea, and the church leaders say they are ashamed that they cannot speak English when they go to the government offices.

[34]Paul Embel, e-mail to Ruth Tipton, June 27, 2011.

[35]Sengi Iruwa, conversation with the author at Embi in January of 2014. Sengi told me that his son who is married and has two or three children of his own enrolled in Ka Community school and was completing his elementary education. He hoped to qualify for high school and beyond. A number of young adults, according to Sengi, have returned to school because an education was denied to them when they were children.

[36]A number of the current PNG missionaries talked about the church losing its youth because they did not want to sit under the teaching of poorly educated pastors. During the summer of 2014 I heard Benji Jenkins speak in church services three different times, and each time he talked about the youth turning away from the church because they thought they had nothing to learn from partially educated pastors.

Christ.[37] Hiebert says that to "meaningfully communicate the gospel in human contexts," the communicator must exegete the scriptures and exegete humans.[38] He says that the gospel and culture are "separate, interrelated realities." The gospel is distinct from culture, but it must be communicated in cultures in order for people to understand it. It is not "simply a message to be affirmed as true." It confronts and transforms culture. There must be both "personal and corporate" transformation.[39] He says further,

> The gospel is not simply information to be communicated. It is a message to which people must respond. Moreover, it is not enough that leaders be convinced that change is needed. They may share their decisions and point out the consequences of various decisions, but they and their people must together make and enforce the decisions that they have arrived at corporately. Only then will the old beliefs and practices not be pushed underground, subverting the gospel.[40]

Higher level theological training for gifted church leaders should help them to exegete the scriptures, but it seems to me that if the trainees are sent overseas to western schools as high school youths and are alienated from their culture for eight to ten years or more they will learn the gospel from a western perspective and will be out of touch with their own culture and unable to exegete it. Those who have trained in Western schools without exposure to cross cultural-studies and training in contextualization bring back little that is relevant to their original cultural setting. It seems to me that students who remain closer to their home communities while they pursue their education will have a better understanding of Melanesian culture. As church leaders, they will be better able to exegete both the scriptures and the culture and lead the church through the contextualization process so that the Gospel confronts their culture and the church becomes a Christ centered Melanesian church.

The challenge for Christian Union Church and Mission is to recognize the need for and sponsor training at all levels—from Pidgin to PhD. Some will seek higher level training in overseas institutions, and should be encouraged to do so after they have gone as far as they can in PNG.

What's Next?

So where do we go from here? I have said that most of the conflict grew out of the different cultural perspectives of the missionaries and the church leaders and the expectations that each had for the other. The missionaries came from an individualistic oriented Western society, and they interacted with the Nembi and people according to their own cultural biases. Melanesian societies are group

---

[37]Kiru, "Christ Supreme," 17-19.

[38]Paul G. Hiebert, *The Gospel in Human Contexts: Anthropological Explorations for Contemporary Missions*. [Grand Rapids, Mich: Baker Academic, 2009], 12.

[39]Hiebert, *The Gospel in Human Contexts*, 31-32.

[40]Hiebert, *The Gospel in Human Contexts*, 32.

oriented, and the church leaders interacted with the missionaries on the basis of their own cultural biases.

Mary Lederleitner, who writes about developing cross-cultural partnerships, says, "Few of us realize how ethnocentric we are. It is only when we encounter people with different beliefs and attitudes that we realize how intensely we hold certain views."[41] Hiebert defines ethnocentrism as "the attitude that our own culture is better...than other cultures."[42] Ethnocentrism develops when we look at others through our own cultural lenses and think that our way of doing things is superior to the other way. It is "a two-way street." We look at others with feelings of superiority, but they look back at us and think that their ways are superior to ours. It "occurs wherever cultural differences are found." Hiebert says further, "The solution to ethnocentrism is empathy. We need to appreciate other cultures and their ways."[43]

Both the Western missionaries and the Melanesian church leaders are ethnocentric. They are convinced that their way is better and fail to understand the perspective of the other. Lederleitner writes about the differences in the perspectives of individualistic societies and group oriented societies which she calls collectivistic societies. She says that in individualistic societies, people define maturity in relation to how well the individual has learned to manage money. Individualistic societies laud persons who have learned to manage money well and are not dependent on others for their existence. In Christian circles, they are told to be good stewards of God's resources. In contrast, persons from group oriented societies are expected to use their resources to ensure that no one in the group lacks. She postulates that individualistic societies develop in richer economies where people have enough to allow them to accumulate goods and resources beyond their minimal needs. Group oriented societies develop where people have to pool their resources so that everyone's minimal needs are met, and accumulating wealth before everyone's basic needs are met is an anathema.[44]

The missionaries' determination to make the CUC of PNG a fully autonomous independent entity flies into the face of the Nembi and Melpa worldview and their cultural expectations. From their perspective, when they accepted the missionaries into their midst and converted to Christianity, they were entering into a long term, on-going relationship with the missionaries and the sending church.

Lederleitner says that the scriptures support and critique both worldviews. The parables of the ten virgins found in Matthew 25:1-13 and the parable of the talents found in Matthew 25:14-30 teach individual responsibility. She also cites Proverbs 13:22 which talks about "saving and leaving an inheritance." She identifies Matthew 6:19-24, that tells us not to store up treasures on earth, and II Corinthians

---

[41]Mary T. Lederleitner, *Cross-cultural Partnerships: Navigating the Complexities of Money and Mission.* [Downers Grove, IL: InterVarsity Press, 2010], 34.

[42]Paul G. Hiebert, *The Gospel in Human Contexts: Anthropological Explorations for Contemporary Missions.* [Grand Rapids, Mich: Baker Academic, 2009], 195.

[43]Hiebert, *The Gospel in Human Contexts,* 196.

[44]Lederleitner, *Cross Cultural Partnerships,* 34-38.

8:13-14. where Paul urged the Corinthians to give to help those in need that there might be equality, as scriptures that support the collectivist view. Paul told the Corinthians that their gift would be reciprocated later when the Corinthian church was in need and the other had plenty. She also says that Acts 2:41-47, where the early believers held everything in common, and James 2:14-17, that tells us that our faith finds expression in our actions, support the collectivist view. Further, she says that God tells the individualist to love God more than money (Matthew 6:24) and the collectivists to love God more than family (Matthew 10:37).[45]

Lederleitner says that "in order to work well together we need to learn to listen to one another. We need to not only deeply grasp how our partners feel and what they believe but also take the additional step to understand why such feelings and beliefs are wholly logical within a given context."[46] The WGM missionaries, regional and stateside officials who work with the PNG church, and missionary candidates have an inadequate understanding of Melanesian cultures in general, and the Nembi and Melpa in particular. They have never prioritized cultural studies. Investing time to talk with the people, to observe, to participate in the cultural activities, and to write up their observations would pay rich dividends. As it is, the ministry demands are high and missionaries are thrust into their "ministry" without having time to learn culture (and sometimes even the language). They fail to recognize their own ethnocentrism and stumble along without having an adequate understanding of the culture. As Rynkiewich says, "Communication of the gospel is handicapped if we do not know with whom we are communicating, what they are thinking and feeling, and how we are being heard."[47]

The missionaries and the church leaders need to learn how to better listen to each other. Lederleitner makes a distinction between high context and low context cultures. Low context cultures rely on the written and spoken words to convey meaning, but in high context cultures the spoken and written words are less meaningful than the context in which they are spoken. Body languages or action portray the communications true meaning.[48] The Nembi communicate with a lot of metaphors and parables. They speak vaguely about issues, and the real meaning remains hidden under the surface. The missionaries tend to speak more directly and no hidden meaning is intended, but the church leaders always suspect an underlying meaning anyway. Both sides misinterpret what the other is saying.

If the church and mission are to move beyond a dysfunctional relationship and really hear what the other says, they must improve their communication skills. Hiebert says that during the current global era effective communication is measured "not by what the sender means or the receptor comprehends, but by the correspondence between what the sender and the receptor experience and understand

---

[45]Lederleitner, *Cross-Cultural Partnerships*, 38-39.

[46]Lederleitner, *Cross-Cultural Partnerships,* 32.

[47]Michael A. Rynkiewich, "Person in Mission: Social Theory and Sociality in Melanesia" *Missiology* XXXI, no. 2, [April, 2003], 155.

[48]Lederleitner, *Cross-Cultural Partnerships*, 47.

about reality."[49] Far too often there has been little correlation between what the missionaries and the church leaders understand about a given situation much to the frustration of both sides.

Melanesian societies are all about relationships built around reciprocal exchange and the exchange of resources. The mission and the sponsoring church in the USA should ask how they can best relate to the Melanesian church. The constitution of Christian Union Church of Papua New Guinea says that the church is a member of the Churches of Christ in Christian Union (CCCU) with international headquarters in Circleville, Ohio.[50] That statement was approved by the General Missionary Board of the Churches of Christ in Christian Union in the late 1970s when the original constitution for Christian Union Church of PNG was written. It means that the denomination agreed to enter into a permanent relationship with Christian Union Church of Papua New Guinea.

One of the concerns raised by the church leaders of CUC of PNG was that they have not been invited to participate in the denomination's general church councils. Several of the church leaders told me that other denominations bring representatives to their international councils, but CCCU has never invited representatives from CUC of PNG to participate. During the summer of 2014, I attended several of CCCU's denominational and district functions. I asked some of the denomination's leaders when and how we were going to fully incorporate CUC of PNG into our denomination. One said, "You mean as a church and not a mission field." CUC of PNG had been a member of the denomination since they first voted to accept the constitution in 1978, but many of the denominational leaders still do not recognize the PNG church as a full-fledged part of the denomination. The tendency throughout the denomination is to freeze frame the PNG field and think of it as it was in the 60s, the 70s, or the 80s. One of the former church leaders of CUC of PNG told me that the mission needs to quit acting like it is the 1970s. He said, "We are in the 2000s, and the church is diminished because the mission failed to move ahead."[51]

The CCCU leaders that I talked to mentioned the high cost of bringing the PNG church leaders to the general council and the fear that there would be problems because the PNG church leaders would expect greater assistance than the denomination is able to give. There are always "problems" that have to be worked through in cross-cultural relationships, but CCCU established a permanent relationship with CUC of PNG in the 1970s and now needs to strengthen that relationship. That may involve bringing representatives to the general council, providing scholarship for qualified leaders to get more advanced training, assisting with the church's ministries of compassion, or reaching out in some other way.

---

[49]Paul G. Hiebert, ""Beyond Anti-Colonialism to Globalism" *Missiology: An International Review*, XIX no. 3 [July, 1991], 273.

[50]"Konstitusen Bilong Christian Union Church Bilong Papua New Guinea," May 2002, 1.

[51]Simon En, interview by author, Mendi, Southern Highlands Province, Papua New Guinea, December 18, 2009.

CUM began its work among the Nembi people in 1964 during the colonial era in an area that was largely isolated from the outside world. The people had no concept of the Western world or of Christ and Christianity. From the perspective of the colonial administration the Nembi people were not yet fully "pacified." In the fifty years since the work began, the world has moved from colonialism to globalism, and both the church and mission have struggled to keep up with the phenomenal change that has occurred. From the perspective of the church leaders, the church has lagged behind the rest of PNG society, and they want to catch up.

Paul Borthwick writes about the role of Western Christians in global mission. He refers to an address that Pastor Oscar Muriu, who pastors a church in Nairobi, Kenya, gave at the Urbana Missions Conference in 2006. Muriu says that it is time for the churches from the majority world and those from the West to move away from independence and individualism to interdependence and that reciprocity means that all contribute for the good of others, and all have something to give. Borthwick says that the time for the North American church "to initiate, lead, control, fund, and direct everything is over."[52] He asks the question, "How can the vast resources of the Western Christianity on the one hand, and the vitality and dynamism of non-Western Christianity on the other, become a powerful synergistic whole for world evangelization?"[53]

Borthwick is talking about worldwide Christianity, but I think the question is equally applicable to the situation with CCCU/WGM and CUC of PNG. The days when the mission led and directed everything are gone. The PNG church must come to the fore and the mission must diminish. How can the two come together and combine their resources (both human and material) and work together in a synergistic interdependent relationship that advances God's Kingdom as it never has before and accomplish together far more than either can accomplish alone?

I don't know the answer, but the story is not finished yet. Andrew Walls' "indigenizing principle" says that God accepts people as they are

> ...on the ground of Christ's work alone, not on the ground of what we are or are trying to become...God accepts us together with our group relations...our 'dis-relations'...those predispositions, prejudices, suspicions, and hostilities whether justified or not, which mark the group to which we belong. He does not wait to tidy up our ideas any more than he waits to tidy up our behavior before he accepts us sinners into his family.[54]

Walls' "pilgrim principal" says that "not only does God take people as they are: he takes them in order to transform them into what he wants them to be."[55] I believe that those two principles apply equally to the missionaries and the church

---

[52] Paul Borthwick. *Western Christians in Global Mission: What's the Role of the North American Church?* [Downers Grove, IL.: InterVarsity Press, 2012], 115.

[53] Borthwick, *Western Christian in Global Mission*, 178.

[54] Andrew F. Walls, "The Gospel as Prisoner and Liberator of Culture" in *Landmark Essays in Mission and World Christianity*, eds. Robert L. Gallagher and Paul Heritg, [Maryknoll, New York: Orbis Books, 2009], 137-138.

[55] Walls, "The Gospel as Prisoner and Liberator of Culture," 139.

leaders. God has taken them as they are and works to make them what he wants them to be. God has accepted both, and he works to change both to make them what God wants them to be.

Both sides need to begin by looking at themselves and critiquing themselves rather than the other. I am reminded of the Lord's words to Solomon in Second Chronicles 7:14. "If my people, who are called by my name, will humble themselves and pray and seek my face and turn from their wicked ways, then I will hear from heaven, and I will forgive their sin and will heal their land." So my final conclusion calls for humility on the part of both the church and the mission as they humble themselves before God, and trust the Holy Spirit to lead them into the interdependent synergistic relationship that He wants them to have.

Appendix One

Pictorial History[1]

1 CUM's Certificate of Incorporation

TERRITORY OF PAPUA AND NEW GUINEA

Companies Ordinance 1912-19 63
of the Territory of Papua

CERTIFICATE OF INCORPORATION

No. 1136

THIS IS TO CERTIFY THAT an association styled

CHRISTIAN UNION MISSION

the Administrator having directed such association to be registered with limited liability without the addition of the word "limited" to its name pursuant to Section 54

was on the   nineteenth   day of   November   , 19 63 ,

incorporated under the Companies Ordinance 1912-1963 of the Territory of Papua

and that the said company is limited   by shares .

GIVEN under my Hand and Seal of Office at Port Moresby, this   twenty-first

day of   November   , 19 63

STAMP DUTY
£5
CANCELLED
ON ORIGINAL
CERTIFICATE

J.C. Redmond,

L.S.

Registrar of Companies

I, John Christopher Redmond, Registrar of Companies of the Territory of Papua hereby certify that the above is a true copy of Certificate of Incorporation of CHRISTIAN UNION MISSION filed in the records of my office.
GIVEN under my hand and seal at Port Moresby this twenty-first day of November 1963

Registrar

Port Moresby : V. P. Blaink, Government Printer

---

[1]All of the images used in this pictorial history are numbered, and their sources are listed at the end of the appendix in numerical order. Some appeared in previous publications, and those publications are cited. All are used with permission.

2 Jim Hummel's hand-drawn map of the Nembi area sent to the home board in 1964

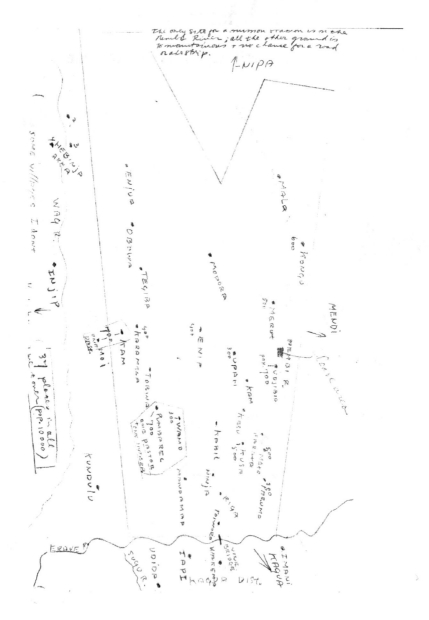

Life in the 1960s

3 Inside a spirit house—the conical shaped platform suggests that this spirit house was associated with the *timp* cult. Each rope hanging from the beam was from pig that had been sacrificed

4 Roasting a pig that had been sacrificed

5 Butchering the sacrificed pig

6 Some spirit stones. Possibly used for the *kepel* cult.

7 Traders—Pearl shells were the most valued item of trade

8 Warriors—The men were the warriors and protectors. Tribal warfare
was endemic.

9 A Nembi man posed for his
pictures in the 1960s

10 Women in the 1960s making a mat

11 The people lived in small hamlets comprised of a man, his wives, and their offspring. Gradens surrounded each home.

12 The women were the providers, caregivers and primary gardeners.

13 Women mourn over a deceased man—The deceased is laid out on a platform. The closest female relatives (wives, sisters, daughters, and mother) sit underneath the platform and keen and wail.

14 A woman in her garden is dressed in mourning garb.

15 Pearl shells ready to be given in some kind of exchange—probably bride wealth, but they could be for a compensation payment.

16 Left. A Nembi bride. Her body glistens from being rubbed with a mixture of tiagaso oil and ashes.

17 Right. A woman harvests reeds for a grass skirt.

18 Vine Bridge

19 Traditional home under construction

20 New Style of house under construction

21 Weaving cane for the walls and floor of the house

22 Weaving cane for the walls and floor of the house

23 New style house in foreground, and frame for traditional style house in background

24 An elderly man carries a load of fire-wood.

25 A traditional *singsing*. Men march around a dance ground. *Singsings* (ceremonial dances) and pig kills were major social events. *Singsings* were held to celebrate victory in warfare and in conjunction with pig kills.

26 Top Left   27 Top Right   28 Below Left   29 Below Right

Everyone—men, women, and children—worked together to make a pig kill success. It was a time of settling debts. Those sponsoring the pig kill invited other groups with whom they had an exchange relationship and/or a political alliance to attend, and they shared the pork with their visitors.

Colonization and Missionization

30 A patrol officer on patrol during the 1960s. After pacification, the patrol officer conducted a census and held court each time that he went out on patrol.

31 When on patrol, the administrative officers required the people to carry in food for the patrol. Notice the pile of sweet potatoes in the foreground that the patrol has purchased from the people.

32 Carriers ready to go on mission patrol.

33 The missionaries slept in the churches or in the patrol officers' rest house when on patrol.

34 Before there were buildings, the pastors and missionaries held church services in the open air.

35 Before the roads and airstrips were built, the people carried everything in. The men carried the heaviest loads, but women and children helped carry the lighter items.

36 Once the mission acquired Ka, the work of development began in earnest. The mission acquired a tractor to help work on the airstrip, but men, women, and children did most of the work by hand.

37 Ka station in June of 1967—the airstrip was almost complete. A few buildings were in place including Ka school, a workshop and missionary housing.

38 The first plane landed at Ka on June 17, 1967. The *Karinj* who were building an airstrip at Ka, and the *Aron* who were building one at Det were racing to see where the first plane would land. *Karinj* won that competition.

39 Ka airstrip and station in 2009—the airstrip closed in 1999 when the mission left Ka.

Land Acquisition

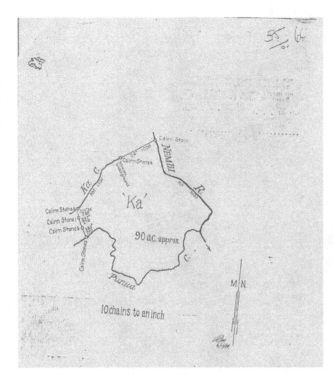

Below are the sketch maps and lease agreements for CUM's stations in the Nembi area:

Ka station was ninety acres in size, and it was the largest piece of ground that the mission acquired. In 1967 and 1968, the administration also approved mission leases at Montanda, Farata, and Embi. Montanda station was opened in January of 1968 when Ted and Florence Meckes settled there. Farata was opened in June or July of 1968 when Don Seymour built the mission house at Farata just before he left for furlough. Bob and Sara Jones arrived

40 Sketch map for Ka Station. Ka was the first large piece of ground that the mission acquired to develop a mission station. Patrol officer Warren R. Read and missionary John Ottway first surveyed the ground in May of 1964. The lease was finalized when the land owners accepted payment in December of 1965.

in the Nembi Valley on August 10, 1968, and they became the first missionary family to reside full time at Farata. In late 1968, Ted and Florence Meckes began making regular trips to Embi to hold weekly classes. In 1969, Shirley Ulman (later Queen) began conducting monthly medical patrols in the Embi area, and in January of 1971 Shirley Ulman and Ruth Tipton became the first missionaries to reside at Embi full time.

Kar

63/1747

TERRITORY OF PAPUA AND NEW GUINEA

Lease Form 6.

Registered in the Register of
Crown/Administration Leases

Volume ...13... Folio ...217...

Land Ordinance 1962 (as amended)

Registrar of Titles
23 / 8 / 1968.

MISSION LEASE UNDER SECTION 66

THE ADMINISTRATOR of the Territory of Papua and New Guinea hereby grants to CHRISTIAN

UNION MISSION in

the Territory of Papua and New Guinea (hereinafter called " the Lessee ") a lease under Section 66 of

the Land Ordinance 1962- 65 of the Territory of Papua and New Guinea (hereinafter called " the

Ordinance ") for a period of   ninety nine (99) years

from the   nineteenth   day of   January   One thousand nine hundred

and   sixty seven   for MISSION purposes, of all that piece or parcel of land

to which the following description applies :—

PORTION ALLOTMENT	MILINCH SECTION	FOURMIL TOWN	AREA	DISTRICT
49	Mendi	Kutubu	90 acres	Southern Highlands
			Be the same a little more or less	

as shown coloured yellow   in the plan   hereon   with all appurtenances thereto
(hereinafter called " the Land "),

EXCEPTING AND RESERVING therefrom the reservations implied in every Administration lease
by the Ordinance TO HOLD unto the Lessee for the said term subject to the terms provisions restric

41 Lease Agreement for Ka

MISSION LEASE UNDER SECTION 66

High Commissioner of Pap~ ~ N~ ~ ~ to

THE ~~ADMINISTRATOR of the Territory of Papua and New Guinea~~ hereby grants to

CHRISTIAN UNION MISSION, a Company incorporated in

~~the Territory of~~ Papua ~~and~~ New Guinea (hereinafter called "the Lessee") a lease under Section 66 of the Land ~~Ordinance~~ *Act* 1962- 1973 ~~of the Territory~~ of Papua ~~and~~ New Guinea (hereinafter called "the ~~Ordinance~~" *Act*) for a period of ninety-four (94) years and twenty-seven (27) days from the seventeenth day of January, One thousand nine hundred and seventy-four for MISSION purposes, of all that piece or parcel of land to which the following description applies:—

PORTION ~~ALLOTMENT~~	MILINCH ~~SECTION~~	FOURMIL ~~TOWN~~	AREA	DISTRICT
38 and 52 (Con-solidated)	Barena	Kutubu	11 · 01 HA Be the same a little more or less	Southern Highlands

as shown coloured yellow in the plan annexed hereto with all appurtenances thereto (hereinafter called "the land").

EXCEPTING AND RESERVING therefrom the reservations implied in every ~~Administration~~ *GOVERNMENT* lease by the ~~Ordinance~~ *Act* TO HOLD unto the Lessee for the said term subject to the terms provisions restrictions and conditions contained in the ~~Ordinance~~ *Act* and the Regulations thereunder and to the reservations covenants terms and conditions hereinafter set forth.

THE LESSEE shall observe and perform the following terms and conditions:--

Other than as provided in clause (i) hereunder the lease shall be used bona fide for Church, Clinic, Mission, Residence and ancillary purposes.

Existing improvements being buildings for Church, Clinic, Mission, Residence and ancillary purposes to a minimum value of Twenty Thousand Dollars ($20,000) or similar improvements to the same minimum value for the same purposes shall be maintained on the land and in good repair during the currency of the lease.

No commercial enterprise shall be undertaken on the land.

Excision of easements for electricity, water, drainage and sewerage reticulation.

Excision of any subsequently necessary roads.

Use of the land for agricultural purposes is permitted in accordance with Section 67(vi) of the Land Ordinance 1962 - 1971 subject however to the following conditions:--

Of the land suitable for cultivation, the following proportions shall be planted in a good and husbandlike manner with a crop, crops or pasture species of economic value

42 Lease Agreement for Montanda Station

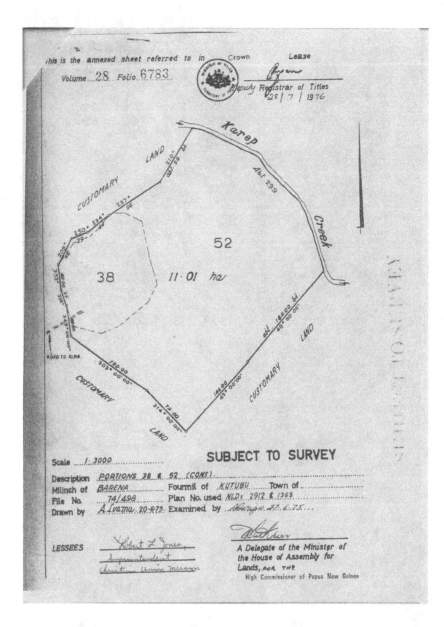

Karep

CUSTOMARY LAND

Abt 299

Creek

52

11·01 ha

38

CUSTOMARY LAND

ROAD TO NIPA

CUSTOMARY LAND

SUBJECT TO SURVEY

Scale ...1: 3000

Description PORTIONS 28 & 52 (CONS).
Milinch of BARENA Fourmil of KUTUBU Town of ....
File No. 74/498 Plan No. used NLDs. 2912 & 1355
Drawn by A.Lvamu. 20·6·75. Examined by .... 27. 6.75...

LESSEES Robert L. Jones
Superintendent
Christian Union Mission

A Delegate of the Minister of
the House of Assembly for
Lands, FOR THE
High Commissioner of Papua New Guinea

43 Sketch Map for Montanda Station

328

MINISTER FOR LANDS
THE ~~ADMINISTRATOR~~ hereby grants to

CHRISTIAN UNION MISSION IN;

Papua New Guinea (hereinafter called "the Lessee") a lease under Section 66 of the Land ~~Ordinance~~ Act

1962- (hereinafter called "the ~~Ordinance~~") ACT for a period of NINETY-NINE (99) YEARS

from the FIRST day of FEBRUARY One thousand nine hundred

and SEVENTY-NINE for MISSION purposes, of all that piece or parcel of land

to which the following description applies:—

~~PORTION~~ ALLOTMENT	~~MILINCH~~ SECTION	~~TOURMIL~~ TOWN	AREA	~~DISTRICT~~ PROVINCE
1	4	POROMA	0.2262 HA Be the same a little more or less	SOUTHERN HIGHLANDS

as shown coloured yellow in the plan annexed hereto with all appurtenances thereto
(hereinafter called "the land").

EXCEPTING AND RESERVING therefrom the reservations implied in every ~~Administration~~ Government lease

by the ~~Ordinance~~ ACT TO HOLD unto the Lessee for the said term subject to the terms provisions restric-

tions and conditions contained in the ~~Ordinance~~ ACT and the Regulations thereunder and to the reservations

covenants terms and conditions hereinafter set forth.

THE LESSEE shall observe and perform the following terms and conditions:—

A) The lease shall be used bona fide for Mission and Ancillary purposes;

B) Provision of any necessary easements for electricity, water, power, drainage and sewerage reticulation;

C) Excision of any necessary roads;

D) No Commercial Enterprises shall be undertaken on the land leased;

44 Lease Agreement for Farata Station

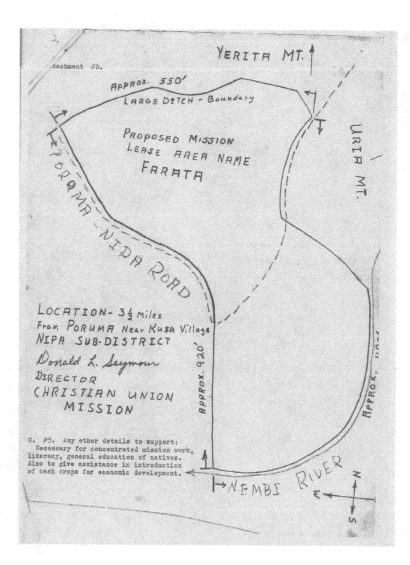

YERITA MT.

attachment #D.

APPROX. 550'
LARGE DITCH - Boundary

PROPOSED MISSION
LEASE AREA NAME
FARATA

URIA MT.

PORAMA - NIPA ROAD

LOCATION - 3½ miles
From PORUMA Near Kusa Village
NIPA SUB-DISTRICT
Donald L. Seymour
DIRECTOR
CHRISTIAN UNION
MISSION

APPROX. 920'

APPROX. ...

C. #5. Any other details to support:
Necessary for concentrated mission work,
literacy, general education of natives.
Also to give assistance in introduction
of cash crops for economic development.

NEMBI RIVER

N
E   W
S

45 Sketch Map for Farata Station

330

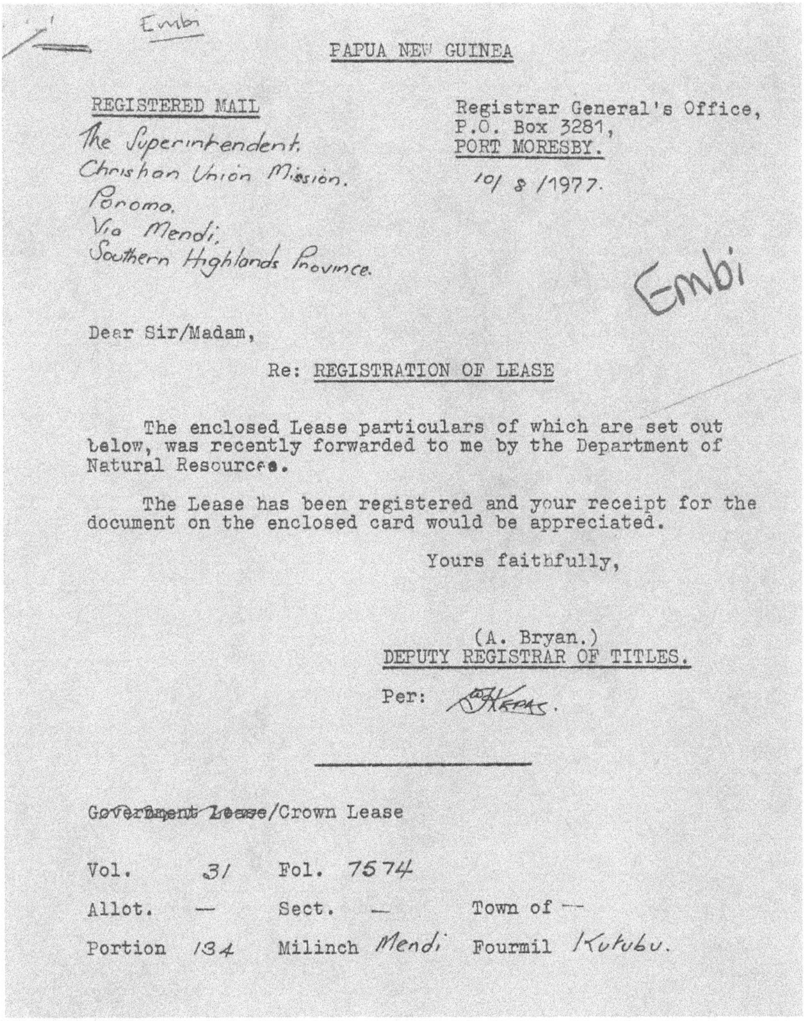

PAPUA NEW GUINEA

REGISTERED MAIL

The Superintendent.
Christian Union Mission.
Poroma,
Via Mendi,
Southern Highlands Province.

Registrar General's Office,
P.O. Box 3281,
PORT MORESBY.

101 8 /1977.

Embi

Dear Sir/Madam,

Re: <u>REGISTRATION OF LEASE</u>

The enclosed Lease particulars of which are set out
below, was recently forwarded to me by the Department of
Natural Resources.

The Lease has been registered and your receipt for the
document on the enclosed card would be appreciated.

Yours faithfully,

(A. Bryan.)
DEPUTY REGISTRAR OF TITLES.

Per:

Government Lease/Crown Lease

Vol.   31   Fol. 7574

Allot.   —   Sect.   —   Town of ---

Portion 134   Milinch Mendi   Fourmil Kutubu.

46 Lease Agreement for Embi Station

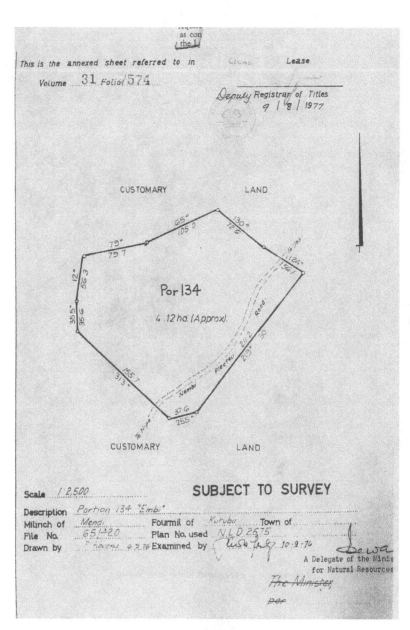

as con
the L

This is the annexed sheet referred to in   Crown   Lease

Volume ....31..Folio..574...

Deputy Registrar of Titles
9 | 8 | 1977

CUSTOMARY   LAND

65°
105.0
130°
72.6
79°
79.7
12°
56.3
16.9ha
12ha
56.1

Por 134

4.12 ha. (Approx).

35.5°
35.6

Road
211.2
30
213°

155.7
313°
Pleateu
Nembi
37.6
255°
To Nipa

CUSTOMARY   LAND

Scale *1,2,500*

SUBJECT TO SURVEY

Description *Portion 134 "Embi"*
Milinch of   *Mendi*   Fourmil of   *Kutubu*   Town of
File No.   *65/420*   Plan No. used *N.L.D. 2675*
Drawn by   *Tororo 6.2.76* Examined by   *10:9:76*

A Delegate of the Minis
for Natural Resources

The Minister

per

47 Sketch Map for Embi Station

48 Montanda station in late 1968 or 1969

49 Another view of Montanda Station. The ground was swampy, but the Meckes with the help of the local people dug drainage ditches and built ponds to drain the water and planted gardens. They introduced a number of new crops into the Nembi area.

50 An open-air service held at Farata in the early 1980s. In the background is the mission/church office. Notice the beautiful casuarinas trees.

Medical Ministry

51 The first clinic opened at Tindom in 1965.

52 At first the people resisted medical treatment, but soon carried their sick to the clinic.

53 The clinic moved to Ka in 1966.

54 The medical team went out on regular well child clinic patrols where they checked every child under the age of five.

55 Giving shots in the 1960s

56 Giving shots in the 2000s

57 The health clinic at Ol in 2014

58 The health clinic at Ka

Christian Union Church now operates health centers at Ol, Tegibo, and Ka and aid posts at Askam, Mont, Tula, and Poroma.

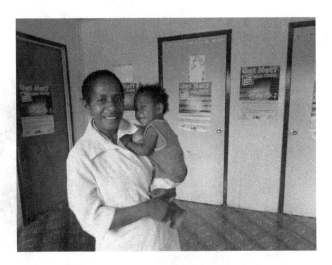

59 Sister-in-charge at Ka health clinic

60 Ol/Pomberel Health Center. The medical ministry of CUC of PNG is fully nationalized, but student nurses from the USA visit the medical work each year to experience nursing in a developing country and to help provide in-service training to the medical staff.

Education Ministries

Ka Community School opened in February of 1966.

61 Ka community school in
1966 or 1967

62 Assembly—The children
salute the Australian flag

63 School children in the
late 1960s or early 1970s.

64 Ka school classroom in 1997

65 The Ka Community school graduation in 2009. The students are graduating from Grade Eight. In 2009 the school had 778 students and twenty teachers.

66 Vernacular literacy class for children before they enrolled in community school around 1993

67 1971—the young men who went to the Lae Pidgin Bible School sponsored by the Swiss Evangelical Mission. From left to right are Pangia Waista, Mapon Ek, Tui Tondpen Ori, Simon En, John Esup, and Jeremaiah Kele.

68 In 1971 six female students went to Yagrumbak School near Wewak run by the South Seas Evangelical Mission. Pictured are two of the young women who went to the school, Sumim Mond and Kibem Peliyap.

69 In 1970 the mission opened a part time Bible School at Ka. It was expanded to a full time Bible school in 1973. After Nembi Bible School became full time, the mission no longer sponsored students to other schools.

70 Farata Bible School girls in 1976 or 1977. Sara Jones (far right second row)

was the principal of the school. Carl Waggoner, the CCCU General missionary Superintendent, and his wife Mary stand at the back.

In 1971 and 1972 the mission sent girls to Yagrumbak School, but in 1973 the general pastors' committee asked the mission to open a Bible school for girls and not to return the girls for their third year at Yagrumbak. The Farata girls for school ran from 1975 to 1979, and then it was move to Ka and became a part of Nembi Bible School.

71 The current Bible College Campus. After the mission withdrew from Ka in 1999, the Bible school was relocated to Mount Hagen.

72 A class at Mount Hagen Bible College

Women's Ministries

73 An early women's class. Women's ministries started in 1967 when Betty Seymour started a class for women. Twenty-two women attended the first class, but by August of 1969 more than eight hundred women attended the weekly classes. At first the classes here held only at Ka, and some of the women walked three or more hours to attend the classes. When the other stations opened they held women's classes and the women did not have to walk quite as far to attend their classes.

Teaching assistants

74 A missionary or pastor taught the lesson to the entire group. The women were then divided into smaller groups and the assistants again taught the lesson to the smaller group.

75 In 1975 the women started accompanying the medical patrols on well-child clinics to witness to the women who were waiting to be seen at the clinic. The missionaries held special classes for the women to teach them Bible stories to use in their witnessing.

Christianity was empowering for the women. In the traditional belief system the women had no direct access to the spirits and were not privy to the cults' secrets. In Christianity they could approach God directly. They were never quiet about their new found faith and actively witnessed to anyone who would listen including their husbands, fathers, sons, and brothers.

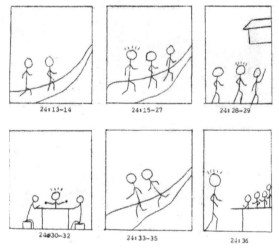

76 Most of the women were non-literates, and so the missionaries used simple stick figure drawings to help the women remember the Bible stories.

77 Top Left   78 Top Right
The women studied and prayed together in preparation for the patrols.

79 Middle   80 Bottom
In the late 1970s and the
1980s the mission spon-
sored retreats for the teachers of the witness women.

81 The retreats grew into an annual women's camp held by and for the women of CUC of PNG.

Service at the 2007 women's camp held at Embi.

82 The women enjoy food and fellowship at their camp.

83 The men are marginalized during the women's camps. They become the cooks and bottle washers.

84 The women leaders count an offering in cash and kind that they took up to support the Bible College in Mount Hagen during the camp.

85 The camp ends with a pig kill.

Church Development

86 People began attending classes and church services in the 1960s. At first they met outdoors.

87 Bush buildings were constructed for churches, and the people met inside, but the crowds overflowed the buildings and many remained outside.

88 Sunday school classes were held for the children. At first missionaries taught the Sunday school classes, but older children soon took over and taught the younger children. Notice the offering that the children brought. It is on the ground behind the teacher.

89 An early baptism
The first baptism took place in 1966 and ten of the pastors from outside the area were baptized. Twelve men, including some local men were baptized at the second baptism. The third baptism took place in December and fifty-seven men and woman were baptized. After that many were baptized.

90 Middle 91 Bottom
The first regional church conference was held at Ka on August 10, 1978. All pastors and delegates from each local church voted whether or not to accept the constitution. Many of the church delegates were non-literates. Missionaries registered the names of the pastors and delegates. Each registered participant was given a slip of paper to put into a container indicating that he or she voted to accept or reject the constitution. Papers were placed over the windows of a mission van to insure that each delegate cast his or her vote in privacy. One by one the delegates walked behind the van and cast his or her paper into a container that approved or rejected the constitution. The pastors selected one person to stand by the containers and make sure that each delegate voted only once and that the delegates understood

that they were voting for or against the constitution. The delegates voted to accept the constitution. During the next few months each district held its own conference and elected their district leaders. The second regional church conference took place on December 18, 1978, and the delegates elected the regional officers. Mapon Ek was elected as the first regional superintendent and Tui Tandopen Ori was elected as the first assistant regional superintendent.

92 Men who led the church in the 1970s and early 1980s. Left to right—James Perek, Kanj Mesmba, Tui Tandopen Ori, Ponjel, Jeremaiah Kele, Simon En and Mapon Ek

Outreach to Port Moresby and Mount Hagen began in the early 1980s, but the Port Moresby area was not formally recognized as a district until 2008, and Mount Hagen area was not formally recognized as a district until 2008.

93 The damaged church at Erima following a fire in 2007. The first CUC church in Port Moresby started in Erima settlement in the 1980s. Now there are churches at Erima, Eight Mile, and Taurama settlements and on Veimaruri and Doa Plantations

94 Church at Eight Mile Settlement, Port Moresby

95 Interior of Eight Mile Church, Port Moresby

96 District Certification, November, 2008

97 Hagen Town Church

98 Worship service at the Mount Hagen Church

99 Mount Hagen Sunday School Class in 2007

100 Mount Hagen District Certificate

The church has started churches at several places near Mount Hagen including Keta, Kimil, Rumbrumb, Tike, Rulna, Kala, Pagl, and Raimb. It was recognized as a district in 2013.

Translation Ministry

101 Translation Committee working at Ka around 1986

102 Angal Enen New Testament Dedication, March 29, 2002

103 Selling the First Angal Enen New Testaments, March 29, 2002

104 Recording the Angal Enen New Testament in 2014

105 Editing the Recorded New Testament in 2014

106 The completed audio New Testaments being charged by the sun before distribution, January of 2015

107 Listening to the audio New Testament in February of 2015

Fifty Year Celebration

108 Top Left   109 Below Left January, 2014 missionaries, pastors and people gathered at Embi station to celebrate fifty years in Papua New Guinea.

110 Top Right   111 Below Right
Pastors led men, women and children in a march to celebrate Christ and the church

112 Top Left   113 Top Right
Women and children join the march.

114 At the end of the march, the marchers broke rank and rushed to the church for the afternoon service.

Church Leaders

115 Some members of the Regional Board in 2014

Front Row from left to Right: Stanley Pesi, Joe Wane, Mapon Ek, Amos Alti-map, Alex Karemal, Rick Pombre

Back Row: David James Mackson Paul, Peter Yaki

Missing: Militus Nuepi, Philip Ayo, and Peter Rapu

Regional Superintendents

116 Simon En
Chairman of Pastor's
Conference 1973

117 Mapon Ek
Regional Superintendent
1978-1981

118 Kanj Mesmba
Regional Superintendent
1981-1990

119 Sengi Iruwa
Regional Superintendent
1990-1992

120 Simon En
Regional Superintendent
1993-1995

121 Jeremaiah Kele
Regional Superintendent
1995-1996

122 Andrew Kir
Regional Superintendent
1996-1999

No Picture

Daniel Pe
Acting
1997, 1998, 2002

123 John Kua
Regional Superintendent
2000-2004 and 2006-2008

124 Timothy Pe
Regional Superintendent
2004-2006

125 William Wop
Regional Superintendent
2008-2011

126 Peter Yaki
Regional Superintendent
2012 to present

Missionaries

127 James and Virginia
Hummel
1963-1966

No Picture

John Ottway
1964

128 Don and Betty Seymour
1964-1973

129 Martha Jean Waugh
1965-1974

No Picture

Don Whittingham
1966

130 Leland and Pearlina Johnson
1966-1979

131 Elsie Conley
1966-1984

132 Ted and Florence Meckes
1967-1975

133 Bob and Sara Jones
1968-1982

134 Shirley Ulman
1968-1978 (Single)

135 Alice Jean Christie
1969-1977

136 Ruth Tipton
1970-2007

137 Ruth McClain
1971-1976

138 Bill and Sandy Tolbert
1972-1983

139 Eva Donahue
1972-1987

140 Winfield Johnson
1973-1977

141 Denny and Juanita Brown
1974-1986

142 Ron and Miriam Hood
1974-1991

143 Mary Hermiz
1974-1983

144 Don and Dorothy Wood
1975-1983

145 Verona Charles
1977-1980

146 Lynda Fosnaugh
1977-1978

147 Bill and Becky Benner
1978-1992

148 Lorin and Linda Martin
1979-1980

149 Dean and Shirley (Ulman)
Queen
1980-2004

150 Bob and Theresa Cody
1981-1984

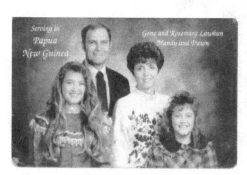

151 Gene and Rosemary Lawhun
1981-1995

152 Ron and Wilma Priest
1982-1985

153 Butch and Leatha Jenkins
1981-1994
2011 to Present

154 Don and Delores Brown
1983-1988

155 Roger and Diana Miller
1984-1987

156 John and Emalie Tipton
1984-1986

157 Al and Helen Owens
1985

158 David and Linda Wright
1985-1986

159 Hope Bowmen
1987-1988, 1992

160 Tim and Diane Bennett
1989-2008

161 Bill and Ruth Price
1991-1992

162 Esther Tipton
1993-1995

163 Jim and Becka Johnson
1993 to Present

164 Linda Bell
1996-1999

No Picture

165 Darin and Lisa Stambaugh
1997-1998

Bruce and Vicki Fivecoat
2001-2002

166 George and Cindy Neal
2003-2004

167 Benji and Erica Jenkins
2003-Present

168 Shawn and Bethany Waugh
2010-Present

169 Denver J Casto
2007, 2012

170 Seth and Veronica Porter
2012 to Present

171 Kevin and Becky Zirkle
WGM Regional Director
2002 to Present
And PNG Field Director
2008 to 2015

Acknowledgement of Picture Sources

Picture

1 - 2	From the files of the Churches of Christ in Christian Union, 1553 Lancaster Pike, Circleville, Ohio, 43113. Used with permission.
3 - 18	From the collection of Martha Jean Waugh Blakeman, currently in the collection of Ruth Tipton. Used with permission.
19	From the files of the Churches of Christ in Christian Union, 1553 Lancaster Pike, Circleville, Ohio, 43113. Used with permission.
20 - 38	From the collection of Martha Jean Waugh Blakeman, currently in the collection of Ruth Tipton. Used with permission.
39	From the collection of Rick Pombre, currently in the collection of Ruth Tipton. Used with permission.
40 - 47	From the files of Christian Union Church of Papua New Guinea. Used with permission.
48 - 49	From the collection of Martha Jean Waugh Blakeman, currently in the collection of Ruth Tipton. Used with permission.
50	From the files of the Churches of Christ in Christian Union, 1553 Lancaster Pike, Circleville, Ohio, 43113. Used with permission.
51 - 55	From the collection of Martha Jean Waugh Blakeman, currently in the collection of Ruth Tipton. Used with permission.
56	From the collection of Leatha Jenkins. Used with permission.
57 - 60	From the collection of Mary Hermiz. Used with permission.
61 - 63	From the collection of Martha Jean Waugh Blakeman, currently in the collection of Ruth Tipton. Used with permission.
64	Photograph taken by the author.
65	From the collection of Rick Pombre, currently in the collection of Ruth Tipton. Used with permission.
66	Photograph taken by the author.
67	From the collection of Simon En, currently in the collection of Ruth Tipton. Used with permission.

68	From the collection of Martha Jean Waugh Blakeman, currently in the collection of Ruth Tipton. Used with permission.
69	From the collection of Leatha Jenkins, 50 Days of Prayer for PNG. Used with permission.
70	Sara Jones, "Farata Girls School" *Missionary Tidings* 29, no 2, [September, 1977]: 11. Used with permission.
71 - 72	From the collection of Leatha Jenkins, 50 Days of Prayer for PNG. Used with permission.
73	Martha Jean Waugh, "Women's Meetings," *Missionary Tidings* XXIII, no. 7 [February, 1972]; 5. Used with permission.
74	From the files of the Churches of Christ in Christian Union, 1553 Lancaster Pike, Circleville, Ohio, 43113. Used with permission.
75	Alice Jean Christie, "They Will Know Christ by Our Love" *Missionary Tidings* XXVII, no 7 [February, 1976]: 11. Used with permission.
76 - 77	Sandy Tolbert, "Patrols For Christ," *Missionary Tidings* XXVII, no 5 [December, 1975]: 8. Used with permission.
78 - 80	Dorothy Wood, "Bung Bilong Witnes (Witnesses Retreat)" *Missionary Tidings* XXIX no. 11 [June, 1978]: 8. Used with permission.
81 - 85	Photographs taken by the author.
86	From the collection of Martha Jean Waugh Blakeman, currently in the collection of Ruth Tipton. Used with permission.
87	Florence Meckes, "I Sat Looking at My Feet," *Missionary Tidings* XXI no. 9 [April, 1970]: 4. Used with permission.
88	From the files of Churches of Christ in Christian Union, 1553 Lancaster Pike, Circleville, Ohio, 43113. Used with permission.
89	From the collection of Martha Jean Waugh Blakeman, currently in the collection of Ruth Tipton. Used with permission.
90 - 91	Bill Tolbert, "The Christian Union Church in Papua New Guinea," *Missionary Tidings* XXX no 3 [October, 1978]: 4. Used with permission.
92 - 95	Photographs taken by the author.
96	From the files of Christian Union Church of Papua New Guinea. Used with permission.

97	Photograph taken by the author.
98	From the collection Sharon Martin. Used with permission.
99	Photograph taken by the author.
100	From the files of Christian Union Church of Papua New Guinea. Used with permission.
101-103	Photographs taken by the author.
104-109	From the collection of Leatha Jenkins. Used with permission.
110 -114	Photographs taken by the author.
115	From the collection of Sharon Martin. Used with permission.
116	From the files of Churches of Christ in Christian Union, 1553 Lancaster Pike, Circleville, Ohio, 43113. Used with permission.
117-125	Photographs taken by the author.
126	From the collection of Sharon Martin. Used with permission.
127	James Hummel. "Greetings From New Guinea," *Missionary Tidings* XV, no 1 [August, 1963]: 3. Used with permission.
128	From the files of Churches of Christ in Christian Union, 1553 Lancaster Pike, Circleville, Ohio, 43113. Used with permission.
129	*Missionary Tidings*, XIX, no 7 [February, 1968]: 11. Used by permission.
130	H. P. Bennett. "Homecoming," *Missionary Tidings*, XXII no 3 [October, 1970]: 8. Used with permission.
131	*Missionary Tidings*, 39, no. 4 [December, 1986]: 4. Used with permission.
132	Ted and Florence Meckes. "Will Bring Them to New Guinea Again," *Missionary Tidings*, XX no. 3 [October, 1968]: 7. Used with permission.
133	Sara Jones. "Only With His Help," *Missionary Tidings*. XXXIII, no. 10 [May, 1982]: 7. Used with permission.
134	Shirley K. Ulman, "Prayer of Thanksgiving," *Missionary Tidings* XX, no. 4 [November, 1968]: 3. Used with permission
135	From the files of Churches of Christ in Christian Union, 1553 Lancaster Pike, Circleville, Ohio, 43113. Used with permission.

136   "Send the Light," *Missionary Tidings*, 41 no. 3 [November, 1988]: 8. Used with permission.

137   Ruth McClain. "What Have You Heard?" *Missionary Tidings*, XXII, no. 10 [May, 1971]: 5. Used with permission.

138   Bill Tolbert. "Telling it as it was—and is," *Missionary Tidings*, XXXIII, no. 10 [May, 1982]: 5. Used with permission.

139   "Profille Eva Donahue," *Missionary Tidings*, 35 no. 7 [April, 1984]: 12. Used with permission.

140   Bill Tolbert, "Wanem Kain Man?" *Missionary Tidings*, XXVIII no. 3 [October, 1976]: 6. Used with permission.

141   From the files of Churches of Christ in Christian Union, 1553 Lancaster Pike, Circleville, Ohio, 43113. Used with permission.

142   "Among The Nations" *Missionary Tidings*, 42, no. 1 [August/September, 1989]: 15. Used with permission.

143   *Missionary Tidings*, 39, no. 4 [December, 1986] 7. From the files of World Gospel Mission. Used with permission.

144   From the files of Churches of Christ in Christian Union, 1553 Lancaster Pike, Circleville, Ohio, 43113. Used with permission.

145   Mary A. Waggoner, "Know Your Missionaries Verona Charles," *Missionary Tidings*, XXVIII, no. 3 [October, 1976]: 10. Used with permission.

146   Mary A. Waggoner, "Know Your Missionaries Lynda Fosnaugh," *Missionary Tidings*, XXVII, no. 8 [March, 1977]: 10. Used with permission.

147   From the files of Churches of Christ in Christian Union, 1553 Lancaster Pike, Circleville, Ohio, 43113. Used with permission.

148   Mary A. Waggoner, "Know Your Missionaries The Lorin Martins," *Missionary Tidings*, XXX, no. 7 [February, 1979]: 10. Used with permission.

149   Mary A. Waggoner, "Know Your Missionaries The Dean Queens," *Missionary Tidings*, XXXI, no. 3 [October, 1979]: 10. Used with permission.

150-152   From the files of Churches of Christ in Christian Union, 1553 Lancaster Pike, Circleville, Ohio, 43113. Used with permission.

153   Betty Seymour, "Profile Leatha and Paul Jenkins," *Missionary Tidings*, 39, no. 2 [January, 1987]: 11. Used with permission.

154   Betty Seymour, "Profile Don and Delores Brown," *Missionary Tidings*, 39, no. 5 [January, 1987]: 11. Used with permission.

155   *Missionary Tidings*, 39 no. 4, [December, 1986]: 7. Used with permission.

156   "Profile: John and Emalie Tipton," *Missionary Tidings*, 35, no. 6 [March, 1984]: 12. Used by permission

157   From the collection of David and Linda Wright. Used with permission.

158   Al and Helen Owens, "Viewpoints," *Missionary Tidings*, 37, no. 7 [April, 1985]: 8. Used with permission.

159   *Missionary Tidings*, 40, no. 4 [December, 1987]: 7. Used with permission.

160   Betty Seymour, "Profile Tim and Diane Bennett," *Missionary Tidings*, 40, no. 3 [November, 1987]: 10. Used with permission.

161   Betty Seymour, "Retired or Re-Fired?" *Missionary Tidings*, 43, no. 6 [June/July, 1991]: 12. Used with permission.

162   "Among The Nations" *Missionary Tidings*, 41, no. 5 [January, 1989]: 11. Used with permission.

163   From the collection of Anatasia Beaver. Used with permission.

164   *Evangelical Advocate*, 91, no. 6 [February, 1996]:18. From the files of World Gospel Mission. Used with permission.

165   "Meet Darin and Lisa Stambaugh," *Evangelical Advocate*, 92 no. 9 [April, 1997], 10. Used with permission.

166   Cindy Neal, "What's up With the Neals?" *Evangelical Advocate*, 98 no. 5 [January, 2002}]: 17. From the filed of World Gospel Mission. Used with permission.

167   From the collection of Sharon Martin. Used with permission.

168   From the collection of Jennifer Perkins. Used with permission.

169   From the collection of Benji Jenkins. Used with permission.

170   From the collection of Jennifer Johnson. Used with permission.

171   From the collection of Kevin Zirkle. Used with permission.

Appendix Two

Nembi Resistance to Administrative Patrols

During the 1950s several of the Nembi groups came under the administration's close scrutiny because of their fighting. The most notorious were the Semin and the Utabia. In December of 1956, officials at Mendi heard reports that the Semin people were the main aggressors in heavy fighting in the Nembi Valley. They were reportedly fighting with all of the surrounding groups except those to the north. Gordon Smith organized a patrol to intervene in the fighting. He approached the Semin area from the north, thinking that the Semin would be unable to flee in any other direction because they were surrounded by enemies. However, the Semin had trading alliances and friends to the south, and as the patrol moved steadily southward the Semin people also moved southward taking their pigs and posses- sions with them and avoiding all contact with the administration. When the Semin fled from the patrol, their enemies rushed in and ravished Semin gardens and burned Semin houses. The patrol then turned its attention to the marauders and arrested seventeen men, all of whom escaped.[1]

The Utabia people caught the administration's attention early because of their frequent clashes with the Det people and other members of the *Aron* alliance. The Det people were a part of the Undiri Census Division and the Mendi sub-district and though they lived on the fringes of the sub-district, patrols from Mendi made regular visits to the Det/Pabaronga area. Few patrols crossed to the western side of the Nembi River where the people were considered to be hostile. In October of 1957 a patrol led by G. J. Hogg moved along the eastern side of the river on its way to Nipa to investigate the proposed airstrip site when it stumbled across fighting near Det between the *Aron* and *Karinj* alliances and decided to remain. Hogg camped at the battle site in the vicinity of Det and stayed there for eight days. The patrol built a rest house and appointed influential men from both Det and Utabia to be village constables in the hope that "having such men in the role of government peacemaker as opposed to that of fight leader" would hasten the

---

[1]Mendi Patrol Report Number 1 of 1956-1957, {NB 54-58 HW 291-297}.

process of pacification.[2] After Hogg moved on, some youths from the *Karinj* alliance burned down the rest house. The *Aron* people killed a village constable of the *Karinj* group and his companions.[3]

When I interviewed Kanj Mesmba he told a story about Porenaik's father, a man named Wonguap from Utabia who had been appointed to serve as a village constable. He and ten other men had slept at Det, and then gone with a government patrol to visit Mendi. As long as they were with the patrol, the men were safe, but after visiting Mendi they started back to their place unaccompanied. The men thought that they were under the government's protection and could safely return home on their own. On the way back to Utabia, *Aron* groups killed the men (ten in all). To reciprocate, men from Utabia killed five or six men from Det. The Utabia people blamed the administration for the deaths of the men. Kanj said that the administration eventually compensated Utabia for the men who had been killed,[4] but at first the administration struggled to understand the increased hostility and animosity that the Utabia people displayed towards the administration.

In November of 1958, two men from Utabia met a patrol led by patrol officer R. N. Desailly and enticed him to the Utabia ceremonial ground with the promise of food, but when the patrol arrived there, it was apparent that it was under threat of attack. Desailly learned that the people blamed the government for "the death of some of their people," but he was unaware of the killings. The patrol made its way cautiously and safely out of Utabia territory and camped on the opposite banks of the river.[5] When reports that the Utabia people were angry with the administration, wanted a fight, and boasted that no one, not even the administration could defeat them filtered back to Mendi, the administration sent patrols to Utabia to learn the reason for the increased animosity.[6] The acting district commissioner D. J. Cancy arrested people from the *Aron* alliance for the murders.[7]

The fights between the Det and Utabia raged on, and a few months later the Det people sent a request for help to the administration in Mendi. A patrol led by S. F. Markwell left Mendi immediately, and went to Pabaronga near Det and with the help of the people of the *Aron* alliance built a rest house and police barracks. Markwell called for the Utabia leaders to come meet him, but they refused and sent instead a delegation of twenty-three younger men who insisted that the Det/Pabaronga people had started the fight. Markwell warned the Utabia contingent not to burn down the rest house as they had in the past. The patrol remained at Pabaronga for five days and then returned to Mendi. Markwell thought that "the patrol's prompt arrival at Pabaronga should convince the people that the adminis-

---

[2]Erave Patrol Number 4 of 1957-1958, 11, {NB 54-58, HW 379}.

[3]Erave Patrol Number 5 of 1957-1958, 4, 17, 18, {NB 54-58 HW 411, 424, 425}.

[4]Kanj Mesmba, interview by author, Port Moresby, Papua New Guinea, November 23, 2009,

[5]Mendi Patrol Report Number 3 1958-59, 3-6 {NB 58-61 HW 20-23}.

[6]B.K. Leen, January 3, 1959, letter written to the District Commissioner in Mendi, in Mendi Patrol Report Number 3 of 1958-1959, {NB 58-61 HW 16}.

[7]I was unable to obtain a copy of the report about the patrol that Clancy led to arrest the murderers, but the other patrol reports mention the arrests.

tration is interested in their problems," but he said nothing about the implication that the administration favored the *Aron* over the *Karinj* alliance.[8]

When the administration opened the Nipa Patrol post in 1959, there was wide spread fighting among the Nembi groups. The administration was determined to stop the fighting, but the Nembi groups did not want to give up their fighting, and most resisted the administration. One by one the warring groups were contacted, told to quit fighting, negotiate a peace settlement with a "*moga*" exchange, and accept administrative control. The Injua (Tembil) people were less resistant than most groups, and were the first to compensate their enemies for a wrongful death. In January of 1960 J. Jordon visited the Injua people and lectured them about "law and order." After that visit the Injua curtailed their fighting, but they were long term enemies of the Semin people, and in March of 1960, an Injua youth killed a Semin youth. A patrol from Nipa went to Semin to investigate. The Injua people paid the Semin compensation, and the next day the patrol moved to the Injua ceremonial ground where it camped for the next four days and conducted a preliminary census of the group, recording 255 names.[9] Injua became a frequent stopping point for patrols on their way to visit other Nembi groups.

The Semin were not so easily pacified. The Merut/Tindom and the Semin/Mobera groups were sworn enemies who had been fighting for generations. When word reached Nipa station in January of 1961 that the two groups were fighting and that two men, one from each side, had been ambushed and killed, R. A. Hoad led a patrol from Nipa to investigate the stories and "enforce the queen's peace." The patrol spent the first few nights at Semin and then moved toward Merut territory accompanied by two of the Semin headmen and followed by a large contingent of Semin warriors who refused to allow their headmen out of their sight. When the patrol entered Merut territory, the Semin turned back, but the Merut observed the patrol's approach, and they fled taking women, children, pigs, and all movable property with them.[10]

Hoad made known his intention of remaining in Merut territory until Merut men came to discuss the situation with him, and he camped on Merut land for two weeks. No Merut man came close, although some came within shouting distance during the day and shouted out obscenities and ordered the patrol to leave their land. They quickly disappeared if the patrol approached them. At night the Semin men made regular trips into Merut territory, destroying houses and raiding gardens, and at times other groups joined in the raids. When the patrol ran short of food, and was unable to purchase enough from other groups, they foraged the Merut gardens.[11]

Finally the Merut were taken by force. Four Merut men were captured on Friday the 27th of January when a youth from a neighboring group across the Nembi River led the patrol to a Merut hiding place. In a pre-dawn raid held on Sunday,

[8]Mendi Patrol Report Number 7 of 1958-1959, {NB 58-61 HW 49-53}.
[9]Nipa Patrol Report Number 4 of 1959-1960, 2-4, 10-11 {NB 58-61, HW 79-81, 87-88}.
[10]Nipa Patrol Report Number 3 of 1960-1961, 3 – 5, {NB 58-61, HW 300-302}.
[11]Nipa Patrol Number 3 of 1960-61, 5 –9, {NB 58-61, HW 302-306}.

the 29th of January, thirteen more Merut men were captured and taken prisoner and led back to the camp in Merut territory. The following morning all seventeen Merut prisoners were taken to the Nipa jail. By then "no person from the Merut group remained in the area." Other groups had given them places of refuge.[12]

The patrol returned to Semin territory where it was "warmly received." Hoad insisted that the Semin surrender the men who had killed the Merut man, and four Semin youth were arrested.[13] Hoad reported that he had "friendly contact" with the Semin people even though the Semin intruded into Merut territory to raid gardens and destroy houses. The Merut had remained "unfriendly" and "uncooperative." From the Nembi perspective, the administration had compromised its neutrality. They believed that the Semin people had brought the administration into the dispute and that the administration favored the Semin over the Merut. The fact that the Semin marauded Merut property while the patrol camped nearby, and that seventeen Merut men, including some of the headmen had been taken prisoner while only four Semin youths were arrested confirmed the perception.[14] Hoad noted that it was the first time that "the Queen's peace had been enforced," and that it was natural for the people to be "unsympathetic...to some foreign power authority that attempted to change their way of life, including their code of justice." [15]

Within a week, all seventeen Murut men escaped from the Nipa prison, and the Semin people attacked and completely destroyed a Merut "hamlet" at Soro.[16] The administration said that the situation in the area was "not good nor improving" and the prison escape had "done inestimable harm to the administration."[17]

During the next few months several patrols tried to apprehend the escaped prisoners. The Semin people continued to harass the Merut, and whenever a patrol entered Merut territory, the women and children fled as the patrol approached. In March Butler reported,

> As the patrol moved on signs of fighting could be seen in the flattened cane-grass, axe marks on the clay banks and occasional broken arrows...

> Throughout the day the patrol saw signs that the Merut people had evacuated their area — tracks of women, children and pigs could be seen along all the roads leading out of the area and these tracks had been obliterated by the men as they followed, however the scuffing feet intended to obliterate the tracks had not always been efficient.[18]

---

[12]Nipa Patrol Number 3 of 1960-1961, 9 – 11, {NB 58-61, HW 306-308}.

[13]Nipa Patrol Report Number 3 of 1960-1961, 11 – 13 {NB 58-61 HW 308-310}.

[14]Nipa Patrol Report Number 4 of 1960-1961, 10 {NB 58-61 HW 347}.

[15]Nipa Patrol Report Number 3 of 1960-1961, 17 – 18 {NB 58-61 HW 314 – 315}.

[16]Nipa Patrol Report Number 4 of 1960-1961, 8 {NB 58-61 HW 345}.

[17]K. W. Dyer, 20 April, 1961, letter to the sub-district office in Mendi in Nipa Patrol Report Number 4 1960-1961, {NB 58-61 HW 335}.

[18]Nipa Patrol Number 4 of 1960-1961, 1 {NB 58-61 – HW 337}.

The administration made it a point to visit the Utabia people frequently. In January of 1960, J. Jordon stayed at Utabia for three days and demanded that all of the men from Utabia come to talk to him. Jordon did not ask to buy food because he wanted to appear to be "self-sufficient" and claimed that food purchases were "normally acts of largesse" on the administration's part. On the third day 120 men gathered, and Jordan gave firearms demonstrations and lectured about the administration's aims and objectives and assured the people of the administration's ability to apprehend any runaways. He informed the Utabia people that the administration would take action against any individual who demonstrated "openly hostile behavior" or showed "signs of recalcitrance" in the future. After the lecture relations between the administration and the people "appeared to be back on a satisfactory basis" and Jordan noted that administrative patrols "were not objects which could be easily forced out of an area, or were so weak as to fall prey to attacks by villagers."[19]

In late 1960 a Mendi patrol arbitrated a peace agreement and a compensation payment between Utabia and Det, and extracted a promise from both sides that they would abide by the agreement. Groups belonging to the *Karinj* alliance were preparing for a major pig kill. The Utabia and Det people promised that they would pay compensation at the pig kill, and they would invite the administration to observe the ceremony.[20] The promise was repeated to every subsequent patrol and reported by every patrol officer who visited Utabia before the pig kill was held. Butler led a patrol through Utabia in July and early August of 1961 just days before the feast was held. Men from both Utabia and Det again assured him that they were going to give the reparation payments at the pig feast and said that it would take place in about four months. Members of the administration would be invited to the dual event. Butler later learned that neither side had done anything toward making the exchange they had agreed to, and no one wanted the administration's presence at the pig feast. They had given Butler false information about the date of the pig kill, saying it would not take place for several months when it was going to be held in just a few days.[21]

In June of 1960 officials at Mendi received reports that the Petum/Kabit groups were fighting, and the Petum people had killed and dismembered one of the fight leaders from Penerop.[22] Arrangements were made for a patrol from Nipa led by D. N. Butler to meet a Mendi patrol at Kabit and the two patrols would work together to intervene in the fighting and negotiate a settlement. However the Mendi patrol was recalled, leaving Butler with a small patrol to handle the situation. At first the Kabit men stood on the surrounding peaks and called out for the patrol to

---

[19]Nipa Patrol Number 2, 1959-60, 3-4, {NB 58-61, HW 63-64}.

[20]Nipa Patrol Report Number 1 of 1961 -1962, 1 {NB 61-64, HW 8}. The payments were arranged by Mendi Patrol Number 10 of 1960-1961. However, I do not have a copy of that patrol report. Either the report was missing from the archives, or it was overlooked either in my reading or in making the photocopies that I requested.

[21]Nipa Patrol Report Number 1 of 1961 -1962, 1-2, 7 {NB 61-64, HW 8-9, 14}.

[22]Nipa Patrol Report Number 5 of 1959-1960, 11-12 {NB – 58-61, HW 104-105}.

leave so they could continue their fight, but Butler refused to leave until the warriors came to camp to talk.[23] After several days a contingent of sixty to eighty Petum/Kabit men came to the camp and admitted that they had killed and dismembered the enemy fight leader, and demanded that the patrol leave. The situation was "ugly" and the men made threatening gestures with their long handled axes, but Butler placed the "arrogant" and "insulting" spokesperson under arrest and demonstrated the power of the patrol's guns. The group "quietened after the arrest of their leader and a severe lecture."[24]

The patrol remained in the Kabit area for the next ten days foraging for food in Petum/Kabit gardens, leaving payment in small trade goods when they were unable to purchase it directly. At one point Petum/Kabit warriors attacked part of the patrol but the attack was repulsed when the patrol members fired over the heads of the attackers and shot two pigs and left them on the track as a demonstration of the strength of the firearms they carried. Finally a large group of Petum/Kabit men visited the camp and listened to the administration's spiel demanding that they quit fighting, and then they invited the patrol to join the fight and help them annihilate the Penerop/Embi. Petum/Kabit leaders finally agreed to meet with the Penerop on neutral ground. The patrol left Kabit accompanied by the Petum/Kabit entourage of about 120 men, and set up camp at Pomberel where one of the Pomberel sub-groups helped persuade the Penerop/Embi men to join in peace negotiations.[25]

Three days of discussion passed before the two groups reached an agreement. The killing was not one-sided. The Penerop/Embi had killed and dismembered three Petum/Kabit men before the Petum/Kabit men killed and dismembered "the most influential Penerop/Embi leader." Butler informed the people that the government came in peace, but it would fight and defeat them if necessary. Three leaders from each group in consultation with the patrol officers reached an agreement on the compensation payment each group would give for six deaths that had occurred in the two groups.[26]

Butler reported that "the patrol had successfully investigated and halted the chain of pay-back killings between the groups involved." The people considered the patrol to be an "unwarranted and unwanted" intruder, and future patrols should expect trouble in the area. The situation in the Emia Valley was not good, and the people were generally "arrogant and resentful of intervention."[27]

The administration did not take it lightly when groups fired arrows at a patrol. I have heard stories from several Nembi people saying the people of Kabit and Ep strongly resisted the patrols. The people say, they launched an attack on the administration, shot a white man, and a battle ensued. The white man was not killed,

[23]Nipa Patrol Report Number 5 of 1959-1960, 2 {NB – 58-61, HW 95}.

[24]Nipa Patrol Report Number 5 of 1959-1960, 3 {NB – 58-61, HW 96}.

[25]Nipa Patrol Report Number 5 of 1959-1960, 7-9 {NB – 58-61, HW 100-102}.

[26]Nipa Patrol Report Number 5 of 1959-1960, 9 {NB – 58-61, HW 100}.

[27]Nipa Patrol Report Number 5 of 1959-1960, 11-12 {NB – 58-61, HW 104-105}.

but a number of the Kabit men died.[28] I was unable to find written confirmation of the incident, but among the Nembi the story is wide spread, and patrol reports confirm that patrols in the area were attacked.[29]

In December of 1960 four patrols from Kagua, Erave, Mendi and Nipa met at Toiwara and conducted a united patrol though the Emia Creek area where they anticipated being given a hostile reception. Many men watched the patrol "from the high vantage points along the valley."[30] At Pomberel, the people seemed anxious to see the last of the patrol, and the Petum/Kabit warriors who had attacked Butler's patrol in June, were extremely reserved.[31] Jensen-Muir comments,

This patrol rendezvoused with a Mendi/Nipa patrol led by Mr. Gordon Smith…on the 7th of December, 1960. It was decided by Mr. Smith and myself that a joint patrol through portion of this troubled area would be most beneficial. Specific comment on this portion of the patrol has been left to the Mendi Patrol Report…

There had been many reports made to me prior to our arrival in the Amia (Emia Creek) area, as to what they, the local people, were going to do to us, viz. attacks… The arrival of the two[32] patrols, both strong, simultaneously from surrounding ridges to the North and to the West quenched such talk most effectively, and the people were duly impressed.[33]

Later patrols found the Penerop/Embi land "devastated by war" and when the first census was taken, the Penerop/Embi were "still in the bush to which they had fled" because of tribal fighting. [34] The Penerop/Embi people had land rights in the Wage Valley and had escaped both their enemies and the administrative patrols by going to the Wage area.

The groups in the lower Nembi/upper Erave Valley living south of the Kuvivi flats (Poroma) "became distinguished for their lack of cooperation." [35] They demanded high prices for the food they sold to the patrols, and on more than one occasion they stole from patrols. In May of 1961, a patrol from Kagua led by G. P. Jensen-Muir visited the groups in the lower Nembi/upper Erave Valleys. As the patrol approached the eastern banks of the river, groups on the western side of the river threatened to cut down the bridge so the patrol could not cross. Jensen-Muir and members of the constabulary rushed to the river to find fully armed men from

---

[28]Kanj Mesmba, interview by author, Port Moresby, Papua New Guinea, January 29, 2010.

[29]There may be some missing records between June and December of 1960.

[30]Erave Patrol Report Number 4 of 1960-1961, 4, {NB 58-61 HW 378}.

[31]Kagua Patrol Report Number 7 of 1960-1961, 4, {NB 58-61, HW 397}.

[32]It was really four patrols. The patrols from Kagua and Earve joined forces at some point on the Eastern side of the Erave River before crossing to Toiwara and entering the Emia Creek area. From the time they joined forces they operated as one patrol with Jensen-Muir, the leader of the combined patrol. At some point before arriving at Toiwara, a Nipa patrol had joined a Mendi patrol lead by Gordon Smith who became the leader of the combined Mendi/Nipa patrol.

[33]Kagua Patrol Report Number 7 of 1960-1961, 6-7, {NB 58-61, HW 400}.

[34]Nipa Patrol Report Number 2 of 1962-1963, 2 {NB 61-64 HW 236, 239}

[35]Mendi Patrol Report Number 4 of 1952-1953, 3, 13, 17 {NB 49-54 HW 198, 208, 212}.

Toiwara, Tiga, Nenja, Wambu and Poroma getting ready to carry out their threat to cut the bridge. Jensen-Muir's later reported,

> My arrival greeted with shouts and brandishing of weapons and cries of 'Go home, we won't let you come over.' Commenced haranguing them. Answered with arrow shots. No one hit. Possible to take bridge by force but decided against this as would have resulted in exchange of fire with possible casualties. Continued to talk at them. After several hours convinced them of our peaceful intentions, and crossed river under cover of rifles.[36]

The following day, the entire patrol crossed the bridge and spent several days camped on the Western side of the river where it made peaceful contacts with a number of groups.[37]

Larger patrols were less likely to face resistance than the smaller patrols. In July and August of 1961 an extremely large patrol that conducted a resource survey visited many Nembi groups. It was accompanied by six Europeans, ten police, and 100 carriers and general laborers. The patrol was so large that it "discouraged open resistance" and "made quite an impression of the people. It was "amicably" received by most groups who readily sold food to the patrol. At Pomberel one man attempted to steel an axe, but was caught in the act and lectured.[38]

However, D. N. Butler led a smaller patrol that visited Pomberel ten days after the large patrol left. His patrol was met by fifty men who demanded that the patrol move on, and informed Butler that the Pomberel people would provide them with no tent poles, firewood or food. Butler immediately decided to camp right there, and sent some men to cut poles from a stand of trees. A Pomberel man threatened to stone the men cutting the poles and stopped only when a rifle was pointed directly at him. Butler scuffled with another man and barely avoided being axed in the leg. When things calmed down, Butler informed the people that "the government required them to abide by its laws and that they were required to co-operate with patrols." Patrols were capable of defending themselves, and the next patrol would begin taking a census, and village constables would be selected.[39]

The next morning another confrontation occurred after a Pomberel man attempted to steal an item of clothing from one of the carriers. Butler and the Pomberel men had a prolonged discussion. The Pomberel people had been undefeated for several generations, and some of the younger men believed that they were strong enough to defeat any patrol that visited their area. Butler claimed that the patrol "had been sent into the area by a higher authority which considered that it had the right and the power to send the patrol." If the patrol were attacked or its belongings taken, there existed a "force or power behind the patrol which would punish the people."[40] The older men compared the wealth that the patrol pos-

---

[36]Kagua Patrol Report Number 12 of 1960-1961, 5 {NB 58-61 HW 415}.

[37]Kagua Patrol Report Number 12 of 1960-1961, 5-6, 9-10 {NB 58-61 HW 415-416, 419-420}.

[38]Kagua Patrol Report Number 2 of 1961-1962, 4, 7 {NB 61-64, HW 29, 32}.

[39]Nipa Patrol Report Number 1 of 1961-1962, 5-8 {NB 61-64, HW 12}.

[40]Nipa Patrol Report Number 1 of 1961-1962, 5-8 {NB 61-64, HW 12}.

sessed with their own, and concluded that any group that possessed the kind of wealth that the patrols possessed had to be strong enough to defend their wealth, but some of the younger men were not convinced. Finally

> an old village leader, with an enormous goiter in his neck (Oball), stood up and told the young men that the elders would move to a distant village and leave youth at Pomberel. The youth would then be free to attack patrols and engage in a trial of strength with the administration while the elders would look on awaiting the outcome.

> This statement by the old man was fully supported by the patrol and the people were told that should this be the only means of convincing the younger men then the patrol was willing to remain in the area until a conclusion was reached...It is realized that this could have been a dangerous move, however, in the situation it was felt that the old and more influential men had to be given support in their public statements and the younger men made to realize that although patrols came in peace they are also willing to defend themselves and their property from attack.[41]

Afterwards the patrols was on "reasonably friendly terms with the people" but Butler cautioned that future patrols to the Pomberel area, must "exercise caution...always take a very firm stand" because conciliatory moves would be interpreted as "weakness" and invite an attack.[42]

By August of 1961, the Mendi officials were losing their patience with the Nembi groups, and K. W. Dyer the District officer demanded that firm action be taken against those who resisted administrative patrols and that "the escapees from the Nipa prison be recaptured and dealt with and for...the people to understand that we intend to administer the law and will exact their compliance."[43] In September three different patrol from Mendi and Nipa converged at Tindom. Alan C. Jeffries led the Mendi Patrol, and was the ranking officer over the conbined patrol. On his way to Tindom he passed through the Det/Pabaronga and Utabia areas where he learned that the groups held their pig kill some time during August, but the people of Utabia and Det/Pabaronga had not made the promised "*moga*" payment. He informed the people that the patrol would return in a week or so to supervise the "*moga*" exchange.[44]

At Tindom yodeling Merut men shouted insults, surrounded the combined patrol, ordered the patrol to leave, and even launched attacks on the patrol. The patrol chased, captured, and imprisoned their attackers.[45] Jeffries, the main leader of the combined patrol, reported that the Semin and Merut people "had an apparent 'hard core' of village elders who did not wish to enjoy the *Pax Britannica*."

---

[41]Nipa Patrol Report Number 1 of 1961 -1962, 9, {NB 61-64, HW 16}.

[42]Nipa Patrol Report Number 1 of 1961 -1962, 9 {NB 61-64, HW 16}.

[43]K. W. Dyer, 31 August, 1961, letter to the assistant district officer at Mendi in Nipa Patrol Report Number 1 of 1961-1962, {NB 61-64 HW 3}.

[44]Mendi Patrol Report Number 4 of 1961-1962, 1, {NB 61-64 HW 43}.

[45]Mendi Patrol Report Number 4 of 1961-1962, 1-2, {NB 61-64 HW 43-44}.

They were aggressive "thugs" who had few friends among the groups that surrounded them.[46]

The patrol then moved to Pomberel with the prisoners in tow to investigate a report of inter-group fighting that had broken out following Patrol officer Butler's visit to Pomberel the previous month. The patrol camped at the Pomberel and when requested, the people brought food and sold it to the patrol, but they denied any knowledge of fighting or barked trees and insisted that naughty children had destroyed the gardens.[47]

The patrol exhumed the body of a woman who had been killed in the fighting to verify the cause of death. The woman's body had several arrow and axe wounds. Her husband provided the patrol with the names and "whereabouts of the woman's killers." Very early the next morning on Sunday the 17th of September, 1961 the patrol divided into four parties, each being led by one of the European officers on the patrol, and went to the homes of the accused killers; arrested them; took them as prisoners; and brought them back to the camp. Butler went to Tobua where one of the warriors broke Butler's leg[48] resisting arrest.[49] The resulting punitive action is not recorded, but it must have been prompt and severe.

The next morning Butler left the patrol, but the other three officers led the patrol on a slow trip to Upa with a long line of prisoners in tow. Angry Pomberel warriors followed the patrol, rushed the police who were guarding the prisoners, and threatened to attack and but held back when the police fired shots into the air. As the patrol entered Upa territory, angry shouting Pomberel men threw stones at the departing party but the stoning stopped when shots were again fired over their heads.[50]

The patrol then passed through Utabia with the prisoners in tow. Jeffries ordered the Utabia people to build a rest house and to come to Det the following day to receive a compensation payment from Det for the Utabia men the Det people had killed.[51] By taking the line of prisoners through Utabia and Det, Jeffries hoped to "impress on the groups concerned that the administration was capable of enforcing law and order in the area." Jeffries thought that his strategy paid off,

---

[46]Mendi Patrol Report Number 4 of 1961-1962, 1-2, 19A {NB 61-64 HW 43-44, 62}.

[47]Mendi Patrol Report Number 4 of 1961-1962, 2-3 {NB 61-64 HW 44-45}.

[48]Shieffelin and Crittenden say that his leg was deliberately broken in 1960 (276). However, it happened in September of 1961. Subsequent patrols make reference to Butler's "accident" at Tobua (Mendi Patrol Report Number 7 of 1961-62, 2, 7 {NB 61-64, 105, 110}, and in a letter dated October 15, 1962, and incuded with Nipa Patrol Number Two of 1962-1963 led by N. D. Lucas, Alan C. Jeffries says that Butler broke his leg at Tobua last year. Tobua was not listed as a separate group until after this patrol, and they are some of Pumberel's nearest neighbors. The early patrols may have identified them with the Pumberel or other nearby groups. I could not find a copy of a patrol that Butler led to meet up with Jeffries in September of 1961, but if he was evacuated to get medical attention, it may not have been written.

[49]Nipa Patrol Number 5 or 1964-1965, 16-17 {NB 61-64, HW 96, 97}.

[50]Mendi Patrol Report Number 4 of 1961-1962, 4-5 {NB 61-64 HW 46-47}.

[51]Mendi Patrol Report Number 4 of 1961-1962, 4-5 {NB 61-64 HW 46-47}.

because after escorting the prisoners to the Lai Valley and leaving them in the care of another patrol officer who took them to Mendi, he returned to Det/Pabaronga where, with the appropriate dances and rituals, the war reparations payments were made. The Utabia people received a compensation payment of twenty-one Mother of Pearl shells, two steel axes, six parcels of indigenous salt, 5 shell necklaces, and 2 oval shaped headbands. The people said that because of the large pig feast that had taken place just three weeks earlier they had no pigs to kill. Jeffries accepted the claim and agreed to delay the pig kill that traditionally accompanied a peace ceremony, but he assured them that the administration was keeping a record and would insist that they hold the pig feast in due time.[52]

After 1961 the groups no longer met the patrols with open resistance. At Pomberel, a follow-up patrol found that the people had built a rest house, kitchen, and barracks, and latrines. When the patrol arrived, the people sat on the ground awaiting the patrols arrival, and had already collected a large pile of food and firewood. The first census was taken, but most people refused to come in to be counted. 230 people, about one-fourth of the total population of Pomberel gave their names at the first census. When the patrol left Pomberel for Upa, "forty Pomberel men volunteered to act as carriers as far as Upa, and their services were accepted."[53]

At Upa, Pe, the head man, met the patrol and informed the patrol officer, that all of the people were away visiting friends. Pe said that a patrol officer from Erave had appointed him to be a "government man" and insisted that the patrol would gain nothing by camping at Upa. Patrol officer Jefferies promptly decided to camp at Upa and build a rest house. The patrol remained at Upa for two days. A few of the men visited the camp, but the women and children, who could be seen watching from nearby garden areas, refused to approach the camp. Only twenty-two people participated in the initial Upa census.[54] Pe insisted that the Upa people were a part of Utabia, and wanted to census with the people of Utabia, but Jefferies decided that Upa should be a separate census point, and that it provided a good stopping place between Pomberel and Utabia, and allowed for direct, "on the spot administration in (an) obviously populous...area".[55]

At Tobua the headman agreed that the patrol could take the initial census of the Tobua people, and a total of 195 people or about one-fourth of the people gave their names at the first census. With the assistance of the Tobua people, the patrol started to build a rest house at Tobua.[56] However, the Tobua people were "still very timid." The people avoided the rest house, and the Tobua village constable resisted joining other village constables from Pomberel, Upa, Utabia, Kongu, and Det who were going to Mendi to get shovels for road work. In the end he agreed

---

[52]Mendi Patrol Report Number 4 of 1961-1962, 13 {NB 61-64 HW 55-56}.

[53]Mendi Patrol Report Number 4 of 1961-1962, 2-3, 15 {NB 61-64 HW 44-45, 57}.

[54]Mendi Patrol Report Number 4 of 1961-1962 4, 8 {NB 61-64 HW 46, 50}.

[55]Mendi Patrol Report Number 4 of 1961-1962 17 {NB 61-64 HW 59}.

[56]Mendi Patrol Report Number 4 of 1961-1962, 8, 15 {NB 61-64 HW 50, 57}.

to go along.[57] In January of 1964, friction again developed between the Tobua people and an administrative patrol led by Patrol Officer Focken. Some of the Tobua men threatened to "cut out the liver" of Focken. The threats were taken seriously enough that Focken withdrew to Nipa and recruited a second Nipa patrol led by Warren R, Read and a Mendi patrol led by Haviland to join Focken's patrol and return to Tobua. The combined patrol remained at Tobua for twelve days. The ringleaders who had confronted Focken were arrested and sentenced to serve time in Bomana jail. Months later, when a follow-up patrol visited the Tobua area in November of 1964, a number of people had gathered, but many remained in hiding.[58]

In late 1961 Semin people became angry when other groups were issued shovels to begin working on roads, but they were not. They threatened to massacre the next patrol, but the administration informed them that it was unwilling to issue any shovels or start them on road work until they accepted administrative control and made peace with the Merut.[59]

The Merut people no longer openly resisted the patrols, but they remained scattered and made themselves scarce whenever a patrol visited the area. Surrounding groups blamed the Merut men for the mass arrests and planned to take action against the Merut people. It was months before enough Merut came out of hiding for the administration to conduct the first census of the group,[60] and as late as December 1964, the administration suspected that many of the Merut had never been censused.[61]

It took almost two years to negotiate a peace settlement between the Semin and the Merut.[62] In December of 1964, Warren R. Read reported that the Semin people were in an "extreme primitive state" and they were "timid and unsure of what to do or say at a census revision," but they were "settling down." It was "pleasing" because just three years earlier they had been "forever clashing with administration patrols and fighting with their neighbours."[63]

In March of 1963, Peter J. Barber visited the groups in the Lower Nembi and Emia Creek areas, and he reported that the Poroma and Mato groups had been helpful but "timid" in the patrol's presence. Toiwara had shown a strange mix of reactions ranging from "timid" to "quite the opposite." The Nenja village constable brought an "alleged murderer" to Toiwara, and the next day Barber went to Nenja to investigate. He saw the "dead man" walking around with only a "dent in his back." Most of the people of Nenja had disappeared into the rocks, crevices, and crannies of the nearby limestone mountains, and they could not be enticed out of their places of hiding. He made no contact with them, conducted no census, and could carry out no investigation.[64]

[57]Mendi Patrol Report Number 7 of 1961-62, 2, 7 {NB 61-64, 105, 110}.
[58]Nipa Patrol Report Number 5 of 1964-65, 16-17 {NB 64-66 HW 96-97}.
[59]Nipa Patrol Report Number 5 of 1961-62, 3-4 {NB 61-64 HW 95- 96}.
[60]Nipa Patrol Report Number 9 of 1961-62, 2{NB 61-64 HW 162, 167}.
[61]Nipa Patrol Report Number 5 of 1964-65, 14 {NB 64-66 HW 101}.
[62]Nipa Patrol Report Number 8 of 1962-63, {NB 61-64 HW 357}.
[63]Nipa Patrol Report Number 5 of 1964-65, 14 {NB 64-66 HW 101}.
[64]Nipa Patrol Report Number 8 of 1962-63, {NB 61-64 HW 357}.

Appendix Three

Push for Independence

In the early 1950s most Australians assumed that the Territory of Papua and New Guinea would eventually become an Australian state,[1] but by the late 1950s Australians anticipated Papua and New Guinea becoming an independent nation. In 1958, J. R. Kerr, who served as a member of the Directorate of Research and Civil Affairs, said that a politically independent Papua and New Guinea with "a close and permanent economic and cultural partnership" with Australia was the only practical goal for the Territory of Papua and New Guinea.[2] At a press conference held in June of 1960, Robert Menzies, who was then the Australian Prime Minister, said that Australia's "ultimate objective" was to bring the people of Papua and New Guinea to independence.[3] The push for independence came from both inside and outside of the territory.

The United Nations was the primary external proponent of independence. Visiting missions from the United Nations came to assess the situation in the Trust Territory of New Guinea every three years, and they pushed Australia to hasten independence. The fifth visit, led by Sir Hugh Foot (later Lord Caradon) took place in 1962.[4] Its report, issued in July of 1962,[5] criticized Australia for not moving more quickly to grant self-government and independence to the Territory of Papua and New Guinea. It called for more rapid educational, political and economic development. The report acknowledged the widespread development of elementary schools, but said that "the time has come...to provide the apex of

---

[1]Brian Jinks, Peter Biskup, and Hank Nelson. *Readings in New Guinea History.* [Sydney: Angus & Robertson, 1973], 354.

[2]J. R. Kerr, "The Political Future" in *New Guinea and Australia,* ed. Australia Institute of Political Science and John Wilkes [Sydney, Australia: Angus and Robertson, LTD, 1958] 160-161.

[3]Jinks, Biskup, and Nelson, 373.

[4]Peter Biskup, Brian Jinks, and H. Nelson. 1968. *A Short History of New Guinea, Revised Edition.* [Angus and Robertson Ltd, Sydney, Australia], 153-154.

[5]W. J. Hudson and Jill Daven. "Papua and New Guinea since 1945" in *Australia and Papua New Guinea,* edited by W. J. Hudson, [Sydney: Sydney University Press, 1971], 161.

the pyramid by a new policy of selection for and encouragement of higher and university education."[6] In response to the criticism, Australia expanded the secondary school system in Papua New Guinea, and in 1965 established the University of Papua New Guinea,[7] bringing an end to the policy of even educational development for all. Much of the Highlands was still restricted and in 1965 had no elementary schools.

The United Nations maintained pressure on Australia to set a target date for independence. On December 14, 1960, the United Nations passed the *Declaration of the Granting of Independence to Colonial Countries and Peoples resolution 1514 (XV)* that affirmed the right of all people to self-determination and declared that inadequate "political, economic, social or educational preparedness" was not legitimate grounds for delaying independence. It called for immediate steps to be taken "to transfer all powers to the people" of all non-independent territories "in accordance with their freely expressed will and desire…in order to enable them to enjoy complete independence and freedom."[8] Beginning in December of 1966, the United Nations passed an annual resolution that affirmed the inalienable right of the people of Papua and New Guinea to self-determination and independence in accordance with the freely expressed wishes of the people and called on Australia to establish a timetable for the granting of independence.[9]

The United Nations sent missions to visit Papua New Guinea in 1965 and again in 1968, to talk with the people. Each mission travelled extensively throughout the territory asking the people about their views on independence. They found it incredible that many Papua New Guineans did not want independence. The Highlanders, who had a short history of colonization, were opposed to the idea. In 1965 they informed the visiting mission that they did not want self-government or early independence, and when they felt ready for it, they would ask for it. They wanted development before independence. They believed that Australia could be trusted more and would do more to bring development to the Highlands than the coastal people of Papua New Guinea. Nathaniel Eastman from Liberia, who was strongly opposed to any form of colonialism, could not believe what he was hearing and wanted to know why anyone would want to delay independence. A Chimbu leader informed him that they still had a lot to learn from the Australians, and wanted them to remain.[10]

---

[6]Jinks, Biskup, and Nelson 382.

[7]"History of the University of Papua New Guinea" http://www.upng.ac.pg-/uni_hist.html [accessed on April 26, 2013].

[8]Jinks, Biskup and Nelson 404-405.

[9]Jinks, Biskup and Nelson 404-407. (Resolution 2227 (XXI) was passed on December 20, 1966. Resolution 2348 (XXII) was passed on December 19, 1967. Resolution 2427 (XXIII) was passed on December 18, 1968. Resolution 2590 (XXIV) was passed on December 16, 1969. Each of these resolutions called for Australia to set a date for self-determination and early determination.)

[10]Bob Connolly and Robin Anderson, *First Contact.* [New York, N.Y., U.S.A.: Viking, 1987], 292-294.

In 1968 a few people spoke out in favor of self-government, but the majority continued to ask that self-government and independence be delayed. Tei Abel was the House of Assembly member for the Enga open electorate, and he informed the visitors that 140,000 Enga people were not ready for and did not want independence. They knew the U.N. was pushing for independence, but they wanted to wait. Phillip Matuakan, a candidate in the Western Highlands told the mission that independence should be delayed for a generation. His son, and not he, would push for independence.[11]

The real impetus for independence came from educated Papua New Guineans who had grown up with colonialism and wanted a change. The 1961 legislative council's select committee on constitutional development recommended that a House of Assembly replace the legislative council. The new House of Assembly would have ten official members, ten representatives from special electorates reserved for expatriates, and forty-four representatives of open electorates for candidates of any ethnicity chosen by a direct vote. The select committee recommendations were accepted and the territory prepared to elect the First House of Assembly in 1964.[12]

By 1963 an increasing number of Papua and New Guineans had joined the public service. They were paid at the same rate as the Australian members. In order to entice overseas officers to Papua New Guinea, the administration paid a relative high salary to public servants in the Territory of Papua and New Guinea. Paul Hasluck, the Australian minister for territories, reasoned that if the indigenous public servants were paid at the same rate as the overseas officers, it would deplete an independent Papua and New Guinea's financial resources and leave little for development.[13]

In November of 1963 during the legislative council's final session, it passed the Public Service Ordinance of 1964 that created a single, integrated public service with all positions open to both indigenous and expatriate officers, but it introduced separate salary scales for overseas and indigenous officers.[14] Papua New Guineans who joined the service before September 10, 1964 would receive the same as their Australian counterparts, but those who joined after that date would receive a lower salary that "related to the future economy of the territory."[15]

The ordinance caused an outcry among both Papua New Guineans and expatriates. It led to angry protests by Papua New Guinean students; sparked the organization of local trade unions; spawned unrest among the European members of the public service who were unsure about their future in the public service; and united educated Papua New Guineans against the administration.[16]

---

[11]Jinks, Biskup and Nelson, 407.

[12]Hudson and Daven, 161.

[13]Biskup, Jinks and Nelson, 165.

[14]Jinks, Biskup and Nelson, 394.

[15]"Upsets Follow P-NG Public Salary Service Reorganization," *Pacific Islands Monthly,* October 1964, 20.

[16]"Upsets Follow P-NG Public Salary Service Reorganization," *Pacific Islands Monthly,* October 1964, 20.

Michael Somare and Albert Maori Kiki, leaders during the drive for independence, wrote autobiographies. Both wrote about the enactment of the Public Service Ordinance of 1964. Somare said, "The new rule angered all of us. ... There was probably no other single issue that made Papua New Guineans more aware of the injustices of colonialism."[17] Kiki, said that when "the Australian minister for territories introduced different wage scales for Papua New Guineans and overseas officers in the public service he made the biggest political blunder the Australian government has ever made in the territory."[18] Kiki saw it as a racist issue,[19] and he was tired of being a second class citizen in his own country.[20]

There were three elected houses of assemblies before Papua New Guinea became an independent nation. The First House of Assembly was formed in June of 1964 with thirty-two expatriate and thirty-eight indigenous representatives. It became a training ground for the newly elected indigenous members. Only four of the indigenous members had an education beyond elementary school, but a number were politically astute. Ten of the indigenous members were appointed to serve as under-secretaries so they could learn administrative roles,[21] and some of the European members of the House of Assembly formed a "study group" that met regularly with twenty-five to thirty-five members of the house to discuss political issues.[22]

-----

[17]Michael Thomas Somare, *Sana: An Autobiography of Michael Somare*. [Port Moresby: Niugini Press, 1975], 42-43.

[18]Albert Maor Kiki, *Kiki; Ten Thousand Years in a Lifetime, a New Guinea Autobiography*. [New York: F.A. Praeger, 1968], 144-145.

[19]An obvious division between the Papua New Guineans and Europeans existed. The native regulations remained in force until the 1960s (Kituai 7). Kiki reported that he had lived with restrictions that applied to him only because he was a Papuan. As he was preparing to go to Fiji for medical training, he was shocked to learn that even though he had been granted an Australian passport, he had to apply for a permit to leave and reenter his own country. Papuans were not permitted to drink or purchase alcohol, and instead of receiving all of their wages in cash, they were paid in part with food rations. Wages were lower than European wages, and housing was not provided for most of the indigenous people who flocked to Port Moresby to work as clerks and laborers. There were separate cinemas for European and Papua New Guineans; separate bus services were provided for the European and the local people; toilets were labeled for gentlemen and ladies for Europeans and *tatau* and *hahine* or *meri* and *man* for indigenous men and women; stores served Papua New Guineans and Europeans from separate counters; and lunch counters served Europeans soft drinks in glasses and Papua New Guineans in blue mugs. There was also a double standard when it came to women. Europeans were free to use Papua New Guinea women as a "sexual outlet," but European women were off limits to the men of Papua New Guinea. Kiki says that there had been no prostitution in Papuan societies until Europeans came on the scene. A European could marry a Papua New Guinea woman if he chose to, but when a New Guinea man married a European woman for the first time in 1962, it created uproar (Kiki 90-95).

[20]Kiki 90-95.

[21]Hudson and Daven, 161-163

[22]Somare, 46-47.

The First House of Assembly appointed a select committee to study Constitutional and Political Development in the territory of Papua and New Guinea. The committee spent eighteen months going around the country talking to numerous groups and seeking recommendations about the future of Papua and New Guiinea. The Highlanders wanted to remain under the Australian administration, but the educated minority wanted to move towards self-government and independence.[23]

Educated Papua New Guineans who were not members of the House of Assembly formed a "committee of ten" who gave input to the committee for constitutional and political development.[24] Some became convinced that the Australian government was not serious about granting self-government to the Papua New Guineans, and so a second group[25] prepared a supplemental "home rule" submission. It called for "immediate limited responsible government or home rule,"[26] a cabinet made of eight ministers, and the immediate appointment of a "chief minister." It demanded that indigenous officers be advanced to senior positions in the public service. The group said that they did not request immediate independence, but wanted Australia to prepare them for the day when they would become independent. They expected the grants in aid from Australia to continue, but that did not entitle Australia to dominate. Grants in aid should not "have strings attached."[27]

The group who had worked on the "home rule" submission became the core of the PANGU Pati[28] formed in June of 1967. They nominated several candidates for the 1968 election for the Second House of Assembly,[29] and their main platform was the "demand for home rule."[30]

---

[23]Biskup, Jinks, and Nelson 163-165.

[24]Kiki (152) identifies the group's members as A. Maori Kiki, J. Karl Nombri, Sinaka Goava, Ilimo Batton, Elliot Elijah, Robin Kumaina, Kamona Walo, Joseph Auna, William Warren, and Cromwell Burau. Cecil Abel who is listed as a sympatherizer but not a member of the group submitted his own proposal separately.

[25]Some of the members of the original committee of ten dropped out of the group, and others joined the newly organized group. Kiki lists the members of the new group as Albert Maori Kiki, Reuben Taureka, Elliott Elijah, Mike Somare, Oala Oala Rarua, J. Karl Nombri, Sinaka Goava, Kamona walo, Gerai Asiba, Cecil Abel, Cromwell Burau, Ilimo, Batton, and Penveli Anakapu (155).

[26]Kiki 152-153.

[27]Kiki, 152-155.

[28]Kiki (157) discusses the debate that settled on the party's name. PANGU was an acronym that stood for Papua and New Guinea United, and Pati is the Pidgin spelling for the word party.

[29]Kiki, 157.

[30]Kiki gives a complete listing of the party's platform that stood for home rule, unity, localization, Pidgin as the main common language, adequate housing for all workers, a road link between Papua and New Guinea, improved laborers, higher subsidies to Christian missions for education and health, the strengthening of local government councils and others (158).

The Second House of Assembly had no seats reserved for expatriates. Instead fifteen regional electorates were reserved for any educated person who held an intermediate certificate or its equivalent regardless of his or her ethnicity. The open electorates were increased from forty-four to sixty-nine. The new House of Assembly was to have seven ministerial members and eight assistant ministerial members.[31]

The Second House of Assembly held its first session in June of 1968. The PANGU Pati had nine elected members who chose to be the opposition in order to have more freedom to work towards independence.[32] The Second House of Assembly appointed another select committee on constitutional development that went around the country gathering peoples' opinions on self-government and independence. Michael Somare served on the committee. The majority of people in PNG did not want early self-government. Most said that "internal self-government should come no sooner than the life of the 1976-1980 House of Assembly." Somare claimed that the people "were not nearly as opposed to self-government as some people thought"[33] and the committee included a statement in its report that allowed for self-government to be established during the 1972 to 1976 House of Assembly if the majority wanted it.[34]

The Nembi, like most Highlanders, opposed early self-government. When the select committee visited Nipa, 5000 people showed up "and told the committee in no uncertain terms that they were not ready for independence."[35] In July of 1970, John Gorton, the Australian Prime Minister, toured Papua and New Guinea and announced that the Australian government had increased the authority of the Papua New Guinea departmental ministers who would make decisions without approval from Australia. When he visited Mendi,

> 2000 people from the Nipa area walked to Mendi to see Mr. Gorton with the intention of informing him of their thoughts on independence... The people feel now that if the House of Assembly does not know how they feel, then they will never know. The majority feel that political education is important but appear to have an underlying fear that independence will be forced upon them[36]

During the Second House of Assembly several more political parties were formed. The most notable was the United Party. It was a conservative group made up mostly of Europeans and Highlanders. During the 1972 elections it was PANGU Pati's main opponent although other smaller parties were active. One of the primary differences in PANGU Pati's and the United Party's platforms was

---

[31]Biskup, Jinks and Nelson, 170.

[32]Somare, 56-57.

[33]Somare, 71.

[34]Somare 71-72.

[35]Nipa Patrol Report Number 1 of 1970-1971, Situation Report Nipa Basin Census Division, 1.

[36]Nipa Patrol Report Number 1 of 1970-1971, Situation Report Nipa Basin Census Division, 1.

the timing of internal self-government. PANGU campaigned for immediate self-government while the United Party favored delaying it.[37]

The final move to independence came after the Third House of Assembly was elected in 1972. The PANGU Pati won twenty-six seats in the new house and the United Party won forty seats. PANGU wasted no time in contacting the minor parties and independent members and formed a coalition made up of the PANGU Pati, the National Party, the People's Progress Party and several independent voters. Somare became the chief minister, and the coalition's primary objective was to bring internal self-government to the territory sooner rather than later.[38] The Australian administration accepted the coalition and supported the move towards early self-government and independence. Australia agreed to provide the newly formed PNG government grants of five hundred million dollars over a three year period.[39]

The coalition immediately formed a constitutional planning committee that included representatives from all regions of Papua New Guinea and all political parties.[40] The committee's primary responsibility was to frame a constitution for the House of Assembly to approve with the eventual goal of becoming a fully independent Papua New Guinea.[41] In September of 1972 the House of Assembly passed legislation declaring December 1, 1973 or as soon as possible thereafter the day that Papua New Guinea would become self-governing. The proposal passed with understanding that the constitution planning committee would complete its work before self-government was implemented.[42]

The constitution was not finished by December 1, 1973, but the coalition agreed that internal self-government would be instituted in two stages. The first stage would be "legal self-government" when the ministers of the Papua New Guinea government officially took over the responsibility for all aspects of government within the territory except for defense and foreign affairs, and the second stage would occur after the constitution planning committee completed its work. The House of Assembly approved the proposal, and on December 1, 1973 Papua New Guinea became legally self-governing.[43]

Somare suggested that December 1, 1974 one year after legal self-government had begun would be the "ideal date" for independence. Two things hindered it. First, the country did not yet have a constitution, and the People's Progress Party, a part of the coalition, insisted that the country finalize its constitution before setting a date for independence. The House of Assembly voted against a motion to hold a referendum on the date of independence and gave Somare, the chief min-

---

[37]Jinks, Biskup and Nelson, 417.
[38]Somare 88-94.
[39]Somare, 95-96.
[40]Jinks, Biskup, and Nelson 430.
[41]Somare, 98.
[42]Somare, 98-101.
[43]Somare 101-102.

ister, the authority to proclaim the date of independence "as soon as practicable after the House had enacted a constitution."[44]

The second hindrance was strong and widespread opposition to early independence. Some regions threatened to withdraw. Bougainvilleans were dissatisfied with the Bougainville Copper Agreement, wanted a greater share in the revenue that was generated from the mine, and threatened secession.[45] "Some Papuan leaders claimed they did not wish to live side by side with New Guineans."[46] Papuans said that "their people had been overlooked and that most of the development had taken place on the New Guinea side.[47] In 1972 Josephine Abaija, who represented the Central district that included Port Moresby, was opposed to rushing into independence without first considering all of the options available to the country. She led the Papua Besena Movement and feared that Papua would become a colony of New Guinea. The only way for Papua to get a fair deal was for Papuans to run an independent Papua. On the streets of Port Moresby, Papuans and New Guineans fought each other over the issue.[48]

Robert M. Glasse, an anthropologist who conducted the first ethnographic studies of the Huli people, reported that "many Huli deplored the approach of independence" and refused to participate in planning for a national celebration. Some of the enterprising Huli "were so adamant that they rolled empty fuel drums across the airstrip to prevent Chief Minister Somare's plane from landing."[49]

From March to July, 1973, Graham Setchell patrolled the Nipa Basin. He wrote an area study and reported on the topic of political development in the Nipa Basin.

> The people have little or no idea of the political system or its personalities. To them 'Maikel Somari' is a name synonymous with the rush to self-government and the reluctant (to their minds) exodus of the white population and replacement of untrustworthy coastal people. One group spoken to at Omdol village told me that somebody from the Southern Highlands would kill Mr. Somare should he ever visit here and would therefore prevent self-government. When questioned further they said that although this was a commonly held thought throughout the Mendi/Nipa area, there had been no-one (sic) appointed to the task and it was just thought that someone 'might – if he felt like it at the time.'[50]

Somare's coalition was determined to bring independence to a united Papua and New Guinea as soon as possible. Independence was delayed beyond December 1, 1974 because the constitution was not ready. The coalition's support was

---

[44]Somare 103-104.

[45]Somare, 114-122.

[46]Jinks, Biskup and Nelson 415.

[47]Somare 128.

[48]Somare 128-137.

[49]Robert M. Glasse, "Time Bilong Mbingi: Syncretism and the Pacification of the Huli" in Biersack, Aletta. 1995. *Papuan Borderlands: Huli, Duna, and Ipili Perspectives on the Papua New Guinea Highlands.* [Ann Arbor: University of Michigan Press, 1995], 61.

[50]Nipa Patrol Report Number 11 of 1972-1973, Area Study Nipa Basin, 21-22.

waning, but in the end Somare and the coalition succeeded in getting the House to approve September 16, 1975 as Independence Day for Papua New Guinea even before the constitution had received its final approval.[51]

[51]Somare, 140-144.

Appendix Four

Nembi Beliefs

The Nembi people followed a number of pre-Christian cults, and they were open to new cults. Some started after a man had an especially vivid dream and was convinced that the spirits had instructed him to start a new cult. Others were passed from one group to the next. *Temo* or ancestral spirits were at the heart of of the cults, and Nembi men related to *temo* through sacrifice and ritual, appeasing them when they were angry, and humoring them when they were pleased. When a group learned that their neighbors possessed a different and more powerful spirit, they wanted access to it. For a price it would be passed from one group to the other. Once a group had purchased all of the secrets and paraphernalia that belonged to a particular cult, they could sell it to the next group bit by bit until the recipient group became fully initiated into the new cult and the priests at the cult's core had learned all of its secrets. The new group was then free to pass it along to the next group. Nembi interviewees referred to the *kepel* and *timp* cults that the Nembi people followed in the 1960s. Alan C. Jeffries reported in 1962 that *Timp* was considered to be "a powerful masculine spirit...and the most feared of all the spirits and ghosts and (was)...responsible for life and death...and (was) replacing the stone cult of *kepel* which (was) associated with one's parents."[1]

The Timp Cult

The fertility cult called *timp*[2] made its way among the Nembi groups in the 1950s and 1960s. The cult originated in the Purari Delta, after an elderly man had dreams in which he was instructed to begin the cult. It slowly made its way northward as it was passed from group to group. It took several generations for it to reach the Mendi and Nembi Valleys.[3] The spirit houses were easily recognized

---

[1]Alan C. Jeffries, Mendi Patrol Report Number 7 of 1961-1962, 11, {NB 61-64, HW 114}.

[2]The patrol officers refer to the *timp* cult as a single cult, but the Nembi speak of two different types of *timp* cults. One was *tundu timp* (short *timp*), and the other was *sollu timp* (long *timp*). I do not know the differences between the two *timp* cults, or if the two were really two separate phases of a single larger cult. The administration spoke of one cult.

[3]Allen C. Jeffries, Mendi Patrol Report Number 7 of 1961-62, 11, {NB 61-64, 114}.

because of their conical roofs,[4] and as Hides and O'Malley crossed the lower Nembi Plateau in 1935, they spotted one of the oddly shaped spirit houses that was square, "built off the ground," and had a conical-shaped roof.[5]

Some of the practices that went with the *timp* cult were anathema to the Australian administration. The recipients paid the donors well to learn the cult's secrets, and hosted the donors for lengthy visits that could last for years until the last of the secrets were passed on to the new group. Word and food taboos were instituted when *timp* was introduced to the recipient group, and any person who violated the taboos, even in ignorance, was severely punished for his or her discretion through beatings and fines. Women who broke the taboos were raped. Whenever a *timp* priest from the donor group was in the area, they played bamboo flutes as a warning to all women, children, and any uninitiated male to hide or suffer the consequences. The fines that violators paid were passed along to the donor group until it yielded the last of its secrets to the recipients. The donor group then surrendered the cult's "key" stone to its new owners who in turn became the donor group and found a new recipient group. The new group paid an even greater price for the cult's secrets and extracted even larger fines from any person who violated the cult's taboos.[6]

Jefferies acknowledged that he had only a superficial knowledge of a highly enigmatic cult that was hard to learn about because the possessors of the knowledge were sworn to silence and faced death if they revealed the cult's secrets. He requested that a competent anthropologist be asked to study the cult, and suggested that

> the greatest care must be taken when handling *Timp* exponents who may infringe the laws of assault, blackmail, theft, damage to property, or riotous behaviour. On the surface *Timp* appears to be anti-social in that it is almost a 'Protection Racket' in some phases, however it had deeper meanings and to 'outlaw' *Timp* in-toto would probably mean that the cult would go underground and punishments would take the form of sorcery or action by sorcery. ...The officer dealing with *Timp* blackmail should use his discretion and only take action when the person blackmailed lays a complaint...

> As *Timp* is a fertility cult and as it is held responsible for life and death, I feel that the true combatants to *Timp* are to be found in the ranks of Christian Missions. The superstition of *Timp* can only be replaced by a mystical belief more powerful than himself.[7]

---

[4]Edward L. Schieffelin, and Robert Crittenden, eds. *Like People You See in a Dream: First Contact in Six Papuan Societies*. [Stanford, Calif: Stanford University Press, 1991], 135.

[5]Jack Gordon Hides, *Papuan Wonderland*. [London: Blackie and Son, 1936], 152-153; Schieffelin and Crittenden, 135 fn, 170.

[6]Alan C. Jeffries, Mendi Patrol Report Number 7 of 1961-1962, 11-13 {NB 61-64, 114-116}.

[7]Alan C. Jeffries, Mendi Patrol Report Number 7 of 1961-1962, 11-13 {NB 61-64, 114-116}.

D'Arcy Ryan an anthropologist who worked in the Mendi area in the 1950s and 1960s, observed the cult being passed on to the group that he studied. He wrote a detailed description of the ceremonies he observed when the recipients were purchasing the cult stones, secrets, rituals, and rights from the donor group.[8] According to Ryan, the *timp* rituals were similar to the rituals performed in other cults, and "pigs were sacrificed to the stones with the primary purpose of placating the ghosts, and a second vaguer purpose of ensuring the general well-being of the community."[9] He considered the ceremonial exchange that took place when the cult was passed form group to group to be "a special adaptation of the elaborate ceremonial exchange which characterized all inter-group relations in the area."[10]

New Cults

As the Nembi coped with staggering economic and social changes in the 1960s and 1970s they sought answers from the spirit world, the most powerful force they knew. In 1965, about two years after Christian missions became active in the Nembi area, a cult that was aimed at procuring wealth and preventing its adherents from being sentenced to prison emerged briefly.[11] Most years, the Nembi area receives abundant rainfall, but in 1965 a drought lasted for four months and created a food shortage. During the drought, "no village was brought to starvation, but the food was certainly meagre."[12]

The cult made its appearance as the drought ended, just before the gardens began to flourish again. A man from Kusa had a dream in which he was told to go and build a spirit house near a pond at Unja. The Nembi people were to discard all other spirits and beliefs that the Nembi relied on and declare allegiance to one spirit who would reveal himself at Unja in the form of a six-headed snake. The snake would appear only after the people had forsaken everything else, gone to Unja, and been cleansed of all badness. The snake would inform the leader of the cult that the people had been cleansed and changed. The people could then go to the government and mission stations where for having become good, the people would be paid with pigs and pearl shells. On Christmas Day, 1965, about 5,000 people gathered along the Lai River below Det to discuss the pros and cons of the revelations. Some rejected them, but many others gathered the materials needed to build the spirit house. Most of the "hard core" groups were from the heart of the Nembi area and included Pumberel, Kum, Nenja (Nainja), Kesu, Kusa, Mato, Poroma, Utabia, Det, Pabaronga, Waramesa, Mala, and Unja.[13] The cult died out

---

[8]D'Arcy Ryan, *Gift-exchange in the Mendi Valley: An Examination of the Socio-political Implications of the Ceremonial Exchange of Wealth among the People of the Mendi Valley,* Southern Highlands District, Papua. Thesis (Ph. D.) [University of Sydney, 1961], 265-296.

[9]Ryan, *Gift Exchange,* 285

[10]Ryan, *Gift Exchange,* 286.

[11]J. S. Hicks, Nipa Patrol Report Nnumber 5 of 1965-1966, 5 [{NB 64-66, HW 295}.

[12]J. S. Hicks, Nipa Patrol Report Nnumber 5 of 1965-1966, 5 [{NB 64-66, HW 295}.

[13]J. S. Hicks, Nipa Patrol Report Nnumber 5 of 1965-1966, 5 [{NB 64-66, HW 295}.

as quickly as it started, but the District Commissioner said that the administration would keep a close watch on the area "to ensure that the cultist movement did not re-occur."[14] One patrol officer suggested that the six headed snake was a legendary figure that was synonymous with a poor crop yield. He speculated that the cult disappeared because the gardens had started to flourish again soon after the drought ended.[15]

Later patrol reports made periodic references to possible cult activity among the Nembi. Patrol officers were determined to stamp out any cult that appeared to be the beginning of a millenarian movement.[16] Although subsequent hints of developing movements surfaced, none grew to a full blown cult. In 1972, rumors said that a cult movement had reached Mala "about six or seven miles northwest of Poroma station" from the Lai Valley. People were supposedly digging up dead bodies, inserting a bamboo in their mouth and reburying them. Later the bodies were to be exhumed a second time, and when they were, each body would produce twenty dollars. If the rumors were true, the people hid it from the patrol officer because when asked, they denied all knowledge of such activities.[17] Sometime after independence, I recall a man from Kusa who exhumed bodies and removed the skulls which he lined on fence posts because he said that a powerful spirit had instructed him to do so in a dream. For a few weeks it created a quite a stir and lot of chatter, and a number of people, including me, went to visit him and see the skulls lined up on the fence, but in a few weeks the skulls disappeared, and the talk died out.

The Sky Beings and *Yeki* the High God

Lawrence and Meggitt noted that many Melanesian belief systems conceived spirit beings that dwelt in some remote location that replicated the earth or attached themselves to the earth.[18] Many of the Highlands cultures believed in sky people. The Dani of the West Papua province of Indonesia said that sky people once lived on earth, but because they refused to work, they were chased away. They climbed into the sky where they now live, and when rain comes as a light

---

[14]D. W. Marsh, 24th February, 1966 in letter to the Department of District Administration in Konedobu, in Nipa Patrol Report Number 5 of 1965 -1966, {NB 64-66, HW 288}.

[15]James W. Kent, 4th February, 1966 in letter to the District Commissioner of the Southern Highlands District in Nipa Patrol Report Number 5 of 1965 -1966, (NB 64-66, HW 289).

[16]J. K. McCarthy, 13 March, 1967, letter to the Southern Highlands District Commissione, in Nipa Patrol Report Number 7 of 1966-1967, {NB 66-68, HW 59}; P. O. Jones, 7th March, 1969, Mendi Patrol Number 5 of 1968-1969, 10, {NB 68-69, HW 98}.

[17]P. J. Puana, 10th May, 1972, Situation Report in Poroma Patrol Report Number 9 of 1971-1972, {NB 71-72, HW 318}.

[18]Peter Lawrence and Mervin J. Meggitt. 1965. *Gods, Ghosts, and Men in Melanesia; Some Religions of Australian New Guinea and the New Hebrides*, [Melbourne: Oxford University Press, 1965], 9.

drizzle, the sky women are urinating on the earth people.[19] Lawrence and Megitt reported that the Mae Enga believed that the sky people colonized the earth, and all the Mae Enga people descended from them. The sky people controlled humankind's fate, and the Mae Enga interacted intermittently with the sky dwellers.[20] The Erave people living in the Southern Highlands southeast of the Nembi had myths about a sky people who granted immortality to a snake, and they say that people killed fighting or assisting warriors during a battle go to live with the sky people.[21] It is generally reported that the Huli do not believe in sky people, but Biersack reports that among the Huli sky beings appear as vague "ascendant figures in cosmogonic genealogies,"[22] and Goldman reported that the Huli do not fear the sky beings, but they sometimes threaten their children with the sky people, but not seriously. It was like telling Western children to be good or the boogey-man will get them.[23]

The Nembi believed in *Yeki*, a high god who resided in the sky. Hood says that there were many *Yekis*. They were territorial localized gods with each group having its own *Yeki* who controlled the weather, was a threat to intruders, but was not very involved in the daily affairs of the people.[24] Paul Embil suggests that *Yeki* was more powerful than the spirits that the people normally related to, and when the spirits failed to respond, the men called out to *Yeki* above the clouds. Immediately things improved and family members, domesticated animals, and garden became healthy.[25]

The Nembi told me that when an infant or small child dies, his spirit goes to *Yeki*. When a mother wailed over her newly deceased child, she called out to *Yeki* to receive the child, take care of it, and protect it as it enters its new abode in the sky. When the sky was ablaze with a colorful sunset, the Nembi said the sky people were burning their bush and getting ready to plant sweet potato gardens. Thunder occurred when the sky people were fighting or participating in a ceremonial dance. Embers of fire falling from the sky caused lightning. Children were instructed never to point at a rainbow because it could cause their mother's milk to

---

[19]Douglas James Hayward, *Vernacular Christianity among the Mulia Dani: an Ethnography of Religious Belief among the Western Dani of Irian Jaya, Indonesia*, [Pasadena, Calif: American Society of Missiology, 1997], 61.

[20]Lawrence and Meggitt, 107-109.

[21]G. W. Trompf, 1991. *Melanesian Religion*. [Cambridge, England: Cambridge University Press, 1991], 71, 73.

[22]Aletta Biersack, *Papuan Borderlands: Huli, Duna, and Ipili Perspectives on the Papua New Guinea Highlands*. [Ann Arbor: University of Michigan Press, 1995], 20.

[23]L. R. Goldman, "The Depths of Deception: Cultural Schemes of Illusion in Huli" in Aletta Biersack, ed. *Papuan borderlands: Huli, Duna, and Ipili Perspectives on the Papua New Guinea Highlands.* [Ann Arbor: University of Michigan Press, 1995], 130-131.

[24]Ronald P. Hood, "Melanesian Paradigm Shifting: Nembi Worldview Change and the Contextualization of the Gospel among Urban Immigrants" [Phd Diss., Fuller Theological Seminary, 1999], 222.

[25]Paul Embel in e-mail to author sent on August 5, 2013.

dry up. The Nembi said that the spirit of a person who died in tribal fighting trying to protect the other members of his group ascended straight to *Yeki*.

When outsiders with light complexions first entered the world of the Highlanders of Papua New Guinea, many thought that they came from the sky.[26] During the early 1970s I recall having some serious conversations with some of the Nembi men as they asked me where my co-workers and I came from. "Did we come from the sky, the ground, or inside the ground? Where did the airplanes come from? How did we arrive on their turf?" They wanted to know if we came from the spirit or material world, but I totally misunderstood the significance of their question. As we talked about my place of origin, I told them that we came from the ground just like they did. We had animals, trees, streams, rain, gardens, mountains and bush areas just like theirs. Humans made everything we possessed from things that either grew in gardens or jungles, or had been harvested from the earth or from within the earth. I talked about airplanes, skyscrapers, basements, subways, caves, and mines, but even with the aid of pictures from National Geographical Magazines, they were unable to visualize the world I tried to tell them about any more than I grasped the implication of their question.

According to Nembi myths, people traveled back and forth between the earth and the sky. One of the myths tells of a man from the ground who married a woman from the sky. When he went to visit her place in the sky, he shot a possum that turned out to be his brother. He returned to his place for the time of mourning and burial, but his father-in-law instructed him not to cry. He did cry, and so travel between the earth and sky came to an end. The myth is included in the section on myths.

The Secret Cult of *Iso* or *Is Pandol*

Iso or *Is Pandol*[27] was a highly secretive cult that believed in spirits or supernatural beings who formerly lived in the area in the form of human beings who had light skins. Everybody knew about the beliefs, but only a few priests who had been initiated and brought into the cult's core knew its secrets. The spirits associated with *Iso* made everything and were responsible for the prosperity of gardens, pigs, pearl shells, and people. During times of famine, or during an epidemic of illness, the spirits associated with *Iso* were thought to be responsible and rituals were performed to alleviate the problem. I first learned about the belief system from my language teacher. I had picked up bits and pieces of information about some of the beliefs when my language teacher told me that there were other beliefs that were very powerful, but the people were not allowed to tell the "white

---

[26]Bob Connolly and Robin Anderson, *First Contact: New Guinea's Highlanders Encounter the Outside World*, [New York, N.Y., U.S.A.: Viking, 1987], 199-198; Bill Gammage. *The Sky Travellers: Journeys in New Guinea, 1938-1939.* [Calton, Vic: Melbourne University Press, 1998], 1-2.

[27]The name of the cult changes according to the dialect area, but the priests from the different areas knew each other, collaborated with one another, and were part of a single belief system.

skins" about them. They were no longer practicing the rituals, but the people still believed very firmly in *Iso*.

I asked some questions, but learned very little from my language teacher. He had an uncle who was an Iso priest, and he agreed to ask his uncle to talk to me. When I talked to the first priest I realized that he was not telling me the truth about the beliefs. He was giving me misinformation about the cult to keep me from learning the real beliefs. About two or three weeks later my language teacher told me that another more important *Iso* priest wanted to talk to me and my language teacher and tell us about the true *Iso* beliefs. He lived at Injua about ten miles from Embi and my language teacher and I went to interview him. He said that when he had been initiated as an *Iso* priest, he had to give up his name. All *Iso* priests are called *More*, and so that is what I call him through the rest of this description. I took notes and recorded everything that he said, and later transcribed it onto paper with my language teacher's assistance. I then wrote a report about the iso beliefs for my missionary colleagues. The original notes and transcriptions were later destroyed in a fire, but I still have the report that I wrote for my missionary colleagues. It is the source for the following discussion of *Iso*.

Like most of the Highlands belief systems, *Iso* beliefs were confined to a particular territory. The belief system extended from Poroma to Margarima. There were a number of specific sacred sites. Most of the places were located in the Wage Valley, but some were on the Nembi plateau and or in the Nembi Valley. There was one near Poroma and Det, some were at Injua, which was near the center of the area that believed in Iso. There were some at Pumberel, and another near Embi. The priest also mentioned some specific places between Nipa and Margarima, but I failed to record those in the report that I wrote for the missionaries. Some of the places were ponds; others were caves with stone faces, and other were bush areas where *Iso* spirit houses had been built.

When the Nembi people tell about their traditional belief systems, the question of authenticity always arises. Goldman says that lies and deception are integral parts of every day life in Melanesian cultures and that the Huli people are masters of deception. It is at the very core of the Huli's ways of being.[28] The Nembi people do not hesitate to deceive when it works to their advantage. Because lies and deception are embedded so deeply in the culture, the outsider needs to explore the question of authenticity when he receives new information about Nembi beliefs. I believe the information that I received from *More* is truly authentic for several reasons.

First, the *More* who talked to me was nearing the end of his life, and he knew it. He showed me a rope with knots tied in it. He was a youth when he was first initiated as an *Iso* priest. He was told that each knot in the rope represented a year, and that he would die when he reached the last knot on the rope. He had used the rope to keep track of events in Nembi history by marking the knots when signifi-

---

[28]L. R. Goldman, "The Depths of Deception; Cultural Schemes of Illusion in Huli." in *Papuan Borderlands,* ed. Aletta Biersack [Ann Arbor, University of Michigan Press, 1995], 111-113.

cant events occurred. When I asked him which knot he was now on, he pointed to the last knot on the rope. He was literally "at the end of his rope," and he did not expect to live much longer. It is worth noting that a few months after my first interview and before I had completed all of the interviews that I hoped to conduct, *More* was helping his brother cut down a tree in a garden when the tree fell on him and he was killed.

During the interview he said that he thought that literacy skills enabled the "white people" to keep permanent records that never change. However the "black people" depend on orality to transmit their stories. The stories change because the storyteller remembers some parts of the myth and forgets others. Other myths die out because the men who know the myths die before they have passed them on to someone else. This was happening to the *Iso* priests. They were not training new priests. The priesthood had been passed from father to son or nephews. Some of the priests of the older generation told the myths to younger men, but they were no longer teaching them the rituals, and most priests had already stopped conducting the *Iso* rites. Some of the stories and myths connected with *Iso* would remain, but the priesthood and rituals would die out with *More*'s generation of priests. I think that he agreed to talk to me because he wanted his stories to be preserved in writing.

Second, there were some known historical events recorded in the information that *More* shared. These events were mentioned in connection with *Iso* predictions about the future. Some had been partially fulfilled and others were waiting to be fulfilled. Not until I read Robert M. Glasse's article about the Huli concept of *mbigini* did I make the connections between *More*'s predictions and some known historical events. Glasse tells about an earthquake that occurred while he was doing fieldwork among the Huli people in the 1950s which sparked a great deal of activity among the people and prompted cries of *Mbigini! Mbigini!* He learned that *mbigini*, a time of darkness followed by renewal, was considered to be an actual historical event that no one living in 1955 could remember. Glasse believed that the original time of darkness could be traced to a volcanic eruption in 1730 on Long Island (now Tabita Island) in the Bismarck Sea. It blew volcanic ash over the island of New Guinea. For the Huli, it had caused a time of darkness to cover the earth.[29]

The Huli predicted that the time of darkness would return to the earth. When the time of *mbigini* approached there would be a series of earthquakes and thunderstorms. The Huli people were to build a house with a steep roof to protect from ash falling from the sky. They were to cover their gardens with kunai grass, and they were to send their wives home to their fathers and brothers to protect against incest. In the shelter they were to build a platform for the men to sleep on. Their pigs were to sleep under the platform, and the wild animals would also seek shel-

---

[29]Robert M. Glasse, "Time Bilong Mbingi: Syncretism and the Pacification of the Huli" in ed. Aletta Biersack, *Papuan Borderlands: Huli, Duna, and Ipili Perspectives on the Papua New Guinea Highlands.* [Ann Arbor: University of Michigan Press, 1995] 67-68.

ter under the platform. The women were to sleep around the platform. The time of darkness would be followed by a time of prosperity.[30]

The Huli concept of *mbigini* reminded me of *More*'s predictions. One of the unfulfilled predictions said that the ground would be destroyed. It was destroyed once before after which they began to count periods of time apparently by generations. Originally, they predicted that the ground would be destroyed again in the seventh generation. However, they had passed the seventh generation and were then living in the thirteenth one. With each passing generation after the seventh, they said that if the ground is not destroyed during this generation, it will be destroyed in the next one. The same volcanic eruption that spread darkness over the Huli area in 1730 would have darkened the Nembi area as well. I collected the *More*'s stories in 1975 or 1976. If a generation is approximately twenty years, then thirteen generations earlier could have been living in 1730 when the eruption occurred.

One prediction about the earth's destruction said that something sharp called *op tos* would fall from the sky and strike the houses. It would be sent by a spirit (or supernatural being) named *Ken Na Mu*. The people were to cover their houses with planks or stones so that these sharp objects will not penetrate the roofs of the houses and destroy the houses and kill the people inside. The houses should be built on top of the mountains and not in the valleys. It would be dark all the time, and the people would not be able to see. The one exception was that a man's only child would be able to see as though it were day, and he or she would be able to go to the gardens and get food for everyone. Stories about a time of darkness, the destruction of the earth, and objects falling from the sky could be related to a major volcanic eruption and the ash and debris that it would spread.

The *Iso* priest told of another prediction that had been partially fulfilled. It said that something would come from a single place and shoot across the sky in a single direction. The Nembi saw the cargo planes that flew over the area during World War Two, and *More* thought the planes were a partial fulfillment of the prophecy about something shooting across the sky in a single direction. He also considered the flash of fire that comes from a gun when it is shot to be a partial fulfillment of the prophecy. *More* would have known of the violent clash with the Hides and O'Malley patrol during first contact, and he would have seen some of the many arms demonstrations that the patrol officers conducted during pacification. The fact that the *more* related the predictions to known historical events gave authenticity to the *Iso* legends.

Rituals were at the center of the *Iso* belief system. The first ritual that the *more* told me about was the initiation rite for the priests. The priesthood was passed down from father to son (or nephew), but it is not clear if the initiate was taught any of the *Iso* secrets before his initiation. Some parts of the initiation rites and the taboos that the priest followed became important during the process of pacification and missionization. First, the aspiring priest was stripped naked during the initiation rites, his hands were tied, and he was led through the bush by the

---

[30]Glasse, 68.

older priests. *More* equated that to the colonial administration propensity to arrest people who had broken the law and lead them off to prison even though they were unwilling to go. Second, the *Iso* priest was permitted to have only one wife. The Christian missions all taught that a man should have only one wife. From *More*'s perspective, the white men followed the custom of having only one wife because they were *Iso* spirits. Third, when a priest defecated he had to bury his excreta in a hole in the ground. He could not leave it exposed to the air. Building pit toilets was one of the first things the patrol officers required the people to do. *More* thought that the digging of toilets was highly significant, and considered it to be a parallel between the *Iso* beliefs and Christianity. Finally, there were many *Iso* priests. In the spirit houses, each priest had his own sleeping area marked off by logs. No one else could sleep in a priest's sleeping area. Each had his own space that could not be violated by the others. *More* equated this with Christian teachings about heaven as a place with many rooms or mansions. Either the many sleeping quarters of the *Iso* priests were symbolic of the many rooms in heaven or the Christian teaching about heaven validated the priests having many rooms.

Certain illnesses were attributed to Iso spirits, and occasionally a red pig was sacrificed to the *Iso* spirits to cure illnesses and to ensure health. Only red pigs were used because they symbolized the spirits who had light skins. The blood of the pig was painted on the post of the spirit house.

In earlier times both light skinned and dark skinned people had lived in the area. However, the light skinned spirits had departed via a hole in the ground. The *Iso* priests blocked it with a sacrificial possum to make sure that the light skinned spirits did not return to the area. *More* said that he had been afraid and had not blocked the hole adequately, and the light skinned spirits had escaped through the hole in the ground, and "white people" now live in the area.

The last *Iso* ritual involving all of the people took place at Embi in the late 1960s. Everyone had taken part—men, women, and children. The people had performed a "snake" dance where they formed a long line and marched to the entrance of an *Iso* forest where the priests had hung a lot of pearl shells. The people remained at the entrance to the forest while the priest went into the spirit house and performed the appropriate ceremonies. One of the chants used while performing rituals for prosperity was the following:

> Everything can come into being!
> Men, women, gardens, greens—everything!
> Salt. cassowaries, cassowary feathers—everything!
> Who has taken this?
> Ollep Yalin or someone else?

The priest told me four Iso myths. One was about Ollep Yalin, from whom all people descended. When I interviewed *More*, there were six single women serving with Christian Union Mission in the Nembi area, and the Catholics had an equal number of sisters working in the area. Before *More* would tell me the legend of Ollep Yalin, he wanted to know why the single white women were not married.

Were they capable of getting married, having husbands, and bearing children? I told him that the single women had either chosen not to marry or had postponed marriage because they wanted to do God's work. They were just like the Nembi women, and were capable of having husbands and bearing children.

Ollep Yalin was a light skinned woman who was a neutral being with no vaginal openings so that she could not urinate, defecate, or have intercourse. Her husband tricked here causing her to be cut with a razor sharp stone axe head so that all of the appropriate openings came. The couple then had intercourse, and all people descended from them—both black and white. Eventually Ollep Yalin entered a blue pond located near Injua where she continued to bear children, but the children she bore after she entered the water all had light skins. The Nembi performed rituals to keep Ollep Yalin and her light skinned descendants inside the water.

Another *Iso* myth is about two cousin/brothers who lived together. One was knowledgable and had great understanding, and the other was ignorant and did the hard work. One day the ignorant cousin warned the knowledgeable cousin that they would soon hear something that sounded like birds calling to each other as they congregated at a feeding place. They were to remain hidden inside their house when they heard the noise, and under no circumstance were they to go outside or even peek outside. However, when they heard the noises, the knowledgeable cousin could not resist peeking out. He saw a lot of white skinned people all over everywhere. One of the white skinned women was sitting on a tree top washing her body by scooting back and forth. Suddenly as the man watched, the white skinned beings all disappeared. He did not know if they went into the sky or into the ground or where they went, but they all vanished. After that the dark skinned people performed rituals to keep the white skinned people from returning, but they were back.

More also told me that God made everything and he divided everything between the black people and the white people. He gave all the good things to the white people including knowledge and the ability to read and write. He gave everything else to the black people. He did not know who got day and who got night, but God had divided everything.

By the time that the priests told me these stories, the missionaries had been working in the area for at least 12 years. *More* had already incorporated some of the Christian stories that he had learned from the missionaries and fit them into the *Iso* belief system. He saw Christianity as a confirmation of the *Iso* behfs. Saying amen at the end of our prayers, digging holes for toilets or septic systems, Christian teachings about monogamy, hand cuffing law-breakers and taking them to jail where they are strip searched, teaching about heaven with its "many rooms," clapping hands while singing, and painting the posts in the churches are all seen as affirmations of the *Iso* belief systems, and the *Iso* priests considered all of the above practices to be a part of Christianity.

One of his comments is worth noting, "Before we believed that the spirits were our enemies and wanted to destroy us. We performed rituals to prevent this. Now we've heard the Gospel and we believe that God will help us."

In 2010 I interviewed a man from Injua who was a young boy in the 1960s.[31] He told me that the people believed that the white people came from the *antap* (the sky) and that at night they did not sleep, but returned to their place *antap*. He then spoke about the belief system known as *Is Pandol* that was led by some powerful men called *more*. The last of the *mores* died two or three years before the 2010 interview, but the stories and remnants to the belief system remain. The interviewee did not know the *more's* secrets or the source of their power, and only a small group of men were *mores*, but they had the power and ability to kill a pig with spoken words. At times they would go to the remote bush areas and be gone for several weeks at a time. On one of their trips they were gone for an especially long time, and when they returned, they told the people that they had seen and fought with a different kind of people. They had seen many white men, and they were going to come to the Nembi area. The *mores* had built a barrier that they hoped the white beings would be unable to penetrate, but the whites were very powerful beings, and they would come sooner or later. When the white people did come, the people said, "Oh, our ancestors told us that they had seen white men, and they built a strong barrier, but the whites have come now. They found their way around the barrier that the *mores* built, and now the whites have come."

My interviewee informed me that the people continue to tell stories about *Ollep Yalin*.[32] The legend has changed to reflect the Nembi people's expanded knowledge of historical events, but the name of the woman and the places associated with her remain the same. In the past, a white woman lived in a cave near the head of the Wage River. Before the people did not know who she was or how she got there, but now they have figured it out. She was traveling with a group of white explorers or soldiers, and she was injured, or her knees hurt. She was unable to keep up with the group, and so they gave her arms and ammunition and left her in a cave where she lived. When the men heard that a white woman was living in a cave near the head of the Wage River, they wanted to go find her and sleep with her. One by one the men went to find her, but when they approached her, they died. The men kept going to her, and they kept dying as they approached her. One by one they went and they died, and died, and died and died. Before the Nembi did not know why the men died, but now they have figured it out. The group that deserted *Ollep Yalin* had left her in the cave made sure she was well armed with guns and ammunition, and every time a man approached she shot and killed him, and she must have eaten them or something.

Finally she ran out of ammunition. She had killed all of the men, but one, and he decided to go to find the woman. He wanted to know what was in the cave. He moved with stealth, as he approached the cave and he saw the woman sitting

---

[31]In December of 2009 and January of 2010 I interviewed a number of people from Injua and Semin at Semin and also in Mendi. I have chosen to withhold the name of the interviewee who shared this story because I am not sure how willing the Nembi groups as a whole would be to share openly the current stories of *Iso* and *Ollep Yalin*.

[32]My interviewee used the name *Owep Salin*, but the change in the name reflects dielectical differences. The two are the same.

inside the cave. Before he went to the cave, he built a fire and heated a stone like the stones that are used to cook food in the ground. When the stone was glowing red hot, the man took a pair of tongs, wrapped the stone and carried it behind his back. The man again approached the cave with stealth, this time holding the stone behind his back. When the woman saw the man, she invited him to come sleep with her. The man went slowly and quietly and when he was close enough to the woman, he thrust the stone onto the woman's stomach, and then fastened it between her legs as he shouted, "You killed many men, but I am the last man, and I am killing you." The woman felt the pain, and the fire had burned her badly. She leaped up and jumped and fell into the water at a pond that they now call *Om Ipa* in the Wage Valley, and then she leaped again and fell into another pond that they call *Hupil*. And she leaped a third time and this time she landed in the pond they call *Howa*. Now they have discovered oil at the place where *Ollep Yalin* lived.

The priests of the belief system have all died, and the places in the bush where they went to perform their rituals are now overgrown, but many of the people still believe the stories that the *mores* told. When the white men came, the people believed that they came from *Iso*. Before, the Nembi were people in the middle, and they traded goods that came from other groups. They traded *tiagaso* oil that came from the people of Lake Kutubu. Salt came from Kandep and Wabi in the Enga province. The red paint that they used to decorate themselves for ceremonial dances came from the Huli people near Tari. Shells came from the Mount Hagen area. All of that has changed, but the items of wealth come from the same directions they came before. Now oil is found at Lake Kutubu; gas has been found in the Tari area; gold comes from the area that salt once came from; and money came from Mount Hagen, and the Nembi remain in the middle,[33] but their position in the middle is no longer an advantage.

Some Nembi Myths

I conclude this section with two of the Nembi myths that I collected in the 1970s. The first is a myth about the sky people, and the second tells about the place of the dead.

A Man Marries a Woman from the Sky (As told by Kopyem from Embi)

Two unmarried brothers shared a house. They were very prosperous, having a large garden and many pigs. One day they killed their largest pig and divided everything equally. One of the brothers only ate a little bit of his meat. He packed the rest in a string bag, and early the next morning, long before the birds called, he went up the mountainside carrying his meat. He was headed for the place where

---

[33]Robert Crittenden, 1982. *Sustenance, Seasonality and Social Cycles on the Nembi Plateau, Papua New Guinea.* [Canberra, Australia: Australian National University, 1982], 210-219.

every day early in the morning the two brothers heard some women laughing and shouting. He arrived long before daybreak and hid both his meat and himself. At daybreak many women came falling from the sky like fruit drops from a tree. They collected red clay, and they sat on the branches of the trees and decorated their faces. One of the women came after all of the others. She had very long hair hanging loose, and very nice white eyes. The brother who was hiding sneaked up on her and grabbed her. OH MY! She turned into a snake, and then she turned into an earthworm, and then she turned into three different kinds of trees with thorns. The man refused to let go, and asked her, "You, this woman of mine that I am holding, why are you doing these things?" She said, "You this man, I changed into many things, but you did not feel it. You let loose now. Let us go." She went with him to the house that he shared with his brother.

When they got back home, he told his brother everything. As the woman instructed, that night they staked pigs out and laid out pearl shells in the clearing around their house. The next morning when they looked, the pigs and pearl shells were gone, and other pigs and pearl shells had been left in their place. The one brother and the woman from the sky were married. They lived there for two weeks.

At the end of the two weeks, the married brother told his wife, I want to go see your place. "Let us go," she said. He pulled his net hat tightly over his head, tied his string bag around his back, and tucked the ends into his bark belt. He tightened his bowstring and was ready to go. The woman also got ready to go. They returned to the place where she had fallen from the sky. They stood at the trunk of the hardwood tree. She carried some wild ginger. They broke it, ate it and swallowed it. Then they closed their eyes and they were transported to the place above the sky. They walked and walked until they came to a lake filled with very blue water.

There was a log bridge across the water, and the bridge very dirty and slimy. The woman said to her husband, "You, this man, we have to cross the bridge. You go first." OH MY BROTHERS! As he stepped on the log bridge, it broke, and he fell into the water. Before he was completely submerged, the woman grabbed him by the head of his hair and pulled him out of the water. She said to him, "You, this man, look at your rotting flesh which is down there in the water." She had pulled him out of the water. Later the two of them traveled on. As they traveled they met many people who offered them the cooked meat from a dove. The people would say, "Here are some sweet potatoes," but instead they gave the two of them some meat.

OH MY BROTHERS, they walked a long way until they came to a nice cleared place with grass, a large fence, trees, and flowers nicely arranged. The man and his wife had arrived at her father's home. They talked and ate together, waiting for the wife's brothers to return home. As the brothers came home they kept shouting out. As they arrived home, the father pulled a set of wooden tongs out of the fire, and he knocked the glowing embers off the end of the tongs, causing lightning to strike a tree.

That night the man from earth slept with his father-in-law who took the man's bow and arrows and loosened the bow's string. He warned his son-in-law that he would hear a lot of possums that night, but he should ignore them. In the middle of the night while his father-in-law was fast asleep, the man heard many possums just outside the house. The temptation was too great. He took his bow, tightened its string, and shot one of the possums. He heard it fall, but he could not find it. He reentered the house and slept again. In the morning, he was awakened by his father-in-law who said, "Son-in-law, you disobeyed me. You must go home now." His father-in-law led him outside, and pulled aside a piece of the ground so they could look down to the earth. The man's brother was laid out on a stretcher with the spear in his heart. The father-in-law gave his daughter and son-in-law many things to take to the funeral, but he warned the young man not to cry and to shed no tears. Instead he was given a bamboo flute and instructed to blow on the flute whenever he felt sad. The man and his wife went to the place of mourning, and neither of them cried. They only blew on the bamboo pipes. The people were taking the corpse to bury it when the leg of the corpse bumped against the chest of the man. It was too much. The brother wept and wailed. He grabbed his head, and walked around in tight circles, shouting and wailing very loudly.

The woman vanished. Did she go here or did she go there, no one knows. When the man came to himself, he tried to return to the sky, but how could he? There was an impenetrable barrier across the sky. He tried to go, but he could not.

When he went into the water and changed his skin, I think that this is what we do when we are baptized.

Up there they said, "Do not cry." If we didn't cry we could go up there. We too would have lived forever. We, too, could go up there and come back down. The end.

A Woman Mourns for her Husband
(As told by Wisup from Embi)

Osisaek's daughter from the line of Yomo was married to Ond Tima Pon from the line of Tellel. They lived at Ullaell Anda. They lived there until the man died. The woman put on mourning beads and rubbed gray clay all over her body. She wore her mourning skirt. She was a widow. She kept her husband's gravesite clean and spotless. After a long time she removed her mourning skirt and her mourning beads and laid them aside, but she always kept crying. She went to her husband's gravesite and she cried saying, "My husband from Ond Tima, my husband from Kesi, my husband from Angara." As she was crying she heard a twig snap and something came close. She turned her head and she saw a man. Her husband had come! You are always crying. I have been to the place of the dead people. I have gone. Why do you always sit and cry? I have come now."

She went inside the house and put on her good grass skirt and she got her good string bag. She rubbed black grease all over her body. After she had done this, she said, "Let's go."

"Where shall we go?"

"Let us go to your house."

He said, "The place where I stay is not a good place. The living don't go there. Now where are you going?"

However, he finally said yes, and they went. They had walked a long time when they came to a long cleared place. "Where is this place?" she asked.

"It is the place where they fight over the fruit of the *pu* tree," he said.

They walked some more and came to another cleared place. "Where is this?" she said.

"This is the cleared place where they struggle over the fruit of the *pengip* tree."

They went and went and went. After they had walked a long time, they came to another very long cleared place. "Where is this cleared place?" she asked.

"This cleared place is the place for forgetting. (When the dead person reaches this cleared place, the living people forget the deceased person.).

They walked and walked and went some more. OH BOY! There was a man's house that looked like dried beans. The two of them walked up to the house. "This is my house," he said.

At the back of the house he had some taro. He dug this up and cooked it for her. There were some very nice ripe bananas. He cut these for her. He let her eat, and then he wrapped her in a blanket and put her where he puts his head when he sleeps. After he fastened her up, he stayed there until the afternoon.

Many men came in and sat down. Many were deformed. Some had only one good eye. Another had only one lip. They kept coming with things to eat until they had nearly filled the house. Finally two light complexioned people—a boy and a girl—came. The man had brought in leaves and firewood. The man cooked all the food and the boy and girl ate and ate. When there stomachs were swollen from the food they had eaten, the boy and girl got a long wooden dish that was stored in the house. They sat on the dish and defecated into it.

The man said to his wife, "You are always crying over me. Now you see the places I go and the food that I eat. Here, you swallow this food," he said referring to the excreta in the huge wooden dish. He had his string bag and a pearl shell. He dug out some roots for her and gave them to her. At daybreak he said, "You go." The people who had come to the house the night before had afready gone out to other places.

He walked with her, and they returned to the land of the living until they saw her father and brothers creating a lot of smoke by burning off some bush to make a garden. He told her, "You go, and take these gifts to your father and your brothers."

She agreed, "Yes, I will go, but wait." She sat down on the ground and scooted over, and she turned into *op tumbeyaem*. (A plant with dried leaves similar to the dried leaves of a banana plant. These leaves are used to wrap up pearl shells.)

He gathered up his things and walked away carrying them as he went.

The end.

Bibliography

Patrol Reports Cited[1]

Erave Patrol Reports

Number 4, 1957-1958, G. J. Hogg, PD 14 to 17 September and 26 September to 19 October, 1957, RD 6 November, 1957, {NB 54-58 HW 369-381}.

Number 5, 1957-1958, G. J. Hogg, PD 14 January to 16 February, 1958, RD 2 March, 1958, {NB 54-58 HW 405-441}.

Number 4 of 1960-1961, N. T. Fairhill, PD 24 November to 16 December; 11 to 22 December, 1960; and 5 to 17 January, 1961, RD 18 February, 1961, {NB 58-61 HW 372-392}.

Kagua Patrol Reports

Number 7 0f 1960-61, Gerald P. Jensen-Muir, PD 24 November to 20 December, 1960, RD 2 February, 1961, {NB 58-61 HW 393-407}.

Number 12 of 1960-1961, Gerald P. Jensen-Muir, PD 3 to 25 May, 1961, RD 8 July, 1961, {NB 58-61 HW 408-428}.

Number 2 of 1961-1962, Gerald P. Jensen-Muir, PD 26 July to 19 August, 1961, RD 25 September, 1961, {NB 61-64 HW 19-36}.

Kutubu Patrol Reports

Number 4 of 1937-38. Central Highlands, 1937, Claude Champion, PD 18 April to 20 September, 1937. http://recordsearch.naa.gov.au-/scripts/Imagine.asp?-B=241575 Series Number A7034, Control Symbol 12, Item Bar Code 241575 [Accessed on October 7, 2014]

Number 2 of 1950-1951, S. S. Smith, PD 23 August to 13 November, 1950. {NB 49-54, HW 23-57} [includes Ivan Champion, 8th August, 1950, Department of

---

[1]The patrol reports are listed by their place of origin (Erave, Kagua, Kutubu, Mendi, Mount Hagen, Nipa, Poroma, and Western Highlands) in alphabetical order. The final sub-section is other archival documents that were either not patrol reports, or are reports prior to 1935. These are listed in alphabetical order. The patrol reports listed under each place of origin are in chronological order. PD means Patrol Date, and RD means Report Date. The patrol reports are stored at the Papua New Guinea National Archives in Port Moresby, Papua New Guinea. I have copies of the patrol reports that are cited in this dissertation, and they will be stored in the Asbury Theological Seminary Information Commons Archives. The information enclosed in curly brackets refers to my personal filing system. NB stands for notebooks, and the numbers that follow refer to the years that the notebooks include. 59-54 stands for the years 1949 to 1954. I numbered the pages in each notebook by hand. HW refers to the hand written page numbers in each notebook.

District Services and Native Affairs, Port Moresby Memorandum to Assistant District Officer at Lake Kutubu {NB 49-54, HW 56}].

Number 1 of 1953-1954, C. E. Terrell, PD 31 July to 27 August, 1953 RD 17 September, 1953 {NB 49-54 HW 346-369}.

Mendi Patrol Reports

Number 1 for 1951-1952, D. P. Sheekley, RD 23 October, 1951, {NB 49-54 HW 168-172}.

Number 4 of 1952-1953, B. R. Haegney, PD 16 August to 29 September, 1952, RD 20 November, 1952 {NB 49-54 HW 196-218} [includes John S. McLeod, 20 November, 1952 letter to District Services and Native Affairs, Port Moresby {NB 49-54 HW 196b, 196c}].

Number 7 of 1952-1953, A. L. Ford, PD 16 to 23 May, 1953. {NB 49-54 HW 280-293}.

Number 3 of 1953-1954, A. L. Ford, PD 4 to 18 September, 1953, RD 24 September, 1953, {NB 49-54, HW 369-383} [includes letter from A. A. Roberts to the District Commissioner of the Southern Highlands Dictrict dated 17 October, 1953 {NB 49-54 HW 370}].

Number 4 of 1953-1954, J. A. Frew, PD 14 to 18 September, 1953, RD 24 September, 1953, {NB 49-54 HW 406-413}.

Number 5 of 1953-1954, J. A. Frew, PD 25 September to 19 October, 1953, RD 14 November, 1953, {NB 1949-1954 HW 414-436}

Number 5 of 1954-1955 A. L. Ford, PD 19 October to 18 December, 1954 RD, 31 December, 1954 {NB 54-58 HW 61-76} [includes letter by Robert C. Cole written to the Director of Department of District Services and Native Affairs, Port Moresby {NB 54-58 HW 64-65}]

Number 11 of 1955-56, J. J. Pickrell, PD 28 May to 3 June, 1956, RD 12 June, 1956, {NB 54-58, HW 269-278}.

Number 3 of 1958-59, R. N Desailly, PD 4 to 14 November, 1958, RD 12 February, 1959, {NB 58-61 HW 14-25} [includes letter from B. K. Leen dated 3rd January, 1959 to the District Commissioner {NB 58-61 HW 16}].

Number 7 of 1958-1959, S. F. Markwell, PD 23 to 29 May, 1959, RD 9 June, 1959, {NB 58-61 HW 45-53}.

Number 2, 1959-1960, J. Jordon, PD 19 January to 2 February, 1960, RD February, 1960, {NB 58-61 HW 63-64}.

Number 5 of 1959-1960, D. N. Butler, PD 2 to 20 June, 1960, RD June, 1960 {NB – 58-61, HW 104-105}.

Number 3 of 1960-61, R. A. Hoad, PD 13 January to 8 February, 1961, RD 4 March, 1961, {NB 58-61, HW 297-332}.

Number 1 of 1961-1962, D. N. Butler, PD 27 July to 11 August, 1961, RD 21 August, 1961, {NB 61-64, HW 1-18} [includes K. W. Dyer, 31 August, 1961, letter to assistant District Officer {NB 61-64 HW 3}].

Number 4 of 1961-1962, Alan C. Jeffries, PD 4 September to 28 October, 1961, RD 24 November, 1961, {NB 61-64 HW 37-63} [includes letter from K. W. Dyer dated 24 November, 1961, {NB 61-64 HW 41-42}].

Number 7 of 1961-62, Alan C. Jefferies, PD 22 November, 1961 to 14 January, 1962 RD 25 January, 1962 {NB 61-64, HW 116}.

Number 3A of 1962-1963, Alan C. Jefferies, PD 7 to 14 July, 1963, RD July, 1963 {NB 61-64 HW 202-207}.

Number 27 of 1963-1964, N. C. McQuilty, PD 23 to 25 March, 1964, RD 1 April, 1964, {NB 61-64 HW 450-460}.

Number 4 of 1966-1967, L. R. Dickson, PD 5 September to 25 November, 1966, RD 20 December, 1966, {NB 66-68 HW 32-50}.

Number 8 of 1966-1967, J. C. Hunter, PD 28 November to 19 December, 1966, RD 26 January, 1966, {NB 66-68 HW 127-153} [includes supplemental reports by N. C. McQuilty, P. N. Sisley and N. J. Cavanage; a letter by M. J. E. Anderson to the District Commissioner at Mendi dated 12 January, 1967; and a letter from J. K. McCarthy, Director of District Services at Konedobu dated 13 March, 1967].

Number 17 of 1966-1967, D. Hoban, PD 17 December, 1966 to 3 March, 1967, RD 16 May, 1967, {NB 66-68 HW 154-177}.

Number 18 of 1966-67, C. P. Dangerfield, PD 4 February to 5 May, 1967, RD 22 June, 1966, {NB 64-68 HW 178-194}.

Number 5 of 1968-69, P. O. Jones, PD 10 to 27 September, 1968, RD 7 March, 1969, {NB 68-69 HW 84-108}.

Mount Hagen Patrol Reports

Number 6, 1950-1951, Allan Timperly, PD 27 February to 3 April, 1951, RD 16 April, 1951, {NB 49-54, HW125-140}.

Nipa Patrol Reports

Number 1 of 1959-1960, J. Jordan, PD 31 August to 28 December, 1959, RD January, 1960 {NB 58-61 HW 54-61} [includes Administration Press Release Number 11, February 26, 1960 {NB 58-61 HW 56}].

Number 4 of 1959-1960, D. N. Butler, PD 11 March to 29 May, 1960, RD June 1960, 9 {NB 58-61 HW 77-92}.

Number 1 of 1961-1962, D. N. Butler, PD 27 July to 11 August, 1961, RD 21 August, 1961, {NB 61-64, HW 1-18} [includes K. W. Dyer, 31 August, 1961, letter to assistant District Officer {NB 61-64 HW 3}].

Number 2 of 1961-1962, R. T. Fairhill, PD 20 September to 6 November, 1961, RD 7 November, 1961, {NB 61-64 HW 64-87}.

Number 5 of 1961-1962, N. D. Lucas, PD 12 to 29 December, 1961, RD January 24, 1962, {NB 61-64 HW 88-98}.

Number 9 of 1961-1962, N. D. Lucas, PD 22 March to 7 April, 1962, RD 28 May, 1962, {NB 61-64 HW 155-172} [includes letter from A. C. Jeffries {NB 61-64 HW 158-159}].

Number 2 of 1962-1963, N. D. Lucas, PD 7 to 17 August, 1962, RD 20 August, 1962, {NB 61-64 HW 230-242} [includes Alan C. Jeffries, 15th October, 1962, letter to Assistant District Officer in Mendi {NB 61-64 HW 232}].

Number 8 of 1962-63, Peter J. Barber, PD 11 to 21 March, 1963, RD 25 March, 1963 {NB 61-64 HW 349-362}.

Number 12 of 1963-64, Warren R. Read, PD 7 to 16 January and 30 January to 6 February, 1964, RD 12 February, {NB 61-64 HW 363-378}.

Number 15 of 1963-1964, Warren R. Read, PD 17 to 19 April; 28 to 30 April; and 25 to 29 May, 1964, RD 1 June, 1964, {NB 61-64 HW 392-401}.

Number 1 of 1964-1965, Warren R. Read, PD 21 to 27 July, 1964, RD 25 September, 1965, {NB 64-66, HW 1-25} [includes letter by R. E. Focken written to the Assistant District Officer in Mendi on 29 September, 1964 Number 1 of 1964-1965, Warren R. Read, PD 21 to 27 July, 1964, RD 25 September, 1965, {NB 64-66, HW 1-25} [includes letter by R. E. Focken written to the Assistant District Officer in Mendi on 29 September, 1964 {NB 64-68 HW 6} and a supplemental report written by Cadet Patrol officer W. R. Patterson on 3 March, 1965, {NB 64-68 HW 15-25}].

Number 5 of 1964-1965, Warren R. Read, PD 2 to 28 November, 1964, RD 22 February, 1965, {NB 64-66 HW 75-106}, [includes D. R. Marsh, letter to the Director of the Department of District administration in Konedobu {NB 64-65 HW 76}].

Number 8 of 1964-1965, J. S. Hicks, PD 8 March to 12 April, 1965, RD 6 July, 1965, {NB 64-66, HW 130-175} [includes letter from A. J. Zweck to the Director of the Department of District Administration at Konedobu on July 5, 1965 {NB 64-66, HW 132-133}].

Number 5 of 1965-1966, J. S. Hicks, PD 10 November to 21 December, 1965, RD 24 February, 1966, {NB 64-66, HW 285-298} [includes letter from D. R. Marsh to the Director of the Deparment of Administation in Konedobu dated 24th February, 1966 {NB 64-66 HW 288} and a letter from James W. Kent to the District Commisssioner {NB 64-66 HW 289-290}].

Number 7 of 1965-1966, J. S. Hicks, PD 10 November to 21 December, 1965, RD 27 December, 1965, [includes letter from J. S. Hicks to the Assistant District Commissioner, Sub-District Office, Mendi and a letter from D.R. Marsh, to the director of the department of District Administration, Konedobu] {NB 64-66, HW 285-298}.

Number 7 of 1966-1967, C.P. Dangerfield, PD 30 August to 17 Sept, 1966, RD 24 September, 1966, {NB 66-68, HW 57-76.} [includes letter from J. K. McCarthy, to the Southern Highlands District Commissioner {NB 66-68 HW 59}].

Number 10 of 1966-1967, C. P. Dangerfield, PD 10 Oct to 1 December, 1966. RD 26 January, 1967, {NB 66-68 HW 77-104.} [includes A. F. McNeill. 28 December, 1966, letter to the District Commissioner of the Southern Highlands District {NB 66-68 HW 82-84}; D. R. Marsh, 26 January, 1967, letter to the Department of Administration in Konedobu {NB 66-68 HW 80-81}; and from J. K. McCarthy, 13 March, 1967, letter to the District Commissioner {NB 66-68 HW 78-79}].

Number 1 of 1967-1968, C. P. Dangerfield, PD 17 July to 5 August, 1967, RD 27 September, 1967, {NB 66-68 HW 256-271}, [includes letter from A. F. McNeill, 16 September, 1967 {NB 66-68 HW 257-258}].

Number 11 of 1967-1968, L. R. Dickson, PD 8 to 21 January and 28 to 31 January, 1968. RD 4 February, 1968, {NB 66-68 HW 284-296}.

Number 13 of 1967-1968, D. H. Agg, PD 30 January to 10 February, 1968, RD 12 February, 1968, [includes A. F. McNeill, 24 February, 1968, letter to The District Commissioner of the Southern Highlands Province] {NB 66-68 HW 297-310}.

Number 2 of 1968-1969, John Sydney Hicks, PD 2 to 21 August, 1968, RD 7 March, 1969, {NB 68-69 HW 11, 13}.

Number 3 of 1968-1969, C. P. Dangerfield, PD 29 August to 16 October, 1968, RD 4 November, 1968, {NB 68-68 HW 16-29}.

Number 7 of 1968-1969: Area Study-Nembi Plateau Census Division 1968, C. P. Dangerfield, PD 28 October to 23 November, 1968, RD 6 March, 1969, {NB 68-69, HW 141-167}, [includes A. F. McNeill, 14 February, 1969, letter to The District Commissioner of the Southern Highlands Province {NB 68-69, HW 144-145}].

Number 2 of 1969-1970: Area Study: Nipa Basin Census Division, nd, {NB 69-70 HW 58-84}.

Number 3 of 1969-1970, A. F. McNeill, PD 8 to 18 August, 1969, RD 17 December, 1969, {NB 69-70 HW 85-136}.

Number 5 of 1969-1970: Situation Report, J. R. Bullock, PD 1 December, 1969 to 30 January, 1970, RD 4 February, 1970, {NB 1969-1970 HW 184-197}.

Number 1 of 1970-1971: Area Study Nipa Basin Census Division , J. R. Bullock, PD 5 August, to 29 October, 1970, RD November 25, 1970, PD 25 November, 1970, {NB 70-74 HW 8-34}.

Number 2 of 1970-1971, N. Wright, PD 2 December 70 to 20 March, 1971, RD 5 April, 1971 {NB 70-74 HW 140] [includes Situation Report by N. Wright, {NB 50-74 HW 131-140}].

Number 2 of 1971-1972, Situation Report, Arthur G. Smedley, PD 14 September to 26 October, 1970, RD 8 November, 1971, {NB 70-74 HW 210-228} [includes letter from M. P. D. Davies to the District Commissioner of the Southern Highlands District, 23 December, 1971 {NB 70-74 HW 214-215}].

Number 2 0f 1972-1973: Area Study – Nembi Plateau, D. C. Ekins, PD 28 September to 19 October, 1972, RD 24 July, 1973, {NB 1970-1974, HW 320-330}.

Number 11 of 1972-1973: Area Study Nipa Basin, Graham Setchell, PD 28 March to 2 July, 1973, RD 24 July, 1973 {NB 70-74 HW 362}.

Poroma Patrol Reports

Number 2 of 1966-1967, N. C. McQuilty, PD 6 March to 1 June, 1967 RD 8 August, 1967, {NB 66-68, HW 210-230}.

Number 5 of 1968-1969: Area Survey—Nembi Census Division, N. Wright, PD 28 November to 19 December, 1968, RD 7 January, 1969, {NB 68-69, HW 169-188}.

Number 7 of 1969-1970: Area Survey—Nembi Valley Census Division, N. Wright, PD 17 November to 11 December, 1969, RD 19 January, 1970, {NB 69-70, HW 198-218}.

Number 3 for 1970-71, N. Wright, PD 3 t0 21 August, 1970, 30 September, 1970,{NB 70-74 HW 1-7} [includes T. W. Ellis, 30 June, 1971, letter to the District Commissioner, Southern Highland District, {NB 70-74 HW 2}].

Number 5 of 1970-1971, W. Hera, PD 4 November to 18 December, 1970, RD 1 January, 1971, [includes John Kabisch, 17 February, 1971, letter to the Assitant District Commissioner at Nipa,], (NB 70-74 HW 64-87).

Number 6 of 1970-1971, Morea K. Veri, PD 19 January to 15 February, 1971, RD 15 March, 1970, {NB 70-74 HW 101}.

Number 9 of 1971-1972, P. J. Puana, PD (not clear) RD 10 May, 1972, {NB 70-74 HW 315-319}.

Number 2 0f 1972-1973: Area Study – Nembi Plateau, D. C. Ekins, PD 28 September to 19 October, 1972, RD 24 July, 1973, {NB 1970-1974, HW 320-330}.

Number 1 of 1973-1974, G. Elimo, PD 23 July to 1 September, 1973, RD 13 November, 1973, [includes letter from John Kabisch to the assistant District Commissioner at Nipa, 6 November, 1973], (NB 70-74 HW 363-384).

Quarterly Reports

Robert R. Cole, July, 1955, *Southern Highlands District Quarterly Report, Period 1st of April to the 30th of June, 1955,* {NB 54-58 HW 204-207}.

Western Highlands Patrol Reports

Number 4 of 1950-1951. A. Timperly, PD 19 October to 25 October, 1950, {NB 49-54, HW 58-68} [includes George Greathead, Letter from District Office, Central Highlands District, Goroka, to The Director, Department of District Services and Native Affairs Port Moresby Dated 21st December, 1950 { NB 49-54, HW 67}].

Other Archival Documents

Champion, Ivan. "The Bamu Purari Expedition" in Hubert Murray, *Territory of Papua Annual Report for the year 1936-1937.* Canberra: Commonwealth of Australia, L. F. Johnston Commonwealth Government Printer, 1937. Australia National Archives: Series Number A981, Control Symbol PAP 1, Papua General Information 1928-1940, Barcode 179669. http://recordsearch.-naa.gov. au/SearchNRetrieve/Interface/ListingReports/ItemsListing.aspx   [Accessed on October 20, 2012].

Champion, Ivan. *Establishment of First Police Camp at Lake Kutubu 1938. Central Highlands.* [1938]. Series Number A7034, Control Symbol 11, Item Bar Code 241574. http://recordsearch.naa.gov.au/SearchNRetrieve/Interface/DetailsReports/ItemDetail.aspx?Barcode=241574 [Accessed on October 23, 2012].

Cleland, D.M., 12 November, 1953, *Administrative Press Release: Policy in Regard to Uncontrolled Areas* [Port Moresby] {NB 49-54 HW 324-325}.

District and Division Boundaries: News Release for South Pacific Post, September 12, 1951, in *Administration New Release to ABC South Pacific Post,* {NB 49-54 HW 331}

Murray, John Hubert Plunkett *Annual Report Papua 1914-1915.* Melbourne, Australia: Commonwealth of Australia, Government Printer, 1915. Australian National Archives 1917/1431, Item Bar Code 36220. http://record-search. naa.gov.au/SearchNRetrieve/Interface/ListingReports/ItemsListing.aspx [Accessed on August 31, 2012].

_____ *Native Administration in Papua.* Port Moresby: [Walter Alfred Black, Acting Government Printer, 1929] Australian National Archives A518, Control Symbol I850/1/5 Item Bar Code 108257. http://recordsearch.naa.-gov.au/ scripts/Imagine.asp?B=108257 [Accessed on October 7, 2014]

_____ *The Machinery of Indirect Rule in Papua.* [Port Moresby: Alfred Gibson, Acting Government Printer, 1935. Australian National Archives A518, Control Symbol M850/1/5 Item Bar Code 108261. http://recordsearch.naa.-gov.au/ SearchNRetrieve/Interface/DetailsReports/ItemDetail.aspx?Barcode=108261 [Accessed on September 15, 2012]

Williams, F. E. "Report on the Grasslanders: Augu—Wage—Wela" in Murray, Sir Hubert. *Territory of Papua Annual Report for the Year of 1938-1939.* [Canberra: Government of the Commonwealth of Australia, 1940], 39-67. Australian National Archives, Series Number M3816, Control Symbol 3 Item Bar Code 1182610 Page 362 of digitalized copy http://recordsearch.-naa.gov.au/ SearchNRetrieve/Interface/ListingReports/ItemsListing.aspx [Accessed on September 24, 2012].

Missionary Reports

Published

"Among The Nations" *Missionary Tidings,* 41, no. 5 [January, 1989]: 11.

"Among The Nations" *Missionary Tidings,* 42, no. 1 [August/September, 1989]: 15.

Benner, Becky, "From Bush to Town" *Missionary Tidings* 36 no 10 [July, 1984]: 9.

Bennett, Diane, "Protection in Time of Trouble" *Missionary Tidings* 44 no. 2, [October/November, 1991]: 6, 11.

_____ "A Story to Tell" *Evangelical Advocate* 99 no. 3 [November 2002], 16.

_____ "Road Blocks" *Evangelical Advocate* 99 no. 9 [May, 2003], 12-13.

_____ "Moving Again" *Evangelical Advocate* 100 no. 12 [August, 2004], 13-14.

_____ "A Meeting with PNG Leaders" *Evangelical Advocate* 101 no. 2 [October, 2004]: 15.

Blankenship, Grover. "The Answer is Already on Its Way," *Missionary Tidings* XVII, no. 8 [March, 1966]:12.

Christie, Alice Jean, "They Will Know Christ by Our Love" *Missionary Tidings* XXVII, no 7 [February, 1976]: 11

Donahue, Eva, "Farewell Greetings," *Missionary Tidings*, XXIV no. 5 [December, 1972]: 11

_____ "Congregation Unwanted" *Missionary Tidings*, XXVII no 7 [February, 1976]: 12.

Estel, Mary, "The Desires of Our Hearts" *Evangelical Advocate* 100 no. 6 [February, 2004]: 9.

Gurwell, Rose. "Highlights Mount of Praise Missionary Services," *Missionary Tidings* XXI, no. 3 [October, 1969]; 6-7.

Hood, Ron, "Target Port Moresby," *Missionary Tidings* 42, no. 5 [April-May, 1990], 8.

Hummel, James. "Greetings From New Guinea," *Missionary Tidings* XV, no 1 [August, 1963]: 3.

Johnson, Becka "In His Hands" *Evangelical Advocate* 91, no. 7 [March, 1996]: 16, 20.

_____ "Utility Right-of-way Update," *Evangelical Advocate* 103 no. 5 [May/June, 2007]: 21.

Johnson, Jim. "A Lae Adventure," *Evangelical Advocate* 94 no. 5 [December, 1998]: 12

Johnson, Jim and Becka, "Look What God is Doing in Papua New Guinea," *Evangelical Advocate* 98 no. 12 [August, 2002], 12.

Johnson, Jim, Becka Johnson, and Ruth Tipton, "It Just Happened" *Evangelical Advocate* 91, no 8 [April, 1996]: 12, 14.

Jones, Sara, "Farata Girls School" *Missionary Tidings* 29, no 2, [September, 1977]: 11.

Lattimer, David, "A New Partnership Agreement With WGM," *The Evangelical Advocate* 91 no. 9 [May, 1996]: 11.

_____ "Why…The New Partnership Agreement With WGM," *The Evangelical Advocate* 91 no.11 [July, 1996]: 11.

_____ "Mission Links" *The Evangelical Advocate* 98 no. 10 [June 2002]: 10.

_____ "A God Moment at Poroma" *The Evangelical Advocate* 98 no. 10 [June 2002]: 9-10.

_____ "Mission Links" *The Evangelical Advocate* 100 no. 10 [June, 2004]: 12.

Lawhun, Gene, "The Mount Hagen Church Papua New Guinea" *Missionary Tidings* 41 no 1 [August-September, 1988]: 7

_____ "God is in Control" *Evangelical Advocate* 91, no. 7 [March, 1996]: 10-11

Lawhun, Rosemary, "From then…to Now" *Missionary Tidings* 44 no. 1 [August/September, 1991]: 7.

_____ "Terror at Night" *Missionary Tidings* 44, no. 5 [April/May, 1992]: 4.

Map, Anna Timothy. "Christian Union Mission's National Women's Convention," *The Evangelical Advocate* 90 no. 12 [August, 1995]: 11.

Map, Timothy. "A Papua New Guineans Testimony," *Missionary Tidings* XXXIV, no. 8 [May, 1983]: 5.

_____ "Return to Papua New Guinea," *Evangelical Advocate* 89 no. 10 [June, 1994], 12.

McClain, Ruth. "What Have You Heard?" *Missionary Tidings*, XXII, no 10 [May, 1971]: 5.

Meade, Thelma. "Let's Help Our Nurse in New Guinea," *Missionary Tidings* XVII, no. 1 [July, 1965], 10.

Meckes, Florence, "I Sat Looking at My Feet," *Missionary Tidings* XXI no. 9 [April, 1970]: 4-5.

Meckes, Ted and Florence. "Will Bring Them to New Guinea Again," *Missionary Tidings*, XX no. 3 [October, 1968]: 6-7.

Meckes, Ted and Florence. "Montanda" *Missionary Tidings* XX, no. 8 [March, 1969]: 7.

"Meet Darin and Lisa Stambaugh," *Evangelical Advocate*, 92 no. 9 [April, 1997], 10

Missionary Tidings XVI, no. 5 [January, 1965]: 1.

Neal, Cindy. "What's up With the Neals?" *Evangelical Advocate*, 98 no. 5 [January, 2002}]: 17.

Owens, Al and Helen. "Viewpoints," *Missionary Tidings*, 37, no. 7 [April, 1985]: 8.

"Prayer Requests," *Missionary Tidings* XV, no. 12, [July, 1963], 7.

"Prayer Requests," *Missionary Tidings* XVI, no 6, [February, 1965], 7.

Priest, Ron. "The Shaping of the Church: Stewardship" *Missionary Tidings* XXXVII no 7, [April, 1985], 5.

Queen, Dean, "Missionary Mama" *Evangelical Advocate* 94 no 10, [May, 1999]: 12-13.

Queen, Dean and Shirley, "Nembi Bible Training Center of Papua New Guinea" *Missionary Tidings* 42 no. 1 [August-September, 1989]: 4.

Sayre, R. L., "Mission Links" *Advocate* 88 no. 6 [February, 1993]: 10.

_____ "General Missionary superintendent's Address Councils, 1995" in *1995 Year Book churches of Christ in Christian Union, Council Addresses and Reports*, 11-16, Circleville, Ohio: Churches of Christ in Christian Union, 1995.

_____ "First Camp Meeting of the Christian Union Church of Papua New Guinea," *Evangelical Advocate* 89 no. 7 [March, 1994]: 12-13.

"Send the Light," *Missionary Tidings*, 41 no. 3 [November, 1988]: 8.

Seymour, Betty. "Godon Angal for New Guinea," *Missionary Tidings* XIX, no. 4 [November, 1967]: 11.

_____ "Thursday Church at Ka Station," *Missionary Tidings* XXIV, no. 8 [March, 1973]: 8, 11.

_____ "Profile: John and Emalie Tipton," *Missionary Tidings*, 35, no. 6 [March, 1984]: 12.

_____ "Profile Leatha and Paul Jenkins," *Missionary Tidings*, 39, no. 2 [October, 1986]: 11.

_____ "Welkam Bek (Welcome Back)," *Missionary Tidings* 39, no. 5 [January, 1987] 6-7.

_____ "Profile Don and Delores Brown," *Missionary Tidings*, 39, no. 5 [January, 1987]: 11.

_____ "Profile Tim and Diane Bennett," *Missionary Tidings*, 40, no. 3 [November, 1987]: 10.

_____ "Retired or Re-Fired?" *Missionary Tidings*, 43, no. 6 [June/July, 1991]: 12

Seymour, Don. "Frontlines of Information and Intercession XXXV no. 7 [April, 1984], 2.

_____ "Frontlines of Information and Intercession" *Missionary Tidings* XXXVII no 2 [October, 1984], 2

_____ "Frontlines of Information and Intercession" *Missionary Tidings* XXXVII no 3 [November, 1984], 2

_____ "Frontlines" *Missionary Tidings* 37 no 5 [January, 1985]: 2.

_____ "The Year in Review" *Missionary Tidings*, 40 no. 1, [August-September, 1987]: 5.

_____ "Frontlines" *Missionary Tidings* 44, no. 5, [April/May, 1992]: 2.

_____ "Frontlines" *Missionary Tidings* 45 no. 1 [August/September, 1992]; 2.

_____ "Let's Go to New Guinea!" *Evangelical Advocate* 99 no. 9 [May 2003, 12-13.

Strouth, Thelma Meade. "Remember Those Coupons," *Missionary Tidings* XVIII, no. 12 [July, 1967]: 8.

Tandopen, Tui. "Tui's Story" *The Evangelical Advocate* 89 no. 10 [June, 1994]: 12-13.

Tipton, Ruth. "Uncertainty...One Certainty!" *The Evangelical Advocate* 90, no. 9 [May, 1995]: 18.

_____ "I Will Never Forget (Part One)" *Evangelical Advocate* 91, no. 7 [March, 1996] 14

_____ "I Will Nevber Forget (Part Two)" *Evangelical Advocate* 91, no 8 [April, 1996] 9, 11, 14.

_____ "2006 PNG Women's Camp (unlike any others!)" *Evangelical Advocate* 103 no. 4 [March/April, 2007]: 19.

Tipton, Ruth and Eva Donahue, "Fire at Farata," *Missionary Tidings* 39 no. 3 [November, 1986], 4-5.

Tolbert, Bill. "Wanem Kain Man?" *Missionary Tidings*, XXVIII no. 3 [October, 1976]: 6.

Tolbert, Bill. "To Everything there Is a Season," *Missionary Tidings* XXIX, no.7 [February, 1978]: 4.

Tolbert, Bill. "The Christian Union Church in Papua New Guinea," *Missionary Tidings* XXX no. 3 [October, 1978]: 4.

Tolbert. Bill. "Telling it as it was—and is, "*Missionary Tidings*, XXXIII, no. 10. [May, 1982]: 5.

Tolbert, Sandy. "Patrols for Christ," *Missionary Tidings* XXVII no. 7 [December, 1975]: 8.

_____ "First Regional Conference," *Missionary Tidings* XXX no. 11, [June, 1979]: 7.

Ulman, Shirley K., "Anniversary Letters" *Missionary Tidings* XXI no. 4 [November, 1969]: 9.

Waggoner, Carl E, "News Flashes" *Missionary Tidings* XXVI no. 3 [October, 1974]: 3.

Waggoner, Mary A. "Know Your Missionaries Verona Charles," *Missionary Tidings*, XXVIII, no. 3 [October, 1976]: 10.

Waggoner, Mary A. "Know Your Missionaries Lynda Fosnaugh," *Missionary Tidings*, XXVII, no. 8 [March, 1977]: 10.

Waggoner, Mary A. "Know Your Missionaries The Lorin Martins," *Missionary Tidings*, XXX, no. 7 [February, 1979]: 10.

Waggoner, Mary A. "Know Your Missionaries The Dean Queens," *Missionary Tidings*, XXXI, no. 3 [October, 1979]: 10.

Waugh, Martha Jean, "Medicine – Stone Age or Modern" *Missionary Tidings* XVI no. 2, [September, 1965], 5.

_____ "Women's Meetings," *Missionary Tidings* XXIII, no. 7 [February, 1972]; 5.

"We were there," *Missionary Tidings*, 39 no. 3 [November, 1986], 7.

Wood, Dorothy "Bung Bilong Witnes (Witnesses Retreat)" *Missionary Tidings* XXIX no. 11 [June, 1978]: 8.

Minutes

Bible School Meeting Minutes, February 5-6, 2004.

Christian Union Mission Annual Field Council Minutes, February 19, 1972.

Christian Union Mission Annual Field Council Minutes, March 8, 9, 13, and 17, 1973,

Christian Union Mission Annual Field Council Minutes, February 15-16, 1974.

Christian Union Mission Annual Field Council Minutes, March 6, 1975.

Christian Union Mission Annual Field Council Minutes, February 19, 21, and 28, 1976.

Christian Union Mission Annual Field Council Minutes, February 11, 18-19, 1977.

Christian Union Mission Annual Field Council Minutes, February 9-10, 1978.

Christian Union Mission Annual Field Council Minutes, May 2-3, 1980.

Christian Union Mission Annual Field Council Minutes, March 16 and April 4 and 25, 1981.

Christian Union Mission Annual Field Council Minutes, January 15-16, 1982.

Christian Union Mission Annual Field Council Minutes, February 10-12, 1983.

Christian Union Mission Annual Field Council Minutes, February 3-4, 1984, 13

Christian Union Mission Annual Field Council Minutes, April 28-29, 1985.

Christian Union Mission Annual Field Council Minutes, March 6, 1986.

Christian Union Mission Annual Field Council Minutes, March, 1987.
Christian Union Mission Annual Field Council Minutes, January, 25, 1988.
Christian Union Mission Annual Field Council Minutes, January 13, 1989.
Christian Union Mission Annual Field Council Minutes, March 10, 1990.
Christian Union Mission Annual Field Council Minutes, November 5-6, 1991.
Christian Union Mission Annual Field Council Minutes, January 11, 1993.
Christian Union Mission Annual Field Council Minutes, July 29-30, 1995.
Christian Union Mission Budget Committee Meeting, December 19, 1986.
Christian Union Mission Executive Committee Minutes, June 10, 1970.
Christian Union Mission Executive Committee Minutes, October 7, 1970,
Christian Union Mission Executive Committee Minutes, October 31, 1970.
Christian Union Mission Executive Committee Minutes, November 12, 1970.
Christian Union Mission Executive Committee Minutes, December 19, 1970.
Christian Union Mission Executive Committee Minutes, January 1, 1971.
Christian Union Mission Executive Committee Minutes, March 6, 1971.
Christian Union Mission Executive Committee Minutes, March 19, 1971.
Christian Union Mission Executive Committee Minutes, July 30, 1971.
Christian Union Mission Executive Committee Minutes, February 12, 1972.
Christian Union Mission Executive Committee Minutes, May 13, 1972.
Christian Union Mission Executive Committee Minutes, November 11, 1972.
Christian Union Mission Executive Committee Minutes, November 10, 1973.
Christian Union Mission Executive Committee Minutes, January 13, 1973.
Christian Union Mission Executive Committee Minutes, October 4, 1975.
Christian Union Mission Executive Committee Minutes, July 31 and August 5,
    1976.
Christian Union Mission Executive Committee Minutes, May 31, 1982.
Christian Union Mission Executive Committee Minutes, September 13-14, 1982.
Christian Union Mission Executive Committee Minutes, December 13, 1983.
Christian Union Mission Executive Committee Minutes, May 1 and 7, 1985.
Christian Union Mission Executive Committee Minutes, December 7, 1990.
Christian Union Mission Executive Committee Minutes, February 14, 1991.
Christian Union Mission Executive Committee Minutes, March 31, 1992.
Christian Union Mission Field Council Minutes, June 15, 1973.
Christian Union Mission Field Council Minutes, September 13-14, 1974.
Christian Union Mission Field Council Minutes, October 26, 1974.
Christian Union Mission Field Council Minutes, February 21, 1975.
Christian Union Mission Field Council Minutes, November 21, 1975.
Christian Union Mission Field Council Minutes, August 12, 1976.
Christian Union Mission Field Council Minutes, July 29, 1978.
Christian Union Mission Field Council Minutes, January 20, 1979.
Christian Union Mission Field Council Minutes, July 28, 1979.
Christian Union Mission Field Council Minutes, October 27, 1979.
Christian Union Mission Field Council Minutes, December 14, 1979.
Christian Union Mission Field Council Minutes, September 27, 1980.
Christian Union Mission Field Council Minutes, November 1, 1980.

Christian Union Mission Field Council Minutes, December 6, 1980.
Christian Union Mission Field Council Minutes, July 25, 1981.
Christian Union Mission Field Council Minutes, October 23, 24, and 31, 1981.
Christian Union Mission Field Council Minutes, January 4, 1982.
Christian Union Mission Field Council Minutes, April 30-May 1, 1982
Christian Union Mission Field Council Minutes, July 16-17, 1982.
Christian Union Mission Field Council Minutes, August 27, 1982.
Christian Union Mission Field Council Minutes, October 8, 1982.
Christian Union Mission Field Council Minutes, January 14, 1983.
Christian Union Mission Field Council Minutes, November 4, 1983.
Christian Union Mission Field Council Minutes, May 4-5, 1984.
Christian Union Mission Field Council Minutes, August 3-4, 1984.
Christian Union Mission Field Council Minutes, November 23, 1984.
Christian Union Mission Field Council Minutes, December 13, 1984.
Christian Union Mission Field Council Minutes, February 8-9, 1985.
Christian Union Mission Field Council Minutes, April 28-29, 1985
Christian Union Mission Field Council Minutes, October 4-5, 1985.
Christian Union Mission Field Council Minutes, December 19, 1986.
Christian Union Mission Field Council Minutes, October 20, 1987.
Christian Union Mission Field Council Minutes, November 17, 1987.
Christian Union Mission Field Council Minutes, September 16, 1988.
Christian Union Mission Field Council Minutes, November 18, 1988.
Christian Union Mission Field Council Minutes, December 28-29, 1989 and January 1, 1990.
Christian Union Mission Field Council Minutes, June 20-21, 1990.
Christian Union Mission Field Council Minutes, July 3, 1990.
Christian Union Mission Field Council Minutes, October 1, 1990.
Christian Union Mission Field Council Minutes, January 15, 1991.
Christian Union Mission Field Council Minutes, June 20-21, 1991.
Christian Union Mission Field Council Minutes, March 20, 1992.
Christian Union Mission Field Council Minutes, June 23, 1993.
Christian Union Mission Field Council Minutes, June 29, 1994.
Christian Union Mission Field Council Minutes, November 9, 10, 13, 1994.
Christian Union Mission Field Council Minutes, March 1, 5, and 6, 1995.
Christian Union Mission Field Council Minutes, January 18, 1996.
Christian Union Mission Field Council Minutes, April 26, 1996.
Christian Union Mission Field Council Minutes, May 13, 1998.
Christian Union Mission Field Council Minutes, August 26, 1998.
Christian Union Mission Field Council Minutes, November 25, 1998.
Christian Union Mission Field Council Minutes, February 5, 1999.
Christian Union Mission Field Council Minutes, February 14, 1999.
Christian Union Mission Field Council Minutes, September 5, 1999.
Christian Union Mission Field Council Minutes, December 1, 2, 3, and 4, 1999.
Christian Union Mission Field Council Minutes, February 18-19, 2000.
Christian Union Mission Field Council Minutes, August 5, 2000.

Christian Union Mission Field Council Minutes, February 13-14, 2001.
Christian Union Mission Field Council Minutes, April 20-21, 2001.
Christian Union Mission Field Council Minutes, May 23, 2001.
Christian Union Mission Field Council Minutes, September 14, 15, and 17, 2001.
Christian Union Mission Field Council Minutes, November 22, 2001.
Christian Union Mission Field Council Minutes, February 13-14, 2002.
Christian Union Mission Field Council Minutes, May 4, 2002.
Christian Union Mission Field Council Minutes, September 8, 10, 2002.
Christian Union Mission Field Council Minutes, October 12, 2002.
Christian Union Mission Field Council Minutes, November 9, 2002.
Christian Union Mission Field Council Minutes, December 11, 12, and13, 2002.
Christian Union Mission Field Council Minutes, April 9, 2003.
Christian Union Mission Field Council Minutes, July 26, 2003.
Christian Union Mission Field Council Minutes, January 30, 2004.
Christian Union Mission Field Council Minutes, February 13, 2004.
Christian Union Mission Field Council Minutes, December 4-8, 2004.
Christian Union Mission Field Council Minutes, June 13, 2005.
Christian Union Mission Field Council Minutes, December 11, 2005.
Christian Union Mission Field Council Minutes, June 29, 2006.
Christian Union Mission Field Council Minutes, January 12, 2007.
Christian Union Mission Field Council Minutes, January 19-25, 2007.
Christian Union Mission Field Council Minutes, October 15, 2007.
Christian Union Mission Field Council Minutes, October 31, 2008.
Christian Union Mission Field Council Minutes, September 9, 2011.
Christian Union Mission Field Council Minutes, March 23, 2012,
Christian Union Mission Field Council Minutes, September 14, 2012.
Christian Union Mission Field Council Minutes, October 9, 2012.
Christian Union Mission Field Council Minutes, January 31, 2013.
Christian Union Mission Field Council Minutes, August 14, 2013.
Christian Union Mission Field Council Minutes, April 20-21, 2013.
Church Mission Coordinating Council Meeting Minutes, January 15, 1996.
Church Mission Coordinating Council Meeting Minutes, November 7, 1994.
Church Mission Coordinating Council Meeting Minutes, January 18, 2007, in
    Christian Union Mission Field Council Minutes, January 19-25, 2007.
Executive Committee of the General Foreign Missionary Board, Churches of
    Christ In Christian Union, October 20, 1960.
Executive Committee of the General Foreign Missionary Board, Churches of
    Christ In Christian Union, September 27, 1961.
Executive Committee of the General Foreign Missionary Board, Churches of
    Christ In Christian Union, November 27, 1962.
Executive Committee of the General Foreign Missionary Board, Churches of
    Christ In Christian Union, August 21, 1963.
Executive Committee of the General Foreign Missionary Board, Churches of
    Christ In Christian Union, October 22, 1963.

Executive Committee of the General Foreign Missionary Board, Churches of Christ In Christian Union, February 3, 1964.

Executive Committee of the General Foreign Missionary Board, Churches of Christ In Christian Union, March 20, 1964.

Executive Committee of the General Foreign Missionary Board, Churches of Christ in Christian Union, April 26, 1974.

General Foreign Missionary Board Meeting, Churches of Christ in Christian Union, August 17, 1962.

General Foreign Missionary Board Meeting, Churches of Christ in Christian Union, June 2, 1964.

General Foreign Missionary Board Meeting, Churches of Christ in Christian Union, June 4, 1964

General Foreign Missionary Board Meeting, Churches of Christ in Christian Union, April 26, 1964.

General Foreign Missionary Board Meeting, Churches of Christ in Christian Union, November 27, 1973.

General Foreign Missionary Board Meeting, Churches of Christ in Christian Union, June 8, 1966.

General Foreign Missionary Board Meeting, Churches of Christ in Christian Union, December 15, 1966.

General Foreign Missionary Board Meeting, Churches of Christ in Christian Union, December 29, 1966.

General Foreign Missionary Board Meeting, Churches of Christ in Christian Union, February 4, 1969.

Regional Board Quarterly Meeting, April 18, 1979 in Christian Union Mission, Field Council Meeting Minutes, July 28, 1979.

Region Board of Trustees Meeting, April 14, 1980, in Christian Union Mission Annual Field Council Minutes, October 23-34, 1981.

Other Unpublished Mission/Church Documents

Benner, Bill, "Personal Activities report in Annual Field Council Minutes, March 10, 1990, 16.

_____ "Personal Report," in Annual Field Council Minutes, November 5-6, 1991, 38.

Brown, Denny, "Hagen Church Planting Report" in Christian Union Mission Field Council Minutes, October 4-5, 1985, 4.

_____ "Activity Report for Denny Brown" in Christian Union Mission Annual Field Council Minutes, March 6, 1986, 5.

Christian Union Church of PNG, letter from RBT to the Christian Union Mission in Christian Union Mission Field Council Minutes, January 19-25, 2007.

Christian Union Church of PNG, letter from RBT to Christian Union Mission Field Council, 24th January, 2014.

Christie, Alice Jean, "CUM Medical Report" in Christian Union Mission Annual Field Council Minutes, February 19, 21, and 28, 1976.

Conley, Elsie, "Farata Girls' School Report" in Christian Union Mission Annual Field Council Minutes, March 6, 1975.

_____ "Nembi Bible School Report" in Christian Union Mission Annual Field Council Minutes February 3-4, 1984

Donahue, Eva, "Medical Report 1985" in Christian Union Mission Annual Field Council Minutes, March 6, 1986.

Foreign Missionary Department of the Churches of Christ in Christian Union, "Co-Laborers Together With God: Handbook of Policy 1980 Revised Edition."

Hermiz, Mary, "Health Secretary's Report" in Christian Union Mission, Annual Field Council Minutes, January 15-16 1982.

Hood, Ron, "Annual Report" in Christian Union Mission Annual Field Council Minutes, February 19, 21, and 28, 1976, 30.

_____ "Port Moresby Urban Ministries Report and Personal Report" in Annual Field Council Minutes, November, 5-6, 1991, 17-18.

Jenkins, Butch "Personal Report by Butch Jenkins" in Christian Union Mission Annual Field Council Minutes, March, 1987, 8.

_____ "Report for Community Development" in Christian Union Mission Annual Field Council Minutes, January 25, 1988.

_____ "Annual Report for 1988," in Christian Union Mission Annual Field Council Minutes, January 13, 1989.

_____ "Field Superintendent and Personal Report" in Christian Union Mission Annual Field Council Minutes, January 11, 1993.

_____ "Report for Sawmill Project" in Christian Union Mission Field Council Minutes, October 9, 2012.

Johnson, Leland, "1974 Annual Report" in Christian Union Mission Annual Field Council Minutes, February 15-16, 1974.

Jones, Bob, "Combined Ka District Advisor and Personal Activities Report" in Christian Union Mission Annual Field Council Minutes, January 15-16, 1982.

Jones, Sara, "Personal Report" in Christian Union Mission Annual Field Council Minutes, January 15-16, 1982.

Ka Eria Komiti, "Letter from Church Leaders" in Christian Union Mission Field Council Minutes, February 21, 1975.

Konstitusen Bilong Christian Union Church of Papua New Guinea (Draft One) in Christian Union Mission Annual Field Council Minutes, February 9-10, 1978.

Konstitusen Bilong Christian Union Church Bilong Papua New Guinea (Na Ol Bailo na Sakremen), 2002.

Kor, Daniel, "Letter from the RBT to the CMCC meeting in December 2002" in Christian Union Mission Field Council Minutes, December 11-13, 2002.

Lawhun, Gene, "Combined Report" in Christian Union Mission Annual Field Council Minutes, February 3-4, 1984, 13.

_____ "Personal Report for Gene Lawhun" in Christian Union Mission Annual Field Council Minutes, March, 1987, 9.

_____ "Personal Report" in Christian Union Mission Annual Field Council Minutes, January, 25, 1988

_____ "Annual Report" in Annual Field Council Meeting Minutes, January 13, 1989, 19.

_____ "Superintendent's Report" in Annual Field Council Meeting Minutes, January 13, 1989.

_____ "My Over View of the PNG Field" in Christian Union Mission Field Council Meeting Minutes, March 1, 5, and 6, 1995.

Lawhun, Rosemary, Personal Report for Rosemary Lawhun in Annual Field Council Minutes, March, 1987, 10.

_____ "Annual Report" in Annual Field Council Meeting Minutes, January 25, 1988,

_____ "Annual Report" in Annual Field Council Minutes, January 13, 1989, 20.

McClain, Ruth, Education Department Report in Christian Union Mission Annual Field Council Minutes, February 19, 1972.

Meckes, Ted and Florence, "Montanda Report" in Christian Union Mission Annual Field Council, February 15-16, 1974.

Miller, Dianna, "Personal Report" in Christian Union Mission Annual Field Council Minutes, April 28-29, 1985.

Miller, Roger, "Personal Report" in Christian Union Mission Annual Field Council Minutes, April 28-29, 1985.

_____ "Annual Personal Report" in Christian Union Mission Annual Field Council, March, 1987, 11.

Missionary Tidings Newsletter, August, 2008.

Missionary Tidings Newsletter, August, 2010.

Missionary Tidings Newsletter, December, 2010.

Missionary Tidings Newsletter, December, 2012.

Missionary Tidings Newsletter, August, 2013.

Missionary Tidings Newsletter, June, 2014.

"Organizational Chart" in Christian Union Mission Field Council Minutes, December 6, 1980.

Papua New Guinea Field Handbook, 1978.

Pombre, Rick and Ruth Tipton, *Histori Bilong Christian Union Church of Papua New Guinea 1963 to 2014.*

Policy Handbook Foreign Missions Department of the Churches of Christ in Christian Union, Revised Edition, 1980.

Queen, Dean, "Annual Report," in Christian Union Mission Annual Field Council Minutes, January 13, 1989.

_____ "Annual Report for Dean Queen and Port Moresby" in Christian Union Mission Annual Field Council Minutes, January 11, 1993, 14.

_____ "Port Moresby Report January-June, 1993," Christian Union Mission Field Council Minutes, June 22, 1993.

Seymour, Don, "Field Superintendent's and Ka Area Report," in Christian Union Mission Annual Field Council Minutes, February 15-16, 1974, Appendix, 6.

Til, Jacob and Daniel Kor, "Stori Bilong Kristen Union Sios Wara Lai District 1963-2007" in *Histori Bilong Christian Union Church of Papua New Guinea 1963 to 2014* eds. Rick Pombre and Ruth Tipton

Tipton, Ruth, "Personal Report for Ruth Tipton" in Christian Union Mission Annual Field Council Minutes, March 6, 1986.

Tolbert, Bill, "Annual Report for Director of Christian Education, in Christian Union Mission Annual Field Council Minutes, February 9-10, 1978, 19.

_____ "Church Report" in Christian Union Mission Field Council Minutes, April 30-May 1, 1982.

Waugh, Martha Jean, "General Medical Report" in Christian Union Mission Annual Field Council Minutes, February 15-16, 1974.

World Gospel Mission Missionary Policy Handbook, March, 2005.

"World Gospel Mission, Manual on Missionary Procedures," November, 2005.

Publications (Books and Articles)

Aerts, Theo. *The Martyrs of Papua New Guinea: 333 Missionary Lives Lost During World War II*. Port Moresby: University of Papua New Guinea Press, 1994.

AISH, "The Cohanim/DNA Collection" aish.com http://www.aish.com/ci/-sam/48936742.html [accessed on August 21, 2014.]

Allen, Roland. *Missionary Methods; St. Paul's or Ours?* Grand Rapids: Eerdmans, 1962.

Allen, Bryant. "The Setting: Land, Economics and Development in the Southern Highlands Province," in *Conflict and Resource Development in the Southern Highlands of Papua New Guinea*, eds. Nicole Haley and Ronald J. May Canberra: Australia National University E Press, 2007.

Allen, Bryant J. and Stephen Frankel. "Across the Tari Furoro," in *Like People You See In a Dream: First Contact in Six Papuan Societies*, eds. E. Schieffelin and R. Crittenden, 88-124. Stanford, CA: Stanford University Press, 1991.

Anderson, Rufus. "The Theory of Missions to the Heathen" in *To Advance the Gospel: Selections from the Writings of Rufus Anderson*, edited by R. Pierce Beaver, 73-88. Grand Rapids Michigan: William B. Erdman's Publishing Company, 1967.

Anderson, Rufus, and R. Pierce Beaver. To Advance the Gospel; Selections from the Writings of Rufus Anderson. Grand Rapids: Eerdmans, 1967.

Australian Department of World Affairs and Trade. "Overview of Australia's Aid Program to Papua New Guinea," Australian Government, http://aid.-dfat.gov.au/countries/pacific/png/Pages/default.aspx [Accessed on January 17, 2015].

Australian Deparment of World Affairs and Trade. "Papua New Guinea Fact Sheet" Australian Government. http://www.dfat.gov.au/geo/fs/png.pdf [accessed on January 19, 2015

Bean, C. E. W. *The story of Anzac: from the Outbreak of war to the End of the First Phase of the Gallipoli Campaign, May 4, 1915*. Sydney: Angus & Robertson, 1941. http://www.awm.gov.au/histories/first_world_war/volume.asp-?levelID=67887 [accessed on September 12, 2014].

Biersack, Aletta. Papuan Borderlands: *Huli, Duna, and Ipili Perspectives on the Papua New Guinea Highlands*. Ann Arbor: University of Michigan Press, 1995.

Biskup, Peter, Brian Jinks, and H. Nelson. *A Short History of New Guinea, Revised Edition.* Sydney, Australia: Angus and Robertson Ltd, 1968.

Bonk, Jon. *Missions and Money: Affluence As a Western Missionary Problem.* Maryknoll, N.Y.: Orbis Books, 1991.

Borthwick, Paul. *Western Christians in Global Mission: What's the Role of the North American Church?* Downers Grove, IL.: InterVarsity Press, 2012.

Bosch, David Jacobus. *Transforming Mission: Paradigm Shifts in Theology of Mission.* Maryknoll, N.Y.: Orbis Books, 1991.

Brinkoff, Thomas. "City Population, Papua New Guinea," http://www.citypopulation.de/PapuaNewGuinea.html [accessed February 26, 2014].

Brooke, C.H. "The Death of Bishop Patteson," Project Canterbury: Mission Life: An illustrated Magazine of Home and Foreign Church Work, ed. Rev. J. Halcombe, M.A., Volume III Part 1 (new series) London: W. Wells Gardner, 1872. Transcribed by the Right Reverend Dr. Terry Brown, Bishop of Malaita Church of the Province of Melanesia, 2006. http://anglicanhis-tory.org/oceania/brooke_patteson1872.html [accessed on September 8, 2014].

Brown, Rev. Kenneth and Rev. P. Lewis Brevard. *A Goodly Heritage, From out of the Past: History of the Churches of Christ in Christian Union.* Circleville, Ohio: Churches of Christ in Christian Union: Circle Press, Inc, 1980.

Burch, Maxie B. *The Evangelical Historians: the Historiography of George Marsden, Nathan Hatch, and Mark Noll.* Lanham, Md: University Press of America, 1996.

Burke, Peter. *New Perspectives on Historical Writing.* University Park, Pa: Pennsylvania State University Press, 2001.

Cahill, Peter. "A Prodigy of Wastefulness, Corruption, Ignorance and Indolence: The Expropriation Board in New Guinea 1920—1927." *The Journal of Pacific History* 32, no 1 [June, 1997]: 3-28.

Carr, Edward Hallett. *What is History?* New York: Knopf, 1962.

Central Intelligence Agency, "The World Factbook" Central Intelligence Agency of the US Government Library, https://www.cia.gov/library/pub-lications/the-world-factbook/geos/pp.html [accessed on January 19, 2015].

Champion, Ivan. "The Bamu Purari Patrol, 1936 (Continued)" *The Geographical Journal* 96:4 [October, 1940]. 243-263. http://www.jstor.org/stable/1787580 [Accessed September 16, 2014].

Champion, Ivan F. *Across New Guinea from the Fly to the Sepik.* Melbourne: Lansdowne, 1966.

Champion, Ivan and A. R. H. "The Bamu Purari Patrol, 1936" *The Geographical Journal* 96:3 [September, 1940]: 190-206. http://www.jstor.org/stable/1788555 [Accessed September 16, 2014].

Clark, Elizabeth A. *History, Theory, Text: Historians and the Linguistic Turn.* Cambridge, Mass: Harvard University Press, 2004.

Clark, Jeffrey, Chris Ballard, and Michael Nihill. *Steel to Stone: A Chronicle of Colonialism in the Southern Highlands of Papua New Guinea.* Oxford, UK: Oxford University Press, 2000.

Connolly, Bob, and Robin Anderson. *First Contact*. New York, NY: Filmakers Library, 1984.

_____ *First Contact*. New York, N.Y., U.S.A.: Viking, 1987.

Cook, James, J. C. Beaglehole, and R. A. Skelton. *The Journals of Captain James Cook on His Voyages of Discovery*, Vol 1. Cambridge: Published for the Hakluyt Society at the University Press, 1955.

Cook, James, and A. Grenfell Price. *The Explorations of Captain James Cook in the Pacific, As Told by Selections of His Own Journals, 1768-1779*. New York: Dover Publications, 1971.

Cooke, C. Kinloch. *Australian Defences and New Guinea*. London: Macmillan and Company, 1887.

Constitution and Bylaws of the Churches of Christ in Christian Union. Circleville, Ohio: The Advocate Publishing House, 1963.

Crittenden, Robert. *Sustenance, Seasonality and Social Cycles on the Nembi Plateau, Papua New Guinea*. Canberra, Australia: Australian National University, 1982.

Crittenden, Robert. "Across the Nembi Plateau" in *Like People You See In a Dream: First Contact in Six Papuan Societies*, eds. E. Schieffelin and R. Crittenden 168-197. Stanford, CA: Stanford University Press, 1991.

Crocombe, Ron and Marjorie Crocombe, eds. *Polynesian Missions in Melanesia: From Samoa Cook Islands and Tonga to Papua New Guinea and New Caledonia*. Suva, Fiji: The Institute of Pacific Studies, 1982.

De Groot, Nick. "Land Acquisition and Use During the Australian Period" in *Land and Churches in Melanesia: Issues and Contexts Point Series No. 25*. edited by Michael Rynkiewich. (277-304). Goroka, EHP, Papua New Guinea: Melanesian Institute, 2001.

Docker, Edward Wybergh. *The Blackbirders, the Recruiting of South Seas Labour for Queensland, 1863-1907*. Sydney: Angus and Robertson, 1970.

Donais, Rosalie M. *To Them Gave He Power: The Gripping Tale of God's Great Love For the Stone Age Waola Highlanders of Papua New Guinea*. Tremont, Illinois: Apostolic Christian Church Foundation, 1987.

Elmer, Duane. *Cross-Cultural Conflict: Building Relationships for Effective Ministry*. Downers Grove, Ill: InterVarsity Press, 1993.

Fernández-Armesto, Filipe. "Epilogue: What is History Now?" in *What is History Now?* edited by David Cannadine, 148-161. [Houndmills, Basingstoke, Hampshire: Palgrave Macmillan, 2002].

Fernández-Armesto, Filipe and K. N. Chaudhuri. *The Times Atlas of World Exploration 3,000 Years of Exploring, Explorers, and Mapmaking*. New York, NY: HarperCollins Publishers, 1991.

Franklin, Karl J., Joice Franklin, and Yapua Kirapeasi. *A Kewa Dictionary with Supplementary Grammatical and Anthropological Materials*. Canberra: Dept. of Linguistics, Research School of Pacific Studies, Australian National University, 1978

Gammage, Bill. *The Sky Travellers: Journeys in New Guinea, 1938-1939*. Calton, Vic: Melbourne University Press, 1998.

Garrett, John. *To Live Among the Stars: Christian Origins in Oceania.* Geneva: World Council of Churches, 1982.

Gibbney, H. J. "Goldie, Andrew (1840 - 1891)." *Australian Dictionary of Biography*, Volume 4, Melbourne University Press, 1972, p. 260 http://www.adb. online.anu.edu.au/biogs/A040293b.htm [accessed on September 9, 2014].

Gilbert, Paul, "What Is Shame? Some Core Issues and Controversies." In *Shame: Interpersonal Behavior, Psychopathology, and Culture*, ed. Paul Gilbert and Bernice Andrews, 3-38. New York, Oxford University Press, 1998.

Glasse, Robert M. "Time Bilong Mbingi: Syncretism and the Pacification of the Huli" in Biersack, Aletta. 1995. *Papuan Borderlands: Huli, Duna, and Ipili Perspectives on the Papua New Guinea Highlands.* [Ann Arbor: University of Michigan Press, 1995] 57-86.

Goddard, Michael. *The Unseen City: Anthropological Perspectives on Port Moresby, Papua New Guinea.* Canberra, ACT: Pandanus Books, Research School of Pacific and Asian Studies, Australian National University, 2005.

Goldman, L. R. "The Depths of Deception: Cultural Schemes of Illusion in Huli" in Biersack, Aletta. *Papuan borderlands: Huli, Duna, and Ipili Perspectives on the Papua New Guinea Highlands.* [Ann Arbor: University of Michigan Press, 1995] 111-138.

Goode, John. *Rape of the Fly.* Melbourne: Nelson, 1977.

Gutch, John. *Martyr of the Islands: The Life and Death of John Coleridge Patteson.* London: Hodder and Stoughton, 1971.

Gray, Geoffrey. "Remembering the War in New Guinea," Australia War Memorial, 2000. http://ajrp.awm.gov.au/AJRP/remember.nsf/Web-Printer/2BA-56E4 6D717A652CA256A99001D9F10?OpenDocument [Accessed on September 16, 2014].

Halligan, J R. 1938. "Administration of Native Races," *Oceania 9* no 3 [March, 1939] 266-285.

Hasluck, Paul. *Papua and New Guinea: Some Recent Statements of Australian Policy on Political Advancement.* Canberra: Minister for Territories, 1960.

_____ *A Time for building: Australian Administration in Papua and New Guinea, 1951-1963.* Carlton, Vic: Melbourne University Press, 1976.

Haley, Nicole and Ronald J. May, *Conflict and Resource Development in the Southern Highlands of Papua New Guinea.* Canberra: Australia National University E Press, 2007.

Hayward, Douglas James. *Vernacular Christianity among the Mulia Dani: an Ethnography of Religious Belief among the Western Dani of Irian Jaya, Indonesia.* Pasadena, Calif.: American Society of Missiology, 1997.

Healey, Alan. *Language Learner's Field Guide.* Ukarumpa, Papua New Guinea: Summer Institute of Linguistics, 1975.

Hesselgrave, David J. *Communicating Christ Cross-culturally.* Grand Rapids: Zondervan, 1978.

Hides, Jack Gordon. *Through Wildest Papua.* London: Blackie & Son, 1935.

_____ *Papuan Wonderland.* London: Blackie and Son, 1936.

Hiebert, Paul G. ""Beyond Anti-Colonialism to Globalism" *Missiology: An International Review*, XIX no. 3 [July, 1991]: 263-281.

_____ *Anthropological Reflections on Missiological Issues.* Grand Rapids, Mich: Baker Books, 1994.

_____ *Transforming Worldviews: An Anthropological Understanding of How People Change.* Grand Rapids, Mich: Baker Academic, 2008.

_____ *The Gospel in Human Contexts: Anthropological Explorations for Contemporary Missions.* Grand Rapids, Mich: Baker Academic, 2009.

Hiebert, Paul G., R. Daniel Shaw, and Tite Tienou. *Understanding Folk Religion: A Christian Response to Popular Beliefs and Practices.* Grand Rapids, Mich: Baker Books, 1999.

Hitt, Russell T. *Cannibal Valley.* New York: Harper & Row, 1962.

Hobsbawm, E. J. *On History.* New York: New Press, 1997.

Hodes, Jeremy Martin. "John Douglas 1828-1904: The Uncompromising Liberal" PhD Thesis." Central Queensland University, 2006.

Hofstede, Geert H., Gert Jan Hofstede, and Michael Minkov. *Cultures and Organizations: Software of the Mind: Intercultural Cooperation and Its Importance for Survival.* New York: McGraw-Hill, 2010.

Hood, Ronald Paul. "Melanesian Paradigm Shifting: Nembi Worldview Change and the Contextualization of the Gospel among Urban Immigrants." PhD diss., Fuller Theological Seminary, 1999.

Hovey, Kevin G. *Before all Else Fails, Read the Instructions: Manual for Cross Cultural Christians.* Brisbane: Harvest Publications, 1995.

Howell, Martha C., and Walter Prevenier. *From Reliable Sources: An Introduction to Historical Methods.* Ithaca, N.Y.: Cornell University Press, 2001.

Hudson, W. J., ed. *Australia and Papua New Guinea.* Sydney: Sydney University Press, 1971.

Hudson, W. J. and Jill Daven. "Papua and New Guinea since 1945" in *Australia and Papua New Guinea*, edited by W. J. Hudson, 151-177. Sydney: Sydney University Press, 1971.

Inglis, Kenneth Stanley. "War Race and Loyalty in New Guinea, 1939-1945" in *The History of Melanesia: Papers Delivered at a Seminar Sponsored Jointly by the University of Papua and New Guinea, the Australian National University, the Administrative College of Papua and New Guinea, and the Council of New Guinea Affairs Held at Port Moresby from 30 May to 5 June 1968*, edited by Waigani Seminar and Kenneth Stanley Inglis, 503-529. Port Moresby: University of Papua and New Guinea, 1971.

International Christian Embassy Jerusalem. "History: The ICEJ's Story and Purpose" International Christian Embassy Jerusalem, http://int.icej.org/history [accessed August 19, 2014].

_____ "International Feast of the Tabernacles Presented by the International Christian Embassy Jerusalem" http://feast.icej.org/about [accessed August 19, 2014]

_____ "Mandate; ICEJ's Scriptural Directive" http://int.icej.org/about/mandate [accessed August 21, 2014].

_____ "Objectives: The ICEJ's Founding Principles" International Christian Embassy Jerusalem, http://int.icej.org/about/objectives [accessed August 19, 2014].

Jinks, Brian, Peter Biskup, and Hank Nelson. *Readings in New Guinea History.* Sydney: Angus & Robertson, 1973.

Joyce, R. B. *Sir William MacGregor.* Melbourne: Oxford University Press, 1971.

Kerr, J. R. 1958. "The Political Future" in *New Guinea and Australia*, ed. Australia Institute of Political Science and John Wilkes, [Sydney, Australia: Angus and Robertson, LTD] 138-175.

Keysser, Christian. *A People Reborn.* Pasadena, Calif: William Carey Library, 1980.

Kiki, Albert Maori. *Kiki: Ten Thousand Years in a Lifetime, a New Guinea Autobiography.* New York: F.A. Praeger, 1968.

Kiru, Cliff "A Critical Evaluation of the Spiritual Harvest Ministry in Poroma, SHP" Essay for R:604.803 Contextualization of the Gospel in Primal Societies, Laidlaw-Carey Graduate School, CLTC Delivery, Banz, Western Highlands Province, Papua New Guinea, 11 August, 2009.

_____ "Footprints of God in Nembi Valley Culture in Light of Acts 17:22-23," [Major Essay: Christian Leaders Training College, Term Four 2014].

_____ "Christ Supreme—An Exposition of the Theological Meaning of 'Image of God' in Colossians 1:15—Its Implications and Significance, Then and Now." Melanesian Journal of Theology 30-2 [2014], 6-19.

King, Joseph. *W.G. Lawes of Savage Island and New Guinea.* London: Religious Tract Society, 1909.

Kituai, August Ibrum K. My Gun, *My Brother: The World of the Papua New Guinea Colonial Police, 1920-1960.* Honolulu: University of Hawai'i Press, 1998.

Knoll, Arthur J., and Hermann Hiery. *The German Colonial Experience: Select Documents on German Rule in Africa, China, and the Pacific, 1884-1914.* Lanham, Md: University Press of America, Inc, 2010.

Koczberski, Gina, George N. Curry, and John Connell. "Full Circle or Spiraling Out of Control? State Violence and the Control of Urbanisation in Papua New Guinea." *Urban Studies* 38:11 [November, 2001] 2017-2022.

Langmore, Diane. *Missionary Lives Papua, 1874-1914.* Honolulu: University of Hawaii Press, 1989.

Lanternari, Vittorio. *The Religions of the Oppressed; A Study of Modern Messianic Cults.* New York: Knopf, 1963.

Lawrence, Peter. *Road Belong Cargo: A Study of the Cargo Movement in the Southern Madang District, New Guinea.* Manchester: Manchester University Press, 1964.

Lawrence, Peter, and Mervin J. Meggitt. *Gods, Ghosts, and Men in Melanesia: Some Religions of Australian New Guinea and the New Hebrides.* Melbourne: Oxford University Press, 1965.

League of Nations Mandate for the Territory of New Guinea 17 December, 1920. *Official Yearbook of the Commonwealth of Australia No 31-1938.* http://www.jje.info/lostlives/transcripts/D00044.html [Accessed on September 12, 2014].

Leahy, Michael J., and Maurice Crain. *The Land That Time Forgot: Adventures and Discoveries in New Guinea.* New York: Funk & Wagnalls, 1937.

Leahy, Michael J., and Douglas E. Jones. *Explorations into Highland New Guinea, 1930-1935.* Tuscaloosa: University of Alabama Press, 1991. http://www.netlibrary.com/urlapi.asp?action=summary&v=1&bookid=20250. [Accessed on October 7, 2014].

Lederleitner, Mary T. *Cross-cultural Partnerships: Navigating the Complexities of Money and Mission.* Downers Grove, IL: InterVarsity Press, 2010.

Lederman, Rena. *What Gifts Engender: Social Relations and Politics in Mendi, Highland Papua New Guinea.* Cambridge [Cambridgeshire]: Cambridge University Press, 1986.

Legge, J. D. *Australian Colonial Policy: A Survey of Native Administration and European Development in Papua.* Sydney: Angus and Robertson, 1956.

Lett, Lewis. *The Papuan Achievement.* Melbourne: Melbourne University Press in association with Oxford University Press, 1944.

Lima, Matthias. "South Sea Evangelical Church Position Paper on the Teaching of Rev. Michael Maeliau" August 19, 2009 http://64.37.52.84/~ssecorgs/wp-content/uploads/2013/06/Position-Paper.pdf [accessed on August 22, 2014].

Limbrock, Eberhard. "Prefecture Apostolic of Kaiserwilhelmsland." *The Catholic Encyclopedia.* Vol. 8. New York: Robert Appleton Company, 1910. http://www.newadvent.org/cathen/08592d.htm [Accessed on September 12, 2014].

Long, Gavin. *The Final Campaigns Series 1, Vol. 7 of Australia in the War of 1939 to 1945.* Canberra: Australia War Memorial, 1963. http://www.aw-m.gov.au/collection/records/awmohww2/army/vol7/awmohww2-army-vol7-ch4.pdf [Accessed on October 9, 2014].

Luzbetak, Louis J. *The Church and Cultures: New Perspectives in Missiological Anthropology.* Maryknoll, N.Y.: Orbis Books, 1988.

MacGreggor, William. "British New Guinea—Administration" in *Proceedings of the Royal Colonial Institute (Great Britian) Volume XXVI.* London: The Institute [1895]: 194-226. http://catalog.hathitrust.org/api/volumes/oclc/177-2110.html [Accessed on September 10, 2014].

MacGreggor, William. "British New Guinea" in *Proceedings of the Royal Colonial Institute (Great Britian) Volume XXX.* London: The Institute [1899]: 238-254. http://catalog.hathitrust.org/api/volumes/oclc/1772110.html [Accessed on September 10, 2014].

Mackenzie, S. S. *The Australians at Rabaul: The Capture and Administration of the German Possessions in the Southern Pacific.* Sydney: Angus and Robertson, 1941. http://www.awm.gov.au/histories/first_world_war/volume.asp?levelID=67896 [Accessed on September 12, 2014].

Maeliau, Michael. *The Deep Sea Canoe Movement: An Account of the Prayer Movement in the Pacific Islands Over the Last Twenty Years.* Canberra: B & M Pub, 2007.

_____ "The Deep Sea Canoe Vision" http://www.ipcprayer.org/upload/resour-ces/items/The_Deep_Sea_Canoe_Vision_1.pdf [accessed on August 22, 2014].

Mair, Lucy. *Australia in New Guinea*. [Melbourne]: Melbourne University Press, 1970.

Mantovani, Ennio, "Traditional Values and Ethics" in *An Introduction to Melanesian Cultures: A Handbook for Church Workers: Book One of a Trilogy*. ed. Darrel Whiteman, 195-212. Goroka, Papua New Guinea: Melanesian Institute, 1984a.

Mantovani, Ennio. "What is Religion" in *An Introduction to Melanesian Religions: A Handbook for Church Workers: Book Two of a Trilogy*. ed. Ennio Mantovanni, 23-48. Goroka, Papua New Guinea: Melanesian Institute, 1984b.

McAuley, James. "Australia's Future in New Guinea" *Pacific Affairs* 26, no. 1 [March 1953]: 59-69. http://www.jstor.org/stable/2752903 [Accessed on October 11, 2014].

McGavran, Donald A. *Understanding Church Growth*. Grand Rapids, Mich: Eerdmans, 1980.

McSwain, Romola. *The Past and Future people: Tradition and Change on a New Guinea Island*. Melbourne: Oxford University Press, 1977.

Miklukho-Maklaĭ, Nikolaĭ Nikolaevich, and C. L. Sentinella. *New Guinea Diaries, 1871-1883*. Madang, P.N.G.: Kristen Pres, 1975.

Moore, Clive. *New Guinea: Crossing Boundaries and History*. Honolulu: University of Hawai'i Press, 2003.

Moresby, John, "Discoveries in Eastern New Guinea by Captain Moresby and the Officers of H.M.S. Basilisk." *Journal of the Royal Geographical Society of London* 45 [1875], 153-170. http://www.jstor.org.ezproxy.asburysemi-nary.edu/stable/1798707 [accessed on September 9, 2014]

Murray, John Hubert Plunkett. *Papua: or, British New Guinea*. London: T. Fisher Unwin, 1912.

_____ *Papua of To-day; or, An Australian Colony in the Making*. London: P.S. King, 1925.

_____ "The Scientific Aspect of the Pacification of Papua." in *Tribal Peoples and Development Issues: A Global Overview*, edited by John H. Bodley, 42-52. [Mountain View, California: Mayfield Publishing Company, 1988].

Narokobi, Bernard. "The Wind is Blowing" in *Land and Churches in Melanesia: Issues and Contexts*, edited by Michael A. Rynkiewich, 5-8. Goroka, EHP, Papua New Guinea: Melanesian Institute, 2001.

Naugle, David K. *Worldview: the History of a Concept*. Grand Rapids, Mich: W.B. Eerdmans Pub, 2002.

Naval History and Heritage Command. n.d. *Battle of the Coral Sea, 7-8 May, 1942 Overview and Special Image Selection* http://www.history.navy.mil-/photos/events/wwii-pac/coralsea/coralsea.htm [Accessed on November 12, 2012].

Neely, Alan, "Saints Who Sometimes Were: Utilizing Missionary Hagiography" *Missiology: An International Review,* XXVII, no. 4 [October, 1999]:441-457.

Nelson, Hank. *Black, White and Gold: Gold Mining in Papua New Guinea, 1878-1930*. Canberra: Australian National University Press, 1976.

_____ "The Australians in Papua New Guinea" in *Melanesia, Beyond Diversity*, edited by Ronald James May and Hank Nelson 143-150 [Canberra: Research School of Pacific Studies, Australian National University, 1982]. http://w-ww.papuaweb.org/dlib/bk1/rspas-1982/ [Accessed on September 13, 2014].

_____ *Taim Bilong Masta: The Australian Involvement with Papua New Guinea.* Crows Nest, NSW: ABC Enterprises for the Australian Broadcasting Corporation, 1990.

Ogan, E. *Business and Cargo: Socio-Economic Change Among the Nasioi of Bougainville*. Port Moresby: New Guinea Research Unit, Australian National University, 1972.

Oliver, Douglas. *A Solomon Island Society: Kinship and Leadership Among the Siuai of Bougainville* Cambridge: Harvard University Press, 1955.

Oram, N. D. *Colonial Town to Melanesian city: Port Moresby 1884-1974.* Canberra: Australian National University Press, 1976.

Ortiz, Manuel. *One New People: Models for Developing a Multiethnic Church.* Downers Grove, Illinois, InterVarsity Press, 1996.

Patteson, J. C. "South Sea Island Labour Traffic" from Appendices to the Journals of the New Zealand House of Representatives, 1871, G-35. Transcribed by the Right Reverend Dr. Terry Brown , Bishop of Malaita Church of the Province of Melanesia, 2006. http://anglicanhistory.org/nz/patteson/traf-fic1871.html [accessed on September 8, 2014].

Pech, Rufus. *Manub and Kilibob: Melanesian models for Brotherhood Shaped by Myth, Dream and Drama.* Papua New Guinea: Melanesian Institute, 1991.

Pók, Attila. *A Selected Bibliography of Modern Historiography.* Bibliographies and indexes in world history, no. 24. New York: Greenwood Press, 1992.

Ranke, Leopold von, Georg G. Iggers, Konrad von Moltke, Wilhelm Humboldt, and Leopold von Ranke. *The Theory and Practice of History.* Indianapolis: Bobbs-Merrill, 1973.

Reithofer, Hans. *The Python Spirit and the Cross: Becoming Christian in a Highland Community of Papua New Guinea.* Münster: Lit, 2006.

Robbins, Joel. *Becoming Sinners: Christianity and Moral Torment in a Papua New Guinea Society.* Berkeley, Calif: University of California Press, 2004.

Robson, R. W. *Queen Emma: the Samoan-American Girl Who Founded an Empire in 19th Century New Guinea.* Sydney: Pacific Publications. 1979.

Roe, Margriet. "Papua New Guinea and War 1941-5," in *Australia and Papua New Guinea,* ed. W. J. Hudson, 138-150. Sydney: Sydney University Press, 1971.

Romilly, Hugh Hastings. *From My Verandah in New Guinea; Sketches and Traditions.* London: D. Nutt, 1889.

Romilly, Hugh Hastings and Samuel Henry Romilly *Letters From the Western Pacific and Mashonaland 1878-1891.* London: D. Nutt, 1893.

Rowell, John. *To Give or Not to Give?: Rethinking Dependency, Restoring Generosity, and Redefining Sustainability.* Tyrone, GA: Authentic Pub, 2007.

Rubel, Paula G., and Abraham Rosman. *Your Own Pigs You May not Eat: A Comparative Study of New Guinea Societies.* Canberra: Australia National University Press, 1978.

Ryan, D'Arcy. "Gift-exchange in the Mendi Valley: An Examination of the Socio-political Implications of the Ceremonial Exchange of Wealth among the People of the Mendi Valley, Southern Highlands District, Papua." PhD diss., University of Sydney, 1961.

Rynkiewich, Michael A. "Big-Man Politics: Strong Leadership in a Weak State" in *Politics in Papua New Guinea: Continuities, Changes and Challenges,* eds. Michael A. Rynkiewich and Roland Seib, 17-43. Goroka, Papua New Guinea: Melanesian Institute, 2000.

_____ "Introduction: The Land and Churches Research Project," in *Land and Churches in Melanesia: Issues and Contexts,* ed. Michael A. Rynkiewich, 9-21, Goroka, EHP, Papua New Guinea: Melanesian Institute, 2001.

_____ "Land Acquisition during the German Period" in *Land and Churches in Melanesia: Issues and Contexts,* ed. Michael A. Rynkiewich, 250-276 Goroka, EHP, Papua New Guinea: Melanesian Institute, 2001.

_____ "Some Practical Advice on Church Land Matters" in *Land and Churches in Melanesia: Issues and Contexts,* ed. Michael A. Rynkiewich, 336-346, Goroka, EHP, Papua New Guinea: Melanesian Institute 2001..

_____ "The World in My Parish: Rethinking the Standard Missiological Model" *Missiology* XXX, no 3, [July 2002], 301-319.

_____ "Person in Mission: Social Theory and Sociality in Melanesia" *Missiology* XXXI, no. 2, [April, 2003], 155-168.

_____ *Cultures and Languages of PNG: The Story of the Origins, Migrations, and Settlement of Melanesian Peoples, Language, and Cultures.* Goroka, Eastern Highlands Province, Papua New Guinea: Melanesian Institute, 2004.

_____ *Soul, Self, and Society: A Postmodern Anthropology for Mission in a Postcolonial World.* Eugene, OR: Cascade Books, 2011.

Sack, Peter G. *Land Between Two Laws: Early European Land Acquisitions in New Guinea.* Canberra: Australian National University Press, 1973.

Sahlins, Marshall D. "Poor Man, Rich Man, Big-Man, Chief Political Types in Melanesia and Polynesia," *Comparative Studies in Society and History 5,* no 3 [April, 1963] 285-303.

Schieffelin, Edward L. and Robert Crittenden, editors. *Like People You See in a Dream: First Contact in Six Papuan Societies.* Stanford, Calif: Stanford University Press, 1991.

Schlatter, Vic. Where Is the Body?: *Discovering the Church in the Heart of Israel.* Shippensburg, Pa: Treasure House, 1999.

Schutt, Russell K. *Investigating the Social World: The Pprocess and Practice of Research.* Thousand Oaks, Calif: Pine Forge Press, 2006.

Schwartz, Glenn "Cutting the Apron Strings" *Evangelical Missions Quarterly* 30 no 1, [January, 1994]; 37-42 reprinted in *Mission Frontiers: The Bulletin of the U. S. Center for World Mission,* January-February, 1997. http://www-.missionfrontiers.org/issue/article/cutting-the-apron-strings (accessed on November 4, 2013).

_____ 2007. *When Charity Destroys Dignity: Overcoming Unhealthy Dependency in the Christian Movement: A Compendium.* Lancaster, Pa: World Mission Associates.

Schweder, Richard A. and Edmund J. Bourne. "Does the Concept of the Person Vary Cross-Culturally." in *Cultural Conceptions of Mental Health and Therapy*, edited by Anthony J. Marsella and Geoffrey M. White, 97-137. Dordrecht: Reidel, 1984.

Shek, Eric "Autralian Aid to Papua New Guinea: Where is This Aid Really Going?" Australia National University, https://eview.anu.edu.au/cross-sec-tions/vol5/pdf/06.pdf--Australian [Accessed on January 17, 2015].

Siilata, Miloalii. "The Prayer Movement Behind the Deep Sea Canoe Vision," http://www.ipcprayer.org/upload/resources/items/The_Deep_Sea_Canoe_Vision_1.pdf [Accessed on August 22, 2014].

Sillitoe, Paul. *Give and Take: Exchange in Wola Society.* New York: St. Martin's Press, 1979.

Sinclair, James Patrick. *The Outside Man.* Melbourne, Australia: Angus and Robertson Ltd, 1969.

_____. 1984. *Kiap: Australia's Patrol Officers in Papua New Guinea.* Bathurst: Brown.

_____. *Last frontiers: The Explorations of Ivan Champion of Papua: A Record of Geographical Exploration in Australia's Territory of Papua between 1926 and 1940.* Broadbeach Waters, Gold Coast, Qld., Australia: Pacific Press, 1988.

Somare, Michael Thomas. *Sana: An Autobiography of Michael Somare.* Port Moresby: Niugini Press, 1975.

Souter, Gavin. *New Guinea: The Last Unknown.* Sydney: Angus and Robertson, 1963.

Spradley, James P., and Michael A. Rynkiewich. *The Nacirema: Readings on American Culture.* Boston: Little, Brown, 1975.

Stanner, W. E. H. *The South Seas in Transition: A Study of Post-war Rehabilitation and Reconstruction in Three British Pacific Dependencies.* Sydney: Australasian Pub. Co, 1953.

Strathern, Andrew. *The Rope of Moka: Big-men and Ceremonial Exchange in Mount Hagen, New Guinea.* Cambridge [Eng.]: University Press, 1971.

Strathern, Marilyn. *Women in Between: Female Roles in a Male World: Mount Hagen, New Guinea.* New York: Seminar Press, 1972.

Stuart, Ian. *Port Moresby, Yesterday and Today.* Sydney: Pacific Publications, 1970.

"The Versailles Treaty June 28, 1919." *The Avalon Project Documents in Law, History and Diplomacy.* Yale Law School, 2008. http://avalon.law.yale.e-du/imt/parti.asp [Accessed on September 12, 2014].

Timmer, Jaep "Straightening the Path from the Ends of the Earth: The Deep Sea Canoe Movement in the Solomon Islands" in *Flows of Faith: Religious Reach*